Fifth Edition

The
HANDY BOOK
For
GENEALOGISTS

REVISED AND ENLARGED

State and County Histories

Maps

Libraries

Bibliographies of Genealogical Works

Where to Write for Records, etc.

Edited By   George B. Everton, Sr.

Published by

The Everton Publishers, Inc.

P. O. Box 368   Logan, Utah 84321

"It is indeed a desirable thing to be
well descended, but the glory belongs to
our ancestors."

Lithographed U. S. A.
Keith Watkins and Sons Printing

Binding
Mountain States Bindery

Fifth Edition of The Handy Book For Genealogists

Eighteen years ago, September 1949, the first copies of the "Handy Book for Genealogists" were distributed to the waiting genealogical world. Since that time over 45,000 copies of this informative research aid have been distributed to genealogists in every corner of the world. The author and publisher of the First Edition of "The Handy Book" was Walter M. Everton, a man who stands alone in his accomplishments in the genealogical world. Not only did he author the first edition of the "Handy Book for Genealogists," but he also authored and originated "The How Book for Genealogists" along with "The Genealogical Helper."

Any degree of success attained by his successors, THE EVERTON PUBLISHERS INC., can to a large extent, be credited to the solid foundation he laid. The dedication of his efforts to "help more people find more genealogy" has been the constant aim of those who have continued his work.

It is with humble pride that this the Fifth Edition of "The Handy Book for Genealogists" is presented. Much of the information found in this edition is the same as the fourth edition; however many corrections and additions have been made. A questionnaire was sent to every county clerk in the United States asking for information about the vital records held by them - the dates of commencement, etc. The information that was printed in the fourth edition was shown them and they were asked to check it for accuracy and to indicate any changes that should be made.

New and larger type has been used in many sections of the book making it much easier to read. Also many of the abbreviations used in former editions have been eliminated making the material presented herein much easier to read and understand.

Many errors of former editions have been eliminated, but undoubtedly some still remain. It is sincerely hoped that readers finding errors in this edition will call them to our attention, as many have done in past editions, which has been greatly appreciated. It is hoped that those who have sent in corrections will find the corrections made in this edition. However in some cases the material sent to us was not documented and we could not find proof of its validity therefore we were unable to use it.

On page 328 there is listed a select bibliography of genealogical reference books. These have been recommended by leading genealogists as representative of their field.

The introduction that follows this foreword has proven to be very successful in helping genealogists to use this book in their ancestor seeking. Here you will find instructions on how to use the information about the counties and states. Once a person learns how to use that information he will seldom, if ever, turn back to the introduction. Many will find it a great help in getting started. Even those who have used former editons until they were threadbare may find pointers to assist them.

George B. Everton, Jr.
for THE EVERTON PUBLISHERS, INC.

15 March 1967

DEDICATION

To
Walter M. Everton
1876 - 1950

and his good wife
Pearl K. Everton
1877 - 1952

Together these two pioneer genealogists founded "The Genealogical Helper", "The Handy Book for Genealogists", and "The How Book for Genealogists".

As you start to gather information for your family tree you will undoubtedly find that your American ancestors migrated from place to place. It is a rare thing to find even two or three generations of a family at one location. If they were not in one of the mass movements from Europe to America or from the eastern seaboard on west, they were nevertheless looking for greener pastures and changing their abodes – sometimes so often it is extremely difficult to follow their trails.

As they moved from one country, state, or county to another they usually left records. You must find those records to verify births, deaths, marriages, and many other facts regarding their lives and loves. You must follow their trails sometimes backward and forward. It is not unusual for genealogists to work on both ends of the trail, finally closing the gap, making a complete record of their movements and many other interesting facts about their lives.

When you start your search for their records you may find some in one state and some in another. It is also possible that you will find some of your progenitors living in one place for many years, yet their records are scattered in several counties. This may have been caused by the original counties being divided and subdivided again and again. How to search for these records at one time presented a great challenge but "The Handy Book For Genealogists" gives answers to thousands of these questions quickly, easily.

Many of the older genealogists have said they wished they had had this aid when they started research. They had to dig the facts regarding the dates of organization of counties and their parent counties from history books, county commission records and legislature minute books and many other kinds of archival material. By trial and error they found where records were kept, what they revealed, etc. These facts must be known in practically all cases before you can get the information needed to establish the connections.

Knowing what records are available and whom to contact for extracts or copies also presents a tremendous problem, as each country, state and county may have different record keeping systems. The county clerk may have the records you need in one county, the city clerk in another, the clerk of the court in another, and the state health department in another. With this book you can quickly decide where to write for what records.

To assist you in the use of the information you have in this volume let us illustrate with some hypothetical cases:

1. STATE HISTORIES

Tradition holds that one of your great grand parents was born in Missouri in 1811. You check the history of Missouri in "The Handy Book" and find it did not become a territory until 1812 - that from 1805 to 1812 it was part of Louisiana Territory. Therefore it would be unlikely that Missouri would have a record about him or his parents in 1811. If you wanted to start a search, the place to look would be in the Louisiana records. Of course, you might find he was not born in Missouri or in 1811 - that his parents brought him from another state as a baby. There may be many other possibilities. One thing for certain is that the Territory of Missouri was not created until 1812, one year after his reported birth, and prior to that time that section of the country belonged to the Territory of Louisiana.

2. COUNTY HISTORIES

Suppose you had a progenitor who was one of the first settlers at Key West, Florida. He took his family there in 1822 but died in 1823, leaving his wife and children. One approach is to learn if there is a will, record of real estate, or any other contemporary record about him in the county records. You find that Key West is the county seat of Monroe County, but none of their records help you. You wonder if something might be found in adjoining counties but your search is fruitless in six or eight neighboring counties. Finally you learn about the "Handy Book for Genealogists". You turn to page 40 and find that Monroe County was formed in 1824 from St. Johns County, one year after the death of your forefather. A further check reveals that St. Augustine is the county seat of St. Johns County and it is almost on the other side of the state, over 375 miles from Key West. You go to the records at St. Augustine and there find just what you want.

Next you search for the records of a forebear who lived and died in Ford County, Illinois. He was 75 years old at his death in 1869 - making his birth date about 1794. There is reason to believe he was born at, or near, his place of death and would like to know everything possible about him from the county records. You check Ford County on page 59 of "The Handy Book" and find it was formed in 1859 from Clark County. Going back it is found that Clark was formed in 1819 from Crawford County, which was formed from Edwards in 1816. In turn Edwards County was formed in 1814 from Madison and Gallatin Counties, they being formed in 1812. St. Clair, which was formed from the N.W. Territory in 1790, was the parent county of Madison. Randolph, formed from St. Clair and the N.W. Territory in 1795, was the parent county of Gallatin.

You must search the records of six or seven counties to be sure you have all that can be found about a man who supposedly lived all his life within the confines of one county: Ford 1869-1814; Clark 1850-1819; Crawford 1819-1816; Edwards 1815-1814.

Then Madison 1814-1812; St. Clair 1812-1794 or Gallatin 1814-1812; Randolph 1812-1795. It might be well to do further investigating to establish whether your research should go to Madison or Gallatin Counties. It undoubtedly would not be both.

3. LIBRARIES

One of your ancestors came from Connecticut. What library might have records on his life? You check the list of libraries on page 28 and find quite a number you can write to for information. You also find several books listed which could be extremely helpful in your progenitor search.

4. MAPS

As you search in many U. S. counties you will find their records do not start until several years after the formation date found in the "Handy Book." This situation undoubtedly arose because the residents failed to take advantage of the enabling act. It is quite certain that people were living there, or the legislature would not have acted. You will find it easy to locate your county and all surrounding counties from maps in the "Handy Book" and it might be well to check with neighboring county clerks to ascertain if they have some record of your ancestor. Occasionally persons would travel to one of the nearby counties for a marriage license or other important business if it could not be taken care of in their own county.

A new feature of this edition is that the maps of all the states show the adjoining counties in neighboring states. Thus you can follow migrations with much greater ease than heretofore.

You follow the trail of one of your ancestors in his westward trek through Virginia. It starts at James City with a year or two or three years stop in each of the following counties: Henrico, Buckingham, Roanoke and Scott. Here you lose the trail. You have reason to believe that he moved across the line to Tennessee. You locate Scott County on the map and find bordering it on the south the Tennessee counties of Hancock, Hawkins and Sullivan - the three counties you will have to search to pick up the trail again.

5. COUNTY RECORDS

A questionnaire was sent to every county clerk or clerk of court in the U. S. asking for information about the records in their custody. About half of them returned the questionnaire. Many gave information which should be helpful in searching county records. This information is included in this edition with the other county data. For instance, you turn to Arkansas on page 11 and find that Arkansas County is the first county listed. Under this county you find: (Co Clk has pro rec from 1809, m rec from 1838; Cir Clk has div & civ ct rec from 1803, War ser discharge from 1917). Interpreted this says: County Clerk has probate records from 1809, marriage records from 1838; Circuit Clerk has divorce and civil court records from 1803, War Service discharge from 1917. The explanations of abbreviations of words with which you may have difficulty are listed on page XI. If this feature proves to be helpful, let us know and we will try to expand it in our next edition.

6. GENEALOGISTS' CHECK LIST OF HISTORICAL RECORDS SURVEY

Surveys of public record archives were conducted in most states during 1936 to 1943 by the Works Progress Administation (WPA), a government agency. For example, inventories were made of the federal archives in all the states, of state, some county and municipal archives, transcripts of some public archives, directories of church archives and religious publications, guides to public vital statistic records and depositories of manuscript collections, check lists of American imprints, and various other surveys and listings of records and archives of interest to different types of researchers.

A great many of these records, as you will note, are vital to genealogical research. But very few WPA publications give full transcripts - they only name the records available in the respective archives. Quite often they tell the condition of the records, where they were stored when the survey was made, and dates of commencement and conclusion of the records. The records themselves must be examined to gain the information.

However, you may save much time in your data search by first consulting the check list, and then the survey, and inventory of transcript to find out the existence of buried or piled up records in some county courthouse basement or attic, which may give contemporary evidence regarding the life of your ancestor.

Of course, only a small portion of all available records and archives were surveyed, but that which was completed is a great help in locating records for research - finding what may be available - what the records contain, etc.

Many times one will find unusual and extremely valuable records for genealogical research in county or other archives which are not common. A search should be made in each place to see if such records as naturalization papers, apprenticeship records, special tax assessments, and many other out-of-the ordinary records are available, as well as the usual wills, deeds, court and vital records.

From the ''Genealogists' Check List of the Historical Records

Survey" you can quickly determine if a survey was made by the WPA. Then you should consult the survey to ascertain what records are available in that archive – the usual and the unusual. You will then know what to look for if you can visit the place personally, or what to write for if you can not.

A check list of these publications was published by the WPA according to the type of publication. Sometimes it takes much searching to find all the records which might be listed of one state or locality. Many of the publications are of little or no value to genealogists, since they pertain to such things as reports and records of the Treasury department and other federal agencies, none of which have any personal records. They are of no value to the genealogist.

At the suggestion of Meredith B. Colket, Jr., for many years director of the Institute for Genealogical Research, sponsored by the American University and the National Archives, George B. Everton, Sr. of The Everton Publishers undertook the assignment of making a rearranged check list of these WPA publications. Almost 2000 books were examined and evaluated as to their genealogical value. The ones of no value to genealogists were eliminated from the list. Then the list was rearranged according to states, putting all publications of a state together. Thus, if you are searching for records of Missouri you can now find them all grouped together, making it possible to quickly determine if the records of any particular county, city, church or federal agency in Missouri was surveyed for records of a genealogical nature. If so, then you should try to get the publication to determine if any records might be available which would assist you.

Of course, as with most records, you will find some of the listed publications of greater value than others. For instance, Ship Registers and Enrollments have only a slight value to genealogists. Nevertheless, the names of the owners and captains of these ships are easy to check in the good indices and at times they may prove to be the only record you can find of these people. You may also find clues as to where other records may be found. So do not be discouraged if some of the publications don't produce the information you need. Persistence is a virtue no genealogist can afford to overlook.

Every state or region had a designated depository of unpublished material which also may have many of the publications. An exchange was made at the time of printing whereby copies were supposed to be sent to each region or state depository. The depositories of unpublished materials – that which were in preparation for publication at the time the project was abandoned – are listed in the rearranged check list. Many libraries also have fair collections of the WPA Historical Records Survey Publications. At one time the Library of Congress acted as an exchange station, distributing surplus copies to other libraries and depositories. The staff of the National Archives Library, Washington D. C. 20025, under the direction of Miss Grace Quimby has also endeavored to gather a complete set, but still lacked some numbers. They also have a few surplus copies they would be happy to exchange with other libraries or depositories, especially if they could fill in the ones they lack.

So you may find a copy of the publication you need close by, or you may have to do some searching. You should check with the local library first and extend your search from there. If you can locate the publications pertinent to the area and time of your ancestor you may save many hours of tedious labor, as they will quickly show what records are available in each archive where surveys were made.

7. ABBREVIATIONS

The following abbreviations have been used to save space – making it possible for us to give you more information.

adpt – adoption; b – birth; bur – burial; ca – about; cen – census; cert – certificate; CH – court house; cir – circuit; civ – civil; clk – clerk; co – county; crim – criminal; ct – court; cts – courts; dept – department; dist – district; div – divorce; incom – incomplete; m – marriage; mtg – mortgage; par – parish; pl – place; pro – probate; rec – record; reg – register or registrar; sup – superior; treas – treasurer; vit stat – vital statistics; vol – volume.

Alabama

Capital, Montgomery - Territory 1817 - State 1819 - (22nd)

The first permanent white settlers to establish homes in Alabama came there in 1702, although some historians say 1699. About one hundred seventy four years earlier the Spanish explorers De Narvaes and Cabeza de Vaca passed through the section on their exploration trips. The first white settlers to move into the territory were Spanish and French. They established Mobile in 1702 as the first community.

To evade participation in the Revolutionary War many British sympathizers living in Georgia moved westward into the Alabama section in 1775. They were followed in 1783 by other planters from Georgia, Virginia and the Carolinas. A group of Scotch-Irish who had tried farming in Tennessee in 1809 settled in the northern part of Alabama, in the rich Tennessee Valley district. In the early 1800's former Carolinians and Virginians came into the central part of the territory. Other groups from the same section came to the western part of Alabama along the Tombigbee and the Black Warrior rivers. But it was not until the end of the War of 1812 that Alabama saw a real influx of settlers. The conclusion of that war was the beginning of a gigantic southward and westward movement which resulted in statehood for four territories between 1816 and 1819. Alabama was the last of the four to gain statehood.

Previously the territory of Alabama had been created from the Territory of Mississippi on 3 March 1817. St. Stephens became the capital of the territory. In November 1818 Cahaba, a community existing only in the blue-print stage, without buildings or a population, was made the capital.

So great had been the influx of people into that south-western section that two years and four months after Alabama had become a Territory a political convention prepared a state constitution. This gathering was held on 5 July 1819 in the temporary state capital, Huntsville, the seat of Madison county, located between the Tennessee River and the southern boundary of the state of Tennessee. Representatives were present from the then existing twenty-two counties of Alabama, namely, Autaga, Baldwin, Blount, Cabela which in 1820 became Biggs, Clarke, Conecuh, Cotaco which in 1821 became Morgan, Dallas, Franklin, Lauderdale, Lawrence, Limestone, Madison, Marengo, Marion, Montgomery, Monroe, St. Clair, Shelby, Tuscaloosa, and Washington.

Alabama officially became a state on 14 December 1819.

1

The official census reports show the Alabama population to be 127,901 in 1820, 309,527 in 1830, 590,756 in 1840, and 771,623 in 1850. It passed the million mark sometime in the 1870-1880 period, and in 1950 had surpassed the three million mark, of which two-thirds was white. All but eight counties of Alabama's first census, taken in 1820, has been lost. All other census records are intact. Less than ten thousand of the 1950 population were foreign born, coming mainly from Italy, Germany, England, Russia, and Greece.

At present Alabama has sixty-seven counties.

The Bureau of Vital Statistics, Department of Public Health, Montgomery, Alabama 36104, has birth and death records since 1908 and incomplete records prior to 1908. The cost of a certified copy is $1.00, the short form $.50. Similar records prior to 1908 are kept in the office of some county clerks. Marriage records are in counties where the Probate Courts also have old records of deeds and wills. Some Alabama counties have court houses in cities or towns in addition to the county seats. The records in those places must be searched as well as those at the county seat. Undoubtedly the Alabama Department of Archives and History, Montgomery, Alabama, may be able to furnish some information or give directions to other sources.

Although not so large as in some states, the Alabama Department of Archives and History, Montgomery, Alabama, has a considerable collection of genealogy and biography pertaining to the south. Copies of the federal census of Alabama are also deposited there.

Among books dealing with Alabama individuals are the following which can be found in many libraries throughout the nation.

Brewer, Willis: "Alabama, Her History and Public Men, 1872."

Owen, Thomas M., Director Alabama Dept. of Archives and History, "Revolutionary Soldiers in Alabama," 132 pp. Montgomery Ala., The Brown Printing Co., 1911.

Owen, Thomas M. "Our State, Alabama," 1927.

Alabama Society of the SAR, "Roster and Roll of Honor, 1903-1952." (Contains names of 263 Revolutionary Soldiers.)

A partial list of Alabama libraries: Anniston Carnegie Library, Anniston 36201, (Calhoun); Birmingham Public and Jefferson County Free Library, 700 N. 21st St., Birmingham 35203, (Jefferson); Muscle Shoals Regional Library, 210 N. Wood Ave., Florence 35630, (Lauderdale); Gadsden Public Library, 701 Forrest Ave., Gadsden 35901, (Etowah); Mobile Public Library, 701 Government St., Mobile 36602, (Mobile); Montgomery County Library, 131 S. Perry St., Montgomery 36104, (Montgomery).

Alabama County Histories

(Population figures to nearest thousand - 1960 Census)

Name	Map Index	Date Formed	Pop. By M	Census Reports Available	Parent County	County Seat
Autauga	D3	1818	19	1830-80	Montgomery	Prattville

(Judge of Pro has m, pro, adpt, and land deed rec)

Name	Map Index	Date Formed	Pop. By M	Census Reports Available	Parent County	County Seat
Baker	(See Chilton)					
Baldwin	F1	1809	49	1820-80	Washington, part of Fla.	Bay Minette
Barbour	D4	1832	25	1840-80	Creek Cession 1812	Clayton & Eufaula

(Judge of Pro has m rec; Clk of cir ct has civ ct rec)

Name	Map Index	Date Formed	Pop. By M	Census Reports Available	Parent County	County Seat
Benton	(See Calhoun)					
Bibb	C2	1818	14	1830-80	Monroe, Montgomery	Centreville

(changed from Cabela 1820)

Name	Map Index	Date Formed	Pop. By M	Census Reports Available	Parent County	County Seat
Blaine	(See Etowah)					
Blount	B3	1818	25	1830-80	Cherokee Cession, Montgomery	Oneonta
Bullock	D4	1866	13	1870-80	Barbour, Macon,	

(Cir ct Clk has div & civ Ct rec)   Montgomery, Pike ...... Union Springs

Name	Map Index	Date Formed	Pop. By M	Census Reports Available	Parent County	County Seat
Butler	E3	1819	25	1830-80	Conecuh, Montgomery	Greenville

(CH burned April 1853 - Judge of Pro has rec since then)

Name	Map Index	Date Formed	Pop. By M	Census Reports Available	Parent County	County Seat
Cahaba	(See Bibb)					
Calhoun	B3	1832	96	1860-80	Creek Cession of 1832	Anniston

(Name changed from Benton 29 Jan 1858)

Name	Map Index	Date Formed	Pop. By M	Census Reports Available	Parent County	County Seat
Chambers	C4	1832	38	1840-80	Creek Cession of 1832	La Fayette
Cherokee	B4	1836	16	1840-80	Cherokee Cession 1835	Centre
Chilton	C2	1868	26	1880	Autauga, Bibb, Perry, Shelby	Clanton

(Changed from Baker 1874)

Name	Map Index	Date Formed	Pop. By M	Census Reports Available	Parent County	County Seat
Choctaw	D1	1847	18	1850-80	Sumter, Washington	Butler
Clarke	E1	1812	26	1830-80	Washington	Grove Hill
Clay	C3	1866	12	1870-80	Randolph, Talladega	Ashland
Cleburne	B4	1866	11	1870-80	Calhoun, Randolph, Talladega	Heflin
Coffee	E3	1841	31	1850-80	Dale	Elba & Enterprise

(Judge of Pro has m rec from 1876, pro rec from 1850)

Name	Map Index	Date Formed	Pop. By M	Census Reports Available	Parent County	County Seat
Colbert	A1	1867	47	1870-80	Franklin	Tuscumbia
Conecuh	E2	1818	18	1820-80	Monroe	Evergreen
Coosa	C3	1832	11	1840-80	Creek Cession of 1832	Rockford
Cotaco	(See Morgan)					
Covington	E3	1821	36	1830-80	Henry	Andalusia
Crenshaw	E3	1866	15	1870-80	Bulter, Coffee, Covington, Lowndes, Pike	Luverne

(Co Clk has m, div, pro, civ ct rec from 1866)

Name	Map Index	Date Formed	Pop. By M	Census Reports Available	Parent County	County Seat
Cullman	B2	1877	46	1880	Blount, Morgan, Winston	Cullman
Dale	E4	1824	31	1830-80	Covington, Henry	Ozark

(Pro Judge has m rec from 1885, pro rec from 1885; Co Clk has civ ct & div rec from 1885; Co health dept has bur rec)

Name	Map Index	Date Formed	Pop. By M	Census Reports Available	Parent County	County Seat
Dallas	D2	1818	57	1820-80	Montgomery	Selma
DeKalb	A3	1836	41	1840-80	Cherokee Cession of 1835	Fort Payne
Elmore	C3	1866	31	1870-80	Autauga, Coosa, Montgomery, Tallapoosa	Wetumpka
Escambia	E2	1868	34	1870-80	Baldwin, Conecuh	Brewton
Etowah	B3	1868	97	1870-80	Blount, Calhoun, Cherokee, Dekalb, Marshall, St. Clair	Gadsden

(Changed from Blaine 1868)

Name	Map Index	Date Formed	Pop. By M	Census Reports Available	Parent County	County Seat
Fayette	B1	1824	16	1830-80	Marion, Pickens, Tuscaloosa	Fayette
Franklin	A1	1818	22	1830-80	Cherokee & Chickasaw Cession of 1816	Russellville

(Co Clk has civ & crim ct rec from 1923; Pro Judge has m & Pro rec from 1896)

Name	Map Index	Date Formed	Pop. By M	Census Reports Available	Parent County	County Seat
Geneva	E3	1868	22	1870-80	Dale, Henry, Coffee	Geneva
Greene	C1	1819	14	1830-80	Marengo, Tuscaloosa	Eutaw

Hale   C2   1867   20   1870-80   Greene, Marengo,
                                            Perry, Tuscaloosa . . . . Greensboro
   (Pro Judge has m, div, pro, civ ct, deeds, and mtg rec from 1868)
Hancock (See Winston)
Henry   E4   1819   15   1830-80   Conecuh . . . . Abbeville
Houston   E4   1903   51   Dale, Geneva, Henry . . . . Dothan
   (m rec from 1903; pro rec from 1903; b, d, & bur recs kept by co Health
   dept; div rec kept by Register, Chancery ct; civ ct rec kept by clk of ct)
Jackson   A3   1819   37   1830-80   Cherokee Cession of 1816 . . . Scottsboro
   (b, d & bur rec kept by co Health dept; m, div & pro rec kept by Pro Judge
   civ ct rec kept by Circuit ct Clerk)
Jefferson   B2   1819   635   1830-80   Blount . . . . Birmingham
Jones (See Lamar)
Lamar   B1   1867   14   1880   Marion, Fayette, Pickens . . . Vernon
   (Jones co formed 4 Feb 1867, abol 3 Nov 1867 & ret to parent cos. Sanford
   Co org 8 Oct 1868 from orig Jones, name changed to Lamar 1877. Co Clk
   has pro rec from 1886 and will rec from 1880)
Lauderdale   A1   1818   62   1830-80   Cherokee & Chickasaw
   (Pro Judge has m & pro Rec)   Cession in 1816 . . . . Florence
Lawrence   A2   1818   25   1830-80   Cherokee & Chickasaw
                                            Cession 1816 . . . . Moulton
   (Pro Judge has incom b & d rec 1881 to 1912, m, div, pro & deed rec from
   1810, also cen of Conf sol)
Lee   C4   1866   50   1870-80   Chambers, Macon,
                                            Russell, Tallapoosa . . . . Opelika
Limestone   A2   1818   37   1820-80   Cherokee & Chickasaw
                                            Cession 1816 . . . . Athens
   (Div rec from 1866; civ ct rec from 1890; b & d rec kept by Co Health
   Dept; m & pro rec kept by Pro Judge)
Lowndes   D3   1830   15   1830-80   Butler, Dallas, Montgomery . . Hayneville
Macon   D4   1832   27   1840-80   Creek Cession of 1832 . . . . . Tuskegee
Madison   A3   1808   117   1830-80   Cherokee & Chickasaw
                                            Cession 1806-7 . . . . Huntsville
Marengo   D1   1818   27   1830-80   Choctaw Cession of 1816 . . . . Linden
Marion   B1   1818   22   1830-80   Tuscaloosa . . . . Hamilton
Marshall   A3   1836   48   1840-80   Blount, Cherokee, Cession 1835,
                                            Jackson . . . . Guntersville
Mobile   F1   1817   314   1830-80   West Florida . . . . Mobile
   (Clk of pro ct has m rec from 1813, pro rec from 1809 & will books 1 to 44)
Monroe   E2   1815   22   1830-80   Creek Cession 1814,
                                            Washington . . . . Monroeville
Montgomery D3   1816   169   1830-80   Monroe . . . . Montgomery
   (Clk of Bd of Revenue has m & pro rec from 1817, div rec from 1852, deeds
   & mtg from 1817, civ ct rec from 1917)
Morgan   A2   1818   60   1830-80   Cherokee Turkeytown Cession . . Decatur
   (Name changed from Cotaco 1821. Judge of Pro has m & pro rec from 1818)
Perry   C2   1819   17   1830-80   Montgomery . . . . Marion
Pickens   C1   1820   22   1830-80   Tuscaloosa . . . . Carrollton
Pike   E3   1821   26   1830-80   Henry, Montgomery . . . . Troy
   (Co Clk has m & pro rec from 1830, deeds from 1828)
Randolph   C4   1832   19   1840-80   Creek Cession 1832 . . . . Wedowee
Russell   D4   1832   46   1840-80   Creek Cession 1832 . . . . . . Phenix City
   (Some rec at Seale)
Sanford (See Lamar)
St. Clair   B3   1818   25   1820-80   Shelby . . . . Ashville
   (m rec from 1819; pro rec from 1800; wills, administration rec from 1800;
   b & d rec kept by Co Health Dept; div & civ ct rec kept by Cir Clks office)
Shelby   C2   1818   32   1820-80   Montgomery . . . . Columbiana
Sumter   C1   1832   20   1840-80   Choctaw Cession of 1830 . . . Livingston
Talladega   C3   1832   65   1840-80   Creek Cession of 1832 . . . . . Talladega
Tallapoosa   C4   1832   35   1840-80   Creek Cession of 1832 . . . . . Dadeville

(b rec from 1881 to 1919; m rec from 1835; d rec from 1881 to 1919; pro rec from 1835; Approx 25% of total co b were put on rec; Approx 10% of total Co d were put on rec; Div & civ ct rec kept by Cir Clk; 90 acres were swapped between Tallapoosa & Coosa Cos in 1963)

Tuscaloosa C2 1818 109 1830-80 Cherokee & Choctaw
                                     Cession 1816 . . . . Tuscaloosa
(Judge of Pro has m & pro rec from 1823)

Walker   B2 1823 54   1830-80 Marion, Tuscaloosa . . . . . . , Jasper
(Judge of Pro has m & pro rec)

Washington E1 1800 15   1830-80 Mississippi Terr., Baldwin . . . Chatom
Wilcox   D2 1819 19   1820-80 Dallas, Monroe . . . . Camden
Winston   B2 1850 15   1860-80 Walker . . . . Double Springs
(Name changed from Hancock 1858)

Note - All 1820 Census records are missing except for eight Counties. More information may be had about this census from the State Archivist, Montgomery, Alabama. The eight counties are as follows: Baldwin, Conecuh, Dallas, Franklin, Limestone, St. Clair, Shelby and Wilcox.

County Map of Alabama

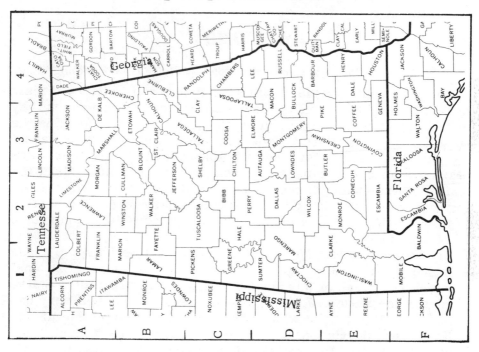

Genealogists' Check List Of The Historical Records Survey, Alabama

Federal Courts, Inventory of County Archives - Clay, Colbert, Conecuh, Cullman, Greene, Hale, Lauderdale, Lowndes, Madison, Marengo, Sumter, Talladega, Wilcox, Winston. Guide to Public Vital Statistics. Guide to Vital Statistic Records, Church Archives. See Louisiana for navigation casualties. Inventory of church archives of Alabama, Protestant Episcopal Church. Check List of Alabama Imprints, 1807-1840. Depository of unpublished material, Dept. of Archives and History, Montgomery, Alabama.

Alaska

Capital, Juneau - Territory 1912 - State 1959 - (49th)

Alaska was purchased from Russia 30 March 1867. At first a district (or unorganized territory), then a Territory in 1912 and a state in 1959. The first federal census was taken in 1880.

First Judicial Dist. . . . . Juneau
Second Judicial Dist. . . . . Nome
Third Judicial Dist. . . . . Anchorage
Fourth Judicial Dist. . . . . Fairbanks

Arizona

Capital, Phoenix - Territory 1863 - State 1912 - (48th)

The first white people to come to Arizona were attracted there by the tale of the fabulous "Seven Cities of Cibola" which they had heard time and again in Mexico City. As early as 1539 the first European explorer came into the region but it was about one hundred fifty years later before Catholic missions were started among the Indians. Tucson became a village about the time the American colonies along the Atlantic coast were fighting their mother country in the Revolutionary War. As a section of New Mexico, Arizona came under the ownership and guidance of Mexico in 1821.

At the close of the Mexican War in 1848, a new dispute arose relative to the ownership of a tract of land at the international border. To alleviate any further difficulties the United States minister to Mexico, James Gadsen, negotiated a deal very unpopular in Mexico, by which the United States paid ten million dollars for slightly less than 50,000 square miles of land, lying south of the Gila River and extending east from the California border to the Rio Grande River.

From the beginning the new territory attracted very few settlers. In 1870, seven years after Arizona became an organized territory, the entire state held less than ten thousand residents. In the forty-year period that followed the Arizona population increased twenty fold, and the following half century more than trebled the 1910 population. The 1950 census placed Arizona with three quarters of a million inhabitants. Since then Arizona stands in the foremost ranks among the states with the highest growth percentage.

The foreign born population of Arizona comes in the following order: Mexico, Canada, England and Wales, Germany, Russia, Italy, Poland, Austria, Sweden, Greece, Ireland, Scotland, Yugoslavia, and Czechoslovakia.

Since 1850 many Mormon families from Utah have settled in Arizona. In fact, in several large agricultural districts, the Mormon population predominates.

Established in July 1909, the Division of Records and Statistics, State Department of Health, Phoenix, Arizona 85007, has birth and death records available since that date, and also similar records originating in the county seats since 1887.

Marriage records are on file with the Clerk of the Superior Court of county in which the license was issued.

Divorce actions are maintained by the Clerk of the Superior Court in county seat where the action was granted.

Citizenship or naturalization papers are filed in the district court of the county where examination was conducted. Also in the office of the clerk of the United States district courts in Tucson, Tombstone, Phoenix, Prescott, and Solomonville.

All real estate records are on file in the office of the recorder of the county in which the land is located.

The 1850 and the 1860 census of Arizona were taken as part of New Mexico. A territorial census of 1864 is in the office of the Secretary of State in the capitol in Phoenix.

The best collection of Arizona history is at the Arizona State Department of Library and Archives in Phoenix 85007 at 309 Capitol Building where microfilm facilities are obtainable. No research is done by staff members. Other libraries with considerable Arizona and southwest history are in the Northern Arizona University Library, Flagstaff Public Library and the Museum of Northern Arizona Library, P.O. Box 402, all of Flagstaff, Arizona 86001. The Maricopa County Free Public Library, 831 North First Ave., Phoenix 85004; The Arizona Pioneers' Historical Society Library, University Stadium, Tucson 85721; and the Genealogical Library, LDS Temple, Mesa 85201. Names of professional researchers may be obtained from the latter if a self-addressed, stamped envelope is enclosed.

Among books of value to the researcher are the following: American Guide Series (1940) "Arizona, a State Guide," gives bibliography on works on Arizona. Bancroft, Hubert Howe, "History of Arizona and New Mexico," (San Francisco 1889). Farish, Thomas E., "History of Arizona," 8 vols., (San Francisco 1915). McClintock, James Harvey, "Arizona, Prehistoric, Aboriginal, Pioneer, Modern," 3 vols., (Chicago 1916). Lockwood,

Francis Cummins, ''Pioneer Days in Arizona,'' (New York 1932).

A partial list of Arizona libraries: Flagstaff Public Library, 212 W. Aspen, Flagstaff 86001, (Coconino); Mesa Public Library, Mesa 85201, (Maricopa); Maricopa County Free Library, 101 E. Roosevelt St., Phoenix 85004, (Maricopa); Prescott Public Library, Gurley and Marina Sts., Prescott 86301, (Yavapai); Tucson Public Library, 200 S. 6th Ave., Tucson 85705, (Pima).

County Map of Arizona

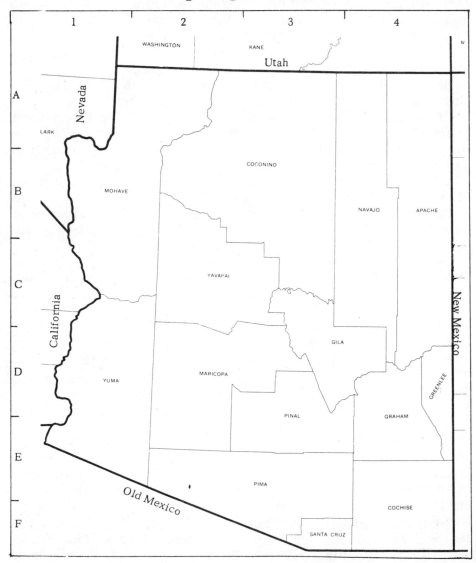

Arizona County Histories

(Population figures to nearest thousand - 1960 Census)

Name	Map Index	Date Formed	Pop. By M	Census Reports Available	Parent County	County Seat
Apache	B4	1872	30	1880	Mohave	St. Johns
Cochise	F4	1881	55		Pima	Bisbee
Coconino	B3	1891	42		Yavapai	Flagstaff
Gila	D3	1881	26		Maricopa, Pinal	Globe
Graham	D4	1881	14		Apache, Pima	Safford

(Clk of Sup Ct has m, div, pro, and civ ct rec; Registrar of Vit Sta has b & d rec)

Name	Map Index	Date Formed	Pop. By M	Census Reports Available	Parent County	County Seat
Greenlee	D4	1909	12		Graham	Clifton
Maricopa	D2	1871	664	1880	Yavapai, Yuma	Phoenix
Mohave	B1	1864	8	1870-80	Original county	Kingman

(Co Clk has m, div, pro and civ ct rec; Bureau of Vit Sta has b & d rec.)

Name	Map Index	Date Formed	Pop. By M	Census Reports Available	Parent County	County Seat
Navajo	B4	1895	38		Apache	Holbrook

(Clk of Sup Ct has m, div, pro and civ ct rec)

Pah Ute (disolved 1895 returned to Mohave)

Name	Map Index	Date Formed	Pop. By M	Census Reports Available	Parent County	County Seat
Pima	E3	1864	266	1870-80	Original county	Tucson
Pinal	D3	1875	63	1880	Pima	Florence
Santa Cruz	F3	1899	11		Pima	Nogales
Yavapai	C2	1864	29	1870	Original county	Prescott

(Clk of Sup Ct has m, div, pro and civ ct rec)

Name	Map Index	Date Formed	Pop. By M	Census Reports Available	Parent County	County Seat
Yuma	D1	1864	46	1870	Original county	Yuma

(Co Clk has m, div, pro and civ ct rec from 1863)

Additional U. S. Census Data: For the 1850 and the 1860 census figures of the following, see New Mexico: Bernalillo, Rio Arriba, Santa Ana, Soccoro, and Valencia.

Genealogists' Check List of the Historical Records Survey, Arizona

Federal Courts (start 1912). Inventory of County Archives, Maricopa, Pima, Santa Cruz. 1864 census of territory. Guide to Public Vital Statistic Records. Directory of Church and Religious Organizations. Private Journal of George Whitewell Parsons. Journal of the Pioneer and Walker Districts. Check List of Arizona Imprints 1860-1890. District Courts of the Territory of Arizona 1864-1912. Depository of unpublished material, Arizona State Library and Archives, Phoenix, Arizona.

Arkansas

Capital, Little Rock - Territory 1817 - State 1836 - (25th)

The Indians had free reign in Arkansas until after the United States completed negotiations with the French for the Louisiana Purchase in 1803. Off and on during the previous two hundred sixty two years several French explorers had come to the region with their parties in search of whatever loot they could find. They came today and were gone tomorrow.

With the land in the ownership of the United States it was immediately thrown open for settlement at attractive low prices.

The new opportunities beckoned thousands of earlier settlers of the mid-east and south-east sections. The first comers were mainly of English, Irish and Scottish stock. Many moved into the new section from nearby Kentucky and Tennessee.

What is now Arkansas became part of the Missouri Territory in 1812. When Missouri applied for statehood in 1819 Congress created the Arkansas Territory included in which was what is now Oklahoma. On 15 June 1836 Arkansas became the twenty-fifth state in the union.

When the Panic of 1837 drained most of the settlers in the older southern and eastern states many of them set out for the newly created state on the west to make a new start in life. Thirty years later the rich lands between the Arkansas and the White Rivers attracted large groups of South European emigrants. Many came direct from Poland to establish themselves in Pulaski County. Italians were attracted to the northwest section of the state where they engaged in fruit raising.

Lawrence County, in the northeast corner of the state, and Arkansas County, in the southeast corner, were settled before most of the other counties in the state.

The Bureau of Vital Statistics, State Health Department, State Health Building, Little Rock, Arkansas, has birth and death records from 1914 and marriage records from 1917. Clerks of counties where license was obtained also have marriage records. The Clerks of Circuit Courts also have records of wills, deeds, divorces, and war service. Naturalization records are on file in the District Courts at Little Rock, Helena, Batesville, Fort Smith, and Texarkana.

All Arkansas federal censuses since 1830 are available. The 1820 census was also taken in the Arkansas Territory but the schedules are missing.

A continuously expanding collection of early Arkansas history and genealogy is to be found in the Public Library, 700 Louisiana Street, Little Rock 72201. Other Arkansas collections are at the Carnegie City Library, 318 North 13th Street, Fort Smith 72901; Arkansas Agricultural, Mechanical and Normal College Library, Pine Bluff 71601; Garland County Public Library, 200 Woodbine, Hot Springs 71901; The University of Arkansas Library, Fayetteville 72701; and the Arkansas History Commission, Little Rock 72200.

State Land Office, State Capitol Bldg., has original plats of U.S. Government surveys of Arkansas and original entries by Township and Range.

Among important books dealing with Arkansas and her people are the following: Josiah Shinn's ''Pioneers and Makers of Arkansas,'' 1908 (recognized in some circles as the most valuable historical record of the state); David Y. Thomas' "Arkansas and Its People," 4 vols. (last two biographical), New York 1931; Arkansas Historical Association's "Arkansas Historical Quarterly," Fayetteville 1942- ; W. F. Pope's "Early Days in Arkansas," 1895; similar to this in popular character, vast in bulk and loose in method, are the "Biographical and Pictorial Histories," covering the different sections of the state. (One volume by J. Hallum in 1887, four others compiled anonymously 1889-1891.)

A partial list of Arkansas libraries: Washington County Library Fayetteville 72701, (Washington); Garland County Public Library, 200 Woodbine St., Hot Springs 71901, (Garland); Little Rock Public Library, 700 Louisiana St., Little Rock 72201, (Pulaski); Pine Bluff and Jefferson County Library, 219 W. 5th Ave., Pine Bluff 71601, (Jefferson).

Arkansas County Histories

(Population figures to nearest thousand - 1960 Census)

Name	Map Index	Date Formed	Pop. By M	Census Reports Available	Parent County	County Seat
Arkansas	C3	1813	23	1830-80	Original county	Stuttgart & De Witt

(Co Clk has pro rec from 1809, m rec from 1838; Cir Clk has div & civ ct rec from 1803, War ser discharge from 1917)

| Ashley | D3 | 1848 | 24 | 1850-80 | Union, Drew . . . . | Hamburg |

(Ashley Co was formed from Chicot Co, Ark. as well as from Union & Drew Cos. More of Ashley Co was taken from Chicot than from Union or Drew)

Baxter	A2	1873	10	1880	Fulton, Izard Marion and Searcy	Mountain Home
Benton	A1	1836	36	1840-80	Washington	Bentonville
Boone	A2	1869	16	1870-80	Carrol, Madison	Harrison

(C o Clk has m & pro rec from 1869)

| Bradley | D3 | 1840 | 14 | 1850-80 | Union . . . . | Warren |
| Calhoun | D2 | 1850 | 6 | 1860-80 | Dallas, Ouachita . . . . | Hampton |

(Co Clk has m, div, pro, civ ct rec)

| Carroll | A1 | 1833 | 11 | 1840-80 | Izard . . . . Berryville & Eureka Springs |

(m rec from 1870; div rec from 1870 kept by Circuit Clk; Pro rec)

| Chicot | D3 | 1823 | 19 | 1830-80 | Arkansas . . . . | Lake Village |

(Co Clk has m & pro rec from 1839; Cir Clk has civ ct rec from 1824)

| Clark | C2 | 1818 | 21 | 1830-80 | Arkansas . . . . | Arkadelphia |
| Clay | A4 | 1873 | 21 | 1880 | Randolph, Green . . . Corning & Pigott |

(Co Clk has m, pro rec from 1881; Div rec & civ ct rec kept by Cir Clk Off)

| Cleburne | B3 | 1883 | 9 | | White, Van Buren, Independence . . . . | Heber Springs |
| Cleveland | C2 | 1873 | 7 | 1880 | Dallas, Bradley, Jefferson, Lincoln . . . . | Rison |

(Changed from Dorsey 5 March 1885)

| Columbia | D2 | 1852 | 26 | 1860-80 | Lafayette, Hempstead, Ouachita . . | Magnolia |
| Conway | B2 | 1825 | 15 | 1830-80 | Pulaski . . . . | Morrilton |

(Co Clk has incom m rec from 1851, pro rec from 1846; Cir clk has div rec from 1842, civ ct rec from 1865, Deed rec from 1825, will rec from 1861)

| Craighead | A4 | 1859 | 47 | 1860-80 | Mississippi, Greene, Poinsett . . . Jonesboro and Lake City |

(Co Clk has Pro rec from 1885; b & d rec kept by Bureau of Vital Statistics; div & civ ct rec kept by Cir Clk)

| Crawford | B1 | 1820 | 21 | 1830-80 | Pulaski . . . . | Van Buren |

(Co Clk has m, div, pro, civ ct and crim ct rec 1883 for eastern dist of co only)

Crittenden   B4   1825   48   1830-80   Phillips . . . . Marion
(Co Clk has m rec filed by dates, also pro rec; b, d & bur rec are kept by Bur
of Vital Statistics in Little Rock; Div rec are kept by Chancery Clk; Civ ct rec
kept by Cir Clk)
Cross   B4   1862   20   1870-80   Crittenden, Poinsett, St. Francis . . . Wynne
(Co Clk has m & pro recs; b & bur rec kept by Bur of Vital Statistics in
Little Rock; Div & civ ct rec kept by Cir Clk)
Dallas   C2   1845   11   1850-80   Clark, Bradley . . . . Fordyce
Desha   C3   1838   21   1840-80   Arkansas . . . . Arkansas City
Dorsey   (See Cleveland)
Drew   D3   1846   15   1850-80   Arkansas, Bradley . . . . Monticello
(Co Clk has m & pro rec from 1850; Board of Health has b & d rec; Cir Clk has
div & civ Ct rec)
Faulkner   B2   1873   24   1880   Pulaski, Conway . . . . Conway
(Co Clk has m, pro, co ct rec from 1873)
Franklin   B1   1837   10   1840-80   Crawford . . . . . . Charleston and Ozark
(Co Clk has m & pro rec from 1901; div & civ Ct rec from 1891)
Fulton   A3   1842   7   1850-80   Izard . . . . Salem
(Part attached from Fulton 1855)
Garland   C2   1873   47   1880   Montgomery, Hotsprings,
                                        Saline . . . . Hot Springs N. P.
Grant   C2   1869   8   1870-80   Jefferson, Hotsprings, Saline . . . Sheridan
(Co Clk has m, div, pro & civ Ct rec from 1877; Bur of Vital Statistics has
b & d rec)
Hempstead   D1   1818   20   1830-80   Arkansas . . . . Hope
Greene   A4   1833   25   1840-80   Lawrence . . . . Paragould
Hot Springs   C2   1829   22   1830-80   Clark . . . . Malvern
(Co Clk has m & pro rec from 1845; Cir Clk has div & civ ct rec)
Howard   C1   1873   11   1880   Pike, Hempstead, Polk, Sevier . . Nashville
Independence A3   1820   20   1830-80   Lawrence, Arkansas . . . . . . Batesville
(Co Clk has m rec from 1826; Pro rec from 1839; b & d rec in Little Rock;
Cir Clk has div & civ ct rec)
Izard   A3   1825   7   1830-80   Independence . . . . Melbourne
(Line between Izard & Sharp changed 9 Mar 1877. Co Clk has m, div, pro,
civ ct rec from 1889; Bur of Vital Statistics has b, d, & bur rec)
Jackson   B3   1829   23   1830-80   Woodruff . . . . Newport
(Co Clk has m rec 1846, pro rec 1845; Cir Clk has div & civ ct rec from 1845)
Jefferson   C3   1829   81   1830-80   Arkansas, Pulaski . . . . Pine Bluff
Johnson   B2   1833   12   1840-80   Pope . . . . Clarksville
(Co Clk has m rec from 1855, div & civ ct rec from 1865, pro rec from 1844,
Deed books from 1836, and will rec from 1844)
Lafayette   D1   1827   11   1830-80   Hempstead . . . . Lewisville
Lawrence   A3   1815   17   1830-80   New Madrid, Mo . . . . Powhatan
(Co Clk has m & Pro rec)   Walnut Ridge (1)
Lee   C4   1873   21   1880   Phillips, Monroe, Crittenden,
(Co Clk has m & pro rec from 1873) St. Francis . . . . Marianna
Lincoln   C3   1871   14   1880   Arkansas, Bradley, Desha, Drew,
                                        Jefferson . . . . Star City
(Co Clk has m, pro, and tax rec from 1871)
Little River D1   1867   9   1870-80   Hempstead . . . . Ashdown
Logan   B1   1871   16   1880   Pope, Franklin, Johnson, Scott,
                                        Yell . . . . Booneville & Paris (1)
(Co Clk (in Paris) has m, div, pro & civ ct rec from 1877; b, d & bur rec are
in Little Rock. There is a book in Logan Co entitled "Biographical Memoriors
of Western Ark", which contains nms of the early settlers of the Co. Dates
from late 1800's, contact Mary Agnew, Rt.#3, Ozark, Ark. Paris CH
burned Oct 1877; all rec destroyed; rec from 1871 to Oct 1877 missing)
Lonoke   B3   1873   25   1880   Pulaski, Prairie . . . . Lonoke
Lovely   1827   Abolished 1828
Madison   A1   1836   9   1840-80   Washington . . . . Huntsville
Marion   A2   1836   6   1840-80   Izard . . . . Yellville
(Co Clk has m, div, pro & civ ct rec from 1890)

Miller   D1   1820   32   1880   Abolished 1836 & ret to Arkansas
                                              Re-established 1874 . . . . . Texarkana
    (Co Clk has m & pro rec from 1875; Cir Clk has div & civ ct rec)
Mississippi   A4   1833   70   1840-80   Crittenden . . . Blytheville & Osceola
Monroe   C3   1829   17   1830-80   Phillips, Arkansas . . . . Clarendon
    (Co Clk has m rec from 1851 and pro rec from 1830; Cir Clk has div rec
    from 1851, Civ ct rec from 1830)
Montgomery   C1   1842   5   1850-80   Hotsprings . . . . Mount Ida
Nevada   D2   1871   11   1880   Hempstead, Columbia, Ouachita . Prescott
    (Co Clk has, div, pro & Civ ct rec from 1871)
Newton   A2   1842   6   1850-80   Carroll . . . . Jasper
    (Co Clk has m rec from 1867, Deed rec from 1870)
Ouachita   D2   1842   32   1850-80   Union . . . . Camden
Perry   B2   1840   5   1850-80   Conway . . . . Perryville
    (Co Clk has m, div, pro, & civ ct rec from 1884)
Phillips   C4   1820   44   1830-80   Arkansas, Hempstead . . . . Helena
Pike   C1   1833   8   1840-80   Clark, Hempstead . . . . . . Murfreesboro
    (Co Clk has m, div, pro & civ ct rec from 1895)
Poinsett   B4   1838   31   1840-80   Greene, St. Francis . . . . . Harrisburg
Polk   C1   1844   12   1850-80   Sevier . . . . Mena
    (Co Clk has m rec from 1887, pro rec from 1889, & Co ct rec from 1873;
    Cir Clk has div rec from 1907, Crim ct rec from 1873, & deed rec from 1882)
Pope   B2   1829   21   1830-80   Crawford . . . . Russellville
    (Co Clk has m & pro rec from 1835)
Prairie   B3   1846   11   1850-80   Pulaski . . . . Des Arc & De Valls Bluff
Pulaski   C3   1818   243   1830-80   Arkansas . . . . Little Rock
    (Co Clk has m rec from 1838, pro rec from 1840, will rec from 1820, civ rec
    from 1846; Early tax & Assessment Books from 1828; Cir Clk has deed rec
    from 1820; Bur of Vital Statistics has d & b rec from 1914)
Randolph   A3   1835   13   1840-80   Lawrence . . . . Pocahontas
    (Co Clk has m & pro rec from 1836, div rec from 1841)
St. Francis   B4   1827   33   1830-80   Phillips . . . . Forrest City
    (Co Clk has m rec from 1875 & Pro rec from 1910; Bur of Vital Statistics has
    b & d rec; Cir Clk has div rec)
Saline   C2   1835   29   1840-80   Pulaski, Hempstead . . . . Benton
Scott   B1   1833   7   1840-80   Pulaski, Crawford, Pope . . . . Waldron
    (Co Clk has m, div, pro & civ ct rec from 1882; Deeds & Mortgages from
    1882 & tax rec from 1932)
Searcy   A2   1838   8   1840-80   Marion . . . . Marshall
    (Co Clk has m, div, pro & civ rec from 1881, deed rec from 1866)
Sebastian   B1   1851   67   1860-80   Scott, Polk, & Crawford . . . Fort Smith &
                                                                                    Greenwood
    (Co Clk has m rec from 1873 & pro rec from 1884; b, d, & bur rec are in
    Little Rock; Cir Clk has div & civ ct rec at Greenwood; Greenwood gives m
    & Pro rec dates as above, Fort Smith gives m rec as 1865 & pro rec as 1866)
Sevier   C1   1828   10   1830-80   Hempstead, Miller . . . . De Queen
    (Co Clk has m rec from 1839, pro rec from 1830)
Sharp   A3   1868   6   1870-80   Lawrence . . . . Evening Shade & Hardy
    (Line between Sharp & Izard changed 1877)
Stone   A3   1873   6   1880   Izard, Independence, Searcy,
                                              Van Buren . . . . Mountain View
    (Co Clk has m, div, pro & civ ct rec from 1873)
Union   D2   1829   50   1830-80   Hempstead, Clark . . . . El Dorado
    (Co Clk has m rec from 1864, also Co ct rec)
Van Buren   B2   1833   7   1840-80   Independence, Conway, Izard . . . . Clinton
    (Co Clk has m, div, Pro & civ ct rec from 1865; State Health Dept has b,
    d, & bur rec)
Washington   A1   1828   56   1830-80   Crawford . . . . Fayetteville
White   B3   1835   33   1840-80   Pulaski, Jackson . . . . Searcy
Woodruff   B3   1862   14   1870-80   Jackson, St. Francis . . . . Augusta
    (Co Clk has m & pro rec from 1865)
Yell   B2   1840   12   1850-80   Pope, Scott . . . . . . Danville & Dardanelle (1)

County Map of Arkansas

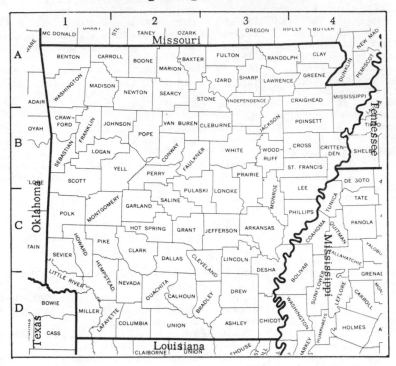

Genealogists' Check List of the Historical Records Survey,
Arkansas

Federal Courts (start 1819). Inventory of County Archives, Baxter, Benton, Carroll, Cleburne, Cleveland, Cross, Faulkner, Hot Springs, Izard, Jackson, Madison, Monroe, Montgomery, Polk, Saline, Scott, Searcy. Guide to Vital Statistic Records, Church Archives. Inventory of the Church Archives of Arkansas, Church of Christ Scientists. Directory of Church and Religious Organizations. Check List of Arkansas Imprints, 1821–1876. Union list of Arkansas newspapers, 1819–1942, a partial inventory of Arkansas newspaper files available in offices of publishers, library and private collection. Depository of unpublished material, University of Arkansas Library, Fayetteville, Ark.

California

Capital, Sacramento - State 1850 - (31st)

Various expeditions from Mexico, Spain, Russia and England visited California from 1540 to 1792. Spain controlled until 1822 when Mexico came into possession and held power until

1848.   It then ceded California to the United States. The fever
that struck all sections of the United States and every country of
Europe with the finding of gold at Sutter's Mill brought people
to California from all parts of the world. The Gold Rush increased the population from 15,000 to 250,000. In 1957 the population was more than eleven million. About one tenth of the
population is foreign born.

The foreign born residents of California, listed in point of
numbers, originated in the following countries: Mexico, Canada,
Italy, England and Wales, Russia, Germany, Sweden, Ireland,
Scotland, Poland, Austria, France, Denmark, Norway, Switzer-
land, Portugal, Greece, Yugoslavia, Hungary, Netherlands, Spain,
Finland, Czechoslovakia, Rumania, Lithuania, and Belgium.

Records of births and deaths since 1905 are on record in office
of the Bureau of Records and Vital Statistics, 1927 Thirteenth
Street, Sacramento, California 95814.   Many of the health
offices of the larger cities have similar records prior to 1 July,
1905, as have also the recorders of the various counties, or the
county clerks. The Department of Health in San Francisco has
early death and cemetery records.

The Bureau of Records and Statistics, address as above, and all
County Clerks have records of marriage licenses issued in the
respective counties.

Divorce records are available in the office of the Clerk of the
Superior Court in the county in which the proceedings were conducted.

Many of the County Recorders have early birth and marriage
records. County Clerks have divorce, probate, civil court and
other records of interest to genealogists.

Naturalization records are kept in the county offices of the
Superior Courts, and also in the United States Circuit Courts in
Los Angeles and San Francisco.

Deeds for real estate and lands are filed in the office of the
County Recorder in the county in which the land concerned is
located.

A communication from the Chief of the Bureau of Records and
Statistics and the Chief of the Vital Records Section of the Department of Public Health says, ''In the case of a request for a search
for an unknown event, we require a fee of $1.00 (may be more now)
per hour of search, paid in advance.'' An example of this kind of
a record search is when a person was last known to be alive on a
given date, and we are asked to search for a death record of the
person from that date foreward.

There are certain items of information which we require in
order to make a search of our records. These items vary with
the type of record sought and the time period involved.

As we now have over ten million records on file, duplication of names is common. It is therefore desirable that secondary identifying data be furnished."

The largest genealogical library on the west coast is that of the Public Library, 630 West Fifth Street, Los Angeles 90017. No research is done by staff members. The next largest genealogical collection on the coast is found in the Sutro Branch of the California State Library. Other California libraries may borrow books from the Sutro Branch for their clients. Names of professional genealogists may be obtained from the library in question if inquiry is made in writing and a self-addressed, stamped envelope is enclosed.

Other valuable genealogical collections are located in California Genealogical Society Library, 2029 Pacific Ave, San Francisco 94109; California Historical Society Library, 2090 Jackson St., San Francisco 94109; Society of Mayflower Descendants Library, 926 DeYoung Bldg., 690 Market St., San Francisco 94104; Society of California Pioneers Library, 456 McAllister St., San Francisco 94102; Sons of the American Revolution Library, 926-928 de Young Bldg., 690 Market St., San Francisco 94104; Swedish American Hall Library, 2174 Market St., San Francisco 94114; Stockton and San Joaquin County Library, Market and Hunter Sts., Stockton 95204; Public Library, 2090 Kittredge St., Berkeley 95204; General Library, University of California, Berkeley 94704; Public Library, 425 E. Olive Ave., Burbank; County Library, 322 S. Broadway, Los Angeles 90013; Library, University of California at Los Angeles, 405 Hilgard Ave., Los Angeles 90024; Public Library, 659 - 14th St., Oakland 94612; Public Library, Hamilton at Bryant, Palo Alto 94306; State Library, Sacramento 95809; County Free Public Library, 364 Mt. View Ave., San Bernardino 92408; Whittier College Library, Whittier 90601; Long Beach Public Library, Long Beach 90800; Sons of Revolution, Hope St., Los Angeles 90012. San Diego Public Library, 820 E Street, San Diego 92101.

Books on California: H. H. Bancroft's "History of California 1542-1890," 7 vols., San Francisco 1884-90; T. H. Hittell's "History of California," 4 vols., San Francisco 1885-97; C. E. Chapman's "A History of California," "The Spanish Period," New York, 1921; J. W. Caughey's "California," New York 1940; R. G. Cleland's "From Wilderness to Empire," New York 1944; R. G. Cleland's "California in Our Time," New York 1847; State of California, Secretary of State, "California Blue Book," Sacramento, irregularly.

California County Histories

(Population figures to nearest thousand - 1960 Census)

Name	Map Index	Date Formed	Pop. By M	Census Reports Available	Parent County	County Seat
Alameda	C2	1853	906	1860-80	Contra Costa & Santa Clara	Oakland

(Co Clk has div, pro & civ ct rec from 1853, Co Recorder has b, m & d rec)

Alpine	C2	1864	397	1870-80	Eldorado, Amador, Calaveras	Markleeville
Amador	C2	1854	10	1860-80	Calaveras	Jackson

(Co Clk has m, div, pro and civ ct rec from 1854 to present. Also has election supervisors, tax rec)

Butte	B2	1850	82	1850-80	Original county	Oroville
Calaveras	C2	1850	10	1850-80	Original county	San Andreas

(Co Clk has b rec from 1860, a few bef 1890; m & d rec from 1882; Div, pro, & civ ct rec from 1866; Bur rec – Various cem districts)

Colusa	C2	1850	12	1850-80	Original county	Colusa
Contra Costa	C2	1850	409	1860-80	Original county	Martinez
Del Norte	A1	1857	18	1860-80	Klamath	Crescent City

(Co Clk has div, pro & civ ct rec; Co Recorder has b, m, d & bur rec)

El Dorado	C2	1850	29	1850-80	Original county	Placerville

(Co Rec has b & d rec 1910 to present; m rec 1852 to present; bur rec (limited) 1910 to 1953; Co Clk has div & pro rec from 1854 (some exceptions); some rec lost in fire 1910)

Fresno	D2	1856	366	1860-80	Merced, Mariposa	Fresno

(Co Rec has b, d & bur rec from 1900, m div, pro & civ ct rec from1860)

Glenn	B2	1891	17		Colusa	Willows

(Co Clk has m, div, pro, & civ ct rec; Co Recorder has b & d Rec)

Humboldt	B1	1853	105	1860-80	Trinity	Eureka
Imperial	G4	1907	72		San Diego	El Centro

(Co Rec has b, m, d rec from 1907; Co Clk has div, pro & civ ct rec from 1907)

Inyo	E3	1866	12	1870-80	Tulare	Independence

(Co Clk has div, pro & civ ct rec from 1866; Co Rec has b & d rec from 1905 & m rec from 1866; Northern area, part of Supervisorial Dist. #1, was purchased from Mono Co 28 Mar 1870)

Kern	E3	1866	292	1870-80	Tulare, Los Angeles	Bakersfield

(Co Clk has div, pro, & civ ct rec from 1866; Co Rec has b, m & d rec; An exchange of territory with San Bernardino Co in 1963; Co Clk has Registration voting rec from 1866)

Kings	E2	1893	50		Tulare	Hanford

(Co Clk has div, pro, civ ct, crim, Juvenile (not open to Public), and voting great register from 1893; Co Rec has b, m & d rec from 1893; Co Clk says they have m licenses issues only; Each cem District has bur rec)

Lake	C1	1861	14	1870-80	Tuoloumne	Lakeport

(Co Clk has b, m, d, bur, div, pro & civ ct rec)

Lassen	B2	1864	14	1870-80	Plumas, Shasta	Susanville

(Co Clk has div, pro, & civ ct rec from 1864; Co Rec has b, m, d & bur rec)

Los Angeles	F3	1850	6039	1850-80	Original county	Los Angeles

(Co Rec has b, m, & d rec; Co Clk has div, pro & civ ct rec from 1850)

Madera	D2	1893	40		Fresno	Madera
Marin	C1	1850	147	1850-80	Original county	San Rafael
Mariposa	D2	1850	6	1850-80	Original county	Mariposa

(Co Clk has div, pro & civ ct rec; Co Rec has b, m, d & bur rec; The dates on all these rec are indefinite)

Mendocino	B1	1850	51	1850-80	Original county	Ukiah

(Co Clk has m rec 1893, div rec 1880, pro rec 1859, civ ct rec 1880)

Merced	D2	1855	90	1860-80	Mariposa	Merced

(Co Clk has div, pro & civ ct rec from 1855; Co Rec has b, m, d & bur rec)

Modoc	A3	1874	8	1880	Siskiyou	Alturas
Mono	D3	1861	2	1870-80	Calaveras, Fresno	Bridgeport

(Co Clk has b & d rec from 1925, m rec from 1861, div rec from 1880, & pro

& civ ct rec from 1875)

Monterey	D2	1850	198	1850–80	Original county . . . . Salinas
Napa	C2	1850	66	1850–80	Original county . . . . Napa

(Co Clk has div, pro, civ ct rec from 1850)

County Map of California

Nevada   C2   1851   21   1860-80   Yuba . . . . Nevada City
   (Co Clk has div, pro & civ ct rec from 1880)
Orange   F3   1889   704   Los Angeles . . . . Santa Ana
Placer   C2   1851   57   1860-80   Yuba, Sutter . . . . Auburn
   (Co Clk has div, pro & civ ct rec from 1851)
Plumas   B2   1854   12   1860-80   Butte . . . . Quincy
   (Co Clk has div, pro, & civ ct rec from 1860)
Riverside   F4   1893   306   San Diego, San Bernardino . . . Riverside
   (Co Clk has div, pro & civ ct rec from 1893; Co Rec has b, m & d rec from 1893)
Sacramento   C2   1850   503   1850-80   Original county . . . . Sacramento
San Benito   D2   1874   15   1880   Monterey . . . . Hollister
   (Co Clk has div, pro, & civ ct rec from 1874; also, b, m & d rec from 1906;
   Co Health Dept has bur rec; Rec less than five years old should be obtained
   from co Health dept)
San Bernardino F4 1853   504   1860-80   Los Angeles . . . . San Bernardino
   (Co Clk has m lic rec from 1887, div & pro rec from 1856, Civ & crim ct rec
   from 1853, Insanity & Inebriate rec from 1887, Guardianship rec from 1856)
San Diego   G3   1850 1033   1850-80   Original county . . . . San Diego
   (Co Clk has div, pro & civ ct rec from 1855)
San Francisco C1   1850   743   1860-80   Original county . . . . San Francisco
   (Co Clk has div, pro & civ ct rec from 1906; Health Officer has b, d & bur rec;
   Co Rec has m rec)
San Joaquin   C2   1850   250   1850-80   Original county . . . . Stockton
   (Co Clk has div, pro & civ ct rec 1850; Art of Inc & Naturalization rec 1851;
   Co Rec has b, m, & d rec)
San Luis Obispo E2 1850   81   1850-80   Original county . . . . San Luis Obispo
                                               and Templeton
San Mateo   D1   1856   444   1860-80   San Francisco . . . . Redwood City
   (Co Clk has div, pro & civ ct rec from 1856; Co Rec has b, m, d & bur rec)
Santa Barbara E2   1850   169   1850-80   Original county . . . . Santa Barbara
Santa Clara   D2   1850   642   1860-80   Original county . . . . San Jose
Santa Cruz   D1   1850   84   1850-80   Original county . . . . Santa Cruz
   (Co Rec has b & d rec 1873, m rec 1852; Co Clk has div, pro & civ ct rec 1850)
Shasta   B2   1850   59   1850-80   Original county . . . . Redding
   (Co Clk has div, pro & civ ct rec from 1880; Co Rec has b, m & d rec)
Sierra   C2   1852   2   1860-80   Yuba . . . . Downieville
   (Co Clk has b, m, d, div, pro & civ ct rec from 1852, also Register of Voters
   from 1852)
Siskiyou   A2   1852   33   1860-80   Shasta, Klamath . . . . Yreka
   (Co Clk has div, pro & civ ct rec from 1852)
Solano   C2   1850   135   1850-80   Original county . . . . Fairfield
   (Co Clk has div, pro & civ ct rec from 1850; Co Rec has b, m, d & bur rec)
Sonoma   C1   1850   147   1850-80   Original county . . . . Santa Rosa
   (Co Clk has div, pro & civ ct rec; Co Rec has b, m, d & bur rec)
Stanislaus   D2   1854   157   1860-80   Tuolumne . . . . Modesto
   (Co Clk has div, pro & civ ct rec from 1854; Co Rec has b, m, & d rec)
Sutter   C2   1850   33   1850-80   Original county . . . . Yuba City
   (Co Clk has div, pro & civ ct rec from 1850)
Tehama   C2   1856   25   1860-80   Colusa, Butte, Shasta . . . . . . Red Bluff
Trinity   B1   1850   10   1860-80   Original county . . . . Weaverville
   (Co Clk has b, m, d, div, pro, bur & civ ct rec from 1890)
Tulare   E2   1852   168   1860-80   Mariposa . . . . Visalia
   (Co Clk has div, pro & civ ct rec from 1852)
Tuolumne   C2   1850   14   1850-80   Original county . . . . Sonora
   (Co Clk has div, pro, civ ct rec from 1850, voting reg from 1866; Co Rec has m
   rec from 1850, d rec from 1857)
Ventura   F2   1872   199   1880   Santa Barbara . . . . Ventura
                                          (San Buenaventura)
   (Co Clk has div, pro and civ ct rec from 1873 also b, m & d rec from 1873)
Yolo   C2   1850   66   1850-80   Original county . . . . Woodland
   (Co Clk has div, pro & civ ct rec from 1850 also has b, m & d rec)

Yuba   C2   1850   34   1850-80   Original county . . . . Marysville
      (Co Clk has m rec from 1865, div, pro & civ ct rec from 1850, Voting rec 1866)

Genealogists' Check List of the Historical Records Survey, California

Federal Courts (start 1850). Ship register and enrollments Port of Eureka, 1859-1920. Inventory of County Archives, Alameda, Fresno, Kern, Los Angeles (4 Vols), Marin, Mono, Napa, San Benito, San Bernardino, San Diego, San Francisco, San Luis Obispo, San Mateo, Santa Barbara, Santa Clara, Ventura. Guide to Public Vital Records, Vol. 1, births; Vol. 2, deaths. Guide to Church Vital Statistic records, six denominations. Directory of Church and Religious organizations in Alameda Co, San Francisco, Los Angeles Co, San Diego Co. Calendar of the Major Rink Snyder collection of manuscripts Collection in the US, Calif. Calendar of the Montana Papers in the William Andrews Clark Memorial Library, University of California at Los Angeles. Calendar of the Francis Bret Harte Letters in the William Andrews Clark Memorial Library, University of California at Los Angeles. Inventory of the Bixby Collection in the Palos Verdes Library and Art Gallery. List of the letters and manuscripts of Musicians in the William Andrews Clark Memorial Library, University of California at Los Angeles. List of the letters and documents of Rulers and Statesmen in the William Andrews Clark Memorial Library, University of California at Los Angeles. Check List of California Non-Documentary Imprints, 1853-1855. Depository of unpublished material, State Archives (No. Calif. material), Sacramento, & Los Angeles County museum (So. Calif. material), Los Angeles.

Colorado

Capital Denver - Territory 1861 - State 1876 - (38th)

Dr. LeRoy R. Hafen, for many years executive director of the State Historical Society of Colorado and the author of several works on Colorado, says, "Colorado was named for the great river that raises in the snowbanks of her western slope. The musical Spanish word meaning 'red' was bestowed on the river by Spanish explorers a century before it was applied to Colorado Territory."

Early Spanish explorers who came to Mexico heard the natives tell exciting tales of cities of gold and silver to the north. To find the precious metals many of these fortune hunters pressed northward, some of them coming into sections of the present New Mexico, Arizona, Utah, and Colorado. Some of these adventurers were the first white men to see the Grand Canyon of the Colorado, the Rio Grande Valley, and other sections of the Rocky Mountain Territory. Escalante the Catholic priest who tried to find a short cut from Santa Fe to the Pacific Coast, came through there on his unsuccessful trip in the summer of 1776.

About fifty years later these sections swarmed with competing trappers and fur traders working for the various large fur companies of eastern United States and Canada.

The real settlers of Colorado didn't come until 1858, thus making the state the last to be occupied by permanent settlers. Many of the first-comers were attracted there by the discovery of gold and other metals. Not too successful in their fortune hunt, they turned to the land and the ranges for their livelihood.

The territory of Jefferson was voted by the residents in 1859 but was never recognized by congress. Thus some of the counties have organization dates and records prior to 28 February 1861 when the Territory of Colorado was recognized.

The 1860 Census showed a population of about 33,000 men, and 1,500 women. This was taken when Colorado was still a part of Kansas.

Colorado was admitted to statehood 1 August 1876. It was called the Centennial State because it became part of the union 100 years after the formation of the United States.

The first territorial assembly created the first 17 counties in September 1861. They were Arapahoe, Boulder, Clear Creek, Costilla, Douglas, El Paso, Fremont, Gilpin, Guadalupe (later named Conejos), Huerfano, Jefferson, Lake, Larimer, Park, Pueblo, Summit and Weld.

A few birth records before January 1907 may be obtained from the respective county clerks, after January 1907 from the State Bureau of Vital Statistics, Denver, Colo.

A few death records before January 1900 may be obtained at the office of the county clerks, after January 1900 at the Bureau of Vital Statistics.

Marriage records are kept by the county clerks. Marriages were not recorded generally until after 1881, but some counties have marriage records as early as 1860.

Probate matters and wills are on file in the office of the county clerk.

All land titles, deeds, mortgages, leases, etc. are kept by the county recorder.

An efficient and congenial staff of librarians is ready to assist all researchers in the rapidly growing genealogical section of the Public Library, 1357 Broadway, Denver 80203. Rocky Mountain region history and lore is available at the University of Colorado Library, Boulder 80301; Public Library, 21 W. Kiowa St., Colorado Springs 80902; McClelland Public Library, 100 Abriendo Ave., Pueblo 81005. Information regarding professional researchers may be obtained by sending self-addressed envelopes to libraries.

Colorado County Histories

(Population figures to nearest thousand - 1960 Census)

Name	Map Index	Date Formed	Pop. By M	Census Reports Available	Parent County	County Seat
Adams	B2	1902	120		Arapahoe	Brighton
Alamosa	D4	1913	10		Costilla, Conejos	Alamosa

(Co Clk has m & land title rec from 1913)

Arapahoe	C2	1861	113	1870-80	Original county	Littleton

(First formed in 1855 as Territorial Co. For Arapahoe 1860 U.S. Census figures see Kansas 1860. Co Clk has m rec from 1902, also those bur rec in co cemeteries; District ct has div, pro & civ ct rec)

Archuleta	E4	1885	3		Conejos	Pagosa Springs
Baca	A4	1889	6		Las Animas	Springfield
Bent	B4	1874	7	1880	Greenwood	Las Animas

(Co Clk has m rec from 1888; bur rec from 1941 (Burial-transit permits); Local Registrar has b & d rec from 1910 but are located in the Co Clks office)

Boulder	C2	1859	74	1870-80	Original county	Boulder

(Co Clk has m rec from 1866)

Chaffee	D3	1879	8	1880	Lake	Salida

(Co Clk has m rec)

Cheyenne	A3	1889	3		Bent, Elbert	Cheyenne Wells
Clear Creek	D2	1859	3	1870-80	Original county	Georgetown
Conejos	D4	1861	8	1880	Original county	Conejos
Costilla	C4	1859	4	1870-80	Original county	San Luis
Crowley	B3	1911	4		Bent, Otero	Ordway
Custer	C3	1877	1	1880	Fremont	Westcliffe

(Co Clk has m & bur rec)

Delta	E3	1883	16		Gunnison	Delta

(Co Clk has b, m, d, & bur rec; Co & Dist Ct has div, pro & civ ct rec)

Denver	C2	1902	494		Arapahoe	Denver

(Has annexed terr from Arapahoe, Adams & Jefferson Cos on several occasions)

Dolores	F4	1881	2		Ouray	Dove Creek

(Co Clk has b, m, d & bur rec from 1894)

Douglas	C2	1859	5	1870-80	Original county	Castle Rock
Eagle	D2	1883	5		Summit	Eagle

(Co Clk has b, m, d, & bur rec from 1883; Dist & Co Ct has div, pro, & civ ct rec)

Elbert	B2	1874	4	1880	Douglas, Greenwood	Kiowa
El Paso	C3	1859	144	1880	Original county	Colorado Springs

(Co Clk has m rec from 1860; also has Sol Discharges from 1919, Real Estate (War Deeds); Health Dept has b, d & bur rec; Dist Ct has div rec; Pro Ct has Pro rec; Co Ct has civ ct rec)

Fremont	C3	1859	20	1870-80	Original county	Canon City

(Co Clk has m rec from 1860)

Garfield	E2	1883	12		Summit	Glenwood Springs

(Co Clk has b, m, d & bur rec; Co or Dist Ct has div, pro & civ ct rec)

Gilpin	C2	1861	.7	1880	Original county	Central City
Grand	D2	1874	4	1880	Summit	Hot Sulphur Spr.

(Co Clk has m rec from 1893)

Gunnison	E3	1874	5	1880	Lake	Gunnison
Hinsdale	E4	1874	.2	1880	Conejos	Lake City

(Co Clk has m rec from 1876, b & d from 1900, deed rec from 1874)

Huerfano	C4	1861	8	1870-80	Original county	Walsenburg

(Co Clk has m & bur rec)

County Map of Colorado

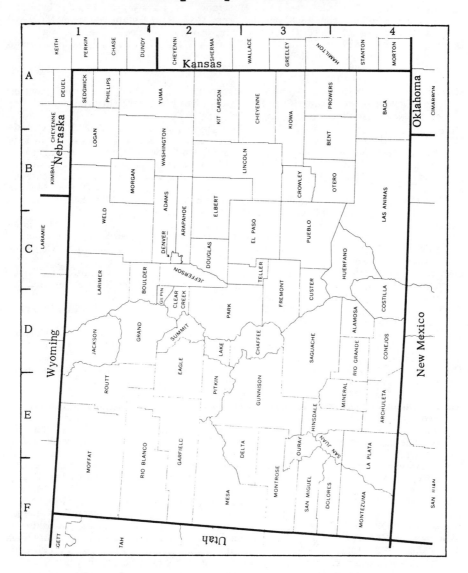

Jackson   D1   1891   2   Grand . . . . Walden
Jefferson   C2   1861   128   1870–80   Original county . . . . Golden
  (Co Clk has m rec from 1861)
Kiowa   A3   1889   2   Cheyenne, Bent . . . . Eads
  (Co Clk has m rec from 1889, b & d rec from 1941)
Kit Carson   A2   1889   7   Elbert . . . . Burlington
Lake   D2   1861   7   1870–80   Original county . . . . Leadville
  (Co Clk has m rec from 1874; Moynohan O'Malia Mortuary has d & bur rec
  Dist Ct has div rec, Co Ct has pro & civ ct rec; b rec are kept by a Miss
  Florence McMahon, 116 E. 7th St., in Leadville)
La Plata   E4   1874   19   1880   Conejos, Lake . . . . Durango
  (Co Clk has m rec; Registrar has b & d rec; Dist Ct has div, pro & civ ct rec)

Larimer   C1   1861   53   1870-80   Original county . . . . Fort Collins
    (Co Clk has m rec from 1865, b & d rec from 1915)
Las Animas   B4   1866   20   1880   Huerfano . . . . Trinidad
    (Co Clk has m rec from 1868, bur rec from 1941; Real Estate rec from 1867;
    Health Dept has b & d rec; Dist Ct has div, pro & civ ct rec)
Lincoln   B3   1889   5   Elbert . . . . Hugo
    (Co Clk has m rec from 1889)
Logan   B1   1887   20   Weld . . . . Sterling
    (Co Clk has m rec from 1887)
Mesa   F3   1883   51   Gunnison . . . . Grand Junction
    (Co Clk has m rec from 1883; Health dept has b & d rec; City Hall has bur
    rec; Dist Ct has div, pro & civ ct rec)
Mineral   E4   1893   .4   Hinsdale . . . . Creede
Moffatt   E1   1911   7   Routt . . . . Craig
    (Mrs. Ellen Robacker has b rec; Dist & Co Ct has div, pro & civ ct rec)
Montezuma   F4   1889   14   La Plata . . . . Cortez
Montrose   F3   1883   18   Gunnison . . . . Montrose
Morgan   B1   1889   21   Weld . . . . Fort Morgan
    (Co Clk has m rec from 1889; Registrar has b & d rec from 1910; Dist Ct has
    div & pro rec from 1889; Co Ct has Civ Ct rec from 1889)
Otero   B4   1889   24   Bent . . . . La Junta
    (Co Clk has m rec from 1892, Real Estate rec from 1889, also Voting rec from
    1938 & Motor Vehicle Titles from 1925; Health Dept has b, d, & bur rec; Co Ct
    has div & pro rec; Dist Ct has civ ct rec)
Ouray   E3   1877   2   1880   Hinsdale . . . . Ouray
    (Co Clk has m rec from 1881 & d & bur rec from 1949; Dist & Co Ct has div,
    pro & civ ct rec; Mildred J. Mager, Reg. has b rec from 1949)
Park   D2   1861   2   1870-80   Original county . . . . Fairplay
    (Co Clk has m rec from 1893)
Phillips   A1   1889   4   Logan . . . . Holyoke
    (Co Clk has m rec from 1888 & some d rec; Registrar has b rec & bur rec;
    Dist Ct has div, pro & civ ct rec)
Pitkin   D2   1881   2   Gunnison . . . . Aspen
Prowers   A4   1889   13   Bent . . . . Lamar
Pueblo   C3   1861   119 1880   Original county . . . . Pueblo
    (Co Clk has m rec from 1880; Health Dept has b, d & bur rec; Dist Ct has div,
    Pro & civ ct rec)
Rio Blanco   E2   1889   5   Summit . . . . Meeker
    (Co Clk has b rec from 1900; m rec from 1889; d rec from 1900; also early day
    Agriculture & stock rec, Bounty books Brand rec registered as Summit Co,
    Garfield Co and finally Rio Blanco; Co Clk also has rec of bur for rural cem
    only, for others see Highland cem assn and Rangely cem assn. Dist Ct has div,
    pro & civ ct rec from 1889)
Rio Grande   D4   1874   11   1880   Conejos, Costilla . . . . Del Norte
Routt   E1   1877   6   1880   Grand . . . . Steamboat Springs
Saguache   D3   1870   4   1880   Costilla . . . . Saguache
San Juan   E4   1876   .8   1880   La Plata . . . . Silverton
San Miguel   F3   1883   3   Ouray . . . . Telluride
    (Co Clk has b & d rec from 1910, m rec from 1883; Dist Ct has div, pro & civ
    ct rec from 1883; Bur rec are kept by the secretary of Lone Tree Cem)
Sedgwick   A1   1889   4   Logan . . . . Julesburg
    (Co Clk has m rec from 1889; Registrar has b & d rec; Co Clk has some bur
    rec; Dist Ct has div, Pro & civ ct rec)
Summit   D2   1861   2   1870-80   Original county . . . . Breckenridge
Teller   C3   1899   2   El Paso . . . . Cripple Creek
    (Co Clk has m rec from 1899)
Washington   B2   1887   7   Weld, Arapahoe . . . . Akron
    (Co Clk has m rec from 1887)
Weld   B1   1861   72   1870-80   Original county . . . . Greeley
Yuma   A2   1889   9   Washington, Arapahoe . . . . Wray
    (Co Clk has m rec from 1900)

Federal Courts (start 1861). Inventory of County Archives, Alamosa, Arapahoe, Bent, Conejos, Costilla, Fremont, Garfield, Hinsdale, Larimer, Logan, Morgan, Phillips, Prowers, San Miguel, Washington, Yuma. Guide to Vital Statistics, Vol. 1 public archives, Vol. 2 Church Archives. Inventory of the Church and Synagogue archives, Jewish. Depository of unpublished material, State Historical Society, Denver.

Connecticut

Capital Hartford - Ninth Colony - State 1788 - (5th)

The settlement of Connecticut began in 1635 by former Massachusetts colonists. Some of them left Massachusetts on order of narrow religious leaders, and others because they had become weary of the intolerant attitude displayed by those leaders. The green Connecticut valley had beckoned them with abundant evidences of opportunities for material prosperity. Most of the settlers in the Massachusetts towns of Newtown, Watertown and Dorchester, all near Boston, moved their families and all of their belongings to the central part of Connecticut, where along the Connecticut River they established three new communities which later came to be called Windsor, Hartford and Wethersfield. It was an attack on these three communities that later caused the Pequot Indian War.

As early as 1614 a Dutch seafarer, Adriaen Block, sailed up the broad river, which he named the Varsche River. The first knowledge of the fertile section of Connecticut the early settlers of Massachusetts learned from the Indians who gave them a highly painted word picture of the section. It was this that brought about the settlement of the three communities mentioned above. Late in 1635 about fifty persons left what is now Cambridge, then called Newtown, and established themselves at Suckiaug, now Hartford. New migrations continued throughout the next few years. While the Dutch remained at the trading posts or forts, the English spread all over the territory.

From 1635 to 1644 another English colony flourished at Saybrook, near the mouth of the Connecticut, but then faded away. In 1643, New Haven was extended as a colony to include Milford (1639), Guilford (1639), and Stamford (1641).

During the ten year period from 1640 to 1650, there was a heavy influx of settlers into Connecticut. The new settlers came almost entirely direct from England. The following forty years saw a tremendous migration away from the newly settled district. The movement was generally westward where fertile fields beckoned those anxious to secure their independence. In many instances the entire population of some of the towns participated in the migration and established themselves again among their old neighbors in a new environment.

In 1772 about 30 English families under the leadership of the Reverend Richard Mosely left Litchfield, Connecticut, for the Kingsborough Patent, Fulton County, New York. (See The Genealogical Helper Vol. 14-4 page 213).

The 1790 Census of Connecticut shows a population of 232,236. All of them with the exception of three and eight-tenths per cent, or 223,437 had come from England proper. Scotland was represented with two and eight-tenths per cent, or 6,425. Ireland with seven-tenths per cent, or 1,589. France, two tenths per cent, or 512. Holland, one-tenth per cent, or 258. There were also five Hebrew, four German, and six from other countries.

During the early days of the American colonies Connecticut had more home industries than any other colony. All kinds of household gadgets were invented and manufactured in the homes. These early necessities were carried all over the eastern section of the present United States, even down to New Orleans, by the so called "Yankee Pedlars". With the heavy migration in the latter part of the eighteenth century away from the state, Connecticut sent lavish invitations to Europe for more families to settle there.

About that time a severe potato crop failure in Ireland brought four million people to the verge of starvation. It didn't take many inducements for them to accept suggestions or invitations to make their homes in Connecticut. Thousands of them came in the late 1850's although many had come for ten years previously. It is estimated that more than 70,000 Irish came during that period who with their descendants now number more than 200,000.

Since 1880 it is estimated that more than 80,000 Germans have sought residence in various sections of the state. Unlike many other nationalities the Germans seldom live in solid nationality groups but are more intermingled with the already existing population.

Canada has always contributed freely to the population of Connecticut. The English-Canadians have generally come to Hartford or some of the other larger cities in the state, while the French-Canadians have been satisfied to cross over the border separating them from the United States and settle down in some of the Northeastern industrial cities where upwards of seventy thousand of them have been employed in the textile industry.

During the past eighty years a heavy influx of Scandinavians has been registered in Connecticut. The earlier migration was much heavier than the later. It is estimated that upwards of fifty-five thousand persons have come from those nations to the Nutmeg State, about eight per cent from Norway, eleven per cent from Denmark, and eighty-one per cent from Sweden. The majority of them have engaged in the mechanical arts, while some have engaged in gardening and farming.

The Italians have been coming to Connecticut in quite a solid stream over the past eighty years. The greatest influx was during the first sixteen years of the twentieth century. The first and second generation of Italians number approximately more than 300,000 in Connecticut today. While good-sized colonies of them live in many of the cities, most of them are centered around Hartford.

With about an equal distribution in agricultural and industrial pursuits there are about 150,000 former residents of Poland in Connecticut. They have concentrated especially around Bridgeport and New Britain. The factories and industrial plants of Waterbury have employed most of the 40,000 Lithuanians who have come here over the years, while about an equal number from Czechoslovakia have centered around the Bridgeport plants. About 30,000 Magyars (Hungarians) are also established in the state, about nine thousand foreign born living there in 1950.

Unlike most states the town clerk, rather than the county clerk, is the custodian of marriage licenses and records, marriage and death records, and land records. Long before the counties were organized, the town clerks were recording these statistics. Record of wills, inventories and administrations of estates are in the probate districts. These are not always identical with the town.

The Church records are still in the respective churches. If information is desired from them, it may be best to write the town clerk and ask him to help you decide where to seek the data desired.

The census records of the state are all complete. The 1790 census is printed in book form and can be found in most libraries. The later census records are in the National Archives in Washington, D.C. and are available for research. In doing research in the Archives, it may be to your advantage to employ a professional researcher. Write to the National Archives, Washington, D.C. state your problem and ask for suggestions how to proceed.

Some Connecticut towns had a census taken in 1776. Information concerning this may be obtained from the Connecticut State Library, Hartford, Conn.

Bureau of Vital Statistics, State Department of Health, State Office Bldg., Hartford, Conn. 06115, has birth, death and marriage records since 1 July 1897. Earlier similar records are on file in the city or town offices of the respective communities.

Information on divorces may be obtained for a fee in the office of the clerk of the Superior Court in the county where the proceedings were heard.

Naturalization records are on file in the office of the United States Circuit court in Hartford, or in the county offices of the Superior Courts.

The Lutheran and the Episcopal churches have available besides the vital statistics, the christening, baptism, confirmation, entrance and departure dates and burials.

The town clerks also have custody of the land records.

The district courts of the counties are the custodians of wills, inventories and administrations of estates. Sometimes a town constitutes a district. Sometimes several smaller towns are grouped into one probate district. There are 118 districts and 169 towns.

Almost every city or town in the state has printed histories containing a great deal of genealogy especially concerning the early inhabitants. Many family genealogies have also been printed.

A wealth of information on early day families of Connecticut may be found in almost every library. Many books have been published, giving the names of the participants in all of the American wars. Numerous family histories have been printed and are available at most of the libraries, and most of the towns and cities have valuable histories of their founding, growth and progress. Many of the family histories in the libraries are in manuscript form. Many of them have been indexed to facilitate research activities. Information regarding these indexes may be obtained from the libraries if self-addressed, stamped envelopes accompany the request. No research is done by library staff members, but information regarding professional researchers may be given by the libraries.

Town and vital records and genealogical information pertaining to the early days of the state may be obtained from the Public Library, 925 Broad St., Bridgeport 06604; Public Library, 215 Greenwich Ave., Greenwich; Connecticut Historical Society, 1 Elizabeth St., Hartford 06105; State Library, Capitol Ave., Hartford 06101; Public Library, 624 Main St., Hartford 06103; Curtis Memorial Public Library, 175 E. Main St., Meriden 06451; Free Public Library, 133 Elm St, New Haven 06511; Yale University Library, 120 High St., New Haven 06520; The Public Library, New London 06320; Otis Public Library, Norwich 06360; Ferguson Public Library, Broad and Bedford Sts., Stamford 06901; Wilbur L. Cross Library, University of Connecticut, Storrs 06268; Silas Bronson Public Library, 267 Grand St.,

Waterbury 06702. The Godfrey Memorial Library, Berlin Ave., Middletown, Conn. 06457 has one of the best collections of Genealogical material in the state. It is solely a genealogical library.

Among books about Connecticut and its people are the following: John Warner Barber's "Historical Collections," 1836; Edgar L. Heermance's "Connecticut Guide"; Samuel Peters, "General History of Connecticut," 1781.

The various counties of Connecticut are at present divided into the following townships: FAIRFIELD: Bethel, Bridgeport, Brookfield, Darien, Danbury, Easton, Fairfield, Greenwich, Monroe, New Canaan, New Fairfield, Newtown, Norwalk, Redding, Ridgfield, Sheldon, Sherman, Stamford, Stratford, Trumbull, Weston, Westport, Wilton.

HARTFORD: Avon, Berlin, Bloomfield, Bristol, Burlington, Canton, East Granby, East Hartford, East Windsor, Enfield, Farmington, Glastonbury, Granby, Hartford, Hartland, Manchester, Marlborough, New Britain, Newington, Plainville, Rock Hill, Simsbury, Southington, South Windsor, Suffield, West Hartford, Wethersfield, Windsor, Windsor Locks.

LITCHFIELD: Barkhamsted, Bethlehem, Bridgewater, Canaan, Colebrook, Cornwall, Goshen, Harwinton, Kent, Litchfield, Morris, New Hartford, New Milford, Norfolk, North Canaan, Plymouth, Roxbury, Salisbury, Sharon, Thomaston, Torrington, Warren, Washington, Watertown, Winchester, Woodbury.

MIDDLESEX: Chester, Clinton, Cromwell, Deep River, Durham, East Haddam, East Hampon, Essex, Haddam, Killingworth, Middlefield, Middletown, Old Saybrook, Portland, Westbrook.

NEW HAVEN: Beacon Falls, Bethany, Branford, Cheshire, Derby, East Haven, Guilford, Hamden, Madison, Meriden, Middlebury, Milford, Naugatuck, New Haven, North Branford, North Haven, Orange, Oxford, Prospect, Seymour, Southbury, Wallingford, Waterbury, West Haven, Woodbridge, Woolcot.

NEW LONDON: Bozrah, Colchester, East Lynne, Franklin, Griswold, Groton, Lebanon, Ledyard, Lisbon, Lyme, Montville, North Stonington, Norwich, Old Lyme, Preston, Salem, Sprague, Stonington, Waterford.

TOLLAND: Andiver, Bolton, Columbia, Coventry, Ellington, Hebron, Mansfield, Somers, Stafford Tolland, Union, Willington.

WINDHAM: Ashford, Brooklyn, Canterbury, Chaplin, Hampton, Eastford, Killingly, Plainfield, Pomfret, Putnam, Scotland, Sterling, Thompson, Windham, Woodstock.

Connecticut Towns organized before 1800:

FAIRFIELD COUNTY -- Brookfield 1788; Danbury 1684; Fairfield 1639; Greenwich 1640; Huntington 1788; New Fairfield 1740;

Newton 1700; Norwalk 1649; Redding 1757; Ridgefield 1709; Stamford 1648; Stratford 1639; Trumbull 1798; Weston 1717.

HARTFORD COUNTY -- Berlin 1785; Bristol 1747; Canton 1740; East Windsor 1680; Enfield 1681; Farmington 1640; Glastonbury 1690; Granby 1786; Hartford 1635; Hartland 1753; Simsbury 1670; Southington 1779; Suffield 1674; Wethersfield 1635; Windsor 1633.

LITCHFIELD COUNTY -- Barkhamsted 1746; Bethlehem 1787; Canaan 1739; Colebrook 1779; Cornwall 1740; Goshen 1739; Harwinton 1731; Kent 1739; Litchfield 1719; New Hartford 1739; New Milford 1712; Norfolk 1744; Plymouth 1795; Roxbury 1796; Salisbury 1730; Sharon 1732-3; Torrington 1740; Washington 1779; Warren 1786; Watertown 1780; Winchester 1771; Woodbury 1674.

MIDDLESEX COUNTY -- Chatham, 1767; Durham 1698; E. Haddam 1685; Haddem 1662; Killingsworth 1667; Middletown 1653; Saybrook 1635.

NEW HAVEN COUNTY -- Branford 1644; Cheshire 1723; Derby, S. 1675; Guilford 1639; Hamden 1786; Meriden 1796; Millford 1639; New Haven 1638; North Haven 1786; Oxford 1798; Seymour 1672; Southbury 1672; Wallingsford 1669; Waterbury 1686; Walcott 1796; Woodbridge 1786.

NEW LONDON COUNTY -- Bozrah 1786; Colchester 1703; Franklin 1786; Groton 1705; Lebanon 1700; Lisbon 1786; Lyme 1664; Montville 1786; New London 1646; Norwich 1660; Preston 1687; Stonington 1649.

TOLLAND COUNTY -- Bolton 1716; Coventry 1709; Ellington 1786; Hebron 1704; Mansfield 1713; Somers 1734; Stafford 1718; Tolland 1700; Union 1727; Vernon 1716; Willington 1720.

WINDHAM COUNTY -- Ashford 1710; Brooklyn 1786; Canterbury 1690; Hampton 1786; Killingly 1700; Plainfield 1699; Pomfret 1686; Sterling 1794; Thompson 1715; Voluntown 1696; Windham 1689; Woodstock 1749.

Connecticut County Histories

(Population figures to nearest thousand - 1960 Census)

Name	Map Index	Date Formed	Pop. By M	Census Reports Available	Parent County	County Seat
Fairfield	F4	1666	654	1790-80	Original county	Danbury & Bridgeport
Hartford	D2	1666	690	1790-80	Original county	Hartford

(Co Clk has b, m, d & bur rec from 1847. Vital Statistics rec are filed with each town or city clk & copies sent to State of Conn. Board of Health each month. Div rec are at Superior Ct, Hartford, Conn. Pro rec are at dist of Berlin, New Britain, Conn)

Name	Map Index	Date Formed	Pop. By M	Census Reports Available	Parent County	County Seat
Litchfield	E2	1751	120	1790-80	Hartford, Fairfield	Litchfield & Winsted
Middlesex	C3	1785	89	1790-80	Hartford, New London, New Haven	Middletown
New Haven	E3	1666	660	1790-80	Original county	Waterbury & New Haven
New London	B3	1666	186	1790-80	Original county	New London & Norwich

(b, m, & d not kept on Co basis in this state; write to town of occurance; b, m, & d rec from 1659; bur rec from 1893; Clk of Superior Ct in Norwich has div rec; Judge of Pro in Norwich has Pro rec; Deeds from 1659; Town meeting rec from 1659)

Tolland	B2	1786	69	1790–80	Windham . . . . Rockville
Windham	A2	1726	69	1790–80	Hartford, New London . . . . . . Putnam
					& Willimantic

County Map of Connecticut

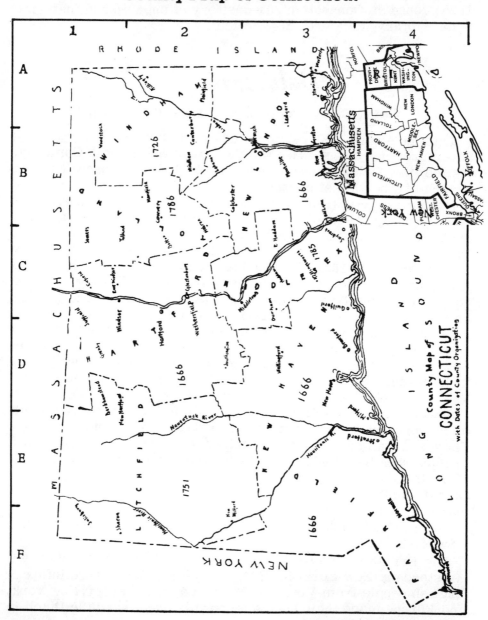

Federal Courts (start 1789). Inventory of Municipal and town Archives, Avon, Berlin, Bloomfield, Newington, North Branford, North Haven, Orange, Oxford, Prospect, Seymour, Southbury, Weston. Guide to Vital Statistics in Church records. Inventory of the Church Archives of Connecticut, Lutheran, Protestant Episcopal. Preliminary Check List of American Portraits 1620-1825, found in Connecticut. Depository of unpublished material, State Library, Hartford, Connecticut.

Delaware

Capital Dover - First State - State 1787 - (1st)

Late in August 1609, Henry Hudson, a British seacaptain and adventurer in the service of the Dutch West India Company, visited the Delaware section en route to the Hudson River in search of a northwest passage.

During a six-year period between 1614 and 1620 a group of sailors under the captaincy of Cornelius Hendricksen, a Dutch navigator, visited the section. As a result of information brought back to Holland by these sailors the Dutch West India Company was organized in 1621. In 1629 this company adopted a charter to grant land in the new world to feudal lords. The following year the company bought land adjoining the Delaware River, and in 1631 David Pietersen de Vries established a camp on Lewes Beach.

Hearing how other European monarchs fostered expeditions and settlements in the new world, the Swedish rulers encouraged the New Sweden Company in outfitting an expedition of two boats. "The Kalmar Nyckel" and "Grip". They arrived at Jamestown, Va., in March 1638, remained there ten days and then continued to Delaware. They established settlements in the rich section south of the present Wilmington, in the extreme north of the colony. They were attacked by the Dutch at different times from 1651 to 1655 when the Swedes were routed from Fort Christina, named after the then twenty-one year old Queen Kristina, daughter of Gustaf Adolf, who lost his life on the battlefield at Lutzen, Germany, in 1632.

The first Finnish colonists came to Delaware in 1656 aboard a Swedish Ship.

The British forces took possession of the Delaware Colony and Amsterdam (New York) in 1664. Two years later a large influx of English people from Virginia, Maryland, New Jersey, New York, and Europe made their homes among the Swedes and the Dutch in

Delaware. From then on conditions among the colonists greatly improved and more unity was established.

Most of the colonists came to the New World for religious as well as material or financial purposes. Churches were among the first buildings erected as each new community was established. The Swedes brought with them religious desires of their groups. The Dutch settlers had in their companies priests of the Reformed church who functioned in chapels erected by their flocks. Many Irish who came after 1698 for the right of worshiping in accordance with the Presbyterian faith gave an early impetus to that body. As early as 1730 many staunch Roman Catholics established themselves in the northern part of Delaware, where the first Catholic chapel was built in 1772 on the Lancaster Pike, going northeast from Wilmington to Philadelphia. Another influx of Catholics came in 1790 when several French families sought rescue here from the West Indies uprisings. Among them were some who since then have played important parts in the financial development of the United States.

Many settlers who first arrived in the northern part of Delaware spread from there into Pennsylvania, Maryland and New Jersey.

When Delaware ratified the Constitution of the United States on 7 December 1787, it became the first state in the Union.

During the Civil War, although a slave state, Delaware was on the side of the regular government.

Because of the slow transportation methods in the early days, the state's three counties were divided into districts, called hundreds. The hundreds correspond to a township.

Among the foreign born the Italians, Poles, Russians, Irish, Germans and English predominate in that order.

The early colonial records of Delaware are scattered. Some are in the archives of the state of New York. After 1681 they were stored in the Archives of Pennsylvania. As the counties exercised full powers as governments, not all of the colonial records went to Pennsylvania. Some are to be found in the Delaware Archives in Dover. Land records after 1785 will be found in the county courthouses and wills also after 1800.

In the Bureau of Vital Statistics, State House, Dover, will be found a record of births, deaths and marriages since 1881. There are some marriages recorded as early as 1847. A record of births was kept from 1861 to 1863.

The State Archivist said in June 1952, ''All extant public records of Delaware and its political subdivisions dated before 1873, other than deeds and mortgages, are in the custody of The Public Archives Commission. Original vital statistics entries to 1913 are also in our custody. It is not possible to list a specific fee for service on these records, since most requests are for photostatic or microfilm copies. Our scale of prices for these is based on the size and number of pages to be copied, and is in line with commercial rates in the area.

"Vital statistics since 1913 are in the custody of the Bureau of Vital Statistics, Dover, Delaware 19901.

"Deeds and mortgages are in the custody of the respective Recorders of New Castle, Kent and Sussex Counties in courthouses in Wilmington, Dover, and Georgetown, Delaware. All service on such records is through those offices.

"The Historical Society of Delaware has a small file of birth, death and marriage records culled from newspaper files which does not in all instances duplicate our own.

"Before 1790 all extant marriage records are from unofficial sources. So also are birth and death records before the Civil War period. Before 1913 coverage was not complete in all catagories for each year."

All Delaware Census records are available with the exception of the entire 1790 Census which is missing.

Books on Delaware:

Israel Acrelius, Swedish Lutheran minister, wrote history of New Sweden about 1714-1791.

Finck, "Lutheran Landmarks and Pioneers in America."

Benjamin Farris, "A History of the Original Settlements on the Delaware." &c," Wilson and Heald, Wilmington, 1846, 312 p.

J. M. Runk & Co., "Biographical and Genealogical History of the State of Delaware" Chambersburg, Pa., 1899, 2 vols.

Amandus Johnson, "The Swedish Settlements on the Delaware, Their History and Relations to the Indians, Dutch and English, 1638-1664," N.Y., U. of Pa. Press per D. Appleton & Co., Agents 1911, 2 vols.

Christopher Ward (Longstreth), "Dutch and Swedes on the Delaware 1609-1664," Philadelphia, University of Pa. Press, 1930, 393 p.

See, "Delaware, The American Guide Series," 1938, pp. 537, 538 for histories of Delaware cities, towns and villages.

Delaware County Histories

(Population figures to nearest thousand - 1960 Census)

Name	Map Index	Date Formed	Pop. By M	Census Reports Available	Parent County	County Seat
Kent	B5	1682	66	1800-80	St. Jones, Name ch in 1682	Dover
New Castle	B5	1673	307	1800-80	Original county	Wilmington
Sussex	C5	1682	73	1800-80	Early 17th Century Horrekill District	Georgetown

See Maryland for Map

Federal Courts (start about 1790). (Delaware has some lists of New Jersey). Inventory of County Archives, Newcastle. Inventory of the Church Archives of Delaware, preprint of Sec. 22. Lutheran Church & 29. Protestant Episcopal. Directory of Church and Religious organizations in Delaware. Depository of unpublished material, Dept. of Archives, State University, Dover, Del.

District of Columbia

Territory of Washington D. C.

organized 1790, Seat of Government 1800

The capital of the United States covers about seventy square miles on the northeast side of the Potomac River, about 38 miles southwest of Baltimore.

The Bureau of Vital Statistics, Health Department, D.C., 300 Indiana Ave, N.W., Washington, D.C. 20001, is the custodian of births from 1871 to the present, and deaths from 1855 to the present, except 1861 and 1862. Custodian of marriages is the Clerk, U. S. District Court for the District of Columbia, Fourth and E Streets, N.W., Washington, D.C. 20001. Custodain of wills is the Register of Wills, Fifth and E Streets, N.W. 20001. In charge of all real estate records and land titles is the Recorder of Deeds, Sixth and D. Streets, N.W. 20004. Census records may be obtained from the U.S. Bureau of the Census, Washington, D.C. 20025. Taxpayer lists are at the office of the Tax Collector, District of Columbia, District Bldg., Washington, D.C. 20004. All cemetery records are kept at the individual cemeteries.

"In 1800," says a historian, "Washington, the new capital, had been recently occupied. It was hardly a village, except on paper, and contained only the Capitol, the White House, two departmental buildings, a few boarding houses. The public buildings were still uncompleted. Mrs. Adams (the wife of President John Adams) found the audience room of the White House convenient for drying clothes, and the representatives met in a temporary building erected in the middle of the unfinished Capitol."

Public buildings in the city were burned by the British during the War of 1812.

The first U.S. Census of the District of Columbia was taken in 1800, but is incomplete. All of the 1810 census records of the district are missing. 1820 and subsequent censuses are available.

The National Society, Daughters of the American Revolution, (DAR) 1176 D. St. N.W., Washington, D.C. 20004 maintain a library of over 40,000 vols., many manuscripts and genealogical records.

The Genealogical Department of the Library of Congress and the National Archives, both Washington, D.C. 20025, are two of the richest sources of genealogical material in the U. S.

The National Genealogical Society, 1921 Sunderland Place, Washington, D.C. 20006, also has considerable material helpful to genealogists.

Genealogists' Check List of the Historical Records Survey, District of Columbia

Inventory of the Church Archives, Protestant Episcopal Church Dio Vol. 1, Washington Cathedral Vol. 2 Roman Catholic Church preprint of inventory of St Patrick's Church and School. Directory of Church and Religious organizations in District of Columbia 1939. Calendar of Alexander Graham Bell correspondence in the Volta Bureau, Washington, D.C. Calendar of the Letters and Documents of Peter Force on the Mecklenburg Declaration of Independence in the Loomis collection. Calendar of the writings of Frederick Douglass in the Frederick Douglass Memorial Home, Anacostia, D.C. Bio-Bibliographical Index of Musicians in the U.S. from Colonial times. Depository of unpublished material, Library of Congress, Washington, D.C.

Florida

Capital Tallahassee - Territory 1822 - State 1845 - (27th)

Maps existing in Spain for nearly five centuries indicate that the contours of the American continent were already then known there. Ponce de Leon, the intrepid Spanish explorer, reached the Florida coast as early as 1513. Landing there on Easter Sunday, he called the new land Florida, from the Spanish name for Easter, Pascua Florida. Attempts to locate Spanish settlers in the new region a few years later failed when the colony was routed by the Indians.

Efforts by the French Huguenots to establish colonies on the south bank of the St. John's river in 1564 had an encouraging beginning but ended in disaster in a couple of years.

In the 1763 peace treaty of Paris, which ended the Seven Years' War, in which the British and the Prussians fought France, Spain and Austria, all her North American possessions east of the Mississippi were ceded by France to Britain. In the same treaty Spain traded Florida to Britain for Havana.

That same year a proclamation by the King of England established among other American provinces, East and West Florida. The two sections were divided by the Chattahoochee and the

Appalachicola rivers.

Twenty years later, the Florida sections were returned to Spain in the treaty ending the Revolutionary War in 1783.

West Florida was taken by the United States in 1810 and 1812, and, after many efforts, finally succeeded in 1819 in getting Florida by promising to pay indemnities to her citizens who had been damaged by Spain. The section embracing West Florida was added to Louisiana, Mississippi, and Alabama.

In 1821 about eight thousand whites lived in Florida, most of them Spaniards, although there were a goodly number of Anglo-Saxons. As early as 1740 many British, Scotch and Irish populated the Cumberland and the Shenandoah valleys and spread through every southern state east of the Mississippi. The early population in the Deep South was predominantly of Irish ancestry. They were the ''Okies'' of the early days. They built Jacksonville in 1822, Quincy in 1825, Monticello in 1828, Marianna and Apalachicola in 1829, and St. Joseph in 1836. Many wealthy people established their homes in Florida, but their bad treatment of the Indians caused the Seminole wars during 1835-42.

A considerable number of Greeks from southern Greece and the Dodecanese Islands moved into Florida as early as 1820. As expert sponge-divers they have established themselves as energetic and successful citizens. Religiously they are affiliated with the orthodox Greek Catholic Church.

The first railroad in the state was built in 1831 and extended from Tallahassee to St. Marks. The middle section of Florida was settled about 1820 by former settlers from Virginia, North Carolina, and South Carolina. Most of the people who came to East Florida from 1845 to 1860 had lived in Georgia, Alabama, and North and South Carolina.

Florida became a territory of the United States on 30 March 1822, from which time her county records begin. She became a state on 3 March 1845, the twenty-seventh state to join the Union.

During the eighteen-forties the population of Florida increased about fifty-six per cent. The census of 1860 shows the white population to have increased to seventy-eight thousand. At that time there were in the state seventy seven plantations embracing more than one thousand acres each. The 1860 census also showed that about half the population was native born while twenty-two per cent had come from Georgia, eleven per cent from South Carolina and five per cent from North Carolina.

In 1912 a large group of Lutheran Slovaks moved from Cleveland, Ohio, onto a large tract of land they had purchased in Seminole county where they established a communal agricultural and poultry business.

The Bureau of Vital Statistics, State Board of Health, P.O. Box

210, Jacksonville, Florida 32201, is custodian of the following records: Incomplete records of births from 1865 to 1917, and births from 1917 to date; incomplete records of deaths from 1877 to 1917, and deaths from 1917, to date. Marriages from June 1927 to date; divorce records also available there.

Some birth and death records are in the city or county health departments from 1893 to 1913 in Jacksonville; from 1897 to 1916 in Pensacola; prior to 1917 in St. Petersburg, and varied records in Ocala, in custody of H. C. Sistrunk, Box 502, Ocala, Florida 32670.

The office of the County Judge of the bride's home county has marriage records prior to June 1927. These offices also have the records of wills of their constituents.

Divorce records before 1927 are filed in the office of the clerk of the Circuit Court where divorce was granted. Similar records before or after 1927 in the mentioned office of the Bureau of Vital Statistics.

Naturalization records are in the federal, circuit and district courts at Pensacola and Jacksonville.

Well-indexed records of land claims, prior to Florida's statehood are at the Land Office, Department of Agriculture, Tallahassee, Florida 32301.

The first U.S. Census of Florida was taken in 1830. Two census records taken by the state in April 1935 and April 1945 are in the office of the Commissioner of Agriculture, Tallahassee, Florida 32301.

Libraries: Fort Lauderdale Public Library, 100 S.E. River Dr., Fort Lauderdale 32202, (Broward); Jacksonville Free Public Library, 101 E. Adams St., Jacksonville 33301, (Duval); Miami Public Library, 1 E Central Ave., Orlando 32801, (Orange); Florida State Library, Supreme Court Bldg., Tallahassee 32301, (Leon); Tampa Public Library, 102 E Seventh Ave., Tampa 33602, (Hillsborough).

Florida County Histories

(Population figures to nearest thousand - 1960 Census)

Name	Map Index	Date Formed	Pop. By M	Census Reports Available	Parent County	County Seat
Alachua	B4	1824	74	1830-80	Duval, St. John	Gainesville

(Co Clk has div & civ ct rec also deeds, etc; b, d rec are kept by Bureau of Vital Statistics in Jacksonville; Co Judge has m & pro rec)

Name	Map Index	Date Formed	Pop. By M	Census Reports Available	Parent County	County Seat
Baker	B4	1861	7	1870-80	New River	MacClenny
Bay	A2	1913	67		Calhoun, Washington	Panama City

(Co Clk has div & civ ct rec from 1913)

Name	Map Index	Date Formed	Pop. By M	Census Reports Available	Parent County	County Seat
Benton		1843		1850	Alachua (Now Hernando)	
Bradford	B4	1861	12	1870-80	"New River" up to 1861	Starke

(Co Clk has div & civ ct rec from 1875)

Name	Map Index	Date Formed	Pop. By M	Census Reports Available	Parent County	County Seat
Brevard	C5	1855	111	1860-80	"St. Lucas" up to 1855	Titusville

Broward   E5   1915   334   Dade, Palm Beach ••••• Ft. Lauderdale
     (Co Judge has m & pro rec from 1915; Clk cir ct has div & civ ct rec from
     1915; Clk Ct of Rec has crim rec from 1915)
Calhoun   A2   1836   7   1840–80   Franklin, Washington, Jackson • Blountstown
Charlotte   D4   1921   13   DeSoto •••••••••••••• Punta Gorda
     (Co Clk has div & civ ct rec from 1921)
Citrus   D4   1887   9   Hernando ••••••••••••••• Inverness
Clay   B4   1858   20   1860–80   Duval •••••••••• Green Cove Springs
Collier   E4   1923   16   Lee, Monroe •••••••••••••• Naples
     (Co Judge has m & pro rec from 1923; Circuit Ct has div rec from 1923 also
     Civil ct rec)
Columbia   B4   1832   20   1840–80   Alachua •••••••••••••••• Lake City
Dade   E5   1836   935   1840–80   Monroe, St. Lucie (1855) •••••• Miami
DeSoto   D4   1887   12   Manatee •••••••••••••••• Arcadia
     (Bureau of vital statistics has b & d rec from 1917, also div rec from 1887;
     Co Judge has m & pro rec from 1887; Clk of Ct has civ ct rec from 1887)
Dixie   B3   1921   4   Lafayette ••••••••••••• Cross City
Duval   B4   1822   455   1830–80   St. John •••••••••••••• Jacksonville
     (Clk cir ct has div, cir ct rec and deeds & mtg from 1921, Soldiers & Sailors
     rec book from 1920; State board of Health has b & d rec; Co Judge, CH, has m
     & pro rec)
Escambia   A1   1821   174   1830–80   One of two original counties ••• Pensacola
Flagler   B5   1917   5   St. John, Volusia •••••••••• Bunnell
     (Co Clk has div and civ ct rec from 1917; Co Judge has m & pro rec from 1917)
Franklin   B2   1832   7   1840–80   Jackson •••••••••••••• Apalachicola
Gadsden   A3   1823   42   1830–80   Jackson ••••••••••••••••••Quincy
     (Clk of Cir ct has div & civ ct rec; Bureau of Vital Statistics has b, d rec; Co
     Judge has m & pro rec)
Gilchrist   B4   1925   3   Alachua ••••••••••••••••• Trenton
     (Clk of Cir Ct has div & civ ct rec)
Glades   D4   1921   3   DeSoto •••••••••••••• Moore Haven
Gulf   B2   1925   10   Calhoun •••••••••••••• Wewahitchka
     (Co Clk has div and civ ct rec from 1925)
Hamilton   A4   1827   8   1830–80   Duval •••••••••••••••••••• Jasper
     (Clk of Cir Ct has div & civ Co rec; Bureau of Vital Statistics has b rec; Co
     Judge has m & pro rec; State Health dept has d rec)
Hardee   D4   1921   12   DeSoto •••••••••••••••• Wauchula
Hendry   D4   1923   8   Lee ••••••••••••••••••• LaBelle
Hernando   C4   1850   11   1870–80   Alachua (Formerly Benton) •••Brooksville
     (Clk of Cir Ct has div rec & civ ct rec; b rec are with Health dept; Co Judge
     has m, d, bur & pro rec)
Highlands   D4   1921   21   DeSoto •••••••••••••••••• Sebring
     (Clk of Cir Ct has div, pro, m, & civ ct rec from 1921; Bureau of Vital
     Statistics has b, d, & bur rec)
Hillsborough C4   1834   398   1840–80   Alachua, Monroe ••••••••••••• Tampa
Holmes   A2   1848   11   1850–80   Walton, Washington, Calhoun ••• Bonifay
Indian Rivers C5   1925   25   St. Lucie •••••••••••••• Vero Beach
     (Clk of Cir Ct has div, civ ct rec also Declarations of Domicile all from
     1925; Co Health dept has b & d rec; Co Judge has m & pro rec)
Jackson   A2   1822   36   1830–80   Escambia ••••••••••••••••• Marianna
     (Clk of Cir Ct has div & civ ct rec from 1850; Co Judge's office has m rec)
Jefferson   A3   1827   10   1830–80   Leon ••••••••••••••••• Monticello
Lafayette   B3   1856   3   1860–80   Madison •••••••••••••••••• Mayo
     (Clk of Ct has div rec from 1902, civ ct rec from 1907; Co Judge has b, m, &
     pro rec; Health Dept has d & bur rec)
Lake   C4   1887   57   Orange, Sumter ••••••••••••• Tavares
Lee   D4   1887   55   Monroe •••••••••••••••••• Ft. Myers
Leon   A3   1824   74   1830–80   Gadsden •••••••••••••••• Tallahassee
Levy   B4   1845   10   1850–80   Alachua, Marion ••••••••••• Bronson
     (Clk of Ct has div & civ ct rec from 1850; Co Judge has m & pro rec from
     1850; Bureau of Vital Statistics has d & bur rec)
Liberty   B2   1855   3   1860–80   Franklin, Gadsden ••••••••••• Bristol

Madison   A3   1827   14   1830-80   Jefferson .... Madison
    (Bureau of Vital Statistics, Jacksonville, Fla. has b, d, & bur rec; Clk of Ct has
    div & civ ct rec also deeds from 1838; Co Judge has m & pro rec)
Manatee   D4   1855   69   1860-80   Hillsboro .... Bradenton
Marion   B4   1844   52   1850-80   Alachua, Hillsboro, Mosquito . . . Ocala
Martin   D5   1925   17   Palm Beach, St. Lucie .... Stuart
    (Clk of cir ct has deeds & mtg from 1925)
Monroe   E5   1824   48   1830-80   St. Johns .... Key West
Mosquito   C3   1824   1830-40   (Changed to Orange, 1845)
Nassau   A4   1824   17   1830-80   Duval .... Fernandina Beach
New River   1858   1860   (Changed to Bradford 1861)
Okaloosa   A1   1915   61   Santa Rosa, Walton .... Crestview
Okeechobee D5   1917   6   Osceola, Palm Beach, St. Lucie ..Okeechobee
    (Clk of Ct has div & civ ct rec)
Orange   C5   1824   264   1850-80   (changed from Mosquito, 1845),
                                        Sumter (1871) .... Orlando
    (Bureau of Vital Statistics has b, m, d, bur & div rec; Co Judge has Pro rec;
    Clk Co Judges Ct & small Claims Ct has civ ct rec)
Osceola   C5   1887   19   Brevard, Orange .... Kissimmee
Palm Beach D5   1909   228   Dade .... West Palm Beach
Pasco   C4   1887   37   Hernando .... Dade City
    (Clk of Ct has div & civ ct rec from 1887)
Pinellas   C4   1911   375   Hillsboro .... Clearwater
Polk   C4   1861   195   1870-80   Brevard, Hillsboro (Boundaries changed
                                        1871) .... Bartow
Putnam   B4   1849   32   1850-80   Alachua, Marion, Orange,
                                        St. Johns .... Palatka
St. Johns   B5   1821   30   1830-80   One of two original cos ... St. Augustine
St. Lucas   C4   1844   (changed to Brevard 1855)
St. Lucie   D5   1844   39   1850   Brevard .... Fort Pierce
    (Clk of Ct has div & civ ct rec from 1905; Co Judge has m & pro rec from
    1905; Bureau of Vital Statistics has b rec)
Santa Rosa A1   1842   30   1850-80   Escambia .... Milton
    (Clk of cir ct has b, div, & civ ct rec from 15 July 1869; Co Judge has m rec
    from 1869) (Ct House burned 1869)
Sarasota   D4   1921   77   Manatee .... Sarasota
    (Clk of Ct has div & civ ct rec from 1921; Health Dept has b, d & bur rec from
    1921; Co Judge has m & pro rec from 1921)
Seminole   C5   1913   55   Orange . . . . Sanford
    (Co Clk has civ ct rec from 1915)
Sumter   C4   1853   12   1860-80   Marion, Orange .... Bushnell
    (Clk of cir ct has div and civ ct rec 1900; Co Judge has m & pro rec 1900)
Suwannee   B4   1858   15   1860-80   Columbia .... Live Oak
    (Clk of Ct has some b rec, m, div & civ ct rec from 1858)
Taylor   B3   1856   13   1860-80   Madison .... Perry
Union   B4   1921   6   Bradford .... Lake Butler
    (Clk of Ct has div & civ ct rec)
Volusia   B5   1854   125   1860-80   St. Lucas . . . . DeLand
    (Clk of Ct has div & civ ct rec; Bureau of Vital Statistics & Health Dept. has
    b, d & bur rec; Co Judge has m & pro rec)
Wakulla   B3   1843   5   1850-80   Leon .... Crawfordville
    (Co Clk has div & civ ct rec from 1843)
Walton   A2   1824   16   1830-80   Jackson .... De Funiak Springs
Washington A2   1825   11   1830-80   Jackson, Walton .... Chipley

Genealogists' Check List of the Historical Records Survey, Florida

Federal Courts (start 1821). Inventory of County Archives,
Charlotte, Clay, Collier, Duval, Flagler, Hardee, Hendry, Leon,
Okaloosa, Pinellas, Sarasota, Wakulla. Transcription of St.

County Map of Florida

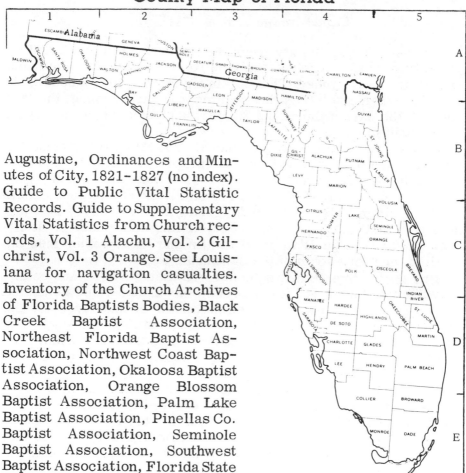

Augustine, Ordinances and Minutes of City, 1821-1827 (no index). Guide to Public Vital Statistic Records. Guide to Supplementary Vital Statistics from Church records, Vol. 1 Alachu, Vol. 2 Gilchrist, Vol. 3 Orange. See Louisiana for navigation casualties. Inventory of the Church Archives of Florida Baptists Bodies, Black Creek Baptist Association, Northeast Florida Baptist Association, Northwest Coast Baptist Association, Okaloosa Baptist Association, Orange Blossom Baptist Association, Palm Lake Baptist Association, Pinellas Co. Baptist Association, Seminole Baptist Association, Southwest Baptist Association, Florida State Association of Old Line Baptist, composed of Missionary Baptist churches. Translation and transcription of church Archives of Florida, Roman Catholic records, St. Augustine Parish white baptisms 1784-1792. A preliminary list of religious bodies in Florida. Guide to Depository of Manuscripts Collection in the U.S. - Florida, a list of the material in the Austin Carey Memorial Collection in the University of Florida. A preliminary Short-Title check list of books, pamphlets and broadsides printed in Florida 1784-1860. Check list of records required of county officials duly appointed or elected. Check list of records required by law in Florida counties. Spanish land grants in Florida, Vol. 1 unconfirmed claims, Vol. 2 confirmed claims A-C, Vol. 3 Confirmed Claims D-J, Vol. 4 Confirmed Claims K-R, Vol. 5 Confirmed Claims S-Z. Depository of Unpublished material, Dept. of Archives, Tallahassee, Florida.

Georgia

Capital Atlanta - State 1788 - (4th)

For one hundred sixty years or more the French and the Spanish were playing a gigantic game of chess with the dominance of Georgia as the prize. This continued from 1540 to about early in 1700. When South Carolina became a royal province, the land between the Savannah and the St. Mary's rivers was set aside for a new British colony.

It was the practice in England at that time to imprison individuals unable to pay their debts. This practice irked a humanitarian army officer and member of Parliament, James Oglethorpe, who conceived the idea of rehabilitating these poor people by taking them to the New World, giving them a tract of land and assisting and guiding them in establishing their homes. He induced King George II to grant to him and twenty other men the English territory south of the Savannah.

With thirty-five families he arrived there in 1733 and established a community at the mouth of the Savannah, which he named after the river. Halfway between the mouth of that river and the southern border of South Carolina they established Augusta in 1734. In the meantime persecuted Protestants in Europe had been invited to come to the colony. At first Roman Catholics were refused to enter the new country.

About 1738 Swiss, German, Italian, Scottish Highlanders, Salzburger, and Moravian settlers had arrived in Georgia. In 1739 another community called Frederica was established on the south banks of the Altamaha. Two years later Georgia was divided into two counties - north of the Altamaha was called Savannah, and south of that river Frederica.

Many of the Moravians had come from North Carolina to Spring Place and New Echota. Unsuccessful in their desire to convert the Indians to their faith, the Moravians later moved from Georgia to Pennsylvania, where they increased rapidly in Bethlehem and Nazareth.

Many of the Presbyterians who came to Georgia as Scottish Highlanders settled in Darien, which they renamed New Inverness In 1752 a group of Massachussetts Puritans came to Midway.

Georgia became a royal province in 1752. The colony claimed all of the land between North Carolina and Florida, and the Atlantic and the Mississippi.

The first counties in Georgia were formed in 1777. These counties covered only a fraction of the land claimed by the province. They covered the section between the Savannah River and the Oconee and the Altamaha Rivers, and a strip about thirty five miles wide extending from the Altamaha to the Florida border. In 1790 there were eleven counties as follows, from north to south: Franklin, Wilks, Greene, Richmond, Burke, Washington, Effingham, Chatham, Liberty, Glyn, and Camden. These counties included the area now occupied by the present counties as follows:

Franklin: the south three-fourths of Stephens, Franklin, Banks, Jackson, all of Oconee but the southern most tip, all of Clarke but the southern fourth, all of Madison but the southeast tip, Hart and Elbert.

Wilks: the southern tip of Clarke, Oglethrope, the southeastern tip of Madison, Wilkes, Lincoln, Columbia, McDuffie, Glascock, Warren, all but west fourth of Taliaferro, and small piece of east corner of Greene.

Greene: small south corner of Oconee, small west corner of Oglethorpe, all of Greene but small north triangle, west fourth of Taliaferro, all of Hancock but south fourth, triangular small northeast corner of Baldwin.

Richmond: triangular northeast fourth of Jefferson and Richmond.

Burke: all of Jefferson but southwest triangular quarter of northeast triangular quarter, Burke, all of Jenkins but southwest third, and northern triangular half of Screven.

Washington: south fourth of Hancock, triangular small southeast corner of Baldwin, Washington, southwest quarter of Jefferson, Johnson, east third of Laurns, east triangular half of Montgomery, Emanual, southeast quarter of Jenkins, Bulloch, Bryan, and west half of Tattnall, and Toombs.

Effingham: the southern half of Screven, and Effingham.

Chatham: Chatham, and southern half of Bryan.

Liberty: eastern half of Tattnall, Liberty Long, and McIntosh.

Glyn: eastern half of Wayne, Glynn, and northeastern third of Brantley.

Camden: southeastern third of Brantley, eastern half of Charlton, and Camden.

Today Georgia has 159 counties. Only nineteen states have a larger area.

In 1798 the Territory of Mississippi was created from the western half of Georgia. Later that territory was formed into the states of Alabama and Mississippi.

Georgia ratified the federal constitution on 2 January 1788 and thus became the fourth state in the union.

Many settlers in Virginia and the Carolinas were attracted to Georgia by the early land lotteries. Families who had lived in the territory for at least one year were permitted to draw for acreages as large as 400 acres. Such lotteries, the participant lists of which are now in the office of the Secretary of State, were held in 1803, 1806, 1819, 1827, and 1832.

Division of Vital Statistics, State Department of Public Health, 1 Hunter St., S.W., Atlanta, Georgia 30303, has on file birth and death records since 1 January 1919. Atlanta and Savannah city health offices have similar records of earlier dates.

The county clerk or the clerk of the Ordinary Court have records of marriages performed in that county.

Records of divorce actions are kept by Superior Court clerk in county where granted. They also have Civil Court records.

Naturalization records are filed in the office of the Superior Court in county where hearing was held. Similar records in the office of the clerk of the federal district courts in Atlanta and Savannah.

The deeds to lands are recorded in the office of the Court of Ordinary where land is located. Abstracts of land grants are furnished for a fee in the office of the clerk of the Secretary of State.

Wills are recorded in the office of the clerk of the Court of Ordinary in county where testator resided.

Libraries: Carnegie Public Library, 215 No. Jackson St., Albany 31701, (Dougherty); Public Library, 126 Carnegie Way, (Genealogy), Atlanta 30303, (Fulton); Georgia State Dept. of Archives and History Library, Rhodes Memorial Hall, 1516 Peachtree Rd., Atlanta 30309, (Fulton), has thousands of valuable early records, deeds, and marriage certificates and personal histories of early residents. Also many volumes of Georgia colonial history; W. C. Bradley Memorial Library, (Chattahoochee Valley History), Bradley Dr., Columbus 31907, (Muscogee); Washington Memorial Library, 1190 Washington Ave., Macon 31204, (Bibb); Georgia Historical Society Library, 501 Whitaker St., Savannah 31401, (Chatham); Savannah Public Library. 2002 Bull St., Savannah 31401, (Chatham).

Georgia County Histories

(Population figures to nearest thousand - 1960 Census)

Name	Map Index	Date Formed	Pop. By M	Census Reports Available	Parent County	County Seat
Appling	D3	1818	13	1820-80	Creek Indian Lands	Baxley

(Rec begin 1879; some 1859; Ordinary office has b, m, d & bur rec; Clk of Ct has div, pro and civ ct rec)

Atkinson	E3	1917	6		Coffee, Clinch	Pearson

(Clk of sup ct has div, pro & civ ct rec from 1919; Clk Ord has b & d rec from 1928, m rec from 1919)

Bacon	D3	1914	8		Appling, Pearce, Ware	Alma

(Clk of Sup Ct has div, civ ct rec & deeds all from 1915; Ord office has b, m, d & pro rec from 1915)

Baker   E1   1825   5   1830-80   Early .... Newton
  (Rec begin 1874)
Baldwin   C2   1803   34   1820-80   Creek Indian Lands .... Milledgeville
  (Co clk has b, m, d, bur, div, pro, civ ct rec from 1861)
Banks   A2   1858   6   1860-80   Franklin, Habersham .... Homer
  (Clk of Sup Ct has d, div, & civ ct rec; Ord office has b & m rec)
Barrow   B2   1914   14   Jackson, Walton, Guinett ...... Winder
Bartow   A1   1861   28   1870-80   Changed from Cass 1861 .. Cartersville
  (Clk of Ct has div rec from 1862, civ ct rec from 1869 & deeds from 1837;
  Some rec destroyed CW)
Ben Hill   D2   1906   14   Irwin, Wilcox .... Fitzgerald
Berrien   E2   1856   12   1860-80   Lowndes, Coffee, Irwin ..... Nashville
  (Clk of Ct has div & civ ct rec from 1856; Ord office has b & d rec from 1919
  & m & pro rec from 1856)
Bibb   C2   1822   141   1830-80   Jones, Monroe, Twiggs, Houston .. Macon
Bleckley   C2   1912   10   Pulaski .... Cochran
  (Clk of Ct has div, pro & civ ct rec)
Brantley   E3   1920   6   Charlton, Pierce, Wayne .... Nahunta
  (Clk of Ct has b, div, pro & civ ct rec from 1921)
Brooks   E2   1851   15   1860-80   Lowndes, Thomas .... Quitman
Bryan   D4   1793   6   1820-80   Effingham, Liberty .... Pembroke
  (Ord Ct rec lost 1866)
Bulloch   C4   1796   24   1820-80   Franklin .... Statesboro
  (Rec believed complete)
Burke   C3   1777   21   1820-80   St. George Parish .... Waynesboro
  (Fire 1870; one will bk, one deed bk saved)
Butts   B2   1825   9   1830-80   Henry, Monroe .... Jackson
Calhoun   D1   1854   7   1860-80   Baker & Early .... Morgan
  (Early rec lost; first m rec begin 1880)
Camden   E4   1777   10   1820-80   St. Mary, St. Thomas ...... Woodbine
  (Fire 1870, only one book lost-Will rec "B" between years 1828-1860 - all
  others intact & legible); Clk of Ct has div & civ ct rec; Ct of Ord has b, m,
  d, and pro rec; Ct of Ord has m, wills rec; Clk of Sup Ct has deed-mortgage
  records)
Campbell   B1   1828   1830-80   Carroll, Coweta - Merged Fulton 1932 ....
Candler   C3   1914   7   Bulloch, Emanuel, Tattnall ..... Metter
  (Clk of Ct has div, civ ct rec and deeds & mortgages from 1915; Ord office has
  m & pro rec from 1915, b from 1919 & d from 1927)
Carroll   B1   1826   36   1830-80   Indian Lands .... Carrollton
  (Clk of Cts has div & civ ct rec; Ord office has b, m, d, bur & pro rec)
Cass   1832   1840-60   Changed to Bartow 1861
Catoosa   A1   1853   21   1860-80   Walker, Whitfield .... Ringgold
  (Clk of Ct has civ ct rec from 1833; div rec from 1853; Office of the Ord has m
  & pro rec from 1853; Health dept. has b & d rec)
Charlton   E3   1854   5   1860-80   Camden, Ware .... Folkston
  (Clk of Ct has div & civ ct rec, also deed rec from 1878; Ord office has b, m, d,
  bur & pro rec)
Chatham   D4   1777   188   1820-80   St. Phillip, Christ Church Parish .Savannah
Chattahoochee C1 1854   13   1860-80   Muscogee, Marion .... Cusseta
Chattooga   A1   1838   20   1840-80   Floyd, Walker .... Summerville
  (Clk of Ct has div rec from early 1900's & civ ct rec; Ord office has b, m, d,
  bur & pro rec)
Cherokee   A2   1832   23   1840-80   Cherokee Lands, Habersham, Hall .. Canton
  (Clk of Ct has div & civ ct rec and deeds from 1833; Ord office has b, m, d,
  bur, and pro rec; deeds comp except bk Q; Wills bks A & B lost)
Clarke   B2   1801   45   1820-80   Jackson, Green .... Athens
  (Clk of Sup Ct has div, deeds & civ ct rec from 1801; Co Dept of Health has
  b, d & bur rec from 1920; Ord Ct has m & pro rec from 1801)
Clay   D1   1854   5   1860-80   Early, Randolph .... Ft. Gaines
Clayton   B2   1858   46   1860-80   Fayette, Henry .... Jonesboro
Clinch   E3   1850   7   1850-80   Ware, Lowndes .... Homerville

(Clk of Sup Ct has ct & deed rec also div & civ ct rec from 1867, voters reg from 1890; Office of Ord has b, m, d, & pro rec)

Cobb   B1   1832   114   1840-80   Cherokee .... Marietta
(Fire 1864; rec lost previously)
Coffee   D3   1854   22   1860-80   Clinch, Irwin, Ware, Telfair ..... Douglas
(Fire 1864 - all lost)
Colquitt E2   1856   34   1860-80   Lowndes, Thomas .... Moultrie
(Clk of Ct has div & civ ct rec; Ord office has b, m, d, bur & pro rec; Fire 1881 - all lost)
Columbia B3   1790   14   1820-80   Richmond .... Appling
Cook   E2   1918   12   Berrien .... Adel
(Clk of Cts has div, pro & civ ct rec from 1919; Ord Ct has b, m, d, & bur rec)
Coweta   B1   1826   29   1830-80   Indian Lands .... Newnan
(Clk of Cts has div & civ ct rec; Office of Ord has b, m, d, bur & pro rec)
Crawford C2   1822   6   1830-80   Houston, Marion, Talbot, Macon . Knoxville
Crisp   D2   1905   18   Dooly .... Cordele
(Clk Sup Ct has div & civ ct rec from 1905)
Dade   A1   1837   9   1840-80   Walker .... Trenton
Dawson   A2   1857   4   1860-80   Lumpkin, Gilmer .... Dawsonville
Decatur   E1   1823   25   1830-80   Early .... Bainbridge
DeKalb   B2   1822   257   1830-80   Fayette, Gwinett, Newton, Henry . Decatur
(Clk of Sup Ct has div & civ ct rec, deed rec from 1842; Ct of Ord has m & pro rec from 1842; CH burned 1842 & 1916)
Dodge   D3   1870   16   1880   Montgomery, Pulaski, Telfair .. Eastman
Dooly   D2   1821   11   1830-80   Indian Lands .... Vienna
(Clk of Sup Ct has div & civ ct rec 1846 & deed rec from 1850; Ord office has b, m, d, bur & pro rec; Fire dest early rec few m left 1848)
Dougherty D2   1852   76   1860-80   Baker .... Albany
(Clk Sup Ct has div & civ ct rec from 1856)
Douglas   B1   1870   17   1880   Carroll, Campbell .... Douglasville
Early   E1   1818   13   1820-80   Creek Indian Lands .... Blakely
(many rec lost; first m bk 1854)
Echols   E3   1858   2   1860-80   Clinch, Lowndes .... Statenville
(most rec burned 1897)
Effingham C4   1777   10   1820-80   St. Mathews, St. Phillips .... Springfield
(Ct of Ord has b & d rec from 1927, m & pro rec from 1790; Clk of Sup Ct has div & civ ct rec from 1777; Some rec lost CW and fire 1890)
Elbert   B3   1790   18   1820-80   Wilkes, Madison .... Elberton
Emanuel   C3   1812   18   1820-80   Montgomery, Bulloch ...... Swainsboro
(Rec believed complete)
Evans   D4   1914   7   Bulloch, Tattnall .... Claxton
(Clk of Cts has b, m, d, bur, div, pro & civ ct rec from 1915)
Fannin   A2   1854   14   1860-80   Gilmer, Union .... Blue Ridge
Fayette   B2   1821   8   1830-80   Indian Lands, Henry ...... Fayetteville
Floyd   A1   1832   69   1840-80   Cherokee, Chattooga, Palding ... Rome
Forsyth   A2   1832   12   1840-80   Cherokee, Lumpkin .... Cumming
Franklin A2   1784   13   1830-80   Cherokee Lands .... Carnesville
(Rec believed complete; prior to 1850 in Ga. Archives)
Fulton   B1   1853   556   1860-80   DeKalb, Campbell .... Atlanta
(Clk of Sup Ct has div & civ ct rec from 1854)
Gilmer   A2   1832   9   1840-80   Cherokee, Union .... Ellijay
Glascock B3   1852   3   1860-80   Warren, Jefferson .... Gibson
(Clk of Ct has div & civ ct rec, also deeds & mortgages)

Glynn   E4   1777   42   1820-80   St. David, St. Patrick ...... Brunswick
(Co Bd of health has b, d & bur rec from 1925; Ct of Ord has m rec from 1845, Administrators, Guardianship & pro rec from 1792; Clk of Sup Ct has div & civ ct rec from 1792; Deeds 1824-1829 burned, all rec to 1818 damaged)
Gordon   A1   1850   19   1850-80   Cass, Floyd .... Calhoun
(Clk of Cts has div & civ ct rec from 1864; Ord office has b, m, d, Bur & pro rec; Rec destroyed 1864)

Grady   E2   1905   18   Decatur, Thomas . . . . Cairo
(Clk of Cts has div & civ ct rec)
Greene   B3   1786   11   1820-80   Washington, Oglethorpe,
                                       Wilkes . . . . Greensboro
(Clk of Sup Ct has div and Civ ct rec from 1786; Ord office has m & pro rec;
Health dept has b & d rec)
Gwinnett   B2   1818   44   1820-80   Cherokee Land, Jackson .. . Lawrenceville
(CH burned 1871; only few rec saved)
Habersham   A2   1818   18   1820-80   Cherokee Lands, Franklin . . . Clarkesville
Hall   A2   1818   50   1820-80   Cherokee Lands, Jackson,
                                       Franklin . . . . Gainesville
(Clk of Cts has div & civ ct rec from 1819; Ct of Ord has m & pro rec;
Health Dept has b, d & bur rec; Tornado leveled CH 1936; many rec lost;
deeds saved)
Hancock   B3   1793   10   1820-80   Greene, Washington . . . . Sparta
(Ct of Ord has b & d rec from 1927, m rec from 1805; Clk of Sup Ct has div
rec from 1879, Pro rec from 1793 & civ ct rec from 1794)
Haralson   B1   1856   15   1860-80   Carroll, Polk . . . . Buchanan
(Clk of Ct has div & civ ct rec)
Harris   C1   1827   11   1830-80   Muscogee, Troup . . . . Hamilton
Hart   A3   1853   15   1860-80   Elbert, Franklin . . . . Hartwell
(Clk of Ct has div & civ ct rec; Office of Ord has b, m, d, bur & pro rec)
Heard   B1   1830   5   1840-80   Carroll, Coweta, Troup . . . . Franklin
(Ct of Ord has b & d rec from 1927 & m & pro rec from 1894; Fire 1894)
Henry   B2   1821   18   1830-80   Indian Lands, Walton . . . . . McDonough
(Some early rec lost; first m 1837)
Houston   C2   1821   39   1830-80   Indian Lands . . . . Perry
(Clk of Sup ct has div & civ ct rec from 1822; Ct of Ord has b, d & bur rec
from 1927 and m rec from 1822)
Irwin   D2   1818   9   1820-80   Indian Land, Coffee, Telfair . . . . Ocilla
Jackson   B2   1796   18   1820-80   Franklin . . . . Jefferson
Jasper   B2   1812   6   1820-80   Baldwin . . . . Monticello
Jeff Davis D2   1905   9   Appling, Coffee . . . . Hazelhurst
(Clk of Sup Ct has div & civ ct rec from 1905)
Jefferson   C3   1796   17   1820-80   Burke, Warren . . . . Louisville
(Rec not complete; deeds 1797-1802; 1865)
Jenkins   C3   1905   9   Bullock, Burke, Emanuel, Screven .. Millen
(Clk of Sup Ct has div & civ ct rec from 1905; Ord office has m & pro rec;
Health dept has b, d & bur rec)
Johnson   C3   1858   8   1860-80   Emanuel, Laurens, Washington. Wrightsville
Jones   C2   1807   8   1820-80   Baldwin, Bibb, Puttnam . . . . Gray
Kinchafoonee   Stewart, changed to Webster 1856
Lamar   C2   1920   10   Monroe, Pike . . . . Barnesville
Lanier   E3   1919   5   Berrien, Lowndes, Clinch . . . Lakeland
(Clk of Sup Ct has div & civ ct rec from 1921; Ord office has b, m, d & pro
rec from 1921)
Laurens   C3   1807   32   1820-80   Montgomery, Washington,
                                       Wilkinson . . . . Dublin
Lee   D2   1824   6   1830-80   Indian Lands . . . . Leesburg
(Clk of Sup ct has m, div & civ ct rec; All rec lost in CH fire 1858)
Liberty   D4   1777   14   1820-80   St. Andrew, St. James, St. Johns . Hinesville
(Early rec lost; first m 1819)
Lincoln   B3   1796   6   1820-80   Wilkes . . . . Lincolnton
Long   D4   1920   4   Liberty . . . . Ludowici
Lowndes   E2   1825   49   1830-80   Irwin . . . . Valdosta
(Ord's office burned, all rec lost to 1869)
Lumpkin   A2   1832   7   1840-80   Cherokee, Habersham, Hall . . . Dahlonega
(Clk of Sup Ct has div & civ ct rec; Ord office has b, m, d & pro rec)
McDuffie   B3   1870   13   1880   Columbia, Warren . . . . Thomson
(Clk of Sup Ct has div rec from 1872; Ord's office has b rec, m rec from 1872;
d rec from 1827 & pro rec from 1872)

McIntosh   D4   1793   6   1820–80   Liberty .... Darien
(Many rec lost during CW; CH fire 1931)
Macon   C2   1837   13   1840–80   Houston, Marion .... Oglethorpe
(CH burned 1857; all rec lost)
Madison   B3   1811   11   1820–80   Clarke, Elbert, Franklin, Jackson,
                                         Oglethorpe .... Danielsville
Marion   C1   1827   5   1830–80   Lee, Muscogee, Stewart ... Buena Vista
(CH fire 1845; all rec lost)
Meriwether   C1   1827   20   1830–80   Troup .... Greenville
Miller   E1   1856   7   1860–80   Baker, Early .... Colquitt
(CH fire 1873, all rec lost)
Milton   B1   1857   1860–80   Cobb, Cherokee, Forsyth
                                         Merged Fulton 1911
Mitchell   E2   1857   20   1860–80   Baker .... Camilla
(Clk of Sup Ct has div rec from 1857 & civ ct rec from 1947; minutes kept
of civ ct rec from 1947 to present not before; CH fire 1869; Sup Ct rec
and some others saved; Address correspondence to Clk of Sup Ct together
with money order in advance & stamped, addressed envelope, or no attention
will be given)
Monroe   C2   1821   10   1830–80   Indian Lands .... Forsyth
(Co Health center has b rec from 1928 & d rec from 1942; Ct of Ord has m &
pro rec from 1824)
Montgomery   D3   1793   6   1820–80   Washington, Laurens, Tattnall,
                                         Telfair .... Mt. Vernon
(Ct of Ord has b & d rec from 1918; m rec from 1807, pro rec from 1793;
Clk of Sup Ct has div & civ ct rec, div rec from time first granted by Sup Ct
instead of legislature to present)
Morgan   B2   1807   10   1820–80   Baldwin, Jasper .... Madison
Murray   A1   1832   10   1840–80   Cherokee .... Chatsworth
(Ct of Ord has b & d rec from 1924, m rec from 1842, pro rec from 1890; Clk
of Sup Ct has civ ct rec from 1834)
Muscogee   C1   1826   159   1830–80   Creek Lands, Harris, Lee,
                                         Marion .... Columbus
Newton   B2   1821   21   1830–80   Henry, Jasper, Morgan, Walton .. Covington
(Clk of Sup Ct has div, civ ct & land deeds 1822, also Army and Navy rec 1917)
Oconee   B2   1875   6   1880   Clarke .... Watkinsville
Ogelthorpe   B3   1793   8   1820–80   Clarke, Green, Wilkes ..... Lexington
(CH fire 1941; Ord & other rec saved; deeds complete) (Original 1800 census
of Oglethorpe Co. Ga. filed in Clk of Sup Ct Office at Lexington, Ga.)
(CH fire 1941; Ord and other rec saved; deeds complete)
Paulding   B1   1832   13   1840–80   Cherokee lands, Carroll, Cobb .. Dallas
(m rec from 1832; wills 1865; deeds from 1848)
Peach   C2   1924   14   Houston, Macon .... Fort Valley
Pickens   A2   1853   9   1860–80   Cherokee, Gilmer .... Jasper
(Clk of Sup Ct has div, pro, & criminal ct rec from 1854)
Pierce   E3   1857   7   1860–80   Appling, Ware .... Blackshear
(Ct of Ord has b rec from 1926, m rec from 1875, d rec from 1924; Clk of
Sup Ct has div & civ ct rec from 1875; CH fire 1874)
Pike   C2   1822   7   1830–80   Monroe .... Zebulon
Polk   B1   1851   28   1860–80   Paulding .... Cedartown
Pulaski   D2   1808   8   1820–80   Laurens, Dodge, Dooly,
                                         Houston ... Wilkerson and Hawkinsville
(Clk of Sup Ct has civ ct rec from 1850 & deeds from 1810; Office of Ord
has m, div & pro rec from 1810, b rec from 1935, d rec from 1920)
Putnam   B2   1807   8   1820–80   Baldwin .... Eatonton
(Clk of Sup Ct has div & civ ct rec from 1807; Office of Ord has b, m, d,
bur & pro rec)
Quitman   D1   1858   2   1860–80   Randolph, Stewart ...... Georgetown
(Rec apparently lost; first m 1919)
Rabun   A2   1819   7   1830–80   Cherokee Lands, Habersham ... Clayton
Randolph   D1   1828   11   1830–80   Baker, Lee .... Cuthbert

Richmond   B3 1777 136 1820-80 St. Paul Parish . . . . Augusta
Rockdale   B2 1870 11   1880   Henry, Newton . . . . Conyers
Schley   D2 1857 3   1860-80 Marion, Sumter . . . . Ellaville
(Clk of Sup Ct has b, d & bur rec from 1927, m rec from 1858 & div & civ ct rec from 1857, also pro rec)
Screven   C4 1793 15   1820-80 Burke, Effingham . . . . Sylvania
(First m list 1822; some deeds 1793; minute bks 1811. Co clk has div and civ ct rec from 1794 to present. Also Land Grant Plats, 1794 to present. Writ bks back to early 1800's and Criminal Crt rec way back. Ordinary's office - H. Lee Moore, Screven Co, Sylvania, Ga 30467 has b, m, d, bur and prob recs. Recs in Clk's and Ordinary's Office are on microfilm in Atlanta archives from beginning of Co to 1900.)

Seminole   E1 1920 7   Decatur, Early . . . . Donalsonville
Spalding   B2 1851 35   1860-80 Fayette, Henry, Pike . . . . Griffin
Stephens   A2 1905 18   Franklin, Habersham . . . . Toccoa
Stewart   D1 1830 7   1840-80 Randolph . . . . Lumpkin
(Ct of Ord has b, d & bur rec from 1927 & m rec from 1828; Clk of Sup Ct has div, pro & civ ct rec from 1830)
Sumter   D2 1831 25   1840-80 Lee . . . . Americus
Talbot   C1 1827 7   1830-80 Crawford, Harris, Marion, Macon,
                                    Muscogee . . . . Talbotton
Taliaferro B3 1825 3   1830-80 Green, Hancock, Oglethorpe,
                                    Warren, Wilkes . . . . . . Crawfordville
(Ct of Ord has b rec from 1927, m & pro rec from 1826, d rec from 1920, Land grants from 1750, Church rec from 1802 Clk of Sup Ct has div & civ ct rec 1826)
Tattnall   D3 1801 16   1820-80 Montgomery, Liberty . . . . Reidsville
Taylor   C2 1853 8   1860-80 Crawford, Macon, Marion,
                                    Talbot, Monroe . . . . Butler
(Clk of Sup Ct has div rec & deeds from 1852, also civ ct rec; Office of Ord has b, m, d, bur & pro rec)
Telfair   D3 1807 12   1820-80 Wilkinson, Appling . . . . . . McRae
Terrell   D2 1856 13   1860-80 Lee, Randolph . . . . Dawson
(Clk of Sup Ct has div & civ ct rec from 1956)
Thomas   E2 1825 34   1830-80 Baker, Decatur, Irwin,
                                    Lowndes . . . . Thomasville
(Co Health Dept has b rec from 1920; Ct of Ord has them prior to 1920; Co Health Dept has d rec from 1920; Ct of Ord has pro rec from 1825; Clk of Sup Ct has div & civ ct rec from 1826)
Tift   D2 1905 23   Berrien, Irwin, Worth . . . . . . Tifton
Toombs   D3 1905 17   Emanuel, Tattnall, Montgomery . . Lyons
(Ct of Ord has b, m, d, bur & pro rec from 1905; Clk of Sup Ct has div and civ ct rec from 1905)
Towns   A2 1856 5   1860-80 Rabun, Union . . . . Hiawassee
Treutlen   C3 1917 6   Emanuel, Montgomery . . . . . Soperton
Troup   C1 1826 47   1830-80 Indian Lands . . . . LaGrange
Turner   D2 1905 8   Dooly, Irwin, Wilcox, Worth . . . Ashburn
(Clk of Sup Ct has div & civ ct rec from 1906; Office of Ord has b, m, d, bur & pro rec)
Twiggs   C2 1809 8   1830-80 Wilkinson . . . . Jeffersonville
Union   A2 1832 7   1840-80 Cherokee Lands, Lumpkin . . Blairsville
Upson   C2 1824 24   1830-80 Crawford, Pike . . . . Thomaston
(Clk of Sup Ct has div & civ ct rec from 1824; Office of Ord has b & d rec from 1920, m rec from 1825 and pro rec)
Walker   A1 1833 45   1840-80 Murray . . . . LaFayette
(Clk of the Sup Ct has div & civ ct rec from 1883; CH fire 1883)
Walton   B2 1803 20   1820-80 Cherokee Lands . . . . Monroe
Ware   E3 1824 34   1830-80 Appling . . . . Waycross
(Rec burned 1854)
Warren   B3 1793 7   1820-80 Columbia, Richmond, Wilkes . . Warrenton
Washington C3 1784 19   1820-80 Indian Lands . . . . Sandersville
(Fire destroyed all rec 1855; Sherman destroyed most all 1864)

County Map of Georgia

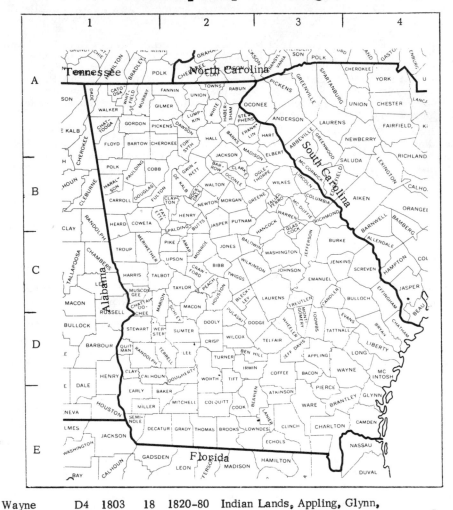

Wayne   D4   1803   18   1820-80   Indian Lands, Appling, Glynn,
                                           Camden .... Jesup
        (Clk of Sup Ct has div & civ ct rec; Office of Ord has b, m, d, bur & pro rec)
Webster   D1   1856   3   1860-80   Changed from Kinchafoonee 1856 . Preston
        (Rec apparently destroyed; first m 1914; Clk of Sup Ct has div & civ ct rec
        from 1903; Office of Ord has b, m, d & bur rec)
Wheeler   D3   1912   5   Montgomery .... Alamo
        (Clk of Sup Ct has div & civ ct rec from 1913; Office of Ord has m & pro rec
        from 1913, b rec from 1927, also d & bur rec)
White   A2   1857   7   1860-80   Habersham .... Cleveland
        (Clk of Sup Ct has div & civ ct rec from 1858, also deeds, mtgs, and discharge
        rec; Office of Ord has b, m, d, bur & pro rec)
Whitfield   A1   1851   42   1860-80   Murray, Walker .... Dalton
        (Office of Ord has b & d rec from 1927, m & pro rec from 1852; Clk of Sup Ct
        has div & civ ct rec from about 1852)
Wilcox   D2   1857   8   1860-80   Dooly, Irwin, Pulaski ..... Abbeville
Wilkes   B3   1777   11   1820-80   Washington .... Washington
        (Early rec perhaps lost; first m rec 1792)

```
Wilkinson   C2   1803    9  1820-80  Creek Cession   . . . . . . . . . . Irwinton
     (CH burned in 1852 and 1924, however property rec were not burned in 1924;
     Clk of Sup Ct has some div rec and property rec from 1852)
Worth       D2   1852   17  1860-80  Dooly, Irwin    . . . . . . . . . . . Sylvester
```

Genealogists' Check List of the Historical Records Survey,
Georgia

Federal Courts (start 1789). Inventory of County Archives, Chatham, Clinch, Cook (includes Tennessee Archives within county), Dougherty, Echols, Jefferson, Lee (Historical sketch Vol. 1, record entries Vol. 2), Muscogee, Richmond. Inventory of municipal & town archives, Adel, Cecil, Lenox, Sparks. Guide to public vital statistic records. Inventory of the Church and Synagogue Archives of Georgia, Atlanta Association of Baptist churches, Fairburn Missionary Baptist association. Classified inventory of Georgia maps. Depository of Unpublished material, University of Georgia, Athens, Georgia.

Hawaii

Capital Honolulu - Territory 1900 - State 1959 - (50th)

Hawaii, 2,100 miles west-southwest of San Francisco, is a 390-mile chain of islets and eight main islands - Hawaii, Kahoolawe, Maui, Lanai, Molokai, Oahu, Kauai, and Niihau. It was discovered in 1778 by Captain James Cook, who named it the Sandwich Islands. It was ruled by native monarchs until 1893, thereafter as a republic until 1898, when it ceded itself to the U.S.

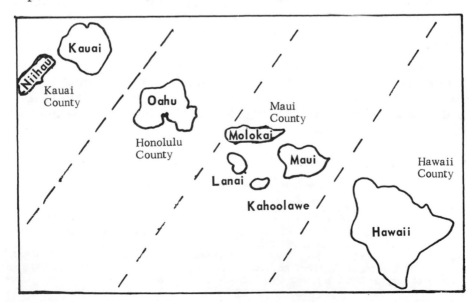

Idaho

Capital Boise - Territory 1863 - State 1890 - (43rd)

Idaho was the last state to be carved from the Oregon Territory. When Idaho became a territory on 3 March 1863, it included all of Montana and nearly all of Wyoming. Montana became a territory in 1864 and Wyoming in 1868. The six original counties of Idaho were formed between 1861 and 1865. It was admitted as a state 3 July 1890, the forty-third state in the union.

The southern part of the state, which borders Utah was the first section to be settled. Mormon emigrants from northern Europe were the first to establish permanent settlements in the region.

A mining boom in 1860 attracted people from the East and Mid-West to the mountainous Idaho valleys. The later construction of large irrigation systems and districts around the long Snake River section about 1910 brought many western and mid-western farm families to take advantage of the farming opportunities in the new state.

Catholic and Protestant churches are represented in most Idaho communities, but more than half of its church membership belongs to the Church of Jesus Christ of Latter-day Saints.

The Division of Vital Statistics, Box 640, Boise, Idaho 83701, has information on births and deaths from 1 July 1911.

The county recorder has records of marriages solemnized in his county. No marriage licenses were required before 11 March 1895.

The county clerk has records of births in that county since 1907. Wills and probate matters are also filed in the clerk's office.

All records pertaining to land transactions are in custody of the county recorder in the respective county court houses.

The first U. S. Census of Idaho was taken in 1870.

Libraries: Public Library, 815 Washington St., Boise 83702, (Ada); Carneigie Library, Nampa 83651, (Canyon); Public Library, Pocatello 83201, (Bannock); Public Library, 434 Second St., E., Twin Falls 83301, (Twin Falls).

Idaho County Histories

(Population figures to nearest thousand - 1960 Census)

Name	Map Index	Date Formed	Pop. By M	Census Reports Available	Parent County	County Seat
Ada	E1	1864	93	1870-80	Boise	Boise
			(Co Clk has m, div & civ ct rec from 1864)			
Adams	D1	1911	3		Washington	Council
			(Co Clk has m, div & civ ct rec from 1911, also some school rec from 1916; Bur of Vit Stat has b & d rec; Pro Judges Office has pro rec)			

County Map of Idaho

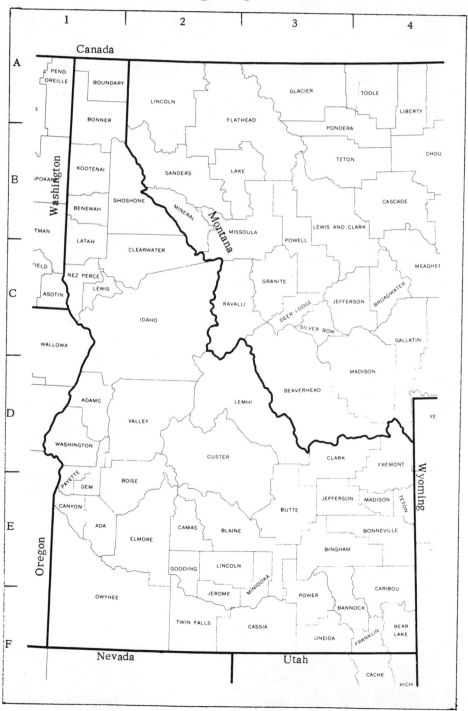

Alturas   1863   1870–80   Original county; discontinued
(Transferred to Lincoln?)
Bannock   F4 1893   49   Oneida, Bear Lake . . . . Pocatello
Bear Lake F4 1875   7   1880   Oneida . . . . Paris
Benewah   B1 1915   6   Kootenai . . . . St. Maries
(Co Clk has m, div & civ ct rec from 1915; Bur of Vit Stat has b & d rec from 1911)
Bingham   E3 1885   28   Oneida . . . . Blackfoot
(Co Clk has b & d rec from 1907, div, pro & civ ct rec from 1895; Bur of Vit Stat has bur rec)
Blaine   E2 1895   5   Alturas . . . . Hailey
(Co Clk has b & d rec from 1907 to 1911, m rec from 1865, div & civ ct rec from 1890)
Boise   E2 1863   2   1870–80 Original county . . . . Idaho City
Bonner   A1 1907   16   Kootenai . . . . Sandpoint
Bonneville E4 1911   47   Bingham . . . . Idaho Falls
(Co Clk has m, div & civ ct rec from 1911)
Boundary A1 1915   6   Bonner . . . . Bonners Ferry
(Co Clk has b, m, d, div & civ ct rec)
Butte   E3 1917   3   Bingham, Blaine, Jefferson . . . . Arco
Camas   E2 1917   .9   Blaine . . . . Fairfield
(Co Clk has m, div & civ ct rec from 1917, bur rec incomplete; Bur of Vit Stat has b & d rec from 1941; Pro Ct has pro rec from 1890)
Canyon   E1 1892   58   Owyhee, Ada . . . . Caldwell
(Co Clk has m, div, pro & civ ct rec from 1891)
Caribou   E4 1919   6   Bannock, Oneida . . . . Soda Springs
(Co Clk has m, div, pro & civ ct rec from 1919; Bur of Vit Stat has b, d & bur rec)
Cassia   F3 1879   16   1880   Oneida . . . . Burley
(Co Clk has m, div & civ ct rec from 1879, also has b rec from 1908 & d rec from 1907; City Clk has bur rec; Pro Judge has pro rec)
Clark   D3 1919   .9   Fremont . . . . Dubois
(Co Clk has m, div, pro & civ ct rec from 1919; Bur of Vit Stat has b, d & bur rec; Pro Ct has pro rec)
Clearwater C2 1911   9   Nez Perce . . . . Orofino
(Co Clk has m, div & civ ct rec from 1911)
Custer   D2 1881   3   Alturas . . . . Challis
(Co Clk has m, div, civ ct & deeds rec from 1872; Bur of Vit Stat has b & d rec; Cem Dist (Challis & Big Lost River) has bur rec; Pro Ct has pro rec)
Elmore   E2 1889   17   Alturus, Ada . . . . Mountain Home
(Co Clk has m rec from 1884, div rec from 1930; Bur of Vit Stat has b & d rec; City has bur rec; Pro Ct has pro rec; Justice Ct has civ ct rec)
Franklin   F4 1913   8   Oneida . . . . Preston
Fremont   D4 1893   9   Bingham, Lemhi . . . . St. Anthony
Gem   E1 1915   9   Boise, Canyon . . . . Emmett
(Co Clk has m, div & civ ct rec from 1915; State House has b & d rec; Pro Ct has pro rec)
Gooding   E2 1913   10   Lincoln . . . . Gooding
Idaho   C2 1864   14   1870–80 Original county . . . . Grangeville
(Co Clk has b & d rec from 1907, div & civ ct rec from 1888, also m rec; Pro Ct has pro rec; Clks of various cem dist have bur rec)
Jefferson E3 1913   12   Fremont . . . . Rigby
(Co Clk has m, div & civ ct rec from 1914, also Deeds and all rec where property is involved from 1886)
Jerome   F2 1919   12   Gooding, Lincoln . . . . Jerome
(Co Clk has m, d & civ ct rec from 1919)
Kootenai   B1 1864   30   1880   Nez Perce . . . . Coeur d'Alene
(Created in 1864, but not organized or officered until 1881. Co Clk has b & d rec from 1907 to 1912, m, div, pro & civ ct rec from 1881)
Latah   B1 1888   21   Nez Perce . . . . Moscow
(Created and organized by U.S. Congressional enactment, said to be the only

Co in the U.S. so created. Co Clk has b & d rec 1907 to 1911, m, div & civ ct rec from 1888; Pro Judge has pro rec)

Lemhi	D3	1869	6	1870-80	Idaho . . . . Salmon
Lewis	C1	1911	4		Nez Perce . . . . Nezperce

(Co Clk has b rec prior to 1911; Bur of Vit Stat since 1911; Co Clk has m, div & civ ct rec from 1911; Pro Judge has pro rec from 1911)

Lincoln	E2	1895	4 ·		Alturas . . . . Shoshone
Madison	E4	1913	9		Fremont . . . . Rexburg

(Co Clk has m, div, pro, & civ ct rec from 1914, also Deeds, Mtgs & Naturalization rec; Dept of Health has b & d rec; Cem Dist has bur rec)

Minidoka	E3	1913	14		Lincoln . . . . Rupert
Nez Perce	C1	1861	28		Original county . . . . Lewiston
Oneida	F3	1865	4		Original county . . . . Malad City

(Co Clk has b rec 1907-1912, m rec 1866, pro rec 1879, div & civ ct rec 1880)

Owyhee	F1	1863	6	1870-80	Original county . . . . Murphy

(Co Clk has b & d rec 1907 to 1913, m rec from 1895, div & civ ct rec from 1864, Naturalization rec 1893-1911)

Payette	E1	1917	12		Canyon . . . . Payette

(Co Clk has div, pro & civ ct rec)

Power	E3	1913	4		Bingham, Blaine, Oneida . . . American Falls
Shoshone	B2	1861	21	1870-80	Original county . . . . Wallace
Teton	E4	1915	3		Madison, Fremont, Bingham . . . Driggs

(Co Clk has m, div & civ ct rec from 1916)

Twin Falls	F2	1907	42		Cassia . . . . Twin Falls
Valley	D2	1917	4		Boise, Idaho . . . . Cascade
Washington	D1	1879	8	1880	Boise . . . . Weiser

(Co Clk has m, div & dist ct rec from 1880)

Genealogists' Check List of the Historical Records Survey, Idaho

Federal Courts (start 1890). Inventory of county archives, Bingham, Boundary, Clark, Kootenai, Lemhi, Minidoka, Nez Perce, Power, Teton. County government in Idaho (Supplementing inventory of county archives). Guide to Public Vital Statistic records, State and county. Directory of churches and religious organizations of Idaho. A check list of Idaho imprints 1839-1890. A short-title check list of books, pamphlets & broadsides printed in Idaho 1839-1890. Depository of unpublished material, Secretary of State, Boise, Idaho.

Illinois

Capital Springfield - American Territory 1783

Territory 1809 - State 1818 - (21st)

Illinois, the transportation center of the United States, was visited by the French explorers in the late sixteen hundreds. Its fertile land appealed to members of various early expeditions passing through during their exploring or hunting or war activities. Many of them returned later and farmed the deep, rich soil along its many rivers and streams.

The southern part was the first to be occupied by permanent settlers. They came from the earlier southern states, including North Carolina, Virginia and Kentucky. Others came from Maryland and Pennsylvania. This condition existed until some years after Illinois had become a state.

Settlers began to arrive in the northern section about 1825. Generally they came from the New England states.

With the beginning of the industrial growth of Illinois, European emigrants flocked there by the thousands every month. They furnished the man-power for the factories and industrial plants that sprung up like mushrooms in the Lake Michigan section. That is one reason why more than forty per cent of the state population centers in that area. They came from Ireland, and the south European countries. Germans flocked there until they formed about one-fourth of the population. They are closely crowded by the Poles, Italians, Swedes and Russians.

Illinois was part of the Northwest Territory which the United States obtained after the Revolutionary War from Great Britain to whom it had been ceded by France in 1763. It became part of the United States in 1783. It was organized as American territory in 1787. It included the land north and west of the Ohio River, east of the Mississippi, and south of Canada. Illinois became the third of five territories and eventual states formed from that area. That was in 1818.

St. Clair became the first county organized in the Illinois Territory. That was in 1790. It extended along the Kaskaskia River. Five years later another county was formed, Randolph, situated farther south along the Kaskaskia and the Mississippi. Farther east, along the Wabash, Edwards county, the third Illinois county, came into existance in 1814. And north of that county, Clark County, also along the Wabash, was formed in 1819. Those four counties were the forerunners of 98 others to be formed in Illinois. The last two of her present 102 counties were formed in 1859, Ford and Douglas.

A communication from the Department of Public Health at Springfield says "Illinois has no provisions for giving genealogical service from the official birth and death records. Our law authorizes the State Department of Public Health, the County Clerks, and the Local Registrars to issue a certified copy of a specified record at the statutory fee of $1.00 per copy. The law forbids us to issue any information from the records except by certified copy as described.

"Marriage records are in sole custody of the County Clerks. Births and deaths from 1877 to 1916 were registered (if at all) by the County Clerks. In a few counties there are some records existing prior to 1877, also in some cities.

"After 1916 all original birth and death certificates have been deposited with this department. A copy of each is deposited with the County Clerk of the county where the event occurred.

"Such genealogical research as is done in the State offices is done in the Illinois State Archives from its miscellaneous historical records. For further information about the services from the Archives communicate with The State Archivist, Archives Building, Springfield, Illinois 62706.

"The best source of the kind of information you request is to be found in a publication by the Historical Records Survey Project of the W. P. A. in May, 1941, entitled, "Guide to Public Vital Statistics Records in Illinois," (137 pp. mimeographed)." (See page VIII)

The United States Census Records are intact from 1820 on. Some schedules are in the State Library in Springfield.

Counties with a population of more than 70,000 have probate courts, in other counties probate matters and wills are handled by the County Clerk. Matters pertaining to real estate are in the offices of the County Recorder of Deeds.

The War Veterans Graves Registration Files contain names of about 350,000 veterans buried in the State of Illinois. It is in alphabetic order, by veterans names, broken down by wars. Also a cemetery listing set up by counties on which veterans' burials are listed and cemeteries in alphabetic order by county. The files carry only those veterans buried within the state. The records are within ninety per cent, possibly more, for veterans buried in Illinois. Each card gives name of veteran, serial, claim, rank, organization, enlistment, discharge, date and place of birth, date and place of death, cemetery where buried, name of town, county, grave description, next of kin and address. A separate index file is carried on peace time soldiers, whose names are not listed on the cemetery listings; also those with service unknown but thought to have had military service. Address: Illinois Veterans Commission, State Office Bldg., 400 Spring St., Springfield, Illinois 62706.

The Newberry Library in Chicago one of the largest in the west, has valuable genealogical volumes. In Springfield the State Historical library is second only to the Newberry Library in genealogical material in Illinois. In most of the counties in the state are libraries with more or less genealogical information.

Libraries: Withers Public Library, 202 E. Washington St., Bloomington 61701, (McLean); Chicago Historical Society Library, North Ave. & Clark St. 60610; Public Library, 78 E. Washington St. 60602; A. N. Marquis Co Library, 210 E. Ohio 60611; (Biographical records); Newberry Library, 60 W. Walton 60606; U. S. Railroad Retirement Board Library, 844 Rush St. 60611; University of Chicago Library, Zone 37, 60637, Chicago (Cook).

Public Library, 457 N. Main St., Decatur 62523, (Macon); Public Library, 9th & State St., East St. Louis 62201, (St. Clair); Public Library, Ill. No. Monroe St., Peoria 61602, (Peoria); Public Library, 215 N. Wyman St., Rockford 61101, (Winnebago); Illinois State Historical Library, Centennial Bldg, (Genealogy), Springfield 62706, (Sangamon).

Illinois County Histories

(Population figures to nearest thousand - 1960 Census)

Name	Map Index	Date Formed	Pop. By M	Census Reports Available	Parent County	County Seat
Adams	C1	1825	68	1830-80	Pike	Quincy

(Co Clk has b & d rec from 1878, m rec from 1825; Cir Clk has div, pro & civ ct rec)

| Alexander | E3 | 1819 | 16 | 1820-80 | Johnson | Cairo |
| Bond | D2 | 1817 | 14 | 1820-80 | Madison | Greenville |

(Co Clk has b, d, pro & civ ct rec from 1877, m rec from 1817)

Boone	A3	1837	20	1840-80	Winnebago	Belvidere
Brown	C2	1839	6	1840-80	Schuyler	Mt. Sterling
Bureau	B2	1837	38	1840-80	Putnam	Princeton

(Co Clk has incom b & d rec from 1848 to 1916, com from 1916, m & deeds rec 1837)

| Calhoun | C1 | 1825 | 6 | 1830-80 | Pike | Hardin |

(Co Clk has b & d rec from 1877, m rec from 1925; Co Registrar has bur rec; Cir Clk has div, pro & civ ct rec)

| Carroll | A2 | 1839 | 20 | 1840-80 | Jo Daviess | Mt. Carroll |
| Cass | C2 | 1837 | 15 | 1840-80 | Morgan | Virginia |

(Co Clk has b rec 1860, m rec 1837, d rec 1878; Cir Clk has div, pro & civ ct rec)

| Champaign | C3 | 1833 | 132 | 1840-80 | Vermilion | Urbana |

(Co Clk has b & d rec from 1916, m & pro rec from 1833)

| Christian | C3 | 1839 | 37 | 1840-80 | Sangamon, Shelby | Taylorville |

(Formerly Dane)

| Clark | C4 | 1819 | 17 | 1820-80 | Crawford | Marshall |

(Co Clk has d rec from 1877, a few b rec from 1877, complete b rec from 1914, m rec from 1820; Cir Clk has div, pro & civ ct rec)

| Clay | D3 | 1824 | 16 | 1830-80 | Wayne, Lawrence, Fayette | Louisville |

(Co Clk has b & d rec from 1878, m rec from 1825; also deeds from 1825 & Veteran Discharges & Entry books; Cir Clk has div, pro & civ ct rec)

Clinton	D2	1824	24	1830-80	Washington, Bond, Fayette, Crawford	Carlyle
Coles	C3	1830	43	1840-80	Clark, Edgar	Charleston
Cook	A4	1831	5130	1840-80	Putnam	Orland Park & Chicago
Crawford	D4	1815	21	1820-80	Edwards	Robinson

(Co Clk has b & d rec from 1878, m rec from 1817, bur rec from 1915; Cir Clk has div, pro & civ ct rec)

Cumberland	C3	1843	10	1850-80	Coles	Toledo
Dane		1839			Name changed in 1840 to Christian County.	
DeKalb	A3	1837	52	1840-80	Kane	Sycamore

(Co Clk has b & d rec from 1878, also Real Estate rec; Cir Clk has div, pro & civ ct rec from 1837)

| DeWitt | A3 | 1839 | 17 | 1840-80 | Macon, McLean | Clinton |

(Co Clk has b & d rec from 1877, m rec from 1839)

| Douglas | C3 | 1859 | 19 | 1860-80 | Coles | Tuscola |

(Co Clk as b, m & d rec from 1870; Cir Clk has div, pro & civ ct rec)

| DuPage | A3 | 1839 | 313 | 1840-80 | Cook | Wheaton |
| Edgar | C4 | 1823 | 23 | 1830-80 | Clark | Paris |

Edwards   D3 1814   8 1820-80 Madison, Gallatin .... Albion
   (Co Clk has m & civ ct rec from 1814, pro rec from 1815, b & d rec from 1877)
Effingham D3 1831   23 1840-80 Fayette, Crawford .... Effingham
Fayette   D3 1821   22 1830-80 Bond, Wayne, Clark, Jefferson .. Vandalia
Ford   B3 1859   17 1860-80 Clark .... Paxton
   (Co Clk has m, pro civ ct rec from 1859, b & d rec from 1878)
Franklin   E3 1818   39 1820-80 White, Gallatin .... Benton
   (Co Clk has b & d rec from 1877, m rec from 1836, pro & civ ct rec from 1838)
Fulton   B2 1823   42 1830-80 Pike .... Lewistown
Gallatin   E3 1812   8 1820-80 Randolph .... Shawneetown
   (Co Clk has b rec 1879, m rec 1830, d rec 1880; Cir Clk has pro rec 1860)

County Map of Illinois

Greene   C2   1821   17   1830-80   Madison . . . . Carrollton
(Co Clk has b & d rec from 1877, m rec from 1821)
Grundy   B3   1841   22   1850-80   LaSalle . . . . Morris
(Co Clk has incom b rec from 1877, incom d rec from 1878, m rec from
1841, pro rec from 1854)
Hamilton   D3   1821   10   1830-80   White . . . . McLeansboro
(Co Clk has b, m, d, bur, div & pro rec from 1821)
Hancock   B1   1825   25   1830-80   Pike, Unorg. Terr. . . . . . . Carthage
Hardin   E3   1839   6   1840-80   Pope . . . . Elizabethtown
Henderson   E3   1841   8   1850-80   Warren . . . . Oquawka
(Co Clk has b & d rec from 1878, few b rec from 1865, m, pro & civ ct rec
from 1841)
Henry   B2   1825   49   1830-80   Fulton . . . . Cambridge
(Co Clk has b & d rec from 1877, m rec from 1843, bur rec from 1839)

Iroquois   B3   1833   34   1840-80   Vermillion . . . . Watseka
(Co Clk has b rec from 1870, m rec from 1876, d rec from 1900, very few
bur rec; Cir Clk has pro & civ ct rec from 1865)
Jackson   E2   1816   42   1820-80   Randolph, Johnson . . . . . Murphysboro
Jasper   D3   1831   11   1840-80   Clay, Crawford . . . . Newton
(Co Clk has b & d rec from 1877, m rec from 1835, also deeds, mortgages
& Original land Entry rec; Cir Clk now has pro rec)
Jefferson   D3   1819   32   1820-80   Edwards, White . . . . Mt. Vernon
Jersey   D2   1839   17   1840-80   Greene . . . . Jerseyville
Jo Daviess A2   1827   22   1830-80   Henry, Mercer, Putnam . . . . . Galena
(Co Clk has b rec from 1877, a few before this date, m rec from 1833, d
rec from 1877; d rec state place of bur; Cir Clk has pro rec from 1830, div
& civ ct rec)
Johnson   E3   1812   7   1820-80   Randolph . . . . Vienna
Kane   A4   1836 208   1840-80   La Salle . . . . Geneva
(Co Clk has b rec from 1870 (Partial), m & d rec from 1837; d rec give place
of bur; Co Clk also has div, pro & civ ct rec)
Kankakee   B3   1853   92   1860-80   Iroquois, Will . . . . Kankakee
(Co Clk has b rec from 1878, m & d rec from 1858; City Clk has bur rec;
Cir Clk has div, pro & civ ct rec)
Kendall   A3   1841   18   1850-80   La Salle, Kane . . . . Yorkville
(Co Clk has b & d rec from 1878, m rec from 1841)
Knox   B2   1825   61   1830-80   Fulton . . . . Galesburg
(Co Clk has b & d rec from 1878, m rec from 1835, pro & civ ct rec from 1832)
Lake   A3   1839 294   1840-80   McHenry . . . . Waukegan
LaSalle   B3   1831 111   1840-80   Putnam, Vermillion . . . . Ottawa
Lawrence   D4   1821   19   1830-80   Crawford, Edwards . . . . Lawrenceville
Lee   A3   1839   39   1840-80   Ogle . . . . Dixon
(Co Clk has b & d rec from 1916, pro and civ ct rec from 1839)
Livingston B3   1837   40   1840-80   LaSalle, McLean . . . . Pontiac
(Co Clk has b rec from 1850, m rec from 1837, d rec from 1877, also bur
rec; b & d rec not compulsory until 1916; Cir Clk has div, pro & civ ct rec)
Logan   C2   1839   34   1840-80   Sangamon . . . . Lincoln
McDonough   B2   1830   29   1830-80   Schuyler . . . . Macomb
(Co Clk has b & d rec from 1877, m rec from 1830; City clk has bur rec;
Cir Clk has div, pro & civ ct rec)
McHenry   A3   1836   84   1840-80   Cook . . . . Woodstock
(Co Clk has b & d rec from 1877, m rec from 1837, div & civ ct rec from
1836, pro rec from 1840)
McLean   B3   1830   84   1840-80   Tazewell, Unorg. Terr. . . . . Bloomington
(Co Clk has b rec from 1860, m rec from 1830, d rec from 1884; City Clk has
bur rec; Cir Clk has div & civ ct rec; Pro Clk has pro rec)
Macon   C3   1829 118   1830-80   Shelby . . . . Decatur
(Co Clk has b rec from 1850, m rec from 1829, d rec from 1877, bur rec
from 1 Jan 1964)
Macoupin   C2   1829   44   1830-80   Madison, Greene . . . . Carlinville
(Co Clk has b, d & bur rec from 1877, m rec from 1829; Cir Clk has div,

pro & civ ct rec)
Madison   D2 1812 225 1820-80 St. Clair .... Edwardsville
(Co Clk has b & d rec from 1868, m rec from 1813; Cir Clk has div, Pro, & civ ct rec)
Marion   D3 1823 39 1830-80 Fayette, Jefferson .... Salem
(Co Clk has b, m, d, pro, civ ct rec from 1850)
Marshall   B2 1839 13 1840-80 Putnam .... Lacon
Mason   C2 1841 15 1850-80 Tazewell .... Havana
Massac   E3 1843 14 1850-80 Pope, Jefferson .... Metropolis
(Co Clk has b, m, d rec)
Menard   C2 1839 9 1840-80 Sangamon .... Petersburg
(Co Clk has b & d rec from 1877, m rec from 1839)
Mercer   B2 1825 17 1830-80 Unorg. Terr., Pike .... Aledo
(Co Clk has b & d rec from 1877, m rec from 1835, bur rec from 1916, Real Estate Ownership rec from 1835; Clk of Ct has div, pro & civ ct rec)
Monroe   D2 1816 16 1820-80 Randolph, St. Clair .... Waterloo
(Co Clk has b rec 1865, m rec 1816, d rec 1878, pro rec 1845, civ ct rec 1843)
Montgomery C2 1821 31 1830-80 Bond, Madison .... Hillsboro
(Co Clk has b & d rec from 1877; Cir Clk has div, pro & civ ct rec)
Morgan   C2 1823 37 1830-80 Sangamon .... Jacksonville
Moultrie   C3 1843 14 1850-80 Shelby, Macon .... Sullivan
(Co Clk has b, m, d & some bur rec)
Ogle   A3 1836 38 1840-80 Jo Daviess .... Oregon
(Co Clk has b rec from 1860, m rec from 1837, d rec from 1878; Cir Clk has div, pro & civ ct rec)
Peoria   B2 1825 189 1830-80 Fulton .... Peoria
(Co Clk has b, m, civ ct rec from 1878, m rec from 1825)
Perry   E2 1827 19 1830-80 Randolph, Jackson .... Pinckneyville
(Co Clk has incom b rec from 1879, com from 1916 to present, m rec incom from 1827, com from 1916 to present, d rec from 1879, com from 1916 to present; Cir Clk has div, pro & civ ct rec from 1827)

Piatt   C3 1841 15 1850-80 DeWitt, Macon .... Monticello
(Co Clk has b & d rec from 1877, m rec from 1878, Deed rec from 1841; Sec of Cemetery assn has bur rec; Cir Clk has div, pro & civ ct rec)
Pike   C1 1821 21 1850-80 Madison, Bond, Clark .... Pittsfield
Pope   E3 1816 4 1820-80 Gallatin, Johnson .... Golconda
(Co Clk has b rec from 1875, m rec from 1816, d rec from 1878, pro rec 1820; City Clk has bur rec; Cir Clk has div, pro & civ ct rec)
Pulaski   E3 1843 10 1850-80 Johnson .... Mound City
(Co Clk has b rec from 1866, m rec from 1861, d rec from 1882, bur rec from 1950, Tax rec from 1851; Cir Clk has div, pro & civ ct rec)
Putnam   B3 1825 5 1830-80 Fulton .... Hennepin
(Co Clk has b & d rec from 1878, m, pro & civ ct rec from 1831)
Randolph   E2 1795 30 1820-80 NW Territory, St. Clair ..... Chester
(Co Clk has b & d rec 1877, m, pro & civ ct rec from 1809)
Richland   D3 1841 16 1850-80 Clay, Lawrence .... Olney
(Co Clk has b & d rec from 1878, m rec from 1841; Cir Clk has div, pro & civ ct rec)
Rock Island B2 1833 151 1840-80 Jo Daviess .. Rock Island & Carbon Cliff
(Co Clk has b & d rec from 1877, m rec from 1833)
St. Clair D2 1790 263 1820-80 NW Territory .... Belleville
(Co Clk has b, m, d & bur rec)
Saline   E3 1847 26 1850-80 Gallatin .... Harrisburg
(Co Clk has b, m, d rec from 1900; Cir Clk has div, pro & civ ct rec)
Sangamon   C2 1821 147 1830-80 Bond, Madison .... Springfield
(Co Clk has b rec from 1870, d rec from 1878, m rec from 1821)
Schuyler   C2 1825 9 1830-80 Pike, Fulton .... Rushville
(Co Clk has b rec from 1877, m rec from 1827)
Scott   C2 1839 6 1840-80 Morgan .... Winchester
(Co Clk has b, m, d, pro & civ ct rec from 1839)
Shelby   C3 1827 23 1830-80 Fayette .... Shelbyville

(Co Clk has b rec from 1849, m rec from 1829, d rec from 1860, pro rec 1839)

Stark	B2	1839	8	1840-80	Knox, Putnam	Toulon
Stephenson	A2	1837	46	1840-80	Jo Daviess, Winnebago	Freeport

(Co Clk has b & d rec from 1878, m rec from 1837, pro & civ ct rec from 1894)

Tazewell	B2	1827	100	1830-80	Sangamon	Pekin

(Co Clk has b & d rec from 1878, m rec from 1827; Cir Clk now has bur, div, pro, & civ ct rec)

Union	E3	1818	18	1820-80	Johnson	Jonesboro
Vermilion	C4	1826	96	1830-80	Unorg. Terr., Edgar	Danville
Wabash	D4	1827	14	1830-80	Edwards	Mt. Carmel

Co Clk has b & d rec from 1878, m rec from 1857, bur info on d rec; Cir Clk has div, pro & civ ct rec)

Warren	B2	1825	22	1830-80	Pike	Monmouth

(Co Clk has b & d rec from 1875, m rec from 1830, pro & civ ct rec from 1825)

Washington	D2	1818	14	1820-80	St. Clair	Nashville

(Co Clk has b & d rec from 1877, m rec from 1832, pro rec from 1850)

Wayne	D3	1819	19	1820-80	Edwards	Fairfield

(Co Clk has b, m, d & bur rec from 1886; Cir Clk has div, pro & civ ct rec)

White	D3	1816	19	1820-80	Gallatin	Carmi
Whiteside	A2	1839	60	1840-80	Jo Daviess, Henry	Morrison
Will	B3	1836	192	1840-80	Cook, Iroquois	Joilet

(Co Clk has b & d rec from 1877, m rec from 1836)

Williamson	E3	1839	46	1840-80	Franklin	Marion

(Co Clk has b rec from 1887, m rec from 1839, d rec from 1877; City Clk has bur rec; Cir Clk has div, pro & civ ct rec)

Winnebago	A3	1836	210	1840-80	Jo Daviess	Rockford

(Co Clk has b & d rec from 1877 and m rec from 1837)

Woodford	B3	1841	25	1850-80	Tazewell, McLean	Eureka

(Co Clk has b & d rec from 1877, m rec from 1841; Cir Clk now has div, pro, and civ ct rec)

Genealogists' Check List of the Historical Records Survey, Illinois

Federal Courts (start before 1850. Fire 1871 destroyed most of records up to that time). Inventory of County Archives, Adams, Brown, Carroll, Champaign, Clark, Cumberland, DeWitt, Douglas, Effingham, Fayette, Franklin, Jackson, Jo Daviess, Knox, Livingston, Logan, Macon, Macoupin, Menard, Montgomery, Morgan, Moultrie, Ogle, Peoria, Piatt, Pike, Rock Island, Saline, Sangamon, Scott, Shelby, St Clair, Stephenson, Vermilion. Guide to public vital statistic records. Guide to church vital statistic records. Inventory of church archives of Illinois, Presbytery of Springfield, Cumberland Presbytery of Cairo, Presbytery of Springfield, Cumberland Presbyterian Church. Directory of Negro Baptist church in the U.S. two vol. Guide to depository of manuscripts collection in Illinois. Calendar of the Robert Weidensall correspondence 1861-1865, at George Williams College, Chicago, Ill. Calendar of the Ezekiel Cooper collection of early American Methodist manuscripts 1785-1839. Check list of Chicago Ante-Fire Imprints 1851-1871. Check list of the Kellogg collection of "Patent Inside," Newspapers of 1876. Depository of unpublished material, University of Illinois, (Lincolniana). State Historical Library, (Inventory of Manuscript Collection). State Archives (all other materials).

Indiana

Capital Indianapolis - Territory 1800 - State 1816 - (19th)

When the French explorers first came into the Indiana region about 1679, the entire territory was more or less a wilderness inhabited by a few Indians. During most of the 1700's, the only white men there were some fur traders.

The first counties to be settled were Knox, Harrison, Switzerland and Clark, in the extreme south end. Settlers in those counties came from Virginia, Kentucky and the Carolinas, although a group of Swiss emigrants established themselves in the southeast part of the state. The Wabash and the Ohio river sections drew many of the first settlers. Many Germans and Irish came there about 1830. About twenty years later New Englanders established themselves in the northern counties. The central part of the state was the last to be settled. Less than seventy years after the settlement of the state, the population had reached more than a million and a half. Abhoring slavery Quakers left Tennessee and the Carolinas and established themselves in Wayne and Randolph counties along the Ohio border mid-way north and south in Indiana.

With the development of the industrial area of the Calumet section, adjacent to the South Chicago area in the northwest part of the state many Central Europeans flocked there to man the rapidly increasing factories.

The marriage records are kept by the clerk of each county where the ceremony was performed.

Birth records before October, 1907 are in the office of the county health officer in the respective county seats; after October, 1907, in the office of the state health department, division of vital records, Indianapolis, Indiana.

Death records before October, 1899 should be in the office of the county health officer; after October 1899, in the office of the division of vital records in Indianapolis.

Records of wills and all probate matters are in the custody of the Clerk of the Circuit Court or County Clerk in most County Seats.

Real estate records, land titles, etc., are in the office of the county recorder in the various counties.

The first U. S. Census taken in Indiana was in 1800.

Libraries: Public Library, 22 S.E. Fifth St., Evansville 47710, (Vanderburgh); Indiana Historical Society, William Henry Smith Memorial Library, 140 N. Senate Ave. 46219, (Northwest Territory data); Public Library of Ft.Wayne, Zone 2, Ft. Wayne, Ind. (Allen), very good genealogical section. Public Library, 301 E.Jackson St., Muncie, 47305, (Delaware); Northern Indiana Historical Soc., 112 S.Lafayette Blvd.,South Bend 46601 (St.Joseph).

Lists of a score or more early day histories of the state and its people may be obtained in most libraries in the state. Most of the census records may be obtained at the State Library.

Highly valuable in all research activities in Indiana ia a compilation by the Indianapolis Public Library, Meridian and St. Clair Sts., Indianapolis 46204, of ''A Consolidated Index to Thirty-Two Histories of Indianapolis and Indiana, 1820-1830''. It also has many volumes, microfilm records and manuscripts from the older counties of Indiana.

For a detailed account of the early settlements of the state, the reader is referred to the 1932 Year Book of the Society of Indiana Pioneers in which Charles Nebeker Thompson has an article dealing with ''The Pioneer Period in Indiana.''

Indiana County Histories
(Population figures to nearest thousand - 1960 Census)

Name	Map Index	Date Formed	Pop. By M	Census Reports Available	Parent County	County Seat
Adams	B3	1835	25	1840-80	Allen, Randolph	Decatur
				(Co Clk has m, div, pro & civ ct rec)		
Allen	A3	1824	232	1830-80	Unorganized Terr, Randolph	Fort Wayne
Bartholomew	C3	1821	48	1830-80	Unorganized Terr, Jackson	Columbus
				(Co Clk has m, div, pro & civ ct rec from 1821; Board of Health has b, d, and bur rec)		
Benton	B2	1840	12	1850-80	Jasper	Fowler
Blackford	B3	1838	15	1840-80	Jay	Hartford City
				(Co Clk has m, div, pro & civ ct rec from 1839; City & Co Health Officers have b rec; Co Coroner has d & bur rec)		
Boone	B2	1830	28	1830-80	Hendricks, Marion	Lebanon
Brown	C2	1836	7	1840-80	Monroe, Bartholomew Jackson	Nashville
				(Co Clk has m rec from 1850, div, pro & civ ct rec; Board of Health has b, d, & bur rec)		
Carroll	B2	1828	17	1830-80	Unorganized Territory	Delphi
				(Co Clk has m, div, pro & civ ct rec from 1828; Co Health Officer has b, d, and bur rec)		
Cass	B7	1829	41	1830-80	Carroll	Logansport
				(Co Clk has m rec from 1829, div & civ ct rec from 1894, pro rec from 1892; Controller's office has bur rec)		
Clark	D3	1801	63	1820-80	Knox	Jeffersonville
Clay	C2	1825	24	1830-80	Owen,Putnam,Vigo,Sullivan	Brazil
Clinton	B2	1830	31	1830-80	Tippecanoe	Frankfort
Crawford	D2	1818	8	1820-80	Orange, Harrison, Perry	English
				(Co Clk has b, m, d, bur, div, pro & civ ct rec)		
Daviess	C2	1817	27	1830-80	Knox	Washington
				(Co Clk has m, div, pro & civ ct rec from 1817)		
Dearborn	C3	1803	29	1820-80	Clark	Lawrenceburg
				(Clk of Cir Ct has m rec, Lic. 1826, Application 1905, div, pro & civ Ct rec; Health Officer has b & d rec)		
Decatur	C3	1822	20	1830-80	Unorganized Territory	Greensburg

DeKalb   A3   1835   28   1840-80   Allen, Lagrange . . . . Auburn
(Co Clk has m, div, pro & civ ct rec from 1837)
Delaware   B3   1827   111 1820-80   Randolph . . . . Muncie
(Co Clk has m, div, pro & civ ct rec from 1827)
Dubois   D2   1818   27   1820-80   Pike . . . . Jasper
Elkhart   A3   1830   107 1830-80   Allen, Cass . . . . Goshen
(Co Clk has m rec from 1831, div, pro & civ ct rec from 1830)
Fayette   C3   1819   24   1820-80   Wayne, Franklin . . . . Connersville
Floyd   D3   1819   51   1820-80   Harrison, Clarke . . . . New Albany
Fountain   B2   1826   19   1830-80   Montgomery, Parke . . . . Covington
Franklin   C3   1811   17   1820-80   Clark,Dearborn,Jefferson . . . . Brookville
Fulton   A2   1835   17   1840-80   Allen, Cass, St. Joseph . . . . Rochester
(Co Clk has m, div, pro & civ ct rec from 1836)
Gibson   D1   1813   30   1820-80   Knox . . . . Princeton
(Co Clk has m rec from 1813, div, pro & civ ct rec from 1820; Co Health
Officer has b, d & bur rec)
Grant   B3   1831   75   1840-80   Delaware,Madison,Cass . . . . Marion
Greene   C2   1821   26   1830-80   Daviess, Sullivan . . . . Bloomfield
(Co Clk has m, div, pro & civ ct rec from 1823)
Hamilton   B2   1823   40   1830-80   Unorganized Terr,Marion . . . Noblesville
Hancock   B3   1828   27   1830-80   Madison . . . . Greenfield
(Co Clk has m rec from 1828, div, pro & civ ct rec from 1840; Health Dept.
has b, d & bur rec)
Harrison   D2   1808   19   1820-80   Knox, Clark . . . . Corydon
(Clk of Cir Ct has m, pro, & Will rec from 1809, div & civ ct rec from 1850)
Hendricks   C2   1824   45   1830-80   Unorganized Terr, Putnam . . . . . Danville
(Co Clk has b rec from 1882 to 1920, Public Health office has b rec from
1920 to present; Co Clk as m, div, pro & civ ct rec from 1823, also tax
receipts, assessor rec & land rec; Public Health Office has d rec from 1882)
Henry   B3   1822   49   1830-80   Unorganized Territory . . . . , New Castle
(Co Clk has div, pro & civ ct rec, also m rec from 1822; Health Officer has
b, d, and bur rec)
Howard   B2   1844   70   1850-80   Carroll, Cass, Miami, Grant, Hamilton
(Orginally Richardville Co.) . . . . Kokomo
Huntington B3   1832   34   1840-80   Allen, Grant . . . . Huntington
Jackson   C2   1816   31   1820-80   Washington,Clark,Jefferson, . . Brownstown
Jasper   A2   1835   19   1840-80   White, Warren . . . . Rensselaer
(Co Clk has m, div, pro & civ ct rec from 1865; Co Health Officer has b & d rec)
Jay   B3   1835   23   1840-80   Randolph, Delaware . . . . Portland
Jefferson   C3   1811   24   1820-80   Dearborn, Clark . . . . Madison
Jennings   C3   1817   17   1820-80   Jefferson, Jackson . . . . Vernon
Johnson   C2   1823   44   1830-80   Unorganized Territory . . . . Franklin
(Co Clk has m, div, pro & civ ct rec from 1830; Health Dept has b, d,
and bur rec from 1883)
Knox   C2   1790   42   1820-80   Northwest Territory . . . . . . Vincennes
(Co Clk has m rec from 1807, pro rec from 1806, div & civ ct rec from 1796)
Kosciusko   A3   1835   40   1840-80   Elkhart, Cass . . . . Warsaw
(Clk of Cir Ct has m rec from 1830, pro rec from 1836, div & civ ct rec from
1838, will rec from 1844; Health Dept has b & d rec from 1882; Sexton of
each cemetery has bur rec)
Lagrange   A3   1832   17   1840-80   Elkhart, Allen . . . . Lagrange
Lake   A2   1836   513 1840-80   Porter, Newton . . . . Crown Point
(Co Clk has m, div, pro, civ ct, crim ct rec from 1837)
LaPorte   A2   1832   95   1840-80   St. Joseph . . . . LaPorte
Lawrence   C2   1818   37   1820-80   Orange . . . . Bedford
Madison   B3   1823   126 1830-80   Unorganized Terr, Marion . . . . Anderson
Marion   C2   1822   698 1830-80   Unorganized Territory . . . . . Indianapolis
Marshall   A2   1835   32   1840-80   St. Joseph, Elkhart . . . . Plymouth
(Co Clk has m, div, pro, civ ct rec from 1836; Co Public Health Office has
b, d & bur rec from 1882)
Martin   C2   1820   11   1820-80   Daviess, Dubois . . . . Shoals

Miami   B2   1832   38   1840-80   Cass . . . . Peru
Monroe   C2   1818   59   1820-80   Orange . . . . Bloomington
Montgomery B2   1823   32   1830-80   Parke, Putnam . . . . Crawfordsville
   (Co Clk has m, div, pro & civ ct rec; Health Officers have b & d rec)
Morgan   C2   1822   34   1830-80   Unorganized Terr. . . . . . . Martinsville
Newton   A2   1859   12   1860-80   Jasper . . . . Kentland
   (Co Clk has m rec from 1850, div, pro & civ ct rec from 1862; Health Dept
   has b & d rec; Town Hall has bur rec)
Noble   A3   1835   28   1840-80   Elkhart, Lagrange, Allen . . . .   Albion
   (Co Clk has m, div, pro & civ ct rec)
Ohio   C3   1844   4   1850-80   Dearborn . . . . Rising Sun
   (Co Clk has m rec from 1882, div, pro, civ ct rec from 1844)
Orange   D2   1816   17   1820-80   Washington, Knox, Gibson . . . . . . Paoli
   (Co Clk has div & civ ct rec from 1874, pro rec from 1817, m & will rec
   from 1816; Dillard Abstract Company has b, d, & bur rec)
Owen   C2   1819   11   1820-80   Daviess, Sullivan . . . . Spencer
Parke   C2   1821   15   1830-80   Unorganized Territory . . . . . . Rockville
   (Co Clk has m, div, pro, civ ct rec from 1833, Health dept has b, d & bur rec)
Perry   D2   1814   17   1820-80   Warrick, Gibson . . . . Cannelton
Pike   D2   1817   13   1820-80   Gibson, Perry . . . . , . . Petersburg
   (Co Clk has m, div, pro, civ ct & will rec from 1817; Co & City Health
   Officer has b, d & bur rec)
Porter   A2   1835   60   1840-80   St. Joseph . . . . , . . . Valparaiso
   (Co Clk has m, div, pro, civ ct rec from 1832; Board of Health has b & d rec)
Posey   D1   1814   19   1820-80   Warrick . . . . Mount Vernon
   (Co Clk has m, div, pro & civ ct rec from 1815; Co Health officer has b,
   d & bur rec)
Pulaski   A2   1835   13   1840-80   Cass, St. Joseph . . . . Winamac
   (Co Clk has m, div & civ ct rec from 1839, pro rec from 1837, b & d rec
   from 1880)
Putnam   C2   1822   25   1830-80   Unorg. Terr, Vigo, Owen . . . Greencastle
   (Co Clk has m rec 1822, div & civ ct rec 1828, pro rec 1825, wills 1844)
Randolph   B3   1818   28   1820-80   Wayne . . . . Winchester
   (Co Clk has m rec from 1819, div & civ ct rec from 1830, pro rec from 1836)
Richardville   (see Howard)
Ripley   C3   1816   21   1820-80   Dearborn, Jefferson . . . . Versailles
   (Co Clk has m, div, pro, civ ct rec from 1818)
Rush   C3   1822   20   1830-80   Unorganized Terr. . . . . Rushville
   (Clk of Ct has m, div, pro & civ ct rec from 1882; Health dept has b,d,
   and bur records)
Saint Joseph A2   1830 239   1830-80   Cass . . . . South Bend
Scott   C3   1820   15   1820-80   Clark, Jefferson, Jennings . . Scottsburg
   (Clk of Ct has m, div, pro & civ ct rec from 1820; Health Dept has b, d,
   and bur records)
Shelby   C3   1822   34   1830-80   Unorganized Territory . . . . . Shelbyville
Spencer   D2   1818   16   1820-80   Warrick, Perry . . . . Rockport
Starke   A2   1835   18   1840-80   St. Joseph . . . . Knox
   (Co Clk has m rec from 1850, div, pro civ ct rec from 1851)
Steuben   A3   1835   17   1840-80   LaGrange . . . . Angola
Sullivan   C2   1817   22   1820-80   Knox . . . . Sullivan
Switzerland C3   1814   7   1820-80   Dearborn, Jefferson . . . . Vevay
   (Co Clk has m & civ ct rec from 1814, pro rec from 1831 and div rec;
   Health officer has b & d rec)

Tippecanoe B2   1826   74   1830-80   Unorganized Terr, Parke . . . . . Lafayette
   (Clk of Cir Ct has m rec from 1830, div rec from 1850, pro & civ ct rec
   from 1832; Health Officer has b & d rec)
Tipton   B2   1844   16   1850-80   Hamilton, Cass, Miami . . . . Tipton
Union   C3   1821   6   1830-80   Wayne, Franklin, Fayette . . . . . . Liberty
   (Co Clk has m, div, pro & civ ct rec from 1821; Co Health Dept has b rec
   from 1882, d rec from 1907)
Vanderburgh D1   1818 166   1820-80   Gibson, Posey, Warrick . . . . . Evansville

County Map of Indiana

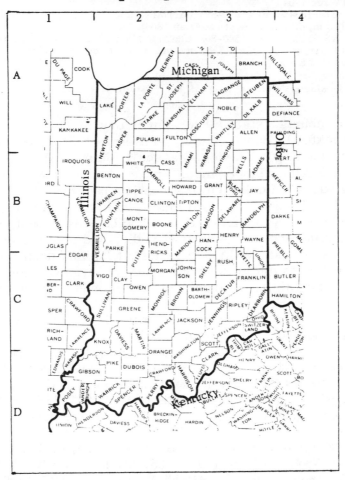

(Co Clk has m, div, pro & civ ct rec from 1835; Health Dept has b & d rec)
Vermillion B2 1824 18 1830-80 Parke . . . . Newport
Co Clk has m, div, pro & civ ct rec from 1824, also Voting rec; Health
Officer has b rec from 1882 & d & bur rec)
Vigo C2 1818 108 1820-80 Sullivan . . . . Terre Haute
(Co Clk has m & pro rec from 1818, div & civ ct rec from 1825)
Wabash B3 1832 33 1840-80 Cass, Grant . . . . Wabash
(Co Clk has m rec from 1943, div, pro & civ ct rec from 1850; Health Dept
has b, d, and bur records)
Warren B2 1827 9 1830-80 Fountain . . . . Williamsport
(Co Clk has b rec 1882 to 1948, m, div, civ ct rec from 1828, pro rec from 1829)
Warrick D2 1813 24 1820-80 Knox . . . . Boonville
Washington D2 1814 18 1820-80 Clark, Harrison, Jefferson . . . . . Salem
(Co Clk has m, div, pro & civ ct rec from 1814, Wills from 1813, Newspaper
(not indexed) from 1891, Co Historical Soc (many family rec); Health Dept has
b & d rec from 1882, bur rec)
Wayne B3 1811 74 1820-80 Clark, Dearborn . . . . Richmond
(Co Clk has m rec from 1811, div & civ ct rec from 1873, pro rec from 1818;
City-Co Health Officer has b, d and bur rec)

Wells   B3   1835   21   1840-80   Allen, Delaware, Randolph . . . . . Bluffton
(Co Clk has m rec 1836, div rec 1850, pro rec 1837, civ ct rec 1853; Co Health
Dept has b rec 1904)
White   B2   1834   20   1840-80   Carroll . . . . Monticello
(Co Clk has m, div, pro, civ ct rec from 1834)
Whitley   A3   1835   21   1840-80   Elkhart, Allen . . . . Columbia City
(Clk of Ct has m rec from 1836, div, pro & civ ct rec from 1839; Board of
Health has b, d & bur rec)

Genealogists' Check List of the Historical Records Survey, Indiana

Federal courts (start 1800). Inventory of County archives, Allen, Blackford, Boone, Clay, Delaware, Fulton, Greene, Howard, Jay, La Porte, Marion, Marshall, Monroe, Morgan, Posey, St Joseph, Shelby, Tippecanoe, Tipton, Vanderburgh, Warrick, Wells. Guide to Public vital statistics records. Directory of churches & religious organizations in Indiana, Vol. 1 Marion Co, Vol. 2 Calumet Region (Lake, Porter and La Porte Counties), Vol. 3 Northern Indiana Pt 1 Adventist bodies and Mennonite bodies, Pt 2 Methodist and YWCA. Check list of Indiana county records with introduction on county government organizations. State Legislation pertaining to archives and records, sample pages for Indiana.

Microfilms were made of the following county records of Indiana. (# indicates the roll number.)

Allen County: #61 Deed record (A,B,C,D) 1824-1842, Commissioners records (A,B.C) 1824-1850. #62 Will records 1831-1855, Probate order book (A,B) 1825-1844, Civil order books (A,B) 1824-1839, marriage records (2 Vol) 1847-1856. #63, marriage records (5 Vol) 1857-1872. #64, marriage records (5 Vol) 1872-1880.

Clark county: #17 Probate Order book (Vol A) 1817-1828, Probate order book (Vol B) 1828-1835, birth records 1882-1893, 1899-1907, 1882-1886, 1886-1890, 1888-1891, 1897-1899, 1900-1901, 1901-1907, Estray book 1802-1818, Court common Pleas 1801-1805, 1806-1808, 1808-1810. #18, order book court common pleas 1810-1817, court records 1802-1813, minute book court common pleas 1801-1805, 1801-1803, 1803-1808, 1808-1814, minute book circuit court & commissioners records 1815-1820, commissioner records 1820-1824, 1824-1828, 1832-1839. #19, commissioners records 1839-1843, 1843-1845, 1845-1852, seminary records 1830-1851, Alien records (Aliens to become citizens of US) 1845-1852, probate order book "C" (Estate of Johathan Jennings) 1836, Appraisal and estates of Jonathan Jennings deceased 1833-1840. #58, minutes board commissioners apportioning lands to Illinois regiment 1785-1820, order book court quarter sessions (2 Vol) 1801-1808, court order book 1807-1813.

Dearborn County: #54 marriage records (Books 8-13) 1846-1879. #54a, marriage records (2 vols) 1880-1889. #55, commissioners records (5 books) 1826-1851, Surveyors book 1799-1805, Deed record book AA prior to 1826. #56, Deed record (BB & CC) prior to 1826, (A to D) 1826-1830, Will records 1824-1832, Probate Court record 1826-1830, order book circuit court (2 Vol) 1824-1829. #57, birth records (7 Vol) 1882-1907.

Floyd County: #13, marriage records 1819-1837, 1837-1845, 1845-1853, 1853-1857, 1858-1864, 1864-1871. #14, marriage records 1871-1878, 1878-1885, 1885-1891, birth records 1882-1885, 1885-1887, 1887-1889, 1889-1891. #15, birth records 1891-1894, 1894-1902, 1897-1903, 1904-1906, 1903-1907, 1900-1907, 1904-1907, deed records (Vol A) 1818-1820, (Vol B) 1820-1825, (Vol C) 1825-1829, Will and Probate records (A) 1818-1829. #16, marriage records general index No. 1, 1808-1878, No. 2 1879-1897, marriage records (Vol A) 1808-1820, (Vol B) 1820-1828, (Vol C) 1828-1834 (Vol D) 1834-1841, Will records (Vol A) 1801-1817, (Vol B) 1817-1833.

Franklin County: #48, Issue Docket 1811, court common Pleas (Minutes of books B & C) 1811-1814, Apprentice records 1831-1853, court common pleas 1814, will records (2 Vol) 1814-1831, Probate order book 1827-1834, probate records 1811-1829, order book circuit court (2 Vol) 1815-1819, (2 Vol) 1823-1828. #49, order book circuit court (4 Vol) 1819-1825, (3 Vol) 1828-1836, minute book circuit court 1815, inventory estates 1811-1820, Fee book circuit court 1811-1816. #50, marriage records (2 Vol, Index) 1811-1824, (8 Vol) 1811-1868. #51, marriage records (4 Vol) 1868-1890, birth records (4 Vol) 1882-1907, Brookville birth records 1894-1907, Stock brands 1811-1839, Estray book 1811-1814, minute book circuit court 1815-1816, reference Docket Circuit court 1813-1816, Execution Docket circuit court 1811-1816. #52, Deed records (7 Vol) 1810-1830. #53, marriage records (Books 1 to 7) 1826-1846.

Gibson county: #34, will records (3 Vol) 1813-1834, probate order book (A) 1817-1830, order book court common pleas & circuit court (A) 1813-1818, order book circuit court (B) 1820-1821, (C) 1821-1828, 1828-1839. #34, common pleas and circuit court 1813-1820, commissioners records 1835-1845. #35 commissioners records 1845-1854, birth records 1882-1907. #36, Princeton birth records 1882-1907, deed records (Vol A, B,C,D) 1813-1833, county tax list 1819-1826, #37 marriage licenses (3 Vol) 1813-1868, marriage records (3 to 7) 1863-1890.

Harrison county: #7, Estray book 1809-1817, tract book 1807-1821, deed records (Vol A) 1809-1817, (Vol B) 1817-1818, (Vol C) 1818-1822, (Vol D) 1822-1826, (Vol E) 1825-1829. #8, birth records (A) 1882-1886, (B) 1886-1888, (C) 1888-1890, (D) 1891-

1893, (E) 1893-1897, (F) 1897-1900, (G) 1900-1904, (H) 1906-1907. Manuscript of William Mitchell 1725. Commissioner record (A) 1817-1824, (B) letters of Corydon Branch Bank 1825-1830, (C) 1831-1838, (D) 1838-1844. #9, commissioners record (Vol E) 1844-1849, (Vol F) 1849-1853, will record book (A) 1809-1832, Seminary record (in possession of the Griffith family, Corydon) 1827-1851, court records (partly probate) 1815-1817, Probate court record 1817-1829, court record 1809-1816, 1814-1817, Circuit court order book (B) 1820-1825, (C) 1817-1820. #10, Court record 1817-1819, McClure Workingmens Institute 1855-1858, Account book of J. B. Slaughter 1818-1830, Minute book court common pleas 1811-1814, Indices to marriage 1809-1817 & part 1842-1846, marriages 1809-1817, 1817-1832, marriage record (Vol B) 1826-1852, (Vol C) 1853-1859, (Vol E) 1859-1866. #11, marriage affidavits (Vol 1) 1866-1875, marriage records (Vol F) 1866-1871, (Vol G) 1872-1875, (Vol H) 1876-1879, (Vol I) 1879-1882. #12, marriage records (Vol J) 1882-1885, (Vol K) 1885-1888, (Vol L) 1888-1892.

Jefferson County: #20, Will records (Vol A) 1811-1822, (Vol B) 1822-1827, (Vol C) 1827-1832. Civil order book 1812-1818, Circuit court records 1811-1819, Treasurers book 1812, license records (by Treasurer) 1816-1837, Commissioners records 1817 1822, 1822-1832, 1836-1838. #21, Commissioners records 1832-1835, 1838-1840, 1840-1843, 1843-1847, 1847-1850, 1850-1854, Tax list 1827. #22, birth records 1882-1896, 1897-1905, 1905-1907, 1882-1890, 1890-1896, 1893-1896, 1896-1900, 1901-1904, 1906-1907, Deed records index for Vol ''A'' to ''F'' (inclusive 1811-1830), Deed records (Vol A) 1811-1817, (Vol B) 1816-1820. #23, Deed records (Vol C) 1820-1823, (Vol D) 1823-1827, (Vol E) 1827-1829, (Vol F) 1829-1830, marriage records 1811-1832, 1831-1836, 1836-1839. #24, marriage records 1839-1841, 1841-1845, 1845-1850, 1850-1853, marriage records indices to men (9 Vol) 1853-1891.

Jennings County: #25, birth records 1882-1884, 1885-1888, 1888-1893, 1893-1898 & 1903-1904, 1899-1902, 1904-1907, Circuit court 1817-1822, Will & Probate records 1818-1829, Probate records 1830-1836, Deed records (Vol A) 1817-1828, (Vol B) 1829-1833. #26, Commissioners records 1824-1836, 1836-1846, Index to marriage records 1818-1845, marriage records 1818-1830, 1830-1837, 1837-1845, 1845-1850. #27, marriage records 1850-1858, 1858-1866, 1866-1873, 1873-1879, 1879-1887, marriage returns 1881-1888.

Knox County: #28, register of Negro Slaves 1805-1807, minutes of Orphans court 1796-1805, minutes of the court of general Quarter sessions 1796-1801, 1801-1805, Chancery Appearance 1806-1810, minute court of Chancery 1807-1811, Court Common

Pleas 1790-1792, minute court Common Pleas 1796-1801, 1796-1799, 1801-1806, 1806-1810, 1807-1010, 1810-1813, Circuit court of Oyer & Terminer, General Jail Deliver, & Nisi Prius held by federal Judge 1795, minutes to Circuit court 1816-1818, Order book Common Pleas 1811-1813 and Order book Circuit court (A) 1814-1820 (B) 1817-1822. #29, Order book Circuit court (Vol C) 1821-1825, (Vol D) 1825-1831, Will records 1806-1852, Probate court records 1790-1805, 1817-1829, 1829-1832, 1832-1839, Poor relief records1821-1832, general index to Deeds 1814-1829. #30, Deed records (Vol A) 1814-1817, (B) 1817-1822, (C) 1822-1826, (D) 1826-1829, Court of Claim 1814-1816 & Commissioners records 1817-1820, Commissioners records (Vol A) 1823-1839, (B) 1839-1847. #31, Commissioners records (Vol A 1827-1855, birth records 1882-1886, 1886-1898, 1897-1899, 1899-1901, 1900-1902, 1902-1903, 1903-1904. #32 birth records 1904-1905, 1905-1906, 1906-1907, minute board Trustees Vincennes U 1806-1836, birth records (Vincennes) 1893-1903, 1903-1906, marriage records (Vol 4) 1838-1854, (Vol E) 1854-1860, (Vol F) 1860-1866. #33, marriage records (G, 8,9,10) 1866-1883, marriage returns 1881-1889, Estate Judge William Clarke 1802, Estate Moses Henry 1790,George Rogers Clark 1796, Jonathan Jennings 1807. #65, Borough of Vincennes: Trustees Proceedings 1815-1816, Ordinary 1816-1836, Treas accounts 1819-1840, Common records 1818-1837, Journal of Borough Trustees 1820-1836, Miscellaneous papers (Vincennes) 1784-1815c.

Perry County: #59, Deed records 1815-1835, Circuit court (Complete records) 1817-1834, Commissioners records 1847-1851, Will records 1813-1843, Circuit Court Order book (2 Vol) 1815-1832, marriage records (2 Vol) 1815-1861. #60, marriage records (4 Vol) 1861-1890, birth records (3 Vol) 1889-1905.

Posey County: #38, Deed records (Vol A to E) 1812-1832, Will record Index (A), (B) 1816-1852, record Circuit Court & Probate Order book 1815-1827. #39, Probate Order 1828-1834, Circuit court Order Book (A,B,C) 1815-1829, General index Commissioners records to Vols. A,B,C,D,E,F,G,H,I,J,K,L, 1817-1855, Commissioners records (A,B,C,D,E,F) 1817-1842. #40, Commissioners records (G,H,I,J,K,L) 1842-1855, birth records (4 Vol) 1882-1900 a. Vol 1887-1893 contains rec of county Mt Vernon & New Harmony. #41, birth records (2 Vol) 1900-1907, marriage records index Vols 1 and 2 1815-1846, marriage records (Vol 1-5) 1815-1868. #42, marriage records (Vol 6-8) 1868-1882, marriage returns 1882-1887, 1887-1900.

Scott County: #1, Deed records (A) 1819-1827, (B) 1826-1828, Land Entry Book, Commissioners records (A) 1820-1840, (B) 1841-1851,Vol 1 1851-1865.

Washington County: #5, Commissioners records (C) 1839-1846,

(D) 1846-1855, Tract book deed records (Vol A) 1814-1817, (Vol B) 1817-1823, (Vol C) 1823-1826. #6 Deed records (Vol D) 1824-1828, (Vol E) 1827-1830, Will records 1821-1830, Circuit court minute book 1814-1818, Probate order book (A) 1814-1824, (B) not photographed, (C) 1837-1841, Appraisement of Benjamin Parks Estate 1834, Sale Bill of Benjamin Parks estate 1835.

Depository of unpublished material, Indiana State Library, Indianapolis, Indiana.

Iowa

Capital Des Moines - Territory 1838 - State 1846 - (29th)

Outside of a few explorers and priests passing by on the Mississippi and some fur traders trapping along the rivers, no white man came to Iowa until about 1788.

Before Iowa became a territory in its own name in 1838, it had been part of the Missouri Territory, 1812-1821; unorganized territory, 1824-1834; the Michigan Territory, 1834-1836, and the Wisconsin Territory, 1836-1838.

Five years prior to becoming a Territory, Iowa had an influx of white settlers after a treaty with some of the numerous Indian tribes inhabiting the country had made it possible for settlements to be established. The first settlers came from the Eastern and the Southern states. Most of them were originally from the British Isles.

Among the thousands of immigrants who flocked to Iowa immediately prior to and after it had gained statehood were Scandinavians to the central and the western sections of the state, Hollanders to the south-central section, Germans along the Mississippi, Scotch and Welch to the mining towns of the southern counties, and many Czechs to the east-central section.

Iowa City, Johnson County, was the capital of Iowa until 1857 when it was moved about 110 miles west to Des Moines, Polk County.

The Divison of Vital Statistics, State Department of Health, State Office Building, Des Moines, Iowa 50319, has birth, marriage and death records. Incomplete birth records available up to 1897, even less complete to January 1819. Death records available in some instances from 1880, and complete from 1905. Marriage records available since 1880.

The offices of the Clerk of the District Court in each County also have similar records of births, marriage and deaths; some marriage records on file since 1832; also records of all probate matters, wills and divorce proceedings of the cases handled in the respective counties.

The Court Auditor is the same as Court Clerk in most states, but the Clerk of the District Court has charge of most of the vital records.

Naturalization information may be obtained from the clerk of the United States Circuit Court in Des Moines and Dubuque, the Superior Courts of Council Bluffs and Cedar Rapids, and the district courts in the various county seats.

Real estate records are in the offices of the county recorder, taxpayers lists in the offices of the county treasurer.

The first federal census was taken in Iowa in 1840. Special state enumerations were taken in 1885, 1895, 1915 and 1925. They are on file at the Department of History and Archives, Historical Bldg., Des Moines, Iowa 50319. Census records are also available for the years 1856 and 1870. The 1856 census is most valuable as it gives the number of years the family has been a resident of the state of Iowa.

War service records of Iowa participants in the Civil War, the Spanish-American War, World War I, and members of the National Guard from 1900 to date are in the office of the Adjutant General, State House, Des Moines, Iowa 50319.

Libraries: Public Library, 321 Main St., Davenport 52801, (Scott); Public Library, 100 Locust St., State Historical & Archive Dept. of Iowa, Des Moines 50309, (Polk); State Historical Society of Iowa Library, Iowa City, 52201, (Johnson); Public Library, 6 & Jackson Sts., Sioux City 51101, (Woodbury); Public Library, 5th & Mulberry St., Waterloo 50703, (Black Hawk).

Among books dealing with historical and genealogical information concerning Iowa are the following:

"Historical Atlas of State of Iowa", A. T. Andreas, Lakeside Press, 1875.

"Biographical History of Pottawattamie County, Iowa." The Lewis Publishing Company, 1891. 172 pp.

"Iowa Old and New" J. E. Briggs, University Publishing Company, 1939.

"Iowa; Its History and Its Foremost Citizens" Brigham Johnson "History of Des Moines."

"Iowa; Through the Years" Cyrenus Cole, Iowa Historical Society. 1940 (Accurate historical account.)

"County Histories and Biographical Histories" every county, 99, in Iowa has had a history written about it, and its people, some counties have as many as five different books.

"Early Algona, The Story of Our Pioneers, 1854-1874" Florence Call Cowles, The Register and Tribune Company, Des Moines, Iowa 1929. 221 pp.

"Iowa Democracy, History of Politics" 1916, John D. Denison, S. J. Clarks Pub. Co.

"History of Iowa" 4 vol. Benjamin F. Gue, Century Historical Co. of N.Y., 1903.

"Narrative, History of People of Iowa", Edgar R. Harlan, five vol. American Historical Society. Chicago, 1931.

"Prominent Iowans" a Deluxe supplement to Iowa, Its History and Foremost citizens.

"Iowa History" Wm. J. Peterson, 4 vols, 1952, and genealogical histories.

"Hawkeye" Herbert Quick, Grosset, 1939. (Iowa life from 1857 to 1858)

"Ioway to Iowa" Irving Richman, Iowa State Historical Society, 1931. (Reliable history of early days in Iowa)

"Progressive Men of Iowa" 1899, "The First Census of the Original Counties of Dubuque and Demoine, Iowa, Taken in July 1836" Benjamin F. Shambaugh, The Historical Department of Iowa, Des Moines, Iowa 1897. 93 pp.

"Notable Lawyers and Public men of Early Iowa to First and Second Generations" Edward Holcom Stiles, Des Moines Homestead Publ. Co. 1916.

"Hawkeyes; a Biography of the State of Iowa" Phillip Duffield Stong, Dodd, 1940.

"An Illustrated History of the State of Iowa from its Exploration down to 1875" Charles R. Tuttle and Daniel S. Durrie, Richard S. Peale and Company 1876. Biographical sketches in the last fifty-five pages.

"U. S. Biographical Dictionary and Portrait Gallery" Iowa Volume 1878.

"Who's Who in Iowa" Iowa Press, 1940.

"A Guide to the Hawkeye State" Works Projects Adminstration, Viking, 1938. (American Guide Series)

Iowa County Histories

(Population figures to nearest thousand - 1960 Census)

Name	Map Index	Date Formed	Pop. By M	Census Reports Available	Parent County	County Seat
Adair	C2	1853	11	1860-80	Cass	Greenfield
(Clk of Dist Ct has b rec from 1880, m, div, & civ ct rec from 1852)						
Adams	C2	1851	7	1860-80	Taylor	Corning
Allamakee	A4	1847	16	1850-80	Clayton	Waukon
(Clk of Dist Ct has b, d, bur, div rec from 1880, m, civ ct & pro rec from 1850)						
Appanoose	C3	1846	16	1850-80	Davis	Centerville
(Clk of Dist Ct has b & d rec from 1880 to 1935 and from 1941 to present; m & pro rec 1846; div & civ ct rec 1848)						
Audubon	B2	1855	11	1860-80	Cass, Black Hawk	Audubon
(Clk of Dist Ct has b, d, bur rec from 1880, m rec from 1856, div rec from 1881, pro rec from 1869, civ ct rec from 1864)						

Benton   B3   1846   23   1850-80   Indian Land Purchase .... Vinton
  (Clk of Dist Ct has b, d & bur rec from 1880, m & civ ct rec from 1856, div rec
  from 1890, pro rec from 1850)
Black Hawk B3   1843 122   1850-80   Delaware .... Waterloo
  (Clk of Dist Ct has m rec from 1854, div & pro rec from 1880, b & d rec from
  1880 to 1935 (rec from 1935 to 1941 are at State Dept., Des Moines) b & d rec
  from 1941 to present)
Boone   B2   1846   28   1850-80   Polk .... Boone
Bremer   A3   1851   21   1860-80   Winnebago, Indian Reserve .... Waverly
Buchanan   B3   1837   22   1850-80   Delaware .... Independence
  (Clk of Dist Ct has b & d rec from 1880, m, pro, civ ct rec from 1845)
Buena Vista A1   1859   21   1860-80   Sac, Clay .... Storm Lake
  (Clk of Dist Ct has b, m, d, pro & civ ct rec from 1880, div rec from 1885)
Butler   A3   1853   17   1860-80   Buchanan, Black Hawk .... Allison
  (Clk of Dist Ct has b & d rec from 1880, m, div, pro & civ ct rec from 1854)
Calhoun   B2   1855   16   1860-80   Formerly Fox County ...... Rockwell City
  (Clk of Dist Ct has b, d, pro rec from 1880; m rec from 1863; bur rec from
  1900; div rec from 1906 and civ ct rec from 1872)
Carroll   B2   1854   23   1860-80   Guthrie .... Carroll
Cass   C1   1853   18   1860-80   Pottawattamie .... Atlantic
  (Clk of Dist Ct has b & d rec from 1880, m rec from 1877, div rec from 1906,
  pro rec from 1870, Dist ct rec from 1865)
Cedar   B4   1838   18   1840-80   Wisconsin Territory .... Tipton
  (Clk of Dist Ct has b, d & bur rec from 1880, m rec from 1841, div rec
  from 1850, pro & civ ct rec from 1838)
Cerro Gordo A3   1855   50   1860-80   Floyd .... Mason City
Cherokee   A1   1857   19   1860-80   Crawford .... Cherokee
Chickasaw   A3   1851   15   1860-80   Fayette .... New Hampton
  (Clk of Dist Ct has b rec from 1880, m, d, bur, div, pro, civ ct rec from 1854)
Clarke   C2   1846   8   1850-80   Lucas .... Osceola
Clay   A1   1858   19   1850-80   Indian Lands .... Spencer
  (Clk of Dist Ct has b & d rec from 1880, m rec from 1864, div rec from
  1906, pro rec from 1871, civ ct rec from 1869)
Clayton   A4   1837   22   1840-80   Dubuque .... Elkader
  (Clk of Dist Ct has b rec from 1880 to 1941, m rec from 1861, d & div
  rec from 1880, pro rec from 1860 & civ ct rec from 1862)
Clinton   B4   1839   55   1840-80   Dubuque .... Clinton
Crawford   B1   1855   19   1860-80   Shelby .... Denison
  (Clk of Dist Ct has b, d & bur rec from 1880, m & civ ct rec from 1856,
  div rec from 1874, pro rec from 1854)
Dallas   B2   1847   24   1850-80   Polk .... Adel
Davis   C3   1844   9   1850-80   Van Buren .... Bloomfield
  (Clk of Dist Ct has b & d rec from 1880, m rec from 1844, div, pro, & civ
  ct rec from 1830)
Decatur   C2   1850   11   1850-80   Appanoose .... Leon
  (Clk of Dist Ct has b, m, d, div, pro, civ ct rec from 1880)(CH burned 1874)
Delaware   B4   1837   18   1840-80   Dubuque .... Manchester
  (Clk of Ct has b & d rec from 1880, m rec from 1851, div & civ ct rec from
  1850, pro rec from 1849, crim rec from 1884, Juvenile rec from 1907)
Des Moines C4   1836   45   1840-80   Wisconsin Territory .... Burlington
  (Clk of Ct has b, m, d, div, pro & civ ct rec)
Dickinson   A1   1857   13   1860-80   Kossuth .... Spirit Lake
  (Clk of Dist Ct has b, m, d, bur, div, pro & civ ct rec from 1880)
Dubuque   B4   1835   80   1840-80   Michigan Territory .... Dubuque
  (Clk of Dist Ct has b & d rec 1880, m rec 1838, div, civ ct, pro rec 1837,
  Land Transfers 1836)
Emmett   A2   1859   15   1860-80   Kossuth, Dickinson .... Estherville
Fayette   A3   1850   29   1850-80   Clayton .... West Union
  (Clk of Dist Ct has b & d rec fom 1880, m, div & civ ct rec from 1860, pro
  rec from 1869)
Floyd   A3   1854   21   1860-80   Chickasaw .... Charles City

(Clk of Dist Ct has b & d rec 1880, m & div rec 1860, pro & civ ct rec 1854)
Fox   (See Calhoun)
Franklin   A3   1855   15   1860-80   Chickasaw . . . . Hampton
Fremont   C1   1847   10   1850-80   Pottawattamie   . . . . Sidney
Greene   B2   1854   14   1860-80   Dallas . . . . Jefferson
  (Clk of Ct has b, d, div & civ ct rec from 1880, m & pro rec from 1854)
Grundy   B3   1856   14   1860-80   Black Hawk . . . . Grundy Center
Guthrie   B2   1851   14   1860-80   Jackson . . . . Guthrie Center
Hamilton   B2   1856   20   1860-80   Webster . . . . Webster City
  (Clk of Ct has b, d, bur, div, pro & civ ct rec from 1880, m rec from 1866)
Hancock   A2   1857   15   1860-80   Wright . . . . Garner
  (Clk of Dist Ct has, b, d, bur rec from 1880, m rec from 1861, div rec from
  1873, pro rec from 1869, civ ct rec from 1865)
Hardin   B3   1853   23   1860-80   Black Hawk . . . . Eldora
  Clk of Dist Ct has b rec from 1880 to 1931 & 1941 to present, m rec from
  1864, d rec from 1880, div rec from 1889, pro rec from 1871, civ ct rec 1877)
Harrison   B1   1853   18   1860-80   Pottawattamie . . . . Logan
  (Clk of Dist Ct has b & d rec from 1880, m & div rec from 1853, pro rec from
  1869, civ ct rec from 1850)
Henry   C4   1836   18   1840-80   Wisconsin Territory . . . . . Mount Pleasant
Howard   A3   1855   18   1860-80   Chickasaw, Floyd . . . . Cresco
Humboldt   A2   1857   13   1860-80   Webster . . . . Dakota City
  (Clk of Dist Ct has b rec from 1880, m rec from 1858, d rec from 1895, div rec
  from 1890, pro rec from 1873, civ ct rec from 1892)
Ida   B1   1858   13   1860-80   Cherokee   . . . . Ida Grove
Iowa   B3   1847   10   1850-80   Washington . . . . Marengo

Jackson   B4   1837   16   1840-80   Wisconsin Territory   . . . . . Maquoketa
Jasper   B3   1846   21   1850-80   Mahaska . . . . Newton
  (Clk of Dist Ct has b, div, pro & civ ct rec from 1880, m rec from 1849,
  d rec from 1880 to 1935 and from 1941 to date)
Jefferson   C3   1839   35   1840-80   Indian Land Purchase . . . . Fairfield
  (Clk of Dist Ct has b, d, div, civ ct rec 1880, m rec 1839, pro rec 1850)
Johnson   B4   1838   16   1840-80   Des Moines . . . . Iowa City
Jones   B4   1837   54   1840-80   Wisconsin Territory . . . . Anamosa
  (Clk of Dist Ct has b & d rec from 1880, m rec from 1840, div rec from 1895)
Keokuk   C3   1844   21   1850-80   Washington . . . . Sigourney
Kossuth   A2   1855   15   1860-80   Webster . . . . Algona
  (Clk of Dist Ct has b & d rec from 1880, m, div, pro, civ ct rec from 1857)
Lee   C4   1836   44   1840-80   Des Moines . . . . Ft. Madison & Keokuk
  (Clk of Dist Ct, Ft. Madison has b rec 1880 to 1921, d rec 1880 to 1919, m
  & civ ct rec 1837, pro rec 1883) (Clk of Dist Ct, Keokuk has most rec from 1880)
Linn   B4   1837   137   1840-80   Wisconsin Territory . . . . . Cedar Rapids
  (Clk of Dist Ct has b rec 1880, d rec 1941, m, div, pro, civ ct rec 1837)
Louisa   C4   1837   10   1840-80   Des Moines . . . . Wapello
  (Clk of Dist Ct has b & d rec from 1880, m, div, pro, civ ct rec from 1837)
Lucas   C2   1849   11   1850-80   Monroe . . . . Chariton
  (Clk of Ct has b, d & civ ct rec from 1880, m & pro rec from 1850, div
  rec from 1900)
Lyon   A1   1851   14   1870-80   Woodbury . . . . Rock Rapids
Madison   C2   1850   12   1850-80   Polk . . . . Winterset
  (Clk of Ct has b & d rec from July of 1880, m rec from 1849, div & civ
  ct rec from 1861, pro rec from 1852)
Mahaska   C3   1844   24   1850-80   Fox, Sac Indian Purchase . . . Oskaloosa
  (Clk of Dist Ct has b & d rec from 1880; m, pro & civ ct rec from 1844;
  div rec from 1850)
Marion   C3   1845   26   1850-80   Washington . . . . Knoxville
  (Clk of Ct has m, div, pro & civ ct rec from 1845; Health Dept. has b, d,
  and bur rec from July 1880)
Marshall   B3   1849   38   1850-80   Jasper . . . . Marshalltown
  (Clk of Dist Ct has b & d rec from 1880, m, pro, & civ ct rec from 1850;
  div rec from 1905)

Mills   C1   1851   13   1860-80   Pottawattamie . . . . Glenwood
   (Clk of Dist Ct has incom b rec 1880, d & div rec 1880, pro & civ ct rec 1851)
Mitchell   A3   1854   14   1860-80   Chickasaw . . . . Osage
   (Clk of Dist Ct has m rec from 1860, b, d, div, pro & civ ct rec from 1880)
Monona   B1   1854   14   1860-80   Harrison . . . . Onawa
   (Clk of Ct has b rec from 1869; m rec from 1865; d rec from 1880; bur rec
   from 1950; div rec from 1906; pro rec from 1858, civ ct rec from 1860)
Monroe   C3   1845   10   1850-80   Wapello . . . . Albia
   (Clk of Dist Ct has b & d rec from 1880, m rec from 1845, div & civ ct rec
   from 1869, pro rec from 1854)
Montgomery C1   1851   14   1860-80   Polk . . . . Red Oak
   (Clk of Ct has b, d, & bur rec from 1880, m rec from 1856, div & civ ct
   rec from 1873, pro rec from 1860; bur rec is part of d rec; City Clk has cem
   records)
Muscatine   A4   1837   34   1840-80   Des Moines . . . . Muscatine
   (Clk of Ct has b & d rec from 1880, m rec from 1837, div & civ ct rec
   from 1861, pro rec from 1866)
O'Brien   A1   1851   19   1860-80   Cherokee . . . . Primghar
   (Clk of Ct has b rec from 1880 to 4 July 1835 & 4 July 1941 to present,
   m, div, pro & civ ct rec from 1880, d rec from July 1941, bur rec is part
   of d rec)
Osceola   A1   1851   10   1870-80   Woodbury . . . . Sibley
   (Clk of Dist Ct has b, m, d, div, pro, civ ct rec from 1880)
Page   C1   1850   21   1850-80   Pottawattamie . . . . Clarinda

Palo Alto   A2   1858   15   1860-80   Kossuth . . . . Emmetsburg
Plymouth   A1   1858   24   1860-80   Woodbury . . . . Le Mars
   (Clk of Dist Ct has b, d, bur rec from 1880, m, div, pro & civ ct rec from 1871,
   nat rec from 1872)
Pocahontas   A2   1859   14   1860-80   Humboldt, Greene . . . . Pocahontas
   (Clk of Dist Ct has b & d rec from 1880, m rec from 1881, div & civ ct rec
   from 1860, pro rec from 1872)
Polk   B2   1836   266   1850-80   Indian Lands . . . . Des Moines
   (Clk of Ct has b & d rec from 1941, m rec from 1870, div rec from 1870, pro
   rec from 1855, and civ ct rec from 1850)
Pottawattamie C1 1848   83   1850-80   Indian Lands . . . . Council Bluffs
   (Clk of Ct has b rec from 1880 to 1921 and 1941 to present, b rec between 1921
   & 1941 are in Des Moines; m rec from 1846, d rec from 1941, div rec from
   1907, pro rec from 1898)
Poweshiek   B3   1848   19   1850-80   Musquaka . . . . Montezuma
   (Clk of Dist Ct has b, m, d, div, pro, civ ct rec from 1880)
Ringgold   C2   1855   8   1860-80   Taylor . . . . Mount Ayr
Sac   B1   1857   17   1860-80   Greene . . . . Sac City
   (Clk of Dist Ct has b, m, d, bur, div, pro, civ ct rec from 1888, Ct house
   burned in 1888)
Scott   B4   1837   119   1840-80   Wisconsin Territory . . . . Davenport
   (Clk of Ct has b, d & bur rec from 1880, m rec from 1837, div & pro rec
   from 1838, civ ct rec from 1851)
Shelby   B1   1853   16   1860-80   Cass . . . . Harlan
   (Clk of Ct has b, m, d, div, pro & civ ct rec from 1880, pro rec are limited
   from 1853, newspapers available at Public Library)
Sioux   A1   1860   26   1860-80   Plymouth . . . . Orange City
   (Clk of Dist Ct has b rec from 1880, m, d, div, pro, civ ct rec from 1870)
Story   B2   1853   49   1860-80   Jasper, Polk, Boone . . . . Nevada
   (Clk of Dist Ct has b & d rec fom 1880, m, div, pro, civ ct, crim ct rec
   from 1854)
Tama   B3   1852   21   1850-80   Boone, Benton . . . . Toledo
   (Clk of Dist Ct has b rec from 1880, m rec from 1853, d rec from 1880, div
   rec from 1908, pro rec from 1895, civ ct rec from 1859)
Taylor   C2   1851   10   1850-80   Page . . . . Bedford
Union   C2   1855   14   1860-80   Clarke . . . . Creston
Van Buren   C3   1836   10   1840-80   Des Moines . . . . Keosauqua

(Clk of Ct has b & d rec from 1880, m, div, pro & civ ct rec from 1837)
Wapello   C3   1844   46   1850-80   Indian Lands .... Ottumwa
Warren   C2   1846   21   1850-80   Polk .... Indianola
      (Clk of Dist Ct has b & d rec from 1880, m, div, pro rec from 1859)
Washington   C4   1837   19   1840-80   Wisconsin Territory ..... Washington
      (Clk of Dist Ct has b & d rec from 1880, m rec from 1846, div rec from 1844,
      pro & civ ct rec from 1836)
Wayne   C2   1850   10   1850-80   Appanoose .... Corydon
      (Clk of Dist Ct has b & d rec from 1880, m rec from 1851, div rec from 1906,
      pro rec from 1891, civ ct rec from 1875, cir ct rec from 1860, guardianship 1895)
Webster   B2   1852   48   1860-80   *Yell, *Risley .... Fort Dodge
                                 *Now known as Hamilton
      (Clk of Ct has b, m, d, pro, civ ct, crim, insane, juvenile & Notary Public rec)
Winnebago   A2   1857   13   1860-80   Kossuth .... Forest City
      (Clk of Ct has b & d rec from 1880, m, div, pro & civ ct rec from 1865; Co
      Registrar has bur rec)
Winneshiek   A3   1847   22   1850-80   Indian Lands .... Decorah
      (Clk of Dist Ct has b & d rec from 1880, m rec from 1851, div rec from 1855,
      civ ct rec from 1855, pro rec from 1853)
Woodbury   B1   1851   108 1860-80   Indian Lands .... Sioux City
      (Clk of Dist Ct has b & d rec 1880, m rec 1854, div, pro, civ ct rec 1857)
Worth   A3   1857   10   1860-80   Mitchell .... Northwood
      (Clk of Ct has b rec from 1880 to 1905, from 1905 to 1921, & from 1941 to
      present. (b rec for 1905 & 1921 to 1941 are at State Dept of Health). Clk has
      m rec from 1858, d rec from 1880 to 1919 (d rec from 1920 to 1941 are at
      State Dept of Health); Div rec from 1879 and pro & civ ct rec from 1857)
Wright   A2   1855   19   1860-80   Webster .... Clarion

County Map of Iowa

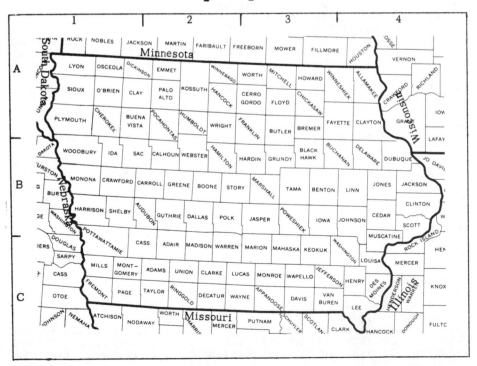

Federal courts (start 1845). Inventory of County Archives, Carroll, Cherokee, Dallas, Dubuque, Ida, Jasper, Montgomery, Polk, Sac, Taylor, Woodbury. Guide to Public vital statistics records. Directory of Church and religious organizations. Guide to Depository of manuscripts in the U.S. - Iowa. Guide to manuscripts collection in Iowa. Diary of E. P. Burton, Surgeon, 7th Regiment, Illinois; A check list of Iowa imprints, 1838-1860. Depository of unpublished material, State Dept. of History and Archives, Des Moines, Iowa.

Kansas

Capital Topeka - Territory 1854 - State 1861 - (34th)

Kansas was part of the Louisiana Purchase when it became annexed to the United States in 1803. It was included in the Missouri Territory until 1821. For 33 years it was known as an unorganized territory, inhabited mainly by Indians. For many years there was constant trouble between them and the settlers, until the Indians were pushed gradually into the Oklahoma area.

Fort Levenworth became the first community in the area in 1827. To thousands en route to the valleys of Utah, the gold fields of California or the beckoning Oregon country, it was a welcome stop-over outfitting place.

Kansas became a state in 1861, the thirty-fourth. The population then was about 110,000, consisting mostly of Southerners and New Englanders with a sprinkling from Missouri, Illinois, Indiana, Ohio and Kentucky. Many Civil War veterans took up homesteads in Kansas following the war. Among the foreign born settlers many came from Germany, Russia, Sweden, and England. Many Mexicans also settled in the state.

Birth records since 1911, marriages since 1913, and death records since 1911 are obtainable at the office of Division of Vital Statistics, State Department of Health, Topeka, Kansas 66603. Most of the records are indexed.

The County Clerk in the county of occurance of birth and death has some records of these events.

The Probate Judge of each county has records of marriages in his county before 1913.

Records of divorces granted before 1951 are on file in the office of the clerk of the District Court handling the matter. Divorces granted after July 1951 are filed in the office of the above mentioned Division of Vital Statistics.

The Naturalization files are kept in the Topeka office of the United States Circuit Court and the district court in each of the counties in the state.

Probate matter and wills are handled by the Probate Judges who also have Civil Court records in most counties.

Real estate property is listed with the county recorder and county assessor in the county where land is located.

The Census Bureau, Memorial Bldg., Topeka, Kansas 66603, has charge of all census records. The first Kansas federal census was taken in 1860. The State census of 1855 is alphabetized.

Libraries: Public Library, 6th & Minnesota Sts., Kansas City 66101, (Wyandotte); University of Kansas (Kansas History), Lawrence 66044, (Douglas); Kansas State Historical Society Library, Memorial Building, (History and Genealogy), Topeka 66603, (Shawnee); Public Library, 220 S. Main St.,(Kansas History), Wichita 67202, (Sedgwick).

The Kansas State Historical Library in the Memorial Building, Topeka 66603, Kansas, has more than 10,000 genealogical volumes including magazines, vital records, war records, family and local histories. Its newspaper collection is second only to that of the Library of Congress. Copies of the Federal Census for 1860,1870 and 1880 are also there, together with the State Census records from 1855 to 1925, inclusive, at ten year periods.

Among books dealing with Kansas histories and genealogical information are the following:

"Biographical History of Central Kansas." The Lewis Publishing Company, New York and Chicago, 1902. Vol. I, 756 pp. Vol. II, 877 pp.

Connelley, William Elsey, "History of Kansas, State and People." American Historical Society, 1928. History and biography.

Green, C. R., "Us and Our Neighbors." A historical and genealogical directory of more than 3,200 men, women and children who lived about Lyndon, Osage county, Kansas, as revealed by the assessor's returns for the years of 1896, 1897 and 1900. Compiled and published by C. R. Green, Lyndon, Kansas, June 1901. 299 pp.

"Genealogical and Biographical Record of North-eastern Kansas." The Lewis Publishing Company, Chicago, 1900. 755 pp.

Isely, Bliss, and Richards, W. M., "Four Centuries in Kansas." McCormick-Mathers Company, Wichita, Kansas, 1936.

Works Projects Administration, "Kansas, a Guide to the Sunflower State." Viking 1939. American Guide Series.

Among available autobiographies or biographies of important

Kansans are the following: Earl Browder, Walter P. Chrysler, John Steuart Curry, Charles Curtis, Amelia Earhart, Dwight D. Eisenhower, Dorothy Canfield Fisher, Frederick Funston, John James Ingalls, Hugh S. Johnson, Martin (Elmer) Johnson and Osa Helen Leighty Johnson, Edgar Lee Masters, Carry Amelia Moore Nation, Fred Andrew Stone, and William Allen White.

Kansas County Histories

(Population figures to nearest thousand - 1960 Census)

Name	Map Index	Date Formed	Pop. By M	Census Reports Available	Parent County	County Seat
Allen	A3	1855	16	1860-80	Original county	Iola
Anderson	A3	1855	9	1860-80	Original county	Garnett
Arapahoe (Disorganized)				1860-80	(1870 census missing) (Inc. some of Colo.)	
Atchison	A2	1855	21	1860-80	Original county	Atchison
Barber	D4	1873	9	1880	Harper	Medicine Lodge
Barton	D2	1867	32	1870-80	Ellsworth	Great Bend
Bourbon	A3	1855	16	1860-80	Original County	Fort Scott

(Clk of Ct has div rec from 1870, pro judges offices has m & pro rec from 1870, civ ct rec from 1963, b & d rec at Topeka, Kans.)

Breckenridge (See Lyon)				1860		
Brown	A1	1855	13	1860-80	Original county	Hiawatha
Butler	B3	1855	38	1860-80	Original county	El Dorado

(Co Clk has b & d rec from 1890 to 1909 incom)

Calhoun		1855			Name changed to Jackson after Civil War	
Chase	B3	1859	4	1860-80	Butler	Cottonwood Falls

(Co Clk has b rec 1886 - 1911, d rec 1886 to 1910)

Chautauqua	B4	1875	6	1880	Howard	Sedan
Cherokee	A4	1855	22	1870-80	Unorganized Territory	Columbus
Cheyenne	F1	1873	5	1880	Kirwin Land District	Saint Francis
Clark	E4	1873	3	1880	Ford	Ashland

(Co Clk has m rec from 1885)

Clay	C2	1856	11	1860-80	Original County	Clay Center

(Clk of Ct has b rec from 1885 to 1911, div rec; Pro Judges Offices has m rec)

Cloud	C2	1860	14	1870-80	Formerly Shirley County	Concordia
Coffey	B3	1855	8	1860-80	Original county	Burlington

(Co Clk has m rec 1859, div rec 1872, pro rec 1857, civ ct rec 1872)

Comanche	D4	1875	3	1880	Kiowa	Coldwater

(Pro Judge has m, div, pro & civ ct rec; City Clk, Coldwater, Kans. has b rec; Co Coroner has d & bur rec)

Cowley	B4	1867	38	1870-80	Formerly Hunter	Winfield

(Clk of Ct has div rec from 1870, civ ct rec; pro ct has m rec & pro rec from 16 Aug 1870; Division of Vit Stat has b & d rec from 1911; Funeral Homes have bur rec)

Crawford	A3	1867	37	1870-80	Bourbon	Girard

(Co Clk has b rec from 1887 to 1911, Board Of Health has b rec from 1911 to present, Co Clk has d rec from 1887 to 1908; Pro Ct has m & pro rec; Clk of Dist Ct has div & civ ct rec)

Davis		1871		1860-80	Riley - See Geary, Junction City	
Decatur	E1	1873	6	1880	Norton	Oberlin

(Pro Judge has m, div, & military rec from 1880, pro rec from 1900, civ ct rec from 1937, and land rec; b & d rec from 1885 and bur rec from 1913 are sent to Topeka, Kans. by the City Clk)

Dickinson	C2	1855	22	1860-80	Original county	Abilene
Doniphan	A1	1855	10	1860-80	Original County	Troy

(Bureau of Vital Statistics, Topeka has b rec; pro Ct has m & pro rec; Clk of Dist Ct has div rec)

Dorn   1860   see Nesho
Douglas   A2   1855   44   1860-80   Original county . . . . Lawrence
Edwards   D3   1874   5   1880   Kiowa . . . . Kinsley
     (Bureau of Vital Statistics has b, d & bur rec; Pro Ct has m & pro rec; Clk of
     Ct has div & civ ct rec)
Elk   B3   1875   5   1880   Howard . . . . Howard
     (Co Clk has b & d rec from 1885 to 1910)
Ellis   D2   1865   21   1870-80   Unorganized Territory . . . . Hays
Ellsworth   C2   1867   8   1870-80   Saline . . . . Ellsworth
Finney   F3   1884   16   Arapahoe, Foote, Sequoyah? . . Garden City
     (Pro Ct has m & pro rec from 1885; Clk Dist Ct has div & civ ct rec from 1885;
     Kans. State Dept of Health, Division of Vital Statistics has b & d rec; City Clk,
     Garden City, Kans. has bur rec) (Formerly Sequoyah County)
Foote   1880
Ford   E3   1873   21   1880   Unorganized Territory . . . . . Dodge City
Franklin   A2   1856   20   1860-80   Original county . . . . Ottawa
Garfield   (Annexed to Finney 1893)
Geary   B2   1889   29   Davis Co. 1875 to 1888 . . . Junction City
     (Pro Ct has m & pro rec from 1860; Clk of Dist Ct has div rec from 1860; Co
     Ct has civ ct rec from 1937)
Godfrey   1860
Gove   E2   1880   4   1880   Lane . . . . Gove
Graham   E2   1880   6   1880   Rooks . . . . Hill City
Grant   F3   1873   5   1880   Finney, Kearney . . . . Ulysses
     (City Clk has b rec 1890 to 1909; Pro Judge has m rec 1892 to 1921, also pro
     rec; Cem Custodian has bur rec; Clk of Ct has div & civ ct rec)
Gray   E3   1887   4   Finney, Ford . . . . Cimarron
     (City Clk has b & d rec; Pro Judge has m, pro & civ ct rec; Clk of Dist Ct has
     div rec) (Gray Co has been named Foote, Buffalo & Sequoia before it became
     Gray Co. Co Clk has Tax Rolls census of 1889 to present, also District school
     rec of pupils with various info on children & parents of real early part of the
     Co. Register of Deeds has deeds from 1886, mtg rec are available from 1887)
Greeley   F2   1873   2   1880   Hamilton . . . . Tribune
     (Pro Ct has m rec from 1888; Clk of Dist Ct has div rec from 1888; Co Clk has
     old newspapers from 1886; City Clk has bur rec; Bureau of Vital Statistics
     has b rec; Co Supt. has school rec)
Greenwood   B3   1855   11   1860-80   Original county . . . . Eureka
Hamilton   F3   1873   3   1880   Unorganized Territory . . . . . Syracuse
Harper   C4   1879   10   1880   Kingman . . . . Anthony
     (Co Clk has m, div, pro & civ ct rec)
Harvey   C3   1872   26   1880   Sedgwick, McPherson, Marion . . . Newton
Haskell   F3   1887   3   Finney . . . . Sublette
     (Dept. of Legal Statistics has b & d rec; Pro Judge has m & pro rec; Clk of
     Dist Ct has div rec)
Hodgeman   E3   1879   3   1880   Indian Lands (Est. 1868) . . . . Jetmore
     (City Clk has b, d & bur rec from 1911; Pro Judge has m & pro rec from 1887;
     Clk of Dist Ct has div & civ ct rec from 1880)
Howard   1875   Taken to form Elk and Chautauqua
Hunter (see Cowley)   1860
Jackson   B2   1855   10   1860-80   (See Calhoun) . . . . Holton
Jefferson   A2   1855   11   1860-80   Original county . . . . Oskaloosa
Jewell   C1   1870   7   1870-80   Mitchell . . . . Mankato
     (Pro Judge has m & pro rec; Pro or Dist Ct has civ ct rec)
Johnson   A2   1855 144   1860-80   Original county . . . . Olathe
     (Clk of Dist Ct has div & civ ct rec from 1861; Pro Ct has m & pro rec; State
     Dept. of Health, Division of Vital Statistics has b & d rec; Bur rec are kept by
     Registration Districts)
Kearny   F3   1873   3   1880   Finney . . . . Lakin
     (Co Clk has b, m & d rec from 1900 to 1910; Board of Cemetery Dist 2 & 3
     has bur rec; Clk of Dist Ct has div rec; Pro Judge has pro & civ ct rec)

Kingman   C3   1874   10   1880   Unorganized Territory .... Kingman
   (Dept of Health has b, d & bur rec; Pro Ct has m rec; Clk of Dist Ct has div rec)
Kiowa   D3   1886   5   Comanche, Edwards ...... Greensburg
   (In 1875 Kiowa County disappeared from map and its territory was divided be-
   tween Edwards and Comanche Counties. Kiowa reappeared in 1886 being formed
   from parts of Edwards and Comanche.)
Labette   A4   1867   27   1870-80   Neosho .... Oswego
Lane   E2   1873   3   1880   Finney .... Dighton
Leavenworth A2   1855   49   1860-80   Original county .... Leavenworth
Lincoln   C2   1870   6   1870-80   Ellsworth .... Lincoln
   (Co Clk has m, d, pro rec from 1870, also div rec)
Linn   A3   1855   8   1860-80   Original county .... Mound City
Logan   F2   1881   4   Wallace .... Oakley
   (Co Treas has tax receipts from 1890; Co Clk has Assessment rec from 1890,
   m, div, pro & civ ct rec; City Clk has b, d, and bur rec; Reg of Deeds has deeds
   from 1890) (Formerly St. John County)
Lykins   1860   (See Miami)
Lyon   B2   1857   27   1870-80   Madison (See Breckenridge) ... Emporia
   (Pro Ct has m rec from 1861, pro rec from 1859; Clk of Dist Ct has div rec
   from 1860, civ ct rec from 1858; Emporia City Clk has b & d rec)
McGhee   1860   (See Cherokee)
McPherson C3   1870   24   1870-80   Unorganized Territory .... McPherson
   (Co Clk has b, d & bur rec from 1888 to 1892, from 1918 these rec are kept in
   Topeka, Kans. McPherson Co early register of births is very incomplete, they
   have less than 10% of the births from 1888 to 1908; Pro Ct has m & pro rec
   from 1870; Clk of Dist Ct has div rec from 1873; Co Ct has civ ct rec)
Madison   1860   Divided to Morris & Lyon Counties
Marion   C3   1860   15   1860-80   Chase .... Marion
   (Co Clk has b rec 1885 to 1911, m rec 1892 to 1899, d rec 1893 to 1903)
Marshall   B1   1855   16   1860-80   Original county .... Marysville
Meade   E4   1873   6   1880   Unorganized Territory .... Meade
Miami   A2   1855   20   1870-80   Formerly Lykins .... Paola
Mitchell   C2   1870   9   1870-80   Kirwin Land District .... Beloit
Montgomery B4   1869   45   1870-80   Labette .... Independence
   (Co Clk has b rec from 1911, m rec 1870 to 1888, d rec 1892 to 1911, div &
   pro rec from 1870, civ ct rec from 1871)
Morris   B2   1858   7   1860-80   Madison (Formerly Wise) .. Council Grove
   (Board of Health has b & d rec; Pro Judge has m, pro & civ ct rec; City Clk has
   bur rec; Clk of Dist Ct has div rec)
Morton   F4   1886   3   Stanton .... Elkhart
Nemaha   B1   1855   13   1860-80   Original county .... Seneca
   (Co Clk has b, d, m rec 1885 to 1911, pro rec 1857, civ ct rec from 1859)
Neosho   A3   1855   19   1870-80   Original County............... Erie
   (originally Dorn - name changed 1861)
Ness   E2   1873   5   1880   Hodgeman .... Ness City
Norton   D1   1872   8   1880   Unorganized Territory .... Norton
Osage   B2   1855   13   1860-80   Formerly Weller .... Lyndon
Osborne   D2   1867   8   1870-80   Mitchell .... Osborne
   (Co Clk has m, div, Pro & civ ct rec)
Otoe   1860
Ottawa   C2   1866   7   1870-80   Saline .... Minneapolis
   (Co Clk has m, div & pro rec; City Officers hav b rec from 1911, d rec)
Pawnee   D3   1872   10   1880   Rush, Stafford .... Larned
Phillips   D1   1872   9   1880   Kirwin Land District ..... Phillipsburg
Pottawatomie B2 1857   12   1860-80   Riley, Calhoun .... Westmoreland
Pratt   D3   1879   12   1880   Stafford .... Pratt
   (Co Clk has b rec from 1887 to 1900)
Rawlins   E4   1873   5   1880   Kirwin Land District .... Atwood
Reno   C3   1877   61   1880   Sedgwick, McPherson ..... Hutchinson

County Map of Kansas

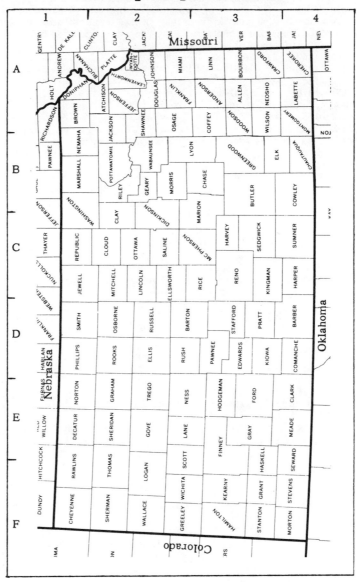

(Co Clk has b, m, d rec from 1890, bur rec from 1901; Clk of Dist Ct has div rec; Pro Ct has pro rec)

Republic	C1	1868	10	1870-80	Washington, Cloud	Belleville
Rice	C3	1867	14	1870-80	Reno	Lyons
Riley	B2	1855	42	1860-80	Unorganized Terr., Wabaunsee .	Manhattan
Rooks	D2	1872	10	1880	Kirwin Land District	Stockton

(Bureau of Vital Statistics has b rec; Pro Judge has m, pro & civ ct rec; Clk of Dist Ct has div rec)

Rush	D2	1874	6	1880	Unorganized Territory	. . . . . La Crosse

(Pro Ct has m rec from 1876)

Russell   D2 1867   11 1870-80 Ellsworth . . . . Russell
    (Co Clk has m, pro & civ ct rec from 1876, also div rec)

Saline   C2 1860   55 1870-80 Original county . . . . Salina

Scott   F2 1873   5 1880   Finney . . . . Scott City
    (City Clk has b & d rec; Pro Judge has m & pro rec; Co Clk has bur rec; Clk
    of Ct has div & civ ct rec)

Sedgwick   C3 1867 343 1870-80 Butler . . . . Wichita
    (Bureau of Vital Statistics has b, d & bur rec; Pro Ct has m & pro rec; Clk of
    Ct has div & civ ct rec)

Sequoyah   1880

Seward   F4 1873   16 1880   Indian Lands . . . . Liberal

Shawnee   B2 1855 141 1860-80 Original county . . . . Topeka

Sheridan   E2 1873   4 1880   Unorganized Territory . . . . Hoxie.
    (Co Clk has incom b rec 1887 to 1910, d rec 1887 to 1910, m, div, pro, civ ct
    rec from 188?)

Sherman   F2 1873   7 1880   Kirwin Land District . . . . Goodland
    (Co Clk has newspaper files from 1898, school and census rec; City Clk has b
    & d rec; Pro Judge has m & pro rec; Clk of Dist Ct has div & civ ct rec;
    morticians have bur rec)

Shirley (See Cloud)

Smith   D1 1872   8 1880   Unorganized Territory . . . . . Smith Center
    (State of Kansas has b, d & bur rec; Pro Judge has m & pro rec from 1875;
    Clk of Dist Ct has div & civ ct rec from 1875)

Stafford   D3 1870   7 1880   Unorganized Territory . . . . Saint John

Stanton   F3 1873   2 1880   Reorganized . . . . Johnson
    (City Clk has b, d & bur rec; Pro Judge has m & pro rec; Clk of Dist Ct
    has div & civ ct rec)

Stevens   F4 1873   4 1880   Indian Lands . . . . Hugoton

Sumner   C4 1867   25 1870-80 Cowley . . . . Wellington

Thomas   F2 1873   7 1880   Kirwin Land District . . . . Colby

Trego   E2 1879   5 1880   Ellis . . . . Wakeeney

Wabaunsee B2 1855   7 1860-80 Riley, Morris . . . . Alma
    (Pro Ct has m, div, pro & civ ct rec; Bureau of Vital Statistics has d & bur rec)

Wallace   F2 1865   2 1870-80 Indian Lands (See Logan) . . Sharon Springs
    (City Clk has b & d rec; Pro Ct has m & pro rec; Townships has bur rec; Dist
    Ct has div rec; Co Ct has civ ct rec)

Washington C1 1856   11 1860-80 Original county . . . . Washington

Weller (see Osage)

Wichita   F2 1873   3 1880   Indian Lands . . . . Leoti

Wilson   B3 1855   13 1860-80 Original county . . . . Fredonia

Wise (see Morris)

Woodson B3 1855   5 1860-80 Original county . . . . Yates Center

Wyandotte A2 1856 185 1860-80 Original county . . . . Kansas City

Genealogists' Check List of the Historical Records Survey, Kansas

Federal courts (Start 1854). Inventory of County archives, Bourbon, Cherokee, Franklin, Gove, Graham, Gray, Greenwood, Johnson, Montgomery, Morris, Osage, Phillips, Seward, Shawnee. Guide to Public Vital Statistic records. Check list of Kansas imprints 1854-1876. Depository of unpublished material, Kansas State Historical Society, Topeka, Kansas.

Kentucky

Capital Frankfort - State 1792 - (15th)

The settling of Kentucky from the mid seventeen-hundreds to the early parts of the eighteen-hundreds included some of the most hazardous and bloody events of America. Several thousand of those early settlers lost their lives in skirmishes with Indians, determined to protect their hunting grounds from the encroachments of the white man.

Long before any white man had explored the entire Kentucky area, it was claimed by Virginia as part of her Augusta County. It was included in the Virginia County of 1584.

Daniel Boone, born in Pennsylvania of English parents, moved his family in September 1773 into the Kentucky area from Rowan County, North Carolina, on the Yadkin River. However, he had previously explored that section some seven years earlier. Neither was Boone the first to investigate the possibilities of Kentucky. The eastern section of the area was explored by Dr. Thomas Walker as early as 1750. Twenty-five years later the Transylvania Company was organized under the leadership of Col. Richard Henderson of North Carolina. From Indian tribes he purchased almost half of what is now the state of Kentucky, all of the land between the Kentucky River, in the central part of the state, and the Cumberland River, in the extreme western part. A multiplicity of law suits and the Revolutionary War completed the activities of the Henderson enterprise in a dismal failure.

Previous to these explorations all of Kentucky had been made part of Fincastle county, Virginia. During Boone's activities in the section, Kentucky was designated as Kentucky County, Virginia. This designation was made in December 1776. In 1780 it was divided into three counties, Fayette, Jefferson, and Lincoln. In 1790 those three counties were subdivided into nine counties, Mason, Bourbon, Woodford, Fayette, Madison, Jefferson, Mercer, Nelson, and Lincoln.

By 1900 those nine 1790 counties had been subdivided into the following present counties:

MASON: The east six-seventh of Pike, Floyd, Martin, Johnson; the east half of each of Magoffin and Morgan; Lawrence, Elliott, Rowan, Carter, Boyd, Greenup, Lewis, Fleming, Mason, Robertson, Bracken, Campbell, and the east third of Pendleton.

BOURBON: East four-fifths of Harlan, Letcher, west one-seventh of Pike, Knott, Perry, east half of Leslie, Breathitt, west half of each of Magoffin and Morgan, Wolfe, north half of each of

Lee and Estill, Bath, Powell, Manifee, Montgomery, east half of Clark, Bourbon, Nicholas, east three-fourths of Harrison, and triangular shaped south one-fifth of Pendleton.

WOODFORD: Woodford, Scott, east half of Franklin, Owen, Grant, Boone, Gallatin and east half of Carroll.

FAYETTE: Fayette, Jessamine and west half of Clark.

MADISON: Madison, east half of Garrard, south half of Estill, Jackson, north-east third of Rockcastle, Owsley, south half Lee, Clay, west half of Leslie, and west one-fifth of Harlan.

JEFFERSON: North half of each of Spencer and Bullit, Jefferson, Shelby, Oldham, Henry, North-west corner of Anderson, Trimble, and west half of Carroll.

MERCER: Triangular south third Franklin, east half of Anderson, Mercer, north two-thirds of Boyle, and northwest third of Garrard.

NELSON: Washington, Marion, Taylor, north half of each of Green, Hart, Edmonson, Butler, and McLean; Ohio, Davies, Hancock, Breckinridge, Meade, Hardin, south half of each of Bullitt and Spencer; Nelson, Larue, and Grayson.

LINCOLN: Henderson, Webster, Hopkins, south half of McLean; Muhlenberg; south half of Butler; Warren, south half of each of Edmonson, Hart, and Green, Adair, Casey, Lincoln, west of Garrard, southwest two-thirds of Rockcastle; Laurel, south one-third of Boyle, Knox, Bell, Whitley, Pulaski, Wayne, Russell, Clinton, Cumberland, Metcalf, Monroe, Barren, Allen, Simpson, Logan, Todd, Christian, Trigg, Caldwell, Lyon, Marshall, Calloway, Graves, Fulton, Hickman, Carlisle, Ballard, McCracken, Livingston, Crittenden and Union.

The extreme western tip of Kentucky, surrounded on three sides by water - the Mississippi on the west, the Ohio and the Tennessee Rivers on the north, and the Kentucky Reservior on the east is sometimes referred to as the Jackson Purchase Region from the fact that it was purchased in 1818 from the Chickasaw Indians during the presidency of Andrew Jackson. It includes the following eight counties, sometimes included in the old Lincoln county: Calloway, Marshall, McCracken, Graves, Fulton, Hickman, Carlisle, and Ballard.

The descriptions of the Kentucky counties carved out of the nine counties existing in 1790 given in earlier paragraphs follow the Kentucky map printed in "A Century of Population Growth - 1790 -1900" by the Bureau of Census, Washington, D.C. 20025. In several instances these descriptions do not harmonize with those on a map arranged by Bayless Hardin of Kentucky State Historical Society and published in Heineman and Brumbaugh's "First Census of Kentucky, 1790" (Kentucky Taxpayers of the Time.) This map is printed on page 45 of the 1953 Handy Book.

Those interested may compare the two maps in question.

On 1 June 1792, Kentucky became the fifteenth state admitted into the union.

It took courageous men and women to make their homes in a country as full of danger and excitement as existed in Kentucky in its early days. They came mostly, to begin with, from Maryland, Norh Carolina, Pennsylvania, Tennessee, and Virginia. Originally they were of German, English, Irish and Scottish descent. As new territories, new states were carved from the large American expanse, many of them were settled by the descendants of the original Kentuckians. With the increased European migration many people have also come to Kentucky from Russia, Italy, Poland and Austria.

Division of Vital Records, State Department of Health, 275 East Main Street, Frankfort, Kentucky 40601, has birth and death records from the beginning of 1911. The City Health Department in some of the larger cities have still earlier records.

Records of births and deaths from some counties as early as 1851 are in the library of the Kentucky Historical Society, Frankfort, Kentucky 40601.

County Clerk of county where transaction was completed may have wills, probate, marriage and divorce records.

Naturalization records are filed in the district courts in Bowling Green, Catlettsburg, Covington, Frankfort, London, Louisville, Owensboro, and Paducah. They may also be obtained in the office of the clerk of the Circuit Court in the various county seats in the state.

Quite complete records of birth, marriages, death, wills, etc., on file on microfilms and written and printed records at the Genealogical Society of Utah, Salt Lake City, Utah 84100. Also the complete 1810 census.

Mimeographed copies of the 1810 Census by counties, and vital statistics by counties may be obtained from Mrs. Anne Walker Burns, P.O. Box 6183 Apex Station, Washington, D.C. 20004.

The federal census records of 1790 and 1800 are missing, but the so called "First Census of Kentucky", supplies a list of taxpayers of those years.

Libraries: Western Kentucky State College Library, (Southern and Western History), Bowling Green 42101, (Warren); Public Library, Scott & Robbins Sts., Covington 41011, (Kenton); Kentucky Historical Society Library, Old State House, Frankfort 40601, (Franklin); Public Library, 2nd & Market Sts., (old Newspapers), Lexington 40508, (Fayette); University of Kentucky Library, (historical manuscripts), Lexington 40508, (Fayette); Filson Club Library, 118 W. Breckenridge St., (Kentucky and Ohio Valley collections), Louisville 40203, (Jefferson); Free Public Library,

301-333 Library Place, (Southern lore), Louisville 40203, (Jefferson).

Among books dealing with Kentucky history and genealogy are the following:

Ardery, Mrs. Wm. Breckenridge. "Kentucky Records - Early Wills and Marriages." The Keystone Printery, Lexington, Ky.,Vol I, 206 pp. 1926; Vol II, 1932.

Biggs, Nina Mitchell and Mackoy, Mabel Lee. "History of Greenup County, Ky." The Franklin Press, Louisville, Ky., 1951, 345 pp.

"Biographical Encyclopedia of Kentucky of the Dead and Living Men of the Nineteenth Century." O. J. Armstrong Company, 1873.

Burns, Annie Walker, P.O. Box 6183, Washington, D. C. 20004. "Kentucky Genealogies and Historical Recorder." Eleven Mimeographed volumes.

Abstracts of Pension Records from most of the Kentucky counties.

Cherry, Thomas C., and Stickles, Arndt M., "Story of Kentucky". Heath, 1940.

Clark, Thomas Doinysius, and Kirkpatrick, Lee. "Exploring Kentucky." American Book Co., 1939.

Clift, G. Glenn. "History of Maysville and Mason County." Transylvania Printing Company, Inc., Lexington, Ky., 1936. Vol I, 461 pp.

"Second Census of Kentucky", 1800. Frankfort, Ky., 1954. 333 pp. A privately compiled list of taxpayers in the forty-two counties of Kentucky of 1800.

Collins, Lewis (1797-1870), "History of Kentucky".

Darnell, Ermina Jett. "Forks of Elkhorn Church." The Standard Printing Co., Inc., Louisville, Ky., 1946. 322 pp.

"Daughters of Colonial Wars, Kentucky Society", Kentucky Pioneers and Their Descendants. Roberts Printing Company, Frankfort, Ky., 1950, 460 pp.

Green, Thomas Marshall. "Historic Families of Kentucky". Robert Clarke and Company, Cincinnati, 1889. 304 pp.

Hall, Mitchell, "Johnson County, Kentucky". The Standard Press, Louisville, Ky., 1928. Vol I, History and Genealogy. 552 pp. Vol. II Genealogy. 708 pp.

Heinemann, Charles Brink. "First Census of Kentucky, 1790", A privately compiled list of taxpayers appearing in the tax lists of Kentucky counties established at time of First Census. Southern Book Company, St. James Hotel, Charles Street at Center, Baltimore, Maryland 21201. 1956. 118 pp.

Jennings, Kathleen. "Louisville's First Families". A series of genealogical sketches. The Standard Printing Company, Louisville, Ky. 1920. 176 pp.

Jillson, Willard Rouse. "The Kentucky Land Grants", 1782-1924. The Standard Printing Co., Inc., Louisville, Ky., 1925. 1,844 pp.

"Old Kentucky Entries and Deeds". The Standard Printing Co., Inc., Louisville, Ky., 1926. 571 pp. State land office records.

McAdams, Mrs. Harry Kennett. "Kentucky Pioneer and Court Records". Abstracts of early wills, deeds and marriages from Anderson, Bourbon, Boyle, Clark, Estill, Fayette, Garrard, Harrison, Jassamine, Lincoln, Madison, Mercer, Montgomery, Nicholas, and Woodford counties. The Keystone Printery, Lexington, Ky., 1929. 382 pp. Indexed.

McGhee, Lucy Kate, Box 7213 Washington, D.C. 20004. "Historical Records of Old Crab Orchard". Lincoln, Ky. 117 pp.

"Pension Abstracts of Maryland Soldiers of the Revolution, War of 1812, and Indian Wars Who Settled in Kentucky". Vol I, 76 pp. Vol. II, 90 pp.

Scott, Hattie Marshall. "Kentucky Court and Other Records". Records from Bourbon, Nicholas, Estill, Fayette, Gallatin, Green, Harrison, Scott, and Woodford counties and other miscellaneous items. The Kentucky Historical Society, Frankfort, Ky., 1953. 251 pp. Excellent index.

Thompson, Ed Porter, "History of the Orphan Brigade". Information on about 5,675 participants in the Civil War. Lewis N. Thompson, Louisville, Ky., 1898. 1,104 pp. Excellent index.

Tibbals, Alma Owens. "History of Pulaski County, Kentucky". The Franklin Press, Louisville, Ky., 1952. 272 pp. Fine index.

Van Meter, Benjamin F. "Genealogies and Sketches of Some Old Families". (Virginia and Kentucky) John P. Morton and Company, Louisville, Ky., 1901. 183 pp.

Wells, J. W. "History of Cumberland County, Kentucky". The Standard Printing Co., Louisville, Ky., 1947. 480 pp.

Wood, Edith. "Middletown's Days and Deeds". (Jefferson County) 1946. 281 pp.

Works Projects Administration. "Kentucky". (American Guide Series) Check List of Historical Records Survey Publications. 1940.

Kentucky County Histories

(Population figures to nearest thousand - 1960 Census)

Name	Map Index	Date Formed	Pop. By M	Census Reports Available	Parent County	County Seat
Adair	C2	1801	15	1810–80	Green	Columbia
Allen	D3	1815	12	1820–80	Barren, Warren	Scottsville
(Co Clk has m & pro rec from 1902; Cir Ct Clk has div rec from 1902)						
Anderson	C2	1827	9	1830–80	Franklin, Mercer, Washington	Lawrenceburg

(Co Clk has m & pro rec from 1857, deeds from 1827, School rec; Cir Clk has civ ct rec from 1857)

Ballard   F3 1842   8 1850-80 Hickman, McCracken .... Wickliffe
(Co Clk has m rec from 1880 & pro rec; Health Center has b rec from 1911 & d rec; Cir Ct has div & civ ct rec; CH burned in 1880, destroyed rec)

Barren   D3 1798   28 1810-80 Green, Warren .... Glasgow
(Co Clk has m & pro rec from 1798; Bureau of Vital Statistics has b & d rec; Cir Ct Clk has div & civ ct rec)

Bath   B2 1811   9 1820-80 Montgomery .... Owingsville

Bell   B3 1867   35 1880   Knox, Harlan .... Pineville
(Co Clk has m rec)

Boone   C1 1798   22 1810-80 Campbell .... Burlington
(Co Clk has m & pro rec from 1799)

Bourbon   B2 1785   18 1810-80 Fayette .... Paris
(Co Clk has m & pro rec from 1786; Co Ct or Cir Ct Clk has civ ct rec from 1786; Board of Health has b & d rec; Cemeteries or undertakers have bur rec; Cir Ct Clk has div rec)

Boyd   A1 1860   52 1860-80 Carter, Lawrence, Greenup ..Catlettsburg
(Co Clk has b, m & d rec from 1911)

Boyle   C2 1842   21 1850-80 Mercer, Lincoln .... Danville
(Co Clk has m, pro, wills from 1842)

Bracken   B1 1796   7 1810-80 Campbell, Mason .... Brooksville

Breathitt   B2 1839   15 1840-80 Clay, Estill, Perry .... Jackson
(Co Clk has m rec from 1875, also div, pro & civ ct rec)

Breckinridge D2 1799   15 1810-80 Hardin .... Hardinsburg

Bullitt   C2 1796   16 1810-80 Jefferson, Nelson ..... Shepherdsville
(Co Clk has m rec from 1797, pro rec, Fiscal Ct Order Books, Co Ct & will rec from 1796; Bureau of Vital Statistics has b, d & bur rec; Cir Clk has div & civ ct rec from 1874)

Butler   D3 1810   10 1810-80 Logan, Ohio .... Morgantown

Caldwell   E3 1809   13 1810-80 Livingston .... Princeton
(State Dept of Health has b, d & bur rec; Co Clk has m & pro rec from 1809; Clk Cir Ct has div rec from 1809 also civ ct rec)

Calloway   E3 1822   21 1830-80 Hickman .... Murray
(Co Clk has m rec; Bureau of Vital Statistics has b & d rec; Cir Clk has div rec; Churchills Funeral Home & Blalock Coleman Funeral home have bur rec)

Campbell   B1 1795   87 1810-80 Harrison, Mason, Scott ......Alexandria
(Co Clk has b, m, pro & civ ct rec)   & Newport

Carlisle   F3 1886   6   Graves, Ballard .... Bardwell

Carroll   C1 1838   8 1840-80 Gallatin, Henry, Trimble ... Carrollton
(Co Clk has b rec from 1911, d rec from 1911 to 1949, also deeds, mortgages, & inventories from 1838; Co Health Dept has bur rec; Cir Ct has div & civ ct rec)

Carter   A1 1838   21 1840-80 Greenup, Lawrence .... Grayson
(Co Clk has b & d rec from 1911 to 1954, m rec from 1838; Cir Ct Clk has div, pro & civ ct rec)

Casey   C2 1806   14 1810-80 Lincoln .... Liberty
(Co Clk has m & pro rec from 1809)

Christian   E3 1797   57 1810-80 Logan .... Hopkinsville
(Co Clk has m & pro rec from 1797; Cir Ct Clk has div & civ ct rec)

Clark   B2 1792   21 1810-80 Bourbon, Fayette ..... Winchester
(Clk of Ct has m & pro rec from 1793, Juvenile rec from 1943, deeds, wills, settlements & mortgages from 1793; Health dept has b & d rec; Cir Clk has div & civ ct rec)

Clay   B2 1806   21 1810-80 Madison, Floyd, Knox .... Manchester
(Co Ct Clk has m & pro rec from 1806; Bureau of Vital Statistics has b, d & bur rec; Cir Ct has div & civ ct rec)

Clinton   C3 1835   9 1840-80 Wayne, Cumberland .... Albany
(Co Clk has m, deeds, mtgs, will, leases from 1865)

Crittenden E2 1842   9 1850-80 Livingston .... Marion

(Co Clk has m & pro rec from 1842)

Cumberland   C3   1796   8   1810–80   Green . . . . Burkesville
(Co Clk has some m rec from 1882)

Daviess   D1   1815   71   1820–80   Ohio . . . . Owensboro

Edmonson   D3   1825   8   1830–80   Grayson, Hart, Warren . . . . . Brownsville
(Co Clk has m rec from 1840)

Elliott   A2   1869   6   1870–80   Carter, Lawrence, Morgan . . . Sandy Hook
(Co Clk has b rec 1882 to 1926, m rec from 1934, pro rec from 1957; Cir Clk
has div rec; Health Office has d & bur rec)

Estill   B2   1808   12   1810–80   Clark, Madison . . . . Irvine

Fayette   B2   1780   132   1810–80   Kentucky Co Virginia . . . . . . Lexington
(Co Clk has m rec from 1820 & pro rec; Bureau of Vital Statistics has b, m,
d & bur rec)

Fleming   B1   1798   11   1810–80   Mason . . . . Flemingsburg

Floyd   A2   1799   42   1810–80   Fleming, Mason,
                               Montgomery . . . . Prestonsburg

Franklin   C2   1794   29   1810–80   Woodford, Mercer, Shelby . . . Frankfort

Fulton   F3   1845   11   1850–80   Hickman . . . . Hickman

Gallatin   C1   1798   4   1810–80   Franklin, Shelby . . . . Warsaw

Garrard   B2   1796   10   1810–80   Madison, Lincoln, Mercer . . . Lancaster

Grant   C1   1820   9   1820–80   Pendleton . . . . Williamstown
(Co Clk has m & pro rec from 1820)

Graves   F3   1823   30   1830–80   Hickman . . . . Mayfield
(Co Clk has m & pro rec from 1887; Cir Clk has div rec from 1887)

Grayson   D2   1810   16   1810–80   Hardin, Ohio . . . . Leitchfield
(Co Clk has m & pro rec from 1896)

Green   C2   1792   11   1810–80   Lincoln, Nelson . . . . Greensburg
(Co Clk has b & d rec 1911 to 1954, m, deeds, ct orders, & pro rec from 1793;
Cir Ct Clk has div & civ ct rec)

Greenup   A1   1803   29   1810–80   Mason . . . . Greenup
(Co Clk as m rec 1803, pro rec 1837, b & d rec from 1911 to 1949; Clk of Cir
Ct has div & civ ct rec 1803)

Hancock   D2   1828   15   1830–80   Daviess, Ohio, Breckinridge .. Hawesville
(Co Clk has m, div, pro, & deeds from 1829; Cir Ct Clk has div & civ ct rec;
Dept of Health has b & d rec)

Hardin   D2   1792   68   1810–80   Nelson . . . . Elizabethtown
(Co Clk has m rec from 1793, also pro rec; Bureau of Vital Statistics has b &
d rec; Cir Clk has div & civ ct rec)

Harlan   B3   1819   51   1820–80   Knox . . . . Harlan
(Co Health Dept or Bureau of Vital Statistics has b & d rec from 1911 also
bur rec; Co Clk has m rec from 1820, pro rec from 1868; Cir Ct Clk has div
and civ ct rec)

Harrison   B1   1793   14   1810–80   Bourbon, Scott . . . . Cynthiana

Hart   D2   1819   14   1820–80   **Hardin, Barren,**
                            possibly Green . . . . Mumfordville

Henderson   E2   1798   34   1810–80   Christian . . . . Henderson
(Co Clk has b & d rec from 1911 to 1950, m rec from 1807, pro rec from 1810,
settlements, inventories & appraisements from 1820; City Clk has bur rec;
Cir Ct Clk has div & civ ct rec)

Henry   C1   1798   11   1810–80   Shelby . . . . New Castle

Hickman   F3   1821   7   1830–80   Caldwell, Livingston . . . . Clinton

Hopkins   E2   1808   38   1810–80   Henderson . . . . Madisonville

Jackson   B2   1858   11   1860–80   Rockcastle, Owsley, Madison,
                            Clay, Estill, Laurel . . . . McKee

Jefferson   C2   1780   611   1810–80   Kentucky Co Virginia . . . . . . Louisville
(Co Clk has m & pro rec; Bureau of Vital Statistics has b & d rec from 1913;
Cir Clk has div rec; Custodian of rec has civ ct rec at CH)

Jessamine   C2   1798   14   1810–80   Fayette . . . . Nicholasville
(Co Clk has m, pro, deeds & mortgages from 1799; Cir Ct Clk has div rec;
Bur of Vital Statistics has b & d rec)

Johnson	A2	1843	20	1850–80	Floyd, Morgan, Lawrence . . . . Paintsville
Josh Bell				1870	
Kenton	B1	1840	121	1840–80	Campbell . . . . Independence
Knott	A2	1884	17		Perry, Breathitt, Floyd
					Letcher . . . . Hindman

(Co Clk has m, pro and civ ct rec from 1886)

Knox	B3	1799	25	1810–80	Lincoln . . . . Barbourville
Larue	C2	1843	10	1850–80	Hardin . . . . Hodgenville

(Co Clk has m rec from 1843, also div, pro & civ ct rec)

Laurel	B3	1825	25	1830–80	Whitley, Clay, Knox, Rockcastle . London
Lawrence	A2	1821	12	1830–80	Floyd, Greenup . . . . Louisa

(Co Clk has m & pro rec from 1825)

Lee	B2	1870	7	1870–80	Owsley, Breathitt, Wolfe, Estill . Beattyville
Leslie	B2	1878	11	1880	Clay, Harlan, Perry . . . . Hyden
Letcher	A3	1842	30	1850–80	Perry, Harlan . . . . Whitesburg
Lewis	B1	1806	13	1810–80	Mason . . . . Vanceburg

(Co Clk has b & d rec from 1911, m, Inv of personal estates, pro rec from 1806)

Lincoln	C2	1780	17	1810–80	Kentucky Co., Va. . . . . Stanford

(Co Clk has m, div, pro, civ ct rec from 1792)

Livingston	E2	1798	7	1810–80	Christian . . . . Smithland

(Co Clk has b rec from 1911, m, pro, surveys, ct orders, deeds, wills from 1800)

Logan	D3	1792	21	1810–80	Lincoln . . . . Russellville

(Co Clk has m rec 1790, pro, real estate conveyances, early land grants & surveys from 1792)

Lyon	E3	1854	6	1860–80	Caldwell . . . . Eddyville
Madison	B2	1785	34	1810–80	Lincoln . . . . Richmond
Magoffin	A2	1860	11	1860–80	Floyd, Johnson, Morgan . . . Salyersville

(Co Clk has m rec from 1860)

Marion	C2	1834	17	1840–80	Washington . . . . Lebanon
Marshall	E3	1842	17	1850–80	Callaway . . . . Benton
Martin	A2	1870	10	1880	Lawrence, Floyd, Pike, Johnson . . **Inez**

(Co Clk has b rec from 1903 to 1949, m rec from 1883, d rec from 1911 to 1949; Health Dept has bur rec; Cir Clk has div, pro & civ ct rec)

Mason	B1	1788	18	1810–80	Bourbon . . . . Maysville

(Co Clk has m rec from 1788, also pro rec; Cir Ct Clk has div & civ ct rec)

McCracken	F3	1824	57	1830–80	Hickman . . . . Paducah

(Co Clk has m & pro rec from 1825, b & d rec from 1911)

McCreary	B3	1912	12		Wayne, Pulaski, Whitley . . . . Whitley City

(Co Clk has m, d, pro rec from 1912)

McLean	D1	1854	9	1860–80	Muhlenberg, Daviess, Ohio . . . . Calhoun

(Co Clk has b & d rec 1911 to 1949, m, div, pro, civ ct rec, deeds from 1854)

Meade	D2	1824	19	1830–80	Hardin, Breckinridge . . . . Brandenburg

(Co Clk has incom b & d rec 1852 to 1911, m, pro, div, civ ct rec from 1824)

Menifee	B2	1869	4	1870–80	Powell, Wolfe, Bath, Morgan,
					Montgomery . . . . Frenchburg

(Co Clk has m rec from 1869; Clk of Cir Ct has div rec from 1869)

Mercer	C2	1785	15	1810–80	Lincoln . . . . Harrodsburg

(Co Clk has m, pro, deeds and ct order bks from 1785; Bureau of Vital Statistics, Frankfort, Ky. has b & d rec; Cir Clk has div rec; Co Judge or Cir Clk has civ ct rec)

Metcalfe	C3	1860	8	1860–80	Monroe, Adair, Barren, Cumberland
					Green . . . . Edmonton
Monroe	C3	1820	12	1820–80	Barren, Cumberland . . . . . Tompkinsville
Montgomery	B2	1796	13	1810–80	Clark . . . . Mount Sterling

(Co Clk has m rec from 1864)

Morgan	B2	1822	11	1830–80	Floyd, Bath . . . . West Liberty
Muhlenberg	D3	1798	28	1810–80	Christian, Logan . . . . Greenville
Nelson	C2	1784	22	1810–80	Jefferson . . . . Bardstown

(Co Clk has m & pro rec from 1784)

County Map of Kentucky

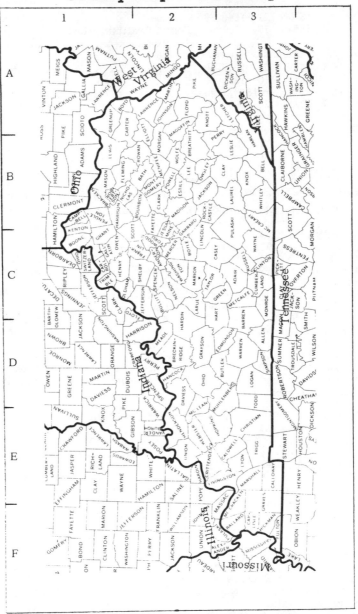

Nicholas	B1	1799	7	1810–80	Bourbon, Mason . . . . Carlisle
Ohio	**D2**	**1799**	**18**	**1810–80**	Hardin . . . . Hartford
Oldham	C1	1823	13	1830–80	Henry, Shelby, Jefferson . . . . LaGrange
Owen	C1	1819	8	1820–80	Scott, Franklin, Gallatin, Pendleton . Owenton

(Co Clk has b & d rec from 1911 to 1949, m & pro rec from 1819; Cir Clk has div rec)

Owsley	B2	1843	5	1850–80	Clay, Estill, Breathitt . . . . Booneville

Pendleton   B1   1798   10   1810-80   Bracken, Campbell . . . . Falmouth

Perry   B2   1820   35   1830-80   Clay, Floyd . . . . Hazard
(Co Clk has m & pro rec from 1821; State Dept of Health has b & d rec; Cir Clk has div & civ ct rec)

Pike   A2   1821   68   1830-80   Floyd . . . . Pikeville

Powell   B2   1852   7   1860-80   Clark, Estill, Montgomery . . . . Stanton

Pulaski   C3   1798   34   1810-80   Green, Lincoln . . . . Somerset
(Co Clk has m & pro rec from 1799; Dept of Health has b & d rec from 1911; Cir Ct Clk has div & civ ct rec)

Robertson   B1   1867   2   1870-80   Nicholas, Bracken, Mason, Fleming, Harrison . . . . Mt. Olivet
(Co Clk has m, pro, civ ct, wills, deeds, settlement of Estates from 1867, Affidavit of descent from 1920; Cir Clk has div rec)

Rockcastle   B2   1810   12   1810-80   Pulaski, Lincoln, Madison . . Mount Vernon
(Co Clk has m rec from 1873; Cir Ct Clk has div rec from 1873, also pro & civ ct rec; Health Dept has b & d rec from 1911)

Rowan   B2   1856   13   1860-80   Fleming, Morgan . . . . Morehead
(Co Clk has m & pro rec from 1890; Health Dept has b & d rec; Cir Ct Clk has div rec & Judges Office has civ ct rec)

Russell   C3   1825   11   1830-80   Cumberland, Adair, Wayne . . . Jamestown
(Co Clk has m & pro rec from 1826; Cir Ct has civ ct rec from 1826)

Scott   C2   1792   15   1810-80   Woodford . . . . Georgetown

Shelby   C2   1792   18   1810-80   Jefferson . . . . Shelbyville
(Co Clk has b rec from 1911 to 1948, also m & pro rec)

Simpson   D3   1819   12   1820-80   Allen, Logan, Warren . . . . . . Franklin
(Co Clk has m rec from 1892)

Spencer   C2   1824   6   1830-80   Shelby, Bullitt, Nelson . . . . . Taylorsville

Taylor   C2   1848   16   1850-80   Green . . . . Campbellsville

Todd   D3   1819   11   1820-80   Christian, Logan . . . . Elkton

Trigg   E3   1820   9   1820-80   Christian, Caldwell . . . . Cadiz
(Co Clk has m & pro rec from 1820, b rec from 1890 to 1911; Cir Clk has div & civ ct rec)

Trimble   C1   1836   5   1840-80   Henry, Oldham, Gallatin . . . . . . Bedford

Union   E2   1811   15   1820-80   Henderson . . . . Morganfield

Warren   D3   1796   45   1810-80   Logan . . . . Bowling Green

Washington   C2   1792   11   1810-80   Nelson . . . . Springfield
(Co Clk has m & pro rec from 1792)

Wayne   C3   1800   15   1810-80   Pulaski, Cumberland . . . . Monticello
(Co Clk has m, pro & deed rec from 1800)

Webster   E2   1860   14   1860-80   Hopkins, Union, Henderson . . . . . Dixon
(Co Clk has m & pro rec from 1860)

Whitley   B3   1818   26   1820-80   Knox . . . . Williamsburg

Wolfe   B2   1860   7   1870-80   Owsley, Breathitt, Powell, Morgan . . . . Campton
(Co Clk has m rec from 1913, deeds from 1860)

Woodford   C2   1788   12   1810-80   Fayette . . . . Versailles

U. S. Census note: The Kentucky census figures for 1790 and 1800 are missing.

Genealogists' Check List of the Historical Records Survey, Kentucky

Federal Courts (start 1789). Inventory of county archives, Anderson, Breckenridge, Carlisle, Fayette, Jessamine, Knox, Laurel, McCreary, Meade. Guide to public vital statistics records.

Preliminary Bibliography of material relating to churches in West Virginia, Virginia, Kentucky and Southern Ohio. Check list of Kentucky imprints 1787-1810. Check list of Kentucky imprints 1811-1820. Supplementary check list of Kentucky imprints 1788-1820. Guide and check list of county government organizations and county record system, Past and present counties. Depository of unpublished material, Kentucky library, Lexington, Kentucky.

Louisiana

Capital Baton Rouge - Territory 1805 - State 1812 - (18th)

Ownership of the Louisiana sector for the first 250 or 300 years of its discovery zig-zagged between France and Spain, until it was sold to the United States as part of the Louisiana Purchase in 1803. Some of the quaint customs of the early French settlers have been perpetuated over the years and gives the state an atmosphere of antiquity.

Every school boy and girl remembers with nostolgic feelings Longfellow's "Evangeline," the poetic story of the transfer of large groups of French settlers from Nova Scotia to Louisiana. Many descendants of these Acadians still live in Louisiana where they are known as Cajuns.

Rather than to fight against the Mother Country during the Revolutionary War, many loyal Britons moved their families from the Atlantic states to Louisiana where they have perpetuated themselves.

On 1 October 1804 Louisiana was divided into two parts by Congressional action. The upper portion was given the name "District of Louisiana" and the lower portion "Territory of Orleans". Immediately after the formation of the Territory of Orleans, large numbers of Americans from south of the Ohio moved into the new acquisition. In 1805 Louisiana was divided into 12 counties and in 1807 the Orleans Territory was partitioned into 19 parishes.

There is nothing different between a Louisiana parish and a county in any other state than the name. Otherwise everythng is the same. Some of the early Church Parish records are now held by the Parish or Court Clerks.

For information regarding wills, deeds, divorces, civil court records and marriages write the clerk of the respective parishes.

The State Registrar, Bureau of Vital Statistics, State Department of Health, Civil Courts Bldg., New Orleans, Louisiana 70112, has records of births since 1914, some since 1870 and deaths since 1914, some since 1899. The Bureau of Vital Statistics, City Health Department of New Orleans, 507 Carondelet St., has some birth, death and marriage records as far back as 1790.

Louisiana Libraries - Rapides Parish Library, P.O. Box 1032, Alexandria 71302, (Rapides); East Baton Rouge Parish Public Library, 700 Laurel St., Baton Rouge 70802 (Baton Rouge); Louisiana State University Library, (Lower Mississippi Valley history), Baton Rouge 70803, (Baton Rouge); Public Library 1031 St. Charles Avenue, New Orleans 70130, (Orleans Parish); Tulane University, Howard-Tilton Memorial Library, Audubon Place at Freret Street, (Southern lore and archives), New Orleans 70118, (Orleans Parish); Shreve Memorial Public Library, 400 Edwards St., Shreveport 71101, (Caddo).

Among available books dealing with Louisiana are the following:

Arthur, Stanley C., "Old New Orleans". A History of the Vieux Carre, its Ancient and Historical Buildings. 246 pp. New Orleans, 1936.

"Baptismal, Marriage and Death Records of Christ Church Episcopal Cathedral, New Orleans". 1849-1900. Obtained at Southern Book Company, Baltimore, Md.

Curtis, Nathaniel C., "New Orleans, Its Old Houses, Shops and Public Buildings". 267 pp. Philadelphia 1933.

Deiler, J. Hanno, "The Settlement of the German Coast of Louisiana and the Creoles of German Descent." 136 pp. Philadelphia, 1909.

"Guide to Public Vital Statistics Records in Louisiana."

"Guide to Vital Statistics Records of Church Archives in Louisiana", Vol. I. "Protestant and Jewish Churches", Vol. II, "Roman Catholic Churches"

King, Grace. "New Orleans, The Place and the People". 402 pp. New York 1922.

Saxon, Lyle. "Old Louisiana". 388 pp. New York, 1941.

Louisiana Parish Histories

(Population figures to nearest thousand - 1960 Census)

Name	Map Index	Date Formed	Pop. By M	Census Reports Available	Parent Parish	Parish Seat
Acadia	C2	1886	50		St. Landry	Crowley
(Par Clk has m, div, pro & civ ct rec from 1886)						
Allen	C2	1912	20		Calcasieu	Oberlin
(Par Clk has m, div, pro & civ ct rec from 1913; Dept of Health has b & d rec)						
Ascension	C3	1807	28	1810-80	St. James	Donaldsonville
(Par Clk has m, div, pro, civ ct, conveyance, mtg, insanity, juvenile, army & navy discharges from 1767)						
Assumption	C3	1807	18	1810-80	Original Parish	Napoleonville
Attakaps				1810	Original Parish - Discontinued	
Avoyelles	C2	1807	38	1810-80	Original Parish - Reorg. 1873	Marksville

(Par Clk has m rec from 1808, div & civ ct rec from 1868, pro rec from 1840,
conveyance, mtg from 1808)
Beauregard C1 1913   19   Calcasieu .... DeRidder
(Par Clk has m, div, pro & civ ct rec from 1913)
Baton Rouge   1810
Bienville   B2 1848   17 1850-80 Claiborne .... Arcadia
(Clk of Ct has m, div, pro & civ ct rec from 1848; Dept of Health has b, d & bur rec)
Bossier   A1 1843   58 1850-80 Claiborne .... Benton
(Par Clk has m, div, pro & civ ct rec from 1843; Bureau of Vital Statistics has
b records)
Caddo   A1 1838 224 1840-80 Natchitoches .... Shreveport
(Par Clk has m, div, pro, civ ct, mtg, conveyance rec from 1835)
Calcasieu   C1 1840 145 1840-80 St. Landry .... Lake Charles
(Par Clk has m, div, pro, and civ ct rec from 1910; Board of Health has b, d,
and bur rec)
Caldwell   B2 1838   9 1840-80 Catahoula, Ouachita......... Columbia
(Par Clk has m, div, pro, civ ct, conveyance, mtg, leases from 1838)
Cameron   C1 1870   7 1870-80 Calcasieu, Vermillion ...... Cameron
(Par Clk has m, div, pro, civ ct rec from 1870; Board of Health has b, d & bur rec)
Carroll   1840-70 See East and West Carroll
Catahoula   B2 1808   11 1810-80 .... Harrisonburg
Claiborne   A2 1828   19 1830-80 Natchitoches .... Homer
(Clk of Ct has m, div, pro, civ ct, deeds, 3 vol of amnesty oaths from 1850;
All Par rec destroyed in fire Nov 1849)
Concordia   B2 1805   20 1810-80 Avoyelles .... Vidalia
DeSoto   B1 1843   24 1850-80 Natchitoches, Caddo .... Mansfield
(Par Clk has m, div, pro, civ ct rec from 1843)
East Baton
  Rouge   C3 1810 230 1820-80 Original Parish .... Baton Rouge
East Carroll A3 1877   14 1880   Carroll .... Lake Providence
East Feliciana C3 1824 20 1830-80 Seceded from Feliciana ..... Clinton
Evangeline   C2 1911   32   St. Landry .... Ville Platte
(Par Clk has m, div, pro, civ ct rec from 1911)
Feliciana   1820
Franklin   B2 1843   26 1850-80 Catahoula,Ouachita,Madison... Winnsboro
(Par Clk has m, div, pro, civ ct rec from 1843)
Grant   B2 1869   13 1870-80 Rapides, Winn .... Colfax
Iberia   C2 1868   52 1870-80 St. Martin, St. Mary ...... New Iberia
(Par Clk has m rec from 1868, div, pro, civ ct rec from 1869; Bureau of
Vital Statistics has b, d & bur rec)
Iberville   C3 1807   30 1810-80 Assumption, Ascension .... Plaquemine
Jackson   B2 1845   16 1850-80 Claiborne, Ouachita, Union ... Jonesboro
Jefferson   D4 1825 209 1830-80 Orleans .... Gretna
(Clk of Ct has m, div, pro, civ ct rec 1825, mtg rec 1892, conveyance rec 1827;
b, d, & bur rec are filed with State of La. Dept of Health, New Orleans, La.)
Jefferson
  Davis   C2 1913   30   Calcasieu .... Jennings
Lafayette   C2 1823   85 1830-80 St. Martin.......... . . . Lafayette

(Par Clk has m, div, pro, civ ct rec, property, crim ct rec from 1823)
Lafourche   D3 1807   55 1810-80   Thibodaux
(Par Clk has m, div, pro, civ ct rec from 1808)
LaSalle   B2 1910   13   Catahoula .... Jena
(Clk of Ct has m, div, pro, civ ct rec from 1910)
Lincoln   A2 1873   29 1880   Bienville, Jackson, Union,
                                   Clairborne .... Ruston
(Par Clk has m, div, pro, civ ct rec from 1873)
Livingston   C3 1832   27 1840-80 St. Helena .... Livingston
Madison   B3 1838   16 1840-80 Concordia .... Tallulah
(Par Clk has m rec 1866, div rec 1839, pro rec 1850, civ ct rec 1882, deeds
1839, mtg 1865; Vital Statistics Bureau has b, d & bur rec)

Morehouse   A2   1844   34   1850-80   Ouachita . . . . Bastrop
    (Par Clk has m, div, pro, civ ct rec 1870, conveyance & mtg 1844, some
    naturalization rec 1871 to 1895; Dept of Health, New Orleans, La has b & d rec)
Natchitoches B2   1807   36   1810-80   Original Parish . . . . Natchitoches
    (Clk of Ct has m rec from 1780, also div, pro & civ ct rec)
Opelousas   1810
Orleans   C4   1807   665   1810-80   Original Parish . . . . New Orleans
    (Bureau of Vital rec, New Orleans, La has b rec from 1790, m rec from 1831,
    & d rec from 1804, pl of bur is on d cert; Clk Civ Dist Ct has div rec from
    1880, pro rec from 1805, civ ct rec from 1880)
Ouachita   A2   1807   102   1810-80   Original Parish . . . . Monroe
    (Clk of Ct has m, div, pro, civ ct rec from 1805)
Plaquemines D4   1807   23   1810-80   Orleans . . . . Pointe a la Hache
    (Par Clk has m rec from 1896, also div, pro & civ & crim rec from 1807,
    conveyance of lands 1807)
Pointe Coupee C2 1807   22   1810-80   Feliciana, Avoyelles . . . . New Roads
    (Clk of Ct has m rec from 1735, div rec from 1800, pro, civ ct, conveyances,
    & mtg from 1780; Board of Health has b, d & bur rec)
Rapides   B2   1807   111   1810-80   Original Parish . . . . Alexandria
    (Par Clk has m, div, pro, civ ct rec from 1864)
Red River   B1   1871   10   Caddo, Bossier, Bienville,
                                       Natchitoches, DeSoto . . . . . . Coushatta
    (Clk of Ct has m & pro rec from 1871, div & civ ct rec from 1904)
Richland   A2   1868   24   1870-80   Ouachita, Carroll, Franklin,
                                       Morehouse . . . . Rayville
Sabine   B1   1843   19   1850-80   Natchitoches . . . . Many
    (Par Clk has m, div, pro, civ ct rec from 1843; State Health Dept. has b,
    d, and burial records)
St. Bernard C4   1807   32   1810-80   Original Parish . . . . Chalmette
St. Charles C3   1807   21   1810-80   Original Parish . . . . Hahnville
St. Helena   C3   1810   9   1820-80   Livingston . . . . Greensburg
    (Par Clk has recs from 1804, Co empoyess do not have time to chk recs)
St. James   C3   1807   18   1810-80   Original Parish . . . . Convent
    (Clk of Ct has m rec from 1846, div, pro & civ ct rec from 1809)
St. John the
    Baptist C3   1807   18   1810-80   Original County . . . . Edgard
    (Par Clk has m, div, pro & civ ct rec; La. State Board of Health has b, d, &
    bur rec)
St. Landry   C2   1807   81   1820-80   Avoyelles, Rapides . . . . . . Opelousas
    (Par Clk has m rec from 1808, div rec from 1813, pro rec from 1809 & civ
    ct rec from 1813; Bureau of Vital Statistics has b, d & bur rec)
St. Martin   C2,3 1807   29   1810-80   Original Parish . . . . St. Martinville
St. Mary   D3   1811   49   1820-80   Assumption . . . . Franklin
St. Tammany C4   1810   39   1820-80   St. Helena . . . . Covington
Tangipahoa   C3   1869   59   1870-80   Livingston, St. Tammany, Wash. . . Amite
    (Par Clk has m, div, pro & civ ct recs, also conveyance & will & donation
    rec from 1869; Dept of Health has b. d & bur rec)
Tensas   B3   1843   12   1850-80   Concordia . . . . St. Joseph
    (Par Clk has m, div, pro, civ ct rec from 1843)
Terrebonne   D3   1822   61   1830-80   La Fourche . . . . Houma
Union   A2   1839   18   1840-80   Ouachita . . . . Farmerville
    (Par Clk has m, div, & pro rec from 1839, also has civ ct rec; Bureau of Vit
    Stat, New Orleans, La. has b rec)
Vermillion   D2   1844   39   1850-80   Lafayette . . . . Abbeville
    (Par Clk has m, div, pro & civ ct rec from 1885; State Dept of Health has
    b, d & bur rec)
Vernon   B1   1871   18   1880   Natchitoches, Rapides, Sabine . . Leesville
    (Clk of Ct has m rec from 1890 and div, pro & civ ct rec from 1871)
Washington   C4   1819   44   1820-80   St. Tammany . . . . Franklinton
    (Clk of Ct has m, div, pro, civ ct rec from 1897; Bureau of Vital Statistics,
    Dept of Health has b, d & bur rec)
Webster   A1   1871   40   1880   Clairborne, Beinville, Bossier. . . . Minden

West Baton
  Rouge   C3 1807   15 1820–80 Baton Rouge . . . . Port Allen
West Carroll A3 1877   14 1880   Carroll . . . . Oak Grove
West Feliciana C3 1824   12 1830–80 Feliciana . . . . Saint Francisville
Winn   B2 1851   16 1860–80 Natchitoches, Catahoula,
                                       Rapides . . . . Winnfield

Parish Map of Louisiana

Genealogists' Check List of the Historical Records Survey,
Louisiana

Federal Courts (start 1804). Ships register and enrollments of
New Orleans 6 Vol 1804–1870. Index of names of owners and mas-
ters. Inventory of Parish archives, Allen, Assumption, Beaure-
gard, Bossier, Calcasieu, Grant, Jefferson, Lafayette, Lafourche,
Morehouse, Natchitoches, Orleans, Ouachita, Plaquemines,
Sabine, St Bernard, St Charles, Terrebonne, Washington, Webster.
Title line inventory of parish archives of Louisiana Parts 1 & 2
Acadia through Winn. Inventory of municipal and town archives,
Franklinton, Thibodaux. Transcription of Public archives, Iber-

ville Parish Police Jury minutes, Vol 1, 1850-1862, Vol 2 1880-1901, Vol 3 1901-1916, Vol 4 1916-1925, Vol 5 1925-1936, general index 1850-1936. Transcription of public archives, Jefferson Parish Police Jury minutes, Vol 1 1834-1843, Vol 3 1858-1870, Vol 3A 1871-1884, Vol 4 1870-1870. Transcription of Public archives, St Bernard Parish Police Jury minutes, Vol 1, 1870-1877, Vol 2 1880-1895, Vol 3 1895-1914, Vol 4 1914-1922, Vol 5 1922-1929, Vol 6 1929-1940. Guide to public vital statistics records. Guide to vital statistics records of church archives, Vol 1 Protestant and Jewish churches, Vol 2 Roman Catholic churches.

A record of Casualties to person and vessels on the Mississippi river and tributaries, U.S. customs district, Port of New Orleans 1873-1924. Navigation casualties on the Mississippi river and tributaries 1866-1910. East Baton Rouge district, third district court cases 1811-1848. Passenger lists taken from manifests of the Customs Service Port of New Orleans. New Orleans, minute books of the U.S. District Court 1808-1876. Inventory of the church and Synagogue archives of Louisiana, Jewish Congregations and organizations. Directory of churchs and religious organizations in New Orleans.

Louisiana manuscripts public: Guide to Depository of manuscripts collection in Louisiana (in the Louisiana Historical Quarterly Vol 24, No. 2). Reprint (51 p Apr 1941, 2nd Ed). Guide to manuscript collection in Louisiana Dept of Archives, La. State University, Vol 1 & Second Edition. Calendar of manuscript collections in Louisiana - Series I. The Dept. of Archives No. 1. Taber collection. An inventory of the collection of the Middle American Research Institute, No. 1 Calendar I. Fayssoux collection of William Walker Papers, No. 2 calendar of the Yucatecan letters, No. 3 maps in the Frederick L. Hoffman collection, No. 4 maps in the library of the Middle American Research Institute. Transcription of manuscripts collection of Louisiana, No. 1 The Favrot Papers, Vol 1 1695-1769, Vol 2 1769-1781, Vol 3 1781-1792, Vol 4 1793-1796, Vol 5 1796-1799, Vol 6 1799-1801, Vol 7 1801-1803, Vol 9 (1812).

Bibliography of the Official Publication of Louisiana 1803-1934. Louisiana newspapers 1794-1940, A Union list of Louisiana newspaper files in the offices of Publishers, Library and private collections. Parish (County) boundaries in Louisiana. Microfilm birth records, City of New Orleans 1847-1901, New Orleans Board of Health. Birth records, state board of health, New Orleans, Louisiana 1911-1941. Depository of unpublished material, Dept. of Archives and History, Louisiana State University, Baton Rouge, Louisiana.

Maine

English and French explorers visited the present Maine region many times from 1598 to 1605. It was not until 1623 that the first permanent settlement was established. A community came into existence that year on the Saco River, in the extreme south-western section. The settlers came into the district as English subjects and they brought with them the laws of England. They came with permission granted them by the English rulers to create for themselves property in American lands.

One hundred Englishmen aboard two vessels left Plymouth on 31 May 1607. At the mouth of the Kennebec, then known as the Sagadahoc, they established a settlement which was disbanded the next year when the remaining settlers returned to England. Some historians maintain that not all of the settlers returned to England. Some, they say, appeared in the present Pemeaquid, Lincoln County, in 1608.

The appetite of many a hard-working low paid, stay-at-home Englishman was whetted by the description of the New Land by one of the returning explorers when he wrote, "Here are no hard landlords to rack us with high rents, or extorted fines to consume us. Here, every man may be master and owner of his own labor and land, or the greatest part, in a small time."

Various small groups brought over from England had settled along the coast of Maine where they engaged in fishing, but the first large contingent to come were the English Pilgrims or Puritans who arrived via Holland and Plymouth off Cape Cod in Massachusetts on 11 November 1620. Most of these so called dissenters came originally from Scrooby, Nottinghamshire.

In 1622 two members of the Plymouth Company in England, Sir Ferdinando Gorges and Captain John Mason where granted all of the land between the Kennebec and the Merrimac rivers. It was about that time that Dover and Portsmouth in New Hampshire were established. Later the grant was divided, Mason taking the part that is now New Hampshire, and Gorges the eastern section called Maine.

Late in sixteen hundred many communities existed along the coast of Maine and the many rivers in that section. Among them were Kittery, York, Kennebunk, Saco, Arundel (Kennebunkport), and several others which in that early period had a population of several thousand. Dissatisfaction among the early settlers toward the aristocratic regime of Gorges and his sons led to

102

Maine's annexation to Massachusetts. After the death of King Charles in 1685, and the brief ascension of James II, Massachusetts suddenly lost all of its former legal standings, and landholders had to resecure their holdings at high fees. The new land titles were recorded in Boston, but Maine also established a special land office in York.

In those early days the population east of the Kennebec River was slim, indeed, most of the settlers gathering on the ocean shore or along the rivers between the Kennebec and the Piscataqua. Among the settlements of those early seventeen hundreds were Biddeford, opposite Saco on the southwest bank of the Saco River; Portland, then known as Falmouth Neck; Berwick, on the east side of the Piscataqua, which is the border between Maine and New Hampshire; Sanford and Alred, north of Berwick and west of Biddeford; and a long line of smaller communities extending north along the western state border, such as Hollis (Little Falls) Newfield (Hubbardstown), Waterborough, (Massabesic), Limington (Ossipee), Baldwin (Flintstown), Bridgton (Bridgetown), Fryeburg (Pequawkett), and Stow.

As a county of Maine, Yorkshire from 1716 until 1760, covered the entire state. In the latter year it was divided into three counties, Lincoln, Cumberland and York. At that time the population was about 17,000, of which 10,000 lived in the cities mentioned in the sixth paragraph above. Above Oxford county, the entire section was a wilderness into which few, if any settlers, had dared to enter. For more than a hundred years transportation was one of the greatest handicaps of the settlements. Travel was mainly along the river courses. The extremely few roads then existing were in such terrible conditions that the limited number of cart roads were a dread to travelers. In many places they were almost impassable. To travel a distance less than sixty miles in those days required two long days. In the winter time when the roads were frozen, they were in better passable condition than in the summer. For many years after settlements were established in the Maine region, most of the roads, or trails, could be used only by the horseback riders.

In 1775 both York and Biddeford were county seats or shire towns of Yorkshire, which at that time had a population of about 15,000 or about half the population of the state. Fryeburg, on the New Hampshire borderline about 65 miles north of Kittery, was made a deed registration office for the section north of the Ossipee River in 1799.

Like York county so Cumberland county had a string of fair sized communities along the coast in those early days, including Scarboro, Cape Elizabeth, Falmouth (Portland), and Yarmouth. These Cumberland County coast towns had a population of a little less than ten thousand. Among the inland plantations, running almost parallel with the coast from twelve to fifteen miles, were Gorham, Windham, New Gloucester, Gray (New Boston), Raymond, Turner (Sylvester Canada), and Harrison (Otisfield). Very few, if any, settlements existed then in the eastern part of the present Oxford County, not even a road or a trail.

From the east boundary of Cumberland extended to the Canadian line, the rest of Maine formed the large county of Lincoln. Only two towns were established along the ocean in all of that territory, Topsham in the west part of the present Sagadahoc County, and Belfast in the present Waldo County. About a dozen other small communities existed along the Kennebec River for a distance of about seventy miles from its mouth. Between the northernmost Norridgewock in the present Somerset County and the coast, some of the other towns then existing were Waterville, Winslow, Sidney, Hallowell, Gardiner (Pittstown), Richmond, and Bowdoinham. Pownalborough (Dresden) was the early county seat of Lincoln County.

Before the first federal census in 1790, the Maine census was taken twice - in 1764 and 1772. The 1764 census showed the population of the three counties to be York, 11,362, Cumberland, 8,291, and Lincoln 4,371. The 1772 census gave these figures York, 13,398; Cumberland, 10,139, and Lincoln, 5,563.

From 1650 to 1819, Maine was under the jurisdiction of Massachusetts. After many attempts Maine finally succeeded in breaking away in 1819. A year later she was admitted into the union as the twenty-third state.

Although the early settlers were mainly from England, many Scotch-Irish and Huguenots came during the first century. Some German families came to Waldoboro, straight west from Rockland on the southeastern Atlantic shore line, from 1740 to 1800. During the nineteenth century many artisans came from England, Scotland and the Scandinavian countries to work in factories and ship yards. About 1870 many Swedes settled in the northeast corner of the state as indicated by such Swedish place-names as New Sweden, Stockholm, Jemtland, and Linneus. The large lumber camps in the northwest section of the state later beckoned many Finns.

Very early in their history, Maine towns began to keep records of births, marriages, and deaths. Notwithstanding the many repeated governmental changes during the first two hundred years the vital statistics of the territory were disturbed but little. Many of the records have been printed and are now in genealogical libraries in most of the states. Unpublished information may be searched in the various city offices in the state. The large majority of the early communities still existing have printed their town histories. Most of those histories contain genealogical information about the early settlers.

Division of Vital Statistics, Department of Health and Welfare, Augusta, Maine 04331, has records of birth, marriage, death, and divorce dating from 1892, adoption records from 1935, and about half a million birth, death, and marriage records of earlier dates. The state census records of 1850, 1860 and 1870 are also available there.

The city clerks of nearly five hundred towns and cities are in possession of the original records of vital statistics long before 1892. Authorities have reported that "the completeness of the early records varies all the way from absent to quite complete. Portland's records, for instance, are very complete and date from 1712."

In the sixteen offices of clerks of court are the records of land titles as well as the divorce records. The sixteen registrars of probate have the settlements of estates and the adoption records. They also have the 1880 census enumerations for their respective counties, but six of the sixteen, it is reported, have strangely mislaid them. The courts are located in the county seats of each county.

War service records, including grave registrations, is under the office of the Adjutant General in Augusta.

The important libraries in the state are located in the following cities: Maine State Library, State House, Augusta 04331, (Kennebec); Public Library, 145 Harlow St., (Genealogies and town histories of Maine, N.H., Vt., and Mass.), Bangor 04401, (Penobscot); Guy Gannett Publishing Company, Press Herald-Express Library, 390 Congress Street, (newspaper references), Portland 04101, (Cumberland); Portland Public Library, 619 Congress St., Portland 04101, (Cumberland).

The following reference books on Maine may help you in your research:

Banks, Charles Edward, "Topographic Dictionary of 2885 English Emigrants to New England", 1620-1650. Publ. 1937. The homes of emigrants, parishes and counties were ascertained in numerous cases.

"Documentary History of the State of Maine", 24 volumes, 1869-1916. Maine Historical Society.

House, Charles J., "Names of Maine Soldiers of the American Revolution". Burleigh and Flynt, Augusta, Me., 1893. 50 pp.

Libby, Charles Thornton; Noyes, Sybil and Davis, Walter Goodwin, "Genealogical Dictionary of Maine and New Hampshire", Five volumes. Total pages 795. Based largely on Col. Banks' two mammoth manuscripts, "Maine Genealogies", which represent a life time of work in all the libraries over the country. The Southworth--Anthoensen Press, Portland, Me., 1928-38.

Libby, Charles Thornton, "Province and Court Records of Maine". Vol. I, 1928. Vol. II, 1931 (index).

Little, George Thomas, "Genealogical and Family History of the State of Maine". About 6,000 individual biographies. Vol. 1, 500 pp. Vol. II, 550 pp. Vol. III, 600 pp. Vol. IV, 633 pp. Lewis Historical Publishing Company, New York, 1909. (Commercial biographies should always be checked carefully.)

"Maine 1790 Census", 105 pp. Bureau of the Census, Government Printing Office, Washington, D. C. 1908.

"Maine Register and State Reference Book", 1852. Masters, Smith and Company, Hallowell, Me., 1852.

Marshall, J. M., "Buxton, Maine, Centennial Anniversary", 288 pp. with 148 pp. of genealogy. Dresser, McLellan & Company, Portland, Me., 1874.

Pope, Charles Henry, "Pioneers of Maine and New Hampshire", 1623-1660, a descriptive list drawn from the records of the colonies, towns, churches, courts, and other contemporary sources. Alphabetically arranged. 1908.

Sargent, William Mitchell, "Maine Wills", 1640-1760, 953 pp. Four indexes: Testators, Other Persons, and Miscellaneous. Brown, Thurston & Company, Portland, Me., 1887.

Scales, John, "Piscataqua Pioneers", 1623-1775. Sketches of early settlers and the first generation of their children, who lived on both sides of the Piscataqua River, including Dover, Oyster River, Kittery, Exeter, Brewick, and Portsmouth.

Spencer, Wilbur Daniel, "Pioneers on Maine Rivers", with lists to 1651. 1930.

Sprague's "Journal of Maine History", 14 vols. Printed 1913-1926.

"The Maine Historical and Genealogical Recorder", 1884-1898. 8 vols. Reprint of vital records, family sketches, etc. (Valuable)

United States, Works Progress Administration, "Bibliography of Research Projects Reports", Check list of historical records survey publications, 1940.

Maine Towns Organized Before 1800

ANDROSCOGGIN COUNTY -- Durham, 1772; E. Livermore, 1780; Greene, 1780; Leeds, 1780; Lewiston, 1768; Lisbon, 1788; Livermore, 1779; Minot, 1769; Turner, 1772; Webster, 1774.

CUMBERLAND COUNTY -- Bridgeton, 1768; Brunswick, 1628; Cape Elizabeth, 1630; Casco, 1729; Cumberland, 1640; Deering 1637; Falmouth, 1632; Freeport, 1658; Gorham, 1732; Gray, 1756; Harpswell, 1659; New Gloucester, 1735; Portland, 1632; Scarborough, 1631; Standish, 1763; Windham, 1735; Yarmouth, 1636.

FRANKLIN COUNTY -- Avon, 1790; Chesterville, 1782; Farmington, 1794; Freeman, 1797; Industry, 1793-4; Jay, 1795; New Sharon, 1794; Philips, 1790; Wilton, 1792.

HANCOCK COUNTY -- Blue Hill, 1762; Brookline S.,1688; Bucksport, 1764; Carline, O. 1626; Demariscotta, S. 1630; Deer Isle, O. 1789; Eastbrook, S. 1800; Eden, 1763; Ellsworth, S. 1763; Gouldsborough, S. 1700; Hancock, S. 1764-5; Penobscot, S. 1765; Fremont, S. 1613.

KENNEBEC COUNTY -- Augustà, 1761-2; Harrington, 1797; Belgrade, 1774; Bingham, 1784; China, 1774; Clinton, 1775; Fayette, 1779; Hallowell, 1771; Litchfield, 1795; Manchester, 1774; Monmouth, 1777; Pittston bef. 1676; Vassalboro, 1760; Wayne, 1773; Waterville, 1760; Windsor, 1790; Winslow, 1771; Winthrop, 1771.

KNOX COUNTY -- Camden, 1770; Cushing, 1789; Friendship, 1750; Hope 1782; Rockland, 1767; St. George, 1635; Thomaston, 1770; Union, 1786; Vinal Haven, 1765; Warren, 1736.

LINCOLN COUNTY -- Boothbay, 1630; Bremen, 1735; Dresden, 1649; Edgecomb, 1744; Jefferson, bef. Rev. New Castle, 1630; Pownalsborough, 1760; Waldoborough, 1733-40; Wiscasset, 1730.

OXFORD COUNTY -- Andover, 1789, Bethel, 1774; Brownsfield, 1770; Buckfield, 1776; Canton, 1790; Denmark, 1788-9; Dixfield, 1793; Fryeburg, 1763; Hanover, 1774; Hartford, aft. Rev. Hebron, 1778; Hiram, 1774; Lovell, 1777; Norway, 1786; Oxford, Dur. Rev. Oxford, 1780; Rumford, 1782; Waterford, 1775.

PENOBSCOT COUNTY -- Bangor, 1769; Carmel, 1695; Charlestown, 1795; Corinth, 1796; Eddington, 1785; Hampden, 1767; Orono, 1770; Orrington, 1770.

SAGADAHOC COUNTY -- Arrowsic, 1679; Bath, 1660; Bowdoin, previous Rev. Bowdoinham, 1762; Georgetown, 1716; Richmond, 1650; Sagadahoe, 1623; Topsham, 1658; Woolwich, 1638.

SOMERSET COUNTY -- Anson, 1798; Athens, 1782; Cannaan, 1770; Concord, aft. Rev.; Cornville, 1794; Embden, 1779; Fairfield, 1774; Harmony, 1796; Norridgewock, aft Rev.; Skowhegan, 1792, Palmyra, 1779; Pittsfield, 1794; Waterville, 1760.

WALDO COUNTY -- Belfast, 1769; Frankfort, 1770; Freedom, 1794; Isleborough, 1769; Jackson, 1708; Monroe, 1760; Montville, 1778-9; Troy, 1778.

WASHINGTON COUNTY -- Calais, bef. 1758; Cutler, 1785; Dennyville, 1786; Eastport, 1780-2; Edmonds, 1775; Harrington, 1762; Lunec, 1776; Machias, 1762-3; Pembroke, 1774.

YORK COUNTY -- Acton, 1776; Alfred, 1764; Berwick, 1624; Biddeford, 1617-18; Buxton, 1772; Cornish, 1794; Dayton, 1664; Eliot, 1632; Hollis, 1753; Kennebunk, 1643; Kennebunkport, 1653; Kittery, 1623; Lebanon, 1746; Limerick, 1775; Lyman, 1778; N.

Berwick, 1630; Parsonfield, 1772; Saco, 1653; Sanford, 1745; S. Berwick, 1624; Waterborough, 1768; Wells, 1640; York, 1663.

Maine County Histories

(Population figures to nearest thousand - 1960 Census)

Name	Map Index	Date Formed	Pop. By M	Census Reports Available	Parent County	County Seat
Androscoggin	D2	1854	86	1860-80	Cumberland, Oxford, Kennebec	Auburn

(Co Clk has div & civ ct rec from 1854; City Clk has m, b, d, & bur rec; Register of Pro has pro rec)

Aroostook	B2	1839	106	1840-80	Washington	Houlton

(Co Clk has div & civ ct rec from 1839; Town Clks keep b, m, d, & bur rec; Pro Ct has pro rec)

Cumberland	D2	1760	183	1800-80	York	Portland

(Co Clk has div & civ ct rec; City or Town Clks have b, m, d & bur rec; Pro Ct has pro rec)

Franklin	C1	1838	20	1840-80	Cumberland	Farmington
Hancock	C3	1789	32	1800-80	Lincoln	Swans Island & Ellsworth

County Map of Maine

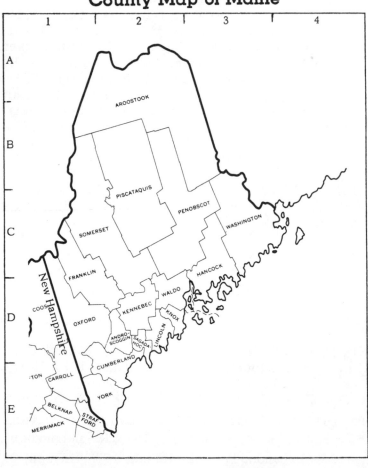

Kennebec	D2	1799	89	1800-80	Lincoln	Augusta
Knox	D2	1860	29	1860-80	Lincoln, Waldo	Rockland
Lincoln	D2	1760	18	1800-80	York	Wiscasset
Oxford	D1	1805	44	1810-80	York, Cumberland	So. Paris
Penobscot	C2	1816	126	1820-80	Hancock	Bangor
Piscataquis	C2	1838	17	1840-80	Penobscot, Somerset . . . Dover & Foxcroft

(Clk of Ct has div & pro rec from 1838, deeds from 1838; Individual towns have b, d, m, & bur rec)

Sagadahoc	D2	1854	23	1860-80	Lincoln	Bath
Somerset	C2	1809	40	1810-80	Kennebec	Skowhegan

(Co Clk has scattered m rec from 1800, div & civ ct rec from 1827, pro & property rec from 1809; Town Clk has b, m, d, & bur rec)

Waldo	D2	1827	23	1850-80	Hancock, Lincoln, Kennebec	Belfast

(Co Clk has m rec from 1828 to 1887 not indexed, also has div & Sup Ct rec from 1828; Town or City Clks have b, m, d, bur rec; Pro Ct has pro rec)

Washington	C3	1789	35	1800-80	Lincoln . . . . Lambert Lake & Machias
York(shire)	E2	1638	99	1800-80	Original county reorg. 1658 . . . . . Alfred

(Part of 1800 cen missing; Clk of Ct has div & civ ct rec; Town & City Clks have b, m, d, & bur rec)

Genealogists' Check List of the Historical Records Survey, Maine

Federal Courts. Inventory of Municipal and Town Archives, Avon, Bar Harbor, Berlin, Brownville, Chesterville, Cranberry Isles, Coplin, Dallas, Eustis, Mt Desert, Seaville, Southwest Harbor, Tremont. Directory of church and religious organizations in Maine. Ship registers and enrollments of Machias 1780-1830, Saco 1791-1915. Index to a Reference list of manuscripts relating to the History of Maine, Part III in the main bulletin Vol XLIII No. 8. American portrait inventory found in the State of Maine 1745-1850. Depository of unpublished material, Works Progress Administration Warehouse, Portland, Maine.

Maryland

Capital Annapolis - State 1788 - (7th)

Depressed by the constant persecution in England of the members of the Roman Catholic church, with which he had become affiliated, Lord Baltimore (George Calvert), a member of Parliament and Secretary of State of James I from 1609 to 1625, sponsored movements to establish colonies in America for the persecuted religionists in his homeland. Failing in his first attempt to build a colony in Newfoundland about 1620, he persuaded the King of England to grant him land for a colony farther south along the Atlantic coast. After the grant was made, but before the charter had been signed, Lord Baltimore died. King

Charles I then transferred the grant to Lord Baltimore's son, Cecilius Calvert, the second Lord Baltimore.

The grant included all of the land between the fortieth parallel and the southern bank of the Potomac River. The first contingent of emigrants to be shipped to the new colony in 1634 consisted of about twenty Catholic gentlemen and two hundred Protestant laborers. They established a settlement about nine miles up the St. George's river, which empties into the north side of the Potomac river, near its mouth.

Already occupying Kent Island in the Chesapeake Bay, just opposite the present site of Annapolis, were William Claiborne, a Virginia planter, and a large group of settlers he had brought there from Virginia several years ahead of the Calvert colonists. Continuous warfare ensued between the two factions, as Claiborne refused to adhere to orders from the British King granting the territory to Lord Baltimore. It was not until Claiborne's death in 1677 that hostilities ceased.

The Maryland colony enjoyed a rapid growth. This was due, in a measure, to the pronouncement of its founder that religious toleration and protection would be extended to all Christians of whatever shade of religious belief who would come there to establish their homes. The Act Concerning Religion, passed by the colony in 1649, declared that "no person professing to believe in Jesus Christ shall henceforth be troubled or molested on account of religion."

This attracted a large group of Puritans who had become disgusted with the activities of the Church of England controlling Virginia. They left Virginia and came into Maryland. They settled and built up what is now Anne Arundel County. This influx increased the population of Maryland to about thirty thousand people.

In 1660 another migration brought many settlers to the so-called Eastern Shore, the land east of Chesapeake Bay. This movement was so great it necessitated the organization of Talbot county. About five years later with the migration continuing steadily, Somerset county was formed south of Talbot.

During the first century of the settlement of Maryland, the settlers clung to the land along the many water courses, the rivers and the bays. No one ventured far away from the streams which provided about the only mode of transportation in those days. It was not until about 1740 that the Appalachian section of Maryland was claimed by settlers. English, Scotch, and Scotch-Irish emigrants came up from St. Mary's, Charles, and Prince George's counties at that time. Joining with them shortly afterward were large groups of Germans who had come down from Pennsylvania. The population increased so rapidly that in 1748 Frederick county was organized in the northwest section of

Maryland.

To Baltimore in 1755 came many Acadians driven from Nova Scotia. Less than forty years later another group of French people, upwards of a thousand, sought refuge in Baltimore from the race riots in Santo Domingo in 1793. From 1817 to 1847 thousands of Irish immigrants came to Baltimore as canal diggers. Later they established themselves as farmers and miners in the Appalachian section. Thousands of people who fled Germany after the 1848 Revolution in that country were given shelter in Baltimore.

The rapid increase in the Maryland population is indicated by the fact that eleven of her twenty-three counties were formed before 1700, and eight of the remaining before 1800.

Concerning vital records of Maryland, the Division of Vital Records and Statistics Department of Health, 2411 N. Charles St., Baltimore, Maryland 21218, says "This office is primarily issuing copies of births, deaths and marriages. Our birth and death records cover the years 1898 to the present time. Our marriage records begin 1 June 1951. Marriage records prior to that date may be obtained from the clerk of the Circuit Court in the county of marriages. Deeds may, in some cases, be found at the Clerk of Court's office in each county. Land grants are only in custody of Land Office, Annapolis, Maryland 21401. Wills are in the Register of Wills' Office in each county."

Libraries to be found in Maryland are as follows: Maryland Historical Society Library, 201 W. Monument St., Baltimore 21201, (Baltimore); Washington County Free Public Library, 21 Summit Ave., Hagerstown 21740, (Washington).

The following books contain valuable genealogical information:

"Archives of Maryland: Muster Rolls and Other Records of Service of Maryland Troops in the American Revolution", 1775-1783. 736 pp. Pub. 1900.

Baldwin, Jane, (Mrs. Cotton), "The Maryland Calendar of Wills", 8 vols. Each volume indexed. 1635-1743. 2,579 pp.

Bromwell, Henrietta Elizabeth, "Old Maryland Families", vital statistics, 1916.

Brumbaugh, Gaius Marcus, "Maryland Records", Colonial, Revolutionary, County and Church, from Original Sources. Vital statistics. Valuable to researchers. Vol. I, 513 pp. Williams & Wilkins Company, Baltimore, 1915. Vol. II, 688 pp. Lancaster Press, Lancaster, Pa., 1928 (Genealogical Book Company, 521-23 St. Paul Place, Baltimore, Maryland 21202.)

Burns, Annie Walker, "Maryland Genealogical and Historical Recorder". Mimeographed. 13 Vol.

. . . ., "Abstract of Wills of Baltimore Co.," 1791-1797, 5 vols.

Hayes, Jr., Robert F., "The Maryland Genealogical Bulletin", 1930-44. Quarterly magazine.

Johnston, Christopher, "Genealogies of the Members and Record of Services of Ancestors, Society of Colonial Wars in the State of Maryland". (Pedigrees of members.) 157 pp. Baltimore, 1905.

Neill, Rev. Edward D., "The Founders of Maryland", 194 pp. Joel Munsell, Albany, 1878.

Parran, Alice Norris, "Register of Maryland's Heraldic Families", 1635 to 1935. Series I, 1935; Series II, 352 pp., 1938 Baltimore. (Genealogical Book Company, 521-23 St. Paul Place, Baltimore, Maryland 21202.)

U. S. Bureau of the Census, "First Census of United States, 1790, Maryland", Government Printing Office, Washington, D.C., 1907.

Maryland County Histories
(Population figures to nearest thousand - 1960 Census)

Name	Map Index	Date Formed	Pop. By M	Census Reports Available	Parent County	County Seat
Allegany	A2	1789	84	1800-80	Washington	Cumberland
Anne Arundel	B4	1650	230	1790-80	Original county	Annapolis

(Clk of Ct has m rec from 1905, div rec, civ ct rec from 1870, land rec from 1851; Reg of Vit Stat has b & d rec; Hall of Rec has m rec 1777 to 1904, also has earlier rec of Civ ct and land rec; Reg of Wills has pro rec)

Name	Map Index	Date Formed	Pop. By M	Census Reports Available	Parent County	County Seat
Baltimore	B4	1659	492	1790-80	Original county	Fullerton & Towson
Baltimore City	B4	1729	939	1800-80	Baltimore	Baltimore
Calvert	C4	1650	16	1800-80	Original county	Prince Frederick
Caroline	B4	1773	19	1790-80	Dorchester, Queen Annes	Denton
Carroll	B3	1836	53	1840-80	Baltimore, Frederick	Westminster

(Clk of Cir Ct has m & div rec from 1837)

Name	Map Index	Date Formed	Pop. By M	Census Reports Available	Parent County	County Seat
Cecil	B4	1674	52	1790-80	Kent	Elkton

(Clk of Ct has m rec from 1777, div & civ ct rec; Health Dept, Ct House has b rec from 1898, d rec from 1898 and bur rec; Actual wills 1674 to 1850 are at Hall of Rec; Clk of Ct has indices only 1674 to present)

Name	Map Index	Date Formed	Pop. By M	Census Reports Available	Parent County	County Seat
Charles	C3	1658	33	1790-80	Original county	La Plata
Dorchester	C4	1669	30	1790-80	Original county	Cambridge
Frederick	B3	1748	72	1790-80	Prince Georges	Frederick

(Clk of Cir Ct has m rec from 1778, div rec from 1807, civ ct & land rec 1748)

Name	Map Index	Date Formed	Pop. By M	Census Reports Available	Parent County	County Seat
Garrett	A1	1872	20	1880	Allegany	Oakland

(Clk of Cir Ct has m, div, civ ct rec, deeds from 1872; b rec are at Health Dept; d rec are at Bureau of Vit Stat, Register of Wills has pro rec)

Name	Map Index	Date Formed	Pop. By M	Census Reports Available	Parent County	County Seat
Harford	B4	1773	95	1790-80	Baltimore	Bel Air

(Clk of Cir Ct has m rec from 1779, div & civ ct rec from 1803, land deeds from 1773, also mtg, bills of sale; Wills are at Register of Wills; Health Dept has b, d & bur rec)

Name	Map Index	Date Formed	Pop. By M	Census Reports Available	Parent County	County Seat
Howard	B3	1851	36	1860-80	Baltimore, Anne Arundel	Ellicott City
Kent	B4	1642	15	1790-80	Original county	Chestertown

(Clk of Cir Ct has m rec from 1796, div rec from 1853, land rec from 1656, civ ct rec from 1728; bur rec are at individual cemeteries; Md State Dept of Health has b & d rec)

Name	Map Index	Date Formed	Pop. By M	Census Reports Available	Parent County	County Seat
Montgomery	B3	1776	341	1790-80	Frederick	Rockville

(Clk of Cir Ct has m rec from 1799, div, civ ct & land rec from 1776) (1830 Census missing)

Name	Map Index	Date Formed	Pop. By M	Census Reports Available	Parent County	County Seat
Prince Georges	B3	1695	357	1790-80	Charles, Calvert	Upper Marlboro

(Many rec with Clk of Cir Ct before 1785 – deeds complete – no fires)(1830 census missing)

QueenAnnes B4 1706 17 1790–80 Talbot . . . . Centreville
(1830 census missing) (Clk of Cir Ct has m rec from 1817, div rec from 1824, also civ ct rec; Bureau of Vit Stat has b, d, bur rec; Register of Wills has pro rec)

Saint Mary's C4 1637 39 1790–80 Original county . . . . Leonardtown
(1830 census missing)

Somerset C4 1666 20 1800–80 Original county . . . . Princess Anne
(1830 census missing) (Clk Cir Ct has m, div, civ ct & land rec from 1666; State Dept of Health has b, d & bur rec; Register of Wills has pro rec)

Talbot B4 1662 22 1790–80 Kent . . . . Easton

Washington A3 1776 91 1790–80 Frederick . . . . Hagerstown

Wicomico C5 1867 49 1870–80 Somerset, Worcester . . . . Salisbury
(Clk of Cir Ct has m, div, civ ct rec from 1867)

Worcester C5 1742 24 1790–80 Somerset . . . . Snow Hill
(Clk of Cir Ct has m rec from 1866, div rec from 1900, civ ct rec from 1916; Hall of rec, Annapolis, Md or Bureau of Vit Stat has b, d & bur rec; Register wills has pro rec)

County Map of Maryland and Delaware

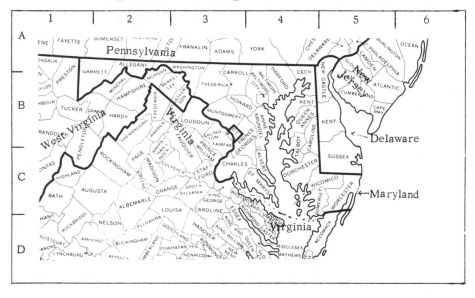

Genealogists' Check List of the Historical Records Survey,
Maryland

Federal Courts (start 1789). Inventory of County Archives, Allegany, Anne Arundel, Carroll, Garrett, Howard, Montgomery, Washington, Wicomico. Inventory of municipal and town archives, Accident, Annapolis, Arundel-on-the bay, Barnesville, Barton, Boonsboro, Brooksville, Chevy Chase, Clearspring, Cumberland, Dear Park, Delmar, Ellicott City, Friendsville, Frostburg, Funkstown, Gaithersburg, Garrett Park, Glen Echo, Grantsville, Hagerstown, Hamstead, Hancock, Hebron, Keddysville, Kensington, Kitzmillersville, Laytonville, Loch Lynn, Lonaconing, Luke,

Manchester, Mardela Springs, Midland, Mt Airy, Moutain Lake Park, New Windsor, Oakland, Poolesville, Rockville, Salisbury, Sharpsburg, Sharpstown, Smithburg, Somerset, Sykesville, Takoma Park, Taneytown, Union Bridge, Washington Grove, Westminster, Willards, Williamsport. Inventory of the church archives of Maryland, Protestant Episcopal Church, Diocese of Maryland. Manuscripts published, calendar of the General Otho Hollard Williams papers in the Maryland Historical Society, Depository of unpublished material, Hall of Records, Annapolis, Maryland.

Massachusetts

Capital Boston - State 1788 - (6th)

It was on 11 December 1620, according to the calendar then in vogue, 21 December, according to our calendar that Massachusetts came into existence with the landing of the Pilgrims on Plymouth Rock. Through the initiative of the Massachusetts Bay Company another colony was formed at Salem in 1628, and two years later more than a thousand colonists arrived founding the towns of Boston, Charleston, Roxbury, Dorchester, Watertown, and Newtown, which later became Cambridge. Within ten years, more than 20,000 immigrants, almost entirely British, had landed in Massachusetts. For the first 200 years or more by far the larger number of immigrants were from England.

Disasters and political troubles of various kinds in Europe from 1850 on brought a large influx from Ireland, Germany and France. A few years later Italians, Russians, Poles, and Portuguese came into the state to work in its rapidly growing factories, mills and fisheries.

Families from Dorchester, England settled in Massachusetts and then migrated to South Carolina. Three separate settlements between Charleston and Georgetown, were settled by New England families.

The people of few states have been of greater assistance to the genealogical researcher than have those of Massachusetts. From its earliest days, records of all vital statistics were kept and preserved. It is said that it is easier to trace genealogy in Massachusetts than in any other state. This because more records are available. Every town not only kept records from its earliest days, but has printed those records for the convenience of the researcher.

The birth and death records since 1850 may be obtained from Registrar of Vital Statistics, 272 State House, Boston, Massachusetts 02133. Some records prior to 1850 are in the offices of the city or town clerks in localities where incidents happened. Similar records for Boston available since 1639 in the office of the City Registrar, Registry Division, Room 1004 City Hall Annex, Boston, Mass. 02108.

Partial marriage records from 1841, and complete from 1848 are in the office of the Division of Vital Statistics, The Secretary of State, Boston, Mass. 02133. Similar records in the offices of the city or town clerk where license was issued. Marriage bans may be found in respective churches in the city.

Divorce records are with the Clerk of the Superior Court or the Register of Probate in the county where divorce was granted.

The state census records at five year intervals from 1850 to 1870, inclusive, are in the office of the Secretary of State.

The record of wills, deeds and land transactions are in the office of the Secretary of State.

The city or county assessors have all records of taxpayers.

The office of the Adjutant General controls all war service records.

Every town library in Massachusetts has vital statistical records from the adjoining communities and numerous biographical and historical books and manuscripts about early residents. Among the most important libraries in the state for genealogical purposes are the following: Public Library, Copley Square, Boston 02116, (Suffolk), (biographies, New England family genealogies, English parish registers and records, heraldry from Great Britain, Ireland, Germany, Italy, Holland, France, and Belgium, early American and Civil War histories, old maps, old newspapers); Massachusetts Historical Society Library, 1154 Boylston St., (New England histories and genealogies), Boston 02215, (Suffolk); Massachusetts State Library, Beacon Hill, (history and newspapers), Boston 02133, (Suffolk); New England Historic Genealogical Society, 101 Newbury St. 02116, (170,000 volumes of history and genealogy, and manuscript family genealogies) Boston 02116, (Suffolk); Public Library, 449 Broadway, (genealogical collection), Cambridge 02138, (Middlesex); Harvard University Library, (early American newspapers), Cambridge 02138, (Middlesex); Dedham Historical Society, (considerable number of historical and family histories and diaries in books and manuscripts, town histories, family genealogies, and newspapers from earliest days), Dedham 02026, (Norfolk); City Library, Merrimac St., (Book and manuscript genealogies), Lowell 01852, (Middlesex); Public Library, North Common St., (New England histories and genealogies), Lynn, 01902, (Essex); Free Public Library, Pleasant St., (southeastern Mass. family genealogies in books and manuscripts), New Bedford 02740, (Bristol); The Berkshire Athenaeum, 44 Bank Row, (biography, Massachusetts history, New England genealogy), Pittsfield 01202, (Berkshire); Essex Institute Library, 132-134 Essex St., (town vital statistics, family histories, and genealogies, printed and in manuscript and genealogical and historical magazines), Salem 01970, (Essex); City Library Association, 220 State St., Springfield 01103, (Hampden); Athenaeum, Elm St., (vital statistic records of the city, cemetery inscriptions, death notices from newspapers, family histories, printed and manuscript), Westfield 01880, (Hampden).

Among the many volumes available to ease the task of the researchers of Massachusetts genealogy are the following:

Banks, Charles Edward. ''The Planters of the Commonwealth'' A study of the Emigrants and Emigration in Colonial Times: to which are added Lists of Passengers to Boston and to the Bay Colony; the Ships which brought them; their English Homes and the Places of their Settlement in Mass. 1620-1640. 229 pp. Houghton Mifflin Company, Boston, 1930.

Boltwood, L. M. ''Genealogies of Hadley Families'', embracing early settlers of the towns of Hatfield, South Hadley, Amherst, and Granby. 168 pp. Metcalf & Company, Northampton, 1862.

''First U.S. Census, 1790 -- Massachusetts'' 363 pp. Government Printing Office, 1908.

Hills, Leon Clark. ''Mayflower Planters and First Comers to Ye Olde Colonie'', 177 pp. Hills Publishing Company, Washington D.C. 1936.

''Massachusetts Enyclopedia of Biography and Genealogy'' Vol. I, 562 pp. Vol. II, 410 pp.

''Massachusetts Soldiers and Sailors of the Revolutionary War'' 17 vols. of abt. 1,000 pp. each. Wright & Potter Printing Company, Boston, 1896-1908.

Nason, Rev. Elias. ''A Gazetteer of the State of Massachusetts'' Map and illustrations 576 pp. B. B. Russel, Boston, 1874.

Rand, John C. ''One of a Thousand'', Biographies of Massachusetts Residents. 707 pp. First National Publishing Company, Boston, 1890.

Stark, James H., ''The Loyalists of Massachusetts and the Other Side of the American Revolution''. With names and biographies. Fully indexed. 510 pp. The Salem Press Company, Salem, Mass., 1910.

The cities and towns of no other state have so many published community histories and vital statistics as has Massachusetts. If your ancestors were there before 1850 it would be well to check with the libraries and town clerks to ascertain what information may be had from the printed records.

The present Massachusetts counties are divided into the following townships:

BARNSTABLE -- Barnstable, Bourne, Brewster, Chatham, Dennis, Eastham, Falmouth, Harwich, Mashpee, Orleans, Provincetown, Sandwich, Truro, Wellfleet, and Yarmouth.

BERKSHIRE -- Adams, Alford, Becket, Cheshire, Clarksburg, Dalton, Edgemont, Florida, Great Barrington, Hancock, Hinsdale, Lanesborough, Lee, Lenox, Monterey, Mount Washington, New Ashord, New Marlborough, North Adams, Otis, Peru, Pittsfield, Richmond, Sandisfield, Savoy, Sheffield, Stocksridge, Tyringham, Washington, West Stockridge, Williamstown, and Windsor.

BRISTOL -- Acushnet, Attleboro, Berkley, Dartmouth, Dighton, Easton, Fairhaven, Fall River, Freetown, Mansfield, New Bedford, North Attleborough, Norton, Raynham, Rehoboth, Seekonk, Swansea, Taunton, and Westport.

DUKES -- Chilmark, Edgartown, Gayhead, Gosnold, Oak Bluffs, Tidbury, and West Tidbury.

ESSEX -- Andover, Amesbury, Beverly, Boxford, Danvers, Essex, Georgetown, Gloucester, Groveland, Hamilton, Haverhill, Ipswich, Lawrence, Lynn, Lynnfield, Manchester, Marblehead, Merrimac, Methuen, Middleton, Nahant, Newburyport, North Andover, Peabody, Rockport, Rowley, Salem, Salisbury, Saugus, Swampscott, Topsfield, Wenham, and West Newbury.

FRANKLIN -- Ashfield, Bernardston, Buckland, Charlemont, Colrain, Conway, Deerfield, Erving, Gill, Greenfield, Hawley, Heath, Leverett, Leyden, Monroe, Montague, New Salem, Northfield, Orange, Rowe, Shelburne, Shutesbury, Sunderland, Warwick, Wendell, and Whately.

HAMPDEN -- Agawam, Blandford, Brimfield, Chester, Chicopee, East Longmeadow, Granville, Hampden, Holland, Holyoke, Longmeadow, Ludlow, Monson, Montgomery, Palmer, Russell, Southwick, Springfield, Tolland, Wales, Westfield, West Springfield, and Wilbraham.

HAMPSHIRE -- Amherst, Belchertown, Chesterfield, Cummington, East Hampton, Goshen, Granby, Hadley, Hatfield, Huntington, Middlefield, Northampton, Pelham, Plainfield, South Hardely, Southampton, Ware, West Hampton, Williamsburg, and Worthington.

MIDDLESEX -- Acton, Arlington, Ashby, Ashland, Ayer, Bedford, Belmont, Billerica, Boxborough, Burlington, Cambridge, Carlisle, Chelmsford, Concord, Dracut, Dunstable, Everett, Framingham, Groton, Holliston, Hopkinton, Hudson, Lexington, Lincoln, Littleton, Lowell, Malden, Marlborough, Medford, Melrose, Natick, Newton, North Reading, Pepperell, Reading, Sherborn, Shirley, Somerville, Stoneham, Stow, Sudbury, Tewksbury, Townsend, Tyngsborough, Wakefield, Waltham, Watertown, Wayland, Westford, Weston, Wilmington, Winchester, and Woburn.

NANTUCKET -- Nantucket.

NORFOLK -- Avon, Bellingham, Braintree, Brookline, Canton, Cohasset, Dedham, Dover, Foxborough, Franklin, Holbrook, Medfield, Medway, Millis, Milton, Needham, Norfolk, Norwood, Plainville, Quincy, Randolph, Sharon, Stoughton, Walpole, Wellesley, Westwood, Weymouth, and Wrentham.

PLYMOUTH -- Abington, Bridgewater, Brockton, Carver, Duxbury, East Bridgewater, Halifax, Hanover, Hanson, Hingham, Hull, Kingston, Lakeville, Marion, Marshfield, Mattapoisett, Middleborough, Norwell, Pembroke, Plymouth, Plympton, Rochester, Rockland, Scituate, West Bridgewater, Wareham, and Whitman.

SUFFOLK -- Boston, Chelsea, Revere, and Winthrop.

WORCESTER -- Ashburnham, Athol, Auburn, Barre, Berlin, Blackstone, Bolton, Boylston, Brookfield, Charlton, Clinton, Douglas, Dudley, East Brookfield, Fitchburg, Gardner, Grafton, Hardwick, Harvard, Holden, Hopedale, Hubbardston, Lancaster, Leicester, Leominster, Lunenburg, Mendon, Milford, Millburg, Millville, New Braintree, North Borough, Northbridge, North Brookfield, Oakham, Oxford, Paxton, Petersham, Phillipston, Princeton, Royalston, Rutland, Shrewsbury, Southborough, South Bridge, Spencer, Sterling, Sturbridge, Sutton, Templeton, Upton, Uxbridge, Warren, Webster, Westborough, West Brookfield, West Boylston, Westminster, Winchendon, and Worcester.

MASSACHUSETTS TOWNS ORGANIZED
Before 1800

BARNSTABLE COUNTY -- Barnstable, 1638, Chatham, 1712; Dennis, 1798; Eastham, 1651; Falmouth 1694; Harwich, 1694; Nauset, 1643; Orleans, 1747; Provincetown from Eastham, Sandwich, 1630; Suckanasset, 1670; Truro, 1709; Wellfleet, 1763; Yarmouth, 1639.

BERKSHIRE COUNTY -- Adams, 1778; Alford, 1773; Becket, 1765; Chesshire, 1793; Clarksburg, 1798; Dalton, 1784; Egremont, 1760; Gagesborough, 1771; Great Barrington, 1761; Hancock, 1776; Lanesborough, 1765; Lee, 1777; Lenox, 1767; Loudon, 1773; Mount Washington, 1779; New Ashford, 1781; New Marlborough, 1759; Partridgefield, 1771; Pittsfield, 1771; Richmont, 1766; Richmond, 1785; Sandisfield, 1762; Savoy, 1797; Sheffield, 1733; Stockbridge, 1739; Tyringham, 1762; Washington, 1777; W. Stockbridge, 1774; Williamtown, 1765; Windsor, 1778.

BRISTOL COUNTY -- Attleboro, 1694; Berkley, 1735; Dartmouth, 1652; Dighton, 1712; Easton, 1725; Freetown, 1683; Mansfield, 1770; New Bedford, 1787; Norton, 1710; Raynham, 1731; Rehoboth, 1645; Somerset, 1790; Swansea, 1668; Taunton, 1639; Westport, 1787.

DUKES COUNTY -- Chilmark, 1695; Edgartown, 1671; Tisbury,

1671; Orig. Middletowne.

ESSEX COUNTY -- Amesbury, 1668, name ch. fr. Salisbury-new-town; Andover, 1646; Beverly, 1668; Boxford, 1694; Bradford, 1675; Danvers, 1752; Gloucester, 1642; Hamilton, 1793; Haverhill, 1641; Ipswick, 1634; Lynn, 1637; Lynnfield, 1782; Manchester, 1645; Marblehead, 1633; Methuen, 1725; Middletown, 1728; Newbury, 1635; Newburyport, 1764; Rowley, 1639; Salem, 1630; Salisbury, 1640; Saugus, 1631, name ch. to Lynn; Topsfield, 1648; Wenham, 1643.

FRANKLIN COUNTY -- Ashfield, 1765; Bernardstown, 1765, Buckland, 1779; Charlemont, 1765; Colrain, 1761; Conway, 1767; Deerfield, 1677; Gill, 1793; Greenfield, 1753; Hawley, 1792; Heath, 1785; Huntstown, 1736; Leverett, 1774; Leyden, 1784; Montague, 1754; New Salem, 1753; Northfield, 1714; Orange, 1783; Rowe, 1785; Sherburne, 1786; Shutesbury, 1761; Sunderland, 1718; Warwick, 1763; Wendall, 1781; Whateley, 1771.

HAMPDEN COUNTY -- Blandford, 1741, Orig. Glasgow; Brimfield, 1714; Chester, 1783; Orig. Murrayfield; Granville, 1754; Longmeadow, 1783; Ludlow, 1774; Monson, 1760; Montgomery, 1780; Murrayfield, 1765; Palmer, 1752; Russell, 1792; South Brimfield, 1762; Southwick, 1770; Springfield, 1641; Westfield, 1669; West Springfield, 1774; Wilbraham, 1763.

HAMPSHIRE COUNTY -- Amherst, 1759; Belchertown, 1761; Chesterfield, 1762; Cummington, 1779; Easthampton, 1785; Goshen, 1781; Granby, 1768; Greenwich, 1754; Hadley, 1661; Hatfield, 1670; Middlefield, 1783; Northampton, 1656; Norwich, 1773; Pelham, 1743; Plainfield, 1785; Southampton, 1753; South Hadley, 1783; Ware, 1761; Westhampton, 1775; Williamsburg, 1771; Worthington, 1768.

MIDDLESEX COUNTY -- Acton, 1755; Ashby, 1767; Bedford, 1729; Billerica, 1655; Boxborough, 1783; Burlington, 1799; Cambridge, 1630; Carlisle, 1780; Charlestown, 1630; Chelmsford, 1655; Concord, 1635; Dracut, 1702, Dunstable, 1680; E. Sudbury, 1780; Framingham, 1675; Groton, 1655; Holliston, 1724; Hopkinston, 1715; Lexington, 1713; Littleton, 1715; Malden, 1649; Marlborough, 1660; Medford, 1630; Natick, 1661; Newton, 1691; Pepperell, 1733; Reading, 1644; Sherburn, 1674; Shirley, 1753; Stoneham, 1725; Stow, 1683; Sudbury, 1639; Tewksbury, 1734; Townsend, 1732; Tynesborough, 1732; Waltham, 1738; Watertown, 1630; Westford, 1729; Weston, 1713; Wilmington, 1730; Woburn, 1642.

NANTUCKET COUNTY Orig. 1695 (Island) -- Nantucket, 1795; Sherburn, 1687.

NORFOLK COUNTY -- Bellingham, 1719; Braintree, 1640; Brookline, 1705; Canton, 1797; Cohasset, 1700; Dedham, 1636; Dorchester, 1630; Dover, 1784; Foxsborough, 1778; Franklin, 1778; Medfield, 1650; Medway, 1713; Milton, 1652; Needham, 1711;

Quincy, 1792; Randolph, 1793; Roxbury, 1630; Sharon, 1783; Stoughton, 1726; Stoughtonham, 1765; Walpole, 1724; W. Roxbury, 1772; Weymouth, 1635; Wrentham, 1673.

PLYMOUTH COUNTY -- Abington, 1712; Bridgewater, 1656; Carver, 1790; Duxbury, 1637; Halifax, 1734; Hanover,1727; Hingham, 1635; Hull, 1644; Kingston, 1726; Marshfield, 1642; Middleborough, 1669; Pembroke, 1712; Plymouth, 1620; Plympton,1707; Rexhame, 1642, name Ch. to Marshfield. Rochester, 1686; Scituate, 1633; Wareham, 1739.

SUFFOLK COUNTY -- Boston, 1630; Chelsea, S. 1739.

WORCESTER COUNTY -- Ashburnham, 1765; Athol, 1762; Barre, 1776; Berlin, 1784; Bolton, 1738; Boyleston, 1786; Brookfield, 1673; Charlton, 1755; Douglas, 1746; Dudley, 1732; Fitchburg, 1764; Gardner, 1785; Gerry, 1786; Grafton, 1735; Hardwick, 1739; Harvard, 1732; Holden, 1741; Hubbardtown, 1767; Hutchinson, 1774; Lancaster, 1653; Leicester, 1713; Leominster, 1740; Lunenberg, 1728; Mendon, 1667; Milford, 1780; New Braintree, 1751; New Sherburn, 1745; Northborough, 1766; Northbridge, 1772; Oakham, 1693; Oxford, 1693; Paxton, 1765; Petersham, 1754; Princeton, 1759; Royalston, 1765; Rutland, 1714; Shrewsbury, 1720; Southborough, 1727, Spencer, 1753; Sterling, 1781; Sturbridge, 1738; Sutton, 1714; Templeton, 1762; Upton, 1735; Uxbridge, 1727, Westborough, 1717; Western, 1742; Westminister, 1759; Winchenden, 1754; Worcester, 1684.

Massachusetts County Histories

(Population figures to nearest thousand - 1960 Census)

Name	Map Index	Date Formed	Pop. By M	Census Reports Available	Parent County	County Seat
Barnstable	B3	1685	70	1790-80	New Plymouth Colony	Barnstable
(Clk of Ct has div & pro rec from 1828 to 1928, civ ct rec from 1828)
Berkshire	E2	1761	142	1790-80	Hampshire	Pittsfield
(Clk of Ct has div rec from 1761 to 1922, civ ct rec from 1761; City or town clks hold b, m, d & bur rec; Pro Ct has pro rec & div rec 1922 to present)
Bristol	C3	1685	398	1790-80	New Plymouth Colony	Taunton / New Bedford & Fall River
(Clk of Cts has civ ct rec from 1796, also naturalization rec; bur rec are at cemeteries; b, m, d rec are at city offices; Pro Ct has div rec from 1921 also pro rec)
Dukes	B4	1695	6	1790-80	(Martha's Vineyard)	Edgartown
(Clk of Cts has div rec & sup ct rec from 1859; Pro Ct has pro rec; Town Clks have b, m, d & bur rec)
Essex	C1	1643	569	1790-80	Original county	Salem
Franklin	E2	1811	55	1820-80	Hampshire	Greenfield
(Clk of Ct has div rec from 1811 in concurrent jurisdiction with Pro ct; Clk of Cts has civ ct rec from 1811 in concurrent jurisdiction with Dist Ct & Sup Judicial Ct)
Hampden	E3	1812	429	1820-80	Hampshire	Springfield
Hampshire	E2	1662	103	1790-80	Middlesex	Northampton
(City Clks have b, m, & d rec; Hampshire Sup Ct or Pro Ct has div rec; Pro Ct has pro rec; Sup Ct has civ ct rec)

County Map of Massachusetts

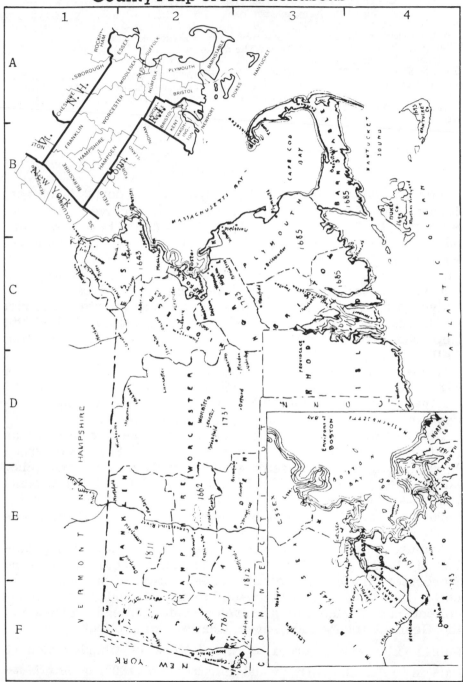

Middlesex   C2   1643 1239   1790–80   Original county . . .   Cambridge, Lowell
(The records from about 1890 or 1895 for the northern part of the county are
at Lowell, while all the county records from 1643 to 1890 or 1895, and then up
to the present for the southern part of the county are at East Cambridge.)

Nantucket   A4 1695   4 1790-80 Original County . . . . Nantucket
    (Clk of Cts has div rec 1890 to 1933, also civ ct rec from 1721; Pro Ct has pro
    rec; Town Clks have b, m, d & bur rec)
Norfolk   C2 1793 510 1800-80 Suffolk . . . . Dedham
    (Originally part of the northeastern section of Massachusetts and some towns
    at present part of New Hampshire. The old records are now at Salem in Essex
    County which originally included most of Norfolk County.)
Plymouth   C3 1685 248 1790-80 New Plymouth Colony . . . . . . Plymouth
    (Clk of Ct has civ ct rec from 1700 also div rec concurrent with Register of Pro)
Suffolk   C2 1643 791 1790-80 Original county . . . . Boston
    (Part of 1800 Census missing.)
Worcester   D2 1731 583 1790-80 Suffolk, Middlesex . . . . Worcester

Genealogists' Check List of the Historical Records Survey, Massachusetts

Federal courts (start 1789). Inventory of county archives, Essex, inventory of municipal and town archives, Agawam, Ashfield, Ashland, Athol, Auburn, Avon, Ayer, Barre, Bellingham, Berlin, Bernardston, Boston (Pt 5 & Pt 9), Braintree, Brookline, Buckland, Chicopee, Clinton, Hampden, Holbrook, Maynard, Pittsfield (Pt 1 & 2), Warwick. Guide to public vital statistics records. Inventory of the church archives of Mass. Universalist churches. Ship register and enrollments of district of Barnstable 1814-1913, Boston & Charlestown 1789-1795, New Bedford (3 Vol) 1796-1939, Plymouth 1789-1808, Dighton, Fall River, 1789-1938.

Indexes to local news in the Hampshire Gazette, Northampton 1786-1937, Vol 1, part 1 Northampton A to M, Vol 2, part 1 Northampton N to Z, part 2 Hampshire & Franklin counties except Northampton, Vol 3 part 3 personal section.

Abstract and index of the records of the Inferior court of Pleas (Suffolk County Court) held in Boston, 1680-1698. Index to Proclamations of Massachusetts issued by Governors and other authorities, Vol 1 1620-1775, Vol 2 1776-1936. Check list of Mass imprints 1801 and 1802. American portraits found in Mass. 1620-1825 (2 Vol). Known early American portrait painters before 1860.

Manuscripts published. Guide to depository of manuscript collection in Mass. Guide to the manuscript collections in the Worcester Historical Society. A description of the manuscript collections in the Mass. Diocesan Library. Calendar of the Ryder collection of Confederate archives at Tufts College. Calendar of the General Henry Knox Paper, Chamberlain collection, Boston Public Library. Calendar of the letters of Charles Robert Darwin to Asa Gray. Diary and journal (1775-1807) of Seth Metcalf. Depository of unpublished material, Forbes Library, Northampton, Massachusetts.

Michigan

Capital Lansing - Territory 1805 - State 1837 - (26th)

For some time after France obtained possession of American territory, a considerable outpost had been maintained at Detroit, This regime came to an end in 1763. Michigan then became part of Quebec territory, under which jurisdiction it remained for twenty years.

It was in 1783 that it was again under the claim of America. For a short time, the Indians, egged on by the British, inflicted considerable damage to the Americans in that section. This ended about 1795 when American troops under the command of General Anthony Wayne cleaned up the situation by herding the Indians farther west.

From 1787 until 1800 the Michigan section was part of the Northwest Territory, and from 1800 to 1805 it was connected with the Ohio and the Indian Territories.

Although the first American settlers began coming to Michigan from New England about 1796, it was not until about twenty-two years later that any appreciable influx of settlers was noted. Many came in 1818 to participate in the first public land sales. The commencing of work on the Erie Canal in that year drew many New Englanders to the Michigan sections. The completion of that important canal in 1825 added new stimula to the migrations. That same year many came to work on the road construction headed toward Chicago.

With the construction of the territorial road through the Kalamazoo Valley in 1829, many New Englanders established themselves in the Jackson, Calhoun, Kalamazoo, and Allegan counties. The following year saw the Saginaw Valley, including the counties of Shiawassee, Saginaw and Bay, beginning to fill up with permanent residents. The growth had been so constant and rapid during the first years of the new century that by 1836 fourteen counties had been established in the territory.

By 1840 the immigration had increased to such an extent that about half of the southern peninsula was cultivated by eager land-seekers who had come from New York, the New England section, and from Germany.

A fifty year boom, from 1840 to 1890, attracted tens of thousands of workers into the lumber camps and the mining camps of Michigan, where they extracted the valuable and plentiful copper and iron ores from the rich mineral deposits of the state.

To secure the needed man-power to work these rich deposits men were induced to come there from Canada, Ireland, Finland, Norway, Sweden, Wales, Poland, Italy and England. The tin mines of Cornwall, England, transplanted hundreds of expert miners into the Michigan mining camps.

Also during that time large groups of religious refugees from Holland settled around Grand Rapids and the western coast of the state.

Birth, marriage, and death records before 1867 are handled by the Clerk of the Circuit Court where incident occured, since then at the State Department of Health, Lansing, Michigan 48933. The Clerk of the Probate Court supervises all court records, such as wills, and probate matters. The Register of Deeds of each county handles all matters pertaining to land titles. County Clerks have many vital records, see county histories.

The Detroit Society for Genealogical Research % Burton Historical Collection, Detroit Public Library, Detroit, Michigan 48202, publish the Detroit Society for Genealogical Research magazine which started as a monthly but later changed to a bi-monthly. Inquiries on Michigan history and genealogy may be sent to the address above.

Michigan State Historical Society, 300 So. Walnut, Lansing 48933, has copies of 1830-50-60-70 and 80 census records.

Following is a partial list of Michigan libraries:

University of Michigan, William L. Clements Library, South University Ave., (early sate histories), Ann Arbor 48104, (Washtenaw); Public Library; County Library, Shelby St., Cadillac 49601, (Wexford); Public Library, 5201 Woodward Avenue, (Historical collections), Detroit 48202, (Wayne); Wayne County Public Library, 3661 Trumbull, Detroit 48208, (Wayne); Public Library, E. Kearsley & Clifford Sts.; County Library, Flint 48502, (Genesee); Public Library, Ill Library St., (state history, genealogical collection), Grand Rapids 49502, (Kent); County Public Library, 1961 Godfrey Ave., SW, Grand Rapids 49509, (Kent); Public Library, 210 W. Shiawassee St., Lansing 48933, (Ingham); State Library, State Office Bldg, Lansing 48933, (Ingham); Bacon Memorial Public Library, 2613 Biddle Ave., (local history), Wyandotte 48192, (Wayne).

Michigan County Histories

(Population figures to nearest thousand - 1960 Census)

Name	Map Index	Date Formed	Pop. By M	Census Reports Available	Parent County	County Seat
Alcona	C4	1869	6	1860-80	Alpena, Cheboygan	Harrisville
(Co Clk has b, m, d, div, pro, civ ct rec from 1870, also bur rec from 1940)						
Alger	B2	1855	9		Schoolcraft	Munising

Allegan   E3   1835   58 1840-80 Kalamazoo . . . . Allegan
(Co Clk has b & d rec from 1867, also m rec from 1836; Cem sextons have bur
rec; Co Clk has div rec from 1835, civ ct rec from 1836)
Alpena   C4   1857   29 1860-80 Cheboygan . . . . Alpena
(Co Clk has b, m, d, div & civ ct rec from 1870; Pro Office has pro rec)
Antrim   C4   1863   10 1860-80 Grand Traverse . . . . Bellaire
(Co Clk has b, m, d, div rec from 1867; pro rec from 1863, civ ct rec from
1865) (Antrim County was formerly named Meguzee)
Arenac   D4   1883   10   Bay, Saginaw . . . . Standish
(Co Clk has b, m, d, div, civ ct rec from 1883, bur rec from 1952)
Baraga   B2   1875   7 1880   Houghton . . . . L'Anse
(Co Clk has b, m, d, div & civ ct rec from 1875; also bur rec from 1950)
Barry   E4   1839   32 1840-80 St. Joseph, Kalamazoo . . . . Hastings
(Co Clk has b & d rec from 1867, m rec from 1839, div rec from 1880 also
cir ct rec; civ ct rec are in City Clks office; City or Village Clk has bur rec;
Pro Ct has pro rec)
Bay   D4   1857   107 1860-80 Saginaw, Midland . . . . Bay City
(Co Clk has b rec from 1868, m rec from 1857, d rec from 1883, bur rec from
1956, div rec from 1869 & civ ct rec from 1963)
Benzie   C3   1869   8 1870-80 Grand Traverse, Leelanau . . . . Beulah
(Co Clk has b & d rec from 1868, m & cir ct rec from 1869, div & pro rec from
1870, Naturalization rec from 1871, bur rec from 1934)
Berrien   E3   1831   156 1830-80 Cass . . . . St. Joseph
(Co Clk has b & d rec from 1867, m rec from 1831, div rec from 1901, civ ct
rec from 1933, bur rec from 1950)
Bleeker (See Menominee)
Branch   E4   1833   35 1840-80 St. Joseph, Lanawee . . . . Coldwater
Calhoun   E4   1833   139 1840-80 St. Joseph, Kalamazoo . . . . Marshall
(Co Clk has b rec from 1868, m rec from 1836, d rec from 1868, bur rec from
1952; div rec from 1847, civ ct (Law) rec from 1838 & crim rec from 1848;
Pro Ct has pro rec)
Cass   E3   1829   37 1830-80 Lenawee . . . . Cassopolis
(Co Clk has b & d rec from 1867, m rec from 1831, div & civ ct rec from 1830)
Charlevoix   C4   1869   13 1870-80 Emmet . . . . Charlevoix
Cheboygan   C4   1853   15 1860-80 Mackinac . . . . Cheboygan
(Co Clk has b, m, d, div, civ ct rec from 1867, also bur rec; Pro Ct has pro rec)
Chippewa   B4   1826   33 1830-80 Mackinac . . . . Sault Ste. Marie
Clare   D4   1871   12 1870-80 Isabella, Midland, Mecosta . . . Harrison
Clinton   D4   1839   38 1850-80 Shiawssee, Kent . . . . St. Johns
(Co Clk has b, m, d rec from 1867, div, civ ct rec from 1839)
Crawford   C4   1869   5 1820-80 Cheboygan, Antrim, Kalkaska . . Grayling
(Co Clk has b rec from 1879, m rec from 1887, d rec from 1878 & div rec from
1883; City Mgr, City Office, has bur rec; Judge of Pro has pro rec)
Delta   B2   1861   34 1860-80 Mackinac . . . . Escanaba
(Co Clk has b, m, d, bur, div & civ ct rec from 1862)
Des Moines   1834   Disorganized
Dickinson   B2   1891   24   Marquette, Menominee . . . Iron Mountain
(Co Clk has m, b, d, div, civ ct, Naturalization rec from 1891; City & Township
Clk has bur rec; Pro Ct has pro rec)
Eaton   E4   1837   50 1840-80 St. Joseph, Kalamazoo, Calhoun . Charlotte
(Co Clk has b, m, d rec from 1867, div and civ ct rec from 1850)
Emmet   C4   1853   16 1860-80 Mackinac . . . . Petoskey
Genesee   D4   1836   374 1840-80 Oakland . . . . Flint
(Co Clk has b & d rec from 1867, m & div rec from 1836, civ ct rec from 1847,
State Health Dept also has b, m, d & div rec; Pro Ct has pro rec)
Gladwin   D4   1875   11 1860-80 Saginaw, Midland . . . . Gladwin
Gogebic   B1   1887   24   Ontonagon . . . . Bessemer
(Co Clk has b, m, d, div, civ ct, Naturalization rec from 1887; Mich, Dept of
Health , Vit Stat also holds b, m & d rec)
Grand Traverse C3 1851   33 1860-80 Mackinac . . . . Traverse City
Gratiot   D4   1855   37 1860-80 Saginaw, Clinton . . . . Ithaca

(Co Clk has b, m, d, div, civ ct rec from 1867)

Hillsdale	E4	1835	35	1840-80	Lenawee	. . . .	Hillsdale
Houghton	B1	1845	36	1850-80	Marquette, Ontonagon,		
					& Schoolcraft	. . . .	Houghton

(Co Clk has b & d rec from 1867, m rec from 1848, some bur rec, div & civ ct
rec from 1853, also naturalization rec from 1848, some military rec)

Huron	D5	1859	34	1850-80	Saginaw, St. Clair, Sanilac	. . . .	Bad Axe

(rec prior 1867 destroyed by fire)

Ingham	E4	1838	211	1840-80	Washtenaw, Jackson, Eaton	. . .	Mason

(Co Clk has b & d rec from 1867, m rec from 1838, div & civ ct rec from 1839;
bur rec are with Township & City Clks; Pro Ct has pro rec)

Ionia	D4	1837	43	1840-80	Kent	. . . .	Ionia
Iosco	C4	1857	17	1860-80	Saginaw, Cheboygan	. . . .	Tawas City

(Co Clk has b, m, d, bur, div, civ ct rec from ca 1880)

Iron	B2	1885	17		Marquette, Menominee	. . .	Crystal Falls

(Co Clk has b, m, d, div, cir ct rec from 1885)

County Map of Michigan

Isabella   D4   1859   35   1860-80   Saginaw, Midland ...... Mt. Pleasant
Isle Royal   1875   1880   Disorganized 1897
  (Attached 1885 to Houghton, 1897 to Keweenaw where records now are held.)
Jackson   E4   1832   132   1840-80   Washtenaw .... Jackson
  (Co Clk has b & d rec from 1867, m rec from 1833, also div & civ ct rec)
Kalamazoo   E3   1830   170   1840-80   St. Joseph .... Kalamazoo
  (Co Clk has b & d rec from 1867, m rec from 1831)
Kalkaska   C3   1871   4   1870-80   Grand Traverse, Antrim .... Kalkaska
  (Co Clk has b, m, d, div rec from 1871)
Kent   D3   1836   363   1840-80   Kalamazoo .... Grand Rapids
  (Co Clk has b, d, div & civ ct rec from 1867, m rec from 1845, bur rec from
  1959; Mich. Dept of Health has originals of all b, d, & m rec)
Keweenaw   A2   1861   2   1870-80   Houghton .... Eagle River
Lake   D3   1871   5   1870-80   Oceana, Mason, Newaygo .... Baldwin
  (Co Clk has b, m, d, bur, div, civ ct rec from 1876)
Lapeer   D5   1835   42   1840-80   Oakland .... Lapeer
  (Co Clk has b & d rec from 1868, m, div, civ ct rec from 1835; also has CW
  rec filed 1865)
Leelanau   C3   1863   9   1860-80   Grand Traverse .... Leland
  (Co Clk has b & d rec from 1867, m rec from 1863; div & civ ct rec from
  1870; Pro Judge has pro rec)
Lenawee   E4   1826   78   1830-80   Wayne .... Adrian
  (Ct house burned 1852, vital rec sketchy up to 1906)
Livingston   D4   1836   38   1840-80   Shiawassee, Washtenaw ...... Howell
Luce   B3   1887   8   Chippewa, Mackinac .... Newberry
  (Co Clk has b, m, d, div, pro, civ ct rec from 1887)
Mackinac   B3   1818   11   1820-80   Wayne and the French .... St. Ignace
  (This Co first called Michilimackinac changed in 1849 to Mackinac. M & land
  rec start 1821)
Macomb   D5   1818   495   1820-80   Wayne .... Mt. Clemens
  (Co Clk has b & d rec from 1867, m rec from 1848, div rec from 1847, civ ct
  rec from 1837, gun permits from 1943, naturalization rec from 1844, and
  business registrations)
Manistee   C3   1855   19   1860-80   Mackinac, Ottawa, Oceana,
                                            Grand Traverse .... Manistee
  (Co Clk has b & d rec from 1867, m rec from 1855, div rec from 1856,
  civ ct rec from 1855)
Manitou   1855   1860-80   Disbanded 1895
Marquette   B2   1848   56   1860-80   Chippewa, Houghton ..... Marquette
  (Co Clk has b, m, & d rec from 1867, div & civ ct rec from 1850, naturali-
  zation rec from 1860; Mich Dept of Health also has b, m, d & div rec)
  (Special 1933 Census of all persons over 21 yrs, census also for yrs 1930-
  40-50-60)
Mason   D3   1855   22   1850-80   Ottawa, Oceana .... Ludington
Mecosta   D4   1859   21   1860-80   Kent, Newaygo .... Big Rapids
Menominee   C2   1861   25   1870-80   Marquette .... Menominee
  (Organized in 1861 as Bleeker, name changed in 1863)
Midland   D4   1850   51   1850-80   Saginaw .... Midland
Missaukee   C4   1871   7   1870-80   Antrim, Grand Traverse ... Lake City
  (Some records destroyed in a fire in 1944)
Monroe   E5   1817   101   1820-80   Wayne .... Monroe
  (Co Clk has b rec 1864, m rec 1818, d rec 1867, div rec 1897, civ ct rec 1857,
  military dis from 1919, crim ct rec from 1859, naturalization from 1913)
Montcalm   D4   1850   36   1850-80   Ionia .... Stanton
Montmorency   C4   1881   4   Cheboygan, Alpena .... Atlanta
  (Most rec lost in fire 1942, still has vital rec others start 1943)
Muskegon   D3   1859   150   1860-80   Ottawa .... Muskegon
  (Co Clk has b & m rec 1860, d rec 1871, div & pro rec 1867, cir ct rec 1859)
Newaygo   D3   1851   24   1850-80   Kent, Muskegon, Oceana .. White Cloud
  (Co Clk has b, m, d, div rec from 1867, civ ct rec from 1853)
Oakland   D5   1820   590   1820-80   Wayne .... Pontiac

(Co Clk has b & d rec from 1867, m & naturalization rec from 1827)
Oceana   D3 1851   17 1840-80 Ottawa .... Hart
(Co Clk has b, m, d rec from 1867, div rec from 1897)
Ogemaw   C4 1875   10 1880   Cheboygan, Midland, Iosco .. West Branch
(Co Clk has b, m, d, bur, civ ct rec from 1878, div rec from 1900)
Ontonagon   B1 1848   11 1850-80 Chippewa, Houghton .... Ontonagon
Osceola   D3 1869   14 1860-80 Mason, Newaygo, Mecosta .... Reed City
Oscoda   C4 1881   3 1870-80 Cheboygan, Alpena, Alcona ..... Mio
(Co Clk has b, m, d, div, civ ct rec from 1881; Pro Ct has pro rec; Township Clks have bur rec)
Otsego   C4 1875   8 1880   Mackinac, Alpena, Cheboygan,
                                     Antrim .... Gaylord
Ottawa   D3 1837   99 1840-80 Kent .... Grand Haven
(Co Clk has b & d rec from 1867, m & civ ct rec from 1847, div rec from 1863, bur rec from 1955)
Presque Isle C4 1871   13 1860-80 Mackinac .... Rogers City
(Co Clk has b & d rec from 1871, m rec from 1872, div rec from 1900)
Roscommon C4 1875   7 1880   Cheboygan, Midland ..... Roscommon
(Co Clk has b & d rec from 1874, m & civ ct rec from 1875, div rec from 1876)
Saginaw   D4 1835 191 1840-80 Oakland .... Saginaw
(Co Clk has b rec 1866, m rec 1867, d rec 1868, div rec 1850, civ ct rec 1843)
St. Clair   D5 1820 107 1830-80 Wayne .... Port Huron
St. Joseph   E4 1829   42 1830-80 Wayne .... Centreville
(Co Clk has d rec from 1865, b rec from 1867, m rec from 1844, div rec from 1850, pro rec from 1832, civ ct rec from 1842)
Sanilac   D5 1848   32 1850-80 Oakland, St. Clair, Lapeer .... Sandusky
(Co Clk has b & d rec from 1867, m rec from 1849, div & civ ct rec; Pro Ct has pro rec)
Schoolcraft B3 1871   9 1850-80 Chippewa, Houghton, Marquette . Manistique
Shiawassee D4 1837   53 1840-80 Oakland, Genesee .... Corunna
(Co Clk has b, d rec 1867, m rec from 1837, Bk A of Co m (1837-1867) was transcribed & indexed, a copy is in Mich. State Lib. at Lansing. d rec 1867, div & civ ct rec 1848, fire destroyed rec in 1867)
Tuscola   D5 1850   43 1850-80 Saginaw .... Caro
(Co Clk has b & d rec 1866, m rec 1851, div rec 1884, civ ct rec 1887)
Van Buren   E3 1837   48 1870-80 Cass .... Paw Paw
(Co Clk has b & d rec from 1867, m rec from 1837, bur rec from 1949, div rec from 1837, civ ct rec from 1844; Village & cities are also holders of b & d rec)
Washtenaw   E4 1822 172 1830-80 Wayne .... Ann Arbor
(Co Clk has m rec from 1827, b & d rec from 1867, naturalization rec from 1833, supervisor's or Commissioners' rec from 1835)
Wayne   E5 1796 2666 1820-80 Original county .... Detroit
Wexford   C3 1869   18 1870-80 Manistee .... Cadillac
(Co Clk has b rec from 1868, m, d, div, civ ct rec from 1869)

Genealogists' Check List of the Historical Records Survey,

Michigan

Federal Courts (start 1805). Inventory of county archives, Alger, Alpena, Baraga, Bay, Calhoun, Cheboygan, Genesee, Iosco, Iron, Jackson, Marquette, Muskegon. Inventory of municipal and town archives, Detroit recorders court, Muskegon list of City Offices. Vital Statistic holding by government agencies. 1. birth records, 2. Marriage records, 3. Divorce records. Guide to church vital statistic records, Wayne county.

Transcription of Public Archives. Bucklin, Dearborn, Pepin, minutes of meetings of townships, 1827-1857, Springwells 1861-1872, Hamtrack minutes of meetings, Charter Comm. 1921-1922,

Village Council 1901–1905 and index to both.

Guide to manuscript depository in the U.S. - Michigan. Guide to manuscript collections in Michigan, Vol 1, Michigan Historical Collections, University of Michigan. Vol. 2 University of Michigan collections. Calendar of the Baptist Collection of Kalamazoo College, Kalamazoo, Michigan. Calendar of John C. Dancey correspondence 1898–1910.

Inventory of the church and synagogue archives of Michigan. African Methodist Episcopal church Michigan conference. Church of the Nazarene, Michigan district assembly. Churches of God, Michigan Assemblies. Dearborn churches. Evangelical and Reformed church, Evangelical Church, Michigan Con. Jewish bodies, Pilgrim Holiness Church, Michigan district, Presbyterian Church in the USA, Presbytery of Detroit, Presbytery of Flint, Protestant Episcopal Church, Diocese of Michigan, Diocese of Northern Michigan, Diocese of Western Michigan. Roman Catholic Church, Diocese of Detroit. Salvation Army in Michigan. Directory of churches and religious organizations in Greater Detroit.

Preliminary check list of Michigan imprints. Depository of unpublished material, Michigan Historical Collection, University of Michigan, Ann Arbor, Michigan.

Minnesota

Capital St. Paul - Territory 1849 - State 1858 - (32nd)

Minnesota, with its more than ten thousand lakes, began to attract sturdy Scandinavian settlers to its borders shortly after 1851 when the land west of the Mississippi was procured from the Indians. Several years prior to that, Yankees from the east and north-east, largely from Maine, had been pulled there by its infant lumber industry, which in succeeding decades drew thousands to its borders. When the Scandinavian influx began, it is estimated that less than 5,000 persons lived in the territory.

The earliest white people to visit the section were the Catholic missionaries and fur traders. Chief among the missionaries was Father Hennepin, who has been honored by having a county and one of the main streets in Minneapolis named after him. He came there about 1680 and floated down the Mississippi in a canoe.

When the northern iron mines began to be developed in the 1880's, Finns and Slavs came there by the tens of thousands. Poland, Lithuania and the Balkans furnished much of the labor for the rapidly growing packing plants around the Twin cities at the beginning of the present century.

The progenitors of the present Minnesota generation came mainly from Sweden, Norway, Denmark, Germany, Canada, Finland, Poland and Russia.

The first United States Census, a special enumeration was taken in Minnesota in 1857, followed by the regular 1860 census. The State Archives, 117 University Ave., St. Paul, Minnesota 55101 has the State census of 1865-1875-1885-1895 and 1905.

Birth and death records before 1900 and all marriage records are in the offices of the clerks of the District Court in the respective counties. The birth and death records after 1900 are in the office of State Department of Health, Division of Birth and Death Records, 469 State Office Bldg., St. Paul, Minn. 55101.

Records of wills, and all probate of estates are in the office of the clerk of the Probate Court in the county court house, while the records of deeds and mortgages are handled by the register of deeds in the county seat.

Some of the libraries of Minnesota which may give you assistance in your search of that area are:

Public Library, 1001 Hennepin Ave., (Scandinavian and local history), Minneapolis 55403, (Hennepin); St. Olaf College, Rolvaag Memorial Library, (Norwegian collections), Northfield 55057, (Rice); Minnesota Historical Society Library, (Minnesota, West, Northwest, Canadian collection, biography, genealogy, local history, Scandinavian-Americans), Cedar & Central Sts., St. Paul 55101, (Ramsey); Public Library, 4th & Washington Sts., St. Paul 55102, (Ramsey); Gustavus Adolphus College, Folke Bernadotte Memorial Library, (Swedish collections), St. Peter 56082, (Nicollet).

Books which may help you in your research are:

Holcombe, Maj. R. I. and Bingham, William H., "Compendium of History and Biography of Minneapolis and Hennepin County Minnesota". Pub. 1914. Henry Taylor & Co. Minneapolis.

"History of Steele and Wasega Counties, Minnesota", Pub. 1887 Union Publishing Co., Chicago, being an album of history and biography, embracing sketches of the villages, cities and townships, portraits of prominent citizens, old settlers, etc.

Minnesota County Histories
(Population figures to nearest thousand - 1960 Census)

Name	Map Index	Date Formed	Pop. By M	Census Reports Available	Parent County	County Seat
Aitkin	C3	1857	12	1860-80	Cass, Itasca	Aitkin
(Clk of Ct has b rec from 1883, m rec from 1885, d & bur rec from 1887, div rec from 1886; Pro Ct has pro rec)						
Anoka	D3	1857	86	1857-80	Ramsey	Anoka
(Clk of Dist Ct has b & d rec from 1870, m, div, pro, civ ct rec from 1857)						
Becker	C2	1858	24	1860-80	Indian Lands	Detroit Lakes

Beltrami   B2   1866   23   1870-80   Unorganized Territory   .... Bemidji
(was attached to Becker Co for many years for rec purposes) (Clk of Ct has b
& d rec from 1895, m, div & civ ct rec from 1897; Minn. Dept. of Health, St.
Paul, also has b & d rec)

Benton   D2   1849   17   1850-80   Original county   .... Foley
(Clk of Dist Ct has b rec from 1871, m rec from 1850, d rec from 1865, div &
civ ct rec from 1852; Judge of Pro Office has pro rec)

Big Stone   D1   1862   9   1870-80   Pierce .... Ortonville
(unorganized until 1881)

Blue Earth   F2   1853   44   1857-80   Unorganized Territory .... Mankato
Breckenridge   1860   (see Clay, Toombs & Wilkin)
Brown   E2   1855   28   1857-80   Nicollett, Blue Earth ...... New Ulm
Buchanan   1857-60   Discontinued
Carlton   C3   1857   28   1857-80   Pine   .... Carlton
(Clk of Ct has b, m, d, div, civ ct rec from 1870; Churches & Clks of Villages
& City have bur rec; Judge of Pro has pro rec)

Carver   E3   1855   21   1857-80   Hennepin .... Chaska
Cass   C2   1851   17   1857-80   Original county   .... Walker
(Clk of Ct has b, m, d, div, civ ct rec from 1900)

Chippewa   E2   1862   16   1870-80   Pierce .... Montevideo
Chisago   D3   1851   13   1857-80   Washington .... Center City
Clay   C1   1862   39   1870-80   Breckenridge .... Moorhead
(Clk of Ct has b, m, d, div, civ ct rec from 1872)

Clearwater   B2   1902   9   Beltrami .... Bagley
Cook   B4   1875   3   1880   Lake .... Grand Marais
(Clk of Dist Ct has b rec from 1879, m, d, div, civ ct rec from 1901)

Cottonwood   F2   1857   16   1857-80   Brown .... Windom
Crow Wing   C2   1857   32   1857-80   Cass, Aitkin .... Brainerd
Dakota   E3   1849   78   1850-80   Original county .... Hastings
(Clk of Dist Ct has b & d rec 1870, m rec 1857, div & civ ct rec 1853)

Dodge   F3   1855   13   1857-80   Olmstead .... Mantorville
Doty (see St. Louis & Lake)
Douglas   D2   1858   21   1860-80   Todd .... Alexandria
(attached to Sterns Co until 1866)

Faribault   F2   1855   24   1857-80   Blue Earth   .... Blue Earth
(Clk of Dist Ct has b & d rec from 1870, m, div, civ ct rec from 1870)

Fillmore   F4   1853   24   1857-80   Wabasha .... Preston
Freeborn   F3   1856   38   1857-80   .... Albert Lea
(Clk of Dist Ct has b & d rec from 1870, m, div, civ ct rec from 1857,
naturalization rec from 1870; Morticians have bur rec; Judge of Pro has pro rec)

Goodhue   E3   1853   33   1857-80   Wabasha .... Red Wing
(Clk of Dist Ct has b & d rec from 1870, m, div, civ ct rec from 1854)

Grant   D1   1868   9   1870-80   Stearns .... Elbow Lake
(Clk of Dist Ct has b & d rec 1877, m rec 1869, div & civ ct rec 1883)

Hennepin   E3   1852   843   1857-80   Dakota .... Minneapolis
(Clk of Dist Ct has b & d rec from 1870, m, div, civ ct rec from 1853)

Houston   F4   1854   17   1857-80   Fillmore .... Caledonia
(Clk of Dist Ct has b & d rec from 1870, m, div, civ ct rec from 1859; Pro Ct
has pro rec)

Hubbard   C2   1883   10   Cass .... Park Rapids
Isanti   D3   1857   14   1857-80   Anoka .... Cambridge
Itasca   B3   1850   38   1850-80   Original county .... Grand Rapids
(Clk of Ct has b, m, d, bur, div, civ ct rec)

Jackson   F2   1857   16   1857-80   Unorganized Territory ..... Jackson
(Clk of Dist Ct has b, m, d, div, civ ct rec, crim, naturalization rec from 1870;
Pro Ct has pro rec)

Johnson (see Wilkin)
Kanabec   D3   1858   9   1860-80   Pine .... Mora
(Clk of Dist Ct has b, m, d, bur, div, civ ct rec, coroner's, naturalization rec
from 1883; Pro Judge has pro rec)

Kandiyohi   E2   1858   30   1860-80   Meeker .... Willmar

(Clk of Dist Ct has b, m, d, div, civ ct rec from 1870)
Kittson   A1   1879   8   1880   Unorganized Territory . . . . . . Hallock
Koochiching B3   1907   18   Itasca . . . . International Falls
  (Clk of Dist Ct has b, m, d, div, & civ ct rec from 1907; Pro Ct has pro rec;
  bur rec are held by funeral directors)
Lac Qui Parle E1 1863   13   1870-80   Formerly Toombs . . . . Madison
Lake   B4   1855   14   1857-80   Formerly Doty . . . . Two Harbors
  (Clk of Dist Ct has b rec from 1898, m & d rec from 1891, div & civ ct rec
  from 1892; City Clk has bur rec; Judge of Pro has pro rec)
Lake of the
  Woods   A1   1922   4   Beltrami . . . . Baudette
Le Sueur   E3   1853   20   1857-80   Unorganized Territory . . . Le Center
  (Clk of Dist Ct has b & d rec from 1870, m rec from 1854, div rec from
  1885 & civ ct rec from 1880; Pro Ct Office has pro rec)
Lincoln   E1   1873   10   1880   Lyon . . . . Ivanhoe
  (Clk of Dist Ct has b & m rec from 1879, d, div & civ ct rec from 1880, also
  crim rec from 1880; Pro Ct has pro rec; bur rec are held by undertakers)
Lyon   E1   1871   23   1880   Redwood . . . . Marshall
McLeod   E2   1883   24   1857-80   Carver . . . . Glencoe
Mahnomen   C1   1906   6   1857-80   Becker . . . . Mahnomen
  (Clk of Dist Ct has b, m, d, div, civ ct & crim rec from 1905; bur rec as part
  of d rec from 1941; Judge of Pro has pro rec)
Markahta   1850   Discontinued
Marshall   B1   1878   14   1880   Kittson . . . . .Warren
  (Clk of Dist Ct has b, m, d, div, civ ct, naturalization rec from 1884, have
  few bur rec)
Martin   F2   1857   27   1857-80   Faribault, Brown . . . . Fairmont
  (Clk of Dist Ct has b rec 1874, m rec 1864, d rec 1871, div rec 1880, civ ct
  rec 1870; State Dept of Health, St. Paul, also holds b, d & bur rec)
Meeker   E2   1856   19   1857-80   Wright, Stearns . . . . Litchfield
Mille Lacs   D3   1857   15   1860-80   Kanabec . . . . Milaca
Monongalia   1860-70   Discontinued
Morrison   D2   1856   27   1857-80   Benton, Stearns . . . . Little Falls
  (Clk of Dist Ct has b & d rec from 1870, m, div, civ ct rec from 1860)
Mower   F3   1855   48   1857-80   Fillmore . . . . Austin
  (Clk of Dist Ct has b & d rec from 1870, m rec from 1865, div rec from 1888,
  civ ct rec from 1888; Pro Ct has pro rec)
Murray   F2   1857   15   1857-80   Lyon . . . . Slayton
Nicollet   E2   1853   23   1857-80   Unorganized Territory . . . . Saint Peter
  (Clk of Dist Ct has b & d rec from 1870, m rec from 1856, div, civ ct rec
  from 1853; Judge of Pro has pro rec; Funeral Homes have bur rec)
Nobles   F2   1857   23   1857-80   Jackson . . . . Worthington
  (Clk of Dist Ct has b, m, d, rec from 1872, div rec from 1882, civ ct & crim
  rec from 1874; Sextons of cem have bur rec; Pro Ct has pro rec)
Norman   C1   1881   11   Polk . . . . Ada
  (Clk of Dist Ct has b, m, d, div, civ ct rec from 1881)
Olmsted   F3   1855   66   1857-80   Unorganized Territory . . . . . Rochester
  (Clk of Dist Ct has incom b & d rec 1871, m rec 1855, div rec 1860, civ ct rec
  1858; Coroner & Dept of Health have bur rec; Pro Ct has pro rec; Dept of
  Health, Div of Vit Stat, St. Paul, also has b, m, & d rec)
Otter Tail   C2   1858   49   1860-80   Pembina, Cass . . . . Fergus Falls
Pembina   1850-70   disorganized
Pennington   B1   1910   12   Red Lake . . . . Thief River Falls
  (Clk of Dist Ct has b, m, d, div, civ ct rec from 1910)
Pierce   1857-60   disorganized
Pine   D3   1857   17   1857-80   Unorganized Lands . . . . Pine City
Pipestone   F1   1857   14   1857-80   Murray . . . . Pipestone
Polk   B1   1858   36   1860-80   Indian Lands . . . . Crookston
Pope   D2   1862   12   1870-80   Pierce . . . . Glenwood
  (Clk of Dist Ct has b & d rec from 1870, m rec from 1868, div rec from 1880,
  civ ct rec from 1871)

County Map of Minnesota

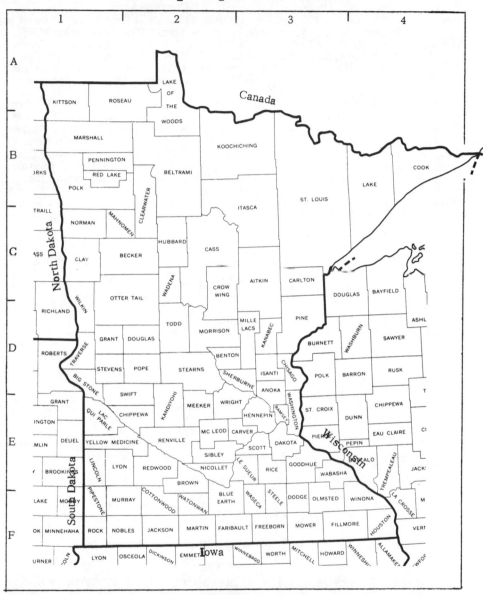

Ramsey   E3 1849 423 1850–80 Original county . . . . Saint Paul
  (Clk of Dist Ct has b & d rec from 1870, m, div, civ ct rec from 1849; Cem
  Assn has bur rec; Pro Ct has pro rec)
Red Lake   B1 1897   6   Polk . . . . Red Lake Falls
Redwood   E2 1862   22 1870–80 Brown . . . . Redwood Falls
  (Clk of Dist Ct has b & d rec from 1870, m rec from 1865, div rec from 1871,
  civ ct rec & citizenship rec from 1867; Judge of Pro has pro rec; Various
  cem hold bur rec)
Renville   E2 1855   23 1857–80 Unorganized Territory . . . . . Olivia
  (Clk of Dist Ct has b, d, div & civ ct rec from 1870, m rec from 1867)

Rice   E3   1853   39   1857-80   Original county . . . . Faribault
    (Clk of Dist Ct has b, d, div, civ ct, crim rec from 1870, m rec from 1856,
    bur rec from 1946, also some notary rec; Pro Ct has pro rec)
Rock   F1   1857   12   1857-80   Nobles as Unorg Co. Brown . . . . . Luverne
    (Clk of Dist Ct has b, m, d & civ ct rec from 1872; div rec from 1870)
Roseau   A1   1895   12   Kittson . . . . Roseau
    (Clk of Dist Ct has b, m, d, div, civ ct rec from 1895, Pro Ct has pro rec 1895)
Saint Louis   B3   1856 232   1857-80   Doty (now Lake) . . . . Duluth
    (Clk of Dist Ct has b, m, d rec from 1857, div rec from 1856, civ ct rec from
    1860)
Scott   E3   1853   22   1857-80   Dakota . . . . Shakopee
Sherburne   D3   1856   13   1857-80   Anoka . . . . Elk River
Sibley   E2   1853   16   1857-80   Unorganized Territory . . . . . . Gaylord
    (Clk of Dist Ct has b & d rec 1870, m rec 1856, div & civ ct rec from 1870)
Stearns   D2   1855   80   1857-80   Indian Lands . . . . Saint Cloud
Steele   F3   1855   25   1857-80   Unorganized Territory, Dodge . Owatonna
    (Clk of Dist Ct has b & d rec from 1870, m, div, civ ct rec from 1856)
Stevens   D1   1862   11   1870-80   Pierce, Big Stone . . . . Morris
Swift   E1   1870   15   1880   Chippewa, Unorg. Lands . . . . . Benson
    (Clk of Dist Ct has b rec from 1870, m, d, bur , civ ct rec from 1871, div rec
    from 1872)
Todd   D2   1856   23   1857-80   Stearns . . . . Long Prairie
Toombs   (see Lac Qui Parle & Wilkin)   Disorganized
Traverse   D1   1862   8   1870-80   Toombs . . . . Wheaton
Wabasha   E3   1849   17   1850-80   Original county . . . . Wabasha
Wadena   C2   1858   12   1870-80   Cass, Todd . . . . Wadena
    (Clk of Dist Ct has b, m, d, rec from 1873, div & civ ct rec from 1881)
Wahnata   1850   Disorganized
Waseca   F3   1857   16   1857-80   Steele . . . . Waseca
    (Clk of Dist Ct has b & d rec from 1870, m, div, civ ct rec 1857, bur rec 1880)
Washington   E3   1845   52   1850-80   Original county . . . . Stillwater
    (Clk of Dist Ct has b & d rec from 1870, m rec from 1845, div & civ ct rec 1847)
Watonwan   F2   1860   14   1870-80   Brown . . . . Saint James
    (Clk of Dist Ct has b & d rec from 1863, m rec from 1871, also div & civ ct
    rec; Sextons of Cem have bur rec; also have school cen rec from 1918-1963)
Wilkin   D1   1858   11   1870-80   Cass, Toombs, Johnson . . . Breckenridge
    (Clk of Dist Ct has b rec from 1874, m & div rec from 1890, d rec from 1875,
    civ ct rec from 1858; Judge of Pro has pro rec)
Winona   F4   1854   41   1857-80   Unorganized Territory . . . . . Winona
    (Clk of Dist Ct has b & d rec from 1870, m, div, & civ ct rec from 1856)
Wright   E3   1855   30   1857-80   Hennepin . . . . Buffalo
    (Clk of Dist Ct has b & d rec from 1871, m rec from 1866, and div & civ ct rec)
Yellow
    Medicine E1   1871   16   1880   Redwood . . . . Granite Falls
    (Clk of Dist Ct has b, m, d, div rec from 1872)

Genealogists' Check List of the Historical Records Survey,

Minnesota

Federal Courts (start 1849). Inventory of County Archives, Aitkin, Anoka, Beltrami, Benton, Big Stone, Blue Earth, Cass, Chippewa, Dakota, Dodge, Douglas, Fairbault, Fillmore, Freeborn,
Goodhue, Grant, Houston, Hubbard, Jackson, Kanabec, Lincoln,
Marshall, Martin, Meeker, Mille Lacs, Morrison, Murray,
Nicollet, Nobles, Olmstead, Otter Tail, Pipestone, Redwood, Renville, Rice, Rock, Scott, Sherburne, Stearns, Traverse, Wabasha,
Washington, Wright, Yellow Medicine. Guide to public vital statistics records. Guide to church vital statistics records, baptisms,

marriages, funerals. Directory of churches and religious organizations in Minnesota. Guide to depository of manuscript collection in the US - Minnesota. Minnesota check list of Minn. imprints 1849-1865. General Legislation concerning counties in Minnesota. Guide to Historic Markers, erected by the State Highway Dept., cooperating with the Minnesota Historical Society. Minnesota Judicial districts. The Cuyuna Range, a history of a Minnesota iron mining district. Depository of unpublished material, State Historical Society, St. Paul, Minnesota.

Mississippi

Capital Jackson - Territory 1798 - State 1817 - (20th)

French and Spanish adventurers, less interested in establishing homes in the New World than in finding easy wealth to take home to their native lands, came to the Mississippi regions in the sixteenth century. Few evidences of their sojourn remain.

The French established colonies on the Gulf Coast at Old Biloxi in 1699 and on the Mississippi River at Natchez in 1716. The province was ceded to Great Britain in 1763 and the British settlers who followed established permanent homes. Land grants in the vicinity of Natchez to retired English army and navy officers spurred a migration of Protestants, land-loving settlers who contrasted greatly with the remaining Roman Catholic settlers of the French period. When the Thirteen Colonies revolted in 1776, the Natchez district remained loyal to the Crown, and a number of Tories of the seaboard colonies, unwilling to participate in the forced resistance, moved their families to the District. Between 1779 and 1781 Spain asserted her authority and took over the government of the Natchez District.

By 1798 pro-American sentiment had overthrown the rule of Spain and on April 7 of that year the Mississippi Territory was created by act of Congress. Natchez was the first Territorial capital, having served also as a seat of government for the District during the British and Spanish regimes.

The opening of the Mississippi River following the completion of the Louisiana Purchase in 1803 and the relinquishment of her claims to the western lands by the State of Georgia, brought about a land boom in the Mississippi Territory. Thousands of settlers came from the eastern and the northern states to claim the new lands. Petitions for statehood soon began and on 10 December 1817 the State of Mississippi was created, the eastern half of the Territory having been sheared off to create the

Alabama Territory.

Another tremendous migration came in 1837, after the last of the Indian lands in Mississippi had been opened for settlement.

By 1850 Mississippi's population was more or less stabilized and is little changed basically today. The white people of the state are mostly Anglo-Saxon who trace their ancestry to the British Isles.   Exceptions to this rule may be found in the families of southern European extraction who were brought to Biloxi as laborers in the fishing industry, and small colonies of thrifty Germans and Italians in various localities. In addition the Greek restaurateur is a fixture in almost every town of any size throughout the state and in the northwest section the Chinese grocer is an institution.

Genealogical information about Mississippi may be gained from records in the Mississippi Department of Archives and History at Dept. of Archives and History, War Memorial Bldg. 120 No. State St., Jackson, Miss. 39201, which has early censuses and tax rolls, newspaper files, microfilm copies of the Federal Censuses of Mississippi, records of Mississippi's Confederate soldiers and an excellent pamphlet ''Research in the Mississippi Department of Archives and History,'' Many helpful suggestions given in foreign, territorial, state and federal archives. Wills, deeds and probate files are held by the Chancery Clerks of the various counties. Marriage records are kept by the Circuit Clerks. Records of births and deaths since 1912 are at the Bureau of Vital Statistics, State Board of Health, Jackson 39201. Land grants are in the National Archives in Washington. The Evans Memorial Library, Aberdeen 39730, has source records pertaining to Monroe County and surrounding territory.

The limited staff of the Department of Archives and History, Jackson, is happy to supply any information that is indexed or readily accessible but cannot undertake detailed research or microfilm census checking due to the time involved. They are glad to recommend persons outside of the Department who do this sort of work for a reasonable fee.

Incomplete birth and death records prior to 1912 are available in some counties at the office of the county clerk where marriage records before 1926 also may be available. Wills, probate files and records of deeds and mortgages are in the office of the clerk of the Court of Chancery.

In several Mississippi counties the date of their formation does not necessarily coincide with the date of the available records. Some counties have valuable genealogical information dating way back earlier than their organization, while in other counties the records on file are of a much later date. Mrs. Margaret Scruggs Carruth, 3715 Turtle Creek Blvd., Dallas, Tex.

75219, one of the leading southern researchers has given the following list of counties and the starting dates of their records, which you will note, are entirely different than their organization dates: Alcorn, 1842; Attala, 1870; Calhoun, 22 Dec. 1922; Chickasaw, 1863; Forest (formed 1906), 1876; Green, 1875; Jackson, 1875; Jasper, 1932; Kemper, 1912; Newton, 1876; Neshola, 1836; Panola, 1870 (newspaper files since 1840); Tishamingo, 1877; Wayne, 1892. Mrs. Carruth also says, "Since the Mississippi law forbids county clerks or anyone employed in their offices to do any research work, it is of no use to contact any of them by letter."

The Evans Memorial Library, Aberdeen, Miss. 39730, has a collection of tens of thousands of manuscripts, old church records, account books, letters, etc., all indexed in a card file. This is their announcement:

"The Manuscript Division of the Evans Memorial Library is inaugurating a "March of Monroe County Familes". The object of this is to have every family represented with a collection of manuscript material in the files. By Manuscript is meant old letters, land grants, bills, paroles, clippings, diaries, account books, copied Bible records, scrapbooks, bulletins, old music, newspapers, etc. A Collection can be two, two hundred or two thousand! Yes, we have some family collections containing over 2,000! The Gifts will be recorded, then placed in manila folders labeled with the family name which the donor prefers, then placed in locked steel filing cabinets. Authors, historians, research people who come to the library, study these materials for facts, descriptions, dates, names, etc., needed in their writing about the South. From time to time, certain items are placed on display in the locked museum case. These materials are never checked out but are used in the library."

Other Mississippi libraries:

Jackson Municipal Library, 301 N. State St., Jackson, 39201, (Hinds); City and County Public Library, 628 25th Ave., Meridian 39301, (Lauderdale).

Books which have been published by genealogical and historical researchers may assist you in your Mississippi research:

Hendricks, Mary Louise Flowers. "Mississippi Court Records from the Files of the High Court of Errors and Appeals", 1799-1859. Pub. 1950.

Welch, Alice Tracy, "Family Records Mississippi Revolutionary Soldiers", Pub. 1953-56 by The Mississippi Society of the Daughters of the American Revolution. State Board of Management.

Mississippi County Histories

(Population figures to nearest thousand - 1960 Census)

Name	Map Index	Date Formed	Pop By M	Census Reports Available	Parent County	County Seat
Adams	E1	1799	38	1820-80	Natchez District	Natchez
Alcorn	A4	1870	25	1870-80	Tippah, Tishomingo, Prentiss	Corinth

(Chancery Ct Clk has div rec from 1913 & Chancery Ct rec; Cir Clk has civ ct & m rec from 1860; Bureau of Vit Stat, Jackson, Miss. has b & d rec from 1912; Funeral homes have bur rec)

Amite	E1	1809	16	1820-80	Wilkinson	Liberty
Attala	C3	1833	21	1840-80	Choctaw Cession	Kosciusko
Benton	A3	1870	8	1880	Marshall, Tippah	Ashland

(Chancery Clk has div, pro, deeds, wills from 1871)

Bolivar	B1	1836	54	1840-80	Choctaw Cession	Rosedale & Cleveland
Calhoun	B3	1852	16	1860-80	Lafayette, Valobusha	Pittsboro
Carroll	B2	1833	11	1840-80	Choctaw Cession	Carrollton & Vaiden

(Co Clk has m, div, pro, civ ct, land rec from 1870)

Chickasaw	B3	1836	17	1840-80	Chickasaw Cession of 1832	Houston & Okolona
Choctaw	C3	1833	8	1840-80	Chickasaw Cession of 1832	Ackerman

(Co Clk has div rec from 1882, pro rec from 1890, civ ct rec from 1890; Co Health Dept has b & d rec from 1913; Cir Ct has m rec from 1881)

Claiborne	D1	1802	11	1820-80	Jefferson	Port Gibson

(Chancery Clk has m rec from 1816, div rec from 1856, pro & civ ct rec 1802)

Clarke	D4	1833	16	1840-80	Choctaw Cession	Quitman

(Chancery Clk has div & pro rec from 1875)

Clay	B4	1871	19	1880	Chickasaw, Lowndes, Monroe, Oktibbeha (Formerly Colfax)	West Point
Coahoma	A2	1836	46	1840-80	Chickasaw Cession 1836	Clarksdale
Colfax		1871			Name changed to Clay, 1876	
Copiah	D2	1823	27	1830-80	Hinds	Hazlehurst

(Co Clk has div, pro, civ ct, mort from 1823)

Covington	E3	1819	14	1820-80	Lawrence, Wayne	Collins

(Chancery Clk has m, div, pro, civ ct rec; Bureau of Vit Stat, Jackson, Miss. has b, d, & bur rec)

DeSoto	A2	1836	24	1840-80	Indian Lands	Hernando
Forrest	E3	1906	53		Perry	Hattiesburg
Franklin	E1	1809	9	1820-80	Adams	Meadville
George	F4	1910	11		Greene, Jackson	Lucedale
Greene	E4	1811	8	1820-80	Amite, Franklin, Wayne	Leakesville
Grenada	B2	1870	18	1870-80	Carrol, Yalobusha, Choctaw, Talahatchie	Grenada

(Chancery Clk has div & pro rec from 1870; Clk of Cir Ct has m rec from 1870)

Hancock	F3	1812	14	1820-80	Mobile District	Bay St. Louis
Harrison	F3	1841	119	1850-80	Hancock, Jackson	Gulfport
Hinds	D2	1821	187	1830-80	Choctaw Cession 1820	Jackson & Raymond

(Chancery Clk has div & pro rec from 1820; Bureau of Vit Stat has b & d rec; Cir Clk has m rec)

Holmes	C2	1833	27	1840-80	Yazoo	Lexington

(Chancery Clk has div & pro rec from 1894, also deeds, wills from 1833 & bur rec; Cir Clk has m, civ ct rec; Bureau of Vit Stat, State Dept of Health, Jackson, Miss has b & d rec)

Humphreys	C2	1918	19		Holmes, Washington, Yazoo, Sunflower	Belzoni
Issaquena	C1	1844	4	1850-80	Washington	Mayersville
Itawamba	A4	1836	15	1840-80	Chickasaw Cession 1832	Fulton

(Chancery Clk has div & pro rec from 1860; Cir Clk has m & civ ct rec)

Jackson	F4	1812	56	1820-80	Mobile Distrcit	Pascagoula

(Chancery Clk has div & pro rec from 1875, also Justice of the Peace Dockets
and licenses of physicians & dentists from 1875; Bureau of Vit Stat, Jackson,
Miss. has b & d rec; Clk of Cir Ct has m rec from 1875)

Jasper   D3   1833   17   1840-80   Indian Lands . . . Bay Springs & Paulding
(Co Clk has div, pro & civ ct rec from 1906; Cir Clk has m rec)

Jefferson   E1   1799   10   1820-80   Natchez, originally Pickering . . . Fayette
(Chancery Clk has div & pro rec; State Board of Health, Jackson, Miss. has
b rec from 1912 and d rec; Cir Clk has m & civ ct rec)

Jefferson
Davis   E2   1906   14   Covington, Lawrence . . . . . . Prentiss
Jones   E3   1826   60   1830-80   Covington, Wayne . . . Ellisville & Laurel
Kemper   C4   1833   12   1840-80   Choctaw Cession, 1832 . . . . . DeKalb
(Chancery Clk has div, pro, civ ct rec from 1912, also has land rec; Bureau
of Vit Stat, Jackson, Miss. has b & d rec; Cir Clk office has m rec)

Lafayette   A3   1836   21   1840-80   Chickasaw Cession . . . . Oxford
(Chancery Clk has m, div, pro & civ ct rec)

Lamar   E3   1904   14   Marion, Pearl River . . . . Purvis
Lauderdale   D4   1833   67   1840-80   Choctaw Cession . . . . Meridian
(Chancery Clk has div, pro, land rec; Co Health has b & d rec; Cir Clk has
m & civ ct rec)

Lawrence   E2   1814   10   1820-80   Marion . . . . Monticello
Leake   C3   1833   19   1840-80   Choctaw Cession . . . . Carthage
(Chancery Clk has div, pro, civ ct rec from 1871, land deeds from 1836 (also
land mtgs), chattel mtgs & discharges from 1918)

Lee   A4   1866   41   1870-80   Itawamba, Pontotoc . . . . Tupelo
(Chancery Clk has div, pro rec from 1866)

Leflore   B2   1871   47   1880   Carroll,Sunflower,Tallahatchie.Greenwood
Lincoln   E2   1870   27   1870-80   Franklin, Lawrence, Copiah, Pike,
                                         Amite . . . . Brookhaven
(Chancery Clk has div, pro & civ ct rec from 1893, Clk Dist Ct has m rec
from 1893; Miss. State Dept of Health, Jackson, has b rec from 1927 & d
& bur rec)

Lowndes   C4   1830   47   1830-80   Monroe . . . . Columbus
Madison   C2   1828   32   1830-80   Yazoo . . . . Canton
Marion   E2   1811   23   1820-80   Amite, Wayne, Franklin . . . . Columbia
Marshall   A3   1836   25   1840-80   Chickasaw Cession of 1832 .. Holly Springs
(Chancery Clk has div, pro, deeds from 1836)

Monroe   B4   1821   34   1820-80   Chickasaw Cession 1821 . . . . . Aberdeen
Montgomery   B3   1871   13   1880   Carroll, Choctaw . . . . Winona
Neshoba   C3   1833   21   1840-80   Choctaw Cession 1830 . . . Philadelphia
(Chancery Clk has div, pro rec from 1890; Clk of Cir Ct has m rec from 1912)

Newton   D3   1836   20   1840-80   Neshoba . . . . Decatur
(Chancery Clk has div, pro, civ ct, wills, deed rec from 1876; State Board
of Health, Jackson, Miss has b, d & bur rec; Cir Ct Clk, has m rec)

Noxubee   C4   1833   17   1840-80   Choctaw Cession 1830 . . . . Macon
(Chancery Clk has div, pro, civ ct, estates, wills, deeds rec from 1834; State
Board of Health, Jackson, Miss has b rec from 1912, also d & bur rec; Cir Clk
has m rec from 1834)

Oktibbeha   B4   1833   26   1840-80   Choctaw Cession 1830 . . . . . Starkville
Panola   A2   1836   29   1840-80   Chickasaw Cession 1832 . Batesville, Sardis
(Chancery Clk has div & pro rec 1836; Clk of Cir Ct has m rec 1885, civ ct rec 1836)

Pearl River   F3   1890   22   Hancock, Marion . . . . Poplarville
(Chancery Clk has div, pro & civ ct rec from 1890; Cir Clk has m rec; State
Board of Health, Jackson, Miss. has b, d & bur rec)

Perry   E3   1820   9   1820-80   Greene . . . . New Augusta
(Chancery Clk has div, pro & civ ct rec from 1882; Cir Clk has m rec 1882)

Pike   E2   1815   35   1820-80   Marion . . . . Magnolia
(Chancery Clk has m, div, pro, civ ct rec from 1882)

Pontotoc   A3   1836   17   1840-80   Chickasaw Cession of 1832 . . . Pontotoc

(Chancery Clk has div rec from 1912, pro rec from 1850, land rec from 1836)

Prentiss   A4   1870   18   1870–80   Tishomingo . . . . Booneville
Quitman   A2   1877   21   1880   Panola, Coahoma . . . . Marks
    (Chancery Ct Clk has div, pro rec from 1877; Cir Clk has m & civ ct rec;
    Bureau of Vit Stat, Jackson, Miss. has b, d & bur rec)
Rankin   D2   1828   34   1830–80   Hinds . . . . Brandon
Scott   D3   1833   21   1840–80   Choctaw Cession 1832 . . . . . . Forest
    (Chancery Clk has div, civ ct rec from 1900, pro, deeds, deeds of trust from
    1835, also land & chattel, Old church & cem plots rec; Cir Clk has m rec;
    State Board of Health, Jackson, Miss. has b, d & bur rec)
Sharkey   C2   1876   11   1880   Warren, Washington,
                                    Issaquena . . . . Rolling Fork
Simpson   D2   1824   20   1830–80   Choctaw Cession of 1820 . . . Mendenhall
Smith   D3   1833   14   1840–80   Choctaw Cession of 1820 . . . . . Raleigh
Stone   F3   1916   7   Harrison . . . . Wiggins

County Map of Mississippi

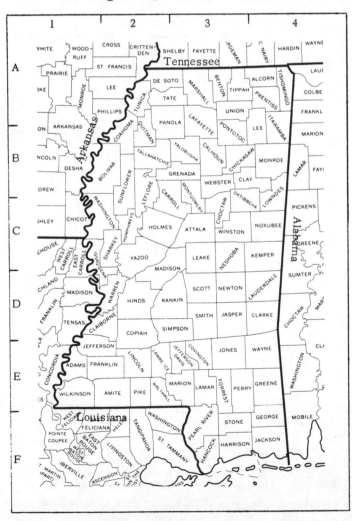

Sunflower   B2   1844   46   1850-80   Bolivar . . . . Indianola
(Chancery Clk has div, pro & civ ct rec, also has land transfers from 1868,
Vets discharges from 1924, Youth Ct rec from 1948 & adoptions from 1868;
Cir Clk has m rec)
Tallahatchie B2 1833   24   1840-80   Choctaw Cession of
                                        1820 . . . . Charleston & Sumner
(Chancery Clk has div, pro, civ ct, deeds 1909; Clk of Cir Ct has m rec 1909)
Tate   A2   1873   18   1880   Marshall, Tunica, De Soto . . . Senatobia
(Cir Clk has m rec from 1873, school rec from 1885 to 1920)
Tippah   A3   1836   15   1840-80   Chickasaw Cession of 1832 . . . . Ripley
(Chancery Clk or Cir Clk has m rec from 1856, also div, pro & civ ct rec from
1856)
Tishomingo   A4   1836   14   1840-80   Chickasaw Cession of 1832 . . . . . Iuka
(Chancery Clk has m, div, pro, civ ct rec from 1887)
Tunica   A2   1836   17   1840-80   Chickasaw Cession of 1832 . . . . Tunica
(Chancery Clk has div, pro rec ; Cir Ct Clk has m rec; Bureau of Vit Stat,
Jackson, Miss. has b & d rec)
Union   A3   1870   19   1880   Pontotoc, Tippah . . . . New Albany
(Chancery Clk has div, pro & civ ct rec; State Health Dept, Jackson, Miss. has
b, d & bur rec; Cir Clk has m rec)
Walthall   E2   1910   14   Marion, Pike . . . . Tylertown
Warren   D2   1809   42   1820-80   Natchez District . . . . Vicksburg
Washington   C1   1827   79   1820-80   Warren, Yazoo . . . . Greenville
(Chancery Clk has div & land rec from 1828, pro rec from 1890; Bureau of
Vit Stat, Jackson, Miss. has b & d rec, also bur rec from 1912; Cir Clk has
m rec from 1858 & civ ct rec from 1890)
Wayne   E4   1809   16   1820-80   Washington . . . . Waynesboro
Webster   B3   1874   11   Montgomery Chickasaw, Choctaw,
                                         Oktibbeha . . . . Walthall
(Originally Summer, name changed 1882)
Wilkinson   E1   1802   13   1820-80   Adams . . . . Woodville
Winston   C3   1833   19   1840-80   Choctaw Cession of 1830 . . . Louisville
Yalobusha   B3   1833   13   1840-80   Choctaw Cession
                                         1830 . . . Coffeyville & Water Valley
Yazoo   C2   1823   32   1830-80   Hinds . . . . Yazoo City
(M rec date from 1820)

Genealogists' Check List of the Historical Records Survey,
Mississippi

Federal Courts (start 1798). Inventory of County Archives, Amite, Forrest, Grenada, Humphreys, Lamar, Pearl River, Tippah, Tunica, Walthall. Transcription of Public Archives Adams county, 1. Minutes of Court of general quarter sessions of the Peace 1799-1801, 2. Minutes of the county court 1802-1804. Guide to Vital Statistic records, Vol. 1 Public Archives, Vol. 2 Church Archives. See Louisiana for navigation casualties. Inventory of the church and synagogue archives of Mississippi, Jewish Congregations and Organizations, Protestant Episcopal Church, Diocese of Mississippi.

A preliminary check list of Mississippi newspaper files available in the Mississippi dept. of Archives and History 1805-1940. A preliminary Union list of Mississippi Newspaper files available in County Archives, offices of publisher, Libraries, and private collections in Mississippi. Sargent's Code, a collection of the

Original Laws of the Mississippi Territory Enacted 1799-1800 by Gov. Winthrop Sargent and the Territory Judges. State and county boundaries of Mississippi. Index to Naturalization records, Mississippi courts. Depository of unpublished material, Department of Archives and History, Jackson, Mississippi.

Missouri

Capital Jefferson City - Territory 1812 - State 1821 - (24th)

The Mississippi, five hundred miles of which is the eastern border of Missouri, was first seen by a white man in 1541 when the Spanish explorer Hernando or Fernando De Soto saw that mighty river. It was 132 years later that two French explorers, Marquette and Joilet, were the first to see the Missouri river. Only nine years later, in 1682, another French explorer, Robert Cavelier de La Salle, took possession of the section as part of Louisiana and claimed it for France. A Catholic mission was established on the present site of St. Louis about 1700. The first permanent Missouri settlement was established about 1750 by the French. It was located along the Mississippi about 50 miles south of St. Louis and was called Sainte Genevieve.

The first actual American settlement in Missouri was in 1787 when one John Dodge established himself in Ste. Genevieve County. He was followed there by Israel Dodge in 1790, and three years later by Dr. Jesse Bryan. A John Moore is said to have made his home in 1790 in what since then has become Perry County which borders Ste. Genevieve County on the southeast. In 1795 American settlements were established on Femme Osage creek in what is now St. Charles County, north of St. Louis. It was then called Upper Louisiana or New Spain. Authority for these statements comes from "Pioneer Families of Missouri," published in 1876 by Wm. S. Bryan and Robert Rose, and reprinted in 1935 with an introduction by W. W. Elwang.

From 1682 until 1803 control over the Missouri section was passed back and forth between France and Spain. In the Louisiana Purchase consummated in 1803 ownership passed into the hands of the United States.

In 1805 Missouri became part of the Territory of Louisiana and remained so until 1812 when it became a Territory in its own name. At that time it claimed a population of 20,000. Most of its early settlers came from Kentucky and Virginia, and some from North and South Carolina, Maryland, Pennsylvania, and Tennessee. In those early days, Indian tribes, enticed by the British, constantly scourged the Missouri settlers in severe plundering raids. It was not until about 1815 that these raids were halted through peace treaties with the various Indian tribes within the territory.

Missouri became a state in 1821. Then it had about 56,000 white settlers. She became the twenty-fourth state in the Union. At present she has 114 counties and one independent city, St. Louis.

For many decades after 1830 a steady stream of European immigrants came into the state, as a result of which St. Louis has a distinct German flavor. Many Irish, English, Polish, Swiss, Bohemian and Italian natives settled in various parts of the state. In his "Creoles of St. Louis," (1893), Paul Beckwith does full justice to the early French immigration, the so called Creoles, the Chouteaus, Gratiots, Cabannes, Papins, Pauls, etc.

Throughout the Civil War, numerous skirmishes and bloody battles were fought in Missouri which was one of the important battle grounds of the conflict, keeping the population in constant excitement and fear.

Birth and death dates after 1910 are obtainable at the State Bureau of Vital Statistics, Jefferson City, Missouri 65101. Births and deaths from 1883 to 1891 may be obtained from the clerk of the respective counties. They also have a census record taken in 1876, it lists the males and females in age groups of under 10, 10 to 16, 16 to 25, 25 to 40, etc. Information on some marriages from 1825 to date may be had at the office of the Recorder of Deeds in each county. In those offices are also the records of deeds. Wills are in the Probate Courts. Tax payer lists are in the offices of the county assessors. War service records are under the care of the Adjutant General at Jefferson City, Mo. 65101. A law originating in 1863 makes it permissible for the Recorder of Deeds in each county to file birth information on request. The first death recording began in St. Louis in 1841.

Many of the county court houses in Missouri have been lost through fire. With them were lost at the same time many old records.

Among organizations and institutions able to give much genealogical information are the Nancy Hunter Chapter, Daughters of the American Revolution, Cape Giardeau 63701, Ann Haynes Chapter, DAR, Kirksville, Mo. 63501,

The following libraries may also be of great assistance: University of Missouri Library, (Western Americana books and manuscripts), Columbia 65201, (Boone); State Library, State Office Bldg., Jefferson City 65101, (Cole); City Public Library, 309 E. 12th St., (local and western history, genealogy), Kansas

City 64106, (Jackson); Missouri Historical Society Library, Jefferson Memorial Bldg., St. Louis 63112; County Library, 6814 Natural Bridge Rd., St. Louis 63121; St. Louis Public Library, Olive, 13th and 14th Sts., (genealogy and local history), St. Louis 63130; Public Library, Central and Jefferson Sts., Springfield 65802, (Green).

From the secretary of State Historical Society of Missouri, corner Hitt and Lowry Streets, Columbia, Mo. 65201, comes this information.

"No official compilation of the vital statistics of Missouri has been issued and for the most part, such records as are still existant are to be found in the archives of the several counties. Registration of births, marriages and deaths began in 1909 and are on file in the Bureau of Vital Statistics of the Missouri State Board of Health at Jefferson City.

"The biographical sections of a number of the general histories of Missouri and those in the histories of Missouri counties contain information of value to persons undertaking genealogical research. And of course, numbers of separate volumes on individual families of the state have been published.

"The greater number of Missouri county histories are now out of print and can only be bought through second-hand book sellers. There are several dealers from whom some of these volumes might be obtained.

"The MISSOURI HISTORICAL REVIEW is a quarterly publication devoted to Missouri and mid-Western history and biography. Since 1906 the Review has served as an outlet for historical scholars, writers and students. In each issue the local historical societies report their activities. We do not maintain a genealogical department or publish genealogical queries in the Review. In certain early volumes a few articles of a genealogical nature were published. Partial unbound sets of the Review are available.

"Our Society has an excellent collection of general genealogical books and periodicals which is made available to anyone visiting our library. Unfortunately, because of the large number of requests we receive and the amount of time required for work of this kind, we find it impossible to undertake genealogical research even for our members.

"To date, there are more than 16,000 members of the Society. For anyone interested in enrolling as a member of the Society, the annual dues are $2.00, which includes a free subscription to the MISSOURI HISTORICAL REVIEW.''

Missouri County Histories

(Population figures to nearest thousand - 1960 Census)

Prepared and published through the courtesy of
MISS NANON L. CARR

6102 the Paseo, Kansas City, Missouri 64110

Name	Map Index	Date Formed	Pop. By M	Census Reports Available	Parent County	County Seat
Adair	C1	1841	20	1850-80	Macon	Kirksville

(Co Clk has b rec ca 1880 to 1903)

Andrew	E1	1841	11	1850-80	Platte Purchase	Savannah

(Co Clk has b & d rec from 1883; Cir Clk has m, div, civ ct rec from 1841; Pro Judge has pro rec from 1841)

Arkansas 1813 New Madrid
(abolished 1819 when Territory of Arkansas was formed)

Atchison E1 1845 9 1850-80 Holt ... Rockport
(Part of Platte Purchase; attached to Holt Co until 1854; lost 10-mile strip to Iowa, 1848)

Audrain C2 1836 26 1840-80 Monroe ... Mexico
(Created in 1831, but remained attached to Callaway, Monroe, and Ralls Cos until 1836. In 1842 gained an additional 31 sq. miles from Monroe Co)

Barry D5 1835 19 1840-80 Greene ... Cassville
(Error in survey, rectified in 1876, established the western line 2 1/2 miles east of previous boundary. In 1872 many rec in cir clks office were destroyed by fire)

Barton D4 1855 11 1860-80 Jasper ... Lamar
(Courthouse burned in 1860; no mention of fate of records)

Bates D3 1841 16 1850-80 Jackson ... Butler
(Feb 22, 1855, the three southern tiers of townships in Cass Co were added to Bates; courthouse burned in 1861; some rec prior to 1861)

Benton D3 1835 9 1840-80 Pettis, St. Clair ... Warsaw
(Remained unorganized until Jan 1837; in 1845, 24 sq miles of n w part of Benton became parts of Pettis, and Hickory Co was created, reducing Benton to its present size) (Co Clk has m rec from 1863, div rec from 1835, pro rec from 1860; Dept of Health Jeff. City, Mo has d & bur rec; Cir Clk has cir ct rec from 1838)

Bollinger A4 1851 9 1860-80 Cape Girardeau, Stoddard, Wayne ... Marble Hill
(In 1866, courthouse destroyed by fire and with it some of the rec; in 1884, courthouse burned while occupied only by the co clks office)

Boone C2 1820 55 1830-80 Howard ... Columbia
Buchanan E2 1839 91 1840-80 Platte Purchase ... Saint Joseph
Butler B5 1849 35 1850-80 Wayne ... Poplar Bluff
Caldwell D2 1836 9 1840-80 Ray ... Kingston
(April 19, 1860, courthouse destroyed by fire, together with all recs except those of the pro ct; Nov 28, 1896, courthouse destroyed by fire)

Callaway C3 1820 24 1830-80 Montgomery ... Fulton
(Co Clk has b, d, bur rec from 1910)

Camden C3 1841 9 1850-80 Benton, Pulaski ... Camdenton
(Organized as Kinderhook, renamed 23 Feb 1843; line between Camden & Miller changed in 1845) (Co Recorder of Deeds has m & div rec; Bureau of Vit Stat has b rec; Pro Judge has pro rec & Cir Clk has civ ct rec)

Cape Girardeau A4 1812 42 1830-80 Original District ... Jackson
(Present size since 5 Mar 1849; in 1870 CH burned; Co Clk has b rec 1883 to 1893, b rec from 1910 to date are in Jefferson City, Mo.; Co Rec has m rec from 1805; Clk of Cir Ct has div & civ ct rec from 1815; Pro Clk has pro rec from 1805)

Carroll D2 1833 14 1840-80 Ray ... Carrollton
Carter B4 1859 4 1860-80 Ripley, Shannon ... Van Buren
Cass D3 1835 30 1850-80 Jackson ... Harrisonville
(Organized as Van Buren renamed Feb 19, 1849; three southern tiers of townships relinquished to Bates Co Feb 22, 1855; Co Clk has partial b rec 1883 to 1890)

Cedar   D4 1845   9 1850–80 Dade, St. Clair . . . . Stockton
Chariton   C2 1820 13 1830–80 Howard . . . . Keytesville
(Courthouse burned Sept 20, 1864; only a few rec lost; Co Clk has b rec 1883 to 1887)
Christian D4 1859 12 1860–80 Greene, Taney, Webster . . . . . . Ozark
(Sources differ on date organized, some say Mar 8, 1859, others Mar 8, 1860;
county seat, Ozark selected May 1859; courthouse burned in 1865; no mention
of fate of records)
Clark (old)   1818   Arkansas . . . .
(Never organized: abolished in 1819 when Terr of Arkansas was created)
Clark   C1 1836   9 1840–80 Lewis . . . . Kahoka
(Co Clk, Rec Office has m, div & civ ct rec; Pro Office has pro rec; Dept
of Health, Jeff. City, Mo. has b & d rec
Clay   D2 1822 87 1830–80 Ray . . . . Liberty
Clinton   D2 1833 12 1840–80 Clay . . . . Plattsburg
Cole   C3 1820 41 1830–80 Cooper . . . . Jefferson City
(Cir Clk has div & civ ct rec from 1821; Clk Pro Ct has pro rec from 1821;
Recorder of Deeds has m rec from 1821; State Board of Health, Jeff. City, Mo.
has b & d rec from 1911)
Cooper   C3 1818 15 1830–80 Howard . . . . Boonville
Crawford   B3 1829 13 1830–80 Gasconade . . . . Steelville
(1829–1835 Co Ct rec lost; courthouse burned Feb 15, 1873; courthouse burned
Jan 5 1884; no mention of fate of rec)
Dade   D4 1841   8 1850–80 Greene . . . . Greenfield
(Lost 10-mile strip on northern boundary to Cedar Co, and 9-mile strip on
southern boundary to Lawrence Co, reducing it to its present limits, Mar 28,
1845; courthouse burned in 1863, but rec had been removed to safety; Co Clk has
m & div rec from 1867)
Dallas   D4 1844   9 1850–80 Polk . . . . Buffalo
(Organized 1842 as Niangua Co; in 1844 boundaries slightly changed and name
changed to Dallas; courthouse burned Oct 18, 1863; second courthouse burned Jul
30, 1864, and rec destroyed; the replaced rec were burned Sept 3, 1867)
Daviess   D1 1836 10 1840–80 Ray . . . . Gallatin
DeKalb   D2 1845   7 1850–80 Clinton . . . . Maysville
(In 1878 CH burned, many rec being destroyed, but rec of cir clks office
were preserved along with a few papers of other offices; Co Clk has b rec
1880 to 1802; Recorder has m & div rec; Registrar has d & bur rec; Judge
of Pro has pro & civ ct rec)
Dent   B4 1851 10 1860–80 Crawford, Shannon . . . . Salem
(Courthouse burned in 1864, destroying some of the ct rec)
Dodge   1851   1850   Putnam . . . .
(Discontinued in 1853; had lost territory when Iowa boundary was established,
bringing its area below the constitutional limit of 400 sq miles; its territory
was added to Putnam Co)
Douglas   C4 1857 10 1860–80 Ozark, Taney . . . . Ava
(Terr increased in 1864 by addition of portions of Taney & Webster Cos)
(Cir Clk & Recorder have m, div, & civ ct rec; Pro & Magistrate Judge have
pro rec)
Dunklin   A5 1845   1850–80 Stoddard . . . . Kennett
(In 1853 a strip one mile wide was taken from Stoddard & added to northern
boundary; CH burned during CW; in 1872 a newly-completed CH burned with
all rec; all rec prior to 1872 are lost) (Bureau of Vit Stat, Jefferson City, Mo.
has b & d rec; Recorder of Deeds has m rec; Cir Clk has div & civ ct rec;
Pro Clk has pro rec)
Franklin   B3 1818 45 1830–80 St. Louis . . . . Union
(Boundaries not accurately defined until 1845; Co Clk has b rec from 1883 to
1892, d rec from 1883 to 1885)
Gasconade B3 1820 12 1830–80 Franklin . . . . Hermann
(In 1869 relinquished 36 sq miles to Crawford Co; Co Clk has b rec 1883 to
1896, m rec from 1850)
Gentry   D1 1841   9 1850–80 Clinton . . . . Albany
(Organization completed 1843; Mar 6, 1885 courthouse burned with all Co rec)

Greene   D4 1833 126 1840–80 Crawford . . . . Springfield
(CH burned in 1861; no mention of fate of rec) (Division of Health, Vit Rec, Jeff. City, Mo has b & d rec; Recorder of Deeds has m rec; Cir Clk has div & civ ct rec; Pro Ct has pro rec; Co Clk has a few old b & d rec)
Grundy   D1 1841 12 1850–80 Livingston . . . . Trenton
(Co Clk has incom b rec from 1870 to 1891)
Harrison   D1 1845 12 1850–80 Daviess . . . . Bethany
(Jan 7, 1874, courthouse destroyed by fire; land books, ct recs, pro recs and most of the Co rec were saved; tax books were destroyed; Co Clk has b rec 1883 to 1893; Clk Cir Ct has m & div rec 1858; civ ct rec from 1845; Pro Clk has pro rec from 1853)
Hempstead   1818   Arkansas . . . .
(Abolished 1819 when Territory of Arkansas was created)
Henry   D3 1834 19 1850–80 Lafayette . . . . Clinton
(Originally Rives Co; name changed Oct 15, 1841)
Hickory   D3 1845 5 1850–80 Benton, Polk . . . . Hermitage
(Courthouses burned 1852 and 1881; many rec destroyed; Co Clk has b rec 1883 to 1898; Clk of Cir Ct has m rec 1872, div rec 1858 civ ct rec 1858; Pro Judge has pro rec from 1845)
Holt   E1 1841 8 1850–80 Platte Purchase . . . . Oregon
(Co Clk has b & d rec 1883 to 1893, Bureau of Vit Stat, Jeff. City, Mo has b & d rec from 1910; Co Recorder has incom m rec from 1899; Clk Cir Ct has div & civ ct rec from 1841; Pro Clk has pro rec from 1849; CH burned 20 Jan 1965 – most all rec in vaults were undamaged, but not having a proper place to file them are very much disorganized)
Howard   C2 1816 11 1830–80 St. Charles, St. Louis . . . . . Fayette
(Courthouse burned 1887; records were saved and some date to 1816)
Howell   C5 1857 22 1860–80 Oregon, Ozark . . . . West Plains
(Courthouse destroyed during CW no mention of fate of rec; Co Clk has b rec 1883 to 1895)
Iron   B4 1857 8 1860–80 Dent, Madison, Reynolds, St. Francis, Washington, Wayne . . . . . . Ironton
(Co Clk has b, d & bur rec from 1910, m, div, pro & civ ct rec from 1857)
Jackson   D2 1826 623 1830–80 Lafayette . . . . Independence
(Nearly all its terr was acquired from Osage & Kansas Indians, June 2, 1825)
Jasper   D4 1841 79 1850–80 Newton . . . . Carthage
(CH destroyed in 1863; rec had been removed were returned in 1865; CH burned in 1883; no mention of fate of rec) (Co Clk has b rec 1883 to 1900 & d rec from 1883 to 1891; Recorder of Deeds has m rec; Pro Ct has pro rec and civ ct rec)
Jefferson B3 1818 66 1830–80 Ste. Genevieve, St. Louis . . . . Hillsboro
Johnson   D3 1834 29 1840–80 Lafayette . . . . Warrensburg
Kinderhook   1841   Benton, Pulaski . . . .
(Renamed Camden Feb 23, 1843)
Knox   C1 1845 7 1850–80 Scotland . . . . Edina
Laclede   C4 1849 19 1850–80 Camden, Pulaski, Wright . . . . Lebanon
Lafayette D2 1820 25 1830–80 Cooper . . . . Lexington
(Originally called Lillard; changed Feb 16, 1825)
Lawrence (old)   1815   New Madrid . . . .
(Abolished 1818)
Lawrence D4 1845 23 1850–80 Barry, Dade . . . . Mount Vernon
(Co Clk has m & div rec from 1860, also pro & civ ct rec)
Lewis   C1 1833 11 1840–80 Marion . . . . Monticello
Lillard   1820   Cooper . . . .
(Changed to Lafayette, Feb 16, 1825)
Lincoln   B2 1818 15 1830–80 St. Charles . . . . Troy
(Co Recorder has m rec from 1825; Pro Judge has pro rec from 1823; Bureau of Vit Stat, Jeff. City, Mo has b rec from 1910; Registrar has d & bur rec; Cir Ct Office has div rec)
Linn   C2 1837 17 1840–80 Chariton . . . . Linneus
Livingston D2 1837 16 1840–80 Carroll . . . . Chillicothe

McDonald   D5   1849   12   1850-80   Newton . . . . Pineville
(In 1876 an error in survey was corrected, establishing a new eastern line which
annexed a 2 1/2 mile strip previously included in Barry Co.; in 1863 courthouse
and rec were burned)

Macon   C2   1837   16   1840-80   Randolph . . . . Macon
(Co Clk has b rec from 1883 to 1893)

Madison   B4   1818   9   1830-80   Cape Girardeau, Ste.
                                         Genevieve . . . . Fredericktown

Maries   C3   1855   7   1860-80   Osage, Pulaski . . . . Vienna
(In 1859 and 1868, small tracts of land were exchanged with Phelps Co; Nov 6,
1868 courthouse burned with nearly all the records)

Marion   C2   1826   30   1830-80   Ralls . . . . Palmyra
(Cir Clk has m & div rec; City Clk, Hannibal, Mo. has b, d & bur rec; Pro Ct
has pro rec; Magistrate Ct has civ ct rec)

Mercer   D1   1845   6   1850-80   Grundy . . . . Princeton
(24 March 1898, CH burned; nearly all rec of the cir clk and recorder, treas,
& sheriff were destroyed or badly damaged; rec in office of pro judge and Co
Clk were saved, but many were badly damaged; Cir Clk has m, div, & civ ct
rec from 1898; Pro Judge has pro rec; b rec in Jeff. City, Mo.)

Miller   C3   1837   14   1840-80   Cole . . . . Tuscumbia
(Line between Camden & Miller changed 1845; terr from Morgan annexed 1860;
minor changes in 1868; Co Clk has b rec from 1883 to 1891; Co Recorders
office has m & div rec; Pro Judge has pro rec; Cir Clk has civ ct rec; State
Dept of Health, Jeff. City, Mo. has b & d rec from 1910)

Mississippi A4   1845   21   1850-80   Scott . . . . Charleston
Moniteau   C3   1845   11   1850-80   Cole, Morgan . . . . California
Monroe   C2   1831   11   1840-80   Ralls . . . . Paris
Montgomery   B3   1818   11   1830-80   St. Charles . . . . Montgomery City
(Co rec burned 1864; Cir Clk has m rec from 1864; div & civ ct rec from
1886; Pro Ct has pro rec from 1890; Magistrate Ct has their rec from 1947;
Division of Health, Jeff. City, Mo. has b, d, & bur rec)

Morgan   C3   1833   9   1840-80   Cooper . . . . Versailles
(CH burned 1887, most records were saved)

New Madrid   A5   1812   31   1830-80   Original district . . . . New Madrid
(State Board of Health, Jeff. City, Mo. has b rec from 1910 & d rec; Local
Undertakers have bur rec; Recorder of Deeds has m rec; Cir Clk has div &
civ ct rec; Pro Clk has pro rec)

Newton   D4   1838   30   1840-80   Barry . . . . Neosho
(In 1846 a strip two miles wide was detached from Newton and attached to
Jasper; courthouse burned 1862; no mention of fate of records)

Niangua   1842   Polk . . . .
(Boundaries slightly changed and name changed to Dallas, Dec 10, 1844)

Nodaway   D1   1845   22   1850-80   Andrew . . . . Maryville
(State Board of Health, Jeff. City, Mo. has b rec from 1910, also d rec;
Funeral Homes have bur rec; Cir Ct Clk has div rec; Pro Ct Clk has pro rec)

Oregon   B5   1845   10   1850-80   Ripley . . . . Alton
(Courthouse burned during Civil War; rec were removed and most of them saved)

Osage   C3   1841   11   1850-80   Gasconade . . . . Linn
(Mar 1, 1855 boundaries between Osage and Pulaski defined Nov 15, 1880,
courthouse burned; fireproof vaults saved records)

Ozark   C5   1841   7   1850-80   Taney . . . . Gainesville
Pemiscot   A5   1851   38   1860-80   New Madrid . . . . Caruthersville
(Courthouse and contents burned 1883)

Perry   A4   1820   15   1830-80   Ste. Genevieve . . . . Perryville
Pettis   D3   1833   35   1840-80   Cooper, Saline . . . . Sedalia
Phelps   C4   1857   35   1860-80   Crawford, Pulaski, Maries . . . . Rolla
(Co Clk has m & div rec)

Pike   B2   1818   17   1830-80   St. Charles . . . . Bowling Green
(Courthouse burned 1864; no mention of fate of records)

Platte   E2   1838   23   1840-80   Platte Purchase . . . . Platte City
(Attached to Clay for civil and military purpose from Dec 1836 to Dec 31, 1838)

Polk   D4   1835   14   1840–80   Greene .... Bolivar
Pulaski (old)   1818   Franklin ....
   (Organization not perfected and much of its terr became Gasconade in 1820;
   abolished 1819 when Terr of Arkansas was created)
Pulaski   C4   1833   47   1840–80   Crawford .... Waynesville
   (Co Clk has m, div, pro, civ ct rec from 1903)
Putnam   C1   1845   7   1850–80   Linn .... Unionville
   (When Iowa boundary was established, the areas of both Putnam and Dodge were
   below the constitutional limit; Dodge disorganized in 1853 and its terr was
   regained by Putnam)
Ralls   B2   1820   8   1830–80   Pike .... New London
Randolph   C2   1829   22   1830–80   Chariton .... Huntsville
   (a few rec lost when courthouse burned 1880)
Ray   D2   1820   16   1830–80   Howard .... Richmond
Reynolds   B4   1845   5   1850–80   Shannon .... Centerville
   (Ch burned in 1872, all rec burned; Co Clk has b rec from 1883, m, div, pro,
   and civ ct rec from 1872)

County Map of Missouri

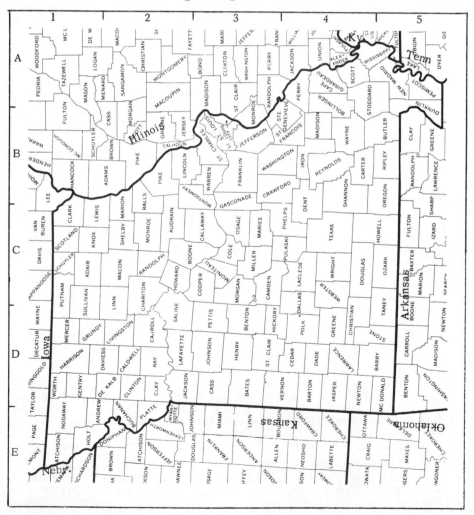

Ripley   B5   1823   9   1840–80 Wayne . . . . Doniphan
Rives   1834   1840   Lafayette . . . .
    (Name changed to Henry Oct 15, 1841)
St. Charles   B3   1812   53   1830–80 Original district . . . . St. Charles
St. Clair   D3   1841   8   1850–80 Rives (later Henry) . . . . Osceola
Ste. Genevieve B4 1812   12   1830–80 Original district . . . . . . Ste. Genevieve
    (Co Clk has b rec from 1883 to 1893; Recorder of Deeds has m rec from 1804;
    Local Registrar has d & bur rec; Cir Clk has div & civ ct rec; Pro Clk has pro
    records)
St. Francois B4   1821   37   1830–80 Jefferson, Ste. Genevieve,
                                        Washington . . . . Farmington
St. Louis   B3   1812 704   1830–80 Original district . . . . Clayton
    (Co Clk has b rec from 1877 to 1910)
St. Louis City B3 1764 750   1830–80 . . . . St. Louis
Saline   D2   1820   25   1830–80 Cooper, Howard . . . . Marshall
    (Courthouse burned 186? but records were saved)
Schuyler   C1   1845   5   1850–80 Adair . . . . Lancaster
    (Co Clk has b & d rec from 1883 to 1893; Cir Clk has m, & div rec; Judge of
    Pro & Magistrate Cts have pro & civ ct rec)
Scotland   C1   1841   6   1850–80 Lewis . . . . Memphis
Scott   A4   1821   33   1830–80 New Madrid . . . . Benton
    (State has b, d & bur rec; Recorder of Deeds had m rec; Cir Clk has div & civ
    ct rec; Pro Judge has pro rec)
Shannon   B4   1841   7   1850–80 Ripley, Washington . . . . . . Eminence
    (Courthouse destroyed during CW; no mention of fate of records)
Shelby   C2   1835   9   1840–80 Marion . . . . Shelbyville
Stoddard   A4   1835   29   1840–80 Cape Girardeau . . . . Bloomfield
    (CH burned 1864 but rec has been removed to safety; Co Clk has b rec
    from 1883 to 1886; Recorder of deeds has m rec; Dept Of Health & Vit
    Stat, Jeff. City, Mo. has d rec; Cir Clk has div rec; Pro Clk has pro rec;
    Magistrate Clk has civ ct rec)
Stone   D5   1851   8   1860–80 Taney . . . . Galena
    (Bureau of Vit Stat, Jeff. City, Mo. has b & d rec; Recorder has m rec;
    Local Registrar has bur rec; Cir Clk has div & civ ct rec; Pro Judge has
    pro rec)
Sullivan   C1   1845   9   1850–80 Linn . . . . Milan
Taney   D5   1837   10   1840–80 Greene . . . . Forsyth
    (Co rec destroyed by fire 1885; Bureau of Vit Stat, Jeff. City, Mo. has b, d,
    and bur rec; Cir Clk has m, div, civ ct rec; Pro Judge has pro rec)
Texas   C4   1845   18   1850–80 Shannon, Wright . . . . Houston
    (Co Clk has b & d rec from 1881 to 1889)
Van Buren   1835   1840   Jackson . . . .
    (Name changed to Cass Feb 19, 1849)
Vernon   D4   1855   21   1860–80 Bates . . . . Nevada
    (Created Feb 15, 1851, but act was declared unconstitutional since its terr was
    exactly that of Bates; legally created Feb 27, 1855; reorganized Oct 17, 1865
    after total suspension of civil order during CW; courthouse destroyed during
    that period but clk had taken the rec with him when he joined the army and all
    rec were later recovered except one deed book; Co Clk has m rec from 1912, div
    rec from 1885, pro rec from 1855)
Warren   B3   1833   9   1840–80 Montgomery . . . . Warrenton
Washington   B3   1813   14   1830–80 Ste. Genevieve . . . . Potosi
Wayne   B4   1818   9   1830–80 Cape Girardeau . . . . Greenville
    (CH burned with all recs 1854, CH burned 2nd time 1892, all rec destroyed)
Webster   C4   1855   14   1860–80 Greene, Wright . . . . Marshfield
    (Courthouse burned 1863 but rec were saved with the exception of tax rolls and
    election returns)
Worth   D1   1861   4   1870–80 Gentry . . . . Grant City
    (Co Clk has b rec from 1883 to 1893, from 1910 b rec available from Bureau
    of Vit Stat, Jefferson City, Mo; Co Clk has m, div, pro & civ ct rec from
    1861)

Wright   C4   1841   14   1850-80   Pulaski . . . . Hartville
(1864 courthouse burned, destroying many rec; 1897 courthouse destroyed with
all its records)

Federal Courts (start 1805). Inventory of County Archives, Cass, Cole, Dallas, Henry (2 Vol), Johnson, Linn, McDonald, Macon, Marion (3 Vol), Jasper, Pettis, Pike, Reynolds, Ripley, Shelby. St. Louis - Transcription of minutes of the Board of Trustees 1808-1809. Guide to Public Vital Statistic records. Guide to Church Vital Statistic records.

Inventory of the church archives of Missouri. Baptist Bodies, No. 1 Tebo Baptist Association. Transcription Bethel Church book minutes of the proceedings of the Bethel Church 1806-1867. Bethel Church minutes (Reprints from records of proceedings of the Bethel Church).

Guide to Depository of manuscript collections in Missouri. Information concerning the Manuscript Depository Collection of the Missouri Baptist Historical Society, Liberty, Missouri (Reprinted with additions from "Guide to Depository of Manuscript Collection in the U.S.-Mo"). Preliminary check list of Missouri imprints 1808-1850. Early History of Missouri. Early Missouri Archives (3 Vol). County Court Records of St Charles County. The organization of Missouri counties. Depository of unpublished material, University of Missouri, Columbia, Missouri.

Books available on Missouri are the following:

Conrad, Howard L. "Encyclopedia of the History of Missouri," 6 vols. New York, 1901.

"Missouri: A Guide to the 'Show Me' State:" American Guide Series. New York, 1941.

Violette, Eugene Morrow. "A History of Missouri." 1918 (Reprint, Cape Girardeau, 1951.

Williams, Walter. "A History of Northwest Missouri." 3 vols. Chicago, 1915.

Montana

Capital Helena - Territory 1864 - State 1889 - (41st)

At least sixteen tribes of Indians roamed over Montana when white explorers first came into the section. Traders from France, Scotland and England were the first whites to visit there.

The eastern part of Montana was part of the Louisiana Purchase in 1803. Members of the Lewis and Clark Expedition crossed the state in 1805 en route west and on the return trip in 1806.

The western part of Montana was included in the section that came to the United States in 1846 through the Oregon Treaty.

The first influx of people really attracted to Montana was in 1862 when gold was discovered in what is now Madison county, southeast of Butte. About twenty years later, copper and silver were found in the Butte region. To work the resulting mines, many workers were shipped in from Ireland, Germany, Austria, Poland, and Czechoslovakia.

In 1864 Montana became an organized Territory. Prior to this, various parts of the section had belonged at sundry times to surrounding Territories, including those of Missouri, Nebraska, Oregon, Washington, and Idaho.

The state has 56 counties. Of the original counties, nine were formed in 1864 and two in 1865. Eleven counties have census reports available from 1860 on.

Birth and death records from June 1907 to the present are at the office of the State Registrar, State Board of Health, Helena, Montana 59601. No birth and death records are available before 1907, with the exception of Bozeman, Great Falls, and Helena at the office of the county clerk. Butte and Missoula have some records in the office of the city health department.

Marriage license information is at the office of the county clerks, where records of wills, probate matters, deeds and land records also are available.

Library facilities in Montana are in keeping with its population. Libraries are established in about seventy-five cities. Among the larger libraries, most of which have fine historical collections, are the Historical Society of Montana at Helena 59601, the public libraries at Billings, Butte, Missoula, and Great Falls, and the Montana State University Library at Missoula 59801.

Montana County Histories
(Population figures to nearest thousand - 1960 Census)

Name	Map Index	Date Formed	Pop. By M	Census Reports Available	Parent County	County Seat
Beaverhead	E4	1864	7	1860-80	Original county	Dillon

(Co Clk has b, d & bur rec; Clk of Dist Ct has m rec, also div, pro & civ ct rec; Co Clk has voting rec)

| Big Horn | B4 | 1913 | 10 | 1860-80 | Rosebud, Yellowstone | Hardin |

(Co Clk has b & d rec from 1913; Clk of Ct has m, div, pro & civ ct rec)

| Blaine | C2 | 1912 | 8 | | Chouteau, Hill | Chinook |

(Co Clk has b & d rec from 1912; Clk of Ct has m, div, pro & civ ct rec; Funeral Directors have bur rec)

| Broadwater | D3 | 1897 | 3 | | Jefferson, Meagher | Townsend |

(Co Clk has b & d rec from 1907; Clk of Ct has m, div, pro & civ ct rec)

| Carbon | C4 | 1895 | 8 | | Park, Yellowstone | Red Lodge |

(Co Clk has b & d rec from 1882, pro rec from 1895)

| Carter | A4 | 1917 | 2 | | Custer | Ekalaka |

(Co Clk has b, d, bur rec from 1917)

Cascade   D2   1887   73   Chouteau, Meagher .... Great Falls
     (Co Clk & Recorder have b, d, bur rec from 1888)
Chouteau   D2   1865   7   1860-80   Original county .... Fort Benton
     (Co Clk has b & d rec from 1895, m rec from 1887, div, pro, civ ct rec 1879)
Custer   A3   1865   13   1880   Original county .... Miles City
     (Co Clk has b rec from 1900, d rec from 1907)
Daniels   A1   1920   4   Valley .... Scobey
     (Co Clk has b, d, & bur rec from 1920; Clk of ct has m, div, pro, civ ct rec)
Dawson   A2   1869   12   1860-80   Original county .... Glendive
     (Clk & Recorder has b & d rec from 1895; Clk of Ct has m rec from 1884,
     div, pro & civ ct rec from 1883)
Deer Lodge   E3   1864   19   1860-80   Original county .... Anaconda
Fallon   A3   1913   4   Custer .... Baker
     (Clk & Recorder has b & d rec)
Fergus   C2   1885   14   Meagher .... Lewistown
Flathead   E1   1893   33   Missoula .... Kalispell
     (Co Clk has b rec from 1885, m rec from 1893, d rec from 1897)
Gallatin   D3   1864   26   1860-80   Original county .... Bozeman
     (Co Clk has b & d rec from 1907)
Garfield   B2   1919   2   Valley, McCone .... Jordan
     (Co Clk has b rec from 1919)
Glacier   E1   1919   12   Teton .... Cut Bank
     (Co Clk has b & d rec from 1919; Clk of Ct has m, div, pro & civ ct rec)
Golden Valley C3 1920   1   Musselshell .... Ryegate
     (Co Clk & Recorder has b & d rec; Clk of Ct has m, div, pro & civ ct rec)
Granite   E3   1893   3   Deer Lodge .... Philipsburg
     (Co Clk & Recorder has b & d rec from 1895; Clk of Ct has m, div, pro & civ
     ct rec)
Hill   D1   1912   19   Chouteau .... Havre
     (Co Clk & Recorder has b & d rec from 1912, partial b rec from 1898 & partial
     d rec from 1907; Clk of Ct has m, div, pro & civ ct rec; Cemetery District has
     bur rec)
Jefferson   E3   1864   4   1860-80   Original county .... Boulder
     (Co Clk has incom b & d rec from 1903)
Judith Basin D2   1920   3   Fergus, Cascade .... Stanford
     (Co Clk & Recorder have b & d rec from 1900, deeds from 1887 & patents from
     1882; Clk of Dist Ct has m, div & civ ct rec)
Lake   E2   1923   13   Flathead, Missoula .... Polson
Lewis & Clark E2 1864   28   1860-80   Original county .... Helena
Liberty   D2   1920   3   Chouteau .... Chester
Lincoln   F1   1909   13   Flathead .... Libby
     (Co Clk has incom b & d rec from 1898)
McCone   A2   1919   3   Dawson, Richland .... Circle
     (Co Clk & Recorder have b, d & bur rec from 1919; Clk of Ct has m, div, pro,
     and civ ct rec)
Madison   E4   1864   5   1860-80   Original county .... Virginia City
Meagher   D3   1867   3   1860-80   Original county ... White Sulpher Springs
     (Co Clk & Recorder have b, d & bur rec from 1905; Clk of Ct has m & div
     rec from 1876 & pro & civ ct rec from 1885)
Mineral   F2   1914   3   Missoula .... Superior
     (Co Clk has b rec from 1914)
Missoula   E2   1864   45   1860-80   Original county .... Missoula
     (On 9 Mar 1943 there was a change of boundaries, land was interchanged
     between Missoula & Granite Cos; Co Clk has b & d rec from 1 July 1895; Clk
     of Ct has m, div, pro & civ ct rec; Cemetery or City Rec have bur rec)
Musselshell C3   1911   5   Fergus, Meagher .... Roundup
Park   D4   1887   13   Gallatin .... Livingston
     (Co Clk has b & d rec from 1907; Clk of Ct has m, div & pro rec; City Clk
     has bur rec)
Petroleum   C2   1925   .9   Fergus, Garfield .... Winnett
     (Director of Rec has b, m, d, bur rec from 1925, also div, pro & civ ct rec)

County Map of Montana

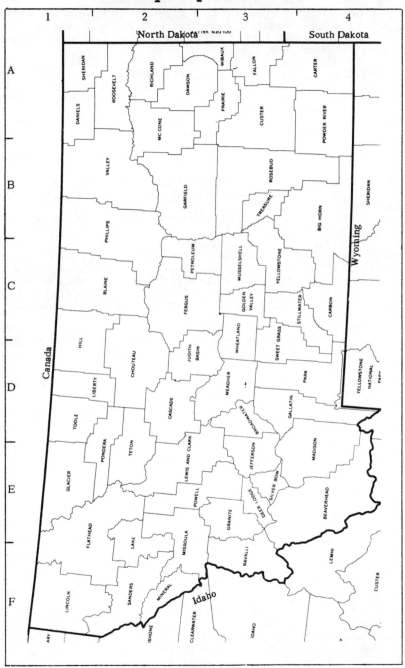

Phillips   B2   1915   6   Valley • • • • • • • • • • • • • • • • • Malta
(Co Clk has b & d rec from 1915; Individual Funeral Homes or Cemetery
Districts have bur rec; Clk of Ct has m, div, pro & civ ct rec)

Pondera   E2 1919   8   Teton · · · · · · · · · · · · · · · Conrad
  (Co Clk has m, div, pro, civ ct rec from 1919)
Powder River A4 1919   2   Custer · · · · · · · · · · · · · · · Broadus
  (Co Clk has b, d, bur rec 1919; Clk of Ct has m, div, pro, civ ct rec 1919)
Powell   E2 1901   7   Missoula · · · · · · · · · · · · Deer Lodge
Prarie   A3 1915   2   Custer · · · · · · · · · · · · · · · · ·Terry
(Co Clk has b & d rec from 1915; Clk of Ct has m, div, pro & civ ct rec from 1915)
Ravalli   F3 1893   12   Missoula · · · · · · · · · · · · Hamilton
  (Co Clk & Recorder has b, d & bur rec from 1911, also deeds, mtgs & Voter
  reg from 1937; Clk of Ct has m, div, pro & civ ct rec)
Richland   A2 1914   11   Dawson · · · · · · · · · · · · · · · Sidney
Roosevelt   A2 1919   12   Valley, Richland · · · · · · · · Wolf Point
  (Co Clk & Recorder have b rec from 1919 & d rec; Clk of Ct has m, div, pro,
  and civ ct rec)
Rosebud   B3 1901   6   Dawson · · · · · · · · · · · · · · Forsyth
  (Co Clk has b & d rec from 1900; Clk of Dist Ct has m, div, pro & civ ct rec)
Sanders   F2 1906   7   Missoula · · · · · · · · · · · Thompson Falls
  (Co Clk & Recorder has b & d rec; Clk of Ct has m, div & pro rec)

Sheridan   A1 1911   6   Custer · · · · · · · · · · · · · · Plentywood
Silver Bow   E3 1881   46   Deer Lodge · · · · · · · · · · · · · · Butte
  (Co Clk & Recorder have b rec from 1900, d & bur rec from 1890; Clk of Dist
  Ct has m, div, pro & civ ct rec)
Stillwater   C4 1913   6   Sweet Grass, Yellowstone
                                    Carbon · · · · · · · · · · · · · · · Columbus
  (Co Clk as b & d rec from 1913; Clk of Dist Ct has m, div, pro & civ ct rec)
Sweet Grass D3 1895   3   Meagher, Park, Yellowstone · Big Timber
Teton   E2 1893   7   Chouteau · · · · · · · · · · · · · · Choteau
  (Co Clk has b, d & bur rec from 1899; Clk of Dist Ct has m, div, pro & civ rec)
Toole   D1 1914   8   Teton · · · · · · · · · · · · · · · · ·Shelby
  (Co Clk & Recorder have b, d & bur rec from 1914)
Treasure   B3 1919   1   Big Horn · · · · · · · · · · · · · · Hysham
Valley   B2 1893   17   Dawson · · · · · · · · · · · · · · · Glasgow
Wheatland   D3 1917   3   Meagher, Sweet Grass · · · · Harlowton
  (Co Clk & Recorder have b, d & bur rec; Clk of Ct has m, div, pro & civ ct rec)
Wibaux   A3 1914   2   Dawson · · · · · · · · · · · · · · · Wibaux
  (Co Clk & Recorder have b, d & bur rec from 1914; Clk of Dist Ct has m, div,
  pro and civ ct rec)
Yellowstone C3 1893   79   Gallatin, Meagher, Custer · · · · Billings

**Genealogists' Check List of the Historical Records Survey,
Montana**

Federal Courts. Inventory of County Archives, Beaverhead, Carbon, Flathead, Galatin, Lake, Lincoln, Madison, Mineral, Missoula, Park, Ravalli, Sanders, Silver Bow, Stillwater, Sweet Grass, Toole. Guide to Public Vital Statistics records. Inventory of Vital Statistic records of churches and religious organizations. Directory of churches and religious organizations in Montana. Manuscript published Bibliography of Graduate Theses in the University of Montana. Depository of unpublished material, State College, Bozeman, Montana.

Nebraska

Capital Lincoln - Part of Mo. Terr. 1812 - State 1867 - (37th)

Nebraska was long a choice spot for several rather belligerent Indian Tribes. The first settlers were stragglers of the California Gold Rush days and the Oregon migration. Others unused to mountain terrain returned to the level lands of Nebraska which had formed a delightful picture in their memory as they were westward bound.

The first settlement was established in 1823. It was called Bellevue, and is situated less than ten miles below Omaha on the Missouri.

Nebraska was part of the Missouri Territory before 1820. In 1834 it was carved into three sections and placed under the supervision of Arkansas, Michigan and the state of Missouri. Twenty years later it became a Territory in its own name, including sections of Colorado, Montana, North and South Dakota, and Wyoming.

All during the 1850's many Germans settled in Nebraska. Twenty years later a large contingent of Germans came out of Russia and settled Lancaster and nearby counties. Many Scandinavians established homes there after the adoption of the Homestead Act of 1862.

In 1867 Nebraska was admitted to the union - the thirty-seventh state. Many Civil War veterans secured cheap land after the close of that struggle.

Most Nebraskans of today are of German, Czech, Swedish or Russian descent.

Birth and death records since 1904 and marriage records since 1909 are at the Bureau of Vital Statistics, State Department of Health, Lincoln, Nebraska 68508. Prior to those dates, the birth, death and marriage records are available at the offices of the county clerks, where wills and probate matters are recorded.

Land records, such as deeds, mortgages and all land titles are recorded in the office of the Register of Deeds in the various county seats.

The earliest census record of any Nebraska county is that of 1860.

Nebraska Libraries: Nebraska State Historical Library, 1500 R St., Lincoln 68508, (Lancaster); Lincoln, (local manuscripts, newspapers of state, midwest lore); University of Nebraska, Don L. Love Memorial Library, (history of Great Plains region), Lincoln 68508, (Lancaster); Public Library, Harney & 19th Sts., Omaha 68102, (Douglas).

Nebraska County Histories

(Population figures to nearest thousand - 1960 Census)

Name	Map Index	Date Formed	Pop. By M	Census Reports Available	Parent County	County Seat
Adams	C3	1870	29	1870-80	Clay	Hastings
Antelope	B2	1875	10	1880	Pierce	Neligh
Arthur	E2	1888	.7		Unorganized Territory	Arthur
Banner	F2	1888	1		Cheyenne	Harrisburg

(Co Clk has b, div, civ ct & real estate rec from 1888, also fairly recent bur & d rec; Co Judge has m & pro rec)

Blaine	D2	1885	1		Custer	Brewster
Blackbird				1870		
Boone	B2	1871	9	1880	Platte	Albion
Box Butte	F2	1886	12		Unorganized Territory	Alliance

(Bureau of Vit Stat, Lincoln, Nebr. has b & d rec; Co Judge Office has m rec; Clk of Dist Ct has div, pro, & civ ct rec)

Boyd	C1	1890	5		Holt	Butte
Brown	D2	1883	4		Unorganized Territory	Ainsworth

(Co Judge has m & civ ct rec from 1883; Clk of Dist Ct has div rec from 1883; Co Clk has Land patent rec from 1883, Co Supt has school cen rec from 1883; Attached to Holt Co Nebr. prior to 1883)

Buffalo	C3	1857	26	1860-80	Original county	Kearney
Burt	A2	1855	10	1860-80	Original county	Tekamah

(Co Clk has bur rec; Bureau of Vit Stat Lincoln, Nebr. has b & d rec; Co Judge has m, pro, civ ct rec; Clk of Dist Ct has div & civ ct rec)

Butler	B3	1857	10	1860-80	Unorganized Territory	David City
Calhoun				1860		
Cass	A3	1855	18	1860-80	Original County	Plattsmouth

(Co Clk has m, pro, civ ct rec from 1855, also div rec from 1853; Bureau of Vit Stat, Lincoln, Nebr. has b & d rec)

Cedar	B1	1855	13	1860-80	Original county	Hartington
Chase	E3	1873	4	1880	Unorganized Territory	Imperial

(Co Clk has div & civ ct rec from 1890; State Register can furnish b, & d rec Co Judge has m & pro rec)

Cherry	E2	1883	8		Unorganized Territory	Valentine
Cheyenne	F3	1867	15	1870-80	Unorganized Territory	Sidney

(Co Clk has bur rec; Bureau of Vit Stat, Lincoln, Nebr. has b & d rec; Co Judge has m & pro rec; Clk of Dist Ct has div & civ ct rec)

Clay	B3	1857	9	1860-80	Original county	Clay Center
Colfax	B2	1865	10	1870-80	Dodge	Schuyler
Cuming	B2	1858	12	1860-80	Burt	Westpoint

(Co Judge has m & pro rec from 1858; Clk Dist Ct has div rec from 1858)

Custer	D3	1875	17	1880	Unorganized Territory	Broken Bow

(Co Judge has m rec from 1878, pro rec from 1887, civ ct rec from 1880; Clk of Dist Ct has div rec from 1881)

Dakota	A2	1854	12	1860-80	Original county	Dakota City
Dawes	F1	1885	10		Sioux	Chadron
Dawson	D3	1871	19	1860-80	Buffalo	Lexington
Deuel	E3	1888	3		Cheyenne	Chappell
Dixon	B2	1853	8	1860-80	Original county	Ponca
Dodge	B2	1855	32	1860-80	Original county	Fremont

(Co Clk has b, d & bur rec from 1919)

Douglas	A3	1854	343	1860-80	Original county	Omaha
Dundy	E4	1873	4	1880	Unorganized Territory	Benkelman

(Co Clk has b rec from 1907, d rec from 1904, also bur, div & civ ct rec; Bureau of Vit Stat, Lincoln, Nebr. has m rec from 1909; Co Judge has pro rec)

Fillmore	B3	1856	9	1860-80	Unorganized Territory	Geneva
Franklin	C4	1867	5	1870-80	Kearney Org. 1871	Franklin
Frontier	D3	1872	4	1880	Unorganized Territory	Stockville

(Co Clk has div rec; Bureau of Vit Stat, Lincoln, Nebr. has b rec from 1910, also d rec; Co Judge has m, pro rec; Co Register has bur rec; Co Supt has school rec)

Furnas   D4 1877   8 1880   Unorganized Territory . . . Beaver City
(State Capitol, Lincoln, Nebr. has b & d rec; Co Judge has m, pro & civ ct rec; Cemetery Assn has bur rec; Clk of Dist Ct has div rec)

Gage   A4 1855   27 1860-80 Original county . . . . Beatrice
Garden   E2 1887   3   Unorganized Territory . . . . Oshkosh
Garfield   C2 1884   3   Wheeler . . . . Burwell
Gosper   D4 1873   2   Unorganized Territory . . . . Elwood
(Co Clk has m & pro rec from 1891; bur rec; div rec from 1880 and civ ct rec from 1923; Bureau of Vit Stat, Lincoln, Nebr. has b & d rec)

Grant   E2 1887   1   Unorganized Territory . . . . Hyannis
(Co Clk has div & civ ct rec from 1890, also bur rec from 1941; Co Judge has m & pro rec; Bureau of Vit Stat, Lincoln, Nebr. has b & d rec)

Greeley   C2 1875   5 1880   Boone . . . . Greeley
Green   1860
Hall   C3 1855   36 1860-80 Original county . . . . Grand Island
(Co Judge has m & pro rec from 1860; Clk of Dist Ct has div rec from 1860; Co Clk has b, d & bur rec from 1904)

Hamilton   B3 1870   9 1870-80 York . . . . Aurora
(Co Judge has b, d rec from 1905, also m, div & pro rec from 1870)

Harlan   C4 1871   5 1880   Unorganized Territory . . . . . . Alma
(Co Clk has m, div, pro, civ ct rec, deeds from 1870's; State Bureau of Vit Stat, Lincoln, Nebr. has b, d & bur rec; Clk of Dist Ct also has div rec; Dist Ct rec & real estate transfers)

Hayes   D3 1873   2 1880   Unorganized Territory . . . . . Hayes Center
(Co Clk has d, div, pro & civ ct rec)

Hitchcock D4 1873   5 1880   Unorganized Territory . . . . . .Trenton
(Co Clk has div rec from 1886; Bureau of Vit Stat, Lincoln, Nebr. has b, d, & div rec; Co Judge has m, pro & civ ct rec; Various cemetery assn have bur rec)

Holt   C2 1876   14 1880   Knox . . . . O'Neill
Hooker   E2 1889   1   Unorganized Territory . . . . . Mullen
(Co Clk has b & d rec from 1919)

Howard   C3 1871   7 1880   Hall . . . . Saint Paul
(Co Judge has m, pro, civ ct rec from 1871; Co Clk has div rec from 1871)

Jackson   1870
Jefferson B4 1865   12 1870-80 Gage . . . . Fairbury
Johnson   A3 1854   6 1860-80 Original county . . . . Tecumseh
Jones   1860
Kearney   C3 1860   7 1860-80 Original county . . . . Minden
(Co Clk has div, pro, civ ct rec from 1872)

Keith   E3 1873   8 1880   Lincoln . . . . Ogallala
Keya Paha D1 1884   2   Brown, Rock . . . . Springview
Kimball   F3 1888   8   Cheyenne . . . . Kimball
(Co Clk has div & pro rec; Co Judge has m, civ ct rec; b, d & bur rec are at Lincoln, Nebr.)

Knox   B1 1854   13 1880   Formerly L'Eau Qui Court . . Center
(Co Clk has b, d & bur rec; Co Judge has m, div, pro & civ ct rec)

Lancaster A3 1854 155 1860-80 Original county . . . . Lincoln
L'Eau Qui Court   1860-70 (see Knox)
Lincoln   D3 1867   28 1870-80 Unorganized Territory . . . . North Platte
Logan   D2 1885   1   Custer . . . . Stapleton
(Co Judge has m & civ ct rec from 1885; Co Clk has div rec from 1885; Bureau of Vit Stat, Lincoln, Nebr. has b, d & bur rec)

Loup   C2 1883   1   Unorganized Territory . . . . . . Taylor
McPherson D2 1887   .7   Lincoln, Keith . . . . Tyron
(Co Judge has div, pro & civ ct rec; Bureau of Vit Stat, Lincoln, Nebr. has b, m, & d rec)

Madison   B2 1856   25 1860-80 Platte . . . . Madison
Merrick   B3 1854   8 1860-80 Original county . . . . Central City

County Map of Nebraska

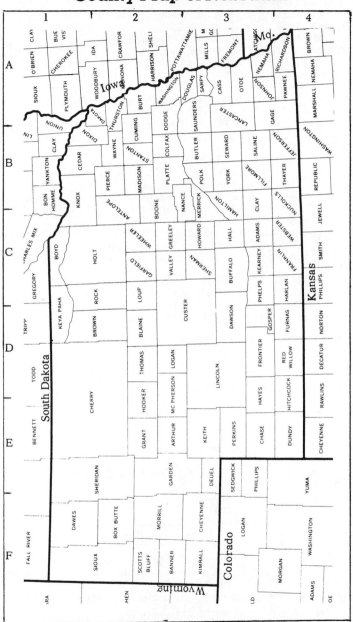

Morrill   F2   1887   7   Cheyenne   • • • • • • • • • Bridgeport
    (Co Clk has b, d, & bur rec from 1919; Bureau of Vit Stat also has b, d, &
    bur rec)
Nance   B3   1879   6   1880   Merrick   • • • • • • • • • • • • Fullerton
    (Co Clk has b & d rec from 1918; Co Judge has m, pro & civ ct rec; Clk of

Dist Ct has div rec)

Nemaha   A3   1855   9   1860-80   Original county .... Auburn
Nuckolls   B4   1860   8   1860-80   Clay .... Nelson
Otoe   A3   1854   17   1860-80   Original county .... Nebraska City
    (Co Clk has chattel mtgs, cartelles, Inc rec)
Pawnee   A4   1854   5   1860-80   Original county .... Pawnee City
    (Co Judge has m rec from 1870)
Perkins   E3   1887   4   Keith .... Grant
    (Co Clk has b & d rec from 1919 and Dist Ct rec from 1888; Co Judge has div,
    pro, civ ct rec)
Phelps   C3   1873   10   1880   Unorganized Territory ..... Holdrege
    (Co Judge has m rec from 1877; pro rec from 1895; Clk of Dist Ct has div rec
    from 1880)
Pierce   B2   1867   9   1870-80   Madison .... Pierce
Platte   B2   1854   24   1860-80   Original county .... Columbus
Polk   B3   1854   7   1860-80   Original county .... Osceola
Red Willow   D4   1873   13   1880   Frontier .... McCook
Richardson   A4   1855   14   1860-80   Original county .... Falls City
Rock   C2   1888   3   Brown   .... Bassett
    (Co Clk has m, div, pro, civ ct rec from 1889)
Saline   B3   1855   13   1860-80   Gage, Lancaster .... Wilber
    (Co Judge has m & pro rec; Clk of Dist Ct has div rec; Local Office has b, d,
    and bur rec)
Sarpy   A3   1854   31   1860-80   Original county .... Papillion
Saunders   A3   1865   17   1870-80   Sarpy, Douglas .... Wahoo
Scotts Bluff   F2   1888   34   Cheyenne .... Gering
    (Co Clk has m, div, pro, civ ct rec from 1889; Bureau of Vit Stat, Lincoln,
    Nebr. has b & d rec)
Seward   B3   1867   14   1870-80   Lancaster .... Seward
    (Co Judge has m rec from 1869, also pro rec from 1870 & civ ct rec; Bureau
    of Vit Stat, Lincoln, Nebr. has b, m, & d rec; Clk of Dist Ct has div rec)
Sheridan   E2   1885   9   Sioux .... Rushville
    (Bureau of Vit Stat, Lincon, Nebr. has b, d, & bur rec; Co Judge has m, pro,
    civ ct rec; Clk of Dist Ct has div rec)
Sherman   C3   1873   5   1880   Buffalo .... Loup City
    (Co Clk has b, d, & div rec, m rec from 1873, pro rec from 1877, civ ct rec
    from 1889; Co Registrar has b, d & bur rec)
Sioux   F2   1877   3   1880   Unorganized Territory ..... Harrison
    (Co Judge has m rec, pro, civ ct rec from 1887; City Clk has bur rec; Clk Dist
    Ct has div rec; State House, Lincoln, Nebr. has b & d rec)
Shorter   1860
Stanton   B2   1865   6   1870-80   Dodge .... Stanton
Taylor   1870
Thayer   B4   1872   9   1880   Jefferson .... Hebron
    (Co Judge office has m, div, pro, & civ ct rec; Bureau of Vit Stat, Lincoln, Nebr.
    has b & d rec; Mortuary has bur rec)
Thomas   D2   1887   1   Blaine .... Thedford
    (Co Judge has m & pro rec; Clk Dist Ct has div & civ ct rec; Bureau of Vit
    Stat, Lincoln, Nebr. has b, d, & bur rec)
Thurston   A2   1865   7   1870-80   Burt (see Blackbird Co) ...... Pender
Valley   C2   1871   7   1880   Unorganized Territory .... Ord
Washington   A2   1854   12   1860-80   Original county .... Blair
Wayne   B2   1867   10   1870-80   Thurston .... Wayne
Webster   C4   1871   6   1880   Unorganized Territory ..... Red Cloud
    (Co Judge has b & d rec from 1919, also m, div, pro, civ ct rec from 1871;
    City keeps bur rec; Co Judge also has land rec)
Wheeler   C2   1877   1   1880   Boone .... Bartlett
Winnebago Indian Reservation 1870
York   B3   1854   14   1860-80   Original county .... York

Genealogists' Check List of the Historical Records Survey, Nebraska

Federal Courts. Inventory of County Archives, Gosper, Greeley, Howard, Loup, Merrick, Seward, Webster. Guide to Public Vital Statistics records. Guide to Depository of Manuscript collections in Nebraska. A check list of Nebraska non-documentary imprints 1847-1876. Depository of unpublished material, State Historical Society, Lincoln, Nebraska.

Nevada

Capital Carson City - Territory 1861 - State 1864 - (36th)

Twelve years after the Mormon Pioneers had reached the Great Salt Lake, gold and silver were found in the Comstock Mine in Virginia City, Nevada, midway - twenty or twenty-five miles - between Reno and Carson City. The strike was rich enough to turn California gold seekers eastward. Almost over-night, the Nevada population, which up to that time had stood a-round a thousand, doubled over and over again. Among Europeans attracted by the rich mineral discovery were people from all sections of Britain, Italy, Scandinavia, Germany, and France. Many Mexicans came also.

Nevada became a territory in 1861 and three years later was admitted into the union as the thirty-sixth state.

Birth and death records from 1887 to 30 June 1911, marriage records from 1864 to date, deeds and land records from 1864 to date are all in the office of the Recorder of each county.

Birth and death files from 1 July 1911 to date are at the Nevada State Department of Health, Division of Vital Statistics, Carson City, Nevada 89701.

Marriage bans are not filed.

Wills from 1864 to date are in the office of the clerk of each county.

The records of the state Census of 1872 are in the custody of the Secretary of State, Carson City, Nevada 89701.

Tax payers lists from 1864 are at the office of the Assessor of each county.

Library - University of Nevada Library, Reno 89507, (Washoe).

Nevada County Histories

(Population figures to nearest thousand - 1960 Census)

Name	Map Index	Date Formed	Pop. By M	Census Reports Available	Parent County	County Seat
Carson				1860	(see Utah) discontinued	

Churchill   C2   1861   8 1870-80 Original County   . . . . Fallon
     (Co Clk has m, div, pro, & civ ct rec from 1905; Bureau of Vit Stat has b,
     d and bur rec)

County Map of Nevada

Clark   F4 1909 127   Lincoln . . . . Las Vegas
  (Co Clk has div, pro & civ ct rec)
Douglas   C1 1861   3 1870-80 Original county . . . . Minden
  (Co Clk has m, div, pro & civ ct rec)
Elko   A4 1869   12 1870-80 Lander . . . . Elko
  (Co Clk has m license, div, pro, civ ct rec from 1875; Co Recorder has m rec
  from 1875, b & d rec from 1875 to 1917; Bureau of Vit Stat, Carson City, Nev.
  has d & bur rec after 1917)
Esmeralda D2 1861   .6 1870-80 Original county . . . . Goldfield
  (Co Clk has b rec from 1900, m, d, bur rec from 1898, div rec from 1908, pro,
  civ ct rec from 1907)
Eureka   B3 1873   .8   Lander . . . . Eureka
  (Co Recorder has b, m, d, bur rec; Co Clk has div, pro & civ ct rec)
Humboldt   A2 1861   9 1860-80 Original county . . . . Winnemucca
  (Co Clk has m rec from 1881, div & civ ct rec from 1863, pro rec from 1900,
  Naturalization rec from 1864, Inquests 1862) See Utah 1860 Cen; Recorder &
  State Dept of Health have b & d rec)
Lander   B3 1861   2 1870-80 Original county . . . . Austin
  (Co Clk has m rec from 1867, div rec, pro, civ ct rec from 1865; Auditor has
  some b rec)
Lincoln   D4 1869   2 1870-80 Nye . . . . Pioche
  (Co Clk has m, div, pro, civ ct rec from 1873)
Lyon   C1 1861   6 1870-80 Original county . . . . Yerington
Mineral   D2 1911   6   Esmeralda . . . . Hawthorne
  (Co Clk has m, pro & civ ct rec from 1911, bur rec from 1930, div rec from
  1863; Division of Vit Stat, Carson City, Nev. has b & d rec)
Nye   D3 1864   4 1870-80 Esmeralda . . . . Tonopah
Ormsby   C1 1861   8 1870-80 Original county . . . . Carson City
  (Co Clk has m, div, pro & civ ct rec)
Pahute   1870   Discontinued
Pershing   B2 1919   3   Humboldt . . . . Lovelock
  (Co Clk has m, div, pro, civ ct rec from 1919)
Roop   1870   Discontinued
St. Mary's   1860   Discontinued (see Utah)
Storey   C1 1861   .6 1870-80 Original county . . . . Virginia City
  (Co Recorder has b, m & d rec from 1875; Co Clk has div, & civ ct rec from
  1861, pro rec from 1875; Dept of Vit Stat, Carson City, Nev. has b rec from
  1912 and d rec from ca 1950)
Washoe   B1 1861 116 1870-80 Original county . . . . Reno
  (Co Clk has m rec from 1871, div, pro & civ ct rec from 1862)
White Pine C4 1864   10 1870-80 Lincoln . . . . Ely

Genealogists' Check List of the Historical Records Survey,
Nevada

Federal Courts. Inventory of County Archives, Douglas,
Elko, Eureka, Mineral, Nye, Ormsby, Washoe. Guide to Public
Vital Statistic Records. Inventory of the Church Archives of
Nevada, Protestant Episcopal Church, Roman Catholic Church.
A check list of Nevada imprints 1859-1890. Depository of un-
published material, Nevada Historical Society, Reno, Nevada.

New Hampshire

Capital Concord - State 1788 - (9th)

New Hampshire, in the northeast corner of the United States,
is one of the thirteen original colonies. Its history dates back to

1603 when an Englishman, Martin Pring anchored in Piscataqua harbor. The French explorer, Samuel de Champlain discovered the Isles of Shoals in 1605 while sailing along the coast of N.H. In 1614 Captain John Smith landed on its shores. It was settled about 1623 at Rye (Little Harbor), Dover and Portsmouth. This was only three years after the landing of the Pilgrim Fathers in Massachusetts. A little later settlements were made at Exeter and Hampton. These places were on or near the coast, or on a river bank near its mouth. After these first settlements, little effort was put forth to establish new settlements for almost a hundred years. The fear of Indians kept the settlers from moving inland.

New Hampshire became part of the Massachusetts colony in 1641, and continued so, with brief interruptions, for about a hundred years. In 1741 it became a Royal British Province and remained so until the Revolutionary War.

A large part of the early settlers came from Massachusetts and Connecticut. The Connecticut River is the western boundary of the state. Apparently it was much easier to go up the river than to cut long roads through the forests from the eastern shore. Many of the river towns, as a result, are much older than those in the interior. If the ancestry of the early settlers of one of those towns is sought, it will more than likely be found in Connecticut or western Massachusetts.

Of New Hampshire, Archibald F. Bennett, former secretary of the Genealogical Society of Utah, has said: "In the great migration to the west, New Hampshire and Vermont were stopping places for a few years for one or more generations of families now established far from there. Many families from their homelands in Massachusetts and Connecticut seemed to pause here briefly, and then resume their westward trek. Their residence in New Hampshire was often during the pioneer period when records were not kept too regularly. Then they removed so early that almost all trace of their presence in those localities is obliterated. Consequently, many ancestral lines of western families are followed back to New Hampshire or Vermont, and then are hopelessly lost. Yet there are actually many sources which can assist in the solution of such problems."

During the first two hundred years or more of its history, it was mainly people from England who came to New Hampshire. During the next seventy-five years, tens of thousands came into the state from the Scandinavian countries and from Greece, Italy and France.

New Hampshire entered the union in 1788, the ninth state to ratify the constitution.

Vital statistics have been kept in the towns since 1640, though they are not complete. Copies of all statistics records since that date have been made. They include town records, church records, cemetery records, and all other available old records. These have all been indexed, and may be searched for a small fee. These records are available at the office of the Registrar of Vital Statistics, State House, Concord, N.H. 03303, and at some of the offices of the town clerks. Wills are in the charge of the clerks of the probate courts of the ten counties. The Registrars of deeds are in charge of deeds and land titles. The State Library at Concord has charge of the Census Records. Cemetery records are handled by the cemetery superintendents or selectmen of the towns. Tax papers are handled by the town and city clerks throughout the state.

Almost all towns have town histories. Many of these contain much genealogical information about the early settlers. In the genealogical departments of the public libraries will be found many books with valuable information about the town families. Many records are available at the New Hampshire State Library and the New Hampshire Historical Society, both in Concord. The Census reports from 1800 are available, as well as those of subsequent years.

New Hampshire libraries - Public Library, 45 Green St., Concord 03301, (Merrimac); New Hampshire Historical Society Library, 30 Park St., (local histories of state, family and genealogical records, old maps, early newspapers), Concord 03303, (Merrimac); New Hampshire State Library, 20 Park St., Concord 03303, (Merrimac); City Public Library, 405 Pine St., (community articles), Manchester 03104, (Hillsboro).

Valuable genealogy records are found in the following books which form only a small part of the many that have been written about this state and its people:

Sterns, Ezra S., "Genealogy and Family History of the State of New Hampshire", 4 vol. Pub. 1908 Lewis Publishing Co., New York, Chicago.

Ayling, Augustus D., "Revised Register of the Soldiers and Sailors of N.H. in the War of Rebellion 1861-1866. Pub. 1895 by the New Hampshire Legislature.

NEW HAMPSHIRE TOWNS
Organized Before 1800

BELKNAP COUNTY -- Alton,-1770; Barnstead, 1727; Belmont; Center Harbor, 1797, Gilmanton, 1761; Meredith, 1748; New Hampton, 1765; Sanbornton, 1764.

CARROLL COUNTY -- Albany, 1766; Bartlett, 1790; Brookfield 1794; Conway, 1764; Chatham, 1767; Eaton, 1760; Effingham, 1749; Hart's Location, 1773; Jackson, 1778; Madison, 1785; Moultonborough, 1763; Ossipee, 1765; Sandwich, 1763; Tamworth,

1771; Tuftonboro, 1750; Wakefield, 1774; Wolfeboro, 1768.

CHESHIRE COUNTY -- Alstead, 1763; Chesterfield, 1761; Dublin, 1752; Fitzwilliam, 1752; Gilsum, 1764; Jaffray, 1752; Keene, 1754; Marlborough, 1752; Marlow, 1753; Nelson, 1767; Rindge, 1754; Richmond, 1758; Stoddard, 1769; Sullivan, 1760; Swanzey, 1753; Surry, 1769; Walpole, 1749; Westmoreland, 1741; Winchester, 1732.

COOS COUNTY -- Berlin, 1771; Colebrook, 1762; Columbia, 1762; Cambridge, 1793; Drummer, 1773; Dalton, 1764; Jefferson, 1765; Lancester, 1763; Milan, 1771; Northumberland, 1767; Randolph, 1772; Stark, 1788; Shelburne, 1770; Stratford, 1775.

GRAFTON COUNTY -- Alexandria, 1782, Benton, 1764; Bath, 1765; Bethlehem, 1799; Bridgewater, 1788; Canaan, 1761; Compton, 1765; Danbury, 1795; Dorchester, 1761; Enfield, 1761; Ellsworth, 1769; Franconia, 1754; Grafton, 1772; Groton, 1761; Hanover, 1765; Haverhill, 1763; Holderness, 1751; Hebron, 1792; Landaff, 1764; Lebanon, 1761; Lisbon, 1763; Littleton, 1764; Lyme, 1764; Lyman, 1761; Lincoln, 1764; Orange, 1790; Oxford, 1765; Pierpont, 1768; Plymouth, 1764; Rumney, 1705; Thornton,1770; Warren, 1767; Wentworth, 1766; Woodstock, 1763.

HILLSBORO COUNTY -- Amherst, 1760; Antrim, 1744; Bedford, 1736; Brookline, 1769; Deering, 1765; Francestown, 1752; Goffstown, 1733; Greenfield, 1771; Hancock, 1765; Hillsboro, 1735; Hollis, 1731; Hudson, 1722; Litchfield, 1720; Lyndeborough, 1759; Manchester, 1751; Mason, 1768; Merrimack, 1722; Milford, 1740; Nashua, 1673; New Boston, 1735; New Ipswich, 1735; Petersboro, 1749; Pelham, 1745; Sharon, 1791; Temple, 1750; Weare, 1735; Wilton, 1749; Windsor, 1798.

MERRIMACK COUNTY -- Allenstown, 1747; Andover, 1761; Boscowan, 1760; Bow, 1727; Bradford, 1771; Canterbury, 1723-50; Chichester, 1727; Concord, 1727; Dunbarton, 1746; Danbury, 1795; Epsom, 1727; Henniker, 1760; Hill, 1768; Hopkinton, 1740; Loudon, 1765; Newbury, 1762; New London, 1758; Northfield, 1760; Pembroke, 1728; Pittsfield, 1782; Salisbury, 1750; Sutton, 1767; Warner, 1773.

ROCKINGHAM COUNTY -- Atkinson, 1728; Auburn, 1734; Brentwood, 1742; Candia, 1748; Chester, 1720; Danville, 1738; Deerfield, 1750; E. Kingston, 1738; Epping, 1741; Exeter, 1638; Fremont, 1764; Greenland, 1704; Hempstead, 1728; Hampton, 1635; Hampton Falls, 1726; Kensington, 1737; Kingston, 1694; Londonderry, 1719; Newcastle, 1693; Newington, 1670; Newfields, 1681; Newmarket, 1727; Newton, 1749; North Hampton, 1690; Northwood, 1763; Nottingham, 1722; Plaistow, 1642; Portsmouth, 1623; Raymond, 1764; Rye, 1635; Sandown, 1756; Seabrook,1758; South Hampton, 1742; Stratham, 1629; Windham, 1741.

STRAFFORD COUNTY -- Barrington, 1762; Dover, 1623; Durham, 1623; Farmington, 1798; Lee, 1766; Madbury, 1755; Middleton, 1778; Milton, 1760; New Durham, 1749; Rochester, 1722; Somersworth, 1754.

SULLIVAN COUNTY -- Acworth, 1767; Charlestown, 1735; Claremont, 1764; Cornish, 1765; Croydon, 1766; Goshen, 1761; Grantham, 1761; Langdon, 1773; Lempster, 1785; Newport, 1765-6; Plainfield, 1765; Springfield, 1772; Unity, 1754; Washington, 1768.

County Map of New Hampshire

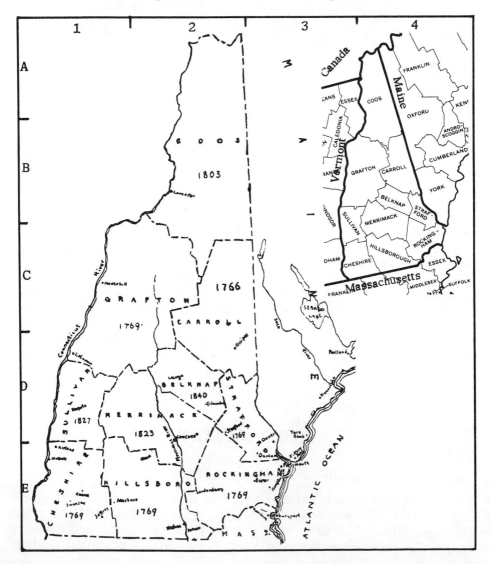

New Hampshire County Histories

(Population figures to nearest thousand - 1960 Census)

Name	Map Index	Date Formed	Pop. By M	Census Reports Available	Parent County	County Seat
Belknap	D2	1840	29	1850-80	Strafford, Merrimac	Laconia
Carroll	C2	1840	16	1850-80	Strafford	Ossipee

(Clk of Ct has div & civ ct rec from 1859; Town Clk of each town has b, m, d & bur rec; Register of Pro has pro rec)

Cheshire	E1	1769	43	1790-80	Original county	Keene
Coos	B2	1803	37	1810-80	Grafton	Lancaster

(Clk of Sup Ct has div, civ ct, naturalization rec from 1887; Town Clk of each town has b, m, d & bur rec; Register of Pro has pro rec)

Grafton	C1	1769	49	1790-80	Original county	Woodsville

(1820 Census missing; Clk of Ct has div & civ ct rec; Pro Ct has pro rec; Vit Stat, Concord, N.H. has b, m, d, and bur rec)

Hillsboro	E1	1769	178	1790-80	Original county	Nashua

(Co Clk has div, & pro rec from 1771)

Merrimack	D1	1823	68	1830-80	Rockingham, Hillsboro	Concord

(Co Clk has div rec from 1840, civ ct rec from 1823; Town or City Clk or Bureau of Vit Stat, Concord, N.H. has b, m, d, & bur rec; Register of Pro has pro rec from 1823)

Rockingham	E2	1769	99	1790-80	Original county	Exeter

(Clk of Ct has div, civ ct rec from 1769)

Strafford	D2	1769	60	1790-80	Original county	Dover
Sullivan	D1	1827	28	1830-80	Cheshire	Newport

Genealogists' Check List of the Historical Records Survey, New Hampshire

Federal Courts. Inventory of County Archives, Belknap, Carroll, Cheshire, Coos, Grafton, Merrimack. Inventory of municipal and town archives, Atkinson, Auburn, Bedford, Candia, Canterbury, Chester, Exeter, Greenland, New Hampton, Sanbornton. Guide to Public Vital Statistics records. Guide to Church Vital Statistic records. Inventory of the Church Archives of New Hampshire, Protestant Episcopal Church, Roman Catholic Church Guide to Depository of manuscript collections in New Hampshire. Preliminary check list of American portraits, 1620-1860, found in New Hampshire. Depository of unpublished material, University of New Hampshire, Manchester, New Hampshire.

New Jersey

Capital Trenton - State 1787 - (3rd)

French explorers sailed along the New Jersey coast as early as 1524. In the service of Holland, Henry Hudson sailed up the Hudson River in 1609. Nine years later the Dutch had settlers opposite the present upper New York City. Commissioned by their King, Swedish adventurers established a colony in the Delaware Valley, shortly after the Dutch came to the area.

With the experience gained in colonizing southern sections of America, two English court favorites, Lord Berkeley and Sir George Carteret, induced the Duke of York to grant them the area between the Hudson and the Delaware rivers. They named the colony New Jersey after the English Channel home of Carteret. Throwing the territory open to land seekers in 1664, the promoters made tempting offers to those willing to come. To the small Dutch communities along the Hudson came folks from every section of Britain. Puritans came down from Connecticut and established Newark. Scotch-Irish Presbyterians poured into the eastern counties, and English Quakers came into the fertile regions of the Delaware.

While differing strongly in their religious convictions, the settlers were solidly united against the tax and monetary ideas of the Crown and the proprietors. Disgusted with the lack of financial returns in the venture, the proprietors sold out to William Penn and his Quaker Friends.

In the intervening years difficulties were erased and more unity ensued. In the early part of the eighteenth century, New Jersey and New York had the same royal governor, but this ended in 1738. During the next 49 years New Jersey had a governor and a legislature of its own.

She became the third state to ratify the constitution of the United States in 1778. Three years later, the first U. S. Census gave New Jersey a population of 184,139. The majority of these were English from the Old World as well as from New England. The Dutch and the Swedes were also represented by large numbers. In the west part of the state were many French and Scotch.

Before William Penn acquired Pennsylvania, he and a company of Quakers settled West Jersey. The early Swedish and Dutch settlers continued to live there. Hence, a New Jersey pedigree may trace back to the English Quakers, the Puritans from New England, the Swedes who waged war on the early English settlers, the Dutch settlers who came from New Amsterdam (New York) and the Huguenots who fled from France in search of religious liberty and peace.

Research conditions are not so favorable in New Jersey as in some other states. Since they were not required by law to keep a record of births and deaths the family Bible was about the only place where these things were recorded. And yet, researchers willing to search into available records can find a wealth of information.

The office of the State Registrar of Vital Statistics, State

Department of Health, Trenton, New Jersey 08607, has birth records from 1848 to 1929 and death records from 1878 to 1929. Marriage information from 1848 to 1939 is also available there, although some are incomplete.

Only in Hudson County does the county clerk issue marriage licenses. In all other counties such licenses are handled by the town or city clerks, the township assessor or the local registrar of vital statistics.

Early marriage records which were kept by the Secretary of State are printed in the Archives.

Divorce records are kept in the Superior Court, Chancery Division, at the State House in Trenton.

The federal circuit and district courts and the State Supreme court, all in Trenton and the county circuit courts have records of naturalization proceedings. Records of Deeds in N. J. may be found as follows: From 1664 to 1703 in New Jersey Archives, Vol. XXI; From 1664 to 1790 in Secretary of State's Office; From 1790 to the present in the County Clerk's Offices (A few of earlier date are included); In Gloucester County deeds recorded before 1786 were destroyed by fire, deeds recorded after that date (even though dated earlier) are extant.

Most of the churches in the state have records of their respective memberships for many years back.

The originals of wills and probate matters, together with early guardianship and orphans' court proceedings are in the custody of the Secretary of State in Trenton. Copies of Wills and administrations of estates beginning in 1804 are at the county court houses. Wills and administrations of estates from 1682 to 1805 have been digested and published in the State Archives. There are ten volumes, each completely indexed. The state also published an index of New Jersey Wills, three volumes. These wills extend to a much later date than those given in the Archives. Many libraries, including the Cache County Library in Logan, Utah, have a complete set of the Archives of New Jersey.

Although thirteen of the twenty-one counties in New Jersey were established before 1790, no federal census schedules are available until the 1830 census. All of the New Jersey schedules for 1790, 1800, 1810, and 1820 are missing. The available schedules are enumerated in the New Jersey County Histories in this sections.

The New Jersey State Library has custody of the state census records taken every ten years since 1855.

More than 275 libraries serve the people of New Jersey. Many of these have valuable genealogical and historical books on their shelves.

Among the libraries are the following: Free Public Library,

Illinois and Pacific Aves., (genealogical material on N.J., N.Y., and Pa., limited number of family histories and family Bible records), Atlantic City 08401, (Atlantic); County Free Public Library, 08101 and City Public Library, 08103, Camden, (Camden), (across the Delaware River from Philadelphia); Free Public Library,472 Jersey Ave.,Jersey City 07302,(Hudson),(Across the river from New York City); County Free Library, Courthouse, (local histories & genealogies), Morristown 07960, (Morris); City Public Library, Miller Road and South St., (family histories and genealogical publications), Morristown 07960, (Morris); Public Library, 5 Washington St., (state and local history), Newark 07102, (Essex); Genealogical Society of New Jersey, 33 Lombardy St., (genealogies and local history), Newark 07102, (Essex); Rutger University Library, (old newspapers and local history), New Brunswick 08903, (Middlesex); Free Public Library, Paterson 07501, Passaic); Princeton University Library, (American History, especially Southern States), Princeton 08541, (Mercer); Free Public Library, 120 Academy St; New Jersey State Teachers College Library, Trenton.

Many books have been printed over the years concerning the history of the various communities and families of New Jersey The following are only a mere mention of a half a dozen available in libraries or book stores:

Barber, John W. "Historical Collections of New Jersey, Past and Present", biographies, the State Census of all the towns in 1865. 543 pp. New Haven, 1868.

Clayton, W. Woodford. "History of Union and Middlesex Counties", with biographies of many pioneers and prominent men. 885 pp. Philadelphia, 1882.

Folsom, Joseph S. "The Municipalities of Essex County", 1666-1924. Four volumes. New York, 1925.

Hatfield, Edwin F. "History of Elizabeth, including the early History of Union County" 701 pp. New York, 1868.

Lee, Francis B. "Genealogical and Personal Memorial of Mercer County." Two volumes. New York 1907.

Stewart, Frank H. "Notes on Old Gloucester County". 342 pp. Camden, 1917.

Wickes, Stephen. "History of the Oranges in Essex County", from 1666 to 1806. 334 pp. Newark, 1892.

New Jersey County Histories

(Population figures to nearest thousand - 1960 Census)

Name	Map Index	Date Formed	Pop. By M	Census Reports Available	Parent County	County Seat
Atlantic	D2	1837	161	1840-80	Gloucester	Mays Landing
Bergen	A3	1675	780	1830-80	Prov East Jersey	Hackensack

Burlington   D2 1681 224 1830–80 Original county . . . . Mt. Holly
    (Co Clk has civ ct rec; Surrogate has pro rec; State House, Trenton, N. J. has
    b rec)
Camden   D2 1844 392 1850–80 Glouc. . . . . Camden
Cape May   E2 1692   49 1830–80 Cumberland . . . . Cape May C.H.
    (Settled 1682; Co Clk has m rec from 1795 to 1826, pro, civ ct rec; also deeds
    and wills from 1692; Surrogate has pro rec)
Cumberland   E2 1748 107 1830–80 Salem . . . . Bridgeton
    (Co Clk has naturalization papers from 1885; newspaper files from 1840, civ ct
    rec from 1880;   Surrogate Office has pro rec; Chancery Ct has div rec;
    Municipalities of Co have bur rec; Bureau of Vit Stat, Trenton, N.J. has b, m,
    and d rec)

County Map of New Jersey

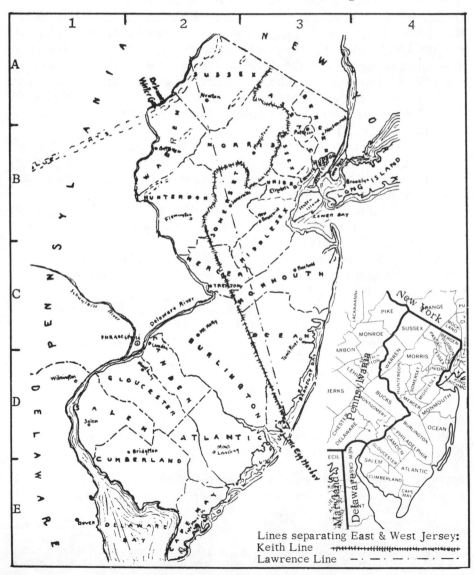

Lines separating East & West Jersey:
Keith Line
Lawrence Line

Essex	B3	1675	924	1830-80	Prov East Jersey	Newark
Gloucester	D2	1686	135	1830-80	Original county	Woodbury

(Co Clk has civ ct rec; Surrogate Ct has pro rec; Superior Ct has div rec; State Registrar of Vit Stat, Trenton, N. J. has b, m, d, and bur rec)

Hudson	E3	1840	611	1840-80	Bergen	Jersey City
Hunterdon	B2	1714	54	1830-80	Burlington	Flemington

(Co Clk has m rec from 1795 to 1875, civ ct rec from 1714, deeds & mtg from 1800; Surrogate Ct has pro rec; Superior Ct has div rec; Bureau of Vit Stat, Trenton, N. J. has b, m, d rec)

Mercer	C2	1838	226	1840-80	Somerset, Middlesex, Hunterdon, Burlington	Trenton
Middlesex	B3	1675	434	1830-80	Prov. East Jersey ...	New Brunswick
Monmouth	C3	1675	334	1830-80	Prov. East Jersey	Freehold
Morris	B2	1739	262	1830-80	Hunterdon	Morristown

(Co Clk has m rec from 1795 to 1887 and civ ct rec from 1740; Bureau of Vit Stat, Trenton, N.J. has b, later m, d rec; Clk of Sup Ct has div rec; Surrogate, has pro rec)

Ocean	C3	1850	108	1850-80	Monmouth	Toms River

(Co Clk has pro, civ ct rec from 1850)

Passaic	A3	1837	407	1840-80	Bergen, Essex	Paterson
Salem	D1	1681	59	1830-80	Original county	Salem

(Co Clk has civ ct rec from 1875, deeds from 1786; Surrogate's office has pro rec; Ct of Chancery has div rec; Municipal Rec of Vit Stat has b, m, d, bur rec)

Somerset	B2	1688	144	1830-80	Middlesex	Somerville

(Co Clk has civ ct rec from 1777, deeds from 1785)

Sussex	A2	1753	49	1830-80	Morris	Newton

(Co Clk has m rec from 1795 to 1878, civ ct rec from 1760)

Union	B3	1857	504	1860-80	Essex	Elizabeth
Warren	B2	1824	63	1830-80	Sussex	Belvidere

Genealogists' Check List of the Historical Records Survey, New Jersey

Federal Courts (listed with Delaware). Inventory of County Archives, Bergen, Morris, Ocean, Passaic, Sussex. Inventory of municipal and town archives, Belmar, Denville, East Newark, Orange, Wharton. Guide to Vital Statistic records, Vol 1 Public Archives, Vol 2 Church Archives. Guide to Naturalization records. Transcriptions, 1. Glouster County RW document, 2. Slave document.

Inventory of the Church Archives of New Jersey, Baha'i Assemblies; Baptist Bodies (Seventh Day Baptist Supplement). Christian Reformed, Congregation Christian, Evangelical Church, Presbyterian Churches, Protestant Episcopal Church, Diocese of New Jersey and Diocese of Newark, Salvation Army, Jersey City. Society of Friends, Unitarian Church. Transcription Colporteur Reports to the American Tract Society, 1841-1846; Transcription John Brainerd's journal 1761-1762, Presbyterian.

Directory of the churches in New Jersey. Vol 1 Atlantic county, 2 Bergen County, 3 Burlington County, 4 Camden County, 5 Cape May Co, 6 Cumberland County, 8 Essex County, 9 Hudson county, 10 Hunterdon County, 11 Mercer County, 12 Middlesex County, 13 Monmouth County, 14 Morris County, 15 Ocean

County, 16 Passaic County, 17 Salem County, 18 Somerset
County, 19 Sussex County, 20 Union Co, 21 Warren County.

Guide to manuscript depository in New Jersey. Calendar of the
New Jersey State Library, Trenton, N.J. Calendar of the Stevens
Family papers, Lieb Memorial Library, Stevens Institute of
Tech., Hoboken, N.J. (Preliminary Vol - Vol 1, 1664-1750, Vol
2 1751-1777). Check list of N.J. imprints 1784-1800. American
portrait inventory, 1440 early American portrait artists 1663-
1860, Manual of N.J. recording acts, Series I, County requirements, Index of the official register of the officers and men of
N.J. in the Revolutionary War.

New Jersey microfilms, (Filmed by N.J. Historical Record
Survey showing location of original records). Films in possession
of American Documentation Institute, Washington, D.C.. Minutes
of the Council of Proprietors of the Eastern division of N.J. (ABI)
1685-1705, 32 Ft, Survey, or General's office, City Hall, Perth
Amboy N.J. Minutes of the Council of Proprietors of the Eastern
division of N.J. 1725-1764, 36 ft, Surveyors General's office, City
Hall, Perth Amboy, N.J. Minutes of the Council of Proprietors of
the Eastern division of N.J. 1764-1794, No. "B" 34 ft., Surveyor
General's office, City Hall, Perth Amboy, N.J. Minutes of the
Council of the Council of the Proprietors of the Eastern division
of N.J. 1794-1866 30 ft., Surveyor General's office, City Hall,
Perth Amboy, N.J. Minutes of the Supreme court 1681-1709
("The Burlington Court Book") 20 ft, Supreme Court Clerk's
office, State House Annex, Trenton, N.J. Minutes of the Supreme
Court 1760-1764, 25 ft., Supreme Court Clerk's office, State
House Annex, Trenton, N.J. Minutes of the Supreme Court 1761-
1765, 30 ft, Supreme Court Clerk's office, State House Annex,
Trenton, N.J. Minutes of the Supreme Court 1767-1768, 30 ft,
Supreme Court Clerk's office, State House Annex, Trenton, N.J.
A Bill in the Chancery on N.J. (Hand printed by James Parker in
N.Y. 1747) 15 ft, Court of Commons Rights of Chancery 1684
(D-2 Liber 2) 35 ft., Section of States Vault, State House, Trenton,
N.J. Early index to Burlington Court Minutes 1681-1709, 25 ft,
Supreme Court Clerk's vault, State House Annex, Trenton, N.J.
Burlington Supreme Court Docket 1731-1737 Feb term, 1 Vol, 30
ft., Supreme Court Clerk's Safe, State House Annex, Trenton, N.J.
Burlington Supreme Court Docket May Term 1742, 14 ft, Supreme
Court Clerk's Safe, State House Annex, Trenton, N.J. Library A
for Judgements 1755-1758, 10 ft, Supreme Court Clerk's Office,
State House Annex, Trenton, N.J. Minutes of the Court of Sessions
and Common Pleas Court 1700-1713, 1713-1731, 1730-1739, 30 ft,
Gloucester County Historical Society, Gloucester County Building, Woodbury, N.J. Supreme Court Docket, May term 1738, Nov
1741 Vol 2, 30 ft, May 1742-45, 15 ft, Nov 1745-1748 No. 4, 22 ft.

Supreme Court Clerk's Vault, State House Annex, Trenton, N.J. Minutes and rules of the Supreme Court, 1704-1715, 10ft; 1716-1731, 14 ft; 1772-1776, 5 ft; 1775-1776, 5 ft; Supreme Court Clerk's Office, State House Annex, Trenton, N.J. Supreme Court Minutes Memoranda 1782-1783, 5 ft, Supreme Court Clerk's Office, State House Annex, Trenton, N.J. Liber AAA of Deeds 1680, 30 ft, Secretary of State's Vault, State House, Trenton, N.J. Deeds-Patents, Liber I, 1666-1682, 30 ft, Secretary of State. State House, Trenton, N.J. Minutes of Gloucester County Freeholders 1700-1812, 2 Vol, 45 ft, Gloucester County Historical Society, Gloucester County Building, Woodbury, N.J. Old Road Book 1745-1775, 30 ft, County Clerk's Office, County Court House, Somerville, N.J. Board of Chosen Freeholders of Somerset County minutes No. 1 1772-1810, 25 ft, Treasurer's Vault, County Court House, Somerville, N.J. Minutes of Piscataway Township Feb. 1, 1682 to July 1933. Township Clerk, Township Hall, New Market, N.J. Woodbridge Township Freeholders Book, Liber A 1668-1757, 28 ft, Clerk's Vault, Woodbridge City Hall, Woodbridge, N.J. Votes and Proceedings of the Common Council of the City of Burington, 25 ft, 104 Vault, Burlington City Hall, Burlington, N.J. Chester Township's "Ponsoking" 1692-1823, 15 ft, David L. Libbincott, 1 East Oak St., Moorestown, N.J. Burlington Town Book 1693-1780, 30 ft, Masonic Home Vault, Masonic Home, Burlington, N.J. Burlington records 1680-1717, 27 ft, Secretary of State's vault, State House, Trenton, N.J. Road Book A Essex Co. 3 Dec. 1698-30, Mary. 1804, 30 ft, Room 228, County Clerk's Vault, Hall of Records, Newark, N.J. Commissions, Acts of Assembly & C, 1682-1898, 40 ft, Secretary of State's vault (Locker No. 12), State House, Trenton, N.J. Commissions AAA 1703-1774, 30 ft, Secretary of State's vault, State House, Trenton, N.J. Declarations of Intentions of Aliens, Feb. 1852, 10 ft, Supreme Court Clerk's office, State House Annex, Trenton, N.J. Records of Naturalization-Minors, 1851, Book No. 1, 5 ft, Supreme Court Clerk's office, State House Annes, Trenton, N.J. Records of Naturalization - Minors 1851-1873, Book 2, 10 ft, Supreme Court Clerk's Office, State House Annex, Trenton, N.J. Minute Book of Government Carteret 1665 (Deeds Liber 3), 30 ft, Secretary of State's vault (Locker 12), State House, Trenton, N.J. The Treasurer of Eastern Division of N.J. to the Commissioner of Loan Office of County of Morris, 27 May 1776-30 Apr. 1838, 10 ft, Surrogate's office Vault, Hall of Records, Morristown, N. J. Proceedings of Justice and Freeholders, County of Morris 10 May 1786-1 Dec. 1823, 10 ft, Surrogate's office vault, Hall of Records, Morristown, N.J. Documentary Evidence, Old Kings Highway, 3 Vol, 45 ft, Gloucester County Historical Society, Gloucester Co. Bldg., Woodbury, N.J. Historic Houses of Woodbury, Gloucester

County, 2 Vol, 30 ft, Gloucester County Historical Society, Gloucester County Bldg., Woodbury, N.J.

Depository of unpublished material, Columbia University Library, New York, N.Y. (Atlas of Congressional Roll Calls, Presidential Message, and Papers and Executive orders) - (All other materials) State Library, Trenton, New Jersey.

New Mexico

Capital Santa Fe - Territory 1850 - State 1912 - (47th)

Until 1821 when the 780-mile Santa Fe Trail was opened from Independence, Mo., to Santa Fe, N.M., few Americans or Europeans had made their homes in New Mexico. For years, the region had belonged to Mexico and was inhabited mainly by Indians and Spanish-Americans. Its main city, Santa Fe, had been the capital of the Mexican territory since 1609. At that early date and for the next 150 years or more, its connections were more with Mexico than the United States. Indians and Spanish-Americans were its only inhabitants until the first part of 1800.

New Mexico became part of the United States in 1848. In 1850 when it was created a territory, it included most of its present domain, plus Arizona and Colorado. The Gadsden Purchase in 1854 included within its boundaries the Gila Valley in Catron and Grant counties.

The Colorado section was taken from New Mexico in 1861 and made into a separate territory. Two years later, Arizona was also withdrawn and created into a separate territory.

After operating for 62 years under territorial laws, New Mexico became a state in 1912, when it was made the forty-seventh in the union.

Birth and death records from 1919 are at the office of the State Health Department, Santa Fe, New Mexico 87501. They are not complete.

The County Clerk in each county seat has marriage records, wills, property deeds, and administration of estates.

Land grants are at the office of the State Land Office in Santa Fe, New Mexico.

Tax payers lists are at the office of the County Assessors, war service records at the office of the Adjutant General, cemetery records with the cemetery boards, and guardianship proceedings with the district courts.

Valuable genealogical information is contained in hundreds of volumes in the Stephen Watts Kearney Chapter of the Daughters of the American Revolution in Santa Fe and the New Mexico Historical Society, Santa Fe, New Mexico 87501. Other libraries in the larger cities have also much genealogical information. Public Library, 423 E. Central Ave., (Southwest lore), Albuquerque 87101, (Bernalillo); University of New Mexico Library, (Mexican and South American publications and history, Southwest lore), Albuquerque 87106, (Bernalillo); New Mexico State Library Commission, 301 Don Gaspar, (Southwestern lore), Santa Fe 87501, (Santa Fe).

New Mexico County Histories

(Population figures to nearest thousand - 1960 Census)

Name	Map Index	Date Formed	Pop. By M	Census Reports Available	Parent County	County Seat
Bernalillo	B2	1852	262	1850-80	Original county	Albuquerque

(Co Clk has m rec from 1885, pro rec from 1895; Dist Ct has div & civ ct rec; Dept Vit Stat, Santa Fe, N.Mex. has b, d & bur rec)

| Catron | C1 | 1921 | 3 | | Socorro . . . . | Reserve |

(Co Clk has m & pro rec from 1921, also b rec)

| Chaves | C3 | 1887 | 58 | | Lincoln . . . . | Roswell |

(Co Clk has m & pro rec from 1887; Dist Clk has div & civ ct rec; Bureau of Vit Stat, Santa Fe, N.Mex. has b & d rec)

| Colfax | A3 | 1869 | 14 | 1870-80 | Mora . . . . | Raton |

(Co Clk has m rec from 1869, pro rec from 1903; Judicial Dist Ct has div & civ ct rec; Public Health Dept, Santa Fe, N.Mex. has b & d rec; Mortician has bur rec)

| Curry | B4 | 1909 | 33 | | Quay, Roosevelt . . . . | Clovis |

(Co Clk has m & pro rec from 1909; Dept of Health, Santa Fe, N.Mex has b & d rec; Dist Ct Clk has div & civ ct rec)

| De Baca | C3 | 1917 | 3 | | Chaves, Guadalupe, Roosevelt . Fort Sumner |

(Co Clk has m, div, pro, civ ct, real estate, deeds & Mtgs from 1917; State Dept of Health, Santa Fe, N.Mex has b, d, & bur rec)

| Dona Ana | D2 | 1852 | 60 | 1860-80 | Original county . . . . | Las Cruces |

(Co Clk has b & m rec from 1816, d rec from 1907, pro rec from 1901, deeds from 1886, liens from 1850, mtgs from 1860)

| Eddy | D4 | 1887 | 51 | | Lincoln . . . . | Carlsbad |

(Co Clk has m, pro and copies of newspapers from 1891; Bureau of Vit Stat Santa Fe, N.Mex. has b & d rec; Dist Ct has div rec; Justices of Peace have civ ct rec)

| Grant | D1 | 1868 | 19 | 1870-80 | Socorro . . . . | Silver City |

(Co Clk has m & pro rec from 1900)

Guadalupe	B3	1905	6		Lincoln, San Miguel	Santa Rosa
Harding	A4	1921	2		Mora, Union	Mosquero
Hidalgo	D1	1920	5		Grant	Lordsburg

(Co Clk has m & pro rec from 1920; Dist Ct has div & civ ct rec; Bureau of Vit Stat, Santa Fe, N.Mex. has b, d & bur rec)

| Lea | D4 | 1917 | 53 | | Chaves, Eddy . . . . | Lovington |

(Co Clk has m rec from 1917, also pro rec; Dist Ct has div & civ ct rec; Dept of Health, Santa Fe, N.Mex. has b, d, & bur rec)

| Lincoln | C3 | 1869 | 8 | 1870 | Socorro . . . . | Carrizozo |

(Co Clk has m rec from 1882, pro rec from 1880, newspapers from 1890)

| Los Alamos | B2 | 1949 | 13 | | Sandoval, Santa Fe . . . . | Los Alamos |

(Co Clk has m & pro rec from 1949, bur rec from 1961)

| Luna | D2 | 1901 | 10 | | Dona Ana, Grant . . . . | Deming |

(Co Clk has m & pro rec from 1901; Dist Ct Clk has div & civ ct rec; Bureau of Vit Stat, Santa Fe, N.Mex. has b & d rec; Co Clk also has from 1901 armed

County Map of New Mexico

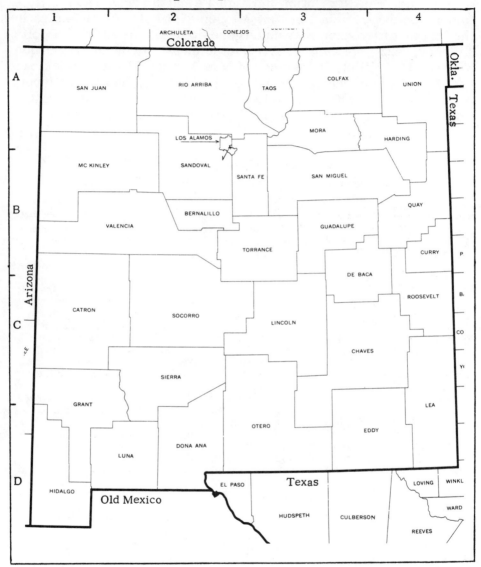

service discharges, bound newspaper pub, voters reg, real estate rec)

McKinley   B1   1899   37   Bernalillo, Valencia, San Juan ... Gallup

Mora   A3   1859   6   1860-80   San Miguel   ₒ ₒ ₒ ₒ ₒ ₒ ₒ ₒ ₒ ₒ Mora
      (Co Clk has m & pro rec from 1891, d rec from 1957; Dist Ct Clk has div
      rec; Health Dept, Santa Fe, N.Mex. has b, early d, bur rec)

Otero   D3   1899   37   Dona Ana, Lincoln, Socorro   ₒ Alamogordo
      (Co Clk has b rec from 1908, m rec from 1899, d & bur rec from 1907, pro
      rec from 1901, voters reg cert from 1939; Dist Ct Clk has div & civ ct rec
      from 1899)

Quay   B4   1903   12   Chaves   .... Tucumcari
      (Co Clk has m rec from 1896, pro, real estate, deeds & mtgs from 1893)

Rio Arriba   A2   1852   24   1850–80   Original county ...... Tierra Amarilla
(Co Clk has m & pro rec from 1852)
Roosevelt   C4   1903   16   Chaves .... Portales
(Co Clk has m, div, pro, civ ct rec from 1903)
Sandoval   B2   1903   14   Rio Arriba .... Bernalillo
San Juan   A1   1887   53   Rio Arriba .... Aztec
(Co Clk has m, div, pro rec from 1887)
San Miguel   B3   1852   23   1850–80   Original county .... Las Vegas
Santa Fe   B3   1852   45   1860–80   Original county .... Santa Fe
(Co Clk has m rec from 1863, pro rec from 1862)
Sierra   C2   1884   6   Socorro .... Truth or Consequences
(Co Clk has m rec from 1905, pro rec from 1919; Co Health Dept has d &
bur rec; Dist Ct Clk has div & civ ct rec)
Socorro   C2   1852   10   1860–80   Original county .... Socorro
Taos   A3   1852   16   1850–80   Original county .... Taos
(Co Clk has b, m, d, bur, pro rec from 1846)
Torrance   B3   1903   6   Lincoln, San Miguel, Socorro,
Santa Fe, Valencia ...... Estancia
(CH burned in July of 1910 and all co rec bef 1910 were destroyed; Co Clk
has b, d, m, pro & real estate transfers rec from 1910; Clk of Ct has div,
adoption, civ & dist pro rec; b & d rec after 1918 are at Bureau of Vit Stat,
Santa Fe, N.Mex)
Union   A4   1894   6   Colfax, Mora, San Miguel ... Clayton
(Co Clk has m, div & pro rec from 1894, civ ct rec from 1915; Bureau of Vit
Stat, Santa Fe, N.Mex. has b & d rec)
Valencia   B1   1852   39   1850–80   Original county .... Los Lunas
(Co Clk has m rec from 1865, pro rec from 1900; Dist ct Clk has div & civ ct
rec; Bureau of Vit Stat, Santa Fe, N.Mex. has b & d rec)

Genealogists' Check List of the Historical Records Survey, New Mexico

Federal Courts. Inventory of County Archives, Bernalillo, Colfax, Dona Ana, Eddy, Grant, Hidalgo, Luna, Mora, Otero. Sandoval, San Miguel, Sierra, Torrance, Union, Valencia. Guide to Public Vital Statistic records. Directory of Churchs and religious organizations in N. Mex. Check List of N.Mex. imprints and publication, 1784-1876. Index to Final Report on investigations among the Indians of the Southwestern U.S., carried on mainly in the years 1880-1885 by A. F. Bandelier. Depository of unpublished material, State Museum, Santa Fe, New Mexico.

New York

Capital Albany - State 1788 - (11th)

The Dutch settled New York in 1624 when they established a colony at Albany, then called Fort Orange. The next year other settlers from Holland came to New York City, then New Amsterdam. Previously, at least two explorers, Hudson and Champlain, had looked over the territory.

In the next few years the Dutch induced individuals from Scandinavia, Great Britain, and Germany to come with them to the New World.

Many Puritan families in Massachusetts and Connecticut drifted south into New York around 1640. Some sixty years later German families came into the Mohawk Valley looking for places in which to build their homes. About the same time French settlers were straggling into the new section from Canada. Other French families, together with some Spaniards and Portuguese, disturbed by the uprisings in the West Indies, where they had been for some time, sought refuge in New York.

The total population of the colony in 1740 was established at only 50,000. About that time many former Connecticut dwellers went across the sound and settled in Long Island. Others came into Dutchess, Westchester and Orange counties. A population check previous to the outbreak of the Revolutionary War would find settlers on Long Isalnd, on the banks of the Hudson River, a few Palatine Germans along the Mohawk River and some New Englanders in the extreme south-eastern part of the state.

In 1776 New York broke with the Mother County, and joined the other colonies in their fight for freedom. This struggle continued until 1781. Seven years later New York became the eleventh state in the Union by ratifying the constitution.

New York is described as a land of many tongues, not less than sixty languages being heard. The predominating nationalities are Italian, Russian, German, Polish, Irish, Austrian, English, Hungarian, Swedish, Norwegian, Czech, Greek, French, Finish, and Danish.

The researcher interested in New York records should first of all, before undertaking any search whatsoever, spend a day or two or more carefully reading Rosalie Fellows Bailey's ''Guide to Genealogical Sources for New York City, 1783-1898.'' The Guide ''is in its field one of the most important, perhaps the most important, in the United States.'' This most worthy appraisal comes from one of the foremost present day genealogists, an individual who has devoted much thought and energy to the science of genealogy. Carefully adhering to Miss Bailey's suggestions in her valuable treatise ''will give reasonable hope that any problem within its limit of time and place may be solved.''

Births, Deaths, and Marriages, from 1880 to present, for the entire state exclusive of all New York City records and certain records of Albany, Buffalo and Yonkers, noted below, are in the charge of the Director, Office of Vital Statistics, State Department of Health, Alfred E. Smith State Office Building, Albany 12200. The records of Albany, Buffalo and Yonkers not on file in the Health Department but available in the registrars' office of the cities concerned are: Births and deaths prior to 1 January 1914; marriages prior to 1 January 1908. The central office for New York City vital records is Board of Health, 125 Worth St., New York City 10013. Registration was not very complete until about 1900. For data on records prior to 1880, when the Department of Health became the central depository for the state, see Historical records survey, New York State, "Guide to Public Vital Statistics in New York State," 1942, 3v. wherein the status of the vital records of each community is given.

Marriage bonds, from 1752 to 1784, originally 40v., are in charge of Associate Librarian, Manuscripts and History Section, New York State Library, Albany 12200. These and other licenses, some as early as 1641 which are contained in other series filed in the State Library, are indexed in Secretary of State, "Names of Persons for Whom Marriage Licenses were Issued by the Secretary of the Province of New York Previous to 1784." 1860. See also "Supplementary List of Marriage Licenses," (State Library Bulletin, History No. 1, April 1898) for list of bonds for years 1752-53, 1755-56, and 1758, formerly bound as v.41 of Marriage bonds.

Wills - usually in county surrogates' office. For other wills see Berthold Fernow ed., "Calendar of Wills on File and Recorded in the Offfices of the Clerk of the Court of Appeals, of the County Clerk at Albany, and of the Secretary of State, 1626-1836,"1896. For abstracts of wills on file in the Surrogate's office. City of New York, 1665-1800, New York Historical Society, "Collections." v.25-41. Included therein are wills for the southern district of New York State. Care should be exercised in the use of the abstracts as many errors have been found - get the original when ever possible.

In the Manuscripts and History Section, New York State Library are wills, 1823-1940, of non-resident property owners.

Deeds and Land Grants - deeds are usually on file in the county clerk's offices.

The following are state records:

Patents, land papers, deeds 1630-64 (Dutch) in New York Colonial Manuscripts, v.GG and HH in custody of Associate Librarian, Manuscripts and History section, New York State Library, Albany.

New York Colonial Manuscripts indorsed Land Papers, 1643-1803. Same custody as preceding.

Deeds, including mortgages and releases to state, 1642 to present, in custody of Secretary, Land Board, Department of State, 164 State St., Albany 12210.

Letters - Patent of Lands, 1664-1878. Custody same as preceding.

Census Records - All schedules of the Federal Census from 1790 to and including 1940 are at Bureau of the Census, Washington D.C.

From the State Librarian, New York State Library, Albany, New York 12200, may be obtained "An Inventory of New York State and Federal Census Records." 1942, showing the available schedules from each county. From one to 14 different schedules are on hand at the office of the County Clerk of each county, In addition to those noted therein, the Manuscripts and History Section, New York State Library has microfilm of the 1800, 1810, and 1830 Federal Censuses for New York State. Originals are on file in the National Archives, Washington, D. C.

Tax Payers Lists - The New York State Library, Manuscripts and History Section, Albany, has some assessment rolls in its collection, both public and private. No inventory of them is available.

Local divisions of government - county, town, etc. - frequently have such records on file.

Church or Parish Records Transferred to State - In custody of the Associate Librarian, Manuscritps and History Section, New York State Library, Albany 12200, is a large collection of Church records, originals and copies. See Historical Records survey, New York State, "Guide to Vital Statistics Records of Churches in New York State," 1942 2v. for information concerning those on file in the State Library and elsewhere.

An invaluable source of basic information has been found in the collections of the Dept. of History and Archives of Montgomery Co. at the old Court House at Fonda, N. Y. 12068. Either original or copied church records of baptisms, marriages and deaths from old churches of the entire county have been preserved and catalogued there.

War Service Records - Colonial and Revolutionary war service records for New York State are in the custody of the Associate Librarian, Manuscripts and History Section, New York State Library, Albany 12200. War of 1812, 1860-65, Spanish-American, World War I and World War II records for this state are in the office of the Adjutant General, Bureau of War Records, 112 State St., Albany 12207.

Cemetery Records - The Manuscripts and History Section, New York State Library, Albany 12200, has a large collection of New York State cemetery records.

Guardianship and Orphan Court Proceedings - In custody of county surrogate's offices.

New York Libraries -- New York State Library (state and local

histories and genealogy), Albany 12200, (Albany);Public Library,
78 Exchange St., Binghamton 13901, (Broome); Public Library,
Grand Army Plaza, (Civil War Records), Brooklyn 11238,(Kings);
Long Island Historical Society, Library, 128 Pierrepont St., (local
and personal histories), Brooklyn 11201, (Kings); St. Johns Uni-
versity Library, 75 Lewis Ave., (Irish History), Brooklyn 11206,
(Kings). Public Library, 120 W. Eagle St, Buffalo, 14221; The
Grosvenor Library, Edward and Franklin Sts., (genealogy and
local history), Buffalo, 14202 (Erie). New York State Association
Library, (community and personal histories), Cooperstown 13326,
(Otsego). Cornell University Library, (collections on Iceland,
history of the states, Civil War), Ithaca 14851, (Tompkins).
American Irish Historical Society Library, 991 Fifth Ave., (Irish
in colonial America and later, genealogy, personal histories),
New York City 10028; Columbia University Libraries, 535 W.
114th St., School of Journalism, (newspaper files), N.Y.C. 10027;
Editor and Publisher Library, 1475 Broadway, (newspaper files),
N.Y.C. 10036; Fordham University, Duane Library, (early
American collections), N.Y.C. 10007; The Holland Society of New
York Library, 90 West St., (genealogical collections), N.Y.C.
10006; National Lutheran Council Library, 50 Madison Ave.,
(history of Lutheran Church in America), N.Y.C. 10038; New
York Genealogical and Biographical Society Library, 122 E. 58th
St., N.Y.C. 10022; New York Herald Tribune Library, 230 W. 41st
St. (newspaper collection), N.Y.C. 10036; The New York Historical
Library, 170 Central Park West, (genealogy, newspapers, local
histories of N.Y. Complete file of N.Y. City directories from 1786
to date), N.Y.C. 10024; The New York Public Library, Fifth Ave.
and 42nd St., (Irish History, Local History, British and American
Genealogies manuscript personal histories) N.Y.C. 10011; New
York Times Library, 229 W. 43rd St., (more than a million bio-
graphical files), N.Y.C. 10036; Sons of the Revolution Library, 54
Pearl St. N.Y.C. 10004; James T. White & Co. Library, 101 Fifth
Ave., (state, county and personal histories), N.Y.C. 10003; All
(New York). Public Library, 115 South Ave., (Rochester Historical
Society collection), Rochester 14604; University of Rochester Li-
brary, (Western New York history collection), Rochester 14627,
(Monroe). Public Library, 335 Montgomery St., (local histories
and genealogies), Syracuse 13202, (Onondaga).

Thousands upon thousands of volumes have been written about
New York people and communities and every library in the nation
has some of them on its shelves. Just to make a mere mention,
consider these, some of which are very valuable:

Barber, John W. and Howe, Henry. ''Historical Collections of
the State of New York.'' 608 pp. New York, 1841.

"Census of New York, 1790," First Federal Census. 308 pp.
Washington, D.C. 1908.

"New York Genealogical and Biographical Record," a quarterly magazine. Eighty seven volumes. 1870-1956.

"New York Historical Society Collections." Sixty six volumes.
1868-1923.

O'Callaghan, E. B. "Th Documentary History of the State of New York." Vol. I, 536 pp. A roll of names and surnames of 1689; N.Y. Army List of 1700; 1702, 1714 and 1720 Census of Orange, Dutches and Albany counties; 1703 Census of N.Y. City; inhabitants of Hempstead in 1673; roll of those taking oath of allegiance in N.Y. in 1687; inhabitants in 1698. Vol. II 1676 Assessement Rolls; 711 pp. Vol. III, Early Immigrants to New Netherlands, 1657-1664, and where they came from; restoration of N.Y. to the English; state of religion in province; names of some residents in 1737; papers relating to the Palatines and the first settlement of Newburgh, Orange Co.; Ulster County Freeholders in 1728; Quakers and Moravians; state of Anglo-American Church, 748 pp. Vol. 4, Journal of New Netherland, 1647; a description of New Netherland in 1644; 1663 massacre of Wildwyck, now Kingston; assessment rolls of the five Dutch towns of Kings Co., L. I. in 1675; census of Flat Bush, Flatt Lands, Gravesend, New Utrecht, Brockland, Bushwyck, Suffolk County, Dutchess County, and soldier lists, all of 1738; 674 pp. Weed, Parsons and Company, Albany, N.Y., 1850.

New York County Histories

(Population figures to nearest thousand - 1960 Census)

Name	Map Index	Date Formed	Pop. By M	Census Reports Available	Parent County	County Seat
Albany	B3	1683	273	1790-80	Original county	Albany
Allegany	D2	1806	44	1810-80	Genesee	Belmont
				(Co Clk has m rec from 1908 - 1935, div, civ ct rec; Clk of Surrogate's Ct has pro rec; Bureau of Vit Stat, Albany, N.Y. has b, m, & d rec)		
Bronx	B4	1914	1425		New York	Bronx
				(Co Clk has m, div, sup civ ct rec from 1914)		
Broome	C3	1806	213	1810-80	Tioga	Binghamton
				(Co Clk has m rec from 1908, div, civ ct rec from 1806)		
Cattaraugus	E2	1808	80	1810-80	Genesee	Little Valley
				(Co Clk has m rec from 1908, div rec from 1880, civ ct rec from 1850, also cen rec; Town & City Clks have b, m, d & bur rec; Surrogate's Ct has pro rec)		
Cayuga	C2	1799	74	1800-80	Onondaga	Auburn
Charlotte		1772			Albany (renamed Washington 1784)	
Chautauqua	E2	1808	145	1810-80	Genesee	Mayville
				(Co Clk has m rec from 1908)		
Chemung	D2	1836	99	1840-80	Tioga	Elmira
Chenango	C2	1798	43	1800-80	Herkimer, Tioga	Norwich
				(Co Clk has m rec from 1908 to 1935, div & civ ct rec from 1885; Surrogate Office has pro rec; Town Clk has b, d, bur rec)		
Clinton	A1	1788	73	1790-80	Washington	Plattsburg

Columbia   B3   1786   47   1790-80   Albany ..../........ Hudson
   (Co Clk has m rec 1908 to 1935, div & civ ct rec 1882, deeds & mtgs 1800)
Cortland   C2   1808   41   1820-80   Onondaga .... Cortland
Delaware   B3   1797   44   1800-80   Ulster, Otsego . . . . Delhi
   (Co Clk has few b rec in 1847, 48, div rec from 1914 & civ ct rec from 1886,
   soldier discharges from 1865 & church cert from 1843; Surrogate's office has
   pro rec)
Dutchess   B3   1683   176   1790-80   Original county . . . . . . Poughkeepsie
   (Co Clk has m rec 1908 to 1935, div rec from 1850, civ ct rec from 1847,
   deed & mtg rec from 1718, also collection of misc ancient documents in-
   dexed by name 1714 to 1800; Local registrars of cities and towns have b,
   m, & d rec)
Erie   D2   1821 1065   1830-80   Niagara . . . . Buffalo
   (Co Clk has m rec 1830 to 1935, div, civ ct rec from 1821)
Essex   A2   1799   35   1800-80   Clinton . . . . Elizabethtown
   (Co Clk has m rec 1908 to 1936, div, pro, civ ct rec from 1799)

County Map of New York

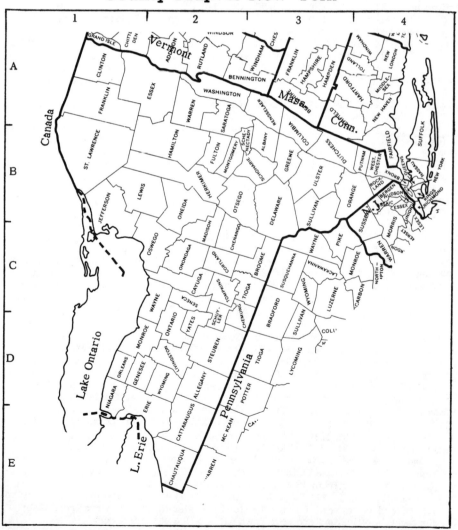

Franklin   A1   1808   45 1810-80 Clinton . . . . Malone
    (Co Clk has m rec from 1908 to 1935, some div rec from 1808 and civ ct
    rec from 1808; Surrogate Ct has pro rec; Various towns hold b, m, d rec)
Fulton   B2   1838   51 1840-80 Montgomery . . . . Johnstown
    (Co Clk has m rec from 1900 to 1926)
Genesee   D1   1802   54 1810-80 Ontario . . . . Batavia
    (Co Clk has m rec 1908 to 1934, div rec from 1802, civ ct rec from 1848,
    deeds and mtgs from 1802)
Greene   B3   1800   31 1800-80 Ulster, Albany . . . . Catskill
    (Co Clk has m rec from 1900 to 1935, div rec from 1800, also civ ct rec;
    Surrogate's office has pro rec; Town Clk have b, other m, d, and bur rec)
Hamilton   B2   1816   4 1820-80 Montgomery . . . . Lake Pleasant
    (Co Clk has m rec from 1908 to 1936, div, civ ct rec from 1835; Surrogate's
    office has pro rec; Registrar of Vit Stat has b rec; Town Clks have other m,
    and d rec)
Herkimer   B2   1791   66 1800-80 Montgomery . . . . Herkimer
    (Co Clk has m rec from 1908 to 1934, div & civ ct rec; Registrar of Vit
    Stat has b rec for village & town of Herkimer only)
Jefferson   B1   1805   88 1810-80 Oneida . . . . Watertown
    (Co Clk has m rec 1908 to 1933, civ ct rec from 1847, deeds Oneida 1795,
    Jefferson 1805, many other rec & censuses)
Kings   B4   1683 2627 1790-80 Original county . . . . Brooklyn
Lewis   B1   1805   25 1810-80 Oneida . . . . Lowville
    (Co Clk has b, d, m rec 1848 to 1850, div rec from 1847, civ ct rec from 1907,
    real estate rec from 1805; Various cem assn have bur rec; Surrogate's office
    has pro rec)
Livingston D2   1821   44 1830-80 Genesee, Ontario . . . . Geneseo
    (Co Clk has m rec 1908 to 1929, div & civ ct rec from 1878)
Madison   C2   1806   55 1810-80 Chenango . . . . Wampsville
    (Co Clk has m rec 1908 to 1935, div & civ ct rec from 1889, deeds from 1806)
Monroe   D1   1821 586 1830-80 Genesee, Ontario . . . . Rochester
    (Co Clk has m rec from 1908 to 1935, div & civ ct rec from 1860)
Montgomery B2   1772   57 1790-80 Albany (as Tryon to 1784) . . . . Fonda
    (Co Clk has m rec from 1908 to 1926, div rec from 1880)
Nassau   B4   1899 1300   Queens . . . . Mineola
    (Co Clk has m rec 1907 to 1935, div & civ ct rec from 1899; Village & Town
    Clks have b & d rec)
New York   B4   1683 1698   1790-80 Original county . . . . New York
Niagara   D1   1808 242 1810-80 Genesee . . . . Lockport
Oneida   B2   1798 264 1800-80 Herkimer (See Jefferson) . . . . Utica
Onondaga C2   1794 423 1800-80 Herkimer . . . . Syracuse
Ontario   D2   1789   68 1790-80 Montgomery . . . . Canandaigua

Orange   B4   1683 184 1790-80 Original county . . . . Goshen
    (Co Clk has m rec from 1908 to 1933, div rec from 1852 & civ ct rec; Town
    or City Clk has b, d & bur rec)
Orleans   D1   1824   34 1830-80 Genesee . . . . Albion
Oswego   C2   1816   86 1820-80 Oneida, Onondaga . . . . Oswego, Pulaski
    (Co Clk has m rec 1907 to 1935)
Otsego   B2   1791   52 1850-80 Montgomery . . . . Cooperstown
    (Co Clk has m rec 1908 to 1936, div rec from 1900, civ ct rec from 1891;
    Surrogate's office has pro rec; City, Town or Village Clk has b & d rec)
Putnam   B4   1812   32 1820-80 Dutchess . . . . Carmel
    (Co Clk has m rec from 1908 to 1935, div rec & civ ct rec from 1812)
Queens   B4   1683 1810 1790-80 Original county . . . . Jamaica
Rensselaer A3   1791 143 1800-80 Albany . . . . Troy
Richmond B4   1683 222 1790-80 Original county . . . . St. George
Rockland   B4   1798 185 1800-80 Orange . . . . New City
    (Co Clk has m rec from 1908 to 1935, also div & civ ct rec)
St. Lawrence B1   1802 111 1810-80 Clinton, Herkimer, Montgomery . Canton
    (Co Clk has m rec from 1908 to 1935, also div & civ ct rec from 1840;
    Surrogate's office has pro rec; Town Clk's office has b & d rec)

Saratoga   A2   1791   89   1800-80   Albany . . . .   Ballston Spa
    (Co Clk has m rec from 1908 to 1935, div & civ ct rec from 1791)
Schenectady B2 1809   153 1810-80   Albany . . . .   Schenectady
    (Co Clk has m rec 1908 to 1935, div & civ ct rec from 1809)
Schoharie   B3   1795   23   1800-80   Albany, Ostego . . . .   Schoharie
    (Co Clk has m rec 1908 to 1935, div & civ ct rec from 1898, deeds & mtgs from
    1797; Town Clk has b, m & d rec; Surrogate's Ct has pro rec)
Schuyler   D2   1854   15   1860-80   Tompkins, Steuben, Chemung . Watkins Glen
    (Co Clk has m rec 1908 to 1943, div, civ ct 1885)
Seneca   C2   1804   32   1810-80   Cayuga . . . . Ovid, Waterloo
    (Co Seat is Waterloo, Ct is held at Ovid in addition to being held at Waterloo.
    No rec are kept at Ovid; Co Clk has m rec from 1908 to 1925, div rec from
    1804, also civ ct rec from 1804; Surrogate's office has pro rec; Cem Com has
    bur rec; Town Clk's have b, m & d rec, they also have 2 vol of Hist rec)
Steuben   D2   1796   98   1800-80   Ontario . . . . Bath
    (Co Clk has m rec from 1908 to 1936, div rec from 1900 and civ ct rec 1796)
Suffolk   B4   1683   667 1790-80   Original county . . . . Riverhead
Sullivan   B3   1809   45   1810-80   Ulster . . . . Monticello
Tioga   C3   1791   38   1800-80   Montgomery . . . . Owego
Tompkins   C2   1817   66   1820-80   Cayuga, Seneca . . . . Ithaca
Tryon   1772   Albany (renamed Montgomery 1784)
Ulster   B3   1683   119 1790-80   Original county . . . . Kingston
Warren   A2   1813   44   1820-80   Washington . . . . Lake George
    (Co Clk has m rec 1908 to 1934, div & civ ct rec from 1813; Town & City Clk
    has b, m & bur rec; Surrogate Clk has pro rec)
Washington A2   1772   48   1790-80   Albany (see Charlotte) . . . Hudson Falls
    (Co Clk has div & civ ct rec from 1796)
Wayne   C2   1823   68   1830-80   Ontario, Seneca . . . . Lyons
    (Co Clk has div & civ ct rec from 1823, naturalization rec from 1855, maps
    from 1823; Town Clks have b, m & d rec; Co Hist has bur rec; Surrogate Ct
    has pro rec from 1823)
Westchester B4   1683   809 1790-80   Original county . . . . White Plains
    (Co Clk has m rec 1908 to 1935, div & civ ct rec from 1847)
Wyoming   D2   1841   35   Genesee . . . . Warsaw
    (Co Clk has m rec 1908 to 1933, div, civ ct, deeds from 1841, town, co, village
    maps from 1853, CW muster rolls from 1861)
Yates   D2   1823   19   1830-80   Ontario, Steuben . . . . Penn Yan

Genealogists' Check List of the Historical Records Survey,
New York

Federal Courts. Inventory of County Archives, Albany, Broome,
Cattaraugus, Chautauqua, Chemung, New York City (Bronx, Kings,
Richmond Borough & Co), Ulster. Inventory of municipal and town
archives, New York City (Bronx, Richmond).

Transcription of Public Archives. N.Y.C. (Newtown). Transcription of Early town records, town minutes of Newtown, Queens
county, Vol 1, 1656-1688, Vol 2, 1653-1734 Part 1 & 2 (Index in
Part 2). Town courts 1656-1690. N.Y.C. (Staten Island) earliest
Vol of records 1678-1813. Ulster County, 1 minutes of the Board
of Supervisors 1710/1 to 1730/1 - 2, records of the Road Commissioners Vol 1, 1722-1769, Vol 2, 1769-1795.

Guide to Public Vital Statistics (Inclusive of N.Y.C.) Vol 1,
birth records, Vol. 2, marriage records, Vol. 3 Death records.
Guide to Vital Statistic records of churches (exclusive of N.Y.C.)
Vol 1 & Vol 2. Guide to Vital Statistic records of churches in

N.Y.C., 1, Borough of Bronx, 2, Borough of Queens, 3, Borough of Richmond, 4, Borough of Manhattan, 5, Borough of Brooklyn.

Inventory of the church archives of New York State. Protestant Episcopal church, Diocese of Western N.Y. Doicese of Rochester. Inventory of the church archives of N.Y.C., Eastern Orthodox Churches and the Armenian Apostolic Church in America, Lutheran Church, Methodist Church, Presbyterian Church in the U.S., Protestant Episcopal Church Diocese of Long Island, Vol. 2 Brooklyn and Queens. Doicese of N.Y., Vol. 2 the Bronx, Manhattan and Richmond. Roman Catholic Church Archdiocese of N.Y. Vol. 2 The Bronx, Manhattan and Richmond. Society of Friends.

Guide to manuscript depository in N.Y.C. Guide to depository of manuscripts collection in N.Y. State. Guide to ten major depositories of manuscript collections in N.Y. State. Calendar of the Gerrit Smith papers in the Syracuse University Library, Vol. 1, 1819-1846, Vol. 2, 1846-1854. Check list of imprints of Sag Harbor, Long Island 1791-1820. Check list of American imprints of Batavia, N.Y. 1819-1876. Check list of Utica N.Y. imprints 1799-1830. A bibliography of books and pamphlets printed at Canadaigua, N.Y. 1799-1850 (Being Vol. 21, No. 4 of Grosvenor Library Bulletin, 62-107 p. printed 1939). Inventory of maps (Partial) located in various state, county, municipal and other public offices in N.Y. State.

Microfilm: (Filmed by N.Y.C. Historical Records Survey) American Loyalists Transcripts 1783-1790, N.Y. Public Library N.Y.C. Subject cards of U.S. History in N.Y., public Library card catalogue.

Depository of unpublished material. N.Y.C. Historical Society, (List & index of Early American Portrait Painters and American Slavery imprints). Columbia University Library (George D. White papers). Cooper Union for the advancement of Society and Art (Calendar of Cooper-Hewitt Papers). American-Jewish Historical Society (Directory of Jewish Cong U.S.A. and Yiddish Anthology). Modern Art Film Library (Film Index). N.Y. Public Library (Negros of N.Y.). N.Y.C. department of Health, Division of Vital Statistics (Public Vital Statistics). Municipal Reference Library, N.Y.C. (all other material on N.Y.C). State Library, Albany, New York (all other New York State material).

North Carolina

Capital Raleigh - State 1789 - (12th)

The first permanent settlement in North Carolina territory was established in 1653 when groups of settlers came south from

Virginia to occupy the section north of the Albermarle Sound. The influx of new settlers was so limited that in an eighty year period the population had increased only to about 14,000.

For several years prior to the Revolution, Highland Scotch immigrants were arriving frequently in the North Carolina section. Most of them established themselves in the southeast section. So rapidly did they arrive that in a few years there were more than 20,000 of them in that territory.

When large groups of Scotch-Irish departed from Pennsylvania down the Shenandoah Valley to settle in Virginia, many continued on into North Carolina. For religious reasons they had been banished from Scotland, where their strong Protestant views irked the religious leaders. Thousands of them were transplanted into Ireland, where they remained long enough to get an opportunity to come to the New World. Many of them established homes in the western section of the state, around the present region of Iredell county.

Many Germans came into North Carolina in the early days. In 1760 there were about 15,000 in Forsyth and Guilford counties. A colony of English speaking Quakers from Virginia, Pennsylvania, and Nantucket, Mass., settled in Rockingham, Guilford, and Chatham counties. Disliking slavery, they later moved to Ohio and Indiana. However, some of them remained and their descendants are still in North Carolina.

Before the Revolution, the Church of England was in "power" in North Carolina as in Virginia. Only the ordained ministers of that church were permitted to perform marriage ceremonies. Those who wished to marry could have their "banns" published or announced from the pulpit or they could buy a license. Those married by license had to furnish a fifty pound bond. Those old marriage bonds, many of which are still in the county court houses, are full of genealogical information. In the parish registers kept by the priests were records of births, deaths and marriages. Some of the old parish records are in the office of the State Historical Commission, though some are still in the offices of the County Clerk or the County Register of Deeds.

The National Archives have the Census schedules for all of the North Carolina counties. Almost half of the hundred counties were represented in the 1790 Federal Census.

North Carolina libraries - Public Library, 310 N. Tryon St., Charlotte 28202, (Mecklenburg); Duke University Library, (Southern history, lore, and newspapers), Durham, 27706, (Durham); North Carolina State Library, Morgan St., (South history and genealogy), Raleigh 27601, (Wake); Carnegie Public Library, Winston-Salem 27101, (Forsyth).

Books on North Carolina:

Allen, W. C. "The Annals of Haywood County, N.C.," historical, socialogical, biographical, and genealogical. 632 pp. 1935.

Crittenden, Charles Christopher and Lacy, Dan. "The Historical Records of North Carolina." Vol. I, 491 pp. County Records of Alamance through Columbus Counties. Vol. II, 568 pp. Craven through Moore Counties Vol. III, 760 pp. Nash through Yancey Counties. North Carolina Historical Commission, Raleigh, 1939.

Griffen, Clarence W. "History of Old Tryon and Rutherford Counties, N. C.," 1730-1936. 640 pp. The Miller Printing Co., Asheville, N. C. 1937.

Grimes, J. Bryan, "North Carolina Wills and Inventories," 587 pp. "Abstract of Wills, 1690-1760." 670 pp. Edwards and Broughton Printing Co., Raleigh, 1912.

Genealogists' Check List of the

Historical Records Survey,

North Carolina

County Map of North Carolina

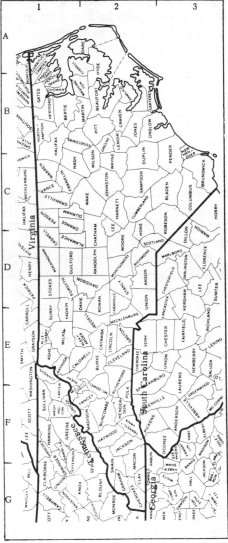

Federal Courts. Inventory of County Archives, Vol. 1 Almace thru Columbus, Vol. 2 Craven thru Moore, Vol. 3 Nash thru Yancey. Guide to Vital Statistic Records, Vol. 1. Inventory of State Archives, N.C. Historical Commission. Inventory of the church archives of N.C. Southern Baptist Convention, Allegany Association, Brunswick Association, Central Association, Flat River Association, Raleigh Association, Stanley, Association, Yancey Association.

Guide to Depository of manuscript collections in N.C. Guide to the manuscript collections in the Archives of the N.C. Historical Commission. Guide to the manuscript collections in Duke University Library. Guide to the manuscripts in the Archives of the Moravian Church in America, Southern Prov, Winston-Salem, N.C. Guide to the manuscripts in the Southern Historical Collection of the University of N.C. A calendar of the Bartlett Yancey Papers in the Southern Historical Collection of the University of N.C. List of the Papeles Procedentes De Cuba (Cuban Papers) in the Archives in the N.C. Historical Commission. Depository of unpublished material, Historical Commission, Raleigh, N.C.

North Carolina County Histories

(Population figures to nearest thousand - 1960 Census)

Name	Map Index	Date Formed	Pop. By M	Census Reports Available	Parent County	County Seat
Alamance	D1	1849	86	1850–80	Orange	Graham

(Clk of Sup Ct has div, pro & civ ct rec from 1849; Reg of Deeds has b, m, & d rec)

Name	Map Index	Date Formed	Pop. By M	Census Reports Available	Parent County	County Seat
Albemarle		1663			1 of 3 original cos. discontinued in 1739	
Alexander	E1	1847	16	1850–80	Iredell, Caldwell & Wilkes	Taylorsville

(Reg of Deeds has b, m, d & bur rec; Clk of Sup Ct has div, pro & civ ct rec)

Name	Map Index	Date Formed	Pop. By M	Census Reports Available	Parent County	County Seat
Alleghany	E1	1859	8	1860–80	Ashe	Sparta

(Clk of Sup Ct has div, pro, civ ct rec from 1863)

Name	Map Index	Date Formed	Pop. By M	Census Reports Available	Parent County	County Seat
Anson	D2	1750	25	1790–80	Bladen	Wadesboro

(CH burned 1868; Reg of Deeds has b & d rec from 1913, m rec from 1869; Clk's Office has div rec from 1868, pro rec from 1750, civ ct rec from 1770)

Name	Map Index	Date Formed	Pop. By M	Census Reports Available	Parent County	County Seat
Ashe	E1	1799	20	1800–80	Wilkes	Jefferson

(Clk has b & d rec from 1913, m rec from 1853, div, pro & civ ct rec from 1800)

Name	Map Index	Date Formed	Pop. By M	Census Reports Available	Parent County	County Seat
Archdale		1705			Changed to Beaufort 1712)	
Avery	E1	1911	12		Caldwell, Mitchell & Watauga	Newland
Bath		1696			Discontinued in 1739	
Beaufort	B2	1712	36	1790–80	Bath (Formerly Archdale)	Washington

(First named Pamtecough, formed 1705 changed to Beaufort 1712)

Name	Map Index	Date Formed	Pop. By M	Census Reports Available	Parent County	County Seat
Bertie	B1	1722	24	1790–80	Chowan	Windsor
Bladen	C3	1734	29	1790–80	New Hanover	Elizabethtown

(Clk of Sup Ct has wills from 1734; CH burned 1800–1893)

Name	Map Index	Date Formed	Pop. By M	Census Reports Available	Parent County	County Seat
Brunswick	C3	1764	20	1790–80	New Hanover, Bladen	Southport

(Reg of Deeds has b, m, d & bur rec; Clk of Sup Ct has div rec from 1900, pro rec & wills from 1858, civ ct rec from 1882)

Name	Map Index	Date Formed	Pop. By M	Census Reports Available	Parent County	County Seat
Buncombe	F2	1791	130	1800–80	Burke, Rutherford	Asheville

(CH burned 1830–1835)

Name	Map Index	Date Formed	Pop. By M	Census Reports Available	Parent County	County Seat
Burke	E2	1777	53	1790–80	Rowan	Morganton

(Reg of Deeds has b, d & bur rec from 1913, m, div, pro & civ ct & wills from 1865)

Name	Map Index	Date Formed	Pop. By M	Census Reports Available	Parent County	County Seat
Bute		1764			Discontinued in 1779	
Cabarrus	D2	1792	68	1800–80	Mecklenburg	Concord

(CH burned 1874)

Name	Map Index	Date Formed	Pop. By M	Census Reports Available	Parent County	County Seat
Caldwell	E1	1841	50	1850–80	Burke, Wilkes	Lenoir

(Clk of Sup Ct has div, pro, civ ct rec from 1841)

Name	Map Index	Date Formed	Pop. By M	Census Reports Available	Parent County	County Seat
Camden	A1	1777	6	1790–80	Pasquotank	Camden

(Clk of Sup Ct has div & civ ct rec from 1896, pro rec from 1912)

Name	Map Index	Date Formed	Pop. By M	Census Reports Available	Parent County	County Seat
Carteret	B2	1722	31	1790–80	Craven	Beaufort
Caswell	D1	1777	20	1800–80	Orange	Yanceyville

(Clk of sup ct has div, pro & civ ct rec)

Name	Map Index	Date Formed	Pop. By M	Census Reports Available	Parent County	County Seat
Catawba	E2	1842	73	1850–80	Lincoln	Newton

Chatham   D2 1771   27 1790-80 Orange .... Pittsboro
(Register of Deeds has b & d rec from 1913, m rec from 1771)
Cherokee   G2 1839   16 1840-80 Macon .... Murphy
Chowan   B1 1670   12 1790-80 Prec. Albermarle .... Edenton
(Chowan Co. was called Shaftesbury from 1671 to 1681)
Clay   G2 1861   6 1870-80 Cherokee .... Brasstown & Hayesville
Cleveland   E2 1841   66 1850-80 Rutherford, Lincoln .... Shelby
(Register of Deeds has b & d rec 1913, m rec 1851; Clk of Sup Ct has div & civ
ct rec 1868, pro rec 1841)
Columbus   C3 1808   49 1810-80 Bladen, Brunswick ...... Whiteville
(Reg of Deeds hav b & d rec from 1913, m rec from 1867; Clk of Sup Ct has
div & civ ct rec from 1868, pro rec from 1817)
Craven   B2 1712   59 1790-80 Prec. Bath Co. .... New Bern
(1810 census missing, was formed in 1705 as one of the precincts of Bath Co.
and was known as Archdale until 1712)
Cumberland   C2 1754 149 1790-80 Bladen .... Fayetteville
Currituck   A1 1671   7 1790-80 Albemarle .... Currituck
(Was called Carteret from 1671 to 1681) (1820 Cen missing CH burned 1842)
Dare   A2 1870   6 1870-80 Tyrrell, Currituck & Hyde ...... Manteo
(Reg of Deeds has b & d rec from 1913, m rec from 1870; Clk of Sup Ct has
div, pro & civ ct rec from 1870)
Davidson   D2 1822   79 1830-80 Rowan .... Lexington
Davie   D1 1836   17 1840-80 Rowan .... Mocksville
(Reg of Deeds has b & d rec from 1913, m rec from 1837; Clk of Sup Ct has
div rec from 1831, pro & civ ct rec from 1837)
Dobbs   1758   Johnston, discontinued 1791
Duplin   C2 1750   40 1790-80 New Hanover .... Kenansville
Durham   C1 1881 112   Orange, Wake .... Durham
(Clk of Sup Ct has div & civ ct rec from 1881)
Edgecombe   B1 1741   54 1790-80 Bertie .... Tarboro
Forsyth   D1 1849 189 1850-80 Stokes .... Winston-Salem
Franklin   C1 1779   29 1800-80 Bute .... Louisburg
(1820 census missing)
Gaston   E2 1846 127 1850-80 Lincoln .... Gastonia
(Clk of Sup Ct has div, pro, civ ct rec from 1846)
Gates   B1 1779   9 1790-80 Chowan, Hertford, Perquimans .. Gatesville
Glasgow   1791   Discontinued 1799
(Was formed from Dobbs Co. 1791, name changed to Green 1799)
Graham   G2 1872   6 1880   Cherokee .... Robbinsville
(Register of Deeds has b & d rec from 1913, m rec from 1872; Clk of Sup Ct has
div, pro, civ ct, wills from 1872)
Granville   C1 1746   33 1800-80 Edgecombe .... Oxford
Greene   B2 1799   17 1800-80 Dobbs or Glasgow .... Snow Hill
(CH burned 1876)
Guilford   D1 1771 247 1790-80 Rowan, Orange .... Greensboro
(CH burned 1872, many older rec still available; Clk of Sup Ct has b, & d
rec from 1913, m rec from 1872, div, judgement rec from 1900 and m bond
book from Nov 1771 to July 1868)
Halifax   B1 1758   59 1790-80 Edgecombe .... Halifax
(Reg of Deeds has b & d rec from 1913, m rec from 1888; Clk of Sup Ct
has div, pro & civ ct rec from 1868, wills from 1759)
Harnett   C2 1855   48 1860-80 Cumberland .... Lillington
Haywood   F2 1808   40 1810-80 Buncombe .... Waynesville
Henderson   F2 1838   36 1840-80 Buncombe .... Hendersonville
Hertford   B1 1759   23 1790-80 Bertie, Chowan, Northampton .. Winton
(Register of Deeds has b, d, bur rec 1913, m rec 1884; CH burned 1832-1862)
Hoke   C2 1911   16   Cumberland, Robeson .... Raeford
(Register of Deeds has b, m, d, bur rec from 1911; Clk of Sup Ct has div, pro,
civ ct rec from 1911)
Hyde   A2 1712   6 1790-80 Wickham, Prcs. Bath Co. ... Swanquarter

(Hyde Co was formed in 1705 and was known as Wickham until 1712 when name was changed to Hyde)

Iredell E2 1788 63 1790-80 Rowan . . . . Statesville
(CH burned 1854; Reg of Deeds has b, m, d & bur rec; Clk of Sup Ct has div, pro & civ ct rec from 1788, plus wills)

Jackson F2 1851 18 1860-80 Haywood, Macon . . . . Sylva
(Clk Sup Ct has div, civ ct, wills, rec of estates from 1851)

Johnston C2 1746 63 1790-80 Craven . . . . Smithfield

Jones B2 1778 11 1790-80 Craven . . . . Trenton
(CH burned 1862)

Lee C2 1907 27 Chatham, Moore . . . . Sanford

Lenoir B2 1791 55 1800-80 Dobbs . . . . Kinston
(Clk of Sup Ct has div, pro, civ ct rec from 1880; CH burned 1878)

Lincoln E2 1779 29 1790-80 Tryon . . . . Lincolnton

Macon F2 1828 15 1830-80 Haywood . . . . Franklin

Madison F2 1851 17 1860-80 Buncombe, Yancey . . . . . . Marshall
(Clk of Sup Ct has div, pro & civ ct rec)

Martin B2 1774 27 1790-80 Halifax, Tyrrell . . . . Williamston
(Clk of Sup Ct has div, pro & civ ct rec from 1885, wills from 1774; CH burned 1884; 1820 cen missing)

McDowell F2 1842 27 1850-80 Burke, Rutherford . . . . Marion
(Reg of Deeds has b, m, d & bur rec; Clk Sup Ct has div, Pro & civ ct rec)

Mecklenburg E2 1762 272 1790-80 Anson . . . . Charlotte

Mitchell F1 1861 14 1870-80 Burke, Caldwell, McDowell
            Watauga, Yancey . . . . Bakersville
(Clk of Sup Ct has div & civ ct rec from 1861)

Montgomery D2 1779 18 1790-80 Anson . . . . Troy
(CH burned 1835; 1820 census missing)

Moore D2 1784 37 1790-80 Cumberland . . . . Carthage
(CH burned 1889)

Nash C1 1777 61 1790-80 Edgecombe . . . . Nashville
(Reg of Deeds has b, m, & d rec; Clk Sup Ct has div, pro rec from 1860, civ ct rec from 1868)

New Hanover C3 1729 72 1790-80 Craven . . . . Wilmington
(CH burned 1798,1819,1840; 1810 cen missing; Reg of Deeds has b,m,d rec; Clk Sup Ct has div, pro & civ ct rec)

Northampton B1 1741 27 1790-80 Bertie . . . . Jackson
(Clk of Sup Ct has div rec from 1800, pro rec & civ ct rec from 1761)

Onslow B2 1834 83 1790-80 New Hanover . . . . Jacksonville
(Reg of Deeds has b & d rec from 1914, m rec from 1893; Clk of Sup Ct has div & civ ct rec from 1867, pro rec from 1792)

Orange C1 1752 43 1800-80 Bladen, Granville, Johnston ... Hillsboro
(CH burned 1789)

Pamlico B2 1872 10 1880 Beaufort, Craven . . . . Bayboro
(Register of Deeds has b & d rec from 1913, m rec from 1872; Clk of Sup Ct has div, pro, civ ct rec from 1872)

Pasquotank B1 1671 26 1790-80 Prec. Albemarle . . . . Elizabeth City
(CH burned 1862)

Pender B3 1875 19 1880 New Hanover . . . . Burgaw

Perquimans B1 1671 9 1790-80 Prec. Albermarle . . . . Hertford
(Perquimans Co was known as Berkeley Precinct from 1671 to 1681)

Person C1 1791 26 1800-80 Caswell . . . . Roxboro

Pitt B2 1760 70 1790-80 Beaufort . . . . Greenville
(CH burned 1857)

Polk F2 1855 11 1860-80 Henderson, Rutherford . . . . Columbus

Randolph D2 1779 61 1790-80 Guilford . . . . Asheboro
(1820 census missing)

Richmond D2 1779 39 1790-80 Anson . . . . Rockingham

Robeson C3 1787 89 1790-80 Bladen . . . . Lumberton
(Co Clk has b & d rec from 1913, m rec from 1868, div & civ ct rec from 1870)

Rockingham D1 1785   70 1790-80 Guilford . . . . Wentworth
  (CH burned 1906; Reg of Deeds has m rec from 1868, deeds from 1787, b &
  d rec from 1913; Clk of Sup Ct has wills from 1804; N.C. Hist Com has m rec
  from 1741 to 1868)
Rowan   D2 1753   83 1790-80 Anson . . . . Salisbury
Rutherford E2 1779   45 1790-80 Tyron . . . . Rutherfordton
  (Clk of Sup Ct has wills from 1790; CH burned 1857)
Sampson   C2 1784   48 1790-80 Duplin, New Hanover . . . . . . Clinton
  (CH burned 1921)
Scotland   D2 1899   25   Richmond . . . . Laurinburg
  (Register of Deeds has b rec from 1913, m, d, bur rec from 1899; Clk of Sup Ct
  has div, pro, civ ct rec from 1899)
Stanly   D2 1841   41 1850-80 Montgomery . . . . Albemarle
Stokes   D1 1789   22 1800-80 Surry . . . . Danbury
Surry   E1 1771   48 1790-80 Rowan . . . . Dobson
Swain   G2 1871   8 1880   Jackson, Macon . . . . Bryson City
  (Register of Deeds has b & d rec 1913, m rec 1907; Clk of Sup Ct has div, civ
  ct rec from 1900)
Transylvania F2 1861   16 1870-80 Henderson, Jackson . . . . Brevard
Tryon   1768   Discontinued 1779. See Lincoln)
Tyrrell   A1 1729   5 1790-80 Bertie, Chowan, Currituck,
                                    Pasquotank . . . . Columbia
  (Register of Deeds has b & d rec from 1913, m rec from 1862; Clk of Sup Ct
  has div rec, pro, wills from 1730 and civ ct rec from 1900)
Union   D2 1842   45 1850-80 Anson Mecklenburg . . . . Monroe
  (Register of Deeds has b, m, d & bur rec; Clk of Sup Ct has div rec, pro & civ
  ct rec from 1843)
Vance   C1 1881   32   Franklin, Granville, Warren . . Henderson
Wake   C2 1771 169 1790-80 Cumberland, Johnston, Orange . . Raleigh
  (1810 and 1820 census missing)
Warren   C1 1779   20 1790-80 Bute, Discontinued 1779 . . . Warrenton
  (Clk of Sup Ct has pro rec from 1776, civ ct rec from 1864)
Washington B2 1799   13 1790-80 Tyrrell . . . . Plymouth
  (Reg. of deeds has b & d rec from 1913, m rec from 1800, deeds from 1799;
  Clk of Sup Ct has div,pro,civ ct rec & wills from 1873)(CH burned 1862,1869,1873)
Watauga   E1 1849   18 1850-80 Ashe, Caldwell, Wilkes, Yancey . . Boone
  (Register of Deeds has b & d rec from 1914, m rec from 1872; Clk of Sup Ct has
  div, pro, civ ct rec from 1872)
Wayne   C2 1779   82 1790-80 Dobbs . . . . Goldsboro
Wilkes   E1 1777   45 1790-80 Surry . . . . Wilkesboro
Wilson   C2 1855   58 1860-80 Edgecombe, Johnston, Nash, Wayne . Wilson
Yadkin   E1 1850   23 1860-80 Surry . . . . Yadkinville
Yancey   F2 1833   14 1840-80 Buncombe, Burke . . . . Burnsville
  (Register of Deeds has b & d rec from 1913, m rec from 1833; Clk of Sup Ct has
  div, pro, civ ct rec from 1833)

North Dakota

Capital Bismarck - Territory 1861 - State 1889 - (39th)

Many Indian tribes roamed the Dakota plains when the white
man began to build the mid-section of the American continent.
Although explorers had visited the section off and on since the
early 1700's it was not until 1851 that the region was thrown
open for settlement.

The first settlers were attracted there by the highly productive Red River district soil. That river is the boundary line between North Dakota and Minnesota. Some hardy Scotch pioneers arrived as early as 1812 in Pembina. Farm folk from the northern European countries, especially from Norway, came there in large numbers in the mid 1800's. In the early days of the section, bloody skirmishes between the Redmen and the settlers were common place occurances.

The Dakota Territory was organized in 1861. It embraced the two Dakotas and Montana and Wyoming. In 1864 the Wyoming and Montana parts of the territory were formed into a separate section as the Montana Territory. The remaining Dakota Territory was divided about equally, north and south, into North Dakota and South Dakota about 1873. In 1889 North Dakota became the thirty-ninth state in the Union.

It was the vision of homes and fertile acres, big barns and cattle, that drew the poor peasants of northern and middle Europe to North Dakota. From Norway they came in the largest numbers, scattering over the state. They were accompanied by large groups of Swedes, Danes, and Icelanders, while numbers of Czechs, Poles and Dutch also came at that time. Previously French-Canadians came down from the north following the Red River. Many Germans and other Europeans settled around Bismarck and the south-central counties indicated by the many German place names in that area, like Leipzig, Strassburg, and Danzig.

Genealogical records are difficult to obtain in North Dakota. Some birth and death records are obtainable from the county offices. But in general they must come from the office of the State Registrar of Vital Statistics, Bismarck, North Dakota 58501. Marriage records are also on file there, but may also be secured from the Judge of the county in which the ceremony was performed, or from the Clerks of the District Courts who have charge of Civil Court, divorce and Probate matters and may also have the above mentioned birth and death records.

The Register of deeds has charge of deeds and land titles.
North Dakota Libraries - State Library, (North Dakota lore), Bismarck 58501, (Burleigh); Public Library, North Dakota Agricultural College Library, Fargo 58101, (Cass); University of North Dakota Library, (North Dakota and Scandinavian lore), Grand Forks 58201, (Grand Forks); Public Library, North Dakota State Teachers College Library, Minot 58701, (Ward).

County Map of North Dakota

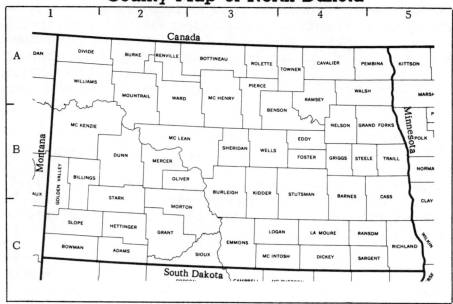

North Dakota County Histories

(Population figures to nearest thousand - 1960 Census)

Name	Map Index	Date Formed	Pop. By M	Census Reports Available	Parent County	County Seat
Adams	C2	1907	4		Hettinger	Hettinger
Barnes	B4	1875	17	1880	Cass	Valley City
Benson	B4	1883	9		Ramsey	Minnewaukan
Billings	B1	1879	2	1880	Unorganized Territory	Medora
Bottineau	A3	1873	11	1884	Unorganized Territory	Bottineau

(Clk of Dist Ct has b, m, d, bur, div, pro, civ ct rec from 1898)

Bowman	C1	1883	4		Billings	Bowman
Buffalo		1880			Disorganized 1873	

(See Burleigh, Kidder, Logan, McHenry, Rolette, & Sheridan.)

Burke	A2	1910	6		Ward	Bowbells
Burleigh	B3	1873	34	1880	Buffalo – discontinued	Bismarck
Cass	B5	1873	67	1880	Original county	Fargo

(Clk of Dist Ct has b, d, div, civ ct rec from 1885)

Cavalier	A4	1873	10		Pembina	Langdon

(Clk of Ct has m, pro, civ ct rec from 1881, div rec from 1888)

Dickey	C4	1881	8		Lamoure	Ellendale
Divide	A1	1910	6		Williams	Crosby

(Clk of Dist Ct has m, div, pro, civ ct rec from 1910)

Dunn	B2	1908	6		Stark	Manning

(Clk of Dist Ct has m rec from 1908, bur rec from 1943 & div, pro & civ ct rec)

Eddy	B4	1885	5		Foster	New Rockford
Emmons	C3	1879	8	1880	Unorganized Territory	Linton
Foster	B4	1873	5	1880	Pembina	Carrington

(Clk of Ct has b, d, bur rec from 1900, m, div, pro, civ ct rec from 1884)

Golden Valley	B1	1912	3		Billings	Beach
Grand Forks	B5	1873	49	1880	Pembina	Grand Forks

(Clk of Dist Ct has b & d rec from 1908, div & civ ct rec from 1878, also adoptions & change of names; Co Judge has m rec from 1887, pro rec 1880)

Grant   C2   1916   6   Morton . . . . Carson
    (Clk of Dist Ct has m, div, pro, civ ct rec from 1916)
Griggs   B4   1881   5   Foster . . . . Cooperstown
    (Clk of Dist Ct has b rec from 1881, d rec from 1904, div & civ ct rec from 1887)
Hettinger   C2   1883   6   Stark . . . . Mott
Kidder   B3   1873   5   1880   Buffalo . . . . Steele
La Moure   C4   1881   9   1880   Pembina . . . . La Moure
    (Clk of Dist Ct has b, m, d, bur, div, pro, civ ct rec from 1881)
Logan   C4   1873   5   Buffalo . . . . Napoleon
    (Clk of Dist Ct has b & d rec from 1940, m rec from 1890, bur rec from 1930,
    div & civ ct rec from 1888, pro rec from 1899, naturalization & citizenship
    rec from 1909)
McHenry   A3   1873   11   Buffalo . . . . Towner
McIntosh   C4   1883   7   Logan . . . . Ashley
McKenzie   B1   1883   7   Howard . . . . Watford City
McLean   B2   1883   14   Stevens . . . . Washburn
Mercer   B2   1875   7   Original county . . . . Stanton
    (Clk of Dist Ct has b rec from 1942, m, div, pro, civ ct rec from 1900 & d &
    bur rec from 1943)
Morton   C2   1878   21   1880   Original county . . . . Mandan
    (Clk of Dist Ct has b, d & bur rec from 1943, div, pro & civ ct rec from 1890;
    Co Judge has m rec from 1890)
Mountrail   A2   1909   10   1880   Ward . . . . Stanley
    (Old Mountrail formed 1873, annexed to Ward in 1891)
Nelson   B4   1883   7   Foster, Grand Forks . . . . . Lakota
Oliver   A2   1885   3   Mercer . . . . Center
    (Clk of Dist Ct has m, bur, div, pro & civ ct rec)
Pembina   A5   1867   13   1880   Indian Lands . . . . Cavalier
    (Clk of Ct has b rec from 1893, m rec from 1872, d rec from 1903, div rec
    from 1889, pro rec from 1875, civ ct rec from 1883)
Pierce   A3   1887   7   De Smet . . . . Rugby
Ramsey   A4   1873   13   1880   Pembina . . . . Devils Lake
Ransom   C5   1873   8   1880   Pembina . . . . Lisbon
    (Clk of Dist Ct has b & d rec from 1943, m rec from 1882, div, pro, civ ct,
    adoptions, name changes & criminal actions from 1881)
Renville   A2   1873   5   Deuel, Pembina . . . . Mohall
    (Co Judge has m & pro rec from 1910; Clk of Dist Ct has div & civ ct rec from
    1910, b, d & bur rec from 1943) (Co Clk says it was formed from Ward 1910)
Richland   C5   1873   19   1880   Original county . . . . Wahpeton
    (Co Judge has m rec from 1890, pro rec from 1876, mental health & feeble
    minded from 1919; Bureau of Vit Stat, Bismarck, N.Dak. has b & d rec; Clk of
    Dist Ct has bur rec from 1943; div & civ ct rec from 1883)
Rolette   A3   1873   11   Buffalo . . . . Rolla
Sargent   C5   1883   7   Ransom . . . . Forman
    (Co Judge has m rec 1887, pro rec 1895; Clk of Dist Ct has div & civ ct rec
    from 1901, b & d rec from 1943 & bur rec from 1948)
Sheridan   B3   1873   4   Buffalo . . . ., McClusky
    (Co Clk has b, m, d, bur, div, pro, civ ct & citizenship rec from 1909)
Sioux   C3   1914   4   Standing Rock Reservation . . . Fort Yates
Slope   C1   1915   2   Billings . . . . Amidon
    (Clk of Dist Ct has b, m, d, bur, div, pro & civ ct rec)
Stark   B2   1879   18   Unorganized Territory   . . . . Dickinson
    (Clk of Dist Ct has b, d, bur, div & civ ct rec)
Steele   B5   1883   5   Grand Forks . . . . Finley
    (Clk of Dist Ct has b & d rec 1894 to 1896, 1900 to 1901, div & civ ct rec 1886;
    Co Judge has m rec from 1883, pro rec from 1886)
Stutsman   B4   1873   25   1880   Pembina . . . . Jamestown
Towner   A4   1885   6   Rolette . . . . Cando
    (Co Clk has m rec from 1885, div rec from 1890, pro & civ ct rec from 1888)
Traill   B5   1875   11   1880   Grand Forks . . . . Hillsboro
    (Clk of Dist Ct has b rec from 1910, m rec from 1887, d rec from 1907, bur rec

from 1915, div rec from 1890, pro rec from 1882)
Walsh   A4 1881   18   Grand Forks   o o o o o o o o o o o Grafton
  (Clk of Dist Ct has bur rec from 1943, div & civ ct rec from 1884; Co Judge
    has m & pro rec; Division of Vit Stat, Bismarck, N.Dak. has b & d rec)
Ward   A2 1885   47   Renville . . . . Minot
Wells   B3 1881   9   Sheridan . . . . Fessenden
Williams A1 1890   22   Mountrail   o o o o o o o o o o o o Williston
  (State Health Dept, Bismarck, N.Dak. has b & d rec; Clk of Dist Ct has bur rec,
    div rec from 1900, also naturalization & veterans' discharges from 1900; Judge
    of Co Ct has m, pro rec)

Genealogists' Check List of the Historical Records Survey, North Dakota

Federal Courts. Inventory of County Archives, Golden Valley, Mercer, Williams. Guide to Public Vital Statistic records. Guide to Church Vital Statistic records. Bibliography of theses prepared at the University of N. Dak. Abstract and check list of Statutory Requisition for County records. Depository of unpublished material, State Library Commission, Bismark, S. Dak.

Ohio

Capital Columbus - State 1803 - (17th)

Prior to the mid-1700s the established American communities were located east of the Alleghenies along the Atlantic Coast. The constantly increasing population was ever on the alert for the best available land at the lowest possible cost. The presence of numerous Indian tribes prevented the land-longing immigrants from going too far away from the colonies established along the Atlantic sea coast.

For a long time the French and the British had quarrelled over the ownership between the Ohio River and Canada. After France had rescinded all claims to the territory and had transferred jurisdiction of the area to Britain, the United States claimed possession by virtue of its victory over the British in the Revolutionary War.

The idea then prevailed for a time that the boundary lines of the original colonies would be extended westward to include the newly acquired territory. After the creation of the Northwest Territory in 1787 that idea was discarded. Instead the central government decided the land should be used as bounty for the soldiers in the Revolutionary War and it was opened for settlement through the Ordinance of 1787 establishing the Northwest Territory.

Within sixty-one years five full states and part of a sixth had been created and admitted into the union from the Northwest Territory.

Massachusetts and Connecticut not-too-ardent Puritans formed the Ohio Company which purchased about a million acres of land for two-thirds of a dollar per acre, including what afterwards became Washington, Noble, Morgan, Athens, Meigs, and Gallia counties.

Known as the Virginia Military Bounty, about four and a quarter million acres were set aside between the Scioto and the Little Miami Rivers for settlement by Virginians and Kentuckians about 1800.

The Chillicote section in Ross county attracted many impatient and unrestrained Kentuckians and Tennesians.

Sometime later two other districts were thrown open to settlers. The first of these movements brought large groups of Scotch-Irish, Germans and Quakers from the neighboring Pennsylvania, across the Ohio to the section from which later were created Columbiana, Carroll, Jefferson, Harrison, Belmont, and Monroe counties.

The second of these migrations brought settlers from New Jersey floating down the Ohio and settling the area between the two Miami Rivers, the Little and the Big. They and some Scotch-Irish and Dutch began the cultivation of some 300,000 acres in that southwestern corner of Ohio. Cincinnati became an important part of that colonization.

After General Anthony Wayne and his United States' forces had driven the hostile Indian tribes westward from the Lake Erie section in 1794, another four million acre tract, known as the Western Reserve, was opened for settlement in the northeast corner of Ohio, along Lake Erie. It was settled mainly by former Connecticut residents. Closely allied with that project was the settlement of the half-a-million acres in what became the Erie and the Huron county just south of Lake Erie. The settlers of that tract were also former Connecticut residents whose holdings had been burned out by the British during the Revolutionary War. For that reason that section was often referred to as ''the Fire Lands.''

The ''Refugee Tract'' was set aside by congress for Canadians who had aided the American cause of the Revolution and had lost their lands in Canada. It was a tract 4 1/2 miles wide (N & S) and extended eastward from the Scioto River to near the Muskingum River. It was the proximity of Franklin, Licking and Perry counties. It was created 1801, effective 1802.

After 1815 the large north-western section of the state was thrown open to settlers who flocked there from east and south. The opening of the Erie Canal in 1825 brought more settlers along the route from the north-eastern states.

In 1799 Ohio was organized as a territory included in which was the Indiana Section. The very next year, Indiana was organized as a Territory, and in 1803 Ohio became a state, the seventeenth in the Union.

Birth and death records before 1909 are in the custody of the Clerks of the Probate Court in the respective counties and in the offices of the City Board of Health. From 1909 to the present the records are in the charge of the Department of Health, Columbus, Ohio 43215.

Marriage records and licenses are on file in each county office of the Clerk of the Probate Court, where are also records of wills and real estate matters.

Each County Recorder has charge of land records within the county.

Much genealogical information is obtainable in the following libraries:

Public Library, 11 Summit St., Akron 44308, (Summit); Public Library Association, 326 Third St., S.W., Canton 44702, (Stark); Chamber of Commerce Library, (historical collections), Public Library, 8th and Vine Sts., (Ohio Valley history and genealogy), Cincinnati 45202, (Hamilton); Pickaway County District Public Library, Main St., (Ohio history and genealogical collections), Circleville 43113, (Pickaway); City Public Library, 325 Superior Ave., (Ohio lore), 44114, County Public Library, 1150 W. Third St., 44113, Western Reserve Historical Soceity Library, 10825 East Blvd., Cleveland 44106, (Cuyahoga); Public Library, 96 Grant Ave., 43215, Ohioana Library, Ohio State Archaeological & Historical Society Library, State Library, State Office Bldg., Columbus 43215, (Franklin); Public Library, 215 E. Third St., (Dayton and Miama Valley collections), Dayton 74515, (Montgomery); Ohio Wesleyan University, (Ohio Methodists Historical Society), Delaware 43015, (Delaware); Miami University Library, (Ohio Valley history), Oxford 45056, (Butler); Public Library, (old Northwest Territory collections), Portsmouth 45662, (Scioto); Public Library, 325 Michigan St., (Northwestern Ohio history and Genealogy), 43624, University of Toledo Library, 2801 West Bancroft St., (American biographies and histories), Toledo 43606, (Lucus); City and County Library, 305 Wick Ave., (local history and genealogy), Youngstown 44503, (Mahoning).

Ohio County Histories

(Population figures to nearest thousand - 1960 Census)

Name	Map Index	Date Formed	Pop. By M	Census Reports Available	Parent County	County Seat
Adams	D2	1797	20	1820-80	1 of 4 Original counties . .	West Union
(Clk of Cts has div rec from 1910; Pro Ct has b & m rec)						
Allen	B1	1820	104	1830-80	Mercer, Indian Terr.	Lima
(Pro Ct has b & d rec 1867, m rec 1831; Clk of Cts has div & civ ct rec 1831)						

Ashland   B3 1846   39 1850-80 Wayne, Richland, Huron, Lorain . Ashland
Ashtabula   A4 1807   93 1820-80 Trumbull, Geauga .... Jefferson
Athens   C3 1805   47 1820-80 Washington .... Athens
Auglaize   B1 1848   36 1850-80 Allen, Logan, Darke, Shelby,
                                     Mercer, Van Wert ..... Wapakoneta
  (Clk of Cts has div, pro, civ ct rec from 1848)
Belmont   C4 1801   84 1820-80 Jefferson, Washington ... St. Clairsville
  (Clk of Cts has div & civ ct rec from 1820; Pro Ct has b, m, d & pre rec; Co
  Health Dept has bur rec)
Brown   D2 1817   25 1820-80 Adams, Clermont .... Georgetown
Butler   C1 1803 199 1820-80 Hamilton .... Hamilton
Carroll   B4 1832   21 1340-80 Columbiana, Stark, Harrison,
                                     Jefferson, Tuscarawas ... Carrollton
  (Clk of Cts has div & civ ct rec from 1833; Pro Ct has b, m, d & pro rec)
Champaign   C2 1805   30 1820-80 Greene, Franklin .... Urbana
Clark   C2 1817 131 1820-80 Champaign, Madison, Greene .. Springfield
Clermont   D2 1800   81 1820-80 Original county .... Batavia
Clinton   C2 1810   30 1820-80 Highland .... Wilmington
  (Clk of Cts has div & civ ct rec from 1810; Pro Ct has b, m & d rec from
  1810 to 1908, rec after 1908 are at Health Office)
Columbiana   B4 1803 107 1820-80 Jefferson, Washington ...... Lisbon
Coshocton   B3 1811   32 1820-80 Muskingum .... Coshocton
Crawford   B2 1820   47 1830-80 Old Indian Territory ...... Bucyrus
  (Clk of Cts has div & civ ct rec from 1834; Pro Ct has b, m & pro rec;
  Health Dept has d & bur rec)
Cuyahoga   A3 1810 1648 1820-80 Geauga .... Cleveland
Darke   C1 1809   46 1820-80 Miami .... Greenville
Defiance   A1 1845   32 1850-80 Williams, Henry, Paulding .. Defiance
  (Clk of Cts has div & civ ct rec from 1845; General Health Dist has d & bur
  rec; Pro Ct has b & m rec from 1845)
Delaware   B2 1808   36 1820-80 Franklin .... Delaware
  (Chancery Ct has div and civ ct rec from 1825)
Erie   A3 1838   68 1840-80 Huron, Sandusky .... Sandusky
Fairfield   C3 1800   64 1820-80 Ross, Washington .... Lancaster
  (Clk of Cts has div, civ ct rec from 1813)
Fayette   C2 1810   25 1820-80 Ross, Highland ...... Washington C. H.
Franklin   C2 1803 683 1830-80 Ross, Wayne .... Columbus
  (Clk of Cts has div rec from 1803)
Fulton   A2 1850   29 1850-80 Lucas, Henry, Williams .... Wauseon
  (Clk of Cts can furnish cert copies of div & civ ct rec; photo copies of b, m, d,
  bur & pro rec)
Gallia   D3 1803   26 1820-80 Washington .... Gallipolis
  (Clk of Cts has div & civ ct rec from 1860; Pro Ct has b & d rec from 1860 to
  1951, m & pro rec from 1803; Co Health Dept has b & d rec from 1951)
Geauga   A3 1805   48 1820-80 Trumbull .... Chardon
  (Clk of Cts has div, civ ct rec from 1806, naturalization rec from 1908; Pro Ct
  & Health Dept has b, m, & d rec)
Greene   C2 1803   95 1820-80 Hamilton, Ross .... Xenia
  (Pro Ct has b rec 1869 to 1908, pro & m rec 1803; Clk of Cts has div, civ ct,
  criminal rec 1802; Recorder has deeds & plat maps 1803; Auditor has tax rec 1803)
Guernsey   C3 1810   39 1820-80 Belmont .... Cambridge
  (Clk of Cts has div rec from 1850, civ ct rec from 1810; Pro Ct has b, m &
  pro rec; City-Co Health Dept has d rec)
Hamilton   D1 1790 864 1820-80 1 of 4 Original counties .... Cincinnati
Hancock   B2 1818   54 1830-80 Wood, Indian Lands .... Findlay
Hardin   B2 1820   30 1820-80 Indian Lands .... Kenton
Harrison   B4 1814   18 1820-80 Jefferson, Tuscarawas ..... Cadiz
  (Clk of Cts has div & civ ct rec; Pro Ct has b rec to 1917, m rec & pro rec;
  Health Office has b rec from 1917, d & bur rec)
Henry   A2 1820   25 1830-80 Wood .... Napoleon
Highland   D2 1805   30 1820-80 Ross, Adams, Clermont ..... Hillsboro

Hocking	C3	1818	20	1820-80	Athens, Ross, Fairfield . . . . . . Logan
Holmes	B3	1824	22	1830-80	Coshocton, Wayne,
					Tuscarawas . . . . Millersburg
Huron	**B3**	**1815**	**47**	**1820-80**	**Indian Lands (Firelands)** . . . . Norwalk
Jackson	D3	1816	29	1820-80	Pike . . . . Jackson
Jefferson	B4	1797	99	1820-80	Original county . . . . Steubenville
Knox	B3	1808	39	1820-80	Fairfield . . . . Mt. Vernon

(Clk. of Cts has div & civ ct rec from 1808; Pro Ct has b rec to 1908, m rec from 1803 & pro rec; City Board of Health has b rec from 1908 & d & bur rec)

Lake	A3	1840	149	1840-80	Geauga, Cuyahoga . . . . . . Painesville
Lawrence	D3	1816	55	1820-80	Gallia . . . . Ironton
Licking	C3	1808	90	1820-80	Fairfield . . . . Newark
Logan	B2	1817	35	1820-80	Champaign . . . . Bellefontaine

(Pro Ct has b & div rec from 1865; Co Recorder has deeds & mtgs from 1818; Histories, Logan Co Dist Library)

| Lorain | A3 | 1822 | 218 | 1830-80 | Huron, Cuyahoga, Medina . . . . . Elyria |
| **Lucas** | **A2** | **1835** | **457** | **1840-80** | **Wood, Sandusky** . . . . Toledo |

(Clk of Cts has div & civ ct rec from 1837; Pro Ct has b rec from 1865 to 1908, also pro rec; Bureau of Vit Stat has b rec after 1908 and d rec before 1935; Pro Ct has d rec after 1935)

| Madison | C2 | 1810 | 26 | 1820-80 | Fayette . . . . London |
| Mahoning | B4 | 1846 | 300 | 1850-80 | Columbiana, Trumbull . . . Youngstown |

(Clk of Cts has div & civ ct rec; Pro Ct has m & pro rec; Dept of Health, City Hall has b & d rec)

| Marion | B2 | 1824 | 60 | 1830-80 | Crawford . . . . Marion |
| Medina | B3 | 1812 | 70 | 1820-80 | Portage . . . . Medina |

(Clk of Cts has div, criminal & civ ct rec)

| Meigs | D3 | 1819 | 22 | 1820-80 | Gallia, Athens . . . . Pomeroy |

County Map of Ohio

Mercer   B1   1820   33   1820-80   Darke .... Celina
(Pro Ct has b & d rec 1867 to 1908, m rec from 1830, pro rec from 1829; Clk of
Cts has div & civ ct rec from 1824)
Miami   C1   1807   73   1820-80   Montgomery .... Troy
(Clk of Cts has div & civ ct rec from 1807; Pro Ct has m, d & pro rec; Health
Dept has b rec)
Monroe   B4   1813   15   1820-80   Belmont, Wash., Guernsey .. Woodsfield
Montgomery C1   1803   527   1820-80   Hamilton, Ross .... Dayton
Morgan   C3   1818   13   1820-80   Washington .... McConnelsville
Morrow   B2   1848   19   1850-80   Knox, Marion, Delaware,
                                         Richland .... Mt. Gilead
Muskingum   C3   1804   79   1820-80   Washington, Fairfield .... Zanesville
(Clk of Co Commissioners has div & civ ct rec from 1847)
Noble   C3   1851   11   1860-80   Monroe, Washington, Morgan,
                                         Guernsey .... Caldwell
Ottawa   A2   1840   35   1840-80   Erie, Sandusky .... Port Clinton
Paulding   B1   1820   17   1830-80   Indian Lands .... Paulding
Perry   C3   1817   28   1820-80   Washington, Fairfield,
                                         Muskingum .... New Lexington
Pickaway   C2   1810   36   1820-80   Ross, Fairfield, Franklin ... Circleville
Pike   D2   1815   19   1820-80   Ross, Highland, Scioto, Adams .. Waverly
Portage   B3   1807   92   1820-80   Trumbull .... Ravenna
(Clk of Cts has div & civ ct rec from 1820; Pro Ct has m rec)
Preble   C1   1808   32   1820-80   Montgomery, Butler .... Eaton
Putnam   B1   1820   28   1830-80   Old Indian Territory .... Ottawa
Richland   B3   1813   118   1820-80   Knox .... Mansfield
Ross   C2   1798   61   1820-80   6th Co. From N.W. Terr. ... Chillicothe
(Clk of Cts has div rec from late 1800 & civ ct rec)
Sandusky   A2   1820   56   1820-80   Huron .... Fremont
Scioto   D2   1803   84   1820-80   Adams, Washington ...... Portsmouth
Seneca   B2   1824   59   1830-80   Wayne, Franklin, Delaware .... Tiffin
Shelby   B1   1819   34   1820-80   Miami .... Sidney
(Clk of Cts has civ ct rec from 1819)
Stark   B3   1809   340   1820-80   Old Indian Lands .... Canton
Summit   B3   1840   514   1840-80   Portage, Medina, Stark ...... Akron
Trumbull   A4   1800   209   1820-80   Jefferson, Western Reserve ... Warren
(Clk of Cts has div, civ ct rec, naturalization & criminal rec from 1800, car
titles from 1937 & juvenile from 1953)
Tuscarawas B3   1808   77   1820-80   Jefferson, Muskingum .. New Philadelphia
Union   B2   1820   23   1820-80   Franklin, Madison, Logan,
                                         Delaware .... Marysville
Van Wert   B1   1820   28   1830-1960 Indian Territory .... Van Wert
(Clk of Cts has div & civ ct rec; Pro Ct has m & pro rec; Dist Board of Health
has b, d & bur rec)
Vinton   C3   1850   10   1850-80   Gallia, Athens, Ross, Jackson,
                                         Hocking .... McArthur
(Pro Ct has b & d rec from 1867 to 1950, m rec from 1850, pro rec from 1867;
Health Dept has b rec after 1950; Clk of Cts has div & civ ct rec)
Warren   C1   1803   66   1820-80   Hamilton .... Lebanon
Washington C3   1788   52   1820-80   Original county .... Marietta
(Clk of Cts has div & civ ct rec from 1795)
Wayne   B3   1808   75   1820-80   Columbian county .... Wooster
(The original Wayne county was established 15 Aug 1796, this county disappears
from Ohio in 1803 when Ohio became a state. It ultimately became Wayne
county Michigan. The present Wayne county Ohio was erected 13 Feb 1808)
Williams   A1   1820   30   1830-80   Henry .... Bryan
Wood   A2   1820   73   1830-80   Indian lands .... Bowling Green
(Clk of Cts has div rec from 1851, also civ ct rec; Pro Ct has b, m & pro rec;
Health Dept has d & bur rec)
Wyandot   B2   1845   22   1850-80   Marion, Crawford, Hardin,
                                         Hancock .... Upper Sandusky

Federal Courts: Inventory of County Archives, Adams, Allen, Ashland, Athens, Belmont, Brown, Columbiana, Cuyahoga, Fayette, Franklin, Geauga, Hamilton, Hancock, Jackson, Knox, Lake, Lorian, Lucas, Madison, Montgomery, Pike, Ross, Scioto, Seneca, Stark, Summit, Trumbull, Washington. Inventory of municipal and town Archives, Cleveland, Also records of Cuyahoga County municipal other than Cleveland.

Roman Catholic Parish of the Diocese of Cleveland. Inventory of the Church Archives of W. Va, Preliminary Bibliograph of material relating to churchs in W. Va., Virginia, Kentucky and Southern Ohio.

Calendar of the Joshua Reed Giddings manuscripts in the Library of the Ohio State Archaelogical and Historical Society, Columbus, Ohio. A check list of Ohio imprints prior to 1820. Historical Sites of Cleveland Hotels and Taverns. Depository of unpublished material, Western Reserve Historical Society, Cleveland, Ohio (Historic sites material). Hayes Memorial Library, Freemont, Ohio (Bibliographical material). Ohio State Archaelogical and Historical Society, Columbus, Ohio (All other material).

Oklahoma

Capital Oklahoma City - Territory 1890 - State 1907 - (46th)

"Westward" for the red man ended with Oklahoma when it became the last gathering place of the displaced Indian. Here the Indian gave up the nomadic existance of his forefathers and accepted the white man's mode of living.

Little significance attaches to the fact that Spanish and French explorers, in search of the proverbial pot of gold at the end of the rainbow, traversed the Oklahoma section time and again from 1590.

While the territory was still dedicated for the use of the Indians, white settlers came there in such hordes to secure land that eventually they had to be driven away by United States soldiers. The clamor for more land became so vociferous that the government purchased from the Indians about two million acres in the section adjacent to Logan and Oklahoma counties.

During the influx of new settlers, Illinois, Iowa and Kansas farmers seemed to favor the western and the northwestern sections of the state, while those from Arkansas, Missouri and Texas preferred the southern and the eastern parts of the state.

After Oklahoma became part of the United States with the Louisiana Purchase in 1803, it was included in the Indiana Territory. In 1812 it was combined with the Missouri Territory, and in 1819 with the Arkansas Territory. For several years, most of Oklahoma was included in what was called the Indian Territory, which continued until about 1893 when the section was divided into the Indian Territory and the Oklahoma Territory, the latter being thrown open to white settlements.

In 1890 the Territorial Government was established with Guthrie as its first capital. 1891 saw two new counties formed and in 1892 six more were formed. The Cherokee Outlet in the Northwest section of the state, next to the panhandle, was opened for white settlers in 1893. A court decision and an act of congress awarded Greer County to Oklahoma in 1896. Prior to that time it had been claimed by both Oklahoma and Texas. In 1906 Congress passed the enabling act. Oklahoma became the forty-sixth state to enter the Union when it was admitted 16 November 1907. The capital was moved from to Guthrie to Oklahoma City in 1910.

The first seven counties of the Oklahoma Territory were designated First, Second, Third, Fourth, Fifth, Sixth and Seventh, thereafter as other counties were added they were named after the letters of the alphabet. Later on by vote of the people they were given their present names. The original seven counties took the following names when this change was accomplished: Logan, Cleveland, Oklahoma, Canadian, Kingfisher, Payne and Beaver.

Birth and death records since 1908 are obtainable at the Department of Health, Division of Vital Statistics, Oklahoma City, Okla. 73105.

Marriage records may be obtained from the respective County Court Clerks, who also have supervision of all court and land records.

Books which might help you:

Johnson, Roy M., "Oklahoma South of the Canadian." Historical and biographical. Published by S. J. Clarke Publishing Co., Chicago, 1925. Three Vols.

Oklahoma libraries - Public Library, Muskogee 74401, (Muskogee); City Public Library, NW at Robinson, Oklahoma City 73102, (Oklahoma), Oklahoma Historical Society Library, Historical Bldg., (historical and genealogical collections), Oklahoma City 73105, (Oklahoma), State Library, 109 State Capital, (biography, genealogy), Oklahoma City 73105, (Oklahoma); Public Library, 220 South Cheyenne Ave., (Tulsa and Okla. histories), Tulsa 74103, (Tulsa).

We are indebted to Mrs. Merlyn Houck, Rt. 2, Stillwater, Okla. 74074, for information on the organization of counties in Oklahoma. In checking it with the information found in the 1953 Handy Book for Genealogists we noted considerable discord. A further check was made with other sources and these sometimes confirmed either one or the other and in some cases gave still different data. In the Oklahoma County Histories which follow you will find printed in parenthesis the data furnished by Mrs. Houck which does not coincide with that found in the 1953 Handy Book for Genealogists. In each case the information from Mrs. Houck is printed under the data in question.

Some additional light on the information of counties in Oklahoma has been forwarded by Sam M. Myers, Box 306, Stillwater, Okla., who writes as follows:

"All of Oklahoma except the extreme southwestern tip (Greer County) and No Man's Land and possibly the Unassigned Lands were Indian Territory until 22 April 1889. On this date the Unassigned Lands were thrown open for settlement in 'Run of 89'. Out of this, 2,000,000 acres were formed Logan, Oklahoma, Cleveland, Canadian, Kingfisher and Payne counties by Act of 2 May 1890 when Oklahoma Territory was authorized and at the same time Beaver County (No Man's Land) was made a part of it.

"The Iowa, Sac, Fox, and Pottawatomie, Shawnee Reservations were opened to form Lincoln and Pottawatomie Counties in the 'Run of 1891'.

"In 1892 the Cheyenne and Arapho Lands were opened and Day, Roger Mills, Beckham, Dewey, Custer, Washita and Blain Counties were organized out of it.

"The 'Strip' (Cherokee Outlet) opened in the 'Run of 1893', to form Woodward, Woods, Grant, Garfield, Kay, Noble and Pawnee Counties. In 1901 the Wichita-Caddo and Comanche, Kiowa and Apache Lands were opened and formed the counties of Caddo, Kiowa and Comanche.

"Generally this is the way things remained until 1907 when Oklahoma was admitted as the 46th state. When this happened there were some readjustments of county boundaries or new counties were added by carving them out of existing counties. In the case of Day County it no longer existed after statehood. A part of it and a part of Woodward County formed the new Ellis County. Roger Mills was formed out of a part of Beckham (and perhaps a part of Day). Woodward and Woods were reduced in area to form Harper, Alfalfa and Major. Out of a part of Comanche, Cotton County was formed also the Jackson County was formed out of Greer. (In 1908 or 1909 Harmon County was also formed out of Greer).

In that part of Oklahoma which has been an Indian Territory, before statehood called the 'Indian Nations', only the Osage and Seminole Nations were designated single counties of the same name. The other four Indian Nations were carved into the following counties:

CHEROKEE NATION: Washington, Rogers, Nowata, Craig, Mayes, Cherokee, Sequoyah, Adair, Delaware and part of Ottawa.

CREEK NATION: Creek, Okfuskee, Hughes, McIntosh, Okmulgee, Muskogie, Wagoner and Tulsa.

CHOCTAW NATION: Bryan, Atoka, Coal, Pittsburg, Haskell, Leflore, Latimer, Pushmataha, Choctaw and McCurtain.

CHICKASAW NATION: Grady, McClain, Pontotoc, Stephens, Murray, Johnston, Marshall, Love, Jefferson, and Carter.

In 1908 as previously stated Harmon County was created out of Greer and Jackson and thus were formed the 77 counties of Oklahoma as they exist today."

Oklahoma County Histories

(Population figures to nearest thousand = 1960 Census)

Name	Map Index	Date Formed	Pop. By M	Census Reports Available	Parent County	County Seat
Adair	A2	1907	13		Cherokee Lands	Stilwell
Alfalfa	D1	1907	8		Woods	Cherokee
Atoka	B3	1907	10		Choctaw Lands	Atoka
Beaver	E1	1890	7		Original county (Public Lands) . .	Beaver

(Co Clk of Cts has m, div & civ ct rec from 1890; pro rec from 1891; Division of Vit Stat, Okla City has b & d rec)

Beckham	E3	1907	18		Roger Mills	Sayre
Blaine	D2	1892	12		Original county	Watonga
					(Cheyenne–Arapaho Lands)	

('Ct Clk has m, div, pro, civ ct rec from 1892)

Bryan	B4	1907	24		Choctaw Lands	Durant

(Ct Clk has m, div, pro, civ ct rec; Co Health Unit has b rec; Funeral Homes have d & bur rec; Bureau of Vit Stat, Okla City has b & d rec)

Caddo	D3	1901	29		Original Lands	Anadarko
					(Wichita–Caddo Lands)	

(Co Ct Clk has m, div, pro, civ ct rec from 1902; State has b & d rec)

Canadian	C2	1889	25		Original county	El Reno

(Co Ct Clk has m rec from 1890, div, pro, civ ct rec from 1900, voting rec 1909)

Carter	C4	1907	39		Chickasaw Lands	Ardmore
Cherokee	A2	1907	18		Cherokee Lands	Tahlequah

(Co Clk of Cts has m, div, civ ct rec from 1907)

Choctaw	B4	1907	16		Choctaw Lands	Hugo
Cimarron	G1	1907	4		Beaver	Boise City
Cleveland	C3	1889	48		Unassigned Lands	Norman
Coal	B3	1907	6		Choctaw Lands	Coalgate
Comanche	D3	1901	91		Kiowa, Comanche, Apache Lands .	Lawton

(Co Ct Clk has m, div, pro, civ ct rec from 1901)

Cotton	D4	1912	8		Comanche	Walters

(Co Ct Clk has m, div, pro, civ ct rec from 1912)

Craig	B1	1907	16		Cherokee Lands	Vinita
Creek	B2	1907	40		Creek Lands	Sapulpa

(Co Clk has m rec from 1907, div, pro & civ ct rec)

Custer	D2	1890–08	21		Cheyenne, Arapaho Lands . . .	Arapaho

(Co Clk has m, div, pro rec from 1899, civ ct rec from 1894, real-estate, deeds, mtgs & releases, Army & U.S. Service rec from 1892, school cen from 1913 & Co Reg of Electors from 1916; Cem Assn has bur rec for each city; Bureau of Vit Stat has b & d rec)

Day		1892			Cheyenne-Arapaho Lands Discontinued 1906	

Delaware   A1   1907   13   Cherokee .... Jay
Dewey   D2   1892   6   Original county .... Taloga
                                  (Cheyenne-Arapaho Lands)
Ellis   E2   1907   5   Day, Woodward .... Arnett
   (Co Ct Clk has m, div, pro, civ ct rec from 1910, deeds & patents from 1898)
Garfield   C2   1893   53   Originally "O" changed to Garfield
                                  1901 (Cherokee Outlet) .... Enid
   (Co Clk has deeds & mtgs, Chattels from 1893, All service men's discharges
   from Spanish American War to present)
Garvin   C3   1907   28   Chickasaw Lands .... Pauls Valley
   (Ct Clk has m, div, pro, civ ct rec from 1908; Bureau of Vit Stat, Okla City has
   b & d rec)
Grady   C3   1907   30   Caddo, Comanche .... Chickasha
                                  (Chickasaw Lands)
   (Ct Clk has m rec from 1907, div & civ ct rec from 1895, pro rec from 1896;
   Division of Vit Stat, Okla City has b & d rec)
Grant   C1   1893   8   Original county .... Medford
                                  (Cherokee Outlet)
   (Ct Clk has m, div, pro, civ ct rec from 1893)
Greer   E3   1890   9   Org. by Texas, to Okla.
                                  by court decision .... Mangum
   (Organized as Greer Co., Texas in 1886. An act of Congress on May 4, 1896 de-
   clared it Greer Co., Okla. A fire in 1901 destroyed the county records. Co Ct
   has m, div, pro, civ ct rec from 1901)
Harmon   E3   1909   6   Greer, Jackson .... Hollis
   (Ct Clk has m, div, pro, civ ct rec from 1909; Bureau Vit Stat, Okla City has
   b rec from 1907 to 1909; m, div, pro, civ ct rec are kept by Greer Co Okla.)
Harper   E1   1907   6   Indian Lands .... Buffalo
                                  (Woods County)
Haskell   A3   1908   9   Choctaw Lands .... Stigler
Hughes   B3   1907   15   Creek Lands .... Holdenville
                                  (Creek and Choctaw Lands)
   (Co Ct Clk has m, div, pro, civ ct rec from 1907)
Jackson   E3   1907   30   Greer .... Altus
Jefferson   C4   1907   8   Comanche .... Waureka
                                  (Chickasaw)
Johnston   C3   1907   9   Chickasaw Lands .... Tishomingo
   (Ct Clk has m, div, pro, civ ct rec from 1907, before 1907 m, div, pro, civ ct
   rec are at Dist Ct Clk office, Ardmore, Okla)
Kay   C1   1895   51   Original county .... Newkirk
                                  (Cherokee Outlet)
Kingfisher   C2   1890   11   Original county .... Kingfisher
Kiowa   D3   1901   15   Original county .... Hobart
                                  (Kiowa-Comanche-Apache Lands)
   (Ct Clk has m, div, pro, civ ct rec; Bureau of Vit Stat, Okla City has b & d rec;
   City Clk office has bur rec)
Latimer   A3   1902   8   Choctaw Lands .... Wilburton
   (Ct Clk has m rec from 1906, also div, pro, & civ ct rec)
Le Flore   A3   1907   29   Choctaw Lands .... Poteau
Lincoln   C2   1891   19   Original county .... Chandler
                                  (Iowa-Kickapoo-Sac-Fox Lands)
   (Ct Clk has m, div, pro, civ ct rec from 1900; State Dept of Health, Okla City
   has b & d rec)
Logan   C2   1890   19   Original county .... Guthrie
Love   C4   1907   6   Chickasaw Lands .... Marietta
McClain   C3   1908   13   Chickasaw Lands .... Purcell
McCurtain   A4   1907   32   Choctaw Lands .... Ibabel
   (Co Ct Clk has m, div, pro, civ ct rec from 1907)
McIntosh   B2   1907   12   Indian Lands .... Eufaula
                                  (Creek Lands)
   (Co Clk has b rec from 1911 to 1948, d rec 1911 to 1918)
Major   D2   1907   8   Woods .... Fairview

County Map of Oklahoma

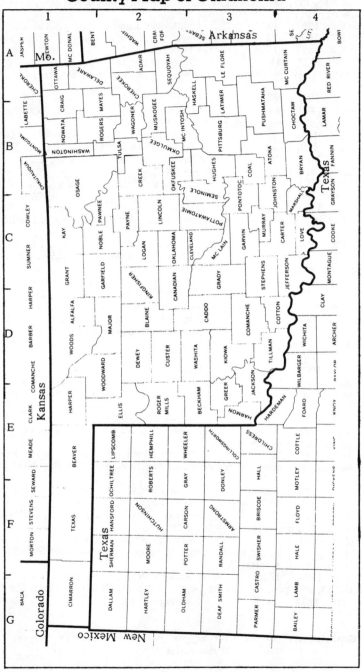

Marshall	C4	1907	7	Chickasaw Lands .... Madill
Mayes	B2	1907	20	Indian Lands .... Pryor

(Cherokee Lands)

(Ct Clk has m, div, pro, civ ct rec from 1907; Bureau of Vit Stat, Okla City has b, d & bur rec)

Murray	C3	1907	11	Chickasaw Lands	Sulphur
Muskogee	B2	1898	62	Creek	Muskogee
Noble	C2	1893	10	Cherokee Outlet	Perry
Nowata	B1	1907	11	Cherokee Lands	Nowata

(Ct Clk has m, div, pro, civ ct rec from 1907; Division of Vit Stat, Okla City has b & d rec)

Okfuskee	B2	1907	12	Creek Lands	Okemah
Oklahoma	C2	1890	440	Original county	Oklahoma City

(Co Clk has m, div, pro, civ ct rec from 1890)

Okmulgee	B2	1907	37	Creek Lands	Okmulgee
Osage	B1	1907	32	Osage Indian Lands	Pawkuska
Ottawa	A1	1907	28	Cherokee Nation	Miami

(Ct Clk has m, div, pro, civ ct rec from 1907)

Pawnee	C2	1893	11	Cherokee Outlet	Pawnee

(Ct Clk has m rec from 1893, div & civ ct rec from 1894, pro rec from 1911)

Payne	C2	1890	44	Original county	Stillwater

(Ct Clk has m, div, pro & civ ct rec from 1894; State Dept of Health has b and d rec)

Pittsburg	B3	1907	34	Choctaw Lands	McAlester
Pontotoc	C3	1907	28	Chickasaw Lands	Ada
Pottawatomie	C3	1891	41	Original county	Shawnee

(Pottawatomie-Shawnee Lands)

Pushmataha	B3	1908	9	Choctaw Lands	Antlers
Roger Mills	E2	1892	5	Cheyenne-Arapaho Lands ...	Cheyenne
Rogers	B2	1907	21	Cherokee Nation	Claremore

(Coo-wee-Scoowee Dist)

(Ct Clk has m, div, pro, civ ct rec from 1907; Bureau of Vit Stat, Okla City has b, d & bur rec)

Seminole	B3	1907	28	Seminole Indian Lands	Wewoka
Sequoyah	A2	1907	18	Cherokee Indian Lands	Sallisaw

(Ct Clk has m, div, pro, civ ct rec from 1907; Bureau of Vit Stat, Okla City has b & d rec)

Stephens	C3	1907	38	Comanche County	Duncan
Texas	F1	1907	14	Beaver	Guymon

(Ct Clk has m, div, pro, civ ct rec)

Tillman	D3	1907	15	Comanche Indian Lands	Frederick

(Ct Clk has m, div, pro, civ ct, criminal rec from 1907; Co Reg has b, d & bur rec)

Tulsa	B2	1905	346	Creek Lands	Tulsa
Wagoner	B2	1908	16	Creek Lands	Wagoner
Washington	B1	1897	42	Cherokee Lands	Bartlesville

(Ct Clk has m, div, pro, civ ct rec from 1907)

Washita	D3	1900	18	Cheyenne-Arapaho Lands ...	Cordell

(Ct Clk has m, div, pro, civ ct rec; Funeral homes have bur rec; State Health Dept, Okla City has b & d rec)

Woods	D1	1900	12	Cherokee Outlet	Alva

(Ct Clk has m, div, pro, civ ct rec; Dept of Vit Stat, Okla City has b & d rec)

Woodward	D2	1893	14	Cherokee Outlet	Woodward

Genealogists' Check List of the Historical Records Survey, Oklahoma

Federal Courts. Inventory of County Archives, Atoka, Beckham, Cherokee, Cimarron, Haskell, Lincoln, McIntosh, Mayes, Muskogee, Pittsburg, Pushmataha. Guide to Public Vital Statistics

Records. Inventory of the Church Archives of Okla. No. 7 Bryan County. Preliminary list of churches and religious organizations in Oklahoma. Check list of various records required by law in Oklahoma. Depository of unpublished material, State Library, Oklahoma City, Oklahoma.

Oregon

Capital Salem - Territory 1848 - State 1859 - (33rd)

John Astor's Pacific Fur Company originally settled the Oregon country in 1811 which was bought out by the Northwest Company of Montreal in 1813. This company was absorbed in the Hudson Bay Company in 1821. The earliest settlers were Canadian British and American who intermarried with the Indian population.

Simultaneously as the Mormon Pioneers were headed for the then uninviting Utah valleys as a refuge from religious persecutions, and the gold-seekers were rushing toward California, thousands of sturdy tillers of the soil who already had broken virgin soil in three or four different states were trekking toward the northwest with the same enthusiasm as those participating in the other movements. A steady stream of these prairie schooners headed toward the Oregon country for several years was attracted by a generous offer. In 1850 the Territorial Legislature of Oregon guaranteed settlers ownership of considerable tracts of land if for four years they would live on and cultivate those farm lands. At the time there were in Oregon slightly more that 13,000 people. The attractiveness of the free land offer is evident in the four-fold increase in population during the following ten-year period. Not only did people from many sections of the United States change their residences to Oregon, but people came there from all parts of the world. Among European countries whose people came there in large numbers are, in order of their numerical contributions to its citizenry, Germany, Sweden, England, Norway, Russia, Finland, Italy, Denmark, Ireland, Austria, Greece, and Czechoslovakia.

Oregon became a territory in 1848 when it also embraced all of the present Washington, Idaho and parts of Montana, Wyoming. It remained so for eleven years and in 1859 became the 33rd state in the Union. At that time it had been shrunk to its present size.

The State Registrar, State Board of Health, 1400 SW 5th Ave., Portland 97204, Oregon, has birth and death records since 1903 and marriage records since 1907. The County Clerks in the respective counties have marriage records since creation of county in some instances. The County Clerk also has custody of the records of wills and the administration of estates, deeds, and matters pertaining to real estate ownership.

Oregon Libraries - Public Library, 100 W. 13th Ave., Eugene 97401, (Lane); University of Oregon Library, (Oregoniana and manuscripts of the Pacific Northwest), Eugene 97403, (Lane); Library Association of Portland, 801 SW 10th Ave, Portland 97205, (Multnomah); Oregon Historical Society Library, 235 SW Market St., (newspapers and manuscripts, Pacific North-west lore), Portland 97201, (Multnomah); The Oregon State Library, State Library Bldg., (genealogy, Northwest History, Oregoniana), Salem 97310, (Marion).

The Genealogical Forum of Portland, Oregon, 2515 N. E. 40th Avenue, Portland, Oregon 97212, "will endeavor to answer queries which involve a limited amount of research if a stamped self-addressed envelope accompanies the request."

Oregon County Histories

(Population figures to nearest thousand - 1960 Census)

Name	Map Index	Date Formed	Pop. By M	Census Reports Available	Parent County	County Seat
Baker	A2	1862	17	1905	Wasco	. Baker
(Co Clk has m, div, pro, civ ct rec from 1862; State Board of Health, Portland has b & d rec)						
Benton	E2	1847	39	1850-80	Polk	Corvallis
(Co Clk has m & div rec from 1850)						
Champoeg		1843			Orig. Co., (Name changed to Marion)	
Clackamas	D1	1843	113	1850-80	Original county	Oregon City
(Co Clk has m rec from 1853, div & civ ct rec from 1850, pro rec from 1844, deeds & mtgs from 1850, terr. from 1842)						
Clark				1850 (Now part of state of Washington)		
Clatsop	E1	1844	27	1850-80	Twality	Astoria
Columbia	E1	1854	22	1860-80	Washington	St. Helens
(Co Clk has m, div, pro, civ ct rec from 1854)						
Coos	F3	1853	55	1860-80	Umpqua, Jackson	Coquille
(Co Clk has m rec from 1864, div, pro, civ ct rec from 1853)						
Crook	C2	1882	9		Wasco	Prineville
Curry	F4	1855	14	1860-80	Coos	Gold Beach
(Co Clk has m, div, pro, civ ct rec; State Board of Health, Portland has b & d rec; Various cem have bur rec)						
Deschutes	D3	1916	23		Crook	Bend
(Co Clk has m, div, pro, civ ct rec from 1916; State Board of Health, Portland has b & d rec)						
Douglas	E3	1852	70	1860-80	Umpqua 1852 & 1862	Roseburg
(Co Clk has m rec from 1852, div & civ ct rec from 1862, pro rec from 1863; State Board of Health, Portland has b & d rec)						
Gilliam	C1	1885	3		Wasco, Morrow	Condon
Grant	B2	1864	8	1870	Wasco, Umatilla	Canyon City
(Co Clk has m, bur, div, pro, civ ct rec from 1864, b & d rec from 1915)						
Harney	B3	1889	7		Grant	Burns
(Co Clk has m, div, pro, civ ct rec from 1889; State Board of Health, Portland has b & d rec)						
Hood River	D1	1908	13		Wasco	Hood River
(Co Clk has m, div, pro, civ ct rec from 1908; State has b, d & bur rec)						

Jackson   E4   1852   87   1860-80   Umpqua   .... Medford
    (Co Clk has m rec from 1855, div & civ ct rec from 1861, pro rec from 1874,
    deeds, mtgs, mining rec from 1854; funeral homes have bur rec; State Board
    of Health, Portland has b & d rec)
Jefferson   D2   1914   7   Crook   .... Madras
    (Co Clk has m, div, pro, civ ct rec from 1915)
Josephine   E4   1856   30   1860-80   Jackson   .... Grants Pass
    (Co Clk has m, civ ct, crim ct rec from 1867, div & pro rec from 1868;
    State Bureau of Vit Stat, Portland has b & d rec)
Klamath   D4   1882   47   West part of Lake Co.   ... Klamath Falls
Lake   C4   1874   7   1880   Jackson, Wasco   .... Lakeview

County Map of Oregon

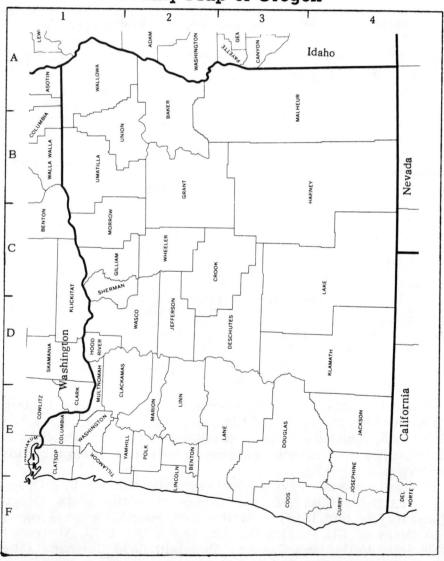

(Co Clk has m, div, pro, civ ct rec from 1875; State Board of Health, Portland has b & d rec)

Lane	E3	1845	163	1860-80	Linn, Benton	Eugene
Lewis					1850 (Now part of state of Washington)	
Lincoln	E2	1893	25		Benton, Polk	Newport

(Co Clk has m, div, pro, civ ct rec from 1893)

Linn   E2   1847   62   1850-80   Champoeg   . . . .   Albany
(Co Clk has m rec from 1850, div, pro, civ ct rec from 1854, military enumeration of 1905; State Board of Health has b & d rec)

Malheur   A3   1887   23   Baker . . . .   Vale
(Co Clk has m, div, pro, civ ct rec from 1887)

Marion   E2   1843   139   1850-80   Orig. Co. Name changed from
                                          Champoeg   . . . .   Salem
(Co Clk has m rec from 1847, also civ ct, pro, div rec; State Board of Health Portland has b & d rec)

Morrow   D1   1865   5   1870-80   Umatilla . . . .   Heppner
(Co Clk has m, pro, div & civ ct rec from 1885; State Board of Health, Portland has b & d rec)

Multnomah   E1   1854   523   1860-80   Washington, Clackamas . . . .   Portland
Polk   E2   1845   27   1850-80   Yamhill . . . .   Dallas
(Co Clk has m rec from 1850, div & pro rec from 1898)

Sherman   C1   1889   2   Wasco . . . .   Moro
(Co Clk has m & pro rec from 1889, b rec from 1904 to 1939, d rec from 1905 to 1952, civ ct rec from 1894)

Tillamook   E1   1853   19   1860-80   Clatsop, Polk, Yamhill . . . . .   Tillamock
(Co Clk has m rec from 1862, div , pro, civ ct rec from 1860)

Twality   Changed to Washington 1849

Umatilla   B1   1862   44   1870-80   Wasco . . . .   Pendleton
(Co Clk has m, div, pro, civ ct rec from 1862)

Umpqua   1851   1860   Benton & Linn (absorbed by Douglas 1863)

Union   B1   1864   18   1870-80   Baker . . . .   La Grande
(Co Clk has m, div, pro, civ ct rec from 1864)

Wallowa   A1   1887   7   Union . . . .   Enterprise

Wasco   D2   1854   20   1860-80   Clackamas, Marion, Linn, Lane,
                                          Douglas, Jackson . . . . The Dalles
(Co Clk has m, div, pro, civ ct rec from 1854; State Board of Health, Portland has b, d & bur rec)

Washington   E1   1843   92   1850-80   Orig Co formerly Twality . . . Hillsboro
(Co Clk has m rec from 1852, div & civ ct rec from 1893, pro rec from 1874)

Wheeler   C2   1899   3   Crook, Gilliam, Grant . . . .   Fossil
(Co Clk has m, div, pro, civ ct rec from 1899)

Yamhill   E2   1843   33   1850-80   Original County   . . . .   McMinnville
(Co Clk has m, div, pro, & civ ct rec from 1857)

Genealogists' Check List of the Historical Records Survey, Oregon

Federal Courts. Inventory of County Archives, Benton, Clatsop, Coos, Hood River, Josephine, Klamath, Linn, Morrow, Multnomah, Tillamock, Umatilla, Wasco, Washington. Guide to Public Vital Statistic records. Directory of church and religious organizations of Oregon.

Guides to depository of manuscript collections in U.S. Oregon and Washington. Guide to manuscript collection of the Oregon Historical Society. Diary of Basil N. Longsworth, Oregon Pioneer, The Diary of Eli Sheldon Glover, Oct - Dec 1875; Abstract of Wilamette Valley and Cascade Mountain Road Company 1864-

1911. Corvallis to Cresent City, Calif. in 1874. Daily Sales of
an Auburn Store in 1868. Letter form Lukiamute Valley in 1846.

Description of County Offices in Oregon and check list of their
records. Guide to the Angelus Studio Collection of Historical
Photos. Records of Married Women's Separate Property in Baker
County. Transportation items from the Weekly Oregonian 1852-
1862. Ship register and enrollments of Marshfield, Oregon 1873-
1941. Ship register and enrollments of Portland, Oregon 1867-
1941. Depository of unpublished material, University of Oregon,
Eugene, Oregon.

Pennsylvania

Capital Harrisburg - State 1787 - (2nd)

Give me your tired, your poor,
  Your huddled masses yearning to breathe free,
The wretched refuse of your teeming shore.
  Send these, the homeless, tempest-tost to me.
I lift my lamp beside the golden door.

Long before the Statue of Liberty had been comtemplated or
Emma Lazarus had written these immortal lines for its pedestal,
William Penn extended an invitation to Europe's religiously persecuted and exiled to come to Pennsylvania where he had established a haven of religious freedom and liberty.

Responding to the earnest solicitation the Society of Friends, or
Quakers, came from England, Scotland, Ireland and Wales; the
severely persecuted Palatines came from the Rhine section; the
Anabaptists, or Mennonites, arrived from Germany and Switzerland; the Church of the Brethren, or Dunkards, so called from
their belief in triple baptism, came from Germany in 1721; the
Roman Catholics from England came there in 1732; the Moravians, or Czech followers of John Huss, came from Moravia
and Bohemia to Pennsylvania via Georgia in 1740 and the so-
called Dutch, who were Germans, not Hollanders.

With the rapidly advancing mineral and business developments
in the early 1800s tens of thousands of workers came from Europe
in the following numerical strength, according to Bureau of
Census figures: Italians, Poles, Russians, Austrians, Germans,
Czechs, English, Irish, Hungarians, Swedes, Greeks, French,
Norwegians, Danes, and Finns.

The Pennsylvania Historical & Museum Commission of Harrisburg has been microfilming early wills, orphans' court, deed and
tax records of Pennsylvania counties. The Division of Public

Records holds copies of these records but they have no staff to search them. Microfilm readers are available, however, for those wishing to do their own research. If certified copies of the records are desired you will have to get them from the county which holds the original record as the films are classed as unofficial.

On the north bank of the Susquehanna River for a distance of 20 miles is the three mile wide Wyoming Valley. Here is the highly industrialized city of Wilkes-Barre and numerous rich anthracite coal mines. In 1778 this section was an incorporated county in the colony of Connecticut. More than 200 settlers were killed that year in the Pennamite-Yankee War fought between the colonists of Connecticut and Pennsylvania. The dispute was finally settled by Congress in 1782 in what is known as the Decree of Trenton. Researchers looking for material from the Wyoming Valley prior to 1782 must search for it in Hartford, Connecticut.

Marriage licenses were first issued in Pennsylvania about 1883. Birth and death records have been kept since 1892. Until 1906 these records were kept in their respective counties, since then they have been under the direction of the Bureau of Vital Statistics at Harrisburg, Pennsylvania. The marriage licenses are kept at the office of the clerks of the respective counties. From 1852 to 1856 birth and death records were also recorded in the counties. The birth records give the names of other children in the family.

Pennsylvania libraries - State Library (genealogical department), Harrisburg 17126, (Dauphin); Franklin and Marshall College, Fackenthal Library, (state history and biography), Lancaster 17603, (Lancaster); American Swedish Historical Foundation Library, 19th and Pattison Ave., (biographies of Swedish American), Philadelphia 19148, (Philadelphia); The Free Library of Philadelphia, Logan Square, (Western manuscripts), Philadelphia 19141, (Philadelphia); The Historical Society of Pennsylvania, 1300 Locust St., (biographies and genealogies), Philadelphia 19107, (Philadelphia); Carnegie Free Public Library of Allegheny, Federal and Ohio Sts., (histories of Pittsburgh and Pennsylvania), Pittsburgh 15212, (Allegheny); Carnegie Library of Pittsburgh, 4400 Forbes St., (histories and biographies, Pittsburgh newspapers from 1768), Pittsburgh 15213, (Allegheny); Public Library, Fifth and Franklin Sts., (material on Pennsylvania Dutch), Reading 19602, (Berks); The Pennsylvania State Library, (histories and genealogies), State College 16801, (Centre); Osterhout Free Public Library, 71 S. Franklin St., (local history), Wilkes-Barre 18701 (Luzerne); Martin Memorial Public & York County Library, 159 E. Market St., York 17401, (York).

Pennsylvania County Histories

(Population figures to nearest thousand - 1960 Census)

Name	Map Index	Date Formed	Pop. By M	Census Reports Available	Parent County	County Seat
Adams	C3	1800	52	1800-80	York	Gettysburg
Allegheny	C1	1788	1629	1790-80	Westmoreland, Washington	Pittsburgh
Armstrong	B1	1800	80	1800-80	Allegheny, Indiana, Clarion, Butler Jefferson, Westmoreland	Kittanning

(Co Clk has div, pro, civ ct, naturalization rec from 1800)

Beaver	B1	1800	207	1800-80	Allegheny, Washington	Beaver

(Co Clk has b rec 1893 to 1907, m rec 1885, d rec 1834, bur rec 1852 to 1855 & 1893 to 1907, div rec 1805, pro rec 1800, civ ct rec 1797)

Bedford	C2	1771	42	1790-80	Cumberland	Bedford

(Clk of Cts has b & d rec 1893 to 1906, m rec 1885, div rec 1804, pro rec 1772, Civ ct rec 1771)

Berks	B4	1752	275	1790-80	Bucks, Chester, Lancaster, Philadelphia	Reading

(Co Clk has b & d rec from 1894 to 1906, div rec from 1800, m rec from 1885, pro & orphan Ct rec from 1752)

Blair	C2	1846	137	1850-80	Huntingdon, Bedford	Hollidaysburg

(Co Clk has b rec 1893 to 1905, m rec 1885, div rec 1846, civ ct rec 1846)

Bradford	A3	1812	55	1820-80	Luzerne, Lycoming	Towanda

(Originally Ontario, changed 1812; Co Clk has b & d rec from 1892 to 1906 m rec, div rec from 1870, pro & civ ct rec from 1850; From 1906 to date, b & d rec are at Harrisburg, Pa.)

Bucks	B4	1682	309	1790-80	Original county	Doylestown

(Orphans Ct has b & d rec 1893 to 1906, m rec 1885; Prothontary has div rec 1878, civ ct rec 1682; Register of Wills has pro rec 1684)

Butler	B1	1800	115	1800-80	Allegheny	Butler

(Chief Co Clk has b rec from 1893 to 1906, m rec 1885, div, pro, civ ct rec 1800)

Cambria	B2	1804	210	1810-80	Somerset, Bedford, Huntingdon	Ebensburg
Cameron	A2	1860	8	1870-80	Clinton, Elk, McKean, Potter	Emporium

(Clk of Ct has m & div rec)

Carbon	B4	1843	53	1850-80	Northampton, Monroe	Jim Thorpe

(Chief Co Clk has m rec from 1883, div, pro, civ ct rec from 1843)

Centre	B2	1800	79	1800-80	Lycoming, Mifflin, Northumberland, Huntingdon	Bellefonte

(Co Clk has b & bur rec 1893 to 1906, m rec from 1885, d rec 1885 to 1906, div, pro, civ ct rec from 1800)

Chester	C4	1682	211	1790-80	Original county	W. Chester

(Co Clk has div rec from 1840, civ ct rec from 1780)

Clarion	B1	1839	37	1850-80	Venango, Armstrong	Clarion
Clearfield	B2	1804	82	1810-80	Huntingdon, Lycoming	Clearfield
Clinton	B2	1839	38	1840-80	Lycoming, Centre	Lock Haven
Columbia	B3	1813	53	1820-80	Northumberland	Bloomsburg

(Co Clk has b rec 1893 to 1905, m rec from 1885, div & civ ct rec from 1813)

Crawford	A1	1800	78	1800-80	Allegheny	Meadville

(Co Clk has b & d rec from 1893 to 1905, m rec from 1885; Reg of Wills & Recorder of Deeds holds pro rec; Bureau of Vit Stat, Harrisburg, Pa. has b & d rec from 1906)

Cumberland	C3	1750	125	1790-80	Lancaster	Carlisle
Dauphin	C3	1785	220	1790-80	Lancaster	Harrisburg
Delaware	C4	1789	553	1790-80	Chester	Media
Elk	A2	1843	37	1850-80	Jefferson, McKean, Clearfield	Ridgway

(Clk of Orphans Ct has b rec 1893 to 1906, m rec from 1895)

Erie	A1	1800	251	1800-80	Allegheny	Erie

(Co Commissioners Clk has b rec from 1893 to 1905, m rec from 1885, estate & pro rec from 1823)

Fayette	C1	1783	169	1790-80	Westmoreland	Uniontown
Forest	A1	1848	4	1860-80	Jefferson, Venango	Tionesta

Franklin   C2   1784   88 1790-80 Cumberland . . . . Chambersburg
   (Co Clk has b rec 1893 to 1906, d rec 1894 to 1906, m & div rec 1885, pro rec
   1784, civ ct rec 1840, deeds 1784)
Fulton   C2   1850   11 1850-80 Bedford . . . . McConnellsburg
   (Clk of Orphans Ct has b & d rec 1895 to 1905, m rec 1885; Prothonotary has
   div & civ ct rec 1850; Register of Wills has pro rec 1850; Recorder of Deeds has
   deeds from 1850)
Greene   C1   1796   39 1800-80 Washington . . . . Waynesburg
   (Clk of Cts has b & d rec 1893 to 1915, m rec 1885, Prothonotary has div & civ
   ct rec 1797; Register has pro rec 1797)
Huntingdon   C2   1787   39 1790-80 Bedford . . . . Huntingdon
   (Co Clk has b rec 1894 to 1906, m rec 1885, d rec 1894 to 1905, div, pro, civ ct
   rec 1787)
Indiana   B2   1803   75 1810-80 Westmoreland, Lycoming . . . . Indiana
   (Clk of the Orphans Ct has b rec 1893 to 1906, m rec 1884, d rec 1852 to 1856,
   pro rec 1805)
Jefferson   B2   1804   47 1810-80 Lycoming . . . . Brookville
Juniata   B3   1831   16 1840-80 Mifflin . . . . Mifflintown
   (Reg & Recorders Office has b, d & bur rec from 1893, m rec from 1885;
   Prothonatary's office has div rec from 1900 & civ ct rec)
Lackawanna   A4   1878   235 1880   Luzerne . . . . Scranton
   (Co Commissioners Office has m, div, pro, civ ct rec from 1878)
Lancaster   C3   1729   278 1790-80 Chester . . . . Lancaster
   (Co Clk has b rec from 1893 to 1906, m, div, pro & civ ct rec from 1729;
   Local Registrars have d rec or also Bureau of Vit Stat, Harrisburg, Pa.)
Lawrence   B1   1849   113 1850-80 Beaver, Mercer . . . . New Castle
Lebanon   C3   1813   91 1820-80 Dauphin, Lancaster . . . . . . Lebanon
   (Clk of Orphans Ct has b rec from 1893 to 1906, m rec from 1885; Prothono-
   tary has div rec from 1888; Register of Wills has pro rec from 1813)
Lehigh   B4   1812   228 1820-80 Northampton . . . . Allentown
   (Co Clk has b rec from 1893 to 1905, m rec from 1885, div & civ ct rec from
   1812; Reg of Wills has pro rec from 1812, d rec from 1874 to 1906, bur rec
   from 1874 to 1906 & b rec from 1873 to 1906)
Luzerne   B3   1786   347 1790-80 Northumberland . . . . Wilkes-Barre
   (Co Clk has b & d rec from 1893 to 1906, m rec from 1885; Prothonatary
   Office has div rec; Reg of Wills has pro rec)
Lycoming   B3   1795   109 1800-80 Northumberland . . . . Williamsport
McKean   A2   1804   55 1810-80 Lycoming . . . . Smethport
Mercer   B1   1800   128 1800-80 Allegheny . . . . Mercer
   (Co Clk has b & d rec from 1893 to 1905, m rec from 1885, pro rec from 1800;
   Prothonotary Officer has div & civ ct rec)
Mifflin   B2   1789   44 1790-80 Cumberland, Northumberland . Lewistown
Monroe   B4   1836   40 1840-80 Pike, Northampton . . . . Stroudsburg
   (Co Clk has m rec from 1885, div rec from 1844, pro & civ ct rec from 1836)
Montgomery   C4   1784   517 1790-80 Philadelphia . . . . Norristown
Montour   B3   1850   17 1850-80 Columbia . . . . Danville
   (Prothonotary has b & d rec 1893 to 1905, m rec 1885, div rec 1865, civ ct rec 1850)
Northampton   B4   1752   201 1790-80 Bucks . . . . Easton
   (Clk of Orphan's Ct has b rec from 1893 to 1936, m rec; Bureau of Vit Stat,
   Harrisburg, Pa. has b rec from 1936, d rec; Prothonotary's Office has div &
   civ ct rec; Reg Of Wills has pro rec; Recorder of Deeds has deeds)
Northumber-
   land   B3   1772   104 1790-80 Lancaster, Bedford, Berks,
                                        Northampton . . . . Sunbury
Ontario (see Bradford)
Perry   C3   1820   27 1820-80 Cumberland . . . . New Bloomfield
Philadelphia C4   1682 2003 1790-80 Original county . . . . Philadelphia
Pike   A4   1814   9 1820-80 Northampton . . . . Milford
   (Clk of Commissioners has b & d rec from 1893 to 1905, m rec from 1885, div
   & civ ct rec from 1815, pro rec from 1828, deeds & mtgs from 1817; Bureau of
   Vit Stat, Harrisburg, Pa. has b & d rec from 1906)

County Map of Pennsylvania

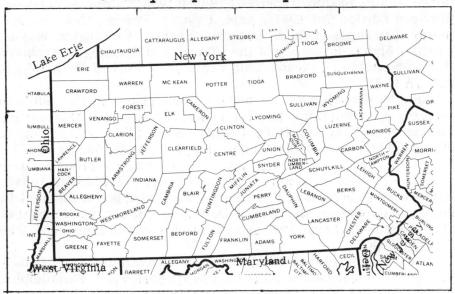

Potter   A2   1804   16   1810-80   Lycoming . . . . Coudersport
  (Prothonotary has b rec 1893 to 1906, div & civ ct rec from 1804; Register of
  Wills has pro rec from 1804)
Schuylkill   B3   1811   173   1820-80   Berks, Northampton . . . . Pottsville
Snyder   B3   1855   26   1860-80   Union   o . . . . o Middleburg
  (Co Clk has b rec from 1892 to 1905; Clk of Cts has m rec from 1885, d rec
  from 1893 to 1905, div & civ ct rec from 1859)
Somerset   C2   1795   77   1800-80   Bedford   . . . . o o. Somerset
  (Co Clk has b & d rec from 1893 to 1906, m rec from 1885, pro rec from 1795;
  Prothonotary has div & civ ct rec)
Sullivan   A3   1847   6   1850-80   Lycoming . . . . Laporte
  (Clk of Orphans Ct has b & d rec 1893 to 1905, m rec from 1885; Prothonotary
  has div rec from 1847, civ ct rec from 1847; Register of wills has pro rec 1847)
Susquehanna A4   1810   33   1820-80   Luzerne . . . . Montrose
  (Co Clk has div and civ ct rec from 1812)
Tioga   A3   1804   37   1810-80   Lycoming . . . . Wellsboro
Union   B3   1813   26   1820-80   Northumberland . . . . Lewisburg
  (Co Clk has b & d rec 1893 to 1905, m rec from 1885, div & civ ct rec from 1813)
Venango   B1   1800   65   1800-80   Allegheny, Lycoming . . . . . Franklin
  (Co Clk has b & d rec from 1893 to 1905, m rec from 1885, div & civ ct rec
  also pro & estate rec from 1806, adoptions prior to 1925)
Warren   A1   1800   46   1800-80   Allegheny, Lycoming . . . . . . Warren
Washington C1   1781   217   1790-80   Westmoreland   . . . . Washington
  (Clk of Ct has b rec to 1905, m, pro rec; Prothonotary has div & civ ct rec,
  also road & Township rec, crim rec)
Wayne   A4   1798   28   1800-80   Northampton . . . . Honesdale
Westmoreland C1   1773   353   1790-80   Bedford . . . . Greensburg
Wyoming   A3   1842   17   1850-80   Luzerne . . . . Tunkhannock
  (Clk of Cts has b & d rec from 1893 to 1906, m & div rec from 1885, civ ct rec
  from 1842; Reg Of Wills has pro rec)
York   C3   1749   238   1790-80   Lancaster . . . . York

Federal Courts. Inventory of County Archives, Adams, Beaver, Berks, Blair, Bradford (printed 1942 & 1946) Cambria, Delaware (Revised Edition Oct 1941), Erie, Fayette, Forest, Greene, Lancaster, Lawrence, Lehigh, Luzerne, Warren, Washington, Wayne, Westmoreland. Inventory of the Church and Synagogue Archives of Pa., Society of Friends. Ship register of Port of Philadelphia Vol. 1A to D.

Guide to depository of manuscript collections in Pa. Guide to manuscript collections in Historical Society of Pa. Descriptive catalog of the Du Simitiere Papers in the Library Company of Philadelphia. Papers of Colonel Henry Bouquet, Series 21631 - 21632- 21634 - 21643 - 21644 - Parts 1 & 2 - 21649 - Parts 1 & 2 - 21650 - 21652 - 21653 - 21654 - 21654A - 21654B. Wilderness Chronicles of Northwest Pa. Calendar of the Joel R. Poinsett Papers in the Henry D. Gilpin collection. Journal of Choussegros de Lery. The Expedition of Baron de Longueuil. The Venengo Trail.

Check list of Philadelphia Newspapers available in Philadelphia (2 Editions). Check list of Pa. newspapers Vo. 1 Philadelphia County. Manual for newspaper transcription. Check list of maps pertaining to Pa. up to 1900. Reprint with supplement to check list of maps to Pa. up to 1900.

Pennsylvania microfilm; (Filmed by New Jersey Historical Records Survey showing location of original records). Court of Common Pleas of Bucks County, Hiram H. Keller, President. Judge, Doylestown, Pa. Minute book Common Pleas and Quarter Sessions, Buck County, Pa. 1684-1730, Clerk of Quarter Sessions Office, Bucks County Court House, Doylestown, Pa. Sessions Docket 1715-1753 Buck County Pa. Clerk of Quarter Sessions Office, Bucks County Court House, Doylestown, Pa. Rules, forms, and fees of Court from 1770-1890, Bucks County, Pa. office of the Clerk of Quarter Sessions, Bucks County Court House, Doylestown, Pa.

Depository of unpublished material, Historical Commission, Harrisburg, Pennsylvania.

Rhode Island

Capital Providence · State 1790 · (13th)

Giovanni de Verazzano, a 44-year-old Florentine navigator, in 1524 visited Block Island and the site of the present Newport on Aquidneck Island, both part of today's Rhode Island. He was then a privateer in the French service.

In 1636 Roger Williams, a 30-year-old Welshman, and some of his followers established the first Rhode Island settlement at Providence. His religious pronouncements, too advanced for the clergy to accept led to his banishment from Massachusetts. An uncompromising advocate of freedom, he held that difference of opinion is not a bar to friendship. All land he settled or tilled was purchased from the Indians.

The banishment of Williams from Massachusetts was soon followed by others including Anne Marbury Hutchinson, John Clarke, and William Coddington. They established a colony at Portsmouth in 1638. Later Clarke and Coddington settled Newport, after their attempt to establish a government based on the Jewish nation had failed. A fourth colony was established at Warwick in 1642.

Many Quakers found a haven in Rhode Island in the early days. The large majority of the people who came into Rhode Island were former residents of Massachusetts.

New England researchers have an abundance of material at their command. Both the state and the cities have large genealogical libraries or genealogical sections in their public libraries. The Rhode Island Historical Society has a wonderful assortment of books at 52 Power St., Providence, 02906, Rhode Island. The Society has one of the largest genealogical collections in New England, probably the third largest. Many people from various sections, searching for the progenitors among Rhode Island families have attained splendid results in the library of the Rhode Island Historical Society.

Among its large numbers of industrial workers are members of almost every nationality. Those with the largest numbers are the Italians, English, Irish, Polish, Russians, Swedes, Germans, and Austrians.

All vital statistics are in the custody of the town or city clerks. Birth and death records since 1853 are in the office of the Registrar of Vital Statistics, Providence, 02903, Rhode Island.

Rhode Island libraries - The Peoples Public Library, Newport 02840, (Newport); Brown University Library, (R. I. history), 02912; Providence Public Library, 229 Washington St., 02903; Rhode Island Historical Society Library, 52 Power St., 02906; Rhode Island State Library, State House, (historical, R.W. records), 02903 Providence, (Providence).

Rhode Island Towns
Organized Before 1800

BRISTOL COUNTY -- Barrington, 1717; Bristol, 1681; Warren, 1746-7.

KENT COUNTY -- Coventry, 1741; East Greenwich, 1677; Warwick, 1642-3; West Greenwich, 1741.

NEWPORT COUNTY -- Jamestown, 1678; Little Compton, 1746-7; Middletown, 1743; Newport, 1639; New Shoreman, 1672; Portsmouth, 1638; Tiverton, 1746-7.

PROVIDENCE COUNTY -- Cranston, 1754; Cumberland, 1746-7; Foster, 1781; Glocester, 1730-1; Johnston, 1759; North Providence, Providence, 1636; Scituate, 1730-1; Smithfield, 1730-1.

WASHINGTON COUNTY -- Charlestown, 1738; Exeter, 1742-3; Hopkinton, 1757; North Kingston, 1641; Richmond, 1747; South Kingston, 1657-8; Westerly, 1669.

Note: The State of Rhode Island does not have the county system of keeping records. For information write to the individual cities.

Rhode Island County Histories

(Population figures to nearest thousand - 1960 Census)

Name	Map Index	Date Formed	Pop. By M	Census Reports Available	Parent County	County Seat
Bristol	C2	1747	37	1790-80		......Bristol, Warren, Barrington

(There is no Co Clk in Bristol Co, the towns of Bristol, Warren & Barrington have b, m, d, bur, & pro rec; Providence, R.I. has div rec, 5th Dist Ct. Warren has civ ct rec)

Name	Map Index	Date Formed	Pop. By M	Census Reports Available	Parent County	County Seat
Kent	B3	1750	113	1790-80	Providence	...........E. Greenwich

(Contact city or town clk in each of 39 towns to get rec)

Name	Map Index	Date Formed	Pop. By M	Census Reports Available	Parent County	County Seat
Newport	D3	1703	82	1790-80	Original County	..........Newport

(City Clk's office, Newport, has b, m, & d rec from 1697; Local cem have bur rec; Office of Sup or Family Cts have div rec; Pro Ct has pro rec; Clk of 1st Dist Ct has civ ct rec) (Town of Newport was founded 1639. Under Royal Charter until 1686, suspended in 1686 when colony became a county of Dominion of New England under Sir Edmund Andros until 1689. Was incorporated as a city in 1784. Incorporated as Rhode Island County in 1703. In 1729 incorporated together with Portsmouth, Middletown, Jamestown & New Shoreham as New-port County. New Shoreham, Tiverton, Little Compton joined later. Transfered to Washington City 1963)

Name	Map Index	Date Formed	Pop. By M	Census Reports Available	Parent County	County Seat
Providence	B1	1703	569	1790-80	Original county	..........Providence
Washington	B4	1729	59	1790-80	Newport (For. Naragannset)	..W. Kingston

(Town Clk of each town or city has b, m, d, bur & pro rec; Family Ct has div rec; Dist Ct has civ ct rec)

Genealogists' Check List of the Historical Records Survey, Rhode Island

Federal Courts. Inventory of municipal and town archives, North Providence, West Greenwich. Summary of Legislation concerning Vital Statistic records. Guide to Public Vital Statistic records in Rhode Island and Providence Plantations. Guide to church vital statistic records in R. I. and Providence Plantations. Ship register and enrollments of Providence, R. I. 2 Vol. 1773-1939. Ship register and enrollments of Bristol - Warren, R.I. 1773-1939. Ship register and enrollments of Newport, R.I. 1790-1939 2 Vol. Inventory of the Church Archives of R.I. - Baptist Churches - Society of Friends. Directory of Churches and Religious organizations of

R.I. Preliminary check list of American portraits 1620-1825 found in R.I. Depository of unpublished material, State Library, Providence, Rhode Island.

County Map of Rhode Island

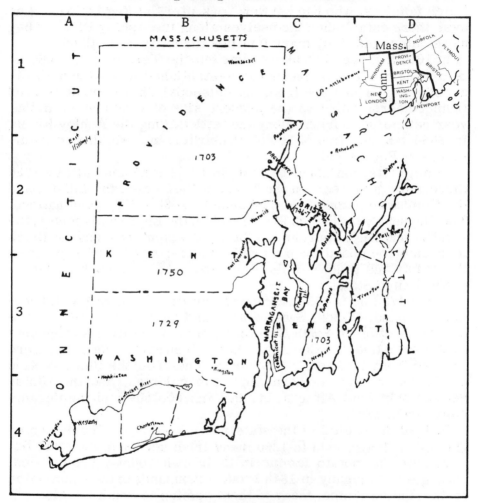

South Carolina

Capital Columbia - State 1788 - (8th)

Several attempts by the Spaniards and the French to establish settlements in what is now South Carolina between 1526 and 1664 failed.

The first colony was established on the Ashley River in the southeastern part of the state in 1671. The settlers were a group of English people direct from the Old World, and another group, the members of which had been living on the Barbados Island, the south-easternmost island in the West Indies group. They called their settlement Charles Town. A few months later some Dutch families, who had left New York after the English had taken over there established themselves along the Ashley River. They were later joined by many families direct from Holland.

In 1675 a group of Quakers came into the Territory. In 1680 about 45 families of Huguenots also established homes there. Quite a colony of dissenters from the Episcopal Church came in 1683 from Somersetshire to the present site of Charleston. In that year came also an Irish colony and settled along the Ashley River. In 1684 ten families of Scotch Presbyterians established themselves at Port Royal.

Immigrants continued to come in large streams until by 1730 there were gathered ''on the banks of the Santee, the Edisto, and the Combahee some of the best elements of the European nations. The Huguenot, the Scotch Presbyterian, the English Dissenter, the loyalist and High Churchman, the Irish adventurer, and the Dutch mechanic composed the powerful material out of which soon grew the beauty and renown of the Palmetto State.'' (Ridpath's History of the United States.)

From 1732 until 1736 a number of families from England, Scotland, Ireland, Wales, Switzerland, and Germany came into the central section of South Carolina. Some of the first settlements in the so-called ''Up Country,'' the western half of the state, were created from 1745 to 1760 by immigrants from the Rhine section of Germany, the northern American colonies, and the Ulster section of Ireland. After the Indian Wars, Scotch-Irish immigrants came about 1761.

In 1790 the capital of the state, was moved from Charleston to Columbia. From 1845 to 1850 many Irish settled in the state because of the potato famine in their own county. The political struggle in Germany in 1848 brought thousands of the expatriates to the United States, many of them coming to South Carolina.

South Carolina was the eighth state to enter the Union, 1788. More than a hundred years before, 1683, the first three counties Berkeley, Colleton, and Craven, were established. All were discontinued and the present Berkeley county is not the original.

By an Act ratified in 1769 the province of South Carolina was divided into seven judicial districts: Charleston, Georgetown, Beaufort, Orangeburg, Ninety-Six, Camden and Cheraws. The first six of these were given the names of the principal towns within their borders and those towns were made the seats of their respective districts. Cheraws District derived its name from the fact that the Cheraw Indians had formerly occupied a considerable portion of the land within its borders and after they had gone elsewhere and white settlers moved in, the section was at first called "the Cheraws' lands", soon simplified into "The Cheraws".

In 1795 Pinckney and Washington Districts were established. Pinckney embraced the present counties of Union and York and a part of Cherokee. Washington embraced the present counties of Greenville, Pickens, Oconee and Anderson.

In 1798 the nine districts then existing were divided up into twenty-four. From Ninety-Six District, Abbeville, Edgefield, Newberry, Laurens, and Spartanburg Districts were formed; from Washington District, Pendleton and Greenville Districts were formed; from Pinckney District, Union and York Districts were formed; from Camden District, Chester, Lancaster, Fairfield, Kershaw and Sumter Districts were formed; from Cheraws District, Chesterfield, Darlington and Marlborough Districts were formed; Ninety-Six, Washington, Pinckney, Camden and Cheraw were discarded as district names; Georgetown District was divided into Georgetown and Marion Districts; Charleston into Charleston and Colleton; and Orangeburg into Orangeburg and Barnwell.

In 1799 Richland District was formed from Kershaw. In 1802 Horry and Williamsburg Districts were formed from parts of Georgetown. In 1804 Lexington was formed from Orangeburg. In 1826 Pendleton District was formed into Pickens and Anderson Districts and the name Pendleton discarded as a district name. In 1855 Clarendon District was formed from a part of Sumter.

From the settlement of South Carolina in 1671 until 1783 all vital statistics and property records were recorded at Charleston where they are still available at the office of the Judge of Probate. Since the Episcopal Church held full sway in the early days of the colony, in 1706 an act was passed making the parishes its legislative units. Regardless of church affilations, all persons were required to register their vital statistics with the church officers. In 1783 offices of Register of Mesne (legal) Conveyance were authorized in all counties.

Archibald F. Bennett, former secretary of the Genealogical Society of Utah, who some years ago made a personal inspection of all record deposits in South Carolina, says that the Judge of Probates office in Charleston has records of wills and estates back to 1692. They are recorded in chronological volumes, with indexes.

Records of deeds and other estate matters are available from 1719 in Charleston. Those prior to 1719 are in the office of the

Historical Commission of South Carolina in Columbia.

What few marriage bonds are available from those early days have been printed in the "South Carolina Historical and Genealogical Magazine." Between 1778 and 1911 no marriage bonds or licenses were required in South Carolina, and only for brief intervals were such records kept.

"Records of land grants earlier than 1695 are in the office of the Historical Commission of South Carolina in Columbia." says Mr. Bennett. "The Secretary of State in Columbia has records of land grants from 1695 to the present time, and a plat to land grants from 1688, warrants for entry and surveys made and certified before the corresponding final grants or patents were issued. The plat records and grant records in the Secretary of State's office are in separate books. There are sets of index books for plats and index books for grants.

'In our Genealogical Library in Salt Lake City, Utah, we have a series of seven printed volumes containing copies of the Stub Entries to Indents for Revolutionary Claims. These contain valuable items for information on the service of soldiers who were paid or received bounty for service."

Birth and death records from 1915 to the present are in the office of the State Health Department, Columbia 29201, South Carolina. Marriage records from 1 July 1950 to the present are also at that office. Marriages from 1 July 1911 to the present are at the office of the Probate Judge, County Court House, in respective county seats.

Birth records kept at the city of Charleston are available since 1877 at the City Health Department, where also are available deaths from 1821 to the present.

The Clerk of the Court in the various counties has charge of wills, deeds, and land grants. Dates will vary with the different counties.

War service records are in the custody of Adjutant General in Columbia, S. C.

Available census records are listed in the "South Carolina County Histories" herewith.

The South Carolina Historical and Genealogical Magazine, a quarterly, has been published regularly since 1900. It contains much valuable information. Many libraries have bound volumes of this magazine.

All schedules of the U. S. Census for 1790 of South Carolina are available, but are not necessarily listed in the names of the present counties, since most of them, with the probable exception of three, have all been formed after the 1790 census.

South Carolina Districts were formed as follows: Abbeville, 1798; Anderson, 1826; Barnwell, 1798; Beaufort, 1769; Berkeley,

1683; Camden, 1769; Cartaret, 1683; Charleston, 1769; Cheraws, 1769; Chester, 1798; Chesterfield, 1798; Clarendon, 1785; Colleton, 1798; Darlington, 1798; Dorchester, 1785; Edgefield, 1798; Fairfield, 1798; Georgetown, 1769; Granville, 1700; Greenville, 1798; Horry, 1802; Kershaw, 1798; Lancaster, 1798; Laurens, 1798; Lexington, 1804; Marion, 1798; Marlboro, 1798; Newberry, 1798; Ninety-Six, 1796; Orangeburg, 1769; Pendleton, 1798; Pickens, 1826; Pickney, 1795; Richland, 1799; Spartanburg, 1798; Sumter, 1798; Union, 1798; Washington, 1798; Williamsburg, 1802; and York, 1798.

South Carolina Libraries - Charleston Free Library, 404 King St., Charleston 29403, (Charleston); Richland County Public Library, 1400 Sumter St., (South Carolina), Columbia 29201, (Richland); South Carolina State Library, Columbia 29201, (Richland); Spartanburg Public Library, 333 S. Pine St., Spartanburg 29301, (Spartanburg).

The 1868 Constitution changed 30 districts to counties. And even after 1868 some recorders continued to use "district" as they felt it has been a "yankee" imposition. Those marked be low with an asterisk (*) are those so changed.

South Carolina books:

Ervin, Sara Sullivan, "South Carolinians in the Revolution", 186 pp. (Index separate) Pub. 1949, DAR.

"Heads of Families At The First Census of the U.S. 1790 South Carolina", Government Printing Office, 1908.

Revill, Janie, "Copy of the Original Index Book Showing the Revolutionary Claims Filed in South Carolina between August 20, 1783 and August 31, 1786". Kept by James McCall, Auditor General.

Sally, A. A. Jr., "Warrants for Lands in South Carolina 1672-1679". Published by the Historical Commission of South Carolina, 1910.

"South Carolina Historical and Genealogical Magazine". Published since 1900 - 57 Vol.

Young, Miss Pauline, "A Collection of South Carolina Wills and Records". 2 Vols. (Vol. 1 printed, vol. 2 mimeographed).

South Carolina County Histories

(Population figures to nearest thousand - 1960 Census)

Name	Map Index	Date Formed	Pop. By M	Census Reports Available	Parent County	County Seat
Abbeville*	B1	1785	21	1800-80	District 96	Abbeville
Aiken	B2	1871	81	1880	Edgefield, Orangeburg, Barnwell Lexington	Aiken
Allendale	C3	1919	11		Barnwell, Hampton	Allendale
Anderson*	A1	1826	98	1830-80	Pendleton District	Anderson

Bamberg   B3   1897   16   Barnwell . . . . Bamberg
   (Clk of Ct has div & civ ct rec; Judge of Pro has pro & m rec; Co Health Dept
   has b & d rec)
Barnwell*   B2   1798   18   1800-80   Orangeburg . . . . Barnwell
   (Co Clk has b & d rec from 1915, div rec from 1950, also civ ct rec; Judge of
   Pro has m & pro rec)
Berkley   1683   (Discontinued)   Original Co not present Berkeley Co
Berkeley   B4   1882   38   Charleston . . . . Moncks Corner
   (Clk of Ct has div & civ ct rec; Pro Judge has m & pro rec; Co Health Dept has
   b, d & bur rec)
Beufort*   C3   1764   44   1790-80   Original county . . . . Beaufort
   (Co Clk has b, d, rec from 1915)
Calhoun   B3   1908   12   Lexington, Orangeburg . . . . St. Matthews
   (Co Health Dept has b & d rec from 1915; Judge of Pro has m rec from 1911,
   pro rec from 1908; Clk of Ct has civ ct rec from 1908, div rec from 1949; His-
   torical Commission has land, Bible, cemetery & gen col from 1735)
Charleston* C4   1769   216 1800-80   Original District . . . . Charleston
Cherokee   A2   1897   35   Union, York, Spartanburg . . . Gaffney
Chester*   A2   1785   31   1800-80   Craven . . . . Chester
   (Judge of Pro has pro rec from 1789; Clk of Ct has deeds from 1785; Dept of
   Vit Stat, Columbia, S.C. has b & d rec from 1915; Pro Judge has m rec from
   1911)
Chesterfield* A3 1798   34   1800-80   Cheraws District . . . . . . Chesterfield
   (Clk of Ct has b, d, bur, div, pro, civ ct rec; Judge of Pro has m rec)
Claremont   1800-10
Clarendon*   B3   1855   29   1800-80   Sumter District . . . . Manning
   (Census schedules missing for 1820, 1830, 1840, 1850) (Clk of Ct has b & d
   rec from 1915, m rec from 1911, div rec from 1947, civ ct rec from 1856)
Colleton*   C3   1798   28   1800-80   Charleston District . . . . . . Walterboro
Darlington* A3   1798   53   1800-80   Cheraws District . . . . Darlington
Dillon   A4   1910   31   Marion . . . . Dillon
   (Clk of Cts has civ ct rec, deeds, real estate, mtgs from 1910)
Dorchester   B3   1897   24   Berkeley, Colleton . . . . St. George
   (Co Clk has b rec from 1915)
Edgefield*   B2   1785   16   1800-80   District 96 . . . . Edgefield
   (Co Clk has b, d, bur rec from 1915)
Fairfield*   A2   1785   21   1800-80   Camden District . . . . Winnsboro
   (Co Clk has civ ct rec, deeds, releases, sale of slaves rec from 1785)
Florence   A3   1888   84   Marion, Darlington, Clarendon
                                           Williamsburg . . . . Florence
Georgetown* B4   1769   35   1790-80   Original District . . . . Georgetown
Greenville* A1   1798   210 1800-80   Washington . . . . Greenville
   (Clk of Ct has b & d rec from 1915, m rec from 1911, div & pro rec)
Greenwood   B2   1897   44   Abbeville, Edgefield . . . . Greenwood
Hampton   C3   1878   17   1880   Beaufort . . . . Hampton
   (Clk of Cts has b rec 1915 to 1957, civ ct rec 1878; Judge of Pro Ct has m rec 1911)
Horry*   A4   1802   68   1810-80   Georgetown . . . . Conway
Jasper   C3   1912   12   Beaufort, Hampton . . . . . Ridgeland
   (Co Clk has b, d & bur rec from 1915, civ ct, deeds, mtgs, judgments from
   1912, div rec from 1949; Pro Judge has pro rec)
Kershaw*   A3   1798   34   1800-80   Camden District . . . . Camden
Lancaster*   A3   1798   39   1800-80   Camden District . . . . Lancaster
   (Co Clk has b & d rec from 1915, civ ct rec from 1866)
Laurens*   A2   1785   48   1800-80   District 96 . . . . Laurens
Lee   A3   1902   22   Darlington, Sumter, Kershaw . . Bishopville
   (Co Clk has b & d rec from 1915, civ ct rec from 1902, div rec from 1949)
Lexington*   B2   1804   61   1800-80   Orangeburg . . . . Lexington
Liberty   1800
McCormick   B2   1916   9   Greenwood, Abbeville . . . . . McCormick
Marion*   A4   1798   32   1800-80   Georgetown . . . . Marion
   (Co Clk has b, d & bur rec from 1915, div rec from 1948, civ ct rec from 1800;

Judge of Pro has m & pro rec)
Marlboro*   A3 1798   29 1800-80 Cheraws District   . . . . . Bennettsville
      (Co Clk has b, d, bur, div, civ ct rec; Pro Judge has m & pro rec)
Newberry*   B2 1785   29 1800-80 District 96 . . . . Newberry
Oconee   A1 1868   40 1870-80 Pickens   . . . . Wahalla
      (Pro Judge has m rec from 1912, pro rec from 1868; Co Clk has civ ct rec
      from 1868, also div rec)
Orange   1800
Orangeburg* B3 1769   69 1800-80 Original district . . . . Orangeburg
Pendleton   1800-20
Pickens*   A1 1868   46 1830-80 Pickens Dist.   . . . . Pickens
      (Clk of Ct has b & d rec from 1915, div rec from 1949, civ ct rec from 1868;
      Office of Pro Judge has m & pro rec)
Richland*   B3 1799 200 1810-80 Kershaw . . . . Columbia
      (Census schedules missing for 1800)
Salem   1800-10
Saluda   B2 1895   15   Edgefield . . . . Saluda
Spartanburg* A2 1785 157 1800-80 District 96 . . . . Spartanburg
      (Pro Judge has m rec from 1911, pro rec 1700; Clk of Ct has civ ct rec 1785)
Sumter*   B3 1798   75 1800-80 Camden District . . . . Sumter
Union*   A2 1798   30 1800-80 District 96 . . . . Union
      (Clk of Ct has civ ct rec from 1785)
Winyaw   1800
Williamsburg* B4 1802 41 1800-80 Georgetown   . . . . Kingstree
      (Clk of Ct has div rec from 1948, civ ct rec from 1806; Health Center has b
      & d rec from 1915; Pro Judge has m rec from 1911, also pro rec)
York*   A2 1798   79 1800-80 Pinckney . . . . York

* See Page 227 - third paragraph.

County Map of South Carolina

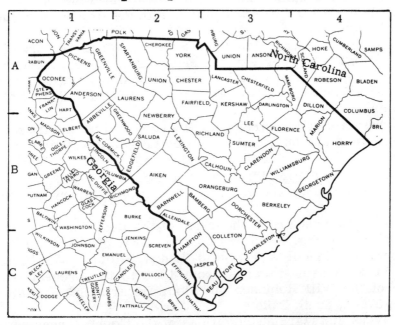

Genealogists' Check List of the Historical Records Survey,
South Carolina

Inventory of County Archives, Abbeville, Aiken, Allendale,

Anderson, Cherokee, Dillon, Florence, Jasper, Lee, McCormick, Oconee, Pickens, Richland, and Saluda.

South Dakota

Capital Pierre - Territory 1861 - State 1889 - (40th)

Part of the Louisiana Purchase in 1803, the Dakotas were wedded to numerous Territories before finally becoming states. Until 1820 they were part of the Missouri Territory. At intervals, the eastern half was tied to the Territories of Minnesota, Iowa, Wisconsin, and Michigan. During those periods, the western parts, or the Dakotas, belonged to the Nebraska Territory. The Dakotas were formed into a Territory by itself in 1861. In 1887 it was divided into two Territories, North and South Dakota.

Attracted by the rich soil between the Big Sioux and the Missouri Rivers, farm families from adjoining states established homes there as early as 1857. Several communities were established, most of them along the Missouri, but two or three along the Big Sioux. The real influx of settlers came about 1863, after the passing of the first Homestead Act in the U. S.

South Dakota became the fortieth state to enter the Union. This was in 1889. All of her 68 counties, with the exception of three were already organized at that time.

The predominating nationality in South Dakota is the Norwegian. Other nationalities represented among its citizenry, in the order of their predominance, are the German, Russian, Swedish, Danish, Czechoslovakian, English, Austrian, Irish, Finnish, Polish, Greek and Italian.

Records of births, marriages, divorces and deaths from 1905 to the present are on file at the office of the State Public Health Department, Pierre, 57501, South Dakota.

Wills and probate matters are in the offices of the Clerk of the Court in each county who also have a record of marriages since 1905.

All land records are at the office of the Register of Deeds in the county of filing. Land grants are at the office of the Commissioner of School and Public Lands, Pierre, 57501, S. D.

The state census records from 1890 to the present are in charge of the Will Robinson Division, Department of History, Pierre, 57501, South Dakota.

Taxpayers lists are at the offices of the County Treasurer of each county.

The war service records are under the direction of the Register of Deeds of each county. The Sexton of each cemetery is supervisor of the records of the respective cemeteries.

Kingsbury, Geo. W., "History of Dakota Territory. Its History and Its People." Vols. four and five, biographical. S. J. Clarke Publishing Co., Chicago, 1915.

Libraries: Alexander Mitchell Public Library, 21 6th Ave., SE, Aberdeen 57401, (Brown); South Dakota Free Public Library Commission, Pierre, 57501, (Hughs); Carnegie Free Public Library, Tenth and Dakota Sts., Sioux Falls 57102, (Minnehaha).

South Dakota County Histories

(Population figures to nearest thousand - 1960 Census)

Name	Map Index	Date Formed	Pop. By M	Census Reports Available	Parent County	County Seat
Armstrong	C2	1883	.05	1880	Merged with Dewey	....
Aurora	B4	1879	5	1880	Brule	.... Plankinton

(Clk of Cts has b & d rec from 1905, m rec from 1883, bur, div, pro, civ ct rec from 1879)

| Beadle | B4 | 1873 | 22 | 1880 | Spink, Clark | .... Huron |
| Bennett | C2 | 1909 | 3 | | Indian Lands | .... Martin |

(Attached to Fall River Co until 1911)

| BonHomme | C4 | 1862 | 9 | 1860-80 | Charles Mix | .... Tyndall |

(Clk of Cts has b, m, d, bur, div, pro & civ ct rec)

| Brookings | B5 | 1868 | 20 | 1860-80 | Unorganized Territory | .... Brookings |

(Clk of Cts has b, d, bur rec from 1905, m rec from 1871, div, pro & civ ct rec from 1890; State Dept of Health, Pierre, S. Dak. also has b, m, d, bur, div rec)

| Brown | A4 | 1879 | 34 | 1880 | Beadle | .... Aberdeen |

(Co Auditor has b & d rec from 1905, m rec 1880, div, pro, civ ct rec 1882)

| Brule | B4 | 1879 | 6 | 1880 | Old Buffalo (disc.) | ...... Chamberlain |

(Clk of Cts has b & d rec from 1905, m rec 1882, div rec 1885, pro & civ ct 1882)

Buffalo	B3	1872	2	1880	Territorial County	...... Gannvalley
Butte	B1	1883	9		Harding	.... Belle Fourche
Campbell	A3	1873	4	1880	Buffalo	.... Mound City

(Clk of Cts has b & d rec from 1905, m rec 1888, pro rec 1885, div & civ ct 1890)

| Charles Mix | C4 | 1865 | 12 | 1860-80 | Original District | ...... Lake Andes |

(Clk of Cts has b, m, d rec from 1905, div, pro, civ ct rec from 1890, bur rec from 1940)

| Clark | B4 | 1873 | 7 | 1880 | Hanson | .... Clark |

(Clk of Cts has b & d rec from 1905, m rec 1886, div rec 1900, pro rec 1885)

| Clay | C5 | 1862 | 11 | 1860-80 | .... | Vermillion |

(Clk of Cts has b, d, div rec from 1905, m rec from 1870, pro rec from 1875, civ ct rec from 1866, bur rec from 1904)

| Codington | B5 | 1878 | 20 | 1880 | Indian Lands | .... Watertown |
| Corson | A2 | 1909 | 6 | | Boreman, Dewey | .... McIntosh |

(Clk of Cts has b, m, d, div, pro, civ ct rec from 1909)

| Custer | C1 | 1877 | 5 | 1880 | Indian Lands | .... Custer |

(Clk of Cts has b & d rec from 1905, m rec 1887, div, pro, civ ct rec 1890)

Davison	B4	1875	17	1880	Hanson	.... Mitchell
Day	A4	1879	11	1880	Clark	.... Webster
Deuel	B5	1878	7	1880	Brookings	.... Clear Lake

(Clk of Cts has b & d rec from 1905, m rec 1879, div rec 1880, pro rec 1889, civ ct rec 1880) (Deuel Co Dakota has 1860-70 Federal Census)

| Dewey | A3 | 1910 | 5 | | Indian Res., Armstrong | ... Timber Lake |

(Clk of Cts has b, m, d, bur, div, pro, civ ct rec from 1910; State Dept of Health, Pierre, S. Dak. also has b & d rec)

County Map of South Dakota

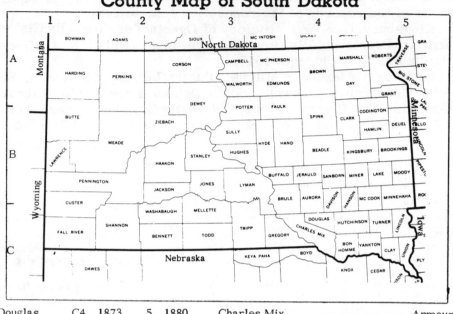

Douglas   C4   1873   5   1880   Charles Mix .... Armour
  (Clk of Cts has b & d rec from 1905, m rec from 1884, bur rec from 1941,
  div & pro rec from 1887, civ ct rec from 1884)
Edmunds   A3   1873   6   Buffalo .... Ipswich
  (Clk of Cts has b & d rec from 1905, m & div rec from 1887, pro & civ ct
  rec from 1884, bur rec from 1941)
Fall River   C1   1883   11   Custer .... Hot Springs
  (Clk of Cts has b & d rec from 1905, m & pro rec from 1890, div & civ ct
  rec from 1890)
Faulk   A4   1873   4   1880   .... Faulkton
  (Clk of Cts has b rec from 1886, m rec from 1885, d rec from 1905, div rec from
  1887, pro rec from 1884, civ ct rec from 1890)
Grant   A5   1873   10   1880   Codington, Deuel .... Milbank
  (Clk of Cts has b & d rec from 1905, m rec from 1890, div rec from 1897, pro
  & civ ct rec from 1888, newspapers from 1880)
Gregory   C3   1889   7   Yankton .... Burke
  (Clk of Cts has b, d, bur, div, pro, civ ct rec from 1905, m rec from 1898, also
  adoption & naturalization rec from 1905)
Haakon   B2   3   .... Philip
  (Clk of Cts has b, m, d, div, pro rec from 1915)
Hamlin   B5   1878   6   1880   Deuel .... Hayti
  (Clk of Cts has b & d rec from 1905, m rec from 1879, div rec from 1885, pro
  rec from 1893, civ ct rec from 1885)
Hand   B4   1873   7   1880   Buffalo .... Miller
Hanson   B4   1871   5   1880   Buffalo, Deuel .... Alexandria
  (Clk of Cts has b, m, d, bur, div, pro, civ ct rec from 1905)
Harding   A1   1881   2   Unorganized Territory .... Buffalo
  (Clk of Cts has b, m, d, bur, div, pro, civ ct rec from 1909)
Hughes   B3   1874   13   1880   Buffalo .... Pierre
  (Clk of Cts has b & d rec from 1905, m, pro rec from 1890, div, civ ct rec
  from 1880)
Hutchinson   C4   1871   11   1860-80   Unorganized Territory .... Olivet
  (Clk of Cts has b & d rec from 1905, m rec from 1887, bur rec from 1895, pro
  rec from 1885, civ ct rec from 1876)
Hyde   B3   1873   3   Hyde .... Highmore

(Clk of Ct has b & d rec from 1905, m rec from 1887, pro rec from 1892, civ ct rec from 1884, bur rec from 1936, also div & adoption rec from 1884)
Jackson   B2 1915   2   Stanley .... Kadoka
Jerauld   B4 1883   4   Aurora .... Wessington Springs
(Clk of Cts has b, d & bur rec from 1905, m & pro rec from 1890, div rec from 1900, civ ct rec from 1895 & cir ct rec from 1889)
Jones   B3 1917   2   Lyman .... Murdo
Kingsbury   B4 1879   9   Hanson .... De Smet
Lake   B5 1873 12 1880 Brookings, Hanson .... Madison
Lawrence   B1 1875 17 1880 Unorganized Territory .... Deadwood
(Clk of Cts has b, d, bur rec from 1905, m rec 1890, div, pro, civ ct rec 1879)
Lincoln   C5 1871 12   Minnehaha .... Canton
(Clk of Cts has b & d rec from 1905, m & pro rec from 1890, bur rec from 1941, div & civ ct rec from 1872)
Lyman   B3 1873   4 1880 Unorganized Territory ...... Kennebec
McCook   B5 1873   8 1880 Hanson .... Salem
(Clk of Cts has b & d rec from 1905, m rec from 1882, bur rec from 1895, div rec from 1887, pro rec from 1881, civ ct rec from 1880)
McPherson   A3 1873   6   Buffalo .... Leola
(Clk of Cts has b & d rec from 1905, m rec from 1887, div rec from 1898, pro rec from 1893, civ ct rec from 1889, naturalization rec from 1884)
Marshall   A4 1885   7   Day .... Britton
(Clk of Cts has b & d rec from 1905, m rec from 1887, div & civ ct rec from 1888, pro rec from 1889)
Meade   B2 1889 12   Lawrence .... Sturgis
Mellette   C3 1909   3   Lyman .... White River
(Clk of Cts has b, m, d, bur, div, pro, civ ct rec from 1912)
Miner   B4 1873   5 1880 Hanson .... Howard
(Clk of Cts has b & d rec from 1905, m, div, pro, civ ct rec from 1886)
Minnehaha   B5 1865 87 1860-80 Territorial County .... Sioux Falls
(Clk of Cts has b & d rec from 1905, m, div, pro, civ ct rec from 1876)
Moody   B5 1873   9 1880 Brookings, Minnehaha ..... Flandreau
(Clk of Cts has b & d rec from 1905, m rec 1873, div rec 1883, pro & civ ct 1881)
Pennington   B1 1877 58 1880 Unorganized Territory . . . Rapid City
(Clk of Cts has b & d rec from 1905, m rec 1887, div & civ ct rec 1877, pro rec 1884)
Perkins   A2 1909   6   Harding, Butte .... Bison
(Clk of Cts has b, m, d, bur, div, pro, civ ct rec from 1909; Bureau of Vit Stat, Pierre, S.Dak. also has b, m, d, bur & div rec)
Potter   A3 1875   5   Buffalo .... Gettysburg
(Clk of Cts has b & d rec from 1905, m rec from 1887, bur rec from 1954, div rec from 1924, pro rec from 1885, civ ct rec from 1884, adoption rec from 1941)
Roberts   A5 1883 13   Grant .... Sisseton
(Clk of Cts has b & d rec from 1905, m & div rec from 1890, civ ct & pro rec from 1889)
Sanborn   B4 1883   5   Miner .... Woonsocket
(Clk of Cts has b, m, d, bur, div, pro, civ ct rec from 1905)
Shannon   C2 1875   6 1880 Terr. Co. - Attached to Fall River County.
Spink   B4 1879 12 1880 Hanson, Walworth .... Redfield
(Clk of Cts has b & d rec from 1905, m rec 1887, bur & pro rec 1880, civ ct rec from 1882)
Stanley   B3 1873   4 1880 Unorganized Territory ...... Ft. Pierre
Sully   B3 1873   3 1880 Potter .... Onida
Todd   C3 1871   5 1860-80 Indian Lands-Attached to Tripp County
Tripp   C3 1873   9   Unorganized Territory .... Winner
(Clk of Cts has b, m, div, pro, civ ct rec from 1909, d rec from 1910, bur rec from 1941)
Turner   C5 1871 11 1880 Lincoln .... Parker
(Clk of Cts has b & d rec from 1905, m rec from 1872, div rec from 1907, pro rec from 1886, civ ct rec from 1900)
Union   C5 1864 10 1880 Unorganized Territory ..... Elk Point

Walworth   A3   1868   8   1880   Territorial County   . . . . Shelby
    (Clk of Cts has b, d, bur rec from 1905, m & div rec from 1889, pro & civ
    ct rec from 1892)
Washabaugh   C2   1883   Indian Lands-Attached to Jackson Co.
Yankton   C5   1884   18   1860-80   Unorganized Territory   . . . . . . Yankton
    (Clk of Cts has b & d rec from 1905, m, div, pro, civ ct rec.from 1900)
Ziebach   B2   1869   2   Pennington   . . . . Dupree

Genealogists' Check List of the Historical Records Survey, South Dakota

Federal Courts. Inventory of County Archives, Bennett, Buffalo, Clark, Faulk, Haakon, Jackson, Mellette, Miner, Washabaugh. Guide to Public Vital Statistic records. Depository of unpublished material, University of South Dakota, Vermillion, South Dakota.

Tennessee

Capital Nashville - State 1796 - (16th)

Four or five hostile Indian tribes inhabited Tennessee up to as late as 1800. Explorers, representing Spain, France, and England, visited the territory intermittently from about 1540 until the early part of the seventeen hundreds.

White settlers moved into what later became Sullivan and Hawkins counties in the northeast corner of the state and established settlements as early as 1772.

The Blue Ridge Mountains, which form the boundary between North Carolina and Tennessee, are barriers to travel. They were so more in the early days than now. For that reason it was easier to come into Tennessee from the north than from the east. Many of the settlers therefore came into Tennessee from Virginia. It was in fact thought by some that it was part of that state.

In those early days came several families into the northeast corner of Tennessee from the Uplands of North Carolina. They banded together as the Watauga Association and spread over the eastern part of the section. North Carolina shortly accepted the district as Washington County which eventually embraced all of the present Tennessee. To secure federal protection for that territory, North Carolina handed it to the national government as a present. But apparently no one in Washington became enthusiastic about the gift, refusing even to acknowledge it. After it had been ignored for four or five years some of the settlers retaliated by organizing the territory into a new state, Franklin. But even that action received cold treatment from Washington, and eventually vanished into the air.

Almost as many early settlers in Tennessee came from North Carolina as came from South Carolina and Virginia. Many of the Tennessee counties were settled by Scotch-Irish immigrants coming into the state via the Shenandoah Valley. Many German families settled in several of the counties west of Chattanooga where still live many of their descendants.

Many present Tennessee counties were settled years before they were formed into counties. Some of those sections and the dates of their earliest settlement are as follows: Johnson, 1770; Washington, 1772, Robertson, 1776; Greene, 1778, Sumner, 1779; Hawkins, Hamilton, Davidson, Montgomery, 1780; Hamblen, Jefferson, Cooke, Jackson, 1783; Grainger, Williamson, 1784; Blount, 1786; Smith 1787; Cheatham, 1790; Dickson, Stewart, 1793; Claiborne, 1794; Hancock, 1795; Campbell, 1796; De Kalb, Wilson, 1797; Houston, Trousdale, 1798; Anderson, Franklin, Humphreys, Moore, Van Buren, 1800; Lincoln, 1806; Morgan, Lewis, Marshall, Maury, 1807; Lawrence, Henderson, 1815; Marion, Meiga, Benton, 1817; McMinn, Gibson, Hardeman, Hardin, Henry, Madison, McNairy, Obion, Shelby, Weakley, 1819; Carroll, Decatur, Lauderdale, 1820; Haywood, 1821; Fayette, 1822; Crockett, 1823; Lake, 1825; Polk, 1836.

In 1790, perhaps earlier, Tennessee had seven counties, each one embracing the following present counties: SULLIVAN - Johnson and Sullivan; WASHINGTON - Washington, Carter and Unicoi; HAWKINS - Hawkins, Hamblen, Grainger, Hancock, Claiborne, Campbell, Union, Anderson, Jefferson, Knox, Roane, Rhea, and Hamilton; GREENE - Greene, Cocke, corner of Jefferson, Blount, Loudon, south-west corner of Roane, Monroe, M'Minn, Polk, Meigs, Bradley, James, south-east corner of Hamilton; SUMNER - eastern third of Robertson, Sumner, Macon, Clay, Pickett, western half of Fentress, Overton, Jackson, Smith, Trousdale, Wilson, DeKalb, western two-thirds of White, Warren, northwest half of Coffee, and Cannon; DAVIDSON - Bedford, Marshall, Maury, Williamson, Rutherford, Davidson, Cheatham, and about middle third of Robertson; TENNESSEE - Stewart, Houston, Humphreys, Hickman, Dickson, Montgomery, and western third of Robertson. The rest of the territory was included in the Indian Country.

It should be noted that the counties to be settled first were in the East and the Middle Tennessee districts, the East district rather leading the Middle. The West Tennessee district was the last to be settled.

"The Colonial and State Records of North Carolina," found in many genealogical libraries, contains many records with much history of the early counties of Tennessee prior to 1790. The State Library at Nashville has one of the largest genealogical sections in the South.

Offical registration of births and deaths began in Tennessee in 1914. Official registration of marriages and divorces began in

County Map of Tennessee

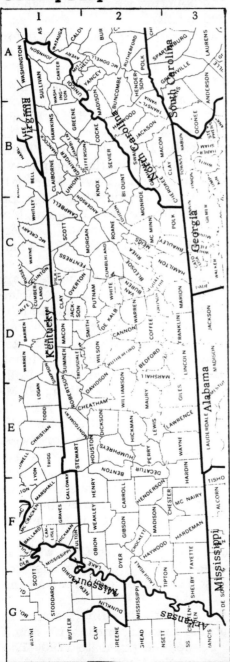

1945. These records may be had from the Division of Vital Statistics, State Dept. of Public Health, Nashville 37203, Tennessee. In the larger cities of Tennessee birth and death records are available for many years back. Check with the office of the City Health Dept. in the particular city in which your ancestors lived as you are ready to conduct your search.

The counties maintain marriage license records and records of wills, deeds, taxpayers lists, guardianship and other court proceedings in the respective county court houses. Some of these records have been transcribed and are in the State Library.

The early land grants are recorded in the Land Grant Office of the State Division of Archives, although these records are far from complete. Although limited in number, there are in the State Library some Church or Parish records as well as cemetery records. There is no full collection of such records in the state.

The most complete collection of war service records in the state is held by the office of Adjutant General, Employment Security Bldg., Nashville 37203 Tenn. There may not be many records of the early wars. There are records of Tennesseans who served in the Union

Forces during the Civil War but not those serving in the Confederate Army. Available are also records of the National Guard, Tennesseans who served in the Spanish-American War and World War I. The State Library has considerable card index of Tennesseans who served in the earlier wars and in the Confederate Army, but they are not complete and not official. They merely indicate the sources from which the information may be obtained.

All of the 1790 census were lost, and all but one county of the 1810 census. Tax lists help fill the gaps.

A letter from the Tennessee State Librarian and Archivist, Mrs. Dan M. Robinson, in 1942 says, "It is my understanding that all the Tennessee records we have and many we do not have were microfilmed back in the 1930's by the Genealogical Society of Utah, the Joseph F. Smith Memorial Building, 80 North Main St., Salt Lake City 84111, Utah. You will probably find there the most complete Tennessee records available in any one place."

Four books which may help you in your Tennessee research are:

Aklen, Jeannette Tillotson and Assistants, "Tennessee Bible Records and Marriage Bonds." Published by Cullom and Ghertner, Nashville, 1933. 2 Vols.

Ray, Worth S., "Tennessee Cousins," A history of Tennessee people. Published by the author. Austin, Texas, 1950.

Temple, O. P., "Notable Men of Tennessee," 1833-1875, Published 1912.

WPA. "Bibliography of Research Projects Reports." Check list of Historical Records Survey Publication, published 1940.

Libraries: Chattanooga Public Library, McCallie Ave., Chattanooga 37403, (Hamilton); Lawson McGhee Public Library, 217 Market St., (Tennessee History and Genealogy), Knoxville 37902, (Knox); Cossitt Public Library, Front and Monroe Sts., Memphis 38103, (Shelby); Nashville Public Library, 222 8th Ave. North, Nashville 37203, (Davidson).

Tennessee County Histories

(Population figures to nearest thousand - 1960 Census)

Name	Map Index	Date Formed	Pop. By M	Census Reports Available	Parent County	County Seat
Anderson	C2	1801	60	1830-80	Knox	Clinton
(Co Clk has m & pro rec)						
Bedford	D2	1807-8	23	1820-80	Rutherford	Shelbyville
(CH has been destroyed by a tornado and by fire in its history)						
Benton	E2	1835	11	1840-80	Henry, Humphreys	Camden
Bledsoe	C2	1807	8	1830-80	Roane	Pikeville
(Co Clk has m & pro rec from 1908) (CH burned 1908 m rec dest.)						
Blount	B2	1795	•58	1830-80	Knox	Maryville
Bradley	C3	1835	38	1840-80	Indian Lands	Cleveland

(Co Clk has m, pro, will from 1864, Cir Ct Clk has div rec)
Campbell　　C1　1806　28　1830-80　Anderson, Claiborne . . . . . .　Jacksboro
(Co Clk has m rec from 1838)
Cannon　　　D2　1836　9　1840-80　Coffee, Warren, Wilson . . . . .　Woodbury
Carroll　　　F2　1821　23　1830-80　Western District . . . .　Huntingdon
Carter　　　A1　1796　42　1830-80　Washington . . . .　Elizabethton
Cheatham　　E2　1856　9　1860-80　Davidson, Dickson,
　　　　　　　　　　　　　　　　Montgomery . . . .　Ashland City
Chester　　　F3　1875　10　1881　Hardeman, Madison, Henderson,
　　　　　　　　　　　　　　　　McNairy . . . .　Henderson
(Co Clk has m, pro rec from 1890; Cir Ct Clk has div & civ ct rec; Division
of Vit Stat, Nashville, Tenn. has b, d & bur rec)
Claiborne　　B1　1801　19　1830-80　Grainger, Hawkins . . . .　Tazewell
Clay　　　　D1　1870　7　1880　Jackson, Overton . . . .　Celina
Cocke　　　B2　1797　23　1830-80　Jefferson . . . .　Newport
(CH burned 1875, most records lost)
Coffee　　　D2　1836　29　1840-80　Franklin, Warren, Bedford . . Manchester
Crockett　　F2　1845　15　1880　Dyer, Madison, Gibson, Haywood . Alamo
(Many early census rec of residents of Crockett Co may be found in sur-
rounding counties) (Co Clk has m & pro rec from 1872; Cir Ct Clk has div &
civ ct rec; Dept of Public Health, Nashville, Tenn. has b, d & bur rec)
Cumberland C2　1856　19　1860-80　Bledsoe, Morgan, Roane . . . Crossville
(Co Clk has m & pro rec from 1905, div rec from 1943)
Davidson　　E2　1783　400　1820-80　Washington . . . .　Nashville
Decatur　　E2　1845　8　1850-80　Perry . . . .　Decaturville
(Co Clk has m & pro rec from 1869, b rec from 1927 to 1939; State of Tenn.
also has b, d & m rec)
DeKalb　　　D2　1837-8　11　1840-80　Cannon, Warren, White . . . Smithville
(Co Clk has m rec from 1848, Chancery Ct has div rec; Division of Vit Stat,
Nashville, Tenn has b & d rec)
Dickson　　E2　1803　19　1820-80　Montgomery, Robertson . . . Charlotte
(CH was destroyed by tornado about 1835, large number of rec destroyed;
Co Clk has m rec from 1839, wills & land rec from 1803)
Dyer　　　　F2　1823　30　1830-80　Western District . . . .　Dyersburg
(Co Clk has m rec from 1850, also div & pro rec)
Fayette　　　F3　1824　25　1830-80　Shelby, Hardeman . . . .　Somerville
Fentress　　C1　1823　13　1830-80　Morgan, Overton . . . .　Jamestown
Franklin　　D3　1807　26　1820-80　Bedford, Warren . . . .　Winchester
Gibson　　　F2　1823　45　1830-80　Western District . . . .　Trenton
Giles　　　　E3　1809　22　1820-80　Maury . . . .　Pulaski
(CH was burned during CW, research is quite difficult; Co Clk has m rec from
1865, deeds from 1809)
Grainger　　B1　1796　13　1830-80　Hawkins, Knox . . . .　Rutledge
Greene　　　B1　1783　42　1830-80　Washington . . . .　Greenville
Grundy　　　D2　1844　12　1850-80　Coffee, Warren . . . .　Altamont
(Co Ct Clk has m & pro rec from 1850)
Hamblen　　B1　1870　33　1880　Grainger, Hawkins . . . . . . Morristown
(Co Ct Clk has m & pro rec; State has b rec; Clk & Master have div rec)
Hamilton　　C3　1819　238　1830-80　Rhea . . . .　Chattanooga
(Co Clk has m rec from 1857 to 1956; Dept of Public Health, Nashville, Tenn.
has b, d & bur rec; Cir Ct has div rec; Clk & Master has pro rec; Sessions
Ct has civ ct rec)
Hancock　　B1　1844　8　1850-80　Claiborne, Hawkins . . . .　Sneedville
Hardeman　　F3　1823　22　1830-80　Western District . . . .　Bolivar
Hardin　　　E3　1819　17　1820-80　Western District . . . . .　Savannah
(Co Ct Clk has m rec from 1860, div, pro & civ ct rec, settlements, wills,
& land grants from 1865)
Hawkins　　B1　1786　30　1830-80　Sullivan . . . .　Rogersville
(Co Clk has m rec from 1865, pro rec from 1865; Clk & Master has b & div
rec; Health Dept has d & bur rec; Civ Ct Clk has civ ct rec)
Haywood　　F2　1823　23　1830-80　Western District . . . .　Brownsville
Henderson　　F2　1821　16　1830-80　Western District . . . . . .　Lexington

(CH burned 1863 & 1895 some rec saved; Co Clk has b rec from 1908 to 1912 and 1925 to 1939, m rec from 1893, d rec from 1908 to 1912, also has pro rec)

Henry   F2   1821   22   1830-80   Western District . . . . Paris
(Co Clk has m rec from 1838)

Hickman   E2   1807   12   1820-80   Dickson . . . . Centerville
(CH burned in 1865, all prior rec destroyed; Co Ct Clk has b rec from 1908 to 1912 and 1920 to 1936, m, div, pro, civ ct rec from 1867)

Houston   E2   1871   5   1880   Dickson, Stewart . . . . Erin

Humphreys   E2   1809   12   1820-80   Stewart, Smith . . . . Waverly
(CH burned in 1876 & in 1898, great lack of rec, land rec are only thing that is complete; Co Clk has deed rec from 1809, m from 1861, wills & inventories from 1838)

Jackson   D1   1801   9   1820-80   Smith . . . . Gainesboro
(Co Clk has m & pro rec from 1870)

Jefferson   B2   1792   21   1830-80   Green, Hawkins . . . . . . Dandridge
(Co Clk has m, pro & wills rec from 1792)

Johnson   A1   1836   11   1840-80   Carter . . . . Mountain City
(Co Clk has m & pro rec from 1836; Chancery & cir ct has div, civ ct rec; Division of Vit Stat, Tenn Dept of Health has b & d rec)

Knox   B2   1792   251   1830-80   Greene, Hawkins . . . . Knoxville

Lake   F2   1870   10   1870-80   Obion . . . . Tiptonville

Lauderdale   G2   1835   22   1840-80   Dyer, Tipton . . . . Ripley

Lawrence   E3   1817   28   1820-80   Hickman, Maury . . . . . . Lawrenceburg
(Co Clk has m rec from 1838, wills & pro rec from 1849; Cir Ct has div rec Dept of Public Health, Nashville, Tenn has b & d rec)

Lewis   E2   1843   6   1850-80   Hickman, Maury, Wayne,
                                         Lawrence . . . . Hohenwald
(This Co completely abolished for one year following the CW, for that year rec will be found in Maury, Lawrence, Hickman & Wayne Cos; Guardian bonds & court minutes begin 1846)

Lincoln   D3   1809   24   1820-80   Bedford . . . . Fayetteville

Loudon   C2   1871   24   1880   Blount, Monroe, Roane . . . . . . Loudon

McNairy   F3   1823   18   1830-80   Hardin . . . . Selmer

McMinn   C2   1819   34   1830-80   Indian Lands . . . . Athens

Macon   D1   1842   12   1850-80   Smith, Sumner . . . . Lafayette

Madison   F2   1821   61   1830-80   Western District . . . . Jackson

Marion   D3   1817   21   1830-80   Indian Lands . . . . Jasper
(Co Clk has m rec from 1919, pro rec from 1874)(CH burned 1922 m rec dest.)

Marshall   D2   1836   17   1840-80   Bedford, Lincoln, Giles, Maury . Lewisburg
(Co Clk has m & pro rec from 1836)

Maury   D2   1807   42   1820-80   Williamson . . . . Columbia
(Deed rec, m license & bonds begin 1807, also wills & inventories)

Meigs   C2   1836   5   1840-80   Hamilton, McMinn, Rhea . . . . . . Decatur

Monroe   C2   1819   23   1830-80   Roane . . . . Madisonville
(Co Clk has m rec from 1838, pro rec 1853, wills 1833, co ct rec 1868)

Montgomery   E1   1796   56   1820-80   Tennessee . . . . Clarksville

Moore   D3   1871   3   1880   Bedford, Franklin . . . . Lynchburg

Morgan   C2   1817   14   1830-80   Roane . . . . Wartburg

Obion   F2   1823   27   1830-80   Western District . . . . Union City

Overton   C1   1806   15   1820-80   Jackson . . . . Livingston

Perry   E2   1818   5   1820-80   Hickman . . . . Linden

Pickett   C1   1879   4   Fentress, Overton . . . . Byrdstown

Polk   C3   1839   12   1840-80   Bradley, McMinn . . . . Benton

Putnam   D2   1842   29   1860-80   White, Jackson, Overton, Dekalb . Cookeville
(Co Clk has m & pro rec; CH burned 1890, m rec begin 1879)

Rhea   C2   1807   16   1830-80   Roane . . . . Dayton
(Co Clk has m rec from 1808)

Roane   C2   1801   39   1830-80   Knox, Blount . . . . Kingston
(Co Clk has m & pro rec from 1801)

Robertson   E1   1796   27   1820-80   Tennessee . . . . Springfield
(Co Clk has m rec from 1839, pro rec from 1796; Cir Ct Clk has div & civ

ct rec; Division of Vit Stat, Nashville, Tenn. has b, d & bur rec)
Rutherford   D2   1803   52   1810–80   Davidson . . . . Murfreesboro
   (Co Ct clk has m & pro rec from 1804)
Scott   C1   1849   15   1850–80   Fentress, Morgan, Anderson . . Huntsville
Sequatchie   C2   1857   6   1860–80   Hamilton . . . . Dunlap
   (Co Clk has b, m, d & pro rec)
Sevier   B2   1794   24   1830–80   Jefferson . . . . Sevierville
   (Co Clk has m rec from 1856, wills from 1850)
Shelby   G3   1819 627   1820–80   Hardin . . . . Memphis
   (Co Ct Clk has m rec from 1820; Memphis & Shelby Co Health Dept has b,
   d & bur rec; Chancery Ct Clk has div rec; Pro Ct Clk has pro rec; Res-
   pective Ct Clks have civ ct rec)
Smith   D2   1799   12   1820–80   Sumner . . . . Carthage
Stewart   E1   1803   8   1820–80   Montgomery . . . . Dover
   (CH burned during CW; Co Clk has deed rec from 1803, m from 1838)
Sullivan   A1   1779 114   1830–80   Washington . . . . Blountville
   (Co Clk has m & pro rec from 1863)
Sumner   D1   1786   36   1820–80   Davidson . . . . Gallatin
Tennessee   1788   Co. surrendered name when state
                                        became Tennessee 1796
Tipton   G3   1823   29   1830–80   Western District . . . . Covington
   (Co Ct Clk has m, div & pro rec; Division of Vit Stat, Nashville, Tenn. has b
   & d rec; funeral homes have bur rec; Cir Ct Clk has civ ct rec)
Trousdale   D1   1870   5   1880   Macon, Smith, Wilson . . . . Hartsville
Unicoi   A1   1875   15   1880   Carter, Washington . . . . Erwin
Union   B1   1850   8   1860–80   Anderson, Campbell . . . . . . Maynardville
Van Buren   D2   1840   4   1850–80   Bledsoe, Warren, White . . . . Spencer
Warren   D2   1807   23   1820–80   White . . . . McMinnville
   (Co Hist has m rec from 1852; Co Ct Clk has div & civ ct rec)
Washington   A1   1777   65   1830–80   Covered present state. Many counties
                                        from section . . . . Jonesboro
   (This county also embraced parts of present N.C Counties) (Co Clk has b
   rec from 1908 to 1912 and from 1925 to 1938, m rec from 1787, pro rec from
   1780, wills from 1779)
Wayne   1785   Abolished 1788
   (This Wayne Co created under the State of Franklin. Included present Carter
   Co and part of Johnson Co.)
Wayne   E1   1819   12   1820–80   Hickman . . . . Waynesboro
Weakley   F2   1823   24   1830–80   Western District . . . . Dresden
White   C2   1806   16   1820–80   Overton, Jackson, Smith . . . . Sparta
   (Co Clk has m rec from 1838, about two dozen before that from 1809, Will,
   settlements, deeds & inventories from 1806)
Williamson   E2   1799   25   1820–80   Davidson . . . . Franklin
   (Co Clk has m rec from 1800, tax, wills, minutes, deeds from 1799)
Wilson   D2   1799   28   1820–80   Sumner . . . . Lebanon
   (Co Clk has m, pro, wills from 1800)

Genealogists' Check List of the Historical Records Survey, Tennessee

Federal Courts. Inventory of County Archives, Anderson, Bedford, Blount, Bradley, Cheatham, Crockett, Hamilton, Haywood, Loudon, Rutherford, Sullivan, Tipton, Wilson. Transcription of Public Archives, minutes of Shelby County Court 1820-1824, minutes of Knox County Court 1792-1795. Guide to Public Vital Statistic records. Guide to Church Vital Statistic records. Inventory of the Church and Synagogue Archives of Tenn. - Tenn. Baptist Convention (Nashville Baptist Association) - Ocoee Baptist

Association - Jewish Congregations - Outline of Development of Methodism in Tenn. Directory of Church, Missions and Religious Institutions of Tenn. Davidson County, Hamilton County, Knox County, Shelby County, Washington County. Guide to depository of manuscript collections in Tenn. Guide to collection of manuscripts in Tenn. Check list of Tenn. imprints 1793-1840 in Tenn. Library. Check list of Tenn. imprints 1841-1850. Check list of Tenn. imprints 1793-1840. Check list of records required or permitted by law in Tenn. Instructions for using county records as source material. Directory of Libraries in Tenn. History and organization of the Shelby County Judiciary. Summary of general highway legislation in Tenn. 1881-1909. Summary of special legislation relating to government of Sullivan County. Check list of acts and codes of the state of Tenn 1792-1939. Depository of unpublished material, State Planning Commission, Nashville, Tenn.

Texas

Capital Austin - State 1845 - (28th)

Texas has been under the jurisdiction of six separate governments since 1685, those of France, Spain, Mexico, The Republic of Texas, The Confederacy, and the United States.

In 1820 the white settlers of Texas could be counted in four digits. Shortly afterwards former residents of Alabama, Louisiana, Mississippi, and Tennessee were brought into the section under the leadership of Moses Austin and his son, Stephen. By 1830 more than 20,000 Americans had become tillers of Texas soil.

Austin has been the capital of Texas since statehood. Other cities which have been the capitals of Texas are Sen Felip de Austin, Washington-on-the-Brazos, Harrisburg, Galveston, Velasco and Columbia during the Revolution, 1835, 1836; Houston, 1837-1839; Austin, 1839; Houston, Washington-on-the-Brazos, 1842-1845; Austin since 1845.

The State Historical Society in Austin has many records of value to the genealogist. Among the public libraries with genealogical sections are those in San Antonio, Dallas, Houston, and Fort Worth. There are collections of material in the museum libraries of the Daughters of the Republic of Texas, and the United Daughters of the Confederacy, both of which are in the Old Land Office Building, Austin 78711, Texas. The Archives section of the Texas State Library, State Capital, Austin 78711, Texas, is a relatively large proportion of the library's holdings.

The Museum Library of San Jacinto Monument has a collection of earlier and colonial period publications. The Cody Memorial Library, Southwestern University, Georgetown, Texas, and the Rosenberg Library in Galveston also cater to researchers. Several Genealogical Societies have sprung up in recent years to assist ancestor searchers. Among the more prominent are:

West Texas Genealogical Society, 3418 Woodridge Dr., Abilene 79605, Texas.

Local History and Genealogical Society, 1954 Commerce St., Dallas, Texas 75201.

Fort Worth Genealogical Society, Box 864, Forth Worth 76101 Texas.

San Antonio Genealogical and Historical Society, P.O. Box 6383, San Antonia 78209, Texas.

Texas State Genealogical Society, 2528 University Drive, So., Fort Worth, Texas 76109.

Central Texas Genealogical Society, 3828 North 22nd St., Waco, Texas.

Other Texas Libraries -- Mary E. Bivins Memorial Library, 10th and Polk St., Amarillo 79101, (Potter); Austin Public Library, 401 W. 9th St. Austin 78701, (Travis); Texas State Library and Historical Commission, State Capital, Austin 78701, (Potter); The University of Texas, Mirabeau B. Lamar Library, (Texas History), Austin 78712, (Potter); Tyrrell Public Library, Pearl & Forsythe, Beaumont 77701, (Jefferson); Dallas Historical Society Library, Hall of Records, 6445 Stichter, Dallas 75230, (Dallas); Dallas Public Library, Commerce & Harwood Sts., Dallas 75201, (Dallas); El Paso Public Library, (Southwest), 501 N. Oregon, El Paso 79901, (El Paso); Fort Worth Public Library, Ninth and Throckmorton St., Fort Worth, 76102, (Tarrant); Rosenburg Public Library, 823 Tremont, Galveston 77550, (Galveston); Harris County Public Library, 1223 Elder St., Houston 77007, (Harris); Houston Public Library, 500 McKinney Ave., Houston 77002, (Harris); San Antonio Public Library, 210 E. Market St., San Antonio 78205, (Bexar); Baylor University Library, Waco 76703, (McLennan).

The Bureau of Vital Statistics, Texas State Department of Health, Austin, Texas 78711 has birth and death records from 1903 to the present, and delayed birth records from about 1850 to 1951, including voluntary registrations made during and since 1929 for births not registered at time of events. The City Clerk of the city, or the County Clerk of the county may have birth or death records prior to 1903.

The County Clerk of each county is custodian of other material of interest to the genealogical researcher.

Johnson, Sid S., ''Texans Who Wore the Gray,'' Names and

deeds of the men who fought for the South in the war between the states.

Texas County Histories

(Population figures to nearest thousand - 1960 Census)

Name	Map Index	Date Formed	Pop. By M	Census Reports Available	Parent County	County Seat
Anderson	B2	1846	28	1850-80	Houston	Palestine

(Co Clk has b & d rec from 1903, m, pro & civ ct rec from 1846; Dist Clk has div rec)

Andrews	E2	1875	13		Bexar	Andrews
Angelina	A2	1846	40	1850-80	Nacogdoches	Lufkin

(m rec available from 1846)

Aransas	B4	1871	7	1880	Refugio	Rockport
Archer	C1	1858	6	1880	Fannin	Archer City
Armstrong	F1	1876	2	1880	Bexar	Claude
Atascosa	C4	1856	19	1860-80	Bexar	Jourdanton
Austin	B3	1837	14	1850-80	Old Mexican Municipality	Bellville
Bailey	E1	1876	9		Bexar	Muleshoe

(Co Clk has b, m, d, div, pro, civ ct rec from 1919)

Bandera	C3	1856	4		Uvalde, Bexar	Bandera

(Co Clk has m, div, pro, civ ct, cattle brands from 1856, b & d rec from 1904)

Bastrop	B3	1836	17	1850-80	Old Mexican Municipality	Bastrop
Baylor	C1	1858	6	1880	Fannin	Seymour
Bee	B4	1857	24	1860-80	Goliad, Refugio, Live Oak, San Patricio	Beeville

(Co Clk has b & d rec from 1903, civ ct rec from 1876, m & pro rec from 1858; Dist Clk has div rec)

Bell	B2	1850	94	1860-80	Milam	Belton

(Co Clk has b & d rec from 1903, m & pro rec from 1850, also civ ct rec)

Bexar	C3	1836	687	1850-80	Old Mexican Municipality established 1718	San Antonio

(Co Clk has b rec from 1838, m rec from 1837, d rec from 1903, div rec from 1910, pro rec from 1836, civ ct rec from 1899, spanish archives from 1729 to 1836)

Blanco	C3	1858	4	1870-80	Gillespie, Comal, Burnet, Hays	Johnson City

(Co Clk has b & d rec from 1903, m, pro rec from 1876, bur rec from 1928, div & civ ct rec from 1877)

Borden	D2	1876	1	1880	Bexar	Gail

(Co Clk has b & d rec from 1903, m, div, civ ct rec from 1891, pro rec from 1894)

Bosque	C2	1854	11	1860-80	McLennan, Milam Dist.	Meridian
Bowie	A1	1840	60	1850-80	Red River	Boston

(Co Clk has b, m, d, bur, pro rec from 1889)

Brazoria	A3	1836	76	1850-80	Old Mexican Municipality	Angelton

(Co Clk has b rec from 1900, m bonds from 1829 to 1836, m licenses from 1838, d rec from 1903)

Brazos	B3	1841	45	1850-80	Washington, Robertson	Bryan

(Originally Navasota Co. - changed to Brazos 1842; Co Clk has m rec from 1841, b & d rec from 1900, pro rec from 1844, civ ct rec from 1959, some civ ct rec earlier)

Brewster	E3	1887	6		Presidio	Alpine

(Co Clk has b & d rec from 1903, m, div, pro, civ ct rec from 1887)

Briscoe	F2	1876	4	1880	Bexar	Silverton

(Co Clk has b rec from 1906, m, div, pro & civ ct rec from 1892, d rec from 1902; Cem assn, has bur rec)

Brooks	F4	1911	9		Starr, Zapata, Hidalgo	Falfurrias

(Co Clk has b, m, d, pro, civ ct rec from 1911)

Brown   C2   1856   25   1860-80   Travis, Comanche   . . . . . . Brownwood
    (Co Clk has b & d rec from 1903, m rec from 1900, civ ct rec from 1930, pro
    and bur rec from 1920; Dist Clk has div rec)
Buchanan   1860   Discontinued
Burleson   B3   1846   11   1850-80   Milam, Washington . . . . Caldwell
    (Co Clk has b & d rec from 1903, m rec 1845, pro rec 1846, civ ct & deeds 1845)
Burnet   C3   1852   9   1860-80   Travis, Bell, Williamson . . . . Burnet
    (Co Clk has b & d rec from 1903, m, pro, civ ct rec from 1852)
Caldwell   B3   1848   17   1850-80   Gonzales . . . . Lockhart
Calhoun   B4   1846   17   1850-80   Victoria, Matagorda, Jackson . Port Lavaca
    (Co Clk has b & d rec from 1903, m & deeds rec from 1846, civ
    ct rec from 1850, criminal rec from 1909, discharge rec from 1919)
Callahan   C2   1858   8   1880   Bexar, Travis, Bosque . . . . Baird
Cameron   E4   1848   151   1850-80   Nueces . . . . Brownsville
    (Co Clk has b rec from 1929, d rec from 1928, m, pro rec from 1848, civ ct
    rec from 1876; Dist Clk has div rec)
Camp   A1   1874   8   1880   Upshur . . . . Pittsburg
    (Co Clk has b & d rec from 1903, m, pro, civ ct rec from 1874; Dist Clk has
    div rec)
Carson   F1   1876   8   Bexar . . . . Panhandle
Cass   A1   1846   23   1850-80   Bowie . . . . Linden
    (Name changed to Davis in 1861 - renamed Cass in 1871)
Castro   F2   1876   9   Bexar . . . . Dimmitt
Chambers   A3   1858   10   1860-80   Jefferson, Liberty . . . . Anahuac
    (Co Clk has b rec from 1903, m rec 1877, d & bur rec 1908, div rec 1910)
Cherokee   A2   1846   33   1850-80   Nacogdoches . . . . Rusk
    (Co Clk has b & d rec from 1903, m, pro, civ ct rec from 1846)
Childress   E2   1876   8   1880   Bexar, Youngland Dist. . . . . Childress
    (Co Clk has b & d rec from 1903, m & pro rec from 1891; Dist Clk has div rec)
Clay   C1   1857   8   1860-80   Cooke   . . . . Henrietta
    (Co Clk has b & d rec from 1903, m rec from 1874, pro rec from 1873, civ ct
    rec from 1876; Dist Clk has div rec)
Cochran   E1   1876   6   Bexar . . . . Morton
    (Co Clk has b, m, d, div, pro, civ ct rec from 1924)
Coke   D2   1889   4   Tom Green . . . . Robert Lee
    (Co Clk has b rec from 1903, m rec 1890, div, pro, civ ct rec 1890, d rec 1906)
Coleman   C2   1858   12   1870-80   Travis, Brown . . . . Coleman
Collin   B1   1846   41   1850-80   Fannin . . . . McKinney
Collingsworth E1 1876   6   1880   Bexar, Youngland Dist. . . . . Wellington
Colorado   B3   1837   18   Old Mexican Municipality . . . Columbus
    (Co Clk has b & d rec from 1903, m & pro rec from 1837; Dist Clk has div &
    civ ct rc)
Comal   C3   1846   20   1850-80   Bexar, Gonzales, Travis . . New Braunfels
    (Co Clk has b & d rec from 1903, m rec from 1846, also pro, naturalization
    and deed rec)
Comanche   C2   1856   12   1860-80   Bosque, Coryell . . . . Comanche
Concho   C2   1858   4   1880   Bexar . . . . Paint Rock
Cooke   B1   1848   23   1850-80   Fannin . . . . Gainesville
    (Co Clk has b & d rec from 1903, m, div, pro, civ ct rec from 1849)
Coryell   C2   1854   24   1860-80   Bell . . . . Gatesville
Cottle   D1   1876   4   1880   Fannin . . . . Paducah
Crane   E2   1887   5   Tom Green . . . . Crane
Crockett   D3   1875   4   1880   Bexar . . . . Ozona
    (Co Clk has b, d, bur rec from 1903, div, pro, civ ct rec from 1892)
Crosby   D1   1876   10   1880   Bexar Dist. (Org 1886) . . . Crosbyton
    (Co Clk has b & d rec from June 1903, m rec from Oct 1886, also pro & civ ct
    rec; Dist Clk has div rec)
Culberson   E2   1911   3   El Paso . . . . Van Horn
Dallam   F1   1876   6   Bexar . . . . Dalhart
    (Co Clk has b, d, pro rec from 1903, m rec 1891, div & civ ct rec 1892)
Dallas   B2   1846   952   1850-80   Nacogdoches, Robertson . . . . Dallas

(Co Clk has b & d rec from 1903, m rec from 1846, pro & civ ct rec; Dist Ct has div rec)

Davis   1870   Discontinued

Dawson   D2   1876-58 19   1860-80   Bexar (Org. 1905) .... Lamesa

Deaf Smith   F1   1876   13   1880   Bexar .... Hereford
(Co Clk has b & d rec from 1903, m, pro, civ ct rec from 1891; Dist Ct has div rec; Funeral Homes have bur rec)

Delta   B1   1870   6   1880   Hopkins, Lamar .... Cooper
(Co Clk has b, pro, civ ct rec from 1903, m rec 1870, d & bur rec 1916)

Denton   B1   1846   47   1850-80   Fannin .... Denton

DeWitt   B3   1846   21   1850-80   Goliad, Gonzales, Victoria .... Cuero
(Co Clk has b & d rec from 1903, m, pro, civ ct rec & cattle brands from 1846)

Dickens   D1   1876   5   1880   Bexar .... Dickens
(Co Clk has b & d rec from 1903, m, div, pro, civ ct rec & deeds from 1891)

Dimmit   C4   1858   10   1880   Uvalde, Bexar, Maverick
             Webb .... Carrizo Springs
(Co Clk has b & d rec from 1903, m & civ ct rec 1881, pro rec 1882)

Donley   E1   1881   4   1881   Jack .... Clarendon
(Co Clk has b, d & bur rec from 1903, m, div, pro, civ ct rc from 1881)

Duval   F4   1858   13   1870-80   Live Oak, Starr, Neuces .... San Diego

Eastland   C2   1858   20   1860-80   Bosque, Coryell, Travis .... Eastland

Ector   E2   1887   91   Tom Green .... Odessa
(Co Clk has b, m, d, bur, pro, civ ct rec)

Edwards   D3   1858   2   1880   Bexar .... Rocksprings

Ellis   B2   1849   43   1850-80   Navarro .... Waxahachie

El Paso   F2   1850   314   1860-80   Bexar .... El Paso

Encinal   1860-70   Discontinued

Erath   C2   1856   16   1860-80   Bosque, Coryell .... Stephenville
(Co Clk has b & d rec from 1903, m rec 1869, pro & civ ct rec 1890)

Falls   B2   1850   21   1860-80   Limestone, Milam .... Marlin
(Co Clk has b & d rec from 1903, m & pro rec from 1854)

Fannin   B1   1837   24   1850-80   Red River .... Bonham
(Co Clk has b & d rec from 1903, m rec from 1850, pro rec from 1838)

Fayette   B3   1837   20   1850-80   Bastrop, Colorado ...... La Grange
(Co Clk has b & d rec from 1903, some b rec from 1866 to 1875, m, pro, civ ct rec from 1838)

Fisher   D2   1876   8   1880   Bexar .... Roby
(Co Clk has b, m, d, rec from 1903, pro & civ ct rec from 1886)

Floyd   D1   1876   12   1880   Bexar (Org. 1890) .... Floydada

Foard   C1   1891   3   Hardman, Knox, King, Cottle .. Crowell

Fort Bend   B3   1837   41   1850-80   Austin .... Richmond
(Co Clk has b & d rec from 1903, m & pro rec from 1838)

Franklin   A1   1875   5   1880   Titus .... Mt. Vernon
(Co Clk has b & d rec from 1903, m, pro, civ ct rec from 1875)

Freestone   B2   1850   13   1860-80   Limestone .... Fairfield
(Co Clk has b & d rec from 1903, m & pro rec from 1851)

Frio   C4   1871   10   1860-80   Atascosa, Bexar, Uvalde .... Pearsall

Gaines   E2   1876   12   1880   Bexar .... Seminole
(Co Clk has b, m, d, bur, pro, civ ct rec from 1905)

Galveston   A3   1838   140   1850-80   Brazoria .... Galveston
(Co Clk has b & d rec from June 1903 to 1910, m & pro rec from 1838, civ ct rec from 1875; City Hall, Registrar of birth has b rec after 1910)

Garza   D1   1907   7   1880   Bexar .... Post
(Co Clk has b, m, d, div, pro & civ ct rec from 1907)

Gillespie   C3   1848   10   1850-80   Bexar, Travis .... Fredericksburg

Glasscock   D2   1887   1   Tom Green .... Garden City
(Co Clk has b, m, d, div, pro, civ ct rec from 1893)

Goliad   B4   1836   5   1850-80   Old Mexican Municipality ...... Goliad

Gonzales   B3   1837   18   1850-80   Old Mexican Municipality ... Gonzales
(Co Clk has b & d rec from 1903, m rec from 1829, also pro & civ ct rec; Dist Clk has div rec)

Gray   E1 1876   32 1880   Bexar . . . . Pampa
    (Co Clk has b, m, d, pro, civ ct rec from 1902, rec not complete between 1902
    and 1930 for b & d rec; Cem Assn has bur rec; Dist Clk has div rec)
Grayson   B1 1846   73 1850-80   Fannin . . . . Sherman
    (Co Clk has b, m, d, pro, civ ct rec & deeds from 1846; Dist Clk has div rec)
Gregg   A2 1873   69 1880   Rusk, Upshur . . . . Longview
    (Co Clk has b, m, d, pro, civ ct rec from 1873; Dist Clk has div rec)
Grimes   B3 1846   13 1850-80   Montgomery . . . . Anderson
Guadalupe   C3 1846   29 1850-80   Bexar, Gonzales . . . . Seguin
    (Co Clk has b, d, bur rec from 1935, m & pro rec from 1838)
Hale   D1 1876   37   Bexar . . . . Plainview
    (Co Clk has m rec from 1888, pro rec from 1889 & civ ct rec from 1900;
    Justice of Peace & City Clk have d & bur rec; Dist Clk has div rec)
Hail   E2 1876   7 1880   Bexar, Young . . . . Memphis
    (Co Clk has b rec from 1901, d rec from 1903, m, pro civ ct rec, deeds from
    1890)
Hamilton   C2 1842   8 1860-80   Bosque, Comanche, Lampasas,
                                      Coryell . . . . Hamilton
    (Co Clk has b & d rec from 1903, m rec from 1880)
Hansford   F1 1876   6 1880   Bexar, Young . . . . Spearman
    (Co Clk has b rec from 1889, also m, d, bur, div, pro & civ ct rec)
Hardeman   C1 1858   8 1880   Fannin . . . . Quanah
    (Co Clk has b & d rec from 1903, m, pro, civ ct rec from 1885)
Hardin   A3 1858   25 1860-80   Jefferson, Liberty . . . . Kountze
Harris   A3 1836 1243 1850-80   Formerly Harrisburg Municipality
                                      (Original county) . . . . Houston
Harrison   A2 1839   46 1850-80   Shelby . . . . Marshall
    (Co Clk has b & d rec from 1903, m & pro rec from 1840, Co Civ ct rec 1900)
Hartley   F1 1876   2 1880   Bexar, Young . . . . Channing
    (Co Clk has b rec from 1903, m, d, div, pro, civ ct rec from 1891)
Haskell   C1 1858   11 1880   Fannin, Milam . . . . Haskell
    (Co Clk has b & d rec from 1903, m rec from 1885)
Hays   C3 1848   20 1850-80   Travis . . . . San Marcos
Hemphill   E1 1876   3 1880   Bexar, Young . . . . Canadian
    (Co Clk has b rec from 1896)
Henderson   B2 1846   22 1850-80   Houston, Nacogdoches . . . . . Athens
    (Co Clk has b & d rec from 1903, m & pro rec from 1860, Voters from 1867 to
    1872, cattle brands from 1846, bur rec from 1903 & civ ct rec from 1909)
Hidalgo   F4 1852   181 1860-80   Cameron . . . . Edinburg
Hill   B2 1853   24 1860-80   Navarro . . . . Hillsboro
    (Co Clk has b & d rec from 1903, m, pro rec from 1874; Dist Clk has div rec;
    CH burned sometime between 1874 and 1878)
Hockley   E1 1876   22   Bexar, Young (Org. 1921) . . . Levelland
    (Co Clk has b, m, civ ct rec from 1921, d & pro rec from 1921; attached to
    Lubbock from 1891 to 1921)
Hood   C2 1866   5 1870-80   Johnson . . . . Granbury
Hopkins   B1 1846   19 1850-80   Lamar, Nacogdoches . . . Sulphur Springs
    (Co Clk has b & d rec from 1903, m rec from 1846, pro rec from 1800's; Dist
    Clk has div rec)
Houston   A2 1837   19 1850-80   Nacogdoches . . . . Crockett
    (Co Clk has b & d rec from 1903, m & pro rec from 1882)
Howard   D2 1876   40 1880   Bexar, Young . . . . Big Spring
Hudspeth   F2 1917   3   El Paso . . . . Sierra Blanca
Hunt   B1 1846   39 1850-80   Fannin, Nacogdoches . . . . Greenville
    (Co Clk has b & d rec from 1903, m rec 1858, pro rec 1896, deeds 1846)
Hutchinson F1 1876   34   Bexar Dist. . . . . Stinnett
Irion   D2 1889   1   Tom Green . . . . Mertzon
    (Co Clk has b, d, bur, div, pro, civ ct rec from 1903, m rec from 1889)
Jack   C1 1856   7 1860-80   Cooke . . . . Jacksboro
    (Co Clk has b & d rec from 1903, also pro, civ ct rec; Dist Clk has div rec)
Jackson   B4 1835   14 1850-80   Old Mexican Municipality . . . . Edna

(Co Clk has b & d rec from 1903, m & pro rec from 1836)

Jasper	A2	1835	22	1850–80	Old Mexican Municipality .... Jasper
Jeff Davis	E3	1887	2		Presidio .... Fort Davis
Jefferson	A3	1836	246	1850–80	Old Mexican Municipality .. Beaumont

(Co Clk has b & d rec from 1904, m, pro, civ ct rec from 1836; Dist Clk has div rec & civ ct rec for suits above $1000.00)

Jim Hogg	F4	1913	5		Brooks, Duval .... Hebbronville
Jim Wells	E4	1911	35		Nueces .... Alice

(Co Clk has b, m, d, pro, civ ct rec from 1911; Dist Clk has div rec)

Johnson	B2	1854	35	1860–80	Ellis, Hill, Navarro ...... Cleburne
Jones	C2	1858–61	19	1880	Bexar, Bosque (Org. 1881) ..... Anson

(Co Clk has b & d rec from 1903, m, pro, civ ct rec from 1882)

Karnes	B4	1854	15	1860–80	Bexar .... Karnes City

(Co Clk has b & d rec from 1903, m rec from 1865, pro rec from 1878, civ ct rec from 1854)

Kaufman	B2	1848	30	1850–80	Henderson .... Kaufman

(Co Clk has b & d rec from 1903, m & pro rec from 1850)

Kendall	C3	1862	6	1870–80	Kerr, Blanco .... Boerne
Kenedy	E4	1921	.9		Willacy, Hidalgo, Cameron ...... Sarita
Kent	D1	1876	2		Bexar, Young .... Jayton

(Co Clk has b rec from 1903, also m, d, bur, div, pro, civ ct rec from 1893)

Kerr	C3	1856	17	1860–80	Bexar .... Kerrville
Kimble	C3	1858	4	1870–80	Bexar .... Junction

(Co Clk has b, d, & bur rec from 1903, m, div, pro & civ ct rec from 1884; Bureau of Vit Stat, Austin, Tex. also has b, d, & bur rec)

King	D1	1876	.6	1880	Bexar .... Guthrie
Kinney	D3	1850	2	1860–80	Bexar .... Brackettville

(Co Clk has b & d rec from 1903, m rec from 1872 & div, pro & civ ct rec; Brackettville Cem Assn has bur rec)

Kleberg	E4	1913	30		Nueces .... Kingsville

(Co Clk has b, m, d, pro & civ ct rec from 1913; Dist Clk has div rec)

Knox	C1	1858	8	1880	Young, Bexar .... Benjamin
Lamar	B1	1840	34	1850–80	Red River .... Paris

(Co Clk has b & d rec from 1903, pro rec from 1840, civ ct rec from 1826, m rec and deeds from 1841; Dist Clk has div rec from 1916)

Lamb	E1	1876	22		Bexar .... Littlefield
Lampasas	C2	1856	9	1860–80	Bell, Travis .... Lampasas
La Salle	C4	1880	6	1870–80	Bexar .... Cotulla

(Co Clk has b, m, d rec from 1900, pro rec from 1880, also div & civ ct rec; com ct rec from 1880)

Lavaca	B3	1846	20	1850–80	Colorado, Victoria, Jackson Gonzales .... Hallettsville
Lee	B3	1874	9	1880	Bastrop, Burleston, Washington Fayette .... Giddings
Leon	B2	1846	10	1850–80	Robertson .... Centervlle

(Co Clk has b & d rec from 1903, m rec from 1885, pro rec from 1846, also has civ ct rec)

Liberty	A3	1836	32	1850–80	Old Spanish Municipality .... Liberty

(All early rec of Liberty Co were destroyed in CH fire on 11 Dec 1874; All of the Co. rec date from 1875)

Limestone	B2	1846	20	1850–80	Robertson .... Groesbeck

(Co Clk has b & d rec from 1903, m, pro, civ ct rec from 1872)

Lipscomb	E1	1876	3	1880	Bexar .... Lipscomb

(Co Clk has b, m, d, bur, div, pro, civ ct rec from 1887)

Live Oak	C4	1856	8	1860–80	Nueces, San Patricio ...... George West

(Co Clk has b & d rec from 1903, m rec from 1856, pro rec from 1857)

Llano	C3	1856	5	1860–80	Bexar .... Llano
Loving	E2	1887	.2		Tom Green .... Mentone
Lubbock	D1	1876	156	1880	Bexar, Crosby .... Lubbock

(Co Clk has b & d rec from 1903, m rec from 1891, pro & civ ct rec from 1904; At one time attached to Crosby)

County Map of Texas

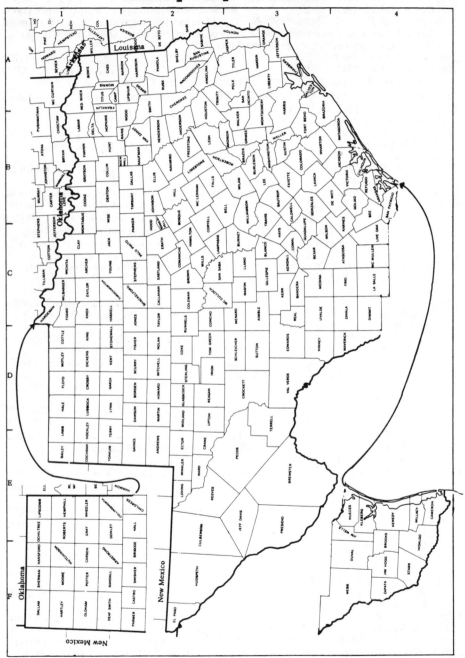

Lynn   Dl   1876   11   1880   Bexar .... Tahoka
(Co Clk has b, m, civ ct rec from 1903, d rec from 1904, pro rec from 1905)
McCulloch   C2   1856   9   1870-80 Bexar   . . . . Brady
(Co Clk has b & d rec from 1903, m rec from 1879, pro rec from 1880, also Co
ct rec & criminal ct rec; Dist Clk has div rec)

McLennan   B2 1850 150 1860-80 Milam .... Waco
McMullen   C4 1858   1   1870-80 Bexar, Live Oak, Atascosa .... Tilden
Madison   B2 1853   7   1860-80 Leon, Grimes, Walker .... Madisonville
Marion   A1 1860   8   1860-80 Cass .... Jefferson
    (Co Clk has b & d rec from 1903, m & pro rec from 1860)
Martin   D2 1876   5   1880   Bexar .... Stanton
    (Co Clk has b & d rec from 1910, m, civ ct, div, & pro rec from 1885)
Mason   C3 1858   4   1860-80 Gillespie .... Mason
    (Co Clk has b & d rec from 1903, m, bur, div, civ ct rec from 1877)
Matagorda   B4 1836 26   1850-80 Old Mexican Municipality ..... Bay City
Maverick   D4 1856 15   1860-80 Kenedy .... Eagle Pass
    (Co Clk has b & d rec from 1903, m rec from 1871 & pro & civ ct rec)
Medina   C3 1848 19   1850-80 Bexar .... Hondo
    (Co Clk has b rec from 1912, d rec from 1903, m, pro & co ct rec from 1848;
    Dist Ct has div rec)
Menard   C3 1858   3   1870-80 Bexar .... Menard
Midland   D2 1885 68   Tom Green .... Midland
    (Co Clk has b rec from 1917, m rec from 1885)
Milam   C3 1836 22   1850-80 Old Mexican Municipality ..... Cameron
Mills   C2 1887   4   Comanche, Brown, Hamilton,
                                    Lampasas .... Goldthwaite
    (Co Clk has b & d rec from 1903, m, div, pro, civ ct rec from 1887)
Mitchell   D2 1876 11   1880   Bexar .... Colorado City
    (Co Clk has b, m, d, pro, civ ct rec)
Montague   C1 1857 15   1860-80 Cooke .... Montague
    (Co Clk has b & d rec from 1903, m, pro, civ ct rec from 1873)
Montgomery B3 1837 27   1850-80 Washington .... Conroe
    (Co Clk has b rec from 1903, m & pro rec from 1838)
Moore   F1 1876 15   Bexar .... Dumas
Morris   A1 1875 13   1880   Titus .... Daingerfield
    (Co Clk has b & d rec from 1903, m & pro rec from 1875)
Motley   D1 1876   3   1880   Bexar (Org. 1891) .... Matador
    (Co Clk has b & d rec from 1903, m, div, pro, civ ct rec from 1891)
Nacogdoches A2 1837 28   1880   Old Mexican Municipality .. Nacogdoches
    (Co Clk has b & d rec from 1903, m, pro, civ ct rec from 1837)
Navarro   B2 1846 34   1850-80 Robertson .... Corsicana
Navasota (Name changed to Brazos in 1842)
Newton   A2 1846 10   1850-80 Jasper .... Newton
    (Co Clk has b & d rec from 1903, m rec from 1846, pro rec from 1870, also civ
    ct rec)
Nolan   D2 1876 19   1880   Young, Bexar .... Sweetwater
    (Co Clk has b & d rec from 1903, m rec from 1881)
Nueces   E4 1846 222 1850-80 San Patricio .... Corpus Christi
Ochiltree   E1 1876   9   Bexar .... Perryton
    (Co Clk has b rec from 1903, m, div, civ ct rec from 1889, d rec from 1904,
    pro rec from 1894; Dist Clk has div rec)
Oldham   F1 1865   2   1880   Bexar (Org. 1880) .... Vega
Orange   A3 1852 60   1860-80 Jefferson .... Orange
    (Co Clk has b & d rec from 1903, m, pro, civ ct rec from 1852)
Palo Pinto C2 1856 21   1860-80 Navarro, Bosque .... Palo Pinto
Panola   A2 1846 17   1850-80 Harrison, Shelby .... Carthage
Parker   C2 1855 23   1860-80 Bosque, Navarro .... Weatherford
Parmer   F2 1876 10   Bexar .... Farwell
    (Co Clk has b rec from 1909, m rec from 1910, d, pro & civ ct rec from 1915;
    Dist Clk has div rec)
Pecos   E3 1871 12   1880   Presidio .... Fort Stockton
Polk   A3 1850 14   1850-80 Liberty .... Livingston
Potter   F1 1876 116 1880   Bexar .... Amarillo
    (Co Clk has b & d rec incom from 1903, m & pro rec from 1888, civ ct rec
    from 1899; Dist Clk has div rec)
Presidio   E3 1850   5   1860-80 Bexar .... Marfa

Rains   B1   1870   3   1880   Hopkins, Hunt, Wood . . . . Emory
Randall   F1   1876   34   Bexar . . . . Canyon
Reagan   D2   1903   4   Tom Green . . . . Big Lake
   (Co Clk has b, m, d, div, pro, civ ct rec from 1903)
Real   C3   1913   2   Bandera, Kerr, Edwards . . . . . Leakey
   (Co Clk has b, m, d, div, pro, civ ct rec from 1913)
Red River   A1   1836   16   1850-80   Old Mexican Municipality . . . Clarksville
Reeves   E2   1883   18   Pecos . . . . Pecos
   (Co Clk has b & d rec from 1903, m, pro, co civ ct rec from-1885)
Refugio   B4   1836   11   1850-80   Old Mexican Municipality . . . . Refugio
   (Co Clk has b & d rec from 1903, m rec 1851, pro rec 1840, co civ ct rec 1881)
Roberts   E1   1876   1   Bexar . . . . Miami
   (Co Clk has b & d rec from 1903, m, div, pro, civ ct rec from 1889)
Robertson   B2   1837   16   1850-80   Milam . . . . Franklin
Rockwall   B1   1873   6   1880   Kaufman . . . . Rockwall
   (Co Clk has b, m, d, pro, civ ct rec some from as far back as 1873)
Runnells   C2   1858   15   1880   Bexar, Travis (Org. 1880) . . . Ballinger
Rusk   A2   1846   36   1850-80   Nacogdoches . . . . Henderson
   (Co Clk has b & d rec from 1903, m rec from 1943, pro & civ ct rec from
   1844; Dist Clk has div rec)
Sabine   A2   1836   7   1850-80   Old Mexican Municipality . . . . Hemphill
San Augustine A2   1835   8   1850-80   Old Mexican Municipality . . San Augustine
San Jacinto   A3   1869   6   1880   Liberty, Polk, Montgomery,
                                          Walker . . . . Coldspring
San Patricio   B4   1836   45   1850-80   Old Mexican Municipality . . . Sinton
   (Co Clk has b rec from 1903, m rec 1858, d rec 1910, pro rec 1847)
San Saba   C2   1856   6   1860-80   Bexar . . . . San Saba
Schleicher   D3   1887   3   Crockett . . . . Eldorado
Scurry   D2   1876   20   1880   Bexar . . . . Snyder
   (Co Clk has b & d rec from 1903, m, pro, civ ct rec from 1884)
Shackelford   C2   1858   4   1860-80   Bosque . . . . Albany
   (Co Clk has b & d rec from 1903, m rec 1886, div, pro, civ ct rec 1887)
Shelby   A2   1836   20   1850-80   Old Mexican Municipality . . . . . Center
Sherman   F1   1876   3   Bexar . . . . Stratford
Smith   A2   1846   86   1850-80   Nacogdoches . . . . Tyler
   (Co Clk has b & d rec fom 1903, m rec from 1848, pro rec from 1847, civ
   ct rec and deed rec from 1846)
Somervell   C2   1875   3   1880   Hood, Johnson . . . . Glen Rose
   (Co Clk has b & d rec from 1903, m rec from 1885, div rec from 1898, pro
   rec from 1875, Co ct rec from 1876 and Dist ct rec from 1898)
Starr   F4   1848   17   1850-80   Nueces . . . . Rio Grande City
   (Co Clk has b & d rec from 1903, m rec from 1858, pro rec from 1870, civ ct
   rec from 1885, naturalization rec from 1883 to 1900; Dist Ct has div rec)
Stephens   C2   1858   9   1870-80   Bosque . . . . Breckenridge
   (Co Clk has b rec from 1903, m rec 1876, pro rec 1886, civ ct rec 1881; Orig.
   Buchanan, name changed in 1861)
Sterling   D2   1891   1   Tom Green . . . . Sterling City
   (Co Clk has b & d rec from 1909, m, pro, civ ct rec 1891, div rec 1892)
Stonewall   D1   1876   3   Bexar . . . . Aspermont
Sutton   D3   1887   4   Crockett . . . . Sonora
Swisher   F2   1876   11   Bexar, Young . . . . Tulia
   (Co Clk has b, d, div, pro rec from 1903, m & civ ct rec from 1890)
Tarrant   B2   1849 538   1850-80   Navarro (1860 census missing) . Fort Worth
   (Co Clk has b, m, pro rec from 1876, d rec from 1900; Dist Clk has div & civ
   ct rec)
Taylor   C2   1858 101   1880   Bexar, Travis . . . . Abilene
Terrell   D3   1905   3   Pecos . . . . Sanderson
Terry   E1   1876   16   Martin, Bexar . . . . Brownfield
Throckmorton   C1   1858   3   1860-80   Fannin (1870 cen missing) . Throckmorton
   (Co Clk has b & d rec from 1903, m, div, pro, civ ct rec from 1879)
Titus   A1   1846   17   1850-80   Red River, Bowie . . . . . Mt. Pleasant

(Co Clk has b, m, d, bur, pro rec from 1895; Dist Clk has div & civ ct rec)
Tom Green   D2   1874   65   1880   Bexar . . . . San Angelo
    (Co Clk has b & d rec from 1903, m, pro, civ ct rec, deeds, mtgs from 1875)
Travis   B3   1840 212   1850-80   Bastrop . . . . Austin
Trinity   A2   1850   8   1860-80   Houston, Polk   . . . . Groveton
    (Co Clk has b & d rec from 1903, m, div, pro, civ ct, deeds, land grants,
    and com ct min from 1876)
Tyler   A3   1846   11   1850-80   Liberty . . . . Woodville
Upshur   A2   1846   20   1850-80   Harrison, Nacogdoches . . . . . Gilmer
    (Co Clk has d rec from 1903, b, & m rec from 1873, pro rec from 1881, civ ct
    rec from 1876; deeds from 1845; Dist Clk has div rec)
Upton   D2   1867   6   Tom Green (Org. 1910) . . . . . . Rankin
    (Co Clk has b, m, d, div, civ ct rec from 1910, pro rec from 1910)
Uvalde   C3   1850   17   1860-80   Bexar . . . . Uvalde
    (Co Clk has b & d rec from 1903, m rec 1856, pro rec 1857, civ ct rec 1876)
Val Verde   D3   1885   24   Crockett, Kinney, Pecos . . . . . Del Rio
Van Zandt   B2   1848   19   1850-80   Henderson . . . . Canton
    (Co Clk has b & d rec from 1903, m, pro, civ ct rec from 1848; Dist Clk has
    div rec)
Victoria   B4   1836   46   1850-80   Old Mexican Municipality   . . . Victoria
    (Co Clk has d rec from 1903, m, pro, civ ct rec from 1838, b rec from 1870)
Walker   B3   1846   21   1850-80   Montgomery . . . . Huntsville
Waller   B3   1873   12   1880   Austin, Grimes   . . . . Hempstead
    (Co Clk has b rec from 1903, d, m, pro, civ ct rec from 1873)
Ward   E2   1887   15   Tom Green . . . . Monohans
    (Co Clk has b & d rec from 1903, m rec from 1893, pro rec from 1895)
Washington   B3   1836   19   1850-80   Texas Municipality . . . . Brenham
Webb   F4   1848   65   1850-80   Bexar . . . . Laredo
    (Co Clk has b rec from ca 1856, m & d rec ca 1850)
Wharton   B3   1846   38   1850-80   Matagorda, Jackson   . . . . . . Wharton
    (Co Clk has b & d rec from 1903, m rec from 1857 & pro rec from 1849)
Wheeler   E1   1876   8   1880   Bexar, Young . . . . Wheeler
Wichita   C1   1858 124   1880   Youngland Dist. . . . . Wichita Falls
Wilbarger   C1   1858   18   1880   Bexar (Org. 1881) . . . . . . Vernon
    (Co Clk has b, m, d, civ ct and pro rec from 1887; City Sec has bur rec; Dist
    Clk has div rec)
Willacy   E4   1911   20   Hidalgo, Cameron . . . . . . Raymondville
Williamson   B3   1848   35   1850-80   Milam . . . . Georgetown
    (Co Clk has b & d rec from 1903, m, pro, co ct rec from 1848; Dist Clk has
    div rec; Local Reg has bur rec)
Wilson   C3   1860   13   1870-80   Bexar, Karnes   . . . . Floresville
    (Co Clk has b & d rec from 1903, m rec from 1860, pro rec from 1862, co ct
    rec from 1876)
Winkler   E2   1910   14   Tom Green   . . . . Kermit
    (Co Clk has b, m, d, pro, co ct rec)
Wise   C1   1856   17   1860-80   Cooke . . . . Decatur
Wood   B2   1850   18   1860-80   Van Zandt . . . . Quitman
Yoakum   E1   1876   8   Bexar . . . . Plains
Young   C1   1856   17   1860-80   Bosque, Fannin   . . . . Graham
    (Co Clk has b & d rec from 1903, m, pro, civ ct, deeds, com ct min, old
    brands from 1856; Dist Clk has div rec; Funeral Home has some bur rec)
Zapata   F4   1858   4   1860-80   Starr, Webb . . . . Zapata
Zavala   C4   1858   13   1860-80   Uvalde, Maverick . . . . Crystal City

Genealogists' Check List of the Historical Records Survey, Texas

Federal Courts. Inventory of County Archives, Bandera, Bastrop, Brown, Caldwell, Calhoun, Denton, DeWitt, Fayette, Gillespie, Gregg, Guadalupe, Hays, Hood, Jackson, Marion, Milam,

Mills, Orange, Robertson, Rockwall, Sabine, Somervell, Uvalde, Wilson. Inventory of municipal and town archives, Brazoria. Guide to Public Vital Statistic records. Index to Probate cases filed in Texas Counties - #7 Atascosa, #19 Bowie, #20, Brazoria, #21 Brazos, #25 Brown, #32 Camp, #36 Chambers, #42, Coleman, #60 Delta, #80 Franklin, #92 Gregg, #94 Guadalupe, #100 Hardin, #105 Hays, #146 Liberty, #155 Marion, #172 Morris, #176 Newton, #177 Nolan, #181 Orange, #198 Robertson, #200 Runnels, #206 San Saba, #210 Shelby, #225 Titus, #228 Trinity, #237 Waller, #246 Williamson, #250 Wood.

Transcription and Translation of San Antonio Spanish minute book 1 & 2, 1815-1835. Journal A record of City of San Antonio 1837-1840. Check list of records required or permitted by law in Texas. A check list of Texas imprints 1848-1860. A check list of Texas imprints 1861-1876. Texas newspapers 1813-1839. A union list of newspaper files available in offices of publishers, libraries and a number of private collectins. See Louisiana for navigation casualties. Depository of unpublished material, University of Texas, Austin, Texas.

Utah

Capital Salt Lake City - Territory 1850 - State 1896 - (45th)

As the Puritans, the Pilgrims, the Quakers, the Huguenots, and many other religious devotees came to the American shore for the opportunity to worship Almighty God according to their conscience, so the members of the Chruch of Jesus Christ of Latter-day Saints, or the so-called ''Mormons,'' came to the then arid forbidding valleys of Utah. When they came the land was barren and desolate, nothing but the bluish gray of the sagebrush and greasewood covered the land. Not a sign of human life, except here and there, scattered along the shores of a small lake or the banks of a tiny mountain stream, a few Indian Wigwams. Not even the hoofprints of the horses that carried Father Escalante and Father Dominguez on a hurried journey through part of the state seventy-one years earlier were anywhere to be found.

It was on 24 July 1847 that the colonization of the Great Salt Lake Basin began with the arrival on the site of the present Salt Lake City of the first Pioneer group 148 - 143 men, three women, and two boys. New groups arrived several times each month. In three years, 1850, there were 11,380.

Most of the early settlers of Utah came from New England,

Ohio, Illinois, Missouri, and Canada, and since then from almost every state in the Union. Most of the Europeans who have come in order of their numerical strength, are English, Germans, Danes, Swedes, Norwegians, Swiss, Hollanders, Welsh, and Scotch, with a sprinkling of Piedmont Italians, and a few Czechs. Many Austrians, Greeks, Mexicans and Italians, not affected by church affiliation, have come to work in the mining and smelting operations of the state. Only about two per cent of the population are Negroes.

The Division of Vital Statistics, State Board of Health, Capitol Bldg., Salt Lake City, 84114, Utah, has records of births since 1890 and deaths since 1848. Marriage records are at the offices of the County Clerks.

The principal sources of genealogical information are the LDS Church records which have been carefully kept and preserved since 1830. Besides that, records have been gathered for years from all over the world and brought to Salt Lake City by the Genealogical Society of the Church of Jesus Christ of Latter-day Saints.

The growth of this society has been astounding. It is now recognized as one of the foremost genealogical libraries in the world, and continues to accelerate its growth by expanding a long time activity of microfilming original records around the world and gathering all types of printed and other records wherever they may be found.

About 95 miles north of Salt Lake City is located the beautiful Cache Valley with its principal city, Logan. A block east of its business section is the Cache County Library. One of the important departments of that Library is the genealogical section, not large, but choice. It is good enough to elicit from a stranger who has visited most of the important libraries on a leisurely auto trip across the nation the remark, ''This is the best Genealogical Library I have seen between the Mississippi and the Pacific, with the exception of course, of your large library in Salt Lake City.''

Any community with an enthusiastic genealogist can do for his or her library what has been done here. Several years ago the late Walter M. Everton, the founder of the GENEALOGICAL HELPER and the HANDY BOOK FOR GENEALOGISTS, opened the genealogical section of the Cache County Library. He brought with him to the library one genealogical book he had purchased some time previously. He appealed for books from those interested, money from those who had no books. He solicited the merchants of Logan for donations and collected about $7,000.00 all of which was spent for books. It is mainly through his efforts and the cooperation of the Board of Directors of the library that there are now about 8,000 genealogical books on the shelves of the department.

Utah County Histories

(Population figures to nearest thousand - 1960 Census)

Name	Map Index	Date Formed	Pop. By M	Census Reports Available	Parent County	County Seat
Beaver	E1	1856	4	1860-80	Iron, Millard	Beaver

(Co Clk has b rec from 1897 to 1905, m rec from 1887, d rec from 1900 to 1905, div rec from 1871, pro rec from 1872, civ ct rec from 1856; Beaver City Office has bur rec)

| Box Elder | A1 | 1856 | 25 | 1860-80 | Unorganized Territory | Brigham City |

(Co Clk has m rec from 1887, div, pro & civ ct rec from 1856; Bureau of Vit Stat, Salt Lake City, Utah has b & d rec; Cities or Towns have bur rec)

| Cache | A2 | 1856 | 36 | 1860-80 | Unorganized Territory | Logan |

(Co Clk has m rec from 1888, div rec from 1883, pro rec from 1857 & civ ct rec from 1893)

Carbon	C3	1894	21		Sanpete	Price
Daggett	B4	1917	1		Uintah	Manila
Davis	B2	1850	65	1850-80	Salt Lake	Farmington

(Co Clk has b & d rec from 1898 to 1905)

| Duchesne | C3 | 1915 | 7 | | Wasatch | Duchesne |

(Co Clk has m rec, div, pro, civ ct rec from 1915; City or Town Recorders have bur rec; Division of Vit Stat, Salt Lake City, Utah has b & d rec)

| Emery | D3 | 1880 | 6 | 1880 | Sanpete, Sevier | Castle Dale |

(Co Clk has div rec from 1900, civ ct rec from 1890)

| Garfield | F3 | 1864 | 4 | | Iron, Sevier, Kane | Panquitch |

(Co Clk has m rec from 1887, div, pro, civ ct rec from 1888) (Garfield Co. boundaries were set up in 1864 but there were no County Officials and they did not function as a County until March 1882)

| Grand | D4 | 1892 | 6 | | Emery, Uintah | Moab |

(Co Clk has m & pro rec from 1890, div & civ ct rec from 1896)

| Iron | F1 | 1852 | 11 | 1850-80 | Unorganized Territory | Parowan |

(Co Clk has m rec from 1880, div, pro, civ ct rec from 1860)

Juab	C1	1849	5	1860-80	Original county	Nephi
Kane	F2	1864	3	1870-80	Washington, Unorganized Terr.	Kanab
Millard	D1	1852	8	1860-80	Juab	Fillmore

(Co Clk has m rec from 1877, div, civ ct rec from 1891, pro rec from 1892, criminal rec from abt 1896)

| Morgan | B2 | 1862 | 3 | 1870-80 | Davis, Summit | Morgan |

(Co Clk has m, div, pro, civ ct rec; Morgan City has d & bur rec)

| Piute | E2 | 1866 | 1 | 1870-80 | Sevier | Junction |

(Co Clk has b & d rec from 1898, m rec from 1887, div, pro, civ ct rec from 1872)

| Rich | A3 | 1864 | 2 | 1870-80 | Formerly Richland | Randolph |

(Co Clk has m, div, pro, civ ct rec from 1888)

| Salt Lake | B2 | 1849 | 383 | 1850-80 | Orig. Co. (Great S.L.) | Salt Lake City |

(Co Clk has m rec from 1887, div, pro, civ ct rec from 1870; State Board of Health has b, d & bur rec)

| San Juan | F4 | 1880 | 9 | 1880 | Kane | Monticello |

(Co Clk has m rec from Nov 1888, div rec from 1891, pro rec from 1888, civ ct rec from 1891)

| Sanpete | D3 | 1849 | 11 | 1850-80 | Original county | Manti |
| Sevier | D2 | 1864 | 11 | 1870-80 | Sanpete | Richfield |

(Co Clk has m rec from 1887, div, pro, civ ct rec from 1896)

| Summit | B3 | 1854 | 6 | 1860-80 | Salt Lake | Coalville |

(Co Clk has some b & d rec from 1898 to 1901, m rec from 1888, div, civ ct rec from 1896; pro rec from 1899)

| Tooele | B1 | 1849 | 18 | 1850-80 | Original county | Tooele |

(Co Clk has b & d rec 1899 to 1904, m rec 1887, div, pro, civ ct rec 1897)

| Uintah | C4 | 1880 | 12 | 1880 | Wasatch | Vernal |
| Utah | C2 | 1849 | 107 | 1850-80 | Original county | Provo |

(Co Clk has b & d rec from 1906, m rec from 1887, div rec & pro rec from 1859, civ ct rec from 1885)

Wasatch   B3   1862   5   1870–80   Summit .... Heber
(Co Clk has b & d rec 1897 to 1905, m rec 1862, div, pro, civ ct rec 1897)

Washington   F1   1852   10   1860–80   Unorganized Territory   ...... St. George
(Co Clk has m rec from 1887, div, pro, civ ct rec from 1856; Cem and City & Towns have d rec; Offices of Cem have bur rec; State Capitol, Salt Lake City has b rec)

Wayne   E3   1864   2   Piute .... Loa
(Co Clk has b rec from 1898, d rec 1899, m, div, pro, civ ct rec 1892)

Weber   A2   1849   111   1850–80   Original county .... Ogden
(Co Clk has m rec from 1887, div & civ ct rec from 1878, pro rec from 1892)

County Map of Utah

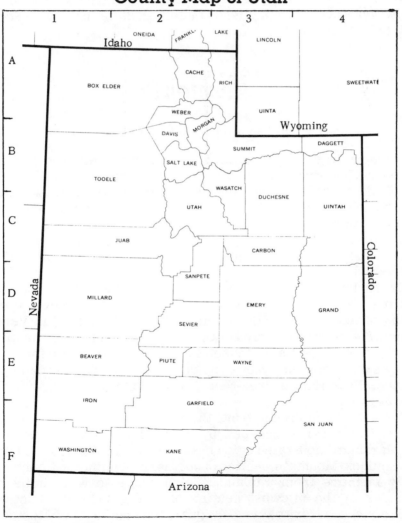

Genealogists' Check List of the Historical Records Survey, Utah

Federal Courts. Inventory of County Archives, Box Elder, Carbon, Daggett, Emery, Grand, Morgan, Sanpete, Tooele, Uintah, Utah, Wasatch, Weber. Inventory of municipal and town archives, a history of Ogden. Census of Weber County (Exclusive of Green River Precinct). Provisional State of Deseret. Guide to Public Vital Statistic records. Inventory of the Church Archives of Utah, Vol. 1 History and Bibliography of Religion, Vol. 2 Baptist Church, Vol. 3 Smaller Denominations. Directory of churches and religious organizations in Utah, except L.D.S. church. Check list of newspapers and magazines published in Ogden. County government of the provisional state of Deseret. Records required of County Officers, State of Deseret 15 March 1849 to 5 April 1851. Depository of unpublished material, State Historical Society, Salt Lake City, Utah.

Vermont

Capital Montpelier - State 1791 - (14th)

Vermont was late in getting settled as compared with other states in New England. One reason was the hostility of the French and Indians in the Quebec district north of Vermont. As soon as the French released all claims on the sections within the American colonies, security was established and settlers felt free to go into the distant and lonely Vermont sections. As early as 1724 English people living along the New England coastline became interested in Vermont.

Massachusetts and Connecticut played the biggest role in the settling of Vermont, although people moved from several of the other states to settle the communities established in Vermont from 1714 on, but mostly between 1740 and 1800. As mentioned, Connecticut and Massachusetts furnished settlers for almost every early community in Vermont, but settlers also came from Canada, New Hampshire, New York, Rhode Island, Maine, and New Jersey.

French Canadians came into the northern counties as late as the 1900s. They were preceded by several years by the Irish. Into the Markham Mountain region in southwestern Windsor county and the Equinox Mountain section of northern Bennington County came many farmers from Finland. Welsh came to work in the slate quarries in the midwest section of Rutland County. Scotch and Italian stone cutters came to the quarries southeast of Montpelier, Russians, Poles, Czechs, Austrians and Swedes came to the granite quarries of Rutland County. About half of the foreign born population of Vermont came from Canada.

Birth, marriage, and death records from approximately 1760 until the present time are on file in the office of the Secretary of State, Division of Vital Records, State House, Montpelier 05601, Vermont. Each month this office receives a group of vital records from the town and the county officers. These records are generally about six months in arrear. It may be well to try the City or Town Clerk if the Secretary of State does not have the record.

Wills are recorded in the twenty probate districts of the state, with each county having one or more probate district. For information write the Registrar, Probate Court, County Seat. Deeds are recorded in 246 Town and fourteen County Clerks offices. Land grants are on file in the offices of the Town Clerk. Census records are available at the State Library in Montpelier. Tax payers lists are with the Town Clerks. War service records are on file in the office of the Adjutant General in Montpelier. Cemetery records are with the church records of the sextons.

Carleton, Hiram, ''Genealogical and Family History of the State of Vermont,'' 2 vols., Lewis Publishing Co., New York, Chicago, 1903.

Clark, Byron N., ''A List of Pensioners of the War of 1812,'' pub. 1904.

Dodge, Prentiss Cutler, ''Encyclopedia, Vermont Biography,'' pub. 1912.

''First Census of the United States, 1790, Vermont,'' Government Printing Office, 1907.

Goodrich, John E., ''Vermont Rolls of the Soldiers in the Revolutionary War,'' Published by authority of the Legislature, The Tuttle Co., Rutland, Vt., 1904.

''Heads of Families, Second Census of the United States, 1800 State of Vermont,'' Published by Vermont Historical Society, Montpelier, Vt., 1938.

WPA, ''Bibliography of Research Projects Reports, Check List of Historical Records Survey Publications,'' 1940.

Vermont Libraries: University of Vermont and State (Agricultural) College Libraries, Billings Library, (Vermont), (Civil War), Burlington, 05401, (Chittenden); Vermont Free Public Library Commission, State Library Bldg., Vermont Historical Society Library, State House, (History, Vermontiana), Montpelier 05601, (Washington).

VERMONT TOWNS ORGANIZED BEFORE 1800

ADDISON, organized 1785. Addison, 1783; Bridport, 1786; Cornwall, 1774; Ferrisburgh, 1769; Leicester, 1774; Lincoln, 1790; Middlebury, 1766; Monktown, 1774; New Haven, 1769; Orwell, 1775; Panton, 1764; Ripton, 1781; Salisbury, 1774; Shoreham, 1766; Starksborough, 1788; Vergennes, 1764; Waltham, S. bef. Rev.; Weybridge, 1775; Whiting, 1773.

BENNINGTON, organized 1779. Arlington, 1763; Bennington, 1761; Dorset, 1768; Glastenbury, 1661; Landgrove, 1761; Manchester, 1764; Peru abt. 1773; Pownal, 1762; Rupert, 1767; Sandgate, 1771; Shaftsbury, 1763; Sunderland, 1766; Winhall, 1761.

CALEDONIA, organized 1796. Barnet, 1770; Burke, 1790; Cabot, 1785; Danville, 1785; Groton, 1787; Hardwick, 1790; Kirby, 1799; Lyndon, 1788; Peacham, 1775; Ryegate, 1774; Sheffield, 1792; St. Johnsbury, 1786; Sutton, 1791; Walden, 1789; Waterford, 1797, Wheelock, 1785.

CHITTENDEN, Organized 1787. Bolton, 1763; Burlington, 1773; Charlotte, 1776; Colchester, 1772; Essex, 1783; Hinesburg, 1774; Huntington, 1786; Jericho, 1774; Milton, 1783; Richmond, 1775; Shelburne, 1768; St. George, 1784; Underhill, 1786; Willistown, 1774.

ESSEX, Organized 1797. Bloomfield, 1762; Brunswick, 1780; Canaan, 1791; Concord, 1783; Guildhall, 1764; Lunenburg, 1770; Maidstone, 1772; Victory, 1781.

FRANKLIN, Organized 1796. Bakersfield, 1799; Berkshire, 1780; Enosburgh, 1797; Fairfax, 1783; Fairfield, 1788; Fletcher, 1781; Franklin, 1789; Georgia, 1784-5; Highgate, 1763; Montgomery, 1780; Richford, 1797; Sheldon, 1790; Swantown, 1787; St. Albans, 1775.

GRAND ISLE, Organized 1802. Alburgh, 1782; Grand Isle, 1783; Isle la Mott, 1785; North Hero, 1783; South Hero, 1779.

LAMOILLE, Organized 1835. Cambridge, 1783; Elmore, 1790; Hyde Park, 1787; Johnson, 1784; Morristown, 1790; Sterling, 1799; Stowe, 1793; Waterville, 1789; Wolcott, 1781.

ORANGE, Organized 1781. Bradford, S. 1765; Braintree, S. 1783; Brookfield, S. 1771; Chelsea, S. 1784; Corinth, O. 1777; Fairlee, S. 1766; Newbury, S. 1763; Orange, O. 1793; Randolph, O. 1781; Stratford, S. 1768; Thetford, S. 1764; Topsham, S. 1781; Turnbridge, S. 1776; Vershire, O. 1780; Washington, O. 1785; W. Fairlee, 1761; Williamtown, 1784.

ORLEANS, Organized 1797. Barton, 1789; Craftsbury, 1788; Derby, 1795; Glover, 1797; Greensborough, 1789; Holland, 1800; Jay, S. bef. Rev.; Salem 1798; Westfield, 1790.

RUTLAND, Organized 1781. Benson, 1783; Brandon, 1772; Castleton, 1767; Chittenden aft. Rev.; Clarendon, 1768; Danby, 1765; Fairhaven, 1779; Hubbardton, 1775; Ira, 1779; Mendon, 1781; Middletown, 1774; Mt. Holly, 1787; Mt. Tabor, 1761; Pawlet, 1761; Pittsford, 1767; Poultney, 1777; Rutland, 1769; Sherburn, 1785; Shrewsbury, 1763; Sudbury, bef. Rev.; Tinsmith, 1770; Wallingsford, 1773; Wells, 1768; West Haven, 1770.

WASHINGTON, Organized 1810. Barre, 1780; Berlin, 1785; Calais, 1787; Duxbury, 1786; Payston, 1798; Marshfield, 1782; Middlesex, 1787; Montpelier, 1786; Moretown, 1790; Northfield,

1785; Plainsfield, 1794; Roxbury, 1789; Waitsfield, 1789; Warren, 1797; Waterbury, 1784; Worcester, 1797.

WINDHAM, 1781. Athens, 1780; Brattleboro, 1724; Brookline, 1777; Dover, 1780; Fullam, 1760; Grafton, 1768; Guilford, 1761; Halifax, 1761; Jamacia, 1780; Londonderry, 1773; Marlborough, 1763; Newfane, 1766; Putney, 1744; Rockingham, 1753; Townsend, 1761; Woodborough, 1780; Westminister, 1741; Whitington, 1771; Wilmington S. bef. Rev.; Windham, 1773.

WINDSOR, Organized before Statehood. Andover, 1776; Baltimore, 1794; Barnard, 1774; Bethel, 1779; Bridgewater, 1779; Cavendish, 1769; Chester, 1764; Hartford, 1763; Hartland, 1763; Ludlow, 1714; Norwich, 1762; Plymouth, 1777; Pomfret, 1770; Reading, 1772; Royalton, 1771; Sharon, 1764; Springfield, 1761; Stockbridge, 1784; Weathersfield, 1761; Weston, 1790; Windsor, 1764; Woodstock, 1768.

Vermont County Histories

(Population figures to nearest thousand - 1960 Census)

Name	Map Index	Date Formed	Pop. By M	Census Reports Available	Parent County	County Seat
Addison	B1	1785	20	1790–80	Rutland	Middlebury
(Co Clk has div & civ ct rec from 1787; Probate Clk has pro rec; Town Clk has b, m, d, & bur rec)						
Bennington	D1	1779	25	1790–80	Original county	Bennington
(Co Clk has div rec from 1899 & civ ct rec from 1861; Clk of Town has b, m, d, & bur rec; Pro Ct has pro rec)						
Caledonia	B3	1792	23	1800–80	Newly Organized Terr.	St. Johnsbury
(Co Clk has div, civ ct, chancery ct rec from 1797; Town Clk has b, m, d & bur rec; Pro Ct has pro rec)						
Chittenden	B1	1787	74	1790–80	Original county	Burlington
Essex	A3	1792	6	1800–80	Unorganized Territory	Guildhall
(Co Clk has b, m, d rec from 1885, div & civ ct rec from 1800)						
Franklin	A1	1792	29	1800–80	Chittenden	St. Albans
(Co Clk has div & civ ct rec from 1900; Reg of Probate Ct has pro rec; Clk of Town has b, m, d, & bur rec)						
Grand Isle	A1	1802	3	1810–80	Franklin	North Hero
Lamoille	A2	1835	11	1840–80	Chittenden, Orleans, Franklin	Hyde Park
(Co Clk has div, civ ct rec from 1837; Town Clks have b, m, d & bur rec; Judge of Probate has pro rec)						
Orange	B2	1781	16	1790–80	Original county	Chelsea
(Co Clk has div & civ ct rec from 1781, pro rec 1793, land rec 1771)						
Orleans	A2	1792	20	1800–80	Original county	Newport
Rutland	C1	1781	47	1790–80	Original county	Rutland
(Co Clk has div, civ ct rec from 1779; Town or City Clk has b, m, d, & bur rec; Judge of Probate has pro rec)						
Washington	B2	1810	43	1820–80	Addison, Orange	Montpelier
(Co Clk has div, pro, civ ct rec from 1791; Vital Records, Montpelier, Vt. has b, m, & d rec; Probate Ct has pro rec)						
Windham	D2	1779	30	1790–80	Bennington	Newfane & Marlboro
Windsor	C2	1781	44	1790–80	Original county	Woodstock
(Co Clk has div & civ ct rec from 1782; Town Clks have b, m, d, & bur rec; Probate Court has pro rec)						

County Map of Vermont

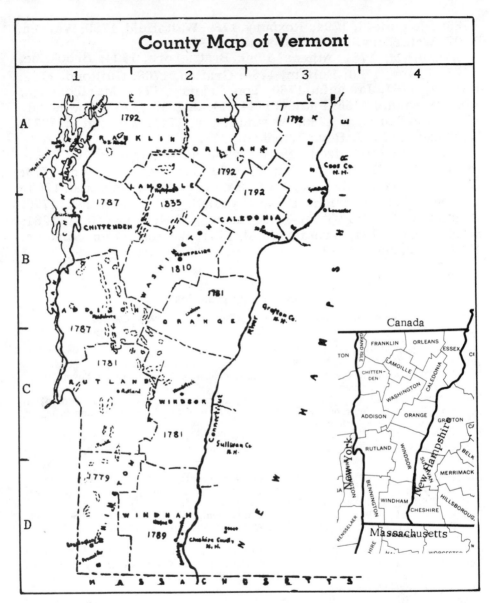

Genealogists' Check List of the Historical Records Survey, Vermont

Federal Courts. Inventory of County Archives, Lamoille. Inventory of municipal and town archives, Albany, Alburgh Village, Belvidere, Benson, Bolton, Bridport, Brookline, Cambridge, Charlotte, Castleton, Cavendish, Clarendon, Coventry, Dandy, Derby (also supplement), Derby Line, Eden, Elmore, Essex, Fairfax, Grafton, Grand Isle, Hubbardton, Hyde Park, Isle La-Motte, Jamaica, Johnson, Mansfield, Morristown, Morrisville,

Mt Tabor, North Hero, Plymouth, Salem, Shrewsbury, South Hero, Sterling Village, Stowe, Walcott, Wallingford, Waterville, Villages of Derby, Tinmouth, Two Heroes.

Inventory of the Church Archives of Vermont, Protestant Episcopal, Diocese of Vermont, Preprint of churches of Hinesburg. Directory of churches and religious organizations in Vt. Calendar of the Ira Allen papers in the Wilburn Library of the University of Vermont. Index to the Burlington Free Press in the Billings Library, University of Vermont, Vol. 1 1848-1852, Vol. 2 1853-1855, Vol. 3 1856-1858, Vol. 4 1859-1861, Vol. 5 1862-1863, Vol. 6 1864-1865, Vol. 7 1866-1867, Vol. 8 1868, Vol. 9 1869, Vol. 19 1870. Depository of unpublished material, State Historical Society, Montpelier, Vermont.

Virginia

Capital Richmond - State 1788 - (10th)

The colonization of the American continent in modern times began with the arrival of three boatloads of English immigrants in May, 1607 on the northeast shore of James River in the present Virginia.

One of the leaders was Captain John Smith, a daring adventurous fellow with an inquisitive mind who had been in many tight situations on the outskirts of civilization. With a score of companions, he sailed into several of the many bays and river openings along the zigzagging east coast, and thus became acquainted with they lay of the land.

Having done nothing to provide food for the winter, more than half of the colony succumbed from illness and lack of nourishing food.

The summer of 1608 brought them new supplies from England and 120 more immigrants.

In the fall of 1608 the colony of 130 or 140 persons was augmented by the arrival of seventy more immigrants in the third expediton to Virginia.

At the beginning of the winter of 1609 the colony consisted of 490 persons. When the spring of 1610 arrived there were only 60 persons left in the colony.

Determined to return to England, the group embarked. The ship was coming out of the mouth of the James River when Virginia bound ships under the command of Lord Delaware came in sight. Against their own judgment, the disgruntled colonists were persuaded to return to their abandoned homes.

Early in 1610 more food and additonal colonists arrived from England.

Virginia became a royal colony in 1624. From then until 1776 when it announced its independence it was in almost constant trouble with the Crown or its representatives. Mainly, the colonists objected to the arbitrary action of the colony officials and their ruthless demands.

Every month in the year, with the exception of the winter months, saw boatloads of new immigrants arriving. More and more settlements were established, some as far north as the Potomac River. By 1700 there were more than 80,000 persons living in the Tidewater region of Virginia. Twenty thousand more had come by 1717. During the next 37 years, the population increased by almost two hundred per cent, reaching 284,000 by 1754.

Even before that time the settlers had scattered over the coastal plain, the Piedmont plateau, and had crossed over the Blue Ridge highlands and settled in the Valley of Virginia, with the Appalachian Plateau at their back. There they had settled along the rivers, hundreds of miles from the coast line.

As early as 1730 there had been a heavy immigration from Pennsylvania into Virginia of Scotch - Irish, Welsh, and Germans, most of whom settled in the upper valleys. Naturally, therefore, it was in that section where flourished the Welsh Baptist Church the English Quakers, and the Scotch Presbyterians. Methodist churches were established about 1800.

Virginia was well settled by 1775. By 1800 it had upwards of 90 counties and a population of nearly a million.

Nine other states had preceded Virginia into the Union when she entered in June 1788. In the first three U.S. Census reports 1790, 1800, 1810, Virginia registered the highest population in the nation. In 1820 she was second to New York. In 1830 she was surpassed by New York and Pennsylvania.

Foreign born residents predominate in the following order in Virginia: Russians, English, Germans, Italians, Greeks, Polish, Czechs, Irish, Austrians and Hungarians.

Until 1786 the Episcopal Church was the state church in Virginia. All children, regardless of religious affiliation, were required to be baptized by the ministers of that church. Dates of their baptism, together with their names, dates of birth, and names of their parents were recorded in the parish registers. The same information was taken of all marriages and burials. All of these church records are preserved, some are printed. They are available in the Virginia State Library in Richmond.

The Quit Rent list is used as a Census Report or Schedule. In 1704 all Virginia landowners, except those in Lancaster, Northumberland, Westmoreland, Richmond and Stafford counties, had to pay the King a Quit Rent of one shilling for each fifty acres bought.

Since the 1790 U. S. Census records were destroyed in a fire, Fothergill and Naugle in "Taxpayers of Virginia" have tried to augment similar lists gathered from other counties by the government.

In the 1790 to 1860 Federal Census schedules for Virginia will be found 50 counties now in West Virginia. These counties withdrew from Virginia in 1861 and in 1863 became our thirty-fifth state.

Excellent service is extended researchers at the Virginia State Library in Richmond 23219, Virginia but you must hire a professional or go there in person to do your researching because their staff does not have the time to research for you. The library has Parish Registers and Vestry Books from 1618 to 1860. Not that all of those records are from that period, but somewhere within the span of time. It also has a collection of State Land Office Records. These records contain patents for land dating from 1623, and a name index has been compiled. However, the nature of the records is such that they give no information as to the date, place of arrival of the patentees in America, or the names of the ships.

The State Bureau of Vital Statistics, Richmond 23219, Virginia, has birth and death records from 1853 to 1896, and after 1912. Marriage records are available from 1853 to the present. Some marriage bonds are in the State Library, Richmomd 23219, Va., others are in the office of the Clerk of the Court or city in which the marriage took place. Several of the so-called independent cities have their own records of birth and deaths. Inquire at the City Board of Health Office.

Virginia's independent cities are Alexandria, Bristol, Buena Vista, Charlottesville, Clifton Forge, Colonial Heights, Covington, Danville, Falls Church, Fredericksburg, Galax, Hampton, Harrisonburg, Hopewell, Lynchburg, Martinsville, Newport News, Norfolk, Petersburg, Portsmouth, Radford, Richmond, Roanoke, South Boston, South Norfolk, Staunton, Suffolk, Virginia Beach, Waynesboro, Williamsburg, and Winchester.

Virginia libraries: University of Virginia, Alderman Library, (Virginiana), Charlottesville 22901, (Albermarle); Danville Public Library, 975 Main Street, Danville 24542, (Pittsylvania); Mary Washington College of the University of Virginia, E. Lee Trinkle Library, (Virginiana, American History), Fredricksburg 22401, (Spotsylvania);   Norfolk Public Library,   345 West Freemason Street, (Local history), Norfolk 23510, (Norfolk); Richmond Public Library, 101 E. Franklin St.,

23219, Union Theological Seminary Library, 3401 Brook Rd., (Presbyterian History), 23227, Virginia Historical Society, 707 E. Franklin St. (mss. Virginia and Colonial Americans Confederate state histories), 23219, Virginia State Library, Capital St., (Virginia and Southern history. Virginia newspapers and public records), 23219, Richmond, (Henrico); Roanoke Public Library, 722 S. Jefferson, St., Roanoke 24011, (Roanoke); College of William and Mary Library, (Virginiana Early Americana), Williamsburg 23185, (James City).

Some of the more important books on Virginia:

Burgess, Louis A., "Virginia Soldiers of 1776," 3 Vol., pub. 1927 Richmond Press, Richmond, Virginia.

DuBellet, Louise Pecquet, "Some Prominent Virginia Families," 4 Vol. pub 1907, Lynchburg.

Gwathmey, John H., "Historical Register of Virginia in the Revolution -- Soldiers, Sailors, Marines, 1775-1783," Pub. 1938 Dietz Press, Richmond, Virginia.

Hayden, Rev. Horace Edwin, "Virginia Genealogies," Reprint 1931. The Rare Book Shop, Washington, D. C.

Nugent, Nell Marion, "Cavaliers and Pioneers, Abstracts of Land Patents and Grants 1623-1800," 5 Vol. pub. 1934, Deitz Printing Co., Richmond, Virginia.

Swem, E. G., "Virginia Historical Index," 2 Vol. pub. 1934, Stone Printing and Mfg. Co., Roanoke, Virginia.

"Virginia Magazine of History and Biography," Published by the Virginia Historical Society, 707 E. Franklin St., Richmond, Va.

"William and Mary Quarterly," (a magazine of early American history, institutions and culture) Published by College of William and Mary, Williamsburg, Virginia.

Virginia County Histories

(Population figures to nearest thousand - 1960 Census)

Name	Map Index	Date Formed	Pop. By M	Census Reports Available	Parent County	County Seat
Accomack	A2	1663	31	1810-80	Northampton	Accomac
Albemarle	C2	1744	31	1810-80	Goochland, Louisa	Charlottesville
Alexandria		1801		1850-80	Prince William Co., Fairfax, became part of Dist. of Columbia	Alexandria

(See Dist. of Columbia for cen rec of 1800-40; 1920 changed to Arlington)

Name	Map Index	Date Formed	Pop. By M	Census Reports Available	Parent County	County Seat
Alleghany	D2	1822	12	1830-80	Bath, Botetourt, Monroe . . .	Covington

(Clk of Cir Ct has div, pro, civ ct rec from 1822)

Name	Map Index	Date Formed	Pop. By M	Census Reports Available	Parent County	County Seat
Amelia	C2	1734	8	1810-80	Brunswick, Prince George . .	Amelia C.H.

(Clk of Cir Ct has m, div, pro, civ ct, & deeds from 1735)

Name	Map Index	Date Formed	Pop. By M	Census Reports Available	Parent County	County Seat
Amherst	D2	1761	23	1810-80	Albemarle	Amherst

(Cir Ct Clk has m, div, pro & civ ct rec from 1761; Va. State Health Dept, Richmond, Va. has b, d & bur rec)

Name	Map Index	Date Formed	Pop. By M	Census Reports Available	Parent County	County Seat
Appomatox	D2	1845	9	1850-80	Buckingham, Campbell, Charlotte, Prince Edward	Appomattox

(Clk of Cir Ct has m, div, pro, civ ct rec from 1892)

Arlington   B1   1801   163   Fairfax ....,... Arlington
Augusta   D2   1738-45 37 1810-80 Orange .... Staunton
   (Clk of Cir Ct has b rec 1853 to 1896, m rec from 1785, div rec from 1745)
Bath   D2   1790-1 5   1810-80 Augusta, Botetourt,
                                        Greenbrier .... Warm Springs
   (Clk of Cir Ct has b rec 1854 to 1880, d rec 1854 to 1870, div, pro, Law &
   Chancery rec from 1791)
Bedford   D2   1753-4 31   1810-80 Albemarle , Lunenburg ..... Bedford
   (Clk of Cir Ct has b & d rec 1854 to 1897, m, div, pro, civ ct, deeds from 1754)
Bland   E3   1861   6   1870-80 Giles, Tazewell, Wythe ...... Bland
   (Clk of Cir Ct has m, pro, civ ct rec from 1861)
Botetourt   D2   1769-70 17 1810-80 Augusta .... Fincastle
   (Clk of Cir Ct has b & d rec 1853 to 1870, m, div, pro, civ ct rec from 1770)
Brunswick   C3   1720-32 18 1810-80 Prince George, Isle of Wight,
                                        Surry .... Lawrenceville
   (Clk of Cir Ct has b rec 1800 to 1896, m & pro rec from 1732)
Buchanan   F3   1858   37 1860-80 Russell, Tazewell .. Big Rock & Grundy
   (Clk of Cir Ct has m, div, pro, civ ct rec from 1885; Ct House burned 1885)
Buckingham   C2   1761   11 1810-80 Albemarle, Appomattox ... Buckingham
   (Clk of Cir Ct has b & d rec 1869 to 1896, m, div, pro rec from 1869)
Campbell   D3   1781-2 33   1810-80 Bedford .... Rustburg
Caroline   C2   1727-8 13   1810-80 Essex, King and Queen,
                                        King William .... Bowling Green
Carroll   E3   1842   23 1850-80 Grayson, Patrick .... Hillsville
Charles City   B2   1634   5 1810-80 Original Shire .... Charles City
Charles River (See York)
Charlotte   C3   1764-5 13   1810-80 Lunenburg ..... Charlotte Court House
Chesterfield   C2   1749   96 1810-80 Henrico .... Chesterfield
   (Clk of Cir Ct has m rec from 1771, also div, pro & civ ct rec)
Clarke   C1   1836   8 1840-80 Frederick, Warren ...... Berryville
Craig   E2   1851   3 1860-80 Botetourt, Giles, Roanoke, Monroe,
                                        Alleghany, Montgomery ... NewCastle
   (Clk of Cir Ct has b rec 1864 to 1896, m, div, pro, civ ct, deeds from 1851)
Culpeper   C1   1748-9 15   1810-80 Orange .... Culpeper
Cumberland   C2   1748-9 6   1810-80 Goochland .... Cumberland
   (Clk of Cir Ct has m, div, pro, civ ct rec from 1749, also b & d rec from 1853
   to 1870)
Dickenson   F3   1880   20   Buchanan, Russell, Wise ... Clintwood
Dinwiddie   C3   1752   22 1810-80 Prince George .... Dinwiddie
   (Clk of Cir Ct has b & d rec from 1867 to 1897, m, pro, div, civ ct rec from 1833)
Dunmore (See Shenandoah)
Elizabeth City   1634   89 1810-80 Original Shire .... Hampton
   (Now Hampton, Independent City)
Essex   B2   1692   7 1810-80 Old Rappahannock .... Tappahannock
Fairfax   C1   1742   275 1810-80 Prince William, Loudoun ..... Fairfax
Fauquier   C1   1759   24 1810-80 Prince William .... Warrenton
Fincastle   1772   Botetourt (Discontinued 1777)
Floyd   E3   1831   10 1840-80 Montgomery, Franklin ...... Floyd
   (Clk of Cir Ct has m, div, pro, civ ct rec from 1831)
Fluvanna   C2   1777   7 1810-80 Albemarle .... Palmyra
   (Clk of Cir Ct has b & d rec 1867 to 1896, m, div, pro, civ ct, deeds from 1777)
Franklin   D3   1785-6 26   1810-80 Bedford, Henry, Patrick ... Rocky Mount
Frederick   C1   1738-43 22 1810-80 Orange, Augusta .... Winchester
Giles   E3   1806   17 1810-80 Montgomery, Monroe, Tazewell, Craig,
                                        Mercer, Wythe .... Pearisburg
Gloucester   B2   1651   12 1810-80 York .... Gloucester
Goochland   C2   1727-8 9   1810-80 Henrico .... Goochland
Grayson   E3   1792-3 17   1820-80 Wythe, Patrick .... Independence
   (Clk of Cir Ct has b & d rec 1853 to 1870, div rec 1792, deeds 1793, wills 1796)
Greene   C2   1838   5 1840-80 Orange .... Stanardsville
   (Clk of Cir Ct has b & d rec 1838 to 1897, m, div, pro, deeds, civ ct rec 1838)

County Map of Virginia

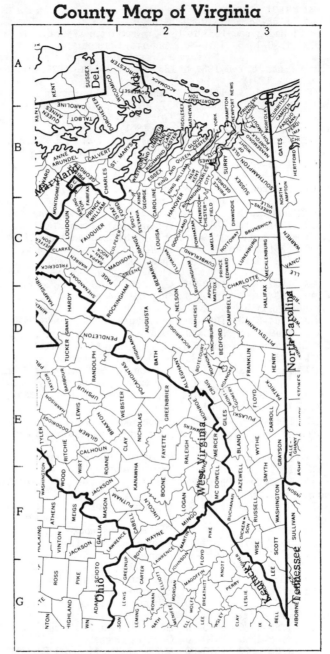

Greensville   C3   1780-1 16   1810-80   Brunswick, Sussex   . . . . Emporia
  (Clk of Cir Ct has m, div, pro, civ ct rec from 1781; State Bureau of Vit Stat,
  Richmond, Va. has b & d rec)
Halifax   D3   1752   34   1820-80   Lunenburg   . . . . Halifax
  (Clk of Cir Ct has m, pro, deeds from 1752)
Hanover   C2   1720-1 28   1810-80   New Kent   . . . . Hanover
  (Clk of Cir Ct has m, div, pro & civ ct rec)

Henrico   C2 1634 117 1810-80 Original Shire . . . . Richmond
(Clk of Cir Ct has m & pro rec from 1781)
Henry   D3 1776-7 40 1820-80 Pittsylvania, Patrick . . . . . Martinsville
Highland   D2 1847   3 1850-80 Bath, Pendleton   . . . . Monterey
(Clk of Cir Ct has b rec from 1847 to 1898, some d rec from 1847, m, div, pro, and civ ct rec from 1847; Bureau of Vit Stat, Richmond, Va. has b rec after 1912, m, d, and div rec)
Illinois   1778   (Discontinued 1784)
Isle of Wight B3 1634   17 1810-80 Original Shire . . . . . . Isle of Wight
(Clk of Cir Ct has b rec 1853 to 1876, d rec 1853 to 1874, m rec from 1772, div rec from 1853, pro rec from 1647, civ ct rec from 1746)
James City B2 1634   12 1820-80 Original Shire . . . . Williamsburg
Kentucky   1777   (Discontinued 1780)
King and Queen B2 1691   6 1810-80 New Kent . . . . King & Queen C. H.
(Clk of Cir Ct has m, div, pro, civ ct rec from 1864, land books from 1782 to 1850)
King George B2 1720-1 7 1810-80 Richmond, Westmoreland . . King George
(Clk of Cir Ct has m rec from 1786, div, pro, civ ct rec from 1721)
King William B2 1701-2 8 1820-80 King and Queen . . . . King William
(Clk of Cir Ct has m, div, pro, civ ct rec from 1885; fire 1885 burned most rec)
Lancaster   B2 1651   9 1810-80 Northumberland, York . . . . . Lancaster
Lee   G3 1792-3 26 1810-80 Russell, Scott . . . . Jonesville
(Clk of Cir Ct has b & d rec 1853 to 1877, m rec 1830, div rec 1832, pro rec 1800, civ ct rec & deeds from 1793)
Loudoun   C1 1757   25 1810-80 Fairfax . . . . , Leesburg
(Clk of Cir Ct has m, pro rec from 1793, d, div rec from 1757; Bureau of Vit Stat, Richmond, Va. has b rec)
Louisa   C2 1742   13 1820-80 Hanover . . . . Louisa
(Clk of Cir Ct has b rec 1867 to 1896, m, div, pro rec from 1742)
Lower Norfolk   1637   New Norfolk (See Princess Anne and Norfolk)
Lunenburg C3 1746   13 1810-80 Brunswick . . . . Lunenburg
(Clk of Cir Ct has m, div, pro, civ ct rec from 1746; Bureau of Vit Stat, Richmond, Va. has b & d rec)
Madison   C2 1792-3 8 1810-80 Culpeper . . . . Madison
(Clk of Cir Ct has m, div, pro, civ ct, chancery ct rec from 1793)
Mathews   B2 1790-1 7 1810-80 Gloucester . . . . Mathews
(Clk of Cir Ct has m, div, pro rec from 1865)
Mecklenburg C3 1764-5 31 1820-80 Lunenburg . . . . . . Boydton & Radcliffe
Middlesex   B2 1673   6 1820-80 Lancaster . . . . Saluda
(Clk of Cir Ct has m, div, pro, civ ct rec from 1668)
Montgomery E3 1776-7 33 1810-80 Fincastle, Botetourt,
                                    Pulaski . . . . Christiansburg
Nansemond B3 1637   31 1820-80 Upper Norfolk . . . . Suffolk
Nelson   D2 1807-8 13 1810-80 Amherst . . . . Lovingston
(Clk of Cir Ct has m, div, pro, civ ct rec from 1808)
New Kent   B2 1654   5 1810-80 York (Pt. James City) . . . . . New Kent
(Clk of Cir Ct has b & d rec 1865 to 1888, m, div, pro, civ ct rec from 1865)
New Norfolk   1636   Elizabeth City
Norfolk   B3 1691   52 1810-80 Lower Norfolk . . . . Portsmouth
Northampton A2 1642   17 1820-80 Original Shire . . . . Eastville
(Clk of Cir Ct has m rec from 1706, pro rec from 1632)
Northumberland B2 1648   10 1810-80 Indian Dist. of Chickacoan . . . Heathsville
Nottoway   C3 1788-9 15 1810-80 Amelia . . . . Nottoway
(Clk of Cir Ct has m, div, pro, civ ct rec from 1865)
Orange   C2 1734   13 1820-80 Spotsylvania . . . . Orange
(Clk of Cir Ct has b rec 1860 to 1895, m rec 1757, pro, civ ct, deeds from 1734)
Page   C1 1831   16 1840-80 Rockingham, Shenandoah . . . . . . Luray
Patrick   E3 1790-1 15 1820-80 Henry . . . . Stuart
(Clk of Cir Ct has b rec 1853 to 1896, m rec from 1791)
Pittsylvania D3 1766-7 58   Halifax . . . . Chatham
(Clk of Cir Ct has m, div, pro, civ ct and accounts current & inventories of

estates from 1767)

Powhatan   C2   1777   7   1810-80   Cumberland, Chesterfield . . . Powhatan

Prince Edward C3 1753-4 14 1810-80   Amelia . . . . Farmville
  (Clk of Cir Ct has b rec 1853 to 1896, d rec 1853 to 1869, m, div, pro, civ ct,
  and deed rec also guardian book from 1754)

Prince George B3 1702-3 20 1810-80   Charles City . . . . Prince George
  (Clk of Cir Ct has partial b rec from 1865 to 1896, m, div, pro rec from 1865;
  civ ct rec from 1945)

Prince William C1 1730-1 50 1810-80   King George, Stafford . . . . . . Manassas
  (Clk of Cir Ct has m rec from 1859, pro rec from 1734)

Princess Anne B3 1691   76 1810-80   Lower Norfolk . . . . Princess Anne
  (Clk of Cir Ct has b rec 1889 to 1895, m rec 1853, div rec 1814, pro rec 1783,
  civ ct rec 1937, min bks 1691)

Pulaski   E3   1839   27 1840-80   Montgomery, Wythe . . . . Pulaski
  (Clk of Cir Ct has m rec from 1882, div, pro, civ ct rec from 1839)

Rappahannock C1   1833   5 1840-80   Culpeper . . . . Washington

Rappahannock (Old, Abolished 1692   Lancaster

Richmond   B2   1692   6 1810-80   Rappahannock (Old) . . . . Warsaw
  (Clk of Cir Ct has b & d rec 1853 to 1895, m rec from 1853, div, pro, deeds,
  wills from 1693)

Roanoke   E2   1838   62 1840-80   Botetourt, Montgomery . . . . . . Salem

Rockbridge   D2   1778   24 1810-80   Augusta, Botetourt . . . . Lexington
  (Clk of Cir Ct has b rec from 1853 to 1896, m, div, pro, land rec and criminal
  rec from 1778; civ ct rec from 1934; Bureau of Vit Stat, Richmond, Va. has d rec)

Rockingham   D1   1778   40 1810-80   Augusta . . . . Harrisonburg
  (Ct rec burned in 1864 some rec lost; Clk of Cir Ct has partial b rec from
  1862 to 1894, partial d rec from 1862 to 1894, m, div, civ ct rec, tax lists,
  execu com bonds from 1778, and pro rec from 1803)

Russell   F3   1787   26 1820-80   Washington . . . . Lebanon

Scott   F3   1814   26 1820-80   Lee, Russell, Washington . . . Gate City

Shenandoah   D1   1772   22 1810-80   Frederick (Dunmore 'til 1778) . Woodstock
  (Clk of Cir Ct has m, div, pro, civ ct, deeds, wills from 1772)

Smyth   F3   1832   31 1840-80   Washington, Wythe . . . . Marion
  (Clk of Cir Ct has m, div, pro, civ ct rec from 1832)

Southampton   B3   1749   27 1810-80   Isle of Wight, Nansemond . . . . Courtland

Spotsylvania C2   1720-1 13 1810-80   Essex, King and Queen,
                                         King William . . . . Spotsylvania
  (Clk of Cir Ct has b rec 1864 to 1895, m rec from 1795, div rec from 1875, pro
  and deeds to real estate from 1722, law cases from 1875) (City of Fredericksburg acquired territory in 1940, 1950 and 1955)

Stafford   C1   1664   17 1810-80   Westmoreland . . . . Stafford
  (Clk of Cir Ct has m rec from 1854, div & civ ct rec 1664, pro & deeds 1699)

Surry   B3   1652   6 1810-80   James City . . . . Surry

Sussex   B3   1753-4 12 1810-80   Surry . . . . Sussex
  (Clk of Cir Ct has m, pro, civ ct rec from 1754)

Tazewell   F3   1799-00 45 1820-80   Russell, Wythe . . . . Tazewell
  (Clk of Cir Ct has m, div, pro & civ ct rec from 1800, b rec from 1800 to
  1840, d rec from 1800 to 1830; Dept of Health, Richmond, Va. has b rec since
  1840 and d rec since 1830)

Upper Norfolk   1637   New Norfolk (See Nansemond)

Warren   C1   1836   15 1840-80   Frederick, Shenandoah . . . . Front Royal

Warrosquoyacke   1634   Changed to Isle of Wight 1637

Warwick   B3   1634   82 1810-80   (Disc. 1953 records in Newport News)

Washington   F3   1776-7 38 1810-80   Fincastle, Montgomery . . . . . Abingdon

Westmoreland B2   1653   11 1810-80   Northumberland . . . . Montross

Wise   F3   1856   44 1860-80   Lee, Russell, Scott . . . . Wise
  (Clk of Cir Ct has m & div rec from 1856)

Wythe   E3   1789-90 22 1810-80   Montgomery (Pt. Grayson) . . Wytheville
  (Clk of Cir Ct has m, div, pro rec from 1790, also civ ct rec)

Yohogania   1776   (Discontinued 1786)

York   B2   1634   22 1810-80   Original Shire . . . . Yorktown
  (Changed from Charles River)

Federal Courts. Inventory of County Archives, Amelia, Brunswick, Chesterfield, Dinwiddie, Isle of Wight, Middlesex, Powhatan, Prince George, Southampton. Guide to manuscripts collection of the Baptist Historical Society, Supplement No. 1. Index to Obituaries in "Religious Herald" Richmond 1828-1938. Supplement No. 2 index to marriage notices in "Religious Herald" Richmond, Vol. 1, A to L, Vol 2, M to Z. Index to marriage notices in "Southern Churchman" 1835-1941, Vol. 1, A to K, Vol. 2, L to Z. Inventory of the Church Archives of Virginia, Dover Baptist Association, Negro Baptist Churches in Richmond. Inventory of the Church Archives of West Virginia, Preliminary Bibliography of material relating to churches in West Virginia, Virginia, Kentucky and Southern Ohio. A check list of New Market, Va. imprints 1806-1876. Depository of unpublished material, Baptist Historical Society, University of Richmond, Richmond, Virginia (Church - Archives), State Library, Richmond, Virginia (all other material).

Washington

Capital Olympia - Territory 1853 - State 1889 - (42nd)

Washington became a Territory in 1853, after having been part of Oregon Territory since 1848. Included in that territorial domain was all of the present Idaho. It was reduced to its present dimensions in 1889 when Washington became the forty-second state to enter the Union.

During the years of its greatest growth, Washington received thousands of former residents of Wisconsin, Minnesota and other western states. Many Canadian farmers flocked there to secure good land at a low price. Most of the newcomers at that time were Canadians, Swedes, Norwegians, English, Germans, Finns, Italians, Russians, Danes, and Scotch. The Scandinavian immigrants felt especially at home since the country and climate reminded them of the place they had previously inhabited.

Since 1907 the State Department of Health, Bureau of Vital Statistics, now located in the General Administration Building, Olympia 98501, Washington, has had control of all birth and death records within the state. Records prior to that time are on file in the offices of the County Auditor of the respective counties. In the cities of Seattle, Spokane, Bellingham and Tacoma, they may be obtained at the city health departments.

Records of marriages are at the offices of the respective County Auditors. All land records are also filed in those offices. The County Clerks have charge of the records of wills and all probate matters.

A partial list of Washington libraries: Bellingham Public Library, 1414 Commercial St., Bellingham 98225, (Whatcom); Regional Public Library, 7th and Franklin Sts., Olympia 98501, (Thurston); King County Library, 906-908 Fourth Ave., 98134, Seattle Public Library, 4th Ave. and Madison St., (Northwest, and the genealogy collection formerly held by Washington State Library), 98134, University of Washington Library, (Pacific Northwest), 98105, Seattle, (King); Spokane Public Library, W. 906 Main, (Pacific Northwest), 99201, Spokane County Library, 1604 W. Riverside, 99201, Spokane, (Spokane); Tacoma Public Library, 1120 S. Tacoma Ave., Washington State Historical Society, Tacoma 98402, (Pierce).

Washington County Histories

(Population figures to nearest thousand - 1960 Census)

Name	Map Index	Date Formed	Pop. By M	Census Reports Available	Parent County	County Seat
Adams	B4	1883	10		Whitman	Ritzville
(Co Clk has div, pro, civ ct rec from 1883)						
Asotin	C4	1883	13		Garfield	Asotin
Benton	C3	1905	62		Yakima, Klickitat	Prosser
Chelan	B3	1899	41		Kittitas, Okanogan	Wenatchee
(Co Auditor has b & d rec from 1900 to 1907, m rec from 1900 ; City Clk has bur rec; Chelan Co Clk has div, pro & civ ct rec)						
Chehalis				1860-80	(Original Co. - Now Grays Harbor .	Chehalis
Clallam	A1	1854	30	1860-80	Jefferson	Port Angeles
Clark	C2	1854	94	1860-80	Original county	Vancouver
Columbia	C4	1875	5	1880	Walla Walla	Dayton
(Co Clk has m, div, pro, civ ct rec from 1876; Co Auditor has b rec from 1892)						
Cowlitz	C2	1854	58	1860-80	Lewis	Kelso
(Co Auditor has b rec from 1890 to 1907, d rec from 1891 to 1907, m rec from 1854; Co Clk has div, pro & civ ct rec)						
Douglas	B3	1884	15		Lincoln	Waterville
(Co Auditor has b rec from 1891 to 1907, m rec from 1885, d rec from 1891 to 1909; Cem Assn has bur rec; Clk of Sup Ct has div, pro & civ ct rec)						
Ferry	A4	1899	4		Stevens	Republic
(Co Clk has div, pro, civ ct rec from 1899)						
Franklin	C3	1883	23		Whitman	Pasco
(Co Auditor has b, d & bur rec from 1891 to 1910; m rec from 1891; Co Clk has div & pro rec from 1891)						
Garfield	C4	1881	3		Columbia	Pomeroy
(Co Auditor has b, m, d & bur rec; Co Clk has div, pro & civ ct rec from 1881)						
Grant	B3	1909	46		Douglas	Ephrata
Gray's Harbor	B1	1854	54		Original county	Montesano
(Co Auditor has b, m, & d rec from 1891; Co Clk has div, pro & civ ct rec from 1860) (Gray's Harbor was first organized as Chelalis County)						
Island	A2	1852	20	1860-80	Original county	Coupeville
(Co Clk has b rec from 1870 to 1907, d rec from 1891 to 1907, m, div, civ ct rec from 1891, pro rec from 1853; State Health Dept. has b & d rec from 1907)						

County Map of Washington

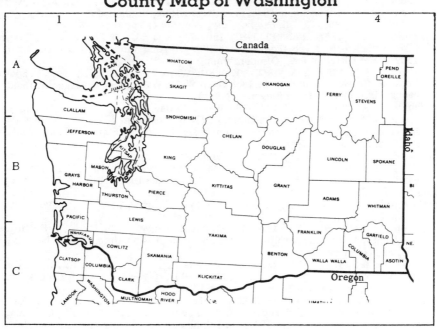

Jefferson   B1   1852   10   1860-80   Original county   . . . . . Port Townsend
(Co Auditor has b & d rec from 1891 to 1907, m rec from 1853; Co Clk has div rec from 1886, pro rec from 1891)

King   B2   1852   935   1860-80   Original county . . . . Seattle

Kitsap   B2   1857   84   1860-80   King   . . . . Port Orchard

Kittitas   B3   1883   20   Yakima   . . . . Ellensburg
(Co Auditor has b rec from 1897 to 1907, m, div, pro, civ ct rec; State Dept Vit Stat, Olympia, Wash. has d rec and b rec from 1907)

Klickitat   C2   1859   13   1860-80   Walla Walla   . . . . Goldendale

Lewis   B2   1845   42   1860-80   Original county   . . . . . . Chehalis
(Co Auditor has b & d rec from 1891 to 1907, m rec from 1850; Co Clk has div, pro, civ ct rec from ca 1870; State Office, Olympia, Wash. has b & d rec after 1 July 1907)

Lincoln   B4   1883   11   Spokane   . . . . Davenport
(Co Clk has b & d rec from 1891 to 1907, m rec from 1884, deeds, mtgs, misc; Co Clk has div, pro, civ ct rec; State Dept of Vit Stat, Olympia, Wash. has b & d rec from 1 July 1907)

Mason   B1   1854   16   1870-80   Thurston   . . . . Shelton
(Mason County was first organized as Sawamish County)

Okanogan   A3   1888   26   Stevens   . . . . Okanogan
(Co Clk has div & civ ct rec from 1899, pro rec from 1888; Co Auditor has m rec; State Dept of Vit Stat, has b & d rec)

Pacific   B1   1851   15   1860-80   Original county   . . . . South Bend

Pend Oreille A4   1911   7   Stevens   . . . . Newport
(Co Auditor has m rec from 1911; Funeral Homes have b, d & bur rec; Co Clk has div, pro & civ ct rec)

Pierce   B2   1852   322   1860-80   Original county   . . . . Tacoma

San Juan   A1   1873   3   1870-80   Whatcom   . . . . Friday Harbor
(Co Clk - Auditor has b rec from 1892 to 1907, d rec from 1890 to 1907, m rec from 1878, div, pro, civ ct rec from 1890)

Sawamish   1860   (See Mason)

Skagit   A2   1883   51   Whatcom . . . . Mount Vernon
(Co Clk has div, pro, civ ct rec from 1883)

Skamania   C2 1854   5 1860-80 Clark .... Stevenson
   (Co Auditor has b rec from 1898, m rec from 1856, deeds, mining claims, U.S.
   Patents from 1856; Co Clk has bur, div, pro, civ ct rec from 1856)
Snohomish   B2 1861 172 1870-80 Island .... Everett
   (Co Clk has b & d rec from 1891 to 1907, m rec from 1891; b & d rec from
   1907 are at Office of Reg, Olmpia, Wash.)
Spokane   B4 1858 278 1860-80 Walla Walla .... Spokane
   (Spokane Co was organized in 1858 from Walla Walla, then disorganized and
   reorganized in 1879 from Stevens County)
Stevens   A4 1863   18 1870-80 Walla Walla .... Colville
   (Co Auditor has b & d rec from 1891 to 1907, m rec from 1891; Co Clk has div
   & civ ct rec from 1882, pro rec from 1887; Dept of Vit Stat, Olympia, Wash.
   has b, d, and bur rec from 1907)
Thurston   B1 1852   55 1860-80 Original county .... Olympia
   (Co Auditor has b & d rec from 1891 to 1907, m rec from 1891; State Dept of
   Vit Stat has b & d rec from 1907; Co Clks Office has div, pro & civ ct rec)
Wahkiakum C1 1854   3 1860-80 Lewis .... Cathlamet
Walla Walla C3 1854   42 1860-80 Original county .... Walla Walla
   (Co Clk has div, pro, civ ct rec from 1860)
Whatcom   A2 1854   70 1860-80 Original county .... Bellingham
   (Co Auditor has b & d rec to June 1907, m rec to present time; Co Clk has div,
   pro, and civ ct rec)
Whitman   B4 1871   31 1880   Stevens .... Colfax
   (Co Auditors have b & d rec from 1891 to 1907, m rec from 1873; Co Clk has
   div, civ ct rec from 1862, pro rec from 1870)
Yakima   C2 1865 145 1870-80 Walla Walla .... Yakima
   (Co Auditor has b & d rec to 1907, m rec; State Dept of Health, Olympia,
   Wash. has b & d rec from 1907; Co Clk has div, pro & civ ct rec from 1890)

Genealogists' Check List of the Historical Records Survey, Washington

Federal Courts. Inventory of County Archives, Adams, Asotin, Benton, Chelan, Cowlitz, Garfield, King, Lewis, Lincoln, Pend Oreille, Skagit, Snohomish, Spokane, Stevens, Yakima. Guide to Public Vital Statistic records. Guide to Church Vital Statistic records. Inventory of the Church Archives of Washington, Survey of Everett, Yakima and Wenatchee church archives, Survey of Seattle Church Archives, Survey of Spokane Church Archives. Guides to depository of manuscript collections in Oregon and Washington. A check list of Washington imprints 1853-1876. Depository of unpublished material, State College, Pullman, Washington.

West Virginia

Capital Charleston - State 1863 - (35th)

West Virginia came into existance as a direct result of the Civil War. That section had always been part of Virginia, even though the two sections never had much in common. One of the main reasons for this, no doubt, is the rugged Allegheny mountain range separating the two sections which made traveling between them rather difficult. When Virginia cast its lot with the Confederacy, the settlers west of the Alleghenies began to murmur. The complaint eventually became so loud and demanding that a separate government for the western section was organized in 1861 under the name of Kanawha. Two years later West Virginia was admitted into the Union as the thirty-fifth state with a total of 50 counties. Since then five counties have been added.

The physical features of the section make West Virginia more accessible from Pennsylvania than from Virginia. At least, it was so in the early days. In those days the Indian trails served as roads and much of the travel was in the direction from Pennsylvania to West Virginia. Germans, Welsh, and Irish came as early as 1670. English in 1671, various nationalities in 1715 and 1725. Some of the early settlers merely crossed over from Maryland and made their homes in the present Berkely and Jefferson counties.

Among different nationalities who have come to West Virginia to man various factories are Italians, Poles, Hungarians, Austrians, English, Germans, Greeks, Russians, and Czechs.

Most of the counties in West Virginia were settled years before they were organized. Here are figures showing the years the respective counties were settled:

Brooke 1744; Pendleton, 1747; Randolph, 1753; Monroe, 1760; Monongalia, 1767; Greenbrier and Ohio, 1769; Harrison, Marion, and Preston, 1772; Kanawha, 1773; Mason and Tucker, 1774; Cabell and Mercer, 1775; Hancock, 1776; Marshall, 1777; Barbour and Wetzel, 1780; Jackson and Wirt, 1796; Wood, 1797; Boone, 1798; Lincoln, 1799; Putnam and Roan, 1800.

The Division of Vital Statistics, State Health Department, State House, Charleston 25301, West Virginia, has the records of births and deaths from 1917 to the present, marriages since 1921. Earlier marriages are recorded in the offices of the respective County Clerks.

The Virginia tax lists, published to replace the fire destroyed 1790 Federal Census, give a record of the taxpayers in the West Virginia counties of those days. A number of West Virginia counties have published the 1850 Census, containing the names, ages, and dates of birth of all family members. The first Federal Census was taken in West Virginia in 1870. Prior schedules of the original 50 counties are lister under Virginia.

The County Clerk has charge of all court and land records.

Books on West Virginia history and genealogy:

Hale, J. P., "Trans-Allegheny Pioneers," Pub. 1886.

Myers, S., "History of West Virginia," 2 Vols. Pub. 1915.

"Sons of the Revolution in the State of West Virginia," published by West Virginia Society, 1941.

West Virginia libraries: Kanawha County Library, Lee and Dickinson Sts. West Virginia Dept. of Archives & History Library, Charleston 25301, (Kanawha); Huntington Public Library, 900 Fifth Ave., Huntington 27501, (Cabell); West Virginia University Library, (West Virginia), Morgantown 26505, (Monongalia)

West Virginia County Histories

(Population figures to nearest thousand - 1960 Census)

Name	Map Index	Date Formed	Pop. By M	Census Reports Available	Parent County	County Seat
Barbour	B3	1843	15	1850-80	Harrison, Lewis, Randolph . . .	Philippi
Berkeley	C4	1772	34	1810-80	Frederick	Martinsburg
(Co Clk has b & d rec from 1865, m rec from 1778, pro rec from 1772)						
Boone	B1	1847	29	1850-80	Kanawha, Cabell, Logan	Madison
(Co Clk has b, m, d rec from 1865, bur rec from 1888)						
Braxton	B2	1836	15	1840-80	Kanawha, Lewis, Nicholas	Sutton
Brooke	A3	1797	29	1810-80	Ohio	Wellsburg
Cabell	A1	1809	108	1820-80	Kanawha	Huntington
(Co Clk has b, m, d, rec from 1809; Clk of Cir Ct has div, pro rec from 1809)						
Calhoun	B2	1856	8	1860-80	Gilmer	Grantsville
(Co Clk has b & d rec from 1855, m rec from 1856)						
Clay	B2	1858	12	1860-80	Braxton, Nicholas	Clay
(Co Clk has b, m, d, pro rec from 1858)						
Doddridge	B3	1845	7	1850-80	Harrison, Tyler, Ritchie, Lewis .	W. Union
(Co Clk has b rec from 1853, m rec from 1850, d rec from 1862)						
Fayette	B2	1831	62	1840-80	Kanawha, Greenbrier, Logan .	Fayetteville
(Co Clk has b & d rec from 1866, m, pro, land rec from 1831)						
Gilmer	B2	1845	8	1850-80	Lewis, Kanawha	Glenville
(Clk of Co Ct has b, m rec from 1845, d rec from 1853, pro rec from 1848)						
Grant	B3	1866	8	1870-80	Hardy	Petersburg
(Co Clk has b, m, d, div, pro, civ ct rec from 1866)						
Greenbrier	B2	1778	34	1820-80	Montgomery	Lewisburg
(Co Clk has b & d rec from 1853, m & pro rec from 1780)						
Hampshire	B4	1753	12	1810-80	Frederick	Romney
(Co Clk has b & m rec from 1865, d rec from 1866, incomplete pro rec from 1780, chancery ct 1831)						
Hancock	A4	1848	40	1850-80	Brooke	New Cumberland
(Co Clk has b, m, d, pro, civ ct rec from 1848; Cir Clk has div rec)						
Hardy	C3	1785	9	1820-80	Hampshire	Moorefield
Harrison	B3	1784	78	1810-80	Monongalia	Clarksburg
Jackson	A2	1831	19		Kanawha, Mason, Wood	Ripley
(Co Clk has b, d, pro rec & wills from 1853, m rec from 1831; Cir Clk has div and civ ct rec)						
Jefferson	C4	1801	19	1810-80	Berkeley	Charles Town
(Co Clk has b & d rec from 1853 except CW years, m & pro rec from 1801)						
Kanawha	B2	1788	253	1810-80	Greenbrier, Montgomery . . .	Charleston
(Co Clk has b, d, bur rec from 1853, m rec from 1854, pro rec from 1838; Cir Clk has div rec)						
Lewis	B3	1816	20	1820-80	Harrison	Weston
(Co Clk has b & d rec from 1853, m, pro rec and deeds from 1816; Cir Clk has div rec)						
Lincoln	A1	1867	20	1870-80	Boone, Cabell, Kanawha	Hamlin
Logan	B1	1824	62	1830-80	Kanawha, Cabell, Giles	Logan
(Co Clk has b, m, d rec from 1872)						

McDowell   B1   1858   71   1860-1960 Tazewell   . . . . Welch
(Co Clk has b rec from 1872, m rec from 1861, d rec from 1894, pro rec from 1897; Cir Clk has div rec)
Marion   B3   1842   64   1850-80   Harrison, Monongalia   . . . . . Fairmont
(Co Clk has b rec from 1860, m rec from 1842, d rec from 1853)
Marshall   A3   1835   38   1840-80   Ohio   . . . . Moundsville
(Co Clk has b & d rec from 1853, m & deed rec from 1835, pro rec from 1850; Cir Clk has div & civ ct rec)
Mason   A2   1804   24   1810-80   Kanawha   . . . . Point Pleasant
Mercer   B1   1837   68   1840-80   Giles, Tazewell   . . . . Princeton
(Co Clk has b, m, d rec from 1853, pro rec from 1860; Clk of Cir Ct has div rec)
Mineral   B4   1866   22   1870-80   Hampshire . . . . Keyser
(Co Clk has b, m, d, pro, land rec, wills, deeds from 1866)
Mingo   B1   1895   40   Logan . . . . Williamson
Monongalia   B3   1776   56   1810-80   Dist of W. Augusta . . . . . Morgantown
Monroe   B2   1799   12   1810-80   Greenbrier   . . . . Union
(Co Clk has b & d rec from 1853, m & pro rec from 1799)
Morgan   C4   1820   8   1830-80   Berkeley, Hampshire   . . Berkeley Springs
(Co Clk has b, m, d rec from 1865, pro rec from 1820; Cir Ct has div & civ ct rec) (Territory taken 12 Jan 1950 to correct boundary – to Hampshre County)
Nicholas   B2   1818   25   1820-80   Greenbrier, Kanawha . . . Summersville
Ohio   A3   1777   68   1810-80   Dist. of W. Augusta   . . . . . . Wheeling
(Co Clk has b, d, & bur rec from 1853, m pro rec from 1777; Clk of Cir Ct has civ ct rec)
Pendleton   C3   1787   8   1810-80   Augusta, Hardy   . . . . Franklin
(Co Clk has b & d rec from 1853, m rec from 1800, also div, pro & civ ct rec)
Pleasants   A3   1851   7   1860-80   Ritchie, Tyler, Wood . . . . . . St. Marys
Pocahontas   B2   1821   10   1830-80   Bath County Virginia   . . . . . . Marlinton
Preston   B3   1818   27   1880   Monongalia   . . . . Kingwood
(Co Clk has b, m, d rec from 1869)
Putnam   A2   1848   24   1850-80   Kanawha, Mason, Cabell . . . . . Winfield

County Map of West Virginia

Raleigh   B1   1850   78   1850-80   Fayette . . . . Beckley
   (Co Clk has b, m, d, pro, wills from 1850)
Randolph   B3   1787   26   1810-80   Harrison . . . . Elkins
   (Co Clk has b rec from 1856, m, pro, wills from 1787, d rec from 1853)
Ritchie   A2   1843   11   1850-80   Harrison, Lewis, Wood . . . Harrisville
   (Co Clk has b & d rec from 1850, m & pro rec from 1843)
Roane   B2   1856   16   1860-80   Kanawha, Jackson, Gilmer . . . . . Spencer
Summers   B1   1871   16   Greenbrier, Monroe, Mercer . . Hinton
Taylor   B3   1844   15   1850-80   Barbour, Harrison, Marion
                     and Preston   . . . . Grafton
    (Co Clk has b, m, d, pro rec from 1853, land rec from 1844)
Tucker   B3   1856   8   1860-80   Randolph . . . . Parsons
Tyler   A3   1814   10   1820-80   Ohio . . . . Middlebourne
Upshur   B3   1851   18   1860-80   Randolph, Barbour, Lewis . . Buckhannon
   (Co Clk has b, m, d, pro rec from 1863; Clk Cir Ct has div & civ ct rc)
Wayne   A1   1842   39   1850-80   Cabell . . . . Wayne
   (Co Clk has b & d rec from 1853, m rec from 1854)
Webster   B2   1860   14   1860-80   Braxton, Nicholas   . . . . Webster Springs
   (Co Clk has b, m, d, pro rec from 1887)
Wetzel   A3   1846   19   1850-80   Tyler . . . . New Martinsville
Wirt   A2   1848   4   1850-80   Wood, Jackson . . . . Elizabeth
Wood   A2   1798   78   1810-80   Harrison . . . . Parkersburg
   (Co Clk has b & d rec from 1850, m rec 1800, land rec 1798)
Wyoming   B1   1850   35   1850-80   Logan . . . . Pineville
   (Co Clk has b & d rec from 1853, m rec from 1854, pro rec from 1851)

Genealogists' Check List of the Historical Records Survey, West Virginia

Federal Courts. Inventory of County Archives, Gilmer, Grant, Lincoln, Marion, Mineral, Monroe, Pendleton, Pocahontas, Putnam, Randolph, Ritchie, Roane, Taylor. Inventory of Public Vital Statistic records. Guide to Church Vital Statistic records. Inventory of the Church Archives of W. Va., Presbyterian Churches, Protestant Episcopal Church, Preliminary Bibliography of material relating to churhes in W.Va, Virginia, Kentucky, and Southern Ohio. Calendar of the Arthur I. Boreman Letters in the State Dept. of Archives and History. Calendar of the William E. Stevenson Letters in the State Dept. of Archives and History. Calendar of the J.J. Jacob letters in West Virginia depository. Calendar of the Francis Harrison Pierpont Letters and Papers in West Virginia depository. Calendar of the Governor Henry Mason Matthews letters and papers in the State Dept. of Archives and History. Check list of W.Va. imprints 1791-1830. West Virginia County formations and boundary changes (2 editions). Cemetery readings in W.Va., Gideon Magisterial District of Cabell County. Cemetery readings, Fairmont and Grant Magisterial District of Marion County. Cemetery readings Lincoln and Paw Paw Magisterial District of Marion County. Calendar of Wills, Upshur County. Depository of unpublished material, Dept. of Archives and History, Charleston, West Virginia (Historical Material), West Virginia University Library, Morgantown, West Virginia (all other material).

Wisconsin

Settlers established themselves in the Wisconsin area as early as 1766. In 1840, according to the first U. S. Census taken, there were 130,945. The real influx of people came about 1848 when tens of thousands of people, mainly from the northern European countries came into the territory. The 1850 Census registered 305,391 and the 1860 Census 775,881.

By far the largest number of these immigrants were Germans.

About 1840 nearly all of the counties facing Lake Michigan had received thousands of settlers. The Rock River Valley in Rock County also had many settlers at that time and earlier.

Wisconsin became a Territory in its own name in 1836. Previously it had been part of several Territories, including Indiana from 1800 to 1809; Illinois, 1809 to 1818; Michigan, 1818 to 1836. In 1848 it became the thirtieth state in the Union.

The leading nationalities represented in Wisconsin, in their numerical order are German (nearly three to one), Polish, Norwegian, Russian, Austrian, Swedish, Czech, Italian, Danish, Hungarian, English, Finnish, Greek, Irish and French.

The Bureau of Vital Statistics, Madison 53702, Wisconsin, has birth and death records from 1860 to date.

Marriage Bans - address church where recorded.

Wills, deeds. land grants, tax payers lists - all of these records are available in the various county court houses. Address inquiries to the County Clerk.

War Service Records - Adjutant General's Office, State Capital, Madison.

Cemetery Records a few have been transferred to the various county clerks, but the practice is not at all general. Contact the local sexton.

Guardianship and Orphan Court Proceedings are held by the issuing court and by the Public Welfare Department, State Capital.

The Library of the State Historical Society of Wisconsin includes some 750,000 volumes, nearly one fifth of which deals with genealogy and local history. Books and pamphlets dealing with every state in the union and collective and individual American genealogies are included. Many church histories and records supplement those volumes generally classified as genealogical.

Wisconsin libraries: Eau Claire Public Library, 217 S. Farwell, (Wisconsin, local history), Eau Claire 54701, (Eau Claire);

Gilbert M. Simmons Public Library, 711 59th Pl., Kenosha 53140, (Kenosha); La Crosse County Public Library, La Crosse 54601, (La Crosse).

Wisconsin County Histories

(Population figures to nearest thousand - 1960 Census)

Name	Map Index	Date Formed	Pop. By M	Census Reports Available	Parent County	County Seat
Adams	D3	1848	8	1850-80	Portage	Friendship
Ashland	A2	1856	17	1860-80	Unorganized Territory	Ashland
Bad Ax				1860	(See Vernon)	
Barron	B1	1868	24	1870-80	Dallas, Polk	Barron
Bayfield	A2	1866	12	1870-80	Ashland, La Pointe	Washburn

(Reg of Deeds has b, m, d rec; Clk of Ct has div, pro & civ ct rec)

Brown	C4	1818	125	1840-80	Territorial county	Green Bay

(Register of Deeds has b rec from 1846, m rec from 1821, d rec from 1834; Clk of Cir Ct has div & civ ct rec 1825; Register of Pro has pro rec 1828; See Mich. for 1820-30 census)

Buffalo	C1	1853	14	1860-80	Trempealeau	Alma

(Reg of Deeds has b, m, d, bur rec; Clk of Ct has div & cir ct rec; Reg in Pro has pro rec)

Burnett	B1	1865	9	1860-80	Polk	Grantsburg

(Register of Deeds has b rec from 1861, m & d rec 1880; Co Clk has div, pro civ ct rec from 1888)

Calumet	D4	1836	22	1840-80	Territorial county	Chilton
Chippewa	C2	1845	45	1850-80	Crawford	Chippewa Falls

(Reg of Deeds has b rec from 1858, m rec from 1855, d rec from 1867; Clk of Ct has div & civ ct rec ffrom 1850; Reg in Probate has pro rec from 1856)

Clark	C2	1853	32	1905	Crawford	Neillsville

(Co Clk has b, m rec from 1880, d rec from 1885, div, civ ct rec & naturalization & criminal rec from 1875, pro rec from 1870)

Columbia	D3	1846	37	1850-80	Portage	Portage
Crawford	E2	1818	16	1840-80	Territorial county	Prairie du Chien

(Co Clk has b rec from 1806, m rec from 1820, d & bur rec 1880, div & civ ct rec 1848, pro rec 1819; See Mich. for 1820-30 census)

Dallas		1859		1860	(Changed to Barron)	
Dane	E2	1838	222	1840-80	Territorial county	Madison

(Co Clk has b, m, d rec from 1904, div & civ ct rec from 1848, pro rec from 1935)

Dodge	D3	1836	63	1840-80	Territoral county	Juneau

(Reg of Deeds has b, m, d, div, pro rec from 1887)

Door	C4	1851	22	1860-1960	Brown	Sturgeon Bay

(Reg of Deeds has b, m, d, bur rec; Co Judge has div, pro rec; Clk of Ct has civ ct rec)

Douglas	A1	1854	45	1860-80	Unorganized Territory	Superior

(Register of Deeds has b, m, d rec from 1878; Clk of Cts has div & civ ct rec 1878; Co Ct has pro rec 1878; Co Treas has prop owners rec 1854)

Dunn	C1	1856	26	1860-80	Chippewa	Menomonie

(Reg of Deeds has b rec from 1858, m rec from 1855, d rec from 1873, div rec from 1870)

Eau Claire	C2	1856	58	1860-80	Chippewa	Eau Claire

(Reg of Deeds has b, d, m rec from 1850 to 1907 (incomplete) and from 1907 (complete); Clk of Cts has div rec from 1856, civ ct rec from 1929)

Florence	B3	1882	3		Marinette, Oconto	Florence
Fond du Lac	D3	1836	75	1840-80	Territorial county	Fond du Lac
Forest	B3	1885	8		Langlade, Oconto	Crandon

(Co Clk has b, m, d, bur, civ, pro, civ ct rec from 1885; State Census 1875-1905)

Grant E2 1836 44 1840-80 Territorial county : . . . . Lancaster
Green E2 1836 26 1880-1905 Territorial county . . . . Monroe
(Reg of Deeds has b rec from 1907, m rec from 1846, d rec from 1878; Clk of Cir Ct has div & civ ct rec; Co Judge has pro rec)
Green Lake D3 1859 15 1860-80 Marquette District . . . . . . Green Lake
Iowa E2 1829 20 1840-80 Territorial county . . . . . Dodgeville
(Register of Deeds has b, d, bur rec from 1867; Co Clk has m rec from 1899; See Mich. for 1830 census)
Iron A2 1893 8 Ashland, Oneida . . . . Hurley
Jackson C2 1853 15 1860-80 LaCrosse . . . . Black River Falls
Jefferson E3 1837 50 1840-80 Milwaukee . . . . Jefferson
(Reg of Deeds has b, m, & d rec; Clk of Cts has div rec; Reg in Probate has pro rec)
Juneau D2 1856 17 1860-80 Adams . . . . Mauston
Kenosha D4 1850 101 1850-80 Racine . . . . Kenosha
(Co Clk has m rec from 1900)
Kewaunee C4 1852 18 1860-80 Manitowoc . . . . Kewaunee
La Crosse D2 1851 72 1860-80 Unorganized Territory . . . . La Crosse
(Reg of Deeds has b, m, & d rec from 1851; Clk of Cts has div & civ ct rec; Reg in Probate has pro rec from 1851)
Lafayette E2 1846 18 1850-80 Iowa . . . . Darlington
La Pointe 1845 1850-60 (See Bayfield)
Langlade B3 1880 20 1880 Oconto . . . . Antigo
Lincoln B3 1866 22 1880 Marathon . . . . Merrill
Manitowoc D4 1836 75 1840-80 Territorial county . . . . Manitowoc
(Reg of Deeds has b, m, d, & bur rec; Clk of Cir Ct has div, pro, civ ct rec)
Marathon C3 1850 89 1850-80 Portage . . . . Wausau
(Reg of Deeds has b, m, d, bur, div, pro & civ ct rec)
Marinette B4 1879 35 1880 Oconto . . . . Marinette
Marquette D3 1836 9 1840-80 Marquette District . . . . Montello
(Register of Deeds has b rec from 1876, m & d rec from 1869; Clk of Ct has div, pro, civ ct rec from 1870)
Menominee 1961 Menominee Indian Reservation. . . Keshena
Milwaukee D4 1834 1036 1840-80 Territorial county . . . . Milwaukee
(Co Clk has m rec from 1834)
Monroe D2 1856 31 1860-80 Unorganized Territory . . . . Sparta
Oconto C4 1851 25 1860-80 Unorganized Territory . . . . . . Oconto
(Reg of Deeds has b, m, d & bur rec; Clk of Cts has div & civ ct rec; Reg in Pro has pro rec; Oconto Historical Society has historical rec)
Oneida B3 1885 22 Lincoln . . . . Rhinelander
Outagamie C3 1851 102 1860-80 Brown . . . . Appleton
(Reg of Deeds has b, m, d rec from 1852; Clk of Cts has div & civ ct rec from 1855; Reg in Probate has pro rec from 1855)
Ozaukee E4 1853 38 1860-80 Milwaukee . . . . Port Washington
(Reg of Deeds has b rec from 1850, m rec from 1845, d & bur rec from 1854; Clk of Cts has div rec from 1853; Clk of Co Cts has pro & co ct rec from 1853; Co Clk has Election rec from 1858; Co Treas has Tax Rolls from 1853)
Pepin C1 1851 7 1860-80 Chippewa . . . . Durand
Pierce C1 1853 23 1880-1905 St. Croix . . . . Ellsworth
(Co Clk has b, d rec from 1876, m rec from 1855, div rec from 1875, pro rec from 1878, civ ct rec from 1869)
Polk B1 1853 25 1860-80 St. Croix . . . . Balsam Lake
(Reg of Deeds has b & d rec from 1862, m rec from 1861; Clk of Ct has div rec; Co Judge has pro rec)
Portage C3 1836 37 1840-80 Territorial county . . . . Stevens Point
(Register of Deeds has b rec from 1844, m rec 1848, d rec 1855; Clk of Cts has div & civ ct rec 1844; Co Judge has pro rec 1890)
Price B2 1878 14 1880 Chippewa . . . . Phillips
Racine D4 1836 142 1840-80 Territorial county . . . . Racine
Richland D2 1842 18 1850-80 Iowa . . . . Richland Center
Rock E2 1836 114 1840-80 Territorial county . . . . . . Janesville
(Reg of Deeds has b rec from 1860, m rec from 1849, d rec from 1873)

County Map of Wisconsin

Rusk	B2	1902	15		Chippewa . . . . Ladysmith

(Register of Deeds has b, m, d rec from 1902)

St. Croix	C1	1840	29	1840–80	Territorial county . . . . Hudson
Sauk	D2	1840	36	1840–80	Territorial county . . . . Baraboo
Sawyer	B2	1883	9		Ashland, Chippewa . . . . . . Hayward

(Reg of Deeds has b, m, d, bur, div, pro, civ ct rec)

Shawano	C3	1856	34	1860–80	Oconto . . . . Shawano
Sheboygan	D4	1836	86	1840–80	Territorial county . . . . Sheboygan

(Co Clk or Reg of Deeds has b, m, d, bur, div, pro, civ ct rec, they are incomplete up to 1910)

Taylor	B2	1875	18	1905	Clark, Lincoln, Marathon, Chippewa . . . . Medford

(Reg of Deeds has b, m, d, & bur rec from 1875; Clk of Cir Ct has div rec from 1875; Clk of Co Ct has pro, civ ct rec from 1875)

Trempealeau	C2	1854	23	1860–80	Crawford, LaCrosse . . . . . . Whitehall

(Reg of Deeds has b, m, d, & bur rec ; Clk of Cir Ct has div & civ ct rec; Reg in Probate has pro rec)

Vernon	D2	1863	26	1870–80	Richland, Crawford, Bad Ax . . . Viroqua
Vilas	B3	1893	9		Oneida . . . . Eagle River
Walworth	E2	1836	52	1840–80	Territorial county . . . . Elkhorn

(Reg of Deeds has b rec from 1900, also d & bur rec; Clk of Cts has div, civ ct rec; Reg in Probate has pro rec)

Washburn   B1   1883   10   Burnett . . . . Shell Lake
(Reg of Deeds has b, m, & d rec from 1883, Clk of Ct has div, pro & civ ct
rec from 1883)

Washington E4   1836   46   1840-80 Territorial county . . . . West Bend
Waukesha   E4   1840 158   1850-80 Milwaukee . . . . Waukesha
(Reg of Deeds has b rec from 1860, m rec from 1846, d rec from 1879; Clk of
Cts has div rec from 1847, civ ct rec from 1962; Reg in Probate has pro rec
from 1847; Co Clk has m applications from 1899)

Waupaca   C3   1851   35   1860-80 . . . . Waupaca
Waushara   D3   1851   13   1860-80 Marquette . . . . Wautoma
Winnebago   D3   1838 108   1840-80 Territorial county . . . . Oshkosh
Wood   C2   1856   59   1860-80 Portage . . . . Wisconsin Rapids
(Register of Deeds has b, m, d rec from 1875; Clk of Cts has div & civ ct rec
from 1875; Register in Pro has pro rec from 1875)

Genealogists' Check List of the Historical Records Survey, Wisconsin

Federal Courts. Inventory of the County Archives, Barron, Buffalo, Chippewa, Clark, Douglas, Dunn, Eau Claire, Grant, Jackson, LaCrosse, Marathon, Monroe, Oneida, Pepin, Polk, Rusk, St Croix, Shawano, Sheboygan, Taylor, Trempealeau, Vernon, Waushara. Inventory of municipal and town archives, Cudahy, Greendale, Wauwatosa. Transcription of the Proceedings of the Iowa County Board of Supervisors 1830-1843, Vol. 2 1843-1850, Vol 3 Index to proceedings of the County Board of Supervisors 1830-1850. Transcription of the proceedings of the St Croix County Board of Supervisors 1840-1849. Guide to Public Vital Statistic records. Guide to Church Vital Statistic records. Outline of Vital Statistic Laws.

Inventory of the Church Archives of Wisconsin. History of the Southern Wisconsin District of the Evangelical Lutheran Synod of Missouri and other states. Protestant Episcopal Church, Diocese of Eau Clair, Diocese of Fond du Lac. Assemblies of God. Church of Nazarene. Disciples of Christ. Jewish Congregations, Moravian Church, Roman Catholic Church Diocese of La Crosse, United Brethren in Christ. Directory of churches and religious organizations in Wisconsin. Directory of Catholic Churches in Wisconsin.

Guide to manuscript depositories in Wisconsin. Guide to manuscript collection in the Wisconsin Historical Society. A check list of Wisconsin imprints, 1833-1849, 1850-1854, 1855-1858, 1859-1863. A guide to Wisconsin newspapers, Iowa County 1837-1940. Abstract and check list of Statutory requirements for County records, supplement to above. Development of Town boundaries in Wisconsin, Chippewa County, Dane County, Manitowoc County, Portage County. Origin and legislative history of County boundaries in Wisconsin. Depository of unpublished material, State Historical Society, Madison, Wisconsin.

Wyoming

Capital Cheyenne - Territory 1868 - State 1890 - (44th)

When Wyoming was organized as a Territory in 1868 it had only six or seven thousand white inhabitants. The middle west and the southern states provided most of the settlers who came into the state to take advantage of the opportunity to get into the cattle business. Hundreds of thousands of cattle roamed the western hills unherded. The eastern section had good agricultural soil.

In 1940 the foreign born population of Wyoming ranked in this order in numbers: England, Germany, Sweden, Russia, Italy, Austria, Greece, Denmark, Norway, Ireland, Poland, Finland, Czechoslovakia, France and Hungary.

The Wyoming State Library in Cheyenne has a genealogical section.

Birth and death records from 1909 to the present, and marriage records from 1 May 1941 are at the office of the Division of Vital Statistics, Cheyenne 82001, Wyoming.

The County Clerk of each county is custodian of the birth and death records from the beginning of the county until 1909, the marriage records from the beginning of the county until 1 May 1941, the wills, probate matters, and all land records.

Wyoming County Histories

(Population figures to nearest thousand - 1960 Census)

Name	Map Index	Date Formed	Pop. By M	Census Reports Available	Parent County	County Seat
Albany	D4	1868	21	1860-80	Original county	Laramie
(Co Clk has m rec from 1869; for 1860 census see Nebr.)						
Big Horn	A3	1890	12		Fremont, Johnson	Basin
(Co Clk has m rec from 1897; Clk of Dist Ct has div, pro, civ ct rec; Dept of Public Health, Cheyenne, Wyo. has b, d, & bur rec)						
Campbell	B4	1911	6		Johnson, Converse	Gillette
Carbon	D3	1868	15	1860-80	Original county	Rawlins
(Co Clk has m rec from 1870; for 1860 census see Nebr.)						
Converse	B4	1888	6		Laramie, Albany	Douglas
Crook	A5	1885	5	1880	Pease	Sundance
(Co Clk has m rec from 1885)						
Fremont	B2	1885	26		Sweetwater	Lander
Goshen	C5	1911	12		Platte, Laramie	Torrington
Hot Springs	B2	1911	6		Fremont	Thermopolis
(Co Clk has m rec from 1913)						
Johnson	B4	1875	5	1880	Pease	Buffalo
Laramie	D5	1868	60	1860-80	Original county	Cheyenne
(Co Clk has m rec from 1868; for 1860 census see Nebr.)						
Lincoln	C1	1913	9		Uinta	Kemmerer
Natrona	C3	1888	50		Carbon	Casper

County Map of Wyoming

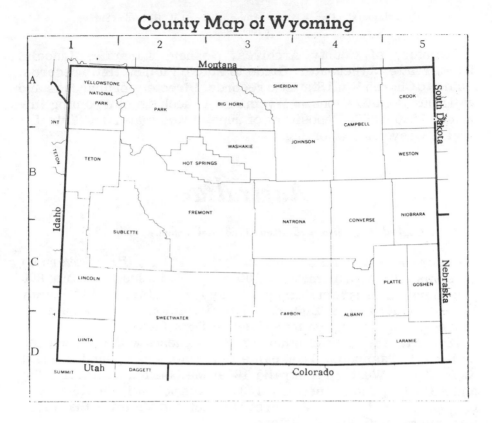

(Bureau of Vit Stat has b rec; Co Clk has m, d & bur rec; Clk of Dist Ct has div, pro & civ ct rec)

Niobrara   B5   1811   4   Converse .... Lusk
(Co Clk has m rec from 1888)

Park   A2   1909   17   Big Horn .... Cody
(Co Clk has m rec from 1911)

Platte   C5   1913   7   Laramie .... Wheatland
(Co Clk has m rec from 1913)

Sheridan   A3   1888   19   Johnson .... Sheridan
   (Co Clk has m rec from 1888; State Dept of Public Health has b, d & bur rec;
   Clk of Ct has div, pro & civ ct rec)

Sublette   C2   1921   4   Fremont .... Pinedale
   (Co Clk has m rec from 1921; Clk of Cts has div, pro, civ ct rec 1921)

Sweetwater   D2   1868   18   1860–80   Original county .... Green River
   (Co Clk has m rec from 1869; Wyo. Dept of Health has b & d rec; Clk of city or
   town has bur rec; Dist Ct Clk has div, pro & civ ct rec) (for 1860 Cen see Nebr)

Teton   B1   1921   3   Lincoln .... Jackson
(Co Clk has m, div, pro & civ ct rec)

Uinta   D1   1868   7   1860–80   Original county .... Evanston
   (For 1860 census see Nebr.) (Co Clk has m rec; Bureau of Vit Stat, Cheyenne,
   Wyo. has b & d rec; Cities have bur rec; Clk of Cts has div & pro rec)

Washakie   B3   1911   9   Big Horn, Fremont .... Worland
(Co Clk has m rec; Clk of Ct has div, pro & civ ct rec)

Weston   B5   1890   8   Crook .... Newcastle
   (Co Clk has m rec from 1890; Bureau of Vit Stat, Cheyenne, Wyo. has b, d,
   and bur rec; Clk of Dist Ct has div, pro & civ ct rec)

Inventory of County Archives, Goshen, Laramie, Lincoln, Park, Platte, Sweetwater. Guide to Public Vital Statistic records. Guide to Church Vital Statistic records. Directory of churches and religious organizations in Wyoming. A check list of Wyoming imprints 1866-1890. Depository of unpublished material, State Library, Cheyenne, Wyoming.

Australia

Capital Canberra - Settled 1788 - Commonwealth 1901

Under the command of Captian Arthur Phillip (first Governor) 11 ships with approximately 1500 persons, including nearly 800 prisoners, sailed from England 13 May 1787 and arrived at Botany Bay 18 January 1788. Eight days later the colony was transferred to the site now occupied by Sydney on Port Jackson.

1803 saw the start of other new settlements with the founding of Hobart, Tasmania. Then came Brisbane, Queensland in 1824; Swan River, Western Australia 1829; Melbourne, Victoria 1835; and Adelaide, South Australia 1836. It was not until the discovery of gold in 1851 in the Bathurst District and Victoria that there was any great influx of settlers.

The capital of Australia is Canberra. It is also the capital of the Australian Capital Territory. Other states and territories with their capitals are as follows: New South Wales, Sydney; Victoria, Melbourne; Queensland, Brisbane; South Australia, Adelaide; Western Australia, Perth; Tasmania, Hobart; Northern Territory, Darwin.

The Australian Society of Genealogists was founded in 1932. They maintain an office and library at 91A Phillip Street, Sydney. Write to them - G. P. O. Box 860, Sydney, Australia - for information regarding their charges for research.

Belgium

Royaume De Belgique - Koninkrijk Belgie. Capital - Brussels

Provinces of Belgium

Province	Map Index	Capital
Antwerpen (Antwerp)	D3	Antwerpen (Antwerp)

Brabrant	E3	*Bruxelles (Brussels)
Hainaut	E2	Mons (Bergen)
Liege	E4	Liege (Luik)
Limbourg (Limburg)	D3	Hasselt
Luxembourg	F4	Aarlon (Arlon)
Namur	F3	Namur (Namen)
Oost Vlaanderen (East Flanders)	E2	Gent (Gand or Ghent)
West Vlaanderen (West Flanders)	E1	Brugge (Bruges)

The history of Belgium dates from 1831 when the South
Netherlands parted from Holland and became an independent
kingdom.

For Map See Page 313

Canada

Capital - Ottawa, Dominion 1867

By virtue of discovery and settlement France claimed possession of Canada as early as 1532. By 1642 Acadia, Quebec, and
Montreal had been founded. Following the French and Indian Wars
extending over a seventy-year period, the Treaty of Paris transferred Canada to British rule in 1763.

After Canada came under British control, many of the early
American colonists, unwilling to sever their British citizenship
rights migrated to Canada where they established their homes.
The French, who had come there earlier, remained in Canada,
later became Canadian citizens, but retained their French language.

Canada is divided into ten provinces, Alberta, British Columbia,
Manitoba, New Brunswick, Newfoundland, Nova Scotia, Ontario,
Prince Edward Island, Quebec, and Saskatchewan; and two terri-
tories, Yukon, created in 1898, and Northwest Territories, which
Canada secured in 1870 from Britain and the Hudson's Bay Co.

Ottawa, located in the province of Ontario on the south side of
the Ottawa River, is the Dominion Capital.

A wealth of genealogical and historical records is on file at the
Public Archives in Ottawa, including a museum, a Library with
books and manuscripts dating back to the earliest days. Most of
the church records are in the provinces. Researchers should
communicate with the Archivists, the Dominion and the Provincial,
to ascertain where information may be obtained. Data regarding
immigration and naturalization papers may be secured from the

Department of Mines and Resources, Citizenship Registration Branch, Ottawa, Canada.

To have the census of Canada searched, write to the Public Archives of Canada, Ottawa, Canada, Census returns since 1871 are not open to the public. The officers in charge give the following explanation:

"Information available from the census returns are: the family name, the age, the country of birth, the religion, the trade or profession, the kind of house and the property. The censuses of 1831 and 1842 give the name of the head of the family only. That of 1851, 1861, and 1871 give the names of the father, mother, and the children of each family. Each census is taken by the province, divided into counties, which are subdivided into townships. In order to obtain information from any census return, the township of the place of residence must be given."

If you do not know the township, ask the Archives for the name of a genealogist.

ALBERTA (D-3)

Edmonton is the provincial capital, with a population of 113,116. Other leading cities are Calgary, 100,044; Lethbridge, 16,522; Medicine Hat, 12,859.

Taken from the Northwest Territories in 1905, Alberta was made a province. The northern half still remains a wilderness. The province is divided into the following counties, Acadia Athabasca, Battle River, Bow River, Calgary East, Calgary West, Camrose, Edmon, Edmonton, Lethbridge, Mac Leod, Medicine Hat, Peace River, Red Deer, Vegerville, and Westaski.

Vital statistics may be secured by inquiring from the Deputy Registrar General, Department of Public Health, Edmonton, Alberta, Canada. Wills are on file at the Court House, Edmonton, Alta, Canada. Deeds are at the Land Titles Office in the same city.

BRITISH COLUMBIA (E-3)   is the westermost province in Canada.

Its counties are Cariboo, Comox-Alberni, East Kootenay, Frazer Valley, Nanalmo, Skeena, Vancouver, North West Kootenay, and Yale.

The Capital of the province is Victoria, on the south-east tip of Vancouver Island. Victoria has a population of 50,744. Other leading cities in the province are Vancouver, 340,272, and New Westminister, 28,390.

British Columbia is the third largest province both in area and in population. More than 1,165,000 people live in the province. It was organized in 1858. The predominating nationalities in the province are British (almost three-fourths of entire population); Scandinavian, German, French, Russian, Italian and Dutch.

For vital statistics since 1874, and incomplete records since 1836, write Division of Vital Statistics, Parliament Bldgs., Victoria, B. C. For wills since 1858 contact Registrar of Supreme Court, Victoria, B. C. For Land records and deeds since 1861 write Land Registry Office, Victoria, B. C.

MANITOBA (C-3)   is the sixth province in area and in population.

Two-thirds of the people of Manitoba are Protestants, belonging to the United Canadian, the Episcopalian, the Lutheran, the Presbyterian, and the Mennonite Church. The other third is Catholic.

Winnipeg is the provincial capital and about the only large city in the province. It has a population of 350,924, which is very little less than one half of the entire population of the province. The population is mainly English, Scottish, German, Swiss, Polish, and Ukranian. The province was created in 1870 when it was cut out of the Northwestern Territories.

The Manitoba counties are Boniface, Brandon, Dauphin, Lisgar, Mac Donald, Marquett, Neepawa, Nelson, which constitutes the northern two-thirds of the provincial area, Portage La Prairie, Provencher, Souris, Springfield, and Winnipeg.

The office of the Registrar General, Vital Statistics Division, Department of Health and Public Welfare, 331 Legislative Bldg., Winnipeg, Canada has vital statistics from 1874, a few scattered perhaps earlier. For wills write the Surrogate Court in the respective district. Some are available from 1891. Land transfers and deeds must also be checked in the district offices of the Registrar of Land Titles.

NEW BRUNSWICK (A-5)   is the eighth largest province in land area and in population. There are a little more than half a million people in the province.

In the days of the American Revolutionary War, English Loyalists moved from the colonies into New Brunswick. Others came over from Yorkshire, England. More recently French Canadians moved south into New Brunswick.

The largest cities are St. John, 51,741, on the south coast; Moncton, in the south-central part of Westmoreland county, 22,763; Fredericton, the provincial capital, in York county, on the St. John River, 10,062.

There are fifteen counties in the province; Albert, Carleton, Charlotte, Gloucester, Kent, Kings, Madawaska, Northumberland, Queens, Restigouche, St. John, Sunbury, Victoria, Westmorland and York.

From 1888 until 1920 all birth, marriage, and death records have been maintained by the County Registrars, since then at the office of the Registrar General, Department of Health and Social

Service, Fredericton, N. B. Fredericton is the provincial capital Records of wills are with the Registrar of Probates of each county. All land titles and real estate transfers are at the office of the Registrar of Deeds of the respective counties.

NEWFOUNDLAND (A-2)   by popular vote, became a province of Canada in 1949.

St. John's the capital, with a population of 52,000, is the only large city in the province. About sixteen other cities have a population between one and six thousand, all others less than a thousand.

The island has been populated since 1750. The English and the French people predominate. The Roman Catholic church is the largest numerically, closely followed by the Episcopalian. The United Canadian Church claims about twenty-five per cent of the population. Other Protestant denominations have smaller memberships.

The vital statistics since 1892 are under the care of the Vital Statistics Division of the Department of Health, St. John's Newfoundland, Canada. The Registrar of the Supreme Court, St. John's, Newfoundland, is the custodian of wills. The Registry of Deeds and Companies, St. John's, Newfoundland, Canada, is in charge of all land title records.

NOVA SCOTIA (A-3)   is the next to the smallest in area of the Canadian provinces and the seventh in population. It has more than 640,000 people. Its southern tip is about 250 miles north-northeast from Boston. It changed from French to British rule about 1750.

A little more than half of the population is English and Scottish. There are still some French, also German, Swiss, Dutch and Irish.

Halifax is the capital. It has a population of about 85,000, with Sydney coming next with about 31,000.

Its eighteen counties are: Annapolis, Antigonish, Cape Breton, Colchester, Cumberland, Digby, Guysborough, Halifax, Hants, Inverness, Kings, Lunenburg, Pictou, Queens, Richmond, Shelburne, Victoria, and Yarmouth.

Vital statistics since 1864 are available at the office of the Deputy Registrar General, Department of Public Health, Halifax, N. S., Canada. The Registrar of Probates, in each probate district has the records of the wills. The Registry of Deeds in each probate district is custodian of deeds and land entries.

ONTARIO (C-4)   is the second largest province in land area and the first in population. It has more than four and a half million people living within its boundaries.

Its counties and county seats are as follows: Algoma, Sault Ste. Marie; Brant, Brantford; Bruce, Walkerton; Carleton, Ottawa; Cochrane, Cochrane; Dufferin, Orangeville; Dundas, Morrisburg; Durham; Elgin, St. Thomas; Essex, Windsor; Front-

enac, Kingston; Glengarry; Grenville; Gray, Owen Sound; Haldi-
mand, Cayuga; Haliburton, Minden; Halton, Milton West; Hastings, Belleville; Huron, Goderich; Kenora, Kenora; Kent,
Chatham; Lambton, Sarnia; Lanark, Perth; Leeds, Brockville;
Lennox and Addington, Napanee; Lincoln, St. Catharines: Mani-
toulin, Gore Bay; Middlesex, London; Muskoka, Bracebridge;
Nipissing, North Bay; Norfolk, Simcoe; Northumberland, Co-
bourg; Ontario, Whitby; Oxford, Woodstock; Parry Sound, Parry
Sound; Peel, Brampton; Perth, Stratford; Peterborough, Peterborough; Prescott, L'Orignal; Prince Edward, Picton; Rainy River,
Ft. Francis; Renfrew, Pembroke; Russell; Simcoe, Barrie; Stor-
mont, Cornwall; Sudbury, Sudbury; Thunder Bay, Port Arthur;
Timiskaming, Hailebury; Victoria, Lindasay; Waterloo, Kitche-
ner; Welland, Welland; Wellington, Guelph; Wentworth, Hamilton;
York, Toronto.

Among the cities of Ontario are Toronto, the capital of the
province, 670,945; Hamilton, 207,544; Ottawa, the Dominion
capital, 198,773, Windsor, 119,550; London, 94,984.

Birth, marriage, and death records since 1869 may be obtained
from the Registrar General, Parliament Bldgs., Toronto, Ontario,
Canada. Copies of wills may be secured from the county or district Registrar of the Surrogate Court. Information on deeds and
land titles may be had from the county office of the Registrar of
Deeds.

PRINCE EDWARD ISLAND (A-3)   one of the most productive
islands and provinces in Canada, is situated between the Gulf of
St. Lawrence and the Northumberland Strait. French colonies
were established as early as 1713. The island was made a British
colony in 1758. Soon after, colonists from Scotland came to the
island. English and Irish settlers followed. There are about 15,000
descendants of the early Acadians.

The island is divided into three districts or counties. The east -
ern section or county is Kings, with Georgetown as the county
seat; the central section or county is Queens, with Charlottetown
the provincial capital also serving as county seat; The West
section or county is Prince, with Summerside as the county seat.
Charlottetown is the largest city on the island with a population
of 15,689; Summerside is the next largest with 6,522, and
Souris, 1,176.

Vital Statistics records since 1906 are available at the office of
the Director of Vital Statistics, Department of Health and Welfare, Charlottetown, P. E. I., Canada. Wills are registered at the
office of the Judge of Probate in the same city. Deeds are recorded with the Registrar of Deeds for King and Queen counties,
Charlotteville, P. E. I., Canada, and the Registrar of Deeds for
Prince County, Summerside, P. E. I., Canada.

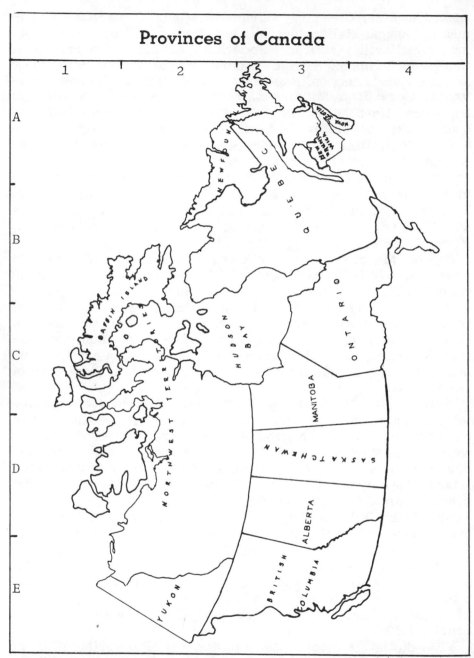

Provinces of Canada

QUEBEC (B-3)   the largest province in area and the second largest in population has more than four million inhabitants.

French settlers came to Quebec in the early sixteen hundreds, and their descendants are now in the majority in the province. More than three-fourths of the population are French and Catholic.

The province has 76 counties, but none of the records in which the genealogical researcher is interested are in any of the county offices.

The most prominent cities are Montreal (Greater) 1,370,044; Quebec, 161,439; Trois-Rivieres (Three Rivers), 45,708.

Vital statistics for Quebec Catholics began about 1622; for Protestants about 1887. The director of the Provincial Bureau of Health, Quebec, Que., Canada has statistics from 1907. The twenty District Notaries have charge of wills and land transfer records.

SASKATCHEWAN' S (D-3)   capital is Regina, located in the south-eastern section of the province. It is fifth among the Canadian provinces in area and population and has more than 800,000 people living mostly in the southern half of the province.

Its largest cities are Regina, 69,928; Saskatoon, 52,732; Moose Jaw, 24,336. Regina is about 700 miles northwest of Minneapolis via Winnipeg.

The Director of Vital Statistics, Department of Public Health, Provincial Health Bldg., Regina, Sask., Canada, has charge of the vital statistics of the province. A few records go back to 1888, but most of them from 1905. A record of all grants made in wills is filed with the Registrar of Surrogate Courts, Court House, Regina, Sask., Canada. The wills are filed in the office of the clerk of the Surrogate Court of the respective counties. Land Titles are filed in the Regina Land Titles Office, but applicant must describe land and give the proper Registration District.

The twenty-one counties of Saskatchewan are Assiniboia, Humboldt, Kindersley, Last Mountain, Long Lake, MacKenzie, Maple Creek, Melfort, Melville, Moose Jaw, North Battleford, Prince Albert, Qu Appelle, Regina, Rosetown, Saskatoon, South Battleford, Swift Current, Weyburn, Willow Bunch, and Yorkton.

Among books dealing with the history and genalogy of Canada are the following:

Grant, W. L., M. A., "History of Canada," Authorized by the Minister of Education for Ontario. The Ryerson press, Toronto, 1922.

McLaughlin, Sara B., "Canadian Educator," The Iroquois Press, Toronto, 1920. Gives much on the geography and history of Canada, also many biographies of prominent men.

Rose, Geo. Maclean, "A Cyclopaedia of Canadian Biography," Rose Publishing Co., Toronto, 1888. A collection of persons distinquished in professional and political life; leaders in commerce and industry of Canada and successful pioneers.

Libraries and genealogical societies include: Hamilton Public Library, Hamilton, Ont.; Public Library and Art Museum, Elsie Perrin Williams Mem. Bldg., London, Ont.; Institute Genealogique Drouin, 4148 St. Denis Street, Montreal, Quebec; Vancouver Dist. LDS Gen. Society, 350 East 55th Ave., Vancouver 15, Bristish Columbia.

Denmark

Capital - Copenhagen (Kobenhavn)

Denmark's (Danmark) principal islands and peninsula: 1. Jutland (Jylland); 2. Fyn Island; 3. Zealand (Sjålland); 4. Falster and Lolland (Laaland) Islands; 5. Bornholm Island.

Jutland (Jylland) Peninsula has the following amter (counties): Asbenraa, Aalborg, Aarhus, Haderslev, Hjoring, Randers, Ribe, Ringkobing (Ringkjöbing), Sonderborg (Skanderborg), Thisted, Tonder, Vejle, and Viborg.

Fyn Island has two amter -- Odense Amt (County) and Svendborg Amt.

Zealand (Sjålland) Island is divided as follows: Copenhagen (Kóbenhavn), Fredriksborg, Holbåk, Prästo and Soró amter.

The islands of Lolland (Laaland) and Falster constitute the amt of Maribo. Bornholm Island with Rönne as the administrative center is Bornholm Amt. The Fäeröe (Fäeröeren) Islands with Thorshavn as its administrative center (750 miles west of Norway and 400 miles north of Scotland) have at times been considered as the Fäeröe Amt.

The amter of Denmark in most cases are named after the cities which are their administrative centers. In fact all follow this pattern except Fredricksborg, which has Hilleröd as its administrative center and Bornholm and Faeroe (mentioned above).

All census records, military levying rolls, civil and government records are gathered into one great central archive at Copenhagen. This is the "Rigsarkivet" or Royal Archive. All church records prior to 1890 are gathered into the three permanent provincial archives located at Copenhagen, Odense, Viborg, and the one temporary provincial archive at Aabenraa. These archives are the most important for genealogical research in Denmark. Of the two kinds of archives the provincial archive is the more important to researchers for it is here that the vital statistics are kept for practically everything prior to 1890.

There are other archives and libraries that furnish valuable information for the genealogist. The Royal Library will probably stand first in this respect. Here will be found all printed records in Denmark and also a few manuscript records. This will, of course, save a researcher a great deal of time, if he should find his records already printed then all he needs to do is check-up on the connections. Other archives worthy of mention are the military archive at Copenhagen, the city and county archives and libraries, the Danish-American Archives at Aalborg which may be of great worth to Danish-Americans in establishing their connections with Denmark; also there are the industrial archives, university archives, etc.

In all of these archives thus mentioned all records that are obtainable for the public are from 1890 and back. None are obtainable after that date except by special permission or rights but for those records that are, there is no charge for the use of them in the reading-rooms of the archives.

CHURCH RECORDS. In Denmark most people belong to the same church, the state or Lutheran church. It used to be required of all to belong to this church and to support it by means of a civil tax, but that is a thing of the past now, as far as it being a requirement of every person regardless of desire or personal creed. However, this church still remains the registrar of certain vital statistics. Thus, regardless of what church you may belong to, all births must be registered with the priest of the state church of that particular parish in which you may be residing. All other vital statistics such as marriages, deaths, etc., are either registered here or with the local civil authorities. For this reason the state church records become the most valuable record for the genealogist in Denmark. The number of Danes not belonging to the state church prior to 1890 is practically negligible, thus making this record most valuable for marriages and deaths as well.

The first church record preserved was made by a priest, Jost Poulsen, in Nakskov for the years 1572-90. Another one was kept by a priest of the same place from 1618-1629. The oldest uninterrupted church record in Denmark is that of Holmen's Church in Copenhagen which began in 1617. Several churches began keeping parish records in 1641, and in 1645 all parishes were asked by the government to keep records of all births, marriages, deaths, etc. It was understood at this time that it became the duty of the parish priest to keep such a record and that this record belonged to the parish and not to the priest. Further enforcement was enacted in 1683 and 1685, such that before the end of the seventeenth century, it was definite and practiced by practically all of the priests.

The birth records generally consists of two separate lists: the male and the female. The information obtainable is the same for both, and consists of: the name of the child, date of birth, date of christening, name of the parents and their occupation, names of the godmother and the sponsors and possibly some remarks.

The confirmation record is also divided into male and female lists. Confirmation generally takes place between fourteen and fifteen years of age. The information obtainable from these records is: name of child, name of parents, date of confirmation, usually the date of either birth or christening, and character testimonials from the school.

The marriage record or list gives the name of the bridegroom and the bride; generally their age or birthdate and the parish they came from, if native of another parish (marriage is performed in the parish which the bride come from), sometimes the names of the fathers are given, the names of the sponsors who are generally fathers or near relatives (male) are always given, date of marriage and possibly remarks and banns.

The removal record or record of incoming and outgoing members from the parish, is a result of the system of character testimonial employed at one time in Denmark.

The death record shows the name of the person deceased, possibly the name of the husband or wife or in the case of a child the name of the father or even both the parents, date of death, date of burial, position or occupation of the deceased, or if a child the position or occupation of the father or mother. The age is also given.

PROBATE RECORDS. Probate records have been in existence since the early part of the sixteenth century in Denmark. In 1874 the old system was done away with entirely. Most of the earliest records have been lost or burned, however, records from 1574 to 1637 are at the archive. These are mostly for cities since this system began much earlier there. After this period there are many more in existence, and as the end of the seventeenth century is approached are found throughout the entire land.

THE ROYAL ARCHIVE

The most important records found at this archive are the census records and the military levying rolls. Other records such as tax lists, customs records, commercial records, postal records, pension records and other governmental records are also available.

CENSUS RECORDS. The first complete census record which has not been destroyed is that taken in 1787. Since that date census records have been taken during the following years: 1801, 1834, 1840, 1845, 1850, 1855, 1860, 1870, 1880, 1890, 1901 and thereafter periodically. Of these all up to and including 1890 census are available to the public for their perusal and study at the reading room at the Royal Archive.

These censuses are listed according to parishes, "hereds," and "Amter." The last two mentioned divisions are comparable to county and state within the United States.

MILITARY LEVYING ROLLS. Beginning with 1789 all males

Norway, Sweden, Finland and Denmark

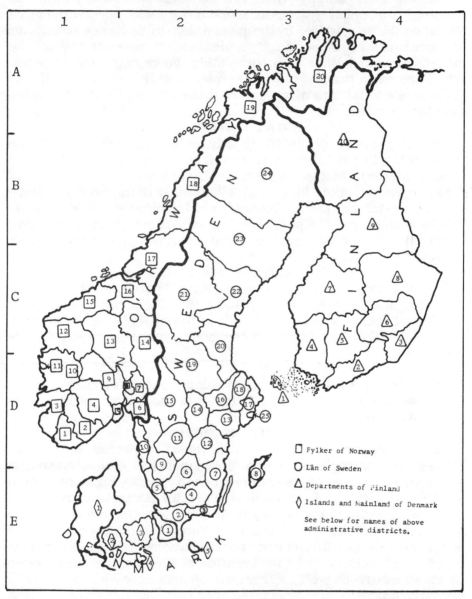

Fylker of Norway

Län of Sweden

Departments of Finland

Islands and Mainland of Denmark

See below for names of above administrative districts.

born outside of the cities in Denmark were entered upon levying rolls so that they could be used for military training when they reached a certain age. It was required of each male individual to ever have his whereabouts known. Thus if he moved he had to report at his new place of residence, where he came from and the one in charge of the records for the place of his original residence was notified in order that his name could be followed through these records at any time.

EXTRA TAX LISTS. Whenever some extraordinary situation arose in the country wherein more money was needed than that which could be supplied by the government by ordinary means, an extra tax was required of the poeple. In most cases it just hit the land-owners and other men with rather large capitals or assets. But there were times when it was required from each family. In such cases a list was made out of all the heads of families which were to be taxed.

ROYAL LIBRARY

Genealogical research is greatly aided through the sources found in the Royal Library. Here will be found all the printed records, history, biography, etc. in Denmark. Various types of directories and short biographical sketches of important or more or less outstanding men of Denmark are found here. Very valuable family histories are also located here which many times can save a researcher a great deal of time when his pedigree connects up with one of these.

MILITARY ARCHIVES

The military archives at Copenhagen will be of great help to any one searching names on a military line. Accurate records are kept of all officers and subofficers in the nation's fighting force. Data generally given is mostly that concerning the person's military career.

'RAADSTUEARKIVER' -- CITY ARCHIVES

The city archives has several valuable records, but that which is of greatest value to the genealogist is the record of marriage permits issued.

OTHER RECORDS

Other records of value are wills, deeds, divorces, civil marriages, death registrations at "Tinghuset," etc. All records pertaining to wills, deeds and divorces in recent years are located at the head office of the Judicial District (Domekontoret) or at least information concerning their whereabouts could be given here. Civil marriages will be with the community government records as well as with the civil confirmations. Deaths are registered at "Tinghuset," so information concerning deaths can also be located here as well as from the church records.

See Scandinavia

(Much of above extracted from an aritcle on Danish research by Henry E. Christensen.)

England

WRITE LETTERS FIRST

You can write letters to find relatives who have genealogy, advertise in newspapers, write to old residents, to postmasters, to city and county officials, to dealers in genealogical books, to names from directories, just the same in England as in America. If you expect to send a number of letters, write to some postmaster and send a money order for some stamps. Because of changing rates we suggest you ask for stamps in denominations for the class of mail you desire your letters to be returned by - air mail or surface mail. You can then send a self-addressed, stamped envelope with your letter to help get a reply. Or for 15 cents you can buy from your postmaster a coupon which can be exchanged in England or any other county for a stamp to pay postage on the answer to your letter.

SEARCHING PARISH REGISTERS

Parish registers, which are the records of the Church of England, are valuable sources of genealogical information. They do not contain the records of Methodists, Quakers, etc. If your ancestors belonged to those religions the records of their churches must be searched for the desired information.

A few parish registers go back as far as 1538, but most of them commence at a later date. Between 1538 and 1 July 1837 they are the principal sources of records of births, deaths, and marriages of every class of people in England. "Burke's Key to the Ancient Parish Registers of England and Wales," by Authur M. Burke, London 1908, lists alphabetically the names of the parishes in England and Wales, giving also the name of the county and the dates of registration. It is not unusual to find gaps in the records - periods when no registrations were made or when they have been lost. Check each register to see if it covers completely the period you are interested in.

If you know the birthplace of your ancestor you can often find his parents and the date of his birth and marriage by searching the parish registers. The record of births or christenings gives only the given name of the mother but by searching the marriage record her surname can often be found. The burial record also gives information that is valuable. There are many thousands of parish registers, only a few of which have been printed.

Parishes may be divided into townships. A small parish may not have a township. A town may have several churches. To be a city in England there must be a cathedral.

THE CENSUS OF ENGLAND AND WALES

For nearly a hundred and fifty years the census has been taken each ten years. The only ones available for genealogical research are those of 1841, 1851 and 1861.

Prior to that time census enumerators listed only the number of people living at a given address. The census of 1841 tells names of family members, the ages of the nearest five years but does not tell the exact place of birth. The census of 1851 gives the names of each member of the family, their relationship to the head of the family, the occupation of each, the age and the parish where born. It is necessary that the approximate address be known before a search can begin.

Information from the 1861 census and later enumerations are not open to the public or their agents. They contain practically the same information as the 1851 census. Upon written application the Register General may make a search for a particular family but it is necessary to give him the precise address, the surname of the person or persons residing there and also signed statement that the information from the census will not be used for litigation. Also state in your letter that it is for genealogical purposes; your relationship to those who might be named in the record; and whether you know of others more closely or equally related to them. Ask for fees for census research. Information from the 1911 and later censuses is not available for genealogy

The following is the address of the office in charge of the census, Public Record Office, Chancery Lane, W. C. 2, London, England. They may suggest a professional genealogist if you enclose an international reply coupon which you may buy for 15 cents at your post office.

ENGLAND VITAL STATISTICS

Previous to 1837 the task of keeping a record of vital statistics of England and Wales was left almost entirely to the churches. Beginning on the first day of July, 1837, the government has kept a record of births, deaths and marriages. These records have been gathered in one 'office and indexed so that anyone born in England or Wales, knowing the date of his birth, can for a small fee obtain a birth certificate, etc. To obtain information from this record write to the Register of Births, Marriages and Death, Somerset House, London, England. The fee for such service is ten shillings one penny, (a shilling is about 15¢). Thus if we know the full name of a person and his exact age but do not know his parents or birthplace, the birth certificate will give this information.

If the date is near 1851, you can refer to the census and find the birthplace of the parents and thus open the way for searching the parish register. If you do not know the exact name and date of birth it will be hard to get information from the record.

A research team of the "Institute of Heraldic and Genealogical Studies" at 58 North Gate, Canterbury, Kent, England has undertaken the monumental task of indexing every entry in all the parish and nonparochial registers in England. It might be well to write them if you would like to know more about their plans and subscription rates.

WILLS IN ENGLAND

Wills are the backbone of genealogical research in England. The information they give us is most reliable, and you can often make up several family group sheets from one will. So far as telling who belongs to which family they are far better than the parish register. After you have examined a will it is well to search a parish register to fill in the dates and complete the record.

NON-PAROCHIAL OR NONCONFORMIST REGISTERS

In England and Wales each church kept its own records. Those who did not belong to the Episcopal Church (Church of England) did not have their names mentioned in the parish registers. The registers of the Nonconformists or Dissenters which included the Methodists, Baptists, Quakers, Presbyterians and some smaller groups were all, as far as possible, gathered up and deposited in Somerset house, London. Most of these records began about 1650 and continued to about 1850. To have these records searched, address: The Registrar General, General Register Office, Somerset House, London, England. When a search is to be made a description of the register must be given, also the name and the location of the chapel. For example, Register of births, from the Baptist Chapel in Dereham, Norfolk, England. Also give the approximate date. Fees vary -- we suggest you ask what charges will be asked for each separate search you request. If your ancestor lived in Dereham and you wish to try the other churches you can send and have the Baptist record searched. If that fails you may try the Quakers, etc. There will be a separate charge for each search.

Your research in England will be eased considerably by a study of the following books. Some may be purchased, others you may find in your public or genealogical library.

Berry, Wm., "County Genealogies Pedigrees of Berkshire", Pub. 1837, Gilbert and Piper, Poternaster Row, London.

Cox, J. Charles, "Notes on the Churches of Derbyshire", 4 Vol., Pub. 1875 by Bemrose and Sons, 10, Paternoster Bld. Gives the early history of the ancient churches and chapelries of Derbyshire County.

Marshal, Dr. G. W., "Marshall's Genealogist's Guide", 1903, gives a list of publications which have, at various times printed material on English families. The families are arranged alphabetically and the publications are coded with the page, volume, etc. listed, enabling a person to quickly discover if genealogical or historical material on that line has appeared in print. This book along with "A Genealogical Guide", which is a continuation of this same idea for the period 1903 to 1953 (see Whitmore, J. B., below), are two of the most important books for English researchers.

Palmer, W. M. "Monumental Inscriptions and Coats of Arms From Cambridge," Pub. by Bowes and Bowes, Cambridge, 1932.

Smith, Frank and Gardner, David E., "Genealogical Research in England and Wales", Vol. 1, Pub 1956 and Vol 2, Pub 1959. Bookcraft Publishers, Salt Lake City, Utah. These books can be purchased through most genealogical supply houses, including The Everton Publishers, prices, $3.50 for Vol. 1 and $3.95 for Vol. 2. The authors have been engaged in professional genealogical work for many years. Both were born in England and handled and searched countless parish and archive records in almost every county in England before coming to America to continue their genealogical careers. Their combined effort has brought forth two books that should be in the hands of every person seeking to do research in England and Wales.

Thompson, T. R., "A Catalogue of British Family Histories", 1928, second edition 1935.

Whitmore, T. R., "A Genealogical Guide", Pub. 1953, John Whitehead & Son Ltd., Leeds. An index to British pedigrees in continuation of Marshall's Genealogist's Guide. (1903).

Worthy, Chas, Esq., "Devonshire Wills", Pub. Benrose & Sons Ltd., London, 1896. A collection of annotated testimentary abstracts, together with the family history and genealogy of many of the most ancient gentle houses of the west of England.

COUNTIES AND/OR SHIRES OF ENGLAND

Name	Abbreviation	Map Index	County Town
Bedfordshire	Beds.	E5	Bedford
Berkshire	Berks.	D6	Reading
Buckinghamshire	Bucks.	D6	Buckingham
Cambridgeshire	Cambs.	E5	Cambridge
Cheshire (Chester Co.)	Ches.	C4	Chester
Cornwall	Cornwall	A8	Bodmin
Cumberland	Cumb.	B2	Carlisle
Derbyshire	Derby	D4	Derby
Devonshire	Devon	B7	Plymouth
Dorsetshire	Dorset	C7	Dorchester
Durham	Dur.	C2	Durham
Essex	Essex	F6	Clemsford
Gloucestershire	Glos. (Gloucs.)	C6	Gloucester
Hampshire	Hants.	D7	Winchester
Herefordshire	Herefs.	C6	Hereford
Hertfordshire	Herts.	E6	Hertford
Huntingdonshire	Hunts.	E5	Huntingdon

COUNTY MAP OF
ENGLAND
AND
WALES

SCALE OF MILES
0 10 20 30 40 50 60 70 80 90 100

Kent	Kent	F6	Maidstone
Lancashire (Lancaster Co.)	Lancs.	C3	Preston
Leicestershire	Leics.	D5	Leicester
Lincolnshire	Lincs.	E4	Lincoln
London	London	E6	London

Middlesex	Mx.	E6	London
Monmouthshire	Mont.	C6	Monmouth
Norfolk	Norfolk	F4	Norwich
Northamptonshire	Northants.	D5	Northampton
Northumberland	Northumb.	C1	Newcastle
Nottinghamshire	Notts.	D4	Nottingham
Oxfordshire	Oxon.	D6	Oxford
Rutlandshire	Rut.	D5	Oakham
Shropshire	Salop. (Shrops.)	C5	Shrewsbury
Somersetshire	Somerset	C7	Bristol
Staffordshire	Staffs.	C5	Stafford
Suffolk	Suffolk	E5	Ipswich
Surrey	Surrey	E6	Guilford
Sussex	Sussex	E7	Lewes
Warwickshire	War. (Warws.)	D5	Warwick
Westmorelandshire	Westmd.	C2	Appleby
Wiltshire	Wilts.	D6	Salisbury
Worcestershire	Worcs.	C5	Worcester
Yorkshire	York	D3	York

Finland

Administrative Departments of Finland (Suomi).

Department	Map Index	Administrative Center
1 Ahvenanmaa (Åland)	D3	Mariehamn (Maarianhamina)
2 Uusimaa	D4	*Helsinki (Helsingfors)
3 Kymi	C4	Kotka
4 Turu-Pori	C3	Turku (Åbo)
5 Häme	C3	Hämeenlinna (Tavastehus)
6 Mikkeli	C4	Mikkeli (Sankt Michel)
7 Vaasa	C3	Vaasa (Vasa)
8 Kuopio	C4	Kuopio
9 Oulu	B4	Oulu (Uleåborg)
10 Lappi	A4	Kemi

Turku is the oldest Finnish City. It was founded by Swedes in 1157 and was the capital of Finland from 1809 to 1819. Helsinki, the present capital of Finland, was founded by Swedes in 1550. Counties are called Iaani; cities and towns are called kyla, kaupala or kaupunki. See Map Page 295

France

The genealogical situation in France is quite different from the conditions in England. We have the noble families in France as in

England but unlike England there was no law to prevent any wealthy family from claiming nobility.

The feudal families, the Quasi-feudal, the noblemen created by the King, and the public office holder of old -- all claiming nobility -- have many descendants. Today it is said that 70,000 Frenchmen assume to be noblemen and not more than 8,000 or 9,000 have any real title to that quality.

The coat of arms, which is so helpful in tracing pedigrees in England, was also greatly overdone in France. The registration of coats of arms was taxed at 20 livres per person. The collector of taxes compelled many persons not connected with the nobility to pay the tax and assume a coat of arms. Over 60,000 coats of arms are recorded.

The earliest parish registers of births, marriages and burials were written about 40 years ago. These registers were kept by the parish priest who, beginning in about 1700 deposited copies of his registers with the Clerk of the Court. At the time of the revolution (1789) the task of recording births, marriages and deaths was transferred to the Mairie (Town Hall) where the parish priests were compelled by law to deposit all the registers in his possession. The new registers (since 1789) are known as Registres de l'Etate Civil. It is therefore to the Town Hall that one should apply to consult the records of births, marriages and deaths either prior to or subsequent to the year 1789. The registers are kept in the Registry Office of the Town Hall Library. Occasionally the Departmental Archivist has insisted on the transfer of the old parish registers to his Muniment rooms when they have not been carefully preserved in the Town Hall. There is usually an index provided for each volume. Only rarely is a register found that dates back to 1600. War fires, floods, and the carelessness of parish priests are all responsible for the loss of many parish registers, in Paris the original registers and the duplicates up to 1860 were destroyed by fire. Copies of a few of these registers had been made and these are still preserved. Registers of the Protestants are, relatively speaking, rare. They are found in the Town Hall along with the other registers.

The Registers of "Insinuations" in which all notorial documents that were subject to a tax had to be recorded is another good source of information.

Besides these, the National Library and the National Archives together with the various departmental archives supply inexhaustable sources of information.

In these public archives are preserved thousands of manuscript volumes extending back into the middle ages where the researcher might spend many months and still continue to find new things.

The above information was gleaned from a six page article in the Genealogists' Magazine, published in London, September, 1946.

Regarding printed genealogies the author has this comment: "Finally we have the printed sources, the genealogical works of the judges of arms and kings genealogists, the monks of St. Maur such as Pere Anselme and a number of professional and amateur genealogists who are more or less reliable, not to say more or less honest or trustworthy . . . . .Unfortunately the only guide to the printed works on heraldry and genealogy is the Bibliotheque heraldique de la France by Joannis Guigard, published in Paris in 1861. For later works one has to wade through the printed or hand written indexes of the National Library, which from my own experiences is a tedious and not very satisfactory process."

He makes no mention at all of the books which form the great bulk of genealogical literature in England and America. Neither does he mention genealogical libraries which play such an important part in genealogical research in both England and America.

In the closing paragraphs he tells us that the Departmental Archivists are most helpful as also as a rule are the secretaries of the town halls in the important towns all over France where the old parish registers and the modern vital statistics are kept. At the National Library and the National Archives one must rely entirely on the manuscript and printed indexes. A letter of introduction from the Embassy is required of those who would examine these indexes.

Incidentally he gives the name of a firm of genealogists in Paris. Pelletier et Pecquet, 18 Rue de Cherche-Midi, Paris 6, France.

DEPARTMENTS OF FRANCE
(Departement)

Departments are listed alphabetical with the map index in parenthisis and the department capital following.

Ain (C4) Bourg; Aisne (A3) Laon; Allier (C3) Moulins; Alpes-Maritimes (D4) Nice; Andorra (Autonomous Republic) (D3) Andorr la Vell; Ardeche (C3) Privas; Ardennes (A3) Mezieres; Ariege (D2) Foix; Aube (B3) Troyes; Aude (D3) Carcassonne; Aveyron (C3) Rodez.

Bas-Rhin (B4) Strasbourg; Basses-Alpes (D4) Digne; Basses-Pryenees (D2) Pau; Belfort (B4) Belfort; Bouches-du-Rhone (D4) Marseille; Calvados (A2) Caen; Cantal (C3) Aurillac; Charente (C2) Angouleme; Charente-Maritime (C2) La Rochelle; Cher (B3) Bourges; Correze (C3) Tulle; Corse (an island SE of Var) Ajaccio; Cote-D'or (B3) Dijon; Cotes-du-Nord (B1) St. Brieuc; Creuse (C3) Gueret.

Map of Departments of France

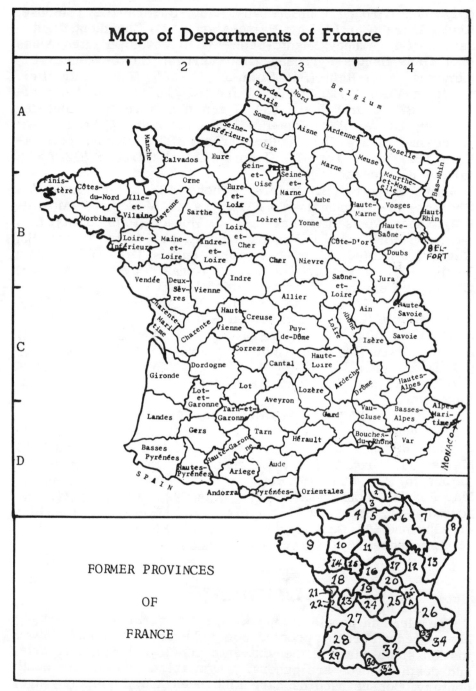

FORMER PROVINCES

OF

FRANCE

Deux-Sevres (B2) Niort; Dordogne (C2) Perigueux; Doubs (B4) Besancon; Drome (C4) Valence; Eure (A2) Evreux; Eure-et-Loir (B2) Chartres; Finistere (B1) Quimper; Gard (D3) Nimes; Gers

(D2) Auch; Gironde (C2) Bordeaux; Haute-Garonne (D2) Toulouse; Haute-Loire (C3) Le Puy; Harte-Marne (B4) Chaumont; Haute-Savoie (C4) Annecy; Haute-Saone (B4) Vesoul; Hautes-Alpes (C4) Gap; Hautes-Pyrenees (D2) Tarbes; Haute-Vienne (C2) Limoges; Haut-Rhin (B4) Colmar; Herault (D3) Montpellier.

Ille-et-Vilaine (B2) Rennes; Indre (B2) Chateauroux; Indre-et-Loire (B2) Tours; Isere (C4) Grenoble; Jura (B4) Lons-le-Saunier; Landes (D2) Mont-de-Marsan; Loire (C3) St. Etienne; Loire-In-ferieure (B2) Nantes; Loiret (B3) Orleans; Loir-et-Cher (B2) Blois; Lot (C3) Cahors; Lot-et-Garonne (C2) Agen; Lozere (C3) Mende.

Maine-et-Loire (B2) Angers; Manche (A2) St. Lo; Marne (A3) Chalons-sur-Marne; Mayenne (B2) Laval; Meurthe-et-Moselle (B4) Nancy; Meuse (A4) Bar-le-Duc; Monaco (Principality) (D4) Monaco; Morbihan (B1) Vannes; Moselle (A4) Metz; Nievre (B3) Nevers; Nord (A3) Lille; Oise (A3) Beauvais; Orne (B2) Alecon; Paris (B3) --; Pas-de-Calais (A3) Arras; Puy-de-Dome (C3) Clermont-Ferrand; Pyrenees-Orientales (D3) Perpignan.

Rhone (C3) Lyon; Saone-et-Loire (B3) Macon; Sarthe (B2) Le Mans; Savoie (C4) Chambery; Seine-et-Marne (B3) Melun; Sein-et-Oise (B3) Versailles; Sein-Inferieure (A2) Rouen; Somme (A3) Amiens; Tarn (D3) Albi; Tarn-et-Garonne (D2) Montauban; Var (D4) Draguignan; Vaucluse (D4) Avignon; Vendee (B2) La Roche-sur-Yon; Vienne (C2) Poitiers; Vosges (B4) Epinal; Yonne (B3) Auxerre.

FORMER PROVINCES OF FRANCE

1, Flanders; 2, Artois; 3, Picardy; 4, Normandy; 5, Ile de France; 6, Champagne; 7, Lorraine; 8, Alsace; 9, Brittany; 10 Maine; 11, Oreanais; 12, Burgundy; 13, Franche-Comte; 14, Anjou; 15, Touraine; 16, Berry; 17, Nivernais; 18, Poitou; 19, Marche; 20, Bourbonnais; 21, Aunis; 22, Saintonge; 23, Angoumois; 24, Limousin; 25, Auvergne; 25A, Lyonais; 26, Dauphin; 27, Guyenne; 28, Gascony; 29, Bearn; 30, Foix; 31, Roussillion; 32, Languedoc; 33, Comtat; 34, Provence.

Germany

The German people during the past several centuries have been a record keeping people. Some church records have information since early in the sixteenth century. Birth, marriage, and death records are generally available since the nineteenth century. Census records have also been kept for many years, as have parish and Protestant church records. In some provinces the real estate records are among the most valuable. Burger rolls, tax lists, and police registers assist in giving accurate identification.   The German police method of keeping track of every individual arriving in any city or locality, is important in tracing individuals or families from one city to another.

To most Americans interested in German genealogy it is necessary to employ researchers in Germany.   They can be located in many German cities.   Care should be taken to secure reliable help, researchers who subscribe to the highest genealogical practices and ideals.

A great deal of information and many records from Germany are now on file in the library of the Genealogical Society of Utah, Salt Lake City, Utah. Those not acquainted with the research situations in Germany may find it advantagous to correspond with that office before employing a researcher.

MILITARY OCCUPATION ZONES OF GERMANY

Some controversy and confusion arises when one attempts to name, locate and establish the capitals of the state and zones of Germany. The accompanying map has the boundaries and capitols similar to those found in ''Hammond's Ambassador World Atlas'', published by C. S. Hammond & Co., Maplewood, N. J., Third Printing 1956. We quote from The New ''Funk & Wagnalls Encyclopedia'', Unicorn Publishers, Inc., N. Y., 36 Vols. 1951, and ''The Columbia-Viking Desk Encyclopedia'', Published by The Viking Press, N. Y., 2 Vols., 1953.

This from Funk and Wagnalls: FRANCE: The French zone comprises parts of the former states of Prussia, Baden, Hessen, and Würtemburg, and all of the Saarland. For administrative purposes, the zone has been divided into four states, namely Rhineland - Palatinate, Baden, Würtemberg - Hohenzollern, and the Saar. The capitals of these states are respectively Coblenz, Frieburg, Tübigen, and Saarbrücken ... UNITED KINGDOM: The British zone consists of the former state of Hamburg, portions of the former state of Prussia, and the former states of Brunswick, Oldenburg, Schaumburg-Lippe, and Lippe. For administrative purposes the zone has been divided into four states, namely Schleswig-Holstein, Lower Saxony, North Rhine-Westphalia, and Hamburg. The capitals of these states are respectively Kiel, Hanover, Düsseldorph, and Hamburg . . . UNION OF SOVIET SOCIALIST REPUBLICS: The Soviet zone consists of the former states of Saxony, Thüringia, Mecklinburg and Anhalt, and portions of the former state of Prussia, including the provinces of Silesia and Pomerania. For Administrative purposes, the zone has been divided into five states, namely Brandenburg, Saxony, Saxony-Anhalt, Thüringia, and Mecklenburg. The capitals of these states are respectively, Potsdam, Dresden, Halle, Weimer, and Schwerin . . . UNITED STATES: The American zone comprises the former states of Bavaria and Bremen and parts of the former states of Prussia, Baden, Würtemberg, and Hessen. For administrative purposes, the zone has been divided into four states, namely Bavaria, which consists of the former state of Bavaria, a part of the former Prussian province, the Palatinate, and the town and district of Lindau; Württemberg-Baden; Hessen; and Bremen.   The capitals of these states are respectively Munich, Stuttgart, Wiesbaden, and Bremen.

This from Columbia-Viking: In 1949 two separate republics came into existance; (1) Federal Republic of (West) Germany, temporary capital, Bonn, under U. S., British, and French

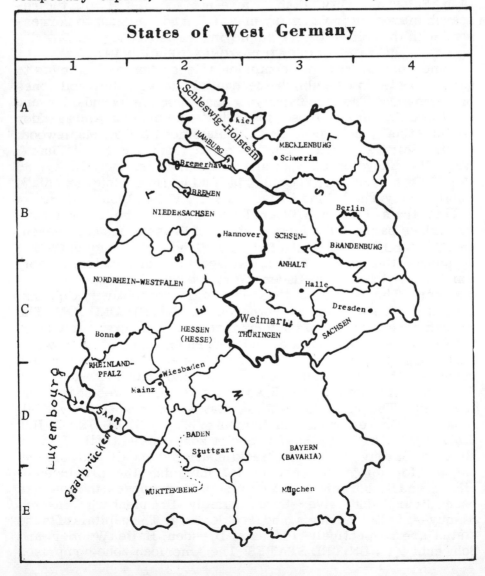

States of West Germany

occupation, consisting of the states of Bavaria, Württemberg-Baden, Hesse, and Bremen (U. S. zone); North Rhine-Westphalia, Lower Saxony, Schleswig-Holstein, and Hamburg (British Zone); Rhineland-Palatinate, Württemberg-Hohenzollern, and Baden (French zone); and W. Berlin. (2) (East) German Democratic Republic, capital E. Berlin, under Russian occupation, consisting of the states of Brandenburg, Mecklenberg, Thüringia, Saxony, and Saxony-Anhalt.

It should be remembered regarding Germany and most of the other European countries that the spelling of many of the place names in their native language is different than the English spelling. For instance in Germany Pflaz means the Palatinate; Bayern is Bavaria; Munchen is Munich; Nordrhein is North Rhine; Sachsen is Saxony; Koblenz is Coblenz, etc.

THE THIRD REICH ADMINISTRATIVE DIVISIONS

The sixteen administrative divisions of the Third Reich in 1937 were Anhalt, Baden, Bavaria, Bremen, Brunswick, Hamburg, Hesse, Lippe, Mecklenberg, Oldenburg, Prussia, Saarland, Saxony, Schaumburg-Lippe, Thüringia, and Württemburg. Lübeck, which had held the status of a city-state, was merged with Prussia in March 1937.

Milton Rubincam, editor of the National Genealogical Society Quarterly, and an expert in many phases of genealogy, has stressed the importance of exhausting both published and unpublished sources in America before attempting research in Germany. The publications of The National Genealogical Society, The New York Genealogical & Biographical Society, The Pennsylvania Genealogical Magazine of History and Biography, and the Pennsylvania Genealogical Magazine abound in material on early German immigrants, as do the very early issues of the publications of the Pennsylvania Dutchman, The Pennsylvania German Folklore Society, The Pennsylvania-German Magazine and the Maryland Historical Magazine, according to Mr. Rubincam.

The National Archives have ship's lists of immigrants of the 19th century; Strassburger & Hinke's "German Pioneers" lists German immigrants in the 18th century; Knittle's Lists gives much information on early Germans to New York State, etc. (See also several chapters in "Genealogical Research Methods and Sources" by the American Society of Genealogists, Edited by Milton Rubincam, 1960, 456 pp.).

Ireland

Capitals: Dublin, Ireland; Belfast, North Ireland

GENEALOGICAL RESEARCH IN IRELAND

Only a very few Irish records have been published. Most of the original records were gathered in Dublin. In 1882 a big fire destroyed them. Others were destroyed in the recent civil war in 1922. The Society of Genealogists in London recently wrote us as follows: "Since the destruction of the Four Courts in Dublin, (the equivalent of the Public Record Office in London) in 1922, Irish records have been so sparse that connected research is out of the question, (except in the case of well known families figuring in the standard reference books.)"

A general index for the vital statistics for all of Ireland is at the Custom House, Dublin, Ireland. There are birth, marriage and death records from 1864. Portestant marriage records available only since 1845. Northern Ireland has kept its registers separately since 1922.

Since 1708 land records and deeds have been filed at the Land Registry, Henrietta Street, Dublin. Two Indexes have been made for these records--one under the surname of the grantor, the other under the township or property name. No index has been made of land owners. These records are being microfilmed.

Indexed records of wills filed in the Prerogative Court of Armagh for all Ireland by testators owning land in more than one diocese are available. They are also microfilmed. Wills relating to property in one diocese only were proved in the diocesan court. Each court file is indexed separately.

Mrs. Margaret D. Falley, 999 Michigan Ave., Evanston, Illinois 60202, has completed two large volumes on Irish research which every serious Irish researcher should have. Write to her for cost. She also has collected an excellent library of many rare volumes on Ireland and her people and can probably give help on many phases of research in the Emerald Isle.

The Ulster-Scot Historical Society, Law Courts Bldg. Chichester Street Belfast, Northern Ireland aims to provide facilities for people of Ulster descent to establish connections there. Write to them and ask for initial registration fee.

IRELAND PROVINCES AND COUNTIES

Ireland is divided into four provinces which in turn are divded into 32 counties and four county boroughs. Each county borough is a separate administrative district and each one is also the county town of one of the counties.

Ulster Province is divided between N. Ireland (counties Antrim, Down, Armagh, Fermanagh, Tyrone, and Londonderry) and republic (counties Monaghan, Cavan, and Donegal). Other three provinces are in republic--Leinster has counties Louth, Meath, Dublin, Kildare, Wicklow, Carlow, Wexford, Longford; Munster Province has Tipperary, Waterford, Cork, Kerry, Limer-

County Map of Ireland

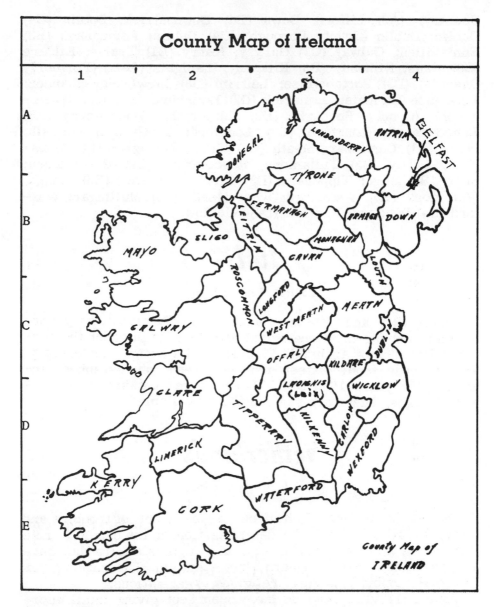

County Map of IRELAND

ick, and Clare; Connaught Province has Leitrim, Roscommon, Galway, Mayo, and Sligo.

COUNTIES AND COUNTY BOROUGHS OF IRELAND

(Counties are listed alphabetical with the map index in parenthisis and the county town following.)

Antrim (A4) Belfast; Armagh (B4) Armagh; Belfast (County Borough) (A4) Belfast; Carlow (D3) Carlow; Cavan (B3) Caven; Clare (D2) Ennis; Cork (E2) Cork; Cork (County Borough) (E2) Cork; Donegal (Ancient Name Tryconnel also O'Donnell's

Country) (A2) Lifford; Down (B4) Downpatrick; Dublin (C4) Dublin; Dublin (County Borough) (C4) Dublin; Fermanagh (B3) Enniskillen; Galway (C1) Galway; Kerry (E1) Tralee; Kildare (C3) Naas; Kilkenny (D3) Kilkenny; Laoighis (Leix) (Formerly Queen's) (D3) Portaoighise; Leitrim (B3) Carwick-on-Shannon; Leix (see Laoighis); Limerick (D2) Limerick; Limerick (Luimneach) (County Borough) (D2) Limerick; Londonderry (A3) Londonderry; Longford (C3) Longford; Louth (B4) Dundalk; Mayo (B1) Castlebar; Meath (C4) Trim; Monaghan (B3) Monaghan; Offaly (C3) Tullamore; Roscommon (C2) Roscommon; Sligo (B2) Sligo; Tipperary (D3) Clonmel; Tyrone (B3) Omagh; Waterford (E3) `Waterford; West Meath (C3) Mullingar; Wexford (D4) Wexford; Wicklow (D4) Wicklow.

Italy

Capital Rome (Roma)

During 1947 and 1948 the records from Piedmont, Italy were microfilmed for the Genalogical Society of Utah under the personal direction of Archibald F. Bennett, its executive secretary. The records from sixteen parishes were photographed, including the years 1690 to 1940. One film contains as many as 11,896 pages. There are several films available.

Netherlands

Capital - Amsterdam

The early history of Holland has been one of troubles and wars, in all of which the determination of the people to rule themselves has been paramount. In religious affairs they have always leaned heavily toward Protestantism. The nation gives financial support to several religious organizations.

Since 1811 vital records have been kept giving detail information about each individual.

Since 1850 the Bevolkingsregister (population register) has kept information as to the movements of each individual.

Many Hollanders have come to the United States and are now living in various parts of the nation. Michigan and Illinois have many of these industrious people within their borders. Since 1861 more than four thousand Hollanders have made their homes in Utah.

The vital statistics of all of the provinces are being micro-

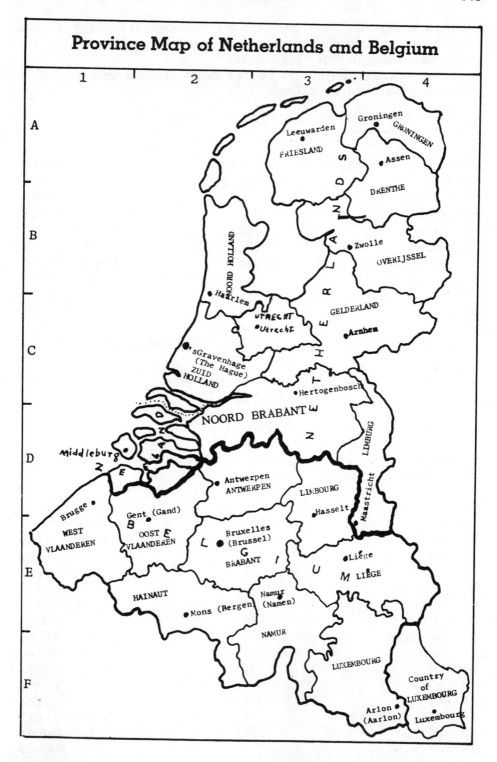

Province Map of Netherlands and Belgium

1 2 3 4

A

Leeuwarden
FRIESLAND

Groningen
GRONINGEN
• Assen
DRENTHE

B

NOORD HOLLAND

• Zwolle
OVERIJSSEL

• Haarlem

UTRECHT
• Utrecht

GELDERLAND

• Arnhem

C

• sGravenhage
(The Hague)
ZUID
HOLLAND

N
E
T
H
E
R
L
A
N
D
S

• Hertogenbosch

NOORD BRABANT

LIMBURG

D

Middleburg

Z
E
E
L
A
N
D

• Antwerpen
ANTWERPEN

LIMBOURG
• Hasselt

• Maastricht

Brugge •
WEST
VLAANDEREN

Gent (Gand)
OOST
VLAANDEREN

B
E
L
G
I
U
M

Bruxelles
(Brussel)
BRABANT

• Liège
LIÈGE

E

HAINAUT

• Mons (Bergen)

Namur
(Namen)

NAMUR

LUXEMBOURG

F

Arlon
(Aarlon) •

Country
of
LUXEMBOURG

• Luxembourg

filmed under the direction of the Genealogical Society of Utah. South Holland and Groningen records have been filmed and work is progressing in other provinces.

Several trained Holland researchers are connected with the Genealogical Society of Utah.

Netherlands is divided into eleven provinces. Each province controls its own archive.

Name	Map Index	Capital
Drenthe	B4	Assen
Friesland	A3	Leeuwarden
Gelderland	C3	Arnhem
Groningen	A4	Groningen
Limburg	D4	Maastricht
Noord (North) Brabant	D3	Hertogenbosch
Noord (North) Holland	B2	Haarlem
Overijssel (Overyssel)	B4	Zwolle
Utrecht	C3	Utrecht
Zeeland	D2	Middleburg
Zuid (South) Holland	C2	*'s Gravenhage (The Hague)

Norway

Capital - Oslo

Administrative Districts (Counties) of Norway (Norge) are called Fylkers as follows:

Fylker	Map Index	Administrative Center
1 Vestager	D1	Kristiansand
2 Aust–Agder	D1	Arendal
3 Rogaland	D1	Stavanger
4 Telemark	D1	Skien
5 Vestfold	D2	Tönsberg
6 Östfold	D2	Moss
7 Akershus	D2	*Oslo
8 Oslo	D2	*Oslo
9 Buskerud	D1	Drammen
10 Hordaland	D1	Bergen
11 Bergen	D1	Bergen
12 Sogn og Fjordane	C1	Hermansverk
13 Opland	C1	Lilliehammer
14 Hedmark	C2	Hamar

15 More og Romsdal	C1	Molde
16 Sör-Tröndelag	C2	Trondheim
17 Nord Tröndelag	C2	Steinkjer
18 Nordland	B2	Bodö
19 Troms	A3	Tromsö
20 Finnmark	A3	Vadsö

See Map Page 295

Some Norwegian Pioneer histories are available in the Norwegian-American Historical Museum at Decorah, Iowa. Norwegian Information Service, Washington, D.C. have booklet, "How to trace you ancestors in Norway."

Scandinavia

Included in this designation should be Sweden, Finland, Norway, Denmark and Iceland. Years ago Finland was part of Sweden and many Swedish families moved there. They have been perpetuated since then in Finland, and the present generations look upon Finland as their original country. There are also Finns and Russians living in Finland, but their names and languages are entirely different. The present Icelanders have descended from the three Scandinavian peoples, but mainly from the Danish.

At different times over the centuries, Norway has been part of either Denmark or Sweden. It wasn't until 1905 that it became a kingdom of its own, when a Danish prince was invited to become King of Norway.

The three languages are enough alike that they can be understood by people of all three countries, although the dialects in different sections of each one of the three countries vary so much that they are not understood in every section of the country. The dialects of the country sections are nothing like the city dialects, and cities vary in different sections of the country.

Until about 1880 the most common method of giving surnames was for the children to take the father's first name or given name and add to it "ssen", or "sson". For instance, if the father's first name was Ronald, his children's surname would be Ronaldssen or Ronaldsson; if Erick, Erickssen or Ericksson; If Johan, Johanssen or Johansson; if Niels or Nils, Nielssen or Nilsson, if Ingvar, Ingvarssen or Ingvarsson, etc.

The patronymic method of naming persons is not so difficult to comprehend as some seem to believe. For instance, if the father's name is Hans Sorensen and son's name is Ola or Jens, or Svend, or Carl, the full name of the son would be Ola Hansen, or Jens Hansen, or Svend Hansen, or Carl Hansen.

The same is true in Swedish families, with the exception that there the name ending is "sson" instead of "sen" as in the Norwegian and the Danish. However, among Scandinavians in America this name ending is not adhered to as strictly as it was years ago. Among Swedish families the "sson" may have become "son," but never "sen". Many Norwegian or Danish name endings are "son" instead of "sen". In Iceland the name endings are like that in Sweden, "sson," as Gislasson, Thordarsson, Sveinsson, Valgardsson, etc.

Books: Nelson, O. N., Ph.D., "History of the Scandinavians in the United States", two Vols, O. N. Nelson & Co., Minneapolis, Minn. 1904.

Hokanson, Nels, "Swedish Immigrants in Lincoln's Time." Harper & Bros, New York.

Scotland

Capital - Edinburgh

RESEARCH IN SCOTLAND

Unlike the conditions in England, the parish registers in Scotland have all been gathered in one building in Edinburgh. Besides the parish registers, there is a wealth of other records in Edinburgh which may be searched. Very few of the Scottish records have been printed. It is usually best to hire a genealogist to do the searching.

Before engaging help perhaps you should inquire from the Genealogical Society of Utah, Salt Lake City, what microfilm records from that country are available and if assistance can be obtained to search them.

THE CENSUS OF SCOTLAND

The census of Scotland was taken the same years and contained the same information as the census of England. In Scotland the census returns of 1841, 1851, 1861 and 1871 may be searched. Written application must be made for permission to search the census. For application blanks write to the Registrar General, New Register House, Edinburgh, Scotland. The fee for a particular search, that is a search for one person or household at one census and at one certain address, is ten shillings. If the address is good enough this search will be made by the office force without extra charge.

Permission for a general search, that is a search that is not limited to one person or to one census will be granted only to responsible officials or local authorities engaged in making search for public purposes, and to other specially approved

County Map of Scotland

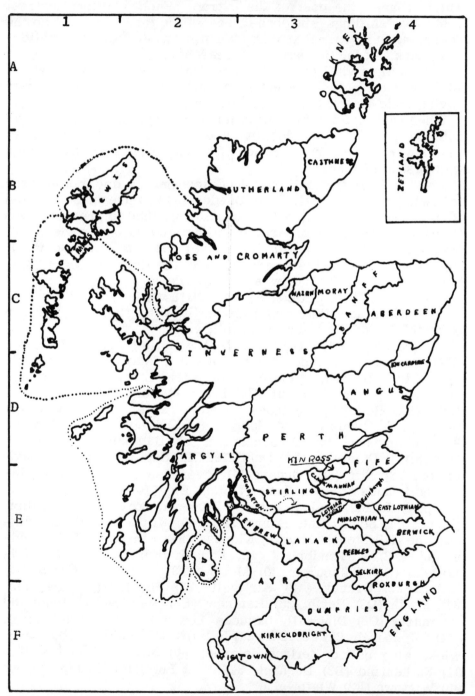

applicants. A general search must not exceed six hours and must be completed within two days. The cost is One Pound (about $3.00) which covers the cost of the extract. Each additional extract costs two shillings six pence. The office force does not do the searching in a general search. When you write for your application blank ask for the name of a searcher.

The earliest vital registers of Scotland have a starting date of 1538 but most of them did not start until much later, the majority having their inception between 1640 and 1700.

When writing for information it is very important that the birth date be given also the locality and occupation of the deceased. The law requiring registration of births, deaths and marriages was passed in 1855.

The Old Registration House in Edinburgh has among others the following records: Wills and Deeds, 1514 to present; Land and Housing records (real estate transfers), 1550 to present; Lyon Court Records (King-of-Arms); Guild registrations (tradesmen); Poll Tax (registration of males of over 16 for military service); Registration of University graduates of the Universities of Edinburgh, Glasgow, St. Andrew's and Aberdeene.

COUNTIES OF SCOTLAND

Counties are listed alphabetically with the map index in parenthisis and the county seat following.

1) Aberdeen (C4) Aberdeen; 2) Angus (D4) Forfar; 3) Argyll (D2) Inveraray, includes islands of Jura, Islay, Colonsay, Mull, Coll, Tiree, Scarba, Luing, Siel, Kerrera, Lismore, and others; 4) Ayr (F3) Ayr; 5) Banff (C4) Banff; 6) Berwick (E4) Duns; 7) Bute (E2) Rothesay, includes islands of Bute, Arran, Gr. Cumbrae, Little Cumbrae, Holy Island, etc.; 8) Caithness (B3) Wick; 9) Clackmannan (E3) Clackmannan; 10) Dumbarton (E2) Dumbarton; 11) Dumfries (F3) Dumfries; 12) East Lothian (E4) Haddington; 13) Fife (D4) Cupar; 14) Inverness (C3) Inverness, includes islands of Skye, Raasay, Muck, Eigg, Rum, Canna, Sanday, Scalpay, Harris, Scalpa, Pabbay, Bernera, Boreray, North Uist, Benbecula, South Uist, Barra, and many little islands; 15) Kincardine (D4) Stonehaven; 16) Kinross (E3) Kinross; 17) Kirkcudbright (F3) Kirkcudbright; 18) Lanark (E3) Lanark; 19) Mid-Lothian (E4) Edinburgh; 20) Moray (C3) Elgin; 21) Nairn (C3) Nairn; 22) Orkney (A3) Kirkwall; 23) Peebles (E4) Peebles; 24) Perth (D3) Perth; 25) Renfrew (E3) Renfrew; 26) Ross and Cromarty (C2) Dingwall, includes Lewis Island; 27) Roxburgh (F4) Jedburgh; 28) Selkirk (E4) Selkirk; 29) Shetland (B4) Lerwick; also called Zetland Islands; 30) Stirling (E3) Stirling; 31) Sutherland (B3) Dornoch; 32) West Lothian (E3) Linlithgow; 33) Wigtown (F3) Wigtown.

South Africa

Capitals - Pretoria and Capetown

The Cape Settlement was established by the Dutch East India Co. as a "half way house" between Europe and India, under the command of Jan van Riebeeck, who arrived in Table Bay on the 6 April 1652. Ten years later van Riebeeck was appointed commander to the Government at Malacca and the muster rolls of the Cape Settlement showed it had grown to several hundred inhabitants during his tenure of office. The Cape settlement continued under the rule of this trading company for about 140 years, gradually growing from within and without. The Netherlands, of course, supplied most of the immigrants but French refugees also came in considerable numbers as well as numerous Germans, a few Swiss and others.

The first British occupation occurred in 1795 but not until 1806 did they wrest it permanently from the Dutch. In 1820 under sponsorship of the British Government over 3,000 English settlers arrived at Algoa Bay (Port Elizabeth), becoming the nucleus of the English speaking people of South Africa. The start of the great trek of the Boers (South African descendants of the Dutch), came in 1836. They traveled north and east with the object of settling outside the sphere of British control. Gradually they found their way to Natal, Orange Free State and Transvaal, which with the Cape Province, after much tribulation and war, now form the Union of South Africa.

PUBLISHED GENEALOGIES

The oldest and largest published genealogical work is that of Christoffel Coetzee de Villiers, "Geslacht-Register der Oude Kaapsche Familien" (Generation Index of the Old Cape Families) which was published in three volumes in 1893-4. This is an excellent reference book but should be checked with original or other sources where possible as it has some mistakes. Another useful genealogical work is "Personalia of the Germans at the Cape, 1652-1806" by Dr. J. Hoge which was published as the 1946 issue of the "Archives Year Book for South African History." This publication attempts to give a complete list of the Germans and Swiss who came to the Cape in the service of the Dutch East India Co. during the period 1652 till 1806. It lists as sources manuscripts in the Cape section of the Government Archives and Archives of the Dutch Reformed Church.

Other good sources are: "The French Refugees at the Cape" by Col. Graham Botha (1919); "Precis of the Archives of the

Cape of Good Hope" in two volumes, consisting of Requesten (Memorials) 1715-1806; "De Afkomst der Boeren" by Dr. H. J. Colenbrander contains a list of many of the early marriages of the settlers, with birthplaces of the wives--sometimes not otherwise obtainable. "The Story of the British Settlers of 1820 in South Africa" lists all the settlers of 1820 and gives their ages as of that year.

The histories and genealogies of some individual families have been compiled, some of them being: "Genealogy Jacob Izaak de Villiers and his wife Johanna Margaretha Muller of Waltevreeden, Dist. of Paarl" by D. F. Bosman; "History of the Malan de Merindol" compiled by Henry Victor Malan (1836) and revised by James John Malan (1950); "Record of the Caldecott Family of South Africa"; "Jan Van Riebeeck Zijn Voor-en Nageslacht" (his ancestors and posterity) published 1952 by the Netherlands government gives many South African descendants of the leader of the first European Colony south of the tropic of Capricorn.

STATE RECORDS

Laws requiring the registration of births, deaths and marriages were passed in Natal in 1868, in the Cape Province in 1895, in the Orange Free State and Transvaal in 1902. Prior to these dates it was optional with parents as to whether they had the births of their children registered or not. Survivors had the same option with the registration of deaths. The registration of marriages started some years before that of births and deaths in all the provinces except Natal. Births, marriage and death certificates may be obtained from the local registrar or from the Registrar of Births, Marriages and Deaths, Dept. of Int. Pretoria, South Africa. Birth certificates are of little value to the genealogists of South Africa, however, as the information given on them is restricted by law to the name, place and date of birth of the registrant--the price is 2s 6d. Full birth certificates, giving the name, place and date of birth, also the names, ages, place of birth and marriage of parents, may be had only by applicants residing outside the Union of South Africa--the price being 5s. (s--Shilling, abt. 15 cents; d--penny, abt. 1 1/2 cents)

The marriage certificate gives the names of each party, the date and place of marriage, the country of birth and the age of each. The death certificate gives the name, date and place of death, age at death and birthplace. In the case of children who died under 10 years of age, it also gives the names of the parents. The cost of a marriage certificate or death certificate is 2s 6d.

In the Union of South Africa they have what they call a "Death Notice" which is completed on the filing of a will or on the settlement of deceased estate. These are very valuable for genealogists as they list, when properly executed, the following information: name, age, birthplace, date and place of death, names of spouse, parents and children. The law requires that all estates over ten pounds sterling be probated, also that all wills of estates under that amount be filed with the Master of the Supreme Court. The charge made for a certified copy of a Death Notice is 6s 6d. If the complete will is wanted, write for cost. Cape Province wills and Deceased Estate records (Death Notices) from 1689 to 1833 are kept in the Union Archives and from 1834 to date in the Master's Office of the Supreme Court--the address of both is Queen Victoria Street, Capetown, C. P. South Africa. In Natal the Master of the Supreme Court has wills dating back to 1852 and Deceased Estates from 1872 to date--the address is Pieter-maritzburg, Natal, South Africa. Deceased Estate records in the Master's Office in the Orange Free State in 1850--the address is Bloemfontein, OFS, South Africa. The address of the Master's Office in the Transvaal is Pretoria, Tvl., South Africa. Their records start in 1872.

It must be remembered that sometimes estates are settled many years after death occurred and that most of the estates are indexed according to the year they are filed. Also, none of the public record offices have facilities for doing research, making it necessary to use care in giving information as to what is wanted and what year it may be found when asking for certificates. In the case of birth certificates, the date and place of birth must be given, also the names of parents. If the record is not found in that year, an additional charge of 2s 6d is made for searching the year before and the year following the one given, but no longer search than for the three years will be made on one application.

CHURCH RECORDS

The church records in the Archives of the Dutch Reformed Church (Nederduits-Hervormde of Gereformeede Kerk claiming 85% of the membership of the Dutch Reformed Church in South Africa) are of great value to historical and genealogical researchers. They have baptism and other records dating back to 1665 and it has been the aim of the church to gather all their church records up to about 1875 to this repository. However, some of the local churches still have their records from inception and, of course, inquiries on recent records must also be made locally. Baptism Certificates may be had for 2s 6d, membership certificates for 2s 6d, and marriage certificates for 6s 6d. Address inquiries to Dutch Reformed Church Archives, 44 Queen Victoria Street, Capetown, C. P., South Africa, or to locality where your people came from.

The records of other churches are kept mostly in the local churches and inquiries should be directed to them.

The Union Archives at Pretoria, Pietermaritzburg, Bloemfontein and Capetown, though not staffed sufficiently to do research, have many wonderful old records which are veritable "gold mines." In some cases the old church records have been removed to the State Archives as in Pietermaritzburg where they have baptismal and marriage records kept by the "Predikants" as they crossed the plains with the Voortrekkers. Also the Marriage Register--1837 to 1912 of the Dutch Reformed Church of that locality.

The South African Mission of the Church of Jesus Christ of Latter-day Saints, with headquarters at "Cumorah" Main Rd., Mowbray, C. P., South Africa, has a card index file of about 15,000 names which is growing continually as members in South Africa send in all information on their personal lines.

Sweden

Capital - Stockholm

The primary sources of genealogical information in Sweden are the church records. They are recognized as among the best in Europe. The Genealogical Association Library in Salt Lake City has more microfilm records from Sweden than from any other nation, except the United States. If your ancestors lived in Sweden within the past century, their records would be in the church in the parish (forsamling) in which they lived. If the desired date is older that that, then the search should be conducted in the particular archive (landsarkiv) to which that parish belongs.

There are more than 2,550 parishes in Sweden. The names of the parish and the county (lan) in which the ancestor lived must be known before any search can be made. The older records from these parishes are in five archives; Lund, Goteborg, Vadstena, Uppsala, and Harnosand.

Among the records kept by the church are birth and baptism, confirmation, marriage banns (lysing), marriages, incoming and outgoing records, catechetical (husförhörslängder), and deaths.

In 184 communities records are kept of 117 district courts in Sweden (domsagor or häradsrätter). Among them are wills (testamenter), land records (jordeböcker), inventories (bouppteckning or lösöreförteckning), and census (mantalslangder).

Most city or community governments maintain a taxoffice (uppbördsverket), which keeps yearly lists of taxpayers and their addresses.

One of the difficulties in Swedish research for the novice researcher is the patronymic name system used until about 1890. The surname of the children in any one family was the given name of the father plus son or dotter (daughter). Since the Swedish possessive is not indicated by an apostrophe, the son of Peter or Peters son gets the surname Petersson. Similarly Hans son is Hansson, Nils son is Nilsson, Magnus son is Magnusson, etc. In the same way the surname of the daughters became Hansdotter, Nilsdotter, Magnusdotter, etc. If the father had adopted a surname not ending in son, as tens of thousands of them did, the children would use the father's adopted name as their surname.

THE COUNTIES OR LANS OF SWEDEN

1	Malmohus	Malmo	Skane	Lund
2	Kristianstad	Kristianstad	Skane	Lund
3	Blekinge	Karlskrona	Blekinge	Lund
4	Kronoberg	Vaxjo	Smaland	Vadstena
5	Halland	Halmstad	Halland	Lund
6	Jönoköping	Jönköping	Smaland	Vadstena
7	Kalmar	Kalmar	Smaland	Vadstena
8	Gotland	Visby	Gotland	Vadstena
9	Älvsborg	Vänersborg	Västergötland	Göteborg
10	Göteborg & Bohus	Göteborg	Bohuslän	Göteborg
11	Skaraborg	Mariestad	Västergötland	Göteborg
12	Ostergötland	Linkoping	Ostergotland	Vadstena
13	Sodermanland	Nyköping	Sodermanland	Uppsala
14	Orebro	Örebro	Närke	Uppsala
15	Värmland	Karlstad	Värmland	Göteborg
16	Västmanland	Vasteras	Västmanland	Uppsala
17	Stockholm	Stockholm	Södermanland	Uppsala
18	Uppsala	Uppsala	Uppland	Uppsala
19	Kopparberg	Falun	Dalarna	Uppsala
20	Gävleborg	Gävle	Gästrikland	Härnösand
21	Jämtland	Östersund	Jämtland	Härnösand
22	Västernorrland	Härnösand	Angermanland	Härnösand
23	Västerbotten	Umea	Västerbotten	Härnösand
24	Norrbotten	Lulea	Norrbotten	Härnösand

See Map Page 295

Switzerland

Capital - Bern

Switzerland, anciently known as Helvetia, covers an area about

Cantons of Switzerland

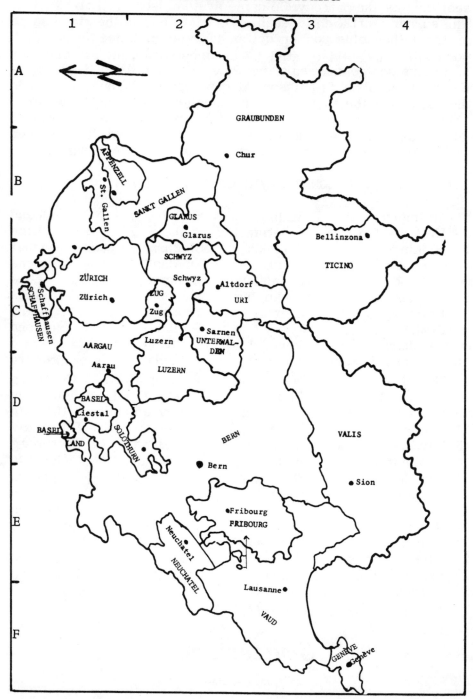

half as large as South Carolina and into that little space is crowded a population twice that of South Carolina plus half a million. The population 4,700,297, as compared to South Carolina's 2,117,027. Switzerland is surrounded by France, Germany, Austria, and Italy. Languages represented are German, French, Italian and Romansch.

Switzerland consists of twenty-two states or cantons which form the Swiss Republic. For administrative purposes three cantons Appenzell, Basel, and Unterwalden, have been divided into two districts each. The cantons are Aargau, Appenzell, Basselland, Bern, Fribourg, Geneve, Glarus, Grisons, Luzern, Neuchatel, St. Gallen, Schaffhausen, Schwyz. Solothurn, Thurgau, Ticino, Unterwalden, Uri, Valais, Vaud, Zug, and Zurich.

Among the available genealogical sources are the church or parish registers, the baptismal, the confirmation, the marriage, and the death books. The confirmation books contain the names and records of the fifteen-year old boys and girls who have prepared themselves in special study groups under the direction of the minister prior to their participation for the first time in the Lord's Supper. Among the non-church records are the Burger Rodel (Citizen Roll) in which is recorded the name of each citizen, together with his parents' and grandparents; names, and the Zivilstandsamt (civilian position), containing about the same information.

Of the many European nationalities represented in Utah, none has been more consistant and energetic in their research activities than have the Swiss. As a result voluminous records have been filed with the Genealogical Society of Utah, For instance, one woman has over the years gathered more than 60,000 names of ancestors, all of whom have been thoroughly identified Several records go back as far as 1520.

People of Swiss descent, regardless of their present residence, may do well to confer with the Genealogical Society of Utah, 80 North Main St., Salt Lake City, Utah 84111, about their research activities before engaging a professional researcher.

Wales

For nearly five hundred years England and Wales have been one country. The Welsh government affairs have been conducted in London just as those of England. In everything else the two peoples are entirely different. The Welsh, or Cymry, have their own traditions, history, language, literature, and songs.

"English and Welsh records were compiled under the same conditions and laws," says David E. Gardner, an untiring Utah student and teacher of genealogy. "This means that parish registers, probate court wills and administrations, and civil registering of vital statistics (since 1837), taxing, militia records, and overseeing of the poor and highways were practically the same."

Mr. Gardner explains that the language is so difficult that names of days, months, and counties often are mistaken for places of birth. Spelling of names is not always uniform. To add to the difficulty of interpreting the old records, some of the parish vicars or ministers have interchanged Latin and English.

Since many of the surnames were taken from the place of residence, you will find many families with the same name who are unrelated.

The patronymics (father's name) changed with each generation just as in the Scandinavian countries. Until 1850 these changes were common in all families. So, for instance, John son Philip Thomas, is the same as John ap Philip Thomas, which becomes John Philip, or David ab Evan Hugh, becomes David Evan or David Bevan.

The only legal form of marriage from 1754 to 1837 was by the parish minister. If births and burials are not found in parish register, search non-parochial registers, many of which, prior to 1837, are at Somerset House.

Because of the changes of names and frequency of common names, wills may give the only real identification.

Wills and administrations are grouped into four probate courts: (1) Llandaff (South Wales and Monmouth); (2) St. David's (West Wales); (3) Bangor (Central and Northwest Wales); (4) St. Asaph (Northwest Wales). All names in the records are indexed under the first given name.

Unless the researcher is well acquainted with the Welsh language, it may be to his advantage to employ a Welsh professional researcher.

COUNTIES OF WALES

Name	Abbreviation	Map Index	County Town
Anglesey	Ang.	A4	Beaurnares
Brecknockshire	Brec.	B6	Brecknock or Brecon
Caernarvonshire (Carnarvon)	Caern.	B4	Caernarvon
Cardiganshire	Card.	B5	Cardigan
Carmarthenshire	Carm.	B6	Carmarthen
Denbighshire	Denb.	B4	Denbigh

Flintshire	Flint.	B4	Flint
Glamorganshire	Glam.	B6	Cardiff
Merionethshire	Meri.	B5	Dolgelly
Montgomeryshire	Mont.	B5	Montgomery
Pembrokeshire	Pemb.	A6	Pembroke
Radnorshire	Rad.	B5	New Radnor

See Map Page 301

A Select Bibliography Of
Genealogical Reference Books

The titles listed below have been recommended by leading genealogists as representive of their field. Many of them have been reprinted by the Genealogical Publishing Company, 521 St. Paul Place, Baltimore, Maryland 21202. This firm is willing to supply a price list upon request.

ALABAMA

"Revolutionary Soldiers in Alabama", 2 vols, by Elizabeth W. Thomas.

"Early Settlers of Alabama" by Col. James E. Saunders. With notes and genealogies by E. S. B. Stubbs.

"Index to Alabama Wills, 1808-1870", compiled by Alabama Society, DAR.

"Alabama: Her History, Resources, War Record, and Public Men, from 1540 to 1872" by W. Brewer.

ARKANSAS

"Reminiscent History of the Ozark Region".

"Pioneers and Makers of Arkansas" by Josiah H. Shinn.

CALIFORNIA

"California Pioneer Register and Index, 1542-1848" by Hubert Howe Bancroft.

CONNECTICUT

"Connecticut, Heads of Families at the First Census of the United States Taken in the Year 1790".

"A Catalogue of the Names of the Early Puritan Settlers of the Colony of Connecticut; with the Time of Their Arrival in the Country and Colony" by Royal R. Hinman.

"Early Connecticut Marriages as Found on Ancient Church Records Prior to 1800" by F. W. Bailey.

"A Digest of the Connecticut Probate Recrods, Hartford District, 1635-1750", 3 vols, by Charles W. Manwaring.

"Rolls and Lists of Connecticut Men in the Revolution, 1775-1783", 2 vols.

"Record of Service of Connecticut Men in the Revolution, War of 1812, Mexican War".

DELAWARE

"Reconstructed 1790 Census of Delaware" by Leon DeValinger, Jr.

"Delaware 1800 Census" by G. and D.O. Maddus.

"Delaware Revolutionary Records", 3 Vols.

"Original Land Titles in Delaware Known as the Duke of York Record, 1646 to 1679".

"Governor's Register, State of Delaware, Appointments and Other Transactions by Executives of the State from 1674 to 1851".

GEORGIA

"Some Early Tax Digests of Georgia" by Ruth Blair.

"A List of the Early Settlers of Georgia" by E. Merton Coulter and Albert B. Saye.

"Georgia's Roster of the Revolution" by Lucian Lamar Knight.

"Reprint of Official Register of Land Lottery of Georgia, 1827" by M.L. Houston.

"Moravians in Georgia, 1735-1740" by Adelaide L. Fries.

"The Cherokee Land Lottery, Containing a Numerical List of the Names of the Fortunate Drawers in Said Lottery" by James F. Smith.

"Roster of Revolutionary Soldiers in Georgia" by Mrs. Howard H. McCall.

"Abstracts of Colonial Wills of the State of Georgia, 1733-1777" by Mary G. Bryan.

"Historical Collections of Georgia" by G. White.

"Revolutionary Records in the State of Georgia", 3 vols, by Allen D. Candler.

"Sketches of Some of the First Settlers of Upper Georgia" by George R. Gilmer.

KENTUCKY

"Kentucky Records: Early Wills and Marriages, Old Bible Records and Tombstone Inscriptions" by Mrs. William (Julia

Hoge) Ardery.

"Kentucky Marriages, 1787-1860" by Glenn G. Clift.

"Second Census of Kentucky, 1800" by Glenn G. Clift.

"Kentucky Pioneers and Their Descendants" by Ila E. Fowler.

"Historic Families of Kentucky" by Thomas Marshall Green.

"History of Kentucky", 2 vols, by Lewis Collins.

"Kentucky Land Grants. Index to All Land Grants Recorded in the State Land Office at Frankfort. 1782-1924" by W. R. Jillson.

"Old Kentucky Entries and Deeds" by Willard Rouse Jillson.

"Kentucky Court and Other Records" by Mrs. William (Julia Hoge) Ardery.

"Kentucky Pioneer and Court Records" by Mrs. Harry Kennett McAdams.

"First Census of Kentucky, 1790" by Charles Brunk Heinemann.

"Abstract of Early Kentucky Wills and Inventories" by J. Estelle Stewart King.

"Revolutionary Soldiers in Kentucky" by Anderson C. Quisenberry.

"A Calendar of the Warrants for Land in Kentucky" by Philip Fall Taylor.

"Catalogue of Revolutionary Soldiers and Sailors of the Commonwealth of Virginia to Whom Land Bounty Warrants Were Granted by Virginia for Military Services in the War for Independence" by Samuel M. Wilson.

LOUISIANA

"Louisiana Colonials: Soldiers and Vagabonds" by Winston DeVille.

"Old Louisiana Plantation Homes and Family Trees", 2 vols, by Herman de Bachelle Seebold.

MAINE

"Maine Wills, 1640-1760" by William M. Sargent.

"An Alphabetical Index of Revolutionary Pensioners Living in Maine" by Charles Alcott Flagg.

"Names of Soldiers in the American Revolution Who Applied for State Bounty Under Resolves of March 17, 1835, March 24, 1836, and March 20, 1836 as Appears of Record in Land Office" by Charles J. House.

"Genealogical Dictionary of Maine and New Hampshire" by Charles Thornton Libby and Sybil Noyes.

"Maine. Heads of Familes at the First Census of the United States Taken in the Year 1790".

"The Pioneers of Maine and New Hampshire, 1623-1660" by Charles Henry Pope.

MARYLAND

"The Maryland Calendar of Wills", 8 vols, by Jane Baldwin.

"Maryland. Heads of Families at the First Census of the United States Taken in the Year 1790".

"Maryland Records. Colonial, Revolutionary, County and Church from Original Sources", 2 vols, by Gaius Marcus Brumbaugh.

"An Index of the Source Records of Maryland. Genealogical, Biographical, Historical" by Eleanor Phillips Passano.

"Sidelights on Maryland History with Sketches of Early Maryland Families" 2 vols, by Hester Dorsey Richardson.

"Old Somerset on the Eastern Shore of Maryland" by Clayton Torrence.

"Index to Maryland Colonial Wills, 1634-1777, at Annapolis", 3 vols, by J.M. Magruder.

"Maryland Records", 2 vols, by Gaius M. Brumbaugh.

"Maryland Revolutionary Records: Data Obtained from 3,050 Pension Claims and Bounty Land Applications" by Harry Wright Newman.

"Register of Maryland's Heraldic Families", 2 vols, by Alice M. Parran.

MASSACHUSETTS

"A List of Alien Passengers, Bonded From January 1, 1847, to January 1, 1851, For the Use of the Overseers of the Poor, in the Commonwealth" by J. B. Munroe.

"Massachusetts. Heads of Families at the First Census of the United States Taken in the Year 1790".

"Records of the Massachusetts Volunteer Militia, Called out by the Governor of Massachusetts to Suppress a Threatened Invasion During the War of 1812-14" by Brigadier General Gardner W. Pearson.

"The Pioneers of Massachusetts" by Charles Henry Pope.

"Massachusetts Soldiers and Sailors of the Revolutionary War", 17 vols.

MICHIGAN

"Mackinac Register of Baptisms and Interments, 1695-1821, as Contained in Collections of the State Historical Society of Wisconsin, Vol. XIX".

"Mackinac Register of Marriages, 1725-1821, as Contained in Collections of the State Historical Society of Wisconsin, Vol. XVIII".

MISSISSIPPI

"Mississippi, As a Province, Territory and State, With Biographical Notices of Eminent Citizens" by J. F. H. Claiborne.

"Mississippi 1820 Census" by Irene S. Gillis and Norman E. Gillis.

"Genealogical Abstract of Goodspeed's Biographical and Historical Memoirs of Mississippi" by Irene S. Gillis and Norman E. Gillis.

"Index to Goodspeed's Biographical and Historical Memoirs of Mississippi" by Norman E. Gillis.

"Mississippi 1830 Census" by Irene S. and Norman E. Gillis.

"The Natchez Court Records, 1767-1805, Abstracts of Early Records" by May Wilson McBee.

"Early Inhabitants of the Natchez District" by Norman E. Gillis.

MISSOURI

"A History of the Pioneer Families of Missouri" by William S. Bryan and Robert Rose.

"History of Southeast Missouri" by Robert S. Douglass.

"Goodspeed's History of Southeast Missouri".

NEW HAMPSHIRE

"New Hampshire. Heads of Families at the First Census of the United States Taken in the Year 1790".

NEW JERSEY

"Index of the Official Register of The Officers and Men of New Jersey in the Revolutionary War".

"State of New Jersey. Index of Wills, Inventories, etc. In the Office of the Secretary of State Prior to 1901", 3 vols.

"New Jersey Marriage Records, 1665-1800" by William Nelson.

"Historical Collections of the State of New Jersey" by J. W. Barber.

"New Jersey Index of Wills, Office of Secretary of State, 1705-1830", 2 vols.

"Calendar of New Jersey Wills, Administrations, etc., 1670-1800", Edited by William Nelson and A. Van Doren Honeyman, 13 vols.

"New Jersey Biographical and Genealogical Notes" by William Nelson.

NEW YORK

"Early Eighteenth Century Palatine Emigration" by Walter Allen Knittle.

"Calendar of Wills on File and Recorded in the Offices of the Clerk of the Court of Appeals, of the County Clerk of Albany, and of the Secretary of State 1626-1836" by Berthold Fernow.

"Refugees of 1776 from Long Island to Connecticut" by F. G. Mather.

"Names of Persons for whom Marriage Licenses were Issued by the Secretary of the Province of New York, Previous to 1784" by Gideon J. Tucker.

"Long Island Genealogical Source Material" by H. F. Seversmith and Kenn. Stryder-Rodda.

"Muster Rolls of New York Provincial Troops, 1755-1764".

"Abstract of Wills on File in the Surrogate's Office, City of New York" 17 vols. (each complete within itself).

"Heads of Families at the First Census of the United States Taken in the Year 1790"

NORTH CAROLINA

"North Carolina. Heads of Families at the First Census of the United States Taken in the Year 1790".

"North Carolina Genealogical Reference" by W. R. Draughon.

"Roster of Soldiers from North Carolina in the American Revolution", (Durham).

"Sketches of Western North Carolina, Historical and Biographical" by C. L. Hunter.

"Abstract of North Carolina Wills, Compiled from Original and Recorded Wills in the Office of the Secretary of State" by Bryan J. Grimes.

"North Carolina Wills and Inventories" by Bryan J. Grimes.

"Western North Carolina" by J. P. Arthur.

"North and South Carolina Marriage Records from the Earliest Colonial Days to the Civil War" by W. M Clemens.

"Old Albemarle and Its Absentee Landlords. Part IV of the Lost Tribes of N.C." by Worth S. Ray.

"Formation of North Carolina Counties, 1663-1943" by David L. Corbitt.

"County Records, The Historical Records of North Carolina", 3 vols, by C. C. Crittenden and D. Lacy.

"The Loyalists in North Carolina during the Revolution" by Robert O. DeMond.

"Colonial Granville County and Its People" by Worth S. Ray.

"North Carolina Historical and Genealogical Register" by James R. B. Hathaway.

"Marriage and Death Notices from the Raleigh Register and North Carolina State Gazette, 1799-1825" by Carrie L. Broughton.

"Mecklenburg Signers and Their Neighbors" by Worth S. Ray.

"Records of the Moravians in North Carolina", 9 vols, by Adelaide L. Fries.

"Records of Emigrands from England and Scotland to North Carolina 1774-1775" A. R. Newsome, ed.

"An Abstract of North Carolina Wills, from About 1760 to About 1800" by Fred A. Olds.

"Index and Digest to Hathaway's North Carolina Historical and Genealogical Registers" by Worth S. Ray.

"Historical Sketches of North Carolina From 1584 to 1851", 2 vols in 1, by John Hill Wheeler.

"Reminiscences and Memoirs of North Carolina and Eminent North Carolinians" by John Hill Wheeler.

OHIO

"Official Roster of the Soldiers of the American Revolution Buried in the State of Ohio".

"Soldiers of the American Revolution Who Lived in the State of Ohio".

"Federal Census Records for Trumbull County, Ohio, 1820" by Doris Wolcott Strong.

PENNSYLVANIA

"Guide to the Published Archives of Pennsylvania, Covering the 138 Volumes of Colonial Records and Pennsylvania Archives, Series I-IX" by Henry H. Eddy.

"Pennsylvania Genealogies; Chiefly Scotch-Irish and German" by William Henry Egle.

"Naturalizations of Foreign Protestants in the American and West Indian Colonies" by M. S. Giuseppi.

"Guide to Genealogical and Historical Research in Pennsylvania" by Floyd G. Hoenstine.

"Names of Persons for Whom Marriage Licenses Were Issued in the Province of Pennsylvania Previous to 1790" .

"Quaker Arrivals at Philadelphia, 1682-1750" by Albert C. Myers.

"Irish Quaker Arrivals to Pennsylvania, 1682-1750" by Albert Cook Myers.

"Pennsylvania German Pionners" by Ralph Beaver Strassburger.

"A Collection of Upwards of Thirty Thousand Names of German, Swiss, Dutch, French, and Other Immigrants in Pennsylvania from 1727 to 1776" by I. Daniel Rupp.

"The German Immigration into Pennsylvania Through the Port of Philadelphia, and the Redemptioners" by Frank Reid Differderffer.

"Welsh Settlement in Pennsylvania" by Charles H. Browning.

"Pennsylvania Marriages Previous to 1810", 2 vols.

"Immigration of the Irish Quakers into Pennsylvania, 1682-1750" by Albert Cook Myers.

"Names of Foreigners Who Took the Oath of Allegiance to the Province and State of Pennsylvania, 1727-1775, with the Foreign Arrivals, 1786-1808" by William Henry Egle.

"William Penn and the Dutch Quaker Migration to Pennsylvania" by William I. Hull.

"Record of Indentures of Individuals Bound Out as Apprentices, Servants, etc, and of German and Other Redemptioners in the Office of the Mayor of the City of Philadelphia, October 3, 1771, to October 5, 1773".

"Welsh Founders of Pennsylvania" 2 vols, by Thomas Allen Glenn.

"Pennsylvania Historical and Museum Commission, Guide to the Published Archives of Pennsylvania Covering 138 vols. of Colonial Records and Pennsylvania Archives" by H. H. Eddy.

"Pennsylvania Genealogies: Scotch-Irish and German" by W. H. Egle.

"Pennsylvania, Heads of Families at the First Census of the United States Taken in the Year 1790".

"Society of Friends in Pennsylvania".

"Pennsylvania German Pioneers. A Publication of the Original Lists of Arrivals in the Port of Philadelphia from 1727 to 1808" by Ralph Beaver Strassburger, 2 vols, Edited by William John Hinke.

"Memorials of the Huguenots in America, With Special Reference to Their Emigration to Pennsylvania" by Ammon Stapleton.

"Bibliography of Pennsylvania History" by Norman B. Wilkinson.

RHODE ISLAND

"Genealogical Dictionary of Rhode Island. Comprising Three Generations of Settlers Who Came Before 1690" by J. O. Austin.

"Rhode Island. Heads of Families at the First Census of the United States Taken in the Year 1790".

"Rhode Island Land Evidences, 1648-1696".

"Vital Records of Rhode Island, 1636-1850. Births, Marriages, and Deaths. A Family Register for the People", 21 vols, by James N. Arnold.

SOUTH CAROLINA

"South Carolina. Heads of Families at the First Census of the United States Taken in the Year 1790".

"Index to Wills of Charleston County, 1671-1863".

"A Compilation of the Original Lists of Protestant Immigrants to South Carolina, 1763-1773" by James Revill.

"South Carolinians in the Revolution" by Sara Sullivan Ervin.

"Indexes to the County Wills of South Carolina" by Martha Lou Houston.

"1800 Census of the Pendleton District" by William C. Stewart.

"South Carolina Colonial Soldiers and Patriots" by Leonardo Andrea.

"Abstracts of the Wills of the State of South Carolina", 2 vols, by Caroline T. Moore.

TENNESSEE

"Tennessee Cousins. A History of Tennessee People" by Worth S. Ray.

"King's Mountain and Its Heroes: History of the Battle of King's Mountain, October 7th, 1780, and the Events Which Led to it" by Lyman C. Draper.

"The King's Mountain Men" by Katherine Keogh White.

"Bible Records and Marriage Bonds" by Jeannette Tillotson Acklen.

"Tombstone Inscriptions and Manuscripts" by Jeannette Tillotson Acklen.

TEXAS

"Austin Colony Pioneers. Including History of Bastrop, Fayette, Grimes, Montgomery, and Washington Counties, Texas and Their Earliest Settlers" by Worth S. Ray.

"First Census of Texas, 1829-1836, To Which Are Added, Texas Citizenship Lists, 1821-1845, and Other Records" by Marion D. Mullins.

"An Abstract of the Original Titles of Record in the General Land Office".

VERMONT

"Census. Heads of Families at the Second Census of the United States Taken in the Year 1800."

"Rolls of the Soldiers in the Revolutionary War, 1775 to 1783" by John E. Goodrich.

"Heads of Families at the First Census of the United States Taken in the Year 1790."

"War of 1812-14. Roster of Soldiers in the State of Vermont."

VIRGINIA

"Virginia Historical Index," 2 vols, by E. G. Swem.

"Gleanings of Virginia History" by William Fletcher Boogher.

"Documents, Chiefly Unpublished Relating to the Huguenot Emigration to Virginia and the Settlement at Manakin-Town" by R. A. Brock.

"Old Churches, Ministers and Families of Virginia" by Bishop William Meade with "Digested Index and Genealogical Guide" by Jennings Cropper Wise, 2 vols.

"History of Southwest Virginia, 1746-1786; Washington County, 1777-1870" by Lewis Preston Summers.

"Virginia Wills and Administrations, 1632-1800" by Clayton Torrence.

"Heads of Families at the First Census of the United States Taken in the Year 1790".

"Chronicles of the Scotch-Irish Settlement in Virginia, Extracted from the Original Court Records of Augusta County, 1745-1800" 3 vols. by Lyman Chalkley.

"Early Virginia Marriages" by William Armstrong Crozier.

"Virginia Colonial Militia, 1651-1776" by William Armstrong Crozier.

"Virginia Heraldica: Being a Registry of Virginia Gentry Entitled to Coat Armor, With Genealogical Notes of the Families" by William Armstrong Crozier.

"English Duplicates of Lost Virginia Records" by Louis Des Cognets.

"List of the Colonial Soldiers of Virginia" by James Hamilton Eckenrode.

"Virginia Tax Payers, 1782-87, Other Than Those Published by the United Census Bureau" by Augusta B. Fothergill and John M. Naugle.

"Virginia Cousins: A Study of the Ancestry and Posterity of John Goode of Whitby" by G. Brown Goode.

"Early Virginia Immigrants, 1623-1666" by George Cabell Greer.

"Historical Register of Virginians, In the Revolution, Soldiers, Sailors, Marines, 1775-1783" by John H. Gwathmey.

"Colonial Families of the Southern States of America" by Stella Pickett Hardy.

"Virginia Genealogies. A Genealogy of the Glassell Family of Scotland and Virginia" by Rev. Horace E. Hayden.

"Kegley's Virginia Frontier. The Beginning of the Southwest. The Roanoke of Colonial Days, 1740-1783" by F. B. Kegley.

"Cavaliers and Pioneers. Abstracts of Virginia Land Patents and Grants, 1623-1666" by Nell M. Nugent.

"Shenandoah Valley Pioneers and Their Descendants." by T. K. Cartmell.

"Spotsylvania County Records, 1721-1800" by William Armstrong Crozier.

"Some Emigrants to Virginia" by William G. Stanard.

"Colonial Virginia Register" by William G. Stanard.

"Index to Printed Virginia Genealogies, Including Key and Bibliography" by Robert Armistead Stewart.

"A Seed-Bed of the Republic: A Study of the Pioneers in the Upper (Southern) Valley of Virginia" by Robert D. Stoner.

"Colonial Surry" by John B. Boddie.

"Virginia Colonial Abstracts", 34 vols. by Beverley Fleet.

"Records of the Virginia Company of London" 4 vols. by Susan M. Kingsbury.

"Virginia Wills Before 1799" by William M. Clemens.

"Virginia's Eastern Shore. A History of Northampton and Accomack Counties" 2 vols. by Ralph T. Whitelaw.

"Adventurers of Purse and Person, Virginia 1607-1625" by Annie Lash Jester.

"Revolutionary War Records" by Gaius Marcus Brumbaugh.

"Cavaliers and Pioneers; Abstracts of Virginia Land Patents and Grants, 1623-1800" by Nell Marion Nugent.

"Early Virginia Immigrants, 1632-1666" by George Cabell Greer.

"Annals of Southwest Virginia, 1769-1800" by Lewis Preston Summers.

"Virginia Valley Records: Genealogical and Historical Materials of Rockingham County, Virginia, and Related Regions" by John W. Wayland.

WEST VIRGINIA

"Chronicles of the Scotch-Irish Settlement in Virginia" by Lyman Chalkley.

"West Virginia Revolutionary Ancestors, Whose Services were Nonmilitary and Whose Names, Therefore, Do Not Appear in Revolutionary Indexes of Soldiers and Sailors" by Anne Waller Reddy.

"Trans-Allegheny Pioneers" by John P. Hale.

"The Soldiery of West Virginia" by Virgil A. Lewis.

NEW ENGLAND

"The English Ancestry and Homes of the Pilgrim Fathers, Who Came to Plymouth on the 'Mayflower' in 1620, the 'Fortune' in 1621, and the 'Anne' and the 'Little James' in 1623" by Charles Edward Banks.

"The Planters of the Commonwealth; A Study of the Emigrants and Emigration in Colonial Times" by Charles Edward Banks.

"Topographical Dictionary of 2885 English Emigrants to New England, 1620-1650" by Charles Edward Banks.

"The Winthrop Fleet of 1630" by Charles Edward Banks.

"A Genealogical Register of the First Settlers of New England" by John Farmer.

"Directory of the Ancestral Heads of New England Families, 1620-1700" by Frank R. Holmes.

"Mayflower Descendants and Their Marriages for Two Generations After the Landing" by John T. Landis.

"A Genealogical Dictionary of the First Settlers of New England Showing Three Generations of Those Who Came Before May, 1692, on the Basis of Farmer's Register" by James Savage.

"Ancestral Roots of Sixty Colonists Who Came to New England Between 1623 and 1650" by Frederick Lewis Weis.

REVOLUTION

"Records of the Revolutionary War, Containing Correspondence, Names of the Officers and Privates of Regiments, with a List of Distinguishing Prisoners of War" by W. T. R. Saffell.

"Index of Revolutionary War Pension Applications".

THE SOUTH

"Historical Southern Families", 9 vols, by John Bennett Boddie.

"A Key to Southern Pedigrees" by William Crozier.

"Colonial Families of the Southern States of America" by Stella Pickett Hardy.

"Notable Southern Families" 6 vols, by Zella Armstrong.

THE GENEALOGICAL HELPER

A quarterly magazine published since 1947, has aided thousands of people all over the world. It is dedicated to helping more people find more genealogy. It is not confined to any particular section of the country but serves people in every state and many foreign countries. It is edited and published by the same concern publishing this book, THE EVERTON PUBLISHERS, INC. - P. O. Box 368 - Logan, Utah 84321.

Three of the four yearly issues contain sixty pages, eight-and-a-half by eleven inches. The September issue contains over 300 pages. The March issue contains a current listing of all the Family Associations with their leaders throughout the United States. The June issue features a current listing of all Genealogical Societies and Libraries, plus a list of professional genealogists giving their qualifications and the areas where they will do research. The September issue has the registrations of approximately 5,000 genealogists with an index of over 11,000 different surnames. The December ''Helper'' contains an index of all surnames found in preceding issues for the year with the exception of those found in the September Genealogists' Exchange which, of course, has its own index.

Besides these special features, in each of the issues you will find such regular sections as: The Question Box (a free query section) - The Book Review Section - Genealogical Miscellany Column - Articles of interest to genealogists. An article published in a recent edition saved many genealogists eight or nine times the cost of a years subscription.

Hundreds of researchers have extended their pedigrees many generations by utilizing the facilities offered in THE GENEALOG-ICAL HELPER. It is the most widely read genealogical magazine published. The subscription price is $5.00 per year; $9.00 for two years and $12.50 for three years, paid in advance. Single copies can be obtained at 75 cents each, with the exception of the Annual Exchange Editions, the September issues, which are $3.50 each.